MILESTONES

Normal Speech and Language Development
Across the Life Span

MILESTONES

Normal Speech and Language Development
Across the Life Span

John W. Oller, Jr., Ph.D.
Hawthorne Regents Professor
Department of Communicative Disorders
University of Louisiana at Lafayette

Stephen D. Oller, Ph.D.
Assistant Professor
Department of Communication and Theater Arts
Texas A&M University at Kingsville

Linda C. Badon, Ph.D., CCC-SLP
Assistant Professor
Department of Communicative Disorders
University of Louisiana at Lafayette

PLURAL
PUBLISHING
INC.

SAN DIEGO
OXFORD
BRISBANE

5521 Ruffin Road
San Diego, CA 92123

e-mail: info@pluralpublishing.com
Web site: http://www.pluralpublishing.com

49 Bath Street
Abingdon, Oxfordshire OX14 1EA
United Kingdom

Typeset in 11/13 Garamond by Flanagan's Publishing Services, Inc.
Printed in Canada by Transcontinental Printing

Library of Congress Cataloging-in-Publication Data:
Oller, John W.
  Milestones : normal speech and language development across the lifespan /
John W. Oller Jr., Stephen D. Oller, Linda C. Badon.
     p. ; cm.
  Includes bibliographical references and index.
  ISBN-13: 978-1-59756-036-8 (hardcover)
  ISBN-10: 1-59756-036-7 (hardcover)
  1. Language acquisition. 2. Child development. I. Oller, Stephen D. II. Badon,
Linda C. III. Title.
P118.O434 2006
  401'.93—dc22
                                                          2006003622

Contents

Preface

We wrote the book you hold in your hand, *Milestones: Normal Speech and Language Development Across the Life Span*, to provide an introduction to cutting-edge theory and research dealing not only with the development of speech forms, which are fairly well represented in other books, but with the full range of sign systems that undergird normal speech and language development across the whole life span. We wanted not only to cover the ground from conception to dissolution, but to do so in a way that would put beginning students in touch with the best of current theory and research in this field. Before the 4D video of the kind provided by Dr. Stuart Campbell, which is incorporated on the *Milestones Student's DVD-ROM* (also, the *Milestones Teacher's DVD-ROM*), could anyone have guessed that a baby could take steps in the womb at a stage of the pregnancy when the baby is so tiny that its mom cannot even distinguish the baby's movements from her own digestive functions? Thanks to Dr. Campbell at the Create Health Clinic in London, we not only see remarkable movements in the first trimester, but during later fetal development we see a clear instance of a full-fledged Duchenne smile with crinkled eyes and upturned cheeks. These milestones occur earlier than almost anyone might have supposed just a few years ago.

The *Milestones* course incorporates more up-to-date research than any other introductory book on this subject-matter and presents it from a user-friendly (teacher and student friendly) multidimensional and multimodal perspective. *Milestones* makes challenging material easy to understand and fun to work through for both teachers and students. The *Milestones* course incorporates resources and study tools that are unprecedented in other course materials on normal speech and language development. It also does something else that introductory textbooks rarely achieve. It introduces certain theoretical predictions for the first time and then provides empirical evidence showing that the predictions, some of them quite necessary to the theory and totally against received wisdom, are nonetheless correct. For instance, with the collaboration of a colleague at a distance, Dr. Robert C. Titzer, we present video showing that normal babies can read printed words with comprehension by about months 6 to 10. This is 5 to 7 years earlier than the standard theories of "reading readiness" suggest should be possible. Students at the introductory level are amazed. As Ramsie Bouzon put it, "That video was so neat! I was in awe how little they were and they could read!" Yet, our theory of abstraction predicted this result before Dr. Titzer provided conclusive evidence that the prediction is correct.

Students of the *Milestones* course are not only exposed to cutting-edge theoretical hypotheses as well as first time evidence showing them in crucial cases to be correct, but they also get the idea that theory and research are fun as well as challenging and absolutely relevant to clinical and educational practice. The story of babbling, to take another example, is more tightly integrated in the *Milestones* course, with the development of primary, secondary, and tertiary referential meanings, leading up to receptive vocabulary, and a few months later, the overt production of the child's first words. This integration is more complete than was possible before the development of our theory of abstraction. That theory also, although available in technical publications for a little more than a decade, is presented for the first time at an introductory level in the *Milestones* book. With the theory of abstraction in place, students are able to explore in greater depth and detail predictions of actual developments that take place from before birth to linguistic maturity and beyond. For instance, the theory helps us to understand the growth in the child's vocabulary from the first year to the "two-word" stage where the child begins to work out the syntax of sequences of words. We follow along as the normal child works up to increasingly complex linguistic systems until the point where, sometime between age 4 and 6 years, the normal child typically begins not only to engage in play, but also to sharply distinguish imaginary scenarios from mistakes. Later, between about 6 and 8 years, unintentional errors will be distinguished from deliberate misrepresentations (lies). The sequence of events is predicted in its entirety by the theory of abstraction and the key milestones along the way are demonstrated, as is shown in the book, in current research findings.

In studying *Milestones*, students develop a deep appreciation for the importance of representations and they begin to see how complex and interesting sign systems actually are in real life and in clinical and educational settings. From the preschool and early school years, we advance through the major achievement of literacy to maturity. We consider the specialized knowledge, culture, and skills that differentiate languages and their varieties, that is, how languages and their dialects vary across geographical, social, and political boundaries. We show that the over-representation of minority language/dialect groups in classes for the mentally retarded, special education, disordered, and so on, as well as their under-representation in classes for the "gifted and talented," can be explained by the fact that minority language/dialect children are commonly assessed, tested, and taught in a language/dialect that is either not known at all or that is not known well by those children. This fact accounts for the disproportionate representation of language/dialect minorities in special education and disordered categories better than any other hypothesis that has been proposed in the existing literature on this problem. We believe that this is an advance that is much needed and easily understood at the introductory level in the *Milestones* course for the first time.

From mature language use, we look forward to the end of the life span where senescence and mortality ensure the ultimate dissolution of communication abilities. To cover the life span it is essential to look ahead to that dissolution, which is part of the natural process of aging. In that part of the story, we also delve not only into the puzzles associated with Alzheimer's, Parkinsonism, and the like, but we also probe the mysteries of the fastest growing class of communication disorders, those that fall on the autism spectrum. One proposal that is being followed closely in the research, and is presented for the first time at an introductory level in the *Milestones* course, concerns the possible impact of certain poisons on the development and course of a large class of neurological problems, diseases, and disorders. Among the suspected possible factors affecting these problems if not causing them, for example, is mercury. It comes out that mercury in several different forms is commonly being placed inside the body through dental and other medical procedures. The *Milestones* course shows students of normal speech and language development for the first time at an introductory level that the neurotoxicity of mercury in all its forms is absolutely uncontroversial. Outside of plutonium, mercury is possibly the most neurotoxic substance on the face of the earth. As a result, it can reasonably be inferred that all neurodegenerative conditions, whether attributed to disease, genetics, or to some combination of factors, are certain to be exacerbated by mercury. On the mercury issue, our student Erving Griffin commented, "That stuff about mercury is the most amazing thing I have ever seen! I would like to thank you for sharing your unpublished book and DVD with the class." He was referring to video materials generously provided to us by Dr. Fritz Lorscheider, Dr. Naweed Syed, and Dr. David Kennedy. Those videos give us a whole new way of thinking about environmental toxins and neurodegenerative conditions.

The *Milestones* book is the result of a team effort by many more people than its three principal authors. It has benefitted from the theory, research, and clinical work of pioneers who came before us. It is based on work in linguistics, psychology, education, and medicine, as well as speech-language pathology and related fields. The roots go back to Charles Sanders Peirce, the mentor of William James, John Dewey, and Christine Alan Ladd. More recently we also draw from the thinking of Lev Vygotsky, A. R. Luria, Jean Piaget, Noam Chomsky, Jerome Bruner, Katherine Nelson, T. G. R. Bower, Elizabeth Bates, Vera John-Steiner, Joan Bybee, Michael Tomasello, and many other of our own contemporaries who have dedicated their lives to the study of language and human development. Our own theory of abstraction provides a basis to bring together a vast amount of research into a coherent chronological story. Our students tell us that the organization of the book, together with the media resources, the PowerPoint presentations, the test materials, Study Questions, Glossary, and Index make the *Milestones* course one of a kind. Sarah Lockhard, one of our many outstanding students moving on to the masters' level commented that she learned more from our course than from any other she has taken. Jolie LeBlanc said that the chronological organization of *Milestones* makes it "easier to learn from and to remember." Christy L. Primeaux said she "learned to take multiple choice tests" by working through the *Milestones* book. Melissa Evans said, "It was great to have a Glossary to turn to if a term was not fully understood" and "the multiple choice test items came directly from the material. There were no trick questions." Kelly Breaux wrote, "I was surprised at how easy it was to understand. I took this class last semester (using a different book), but dropped because I didn't understand." She went on to say that the *Milestones* book enabled her to succeed in the course. Kelly Simon pointed out that it changed the way she saw herself in early pictures. "When I was born, my dad took a picture of me and I was smiling. My mom always said it was gas. I am so excited to tell her that it was actually a smile!" The video of the baby in the womb, one of the impressive pieces on the *Milestones Student DVD-ROM*, from Dr. Stuart Campbell's work, showed Kelly that a Duchenne smile is not only a social phenomenon that is universal across cultures, but that it occurs even before birth. Her smile at birth, therefore, was probably a sign of social togetherness, security, and well-being. The *Milestones* course will change the way students see themselves, their siblings, children, and grandchildren.

We started work on this book to meet the need for a richer, more comprehensive, deeper, and better organized story of milestones across the life span. We also wanted to provide a sound basis for our next book, which is to be an introduction to a more comprehensive treatment of the classification and description of communication difficulties and disorders. See J. Oller, L. Badon, and S. Oller (in press), *Communication Disorders: A Survey Across the Life Span*, San Diego, Plural Publishing. Our intended readership for *Milestones*, and for its planned sequel, includes all students in speech-language pathology, special education, linguistics, psychology, and related fields who need or want to take an introductory course about language acquisition and development. We lay out the milestones of development here in the order in which they are normally achieved by children. They are easier for children and for us to understand in that order. Students see why it is that normal children, no matter how precocious they may be, often fall back to earlier stages of development, but seldom leap ahead to much more advanced stages of development. That is, the sequence spelled out in *Milestones* cannot easily be violated. We tell the story in the chronological order of the normal achievement of the milestones for two reasons: for one, this is the way all of us learned when we were children, and, for another, the best research on discourse processing shows that this is also how we adults continue to learn best. Learners do, as Jolie LeBlanc and other students, notably Kayla Zagar, have observed, understand, remember, and recall the facts of a story better when it is told in a chronological order.

As we study the milestones of normal speech and language development, it becomes increasingly obvious that they themselves really do provide a good basis for understanding difficulties and disorders of communication. If communication did not commonly succeed, breakdowns would not be as evident and noteworthy as they are. Also, to understand how processes of communication breakdown, it is essential to understand how they commonly succeed.

As we note in our acknowledgments of collaborators and colleagues from around the world, we have all been amazed and encouraged at the enthusiastic response with which the book and its accompanying resources have already been received. Most of the materials we cite from other authors, including nearly all of the videos, audio files, animations, and pictures were enthusiastically given to us. Individuals pictured, filmed, recorded, or otherwise represented in the book, in addition to the students we have quoted, as well as the parents, grandparents, and our publishers, all of them without exception have been eager and willing to offer their support, their knowledge, their resources, and their names to this project. They have freely given of themselves, their life experiences, the pictures of themselves and their children, as well as their words, and their own work. As a result our project has been and remains a wholehearted undertaking that has been both challenging and rewarding in every way. We offer it to you, dear reader, teacher, student, user, colleague, in the hope and confidence that it will not only introduce you to current theory and research in this subject area but that it will excite, inspire, and enrich the way you view the remarkable human achievements of normal speech and language development across the life span.

The Authors

Acknowledgments

The persons to be thanked in the *Milestones* project are so many that we cannot mention all of them by name. However, there are some folks that we must not overlook. To start with, we thank our students who generously gave of their time, their effort, their enthusiasm, their ideas, and their spoken and written words. As we worked through this material, our students were indispensable in the development, pretesting, rewriting, and retesting of the 600 multiple-choice items that are provided in the *Milestones Teacher's DVD-ROM*. Some of our students are mentioned by name on the book jacket, in our web pages, and in the book itself. We could not have done this project without them. We are grateful to every one of them. Please remember as you read these words that every student who came to class, read a chapter, wrote a reaction or suggestion, took a test, or participated in a discussion, contributed to the inspiration and energy necessary to the completion of the *Milestones* project. To our former students and theirs, and to the ones yet to come, as well as their teachers, we can honestly say, this book is for you. Thank you for sharing the journey with us.

We also thank our colleagues near at hand who have contributed their resources, time, wisdom, inspiration, and courage with us. Thanks especially to the following doctoral students, staff, and faculty (given here in alphabetical order without distinctions between students and faculty) who helped to advance some aspect of this work: Katie Johnson Abendroth, Shalini Arehole, Brooke Breaux, Liang Chen, Claude Čech, Don Fischer (Defense Language Institute), Heather Grossman, J. Guo (California State University, Hayward), Mark Honegger, Kunok Kim (Chung Ang University, Seoul), Stephanie Landry, Kathryn Listi, Brandi Ortego, Ning Pan, Danny Povinelli, Claiborne Rice, Ben Rutter, Tom Scovel (San Francisco State University), John A. Tetnowski, Mitchell Trichon, and Ruixia Yan. We are also grateful for invitations to present highlights of the *Milestones* course to doctorate students and professors associated either directly or indirectly with the Institute of Cognitive Sciences. We benefitted from conversations (again giving names in alphabetical order and not distinguishing students from faculty) with Istvan S. N. Berkeley, Julie Boland (now at the University of Michigan), Robert Bothwell, Subrata Dasgupta, Sally Donlon, Michele I. Feist, M. Babette Fontenot, Mike Kalish, Cheryl S. Lynch, Anthony S. Maida, Valanne MacGyvers, and John Troutman, to mention only a few.

Additionally, we have received assistance in too many ways to count from colleagues at a distance. So many generously and graciously provided resources that, again, we really cannot name all of them here, but we do want to mention Laverne Baker, Shari Schlehuser Beams, Joan Bybee, Thomas Field, Phebe A. Hayes, Paul Hoffman, Ronald Hy, R. C. Major, Janet A. Norris, D. K. Oller, Dan I. Slobin, Orlando Taylor, Michael Tomasello, and Sherman Wilcox.

Finally, we are indebted to those who generously provided video materials for the *Milestones DVD-ROM*s, or recordings, photographs, and illustrations:

> For the picture of the newborn infant walking in Figure 1-2 along with several other diagrams, especially those of Figures 3-4, 3-5, 5-3, and 5-8, and for critical papers, countless pieces of data, much inspiration, and enjoyment, we thank Thomas G. R. Bower, our esteemed colleague at the University of Texas in Dallas.

> The model in Figure 1-3 is Stacy Alana Oller. We thank her for letting us use her picture there.

> For the picture of an 18-month-old child who is a head taller than himself, Figure 1-4, we thank the Riley family, especially, Luke, Steve and Teena.

> The Video of a Fetus at 12 Weeks of Gestation is due to the gracious generosity and excellent work of Dr. Stuart Campbell at London's Create Health Clinic.

> We thank Dr. Dava Newman and Dr. Charles M. Oman for pointing us to the diagrams of the semicircular canals of the inner ear and of the angular orientation of the semicircular canals of the inner ear at http://paperairplane.mit.edu/16.423J/ Space/SBE/neurovestibular/NeuroVestibular/2_Physiology/ PhysSub3.html at the Massachusetts Institute of Technology.

> Mr. J. D. Lasica, world class photographer, provided the still picture of his son, in Figure 3-1, a newborn baby delivered at 9 pounds 22 inches by Cesarean. We also thank the generous folks at http://www.babycenter.com/general/pregnancy/ newbornprep/8337.html for graciously providing information and access to the photo and the linked video of the Apgar procedure.

> For the excellent video titled Sound Beginnings, associated with Figure 3-2, showing the procedures for testing oto-acoustic

emissions, brainstem auditory response in newborn infants, and interactions between mothers and their infants, we thank Mr. Bruce Hansen at http://www.raisingdeafkids.org and the National Center for Hearing Assessment and Management (NCHAM) at http://www.raisingdeafkids.org/hearingloss/testing/nhs.jsp). We also thank Dr. Karl White at Utah State University for his permission and for pointing us to the latest version of this excellent video.

For appearing as the mom in Figures 3-3 and 4-5, we thank Robin Badon Brookter.

The diagram of the vowel space appearing as Figure 3-4 was provided thanks to Michelle A. Aldridge, R. D. Stillman, and T. G. R. Bower.

We are grateful to T. G. R. Bower and the American Psychological Society for the material reconstructed in Figure 3-5.

The McGurk effect video and the picture of Figure 3-6 were given to us freely by Professor Arnt Maasø. Many thanks to him for the remarkably convincing demonstration of the McGurk effect.

Thanks go to Professor Margaret W. Sullivan and M. Lewis who generously gave us the pictures of the baby smiling in Figure 4-1 and the baby grimacing in Figure 4-3.

Ruth Marie Oller and Ashley Grogan are to be thanked for Figure 4-2 of the two of them demonstrating a genuine shared Duchenne smile.

Thanks go to the Brookter family for the picture of Cole Noah Brookter in Figure 4-6 and his grandfather Ronnell B. Badon for letting us interfere with the normal peace and quiet at his house as much and as often as we did.

Gabrielle Alana Oller is thanked for her picture as the infant in Figure 5-5 diagraming the sign cycle from icon to index to symbol.

Abigail Chen along with Ning Pan Chen and Liang Chen are to be thanked for the picture of the baby at 10 months studying and "reading" a book in Figure 6-1.

For the little boy in Figures 7-1, 7-2, and 8-3 we are grateful to Brenden David Oller who served as the model and provided the marvelous examples of his own language learning.

The pictures and video associated with Figure 10-1 and 10-3 of Aleka and Other Early Readers was generously provided by Dr. Robert C. Titzer. We are grateful for this excellent and deeply original material.

W. W. Norton & Company, Inc., along with Mercer Mayer and our colleagues Diane Whittington and Liang Chen are to be thanked for the material appearing in Figure 10-5.

For the maze cartoon of Figure 11-2 we thank Bruce Beattie and Copley News Service.

We are grateful to Bob Rothman, photographer and proud grandfather, as well as Dr. Ellen Rothman, M.D. for permission to use the picture in Figure 12-1 of little Macy at her "first laugh" ceremony. We also thank the President and Fellows of Harvard College for releasing this picture for our use. See the article at http://webweekly.hms.harvard.edu/archive/2004/12_13/student_scene.html.

For the adaptation shown as Figure 12-3 of Reason's "Swiss cheese" model we thank Dr. James Reason himself who granted permission for us to use his model in this way.

The video of Smoking Teeth was graciously provided to us by Dr. David Kennedy on behalf of the International Academy of Oral Medicine and Toxicology.

Figure 12-4 and the high quality animated video associated with it, How Mercury Damages Nerve Fibrils, was provided by Dr. Fritz Lorscheider and Dr. Naweed Syed of the University of Calgary Medical School. Many thanks to them.

For audio recordings we are grateful to Ruixia Yan for the Mandarin example; to Yvonne Chan for the example of Cantonese; to Mary Anne Chavez-Oller for the English recording; to Brenden David Oller for the fine recording of "MIMI house"; and to Bernice Harrison for the Cajun/Creole example.

For the picture of Eric Gallup in Figure 12-5, we thank his father, Ray, his sister Julie, and Eric himself.

Finally the cartoon shown as Figure 12-7 was purchased from W. W. Norton, Inc.

Introduction to the *Milestones* Student DVD-ROM

This DVD-ROM is intended as a supplement to the book *Milestones: Normal Speech and Language Development Across the Lifespan.* It does not contain all of the *Milestones* text but it does contain some useful searchable resources. The DVD-ROM contains a searchable Adobe Acrobat .pdf file which includes:

1. An expanded Table of Contents, containing searchable introductions and summaries for each chapter along with hyperlinks to the URL's (i.e., Uniform Resource Locators for the Internet) and other digital resources referred to in the book.

2. Figures, illustrations, pictures, and diagrams from the *Milestones* text in the same order in which they appear in this book. However, the materials on the DVD are generally in color.

3. A searchable version of the Glossary, including the Key Words that appear at the head of each chapter.

4. A complete searchable list of References.

5. An Index of Authors, Subjects, and Technical Terms that are found throughout the *Milestones* book.

The searchable text on the DVD-ROM includes all paragraphs from the text that refer to URLs or to video and audio resources.

The DVD-ROM requires Adobe Acrobat Reader version 6.0 or later. It will not run correctly on Acrobat 5.0 or earlier. If you experience any problems in seeing all the materials in the file, you may be using an old version of Acrobat. If so, try removing that software from your computer completely and visit: http://www.adobe.com/products/acrobat/readstep2.html to download the latest edition of the free Adobe Reader.

In order to play all of the video files that are included on the DVD-ROM, you will need the following software installed on your computer. All of these programs are available freely from the Internet and usually only require that you register with the publisher of the program. Please visit the following websites and follow the directions for downloading these players.

Quicktime

http://www.apple.com/quicktime/download/win.html (for Windows)

http://www.apple.com/quicktime/download/mac.html (for Mac)

RealPlayer®

http://www.real.com/ (for Windows)

https://order.real.com/pt/order.html?country=US&language=EN&mppi=0 &mppos_list=0&mpst=0&ppath=cpmacpl060204a&pageregion=player_ button&pcode=rn&opage=sp_os_mac&src=realhome_bb_1_3_1_0_0_1_ 0%2Crealplayer_8020,sp_os_mac (for Mac)

Windows Media Player

http://www.microsoft.com/windows/windowsmedia/download/All Downloads.aspx?displang=en&qstechnology= (for Windows or Mac)

Microsoft PowerPoint Viewer (if you do not have Microsoft PowerPoint on your computer)

http://www.microsoft.com/downloads/details.aspx?FamilyID=428d5727- 43ab-4f24-90b7-a94784af71a4&displaylang=en (for Windows)

http://www.microsoft.com/downloads/details.aspx?FamilyID=e25cb1e5- 209c-4a58-b283-23e84b616477&DisplayLang=en (for Mac)

Dedication

To the memory of
Reverend Rogers Cain,
the father of Linda Cain Badon,
a man who loved God, dedicated his life to mankind,
and respected and valued education

CHAPTER 1

Why We Start at the Beginning

═══════════════════ **OBJECTIVES** ═══════════════════

In studying this chapter you will:

1. Overview key milestones across the lifespan;

2. See that complex sign systems are built up out of simpler sign systems;

3. Consider the nature versus nurture controversy and see that both are involved;

4. Distinguish points of view in human interactions—first person, second person, and the rest of the world;

5. Understand the special role of doubt, conflict, and surprise in driving development; and

6. Begin to see how understanding normal milestones of speech and language development can help us understand, treat, and sometimes cure communication difficulties and disorders.

═══════════════════ **KEY TERMS** ═══════════════════

Here are some key terms of this chapter. (Many of them you may already know.) It may help to review them. These terms are explained in the text and defined in the Glossary at the end of the book. They appear in **bold print** on their first appearance in the text.

abstraction   agent
adrenoleukodystrophy   approximant

1

articulators
autism spectrum disorders
backsliding
breath group
categorical imperative
coda
concept
concrete operational stage
consonant
consonantal sound
construction
convention
deep structure
diagnosis
dialect
diphthong
direct object
discourse
disequilibration
embryo
entrainment
feature
fetus
first position (or person)
foreign language
formal operational stage
fricative
generalization
genome
gestation
glide
icon
index
interlocutor
intonation
language acquisition device
language acquisition support structure
language community
language faculty
lexicon
liquid
logical form
myelin
nasal

native language
normative
object
onset
patient
percept
phonology
pragmatic
preoperational stage
prognosis
prosody
protein
representation
resonance
reversibility
rhythm
rime
second position (or person)
self-awareness
semantic
sensorimotor stage
sign
sign system
signed language
stress pattern
subject
surface-form
syllabic sequences
syllable
symbol
syntax
target language
third position (or person)
transitive
transitive relation
trimester
turn-taking
ultrasound video
verb
vocalic sound
voicing
vowel
zone of proximal development

Every story has a beginning. So does every person. In this book we explore developmental milestones leading from infancy to adulthood and throughout the lifespan. You may already know what some of the major milestones are, but with new technologies and more rigorous methods of research we are learning that many of the milestones that were previously thought to occur after birth actually occur while the child is still in its mother's womb. For instance, you probably already knew that human babies, while they are at the **fetus** stage, suck their thumbs before they are born as shown in Figure 1–1. Every mother knows that the fetus can kick, punch, and do somersaults in the womb, but did you know that a newborn infant can sometimes walk with a little help from the doctor during the first few minutes of life? It is true as shown in Figure 1–2. Amazingly, normal human infants can often stand and even take a few steps fresh from the womb. With moving **ultrasound video** today we also know that by 12 weeks of **gestation** normal infants can move their fingers, by 18 weeks they yawn and smile, and by 26 weeks they blink and cry (see the BBC story retrieved January 28, 2006 from http://news.bbc.co.uk/2/hi/health/ 3846525.stm; also see the Video of a Fetus at 12 Weeks of Gestation on the *Milestones Student DVD-ROM* reproduced by permission from Dr. Stuart Campbell at Create Health Clinic in London).[1] Because of technological advances, knowledge of human development is advancing rapidly. Infants continue to surprise us with what they can do.

Mothers regularly report that their unborn babies are responsive to human voices especially during the last three months (the third **trimester**) of pregnancy. The research shows that infants before birth also respond differently to mom's language (the **native language**) as contrasted with a **foreign language.** Even in the womb the baby seems to distinguish the

---

[1]Throughout the book, websites referred to by a URL (a Uniform Resource Locator for the world wide web) are hyperlinked in the *Milestones Student DVD-ROM* as well as the *Milestones Teacher DVD-ROM*. The student DVD-ROM is packaged with every book. When a video or audio resource referred to in the book can be played directly from the *Milestones DVD-ROM*, it is shown by a descriptor underlined and printed like this: An Example Descriptor Hyperlinked to a Resource on the *Milestones Student (and/or Teacher) DVD-ROM*. These files can be played from a DVD drive without an Internet connection. If the user is connected to the Internet, provided that the sites have been maintained, the other URLs in the textbook are also accessible from the DVD-ROM by clicking the appropriate hyperlink in the Microsoft Word "Read Me" file on either the student's or teacher's version. Hyperlinked URLs and other resources all appear in underlined blue print in the "Read Me" files. Both versions contain (1) introductions and summaries for each chapter along with an Expanded Table of Contents with hyperlinks to the URLs and other digital resources referred to in the book, (2) figures from the text, (3) the Glossary, (4) References, and (5) an Index of Authors, Subjects, and Technical Terms. The teacher DVD-ROM, available to any qualified instructor as a bonus for course adoption, contains (7) a Teacher's Manual with test materials (600 items, along with item statistics concerning reliability, and validity), and (8) a separate Microsoft PowerPoint presentation for each chapter.

Figure 1–1. Infant after 4.5 months of gestation sucking its thumb in the womb (from http://www.dushkin.com/connectext/psy/ch03/fetus.mhtml. Copyright © 2005. The McGraw-Hill Companies).

Figure 1–2. Newborn infant walking with assistance. Reprinted with permission of Wayne State University Press and T. G. R. Bower from: Bower, T. G. R. (1973). Repetition in human development. *Merrill-Palmer Quarterly, 19,* p. 304. Copyright 1973 Wayne State University Press

rhythms, **stress patterns**, and **intonation**—the so-called **prosody** of their native language. At birth infants can distinguish **syllables** such as "ba" and "pa" (Dehaene-Lambertz & Pena, 2001) and probably you have observed that by about their seventh month human infants begin to babble in repetitive **syllabic sequences**, saying, things like "bababa" or "dadada," but did you know that human infants are able to engage in **turn-taking** vocal exchanges that resemble a conversation at birth? Did you know that the movements of a normal human newborn tend to fall into rhythm with the sounds, syllables, words, phrases, and turn changes of adults who speak within the hearing of the infant (Condon & Sander, 1974)? This phenomenon, known as **entrainment**, is among the milestones achieved by normal human babies either at birth or soon after.

Milestones

In this book we introduce the full spectrum of such milestones across the human lifespan. We cover the gamut starting with the developing **embryo**. We consider the maturation of the baby's body, the brain, and the delicately articulated hearing system up to the baby's birth. From there we work our way forward through the first voluntary vocalizations through the stages of infant babbling, where the building blocks of the **phonology** or sound system of the baby's first language are established. From there we move on to the first words. We explore the growth in the child's vocabulary, also called the **lexicon**, from the first year and the progression to the so-called "two word" stage where the child begins to work out the structure of sequences of words, that is, their **syntax**. We follow along as the normal child works up to increasingly complex linguistic **sign systems** until sometime between age four and six, for most normal children, when the child begins not only to engage in play, but to distinguish imaginary **representations** (pretend scenarios and worlds) from representations of the real world. A representation is any thing, thought, or mark of any kind that is used to stand for something else. To create representations we require **signs** of various kinds that are noticeable and that are used to stand for things other than themselves.

From the preschool and early school years we advance through the major achievements of literacy and on to maturity. Along the way we consider the specialized knowledge, culture, and skills that differentiate languages and their varieties, in other words, **dialects**. We consider how languages and their dialects vary across regions, communities, and so on. Some of the differences encountered are so great that the speakers of the distinct dialects and languages cannot understand each other's speech, writing, or signs. We consider how children acquire different languages or dialects. As the child grows to maturity he or she will also learn a great deal about the meanings of representations and how they are used. The child will learn not only to distinguish ordinary factual representations about the here and now, for example, "Here is your bottle," from playacting imaginary roles, "I'll be the mommy! You can be the baby!" but the child will also learn to identify errors, "That's not my dog!" and to tell the difference between an error and a deliberate deception, for example, Jimmy may say, "I didn't bite Suzie!" but Jimmy's teeth marks may have left an impression on Suzie's arm.

From the simplest acts of an unborn infant, such as sucking a thumb, to the special interest of human infants in speech both before and after birth, the forms of speech and language grow in complexity. From the first voluntary vocal acts of earliest infancy, the baby progresses to babbling, then the first word, and from there on to adult **discourse**. For example, mature adults can normally understand the complex conversations that take place at a committee meeting, or in a congressional caucus, or, say, at the United Nations. Compare the level of complexity of behaviors shown by a prebirth infant as seen in the four-dimensional ultrasound Video of a Fetus at 12 Weeks of Gestation on the *Milestones Student DVD-ROM* (also seen on BBC News, 2004, retrieved January 28, 2006 from http://news.bbc.co.uk/2/hi/health/3846525.stm; click on "The BBC's Vicki Young") with a press conference at the United Nations involving Kofi Annan and Colin Powell (UN Webcast Archives, December 31, 2004, retrieved January 28, 2006 from http://www.un.org/webcast/sg2004.html; click on the box labeled "31 December 04"). The baby's actions are interesting and complex, but none of the acts of the baby come near the complexity of adult discourse. However the baby's actions from before birth are already beginning to reveal key building blocks for the **surface-forms** of speech and language, that is, the forms of syllables and signs that we notice with our senses. The baby's actions also reveal how it is beginning to take account of aspects of the meanings that those surface-forms will come to represent as the baby acquires a language. The meanings that the baby will learn to deal with eventually are commonly referred to as **deep structures**, **logical forms**, or **concepts**.

Sign Systems Have Grammatical Structure

Consider the baby's act of sucking the thumb in the womb (see Figure 1–1). Think about the grammatical (and logical) complexity, the deep structure, of this act. For example, from grammar school days you may recall the difference between **subject**, **verb**, and **object**. Think about the fact that the infant is the subject. More accurately, we could say that the baby is a special kind of subject, the **agent**, who performs the action of thumb-sucking. The act itself is the underlying meaning of the **transitive** verb that relates the baby as agent through that action, for example, putting the thumb in the mouth and sucking on it, with the baby's thumb. The baby's thumb is the **direct object** (also the grammatical **patient**) that receives the action of sucking. When it comes to fetal development, the milestone of thumb-sucking is especially interesting because it foreshadows things the infant must do later on to survive.

The act of thumb-sucking arguably anticipates the fact that the baby will later on be supplied with nourishment through the sucking action. The baby's action as seen in Figure 1-1 shows in a kind of pretend version the very action that will be necessary for the infant to get milk and nourishment. It shows the prior design of the baby's body to perform the important act of sucking. It shows that the baby's lips, for instance, are shaped in such a way that the baby's mouth will fit the mother's nipple to gain nourishment. It also presupposes that the breast or a suitable substitute (say, a bottle with a nipple) will be provided to the baby. Similarly, in Figure 1-2, we can see that the baby as agent uses its feet and legs for walking. Again, it appears that the lower limbs and their extremities, the baby's legs and feet were made for walking, as the newborn in the photo demonstrates with a little help from the doctor.

A Place to Begin

The constructive process of building up progressively more adequate and complex representations is not just a matter of trial and error. The child must begin in the here and now and work outward from there because that is where the child is situated. The newborn child does not have the option of deciding, "Oh well, I'll just think about the distant past or the future before I bother with the present." The baby cannot just decide to speak Russian, or to try algebra or the piano for kicks on its first day of life. Those options are not open to the infant. The child has to start with events that are present when the baby begins to be capable of sensations and movement. For instance, for the sounds of the speech of one language, say, English, to be differentiated from speech in some other language, say, Japanese, the hearing system must be sufficiently developed. In Chapter 2, we consider the prebirth experience of the human infant and work our way through the child's initial discovery of its own person and body parts. To represent objects (including persons) and their relations to abstract signs, Charles S. Peirce showed that humans rely on three major kinds of sign systems. These different kinds of signs undergird speech and language development.

Icons

A sign, of course, is any thing, thought, or marker of any kind that represents something other than just itself. The first and most basic system of relatively complete signs (as distinct from mere qualities of signs) are **icons**. These can be **percepts** of objects, persons, things, and whole scenes. They are associated through our senses with bounded bodily things, especially the persons that move around and talk. A visual image, for instance, is an icon. The feel of the apple we hold in our hand, its weight, its smooth surface, its firmness, coolness, and roundness are all **features** (qualities or aspects) of the icon of the apple that we may perceive if we are holding one or that we may imagine on the basis of past experiences with apples. The key characteristic of an icon is that it resembles its object. The image of a person in a photograph, for instance, is a valid icon of that person only to the extent that the image in the photo looks like that person. In the experience of a newborn infant, as we will see in the next chapter, the most interesting icons in the infant's experience, besides its own self, are those other bodies that move and talk. The talking icons, that is, the persons in the infant's experience, are evidently interesting *because* they talk. The infant perceives the talk as marking them as important.

Indexes

The signs associated with the movements or the spatial relations between bodily things and persons are **indexes**. An index is the sort of sign that connects at least two icons, just as a line segment connects the points at its ends. We can say that the line points to both of its ends, and it connects them. This is all that an index does. For example, suppose someone drops a cup on a hard floor and it shatters. The cup is connected with the floor through the action of its being dropped and its falling. Suppose an infant observes the falling of the cup and its breaking to pieces when it hits the floor. Or, suppose it observes the releasing of the cup by the person holding it, the falling of the cup from the person who drops it to the floor, and the shattering of the cup after it strikes the floor. All these event relations are represented by indexes. Every index is like a line or path of movement.

The main characteristic of indexes is that they connect icons. For instance, they connect observers with other things through icons. For this reason, without first distinguishing some icons, it will be impossible to notice any indexes. We cannot notice the movement of an object without also noticing the moving object to some extent. To see a movement as a connection between two locations, we must notice the object that moves and the place where it starts and where it ends up. To notice one thing bumping into another, we need to notice the two things and their relative movements. We can see, therefore, that the **construction** of at least a few iconic signs is essential before any meaningful indexical signs can be built up. Also, we can see that some signs must be built up with the assistance of other signs. This is why it is widely agreed that building signs is a constructive process.

Among the first indexes of early infancy are those associated with bodily persons. As we will see in Chapter 3, even newborn infants are sometimes observed to respond with their own vocalizations to cooing noises made by the adult holding the infant. It seems as if the infant is repeatedly announcing its own presence by vocalizing in response to the vocal noises of the other person. Could the infant intend something like, "I hear you over there and I'm over here"? These first vocalizations seem to be the infant's first indexical signs connecting distinct icons. They seem to announce the person speaking and to call out to the person spoken to. Is this possible for a newborn infant?

Symbols

The signs of greatest interest to us in this book are **symbols**. These signs are distinguished by the fact that they are associated with their objects only by the way they are used. Consistent applications or uses of such signs are called **conventions**. They are largely arbitrary. Our parents could have called any one of us by a different name than they chose. The name assigned is mainly a matter of convention. A person called "Stacy" or "Shirley" or "Kofi" could have been called any one of a thousand or more other names. It is only the fact that other people also use the name "Stacy" to refer to the person who goes by that name that makes it that person's name. Such an arbitrary use is what is meant by a convention. It is a special kind of rule. It is a **pragmatic**, social rule of usage. It connects an abstract symbol, for example, the word "Stacy" through one or many indexes with the icon of the particular bodily person who goes by that name. The pragmatic meaning of a symbol is found in the particular object or objects with which it is associated through an index on any given occasion.

The whole dynamic process connecting icons, through indexes, with symbols, can be shown in the simple diagram of Figure 1–3. The symbol, *Stacy*, for instance, is connected through one or many indexes as shown by the arrow in the diagram, with the person who is represented by the icon of that person. So, we have all three sign systems, symbol-index-icon, in pragmatic relation. If we already know the language and we happen to be introduced to Stacy, we can understand the whole relation easily and from any angle. If we meet her at the coffee shop we are apt to think of her name. If someone mentions the name, we may think of the person. If someone points her out in a crowd, we may understand the index that points to her, will perceive the icon of the person, and think of the symbol, *Stacy* all more or less at the same time.

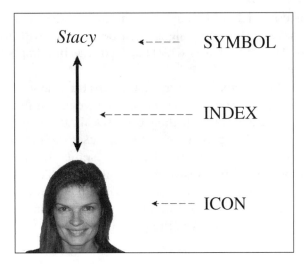

Figure 1–3. A diagram of the most common relations between a symbol, index, and icon.

Symbols also have general, **semantic**, meanings that are abstracted and generalized from their particular objects and occasions of use. If we meet Stacy on Monday, by generalizing we can expect her to still be called Stacy on Tuesday, Wednesday, and so on. We may suppose she was Stacy on the previous Monday and will still be called that years from now. Because of their general applicability in new contexts and even in imaginary settings, by **abstraction** and **generalization**, a symbol like "Stacy" can be combined with other symbols to form more complex syntactic structures. For instance,

(1) Stacy is a brunette.

sounds fine, though it may be false if Stacy is a blonde. On the other hand,

(2) Stacy is a Tuesday morning.

sounds strange, and

(3) Stacy of the went.

does not seem to be a possible syntactic construction in English. In fact, as we can already see from the examples just given (items 1–3), combinations of symbols are conventional. They are constrained only by the ways they are commonly used.

As we will see in subsequent chapters symbols form the essential building blocks for all higher linguistic structures. Interestingly, symbols are by far the most versatile of all signs. They can represent other symbols and they can be used to refer to icons and indexes as well. What is more, symbols can be combined to form uncountably many complex discourse structures that are also symbols.

Development Is Constructive

No infant can begin to develop an understanding of complex phrases without first discovering the meanings of certain words within those phrases. For these reasons, human speech and language development, and in fact all neuromuscular manifestations of sign systems in human experience are constructive. Every product of discourse is a complex construction. It must be built up from signs that have been developed beforehand. Educators often say that more complex forms are built up from less complex ones. This is a little misleading because the sign systems the infant works with are always complex from the very beginning. However, they do become relatively *more* complicated as time goes on right up to the point where, owing to the accumulation of injuries, poisons, and disease, the sign systems (and the neuromuscular systems) of the aging adult begin to break down.

The important thing to remember about the constructive process by which sign systems are built up from infancy, however, is that certain building blocks must be in place before the higher structures that depend on those building blocks can be put together. Wittgenstein (1958) observed concerning what he called "language games" that they involve a progression from simpler to more complex forms. He said, "we recognize in these simple processes, forms of language not separated by a break from our more complicated ones. We see that we can build up the complicated forms from the primitive ones by gradually adding new form" (p. 17).

Before we can build a wall of blocks, we must first have (or construct) the blocks. The blocks may consist of rocks, wood, cement, water, sand, clay, or whatever. Before we can put a roof on a building, we need to have the walls in place. The roof cannot normally be set in place before the walls are erected. These analogies are not perfect, but they make the point that development is constructive. While there are enormous differences of opinion between researchers and theoreticians about theories of human development from infancy to maturity, one point where nearly all theoreticians agree is that *the development of speech and language in particular is a dynamic constructive process* (Gogate, Walker Andrews, & Bahrick, 2001; MacWhinney, 1998; Thelen, 2005; Thelen & Smith, 1994). We can see this fact in the very nature of every sentence in any language: syllables are combined to form words which are combined to form the higher structures that we call phrases which are combined to form clauses, sentences, and higher discourse.

Because some developments have to occur before others will become possible, the milestones that the normal human infant comes to over the course of time fall into a predetermined sequence. They are like a series of steps that must be climbed in a certain order. The infant must proceed on a schedule. The milestones tend to occur in a particular, necessary order. The rate of progress may vary quite a lot, but the sequence cannot easily be violated. We are not surprised that the child starts babbling in fairly distinct syllables prior to uttering his or her first meaningful word. We are not surprised by this because words are constructed from syllables. How will the child differentiate distinct words such as "mama" (say as a term to refer to the infant's mother), from "dada" (as a term to refer to the baby's father), from "baba" (as a term to refer to the baby's bottle, or to the act of waving bye-bye)?

What is more, syllables are structured. In all the 6,912 languages of the world that are catalogued in the latest edition of the *Ethnologue* (Gordon, 2005) the syllables of speech tend to conform to certain preferred structural arrangements (Blevins, 1995). A syllable has at least a **vowel** (or vowel-like sound) as its center, peak, or nucleus. This part of the syllable is sometimes referred to as a **vocalic sound**. It is the part that resonates when we produce the vocal noise we call **voicing**, or the humming sound of the voice when we sing a note. The vocalic nucleus is the part of syllables that receive the beats or pulses in the rhythm of speech. Say the word "syllable" out loud and you will hear three distinct beats, roughly, "syl-la-ble." The nucleus of any syllable is the part that we can sing on a continuing musical note. We cannot hum the "b" part of the "ble" of "syllable," for instance, or at least we cannot hum it or produce it for very long. Consonants tend to function as markers of the boundaries of syllables while vowels take center stage. For this reason consonants of a syllable are called its **onset** if they come at the beginning as in the "s" of "syl" or "str" of "strike," and they are the **coda** if they come at the end as does the "l" of "syl" or the "ngths" of "strengths." If we combine the nucleus of the syllable with its coda, we get the part of the syllable that is called the **rime** of the syllable. For instance, "engths" would be the rime in "strengths" or "lengths."

Typically consonants involve a movement that constricts or shuts off the passage of air from the lungs through the larynx, mouth, and nose. By producing a few examples in speech, we can tell that consonants, by contrast with vowels, are typically transitional. We can only sing the sound represented by "b" for a very brief moment. However, we can sing, or continue to voice, the "a" part, "ahhhhhhhh," until we run out of breath. Incidentally, the sequence of syllables that occur between pauses, or between breaths, are unsurprisingly called a **breath group**. Unlike the vowel at the center of any syllable, which can be extended throughout a single breath, until we run out of air, consonants typically involve either rapid movement from one position to another, as in the sound represented by "b" in "bat" or "m" in "mat," or they involve the constriction of the passage of air, as in the sounds typically represented by "h" in "hot," or "s" in "sad." Consonants are distinguished from vowels mainly by movements that close or constrict the passage of air through the throat, mouth, and nose. Vowels on the other hand are identified mainly by the contrast in resonant qualities. For instance, notice the difference in the vocalic sounds of the words "read," "rod," and "rude."

Consonantal sounds usually involve distinct movements or constrictions of the mouth, throat, and lungs. The movable parts of the body that enter into speech production are called the **articulators**. They not only include the tongue, lips, and lower jaw, but also the muscles of the throat, and the voice box. They even extend to the complex system of muscles and structures that enable us to control the expulsion of air from our lungs.

Vowels are characterized mainly by relatively continuous **resonance** whereas consonants are typically distinguished by transitions and often by near or complete closure of one or more air passages of the mouth and nose. Compare the vowel sounds typically represented by "a" "I," and "u" and consonants such as the sounds represented by "b," "d," "g," "p," "t," "k," "f," "th," "h," and so on. Some consonants can be lengthened indefinitely, such as the **nasals** represented by "m," "n," and "-ng" as in "mat," "nat," and "sang." Still these sounds involve complete stoppage of any continuing flow of air through the mouth. Try humming the nasals one by one. Then try the same experiment (gently) while holding your nose shut and you will see that air is normally passing through the nose when we produce the sounds represented by "m," "n," and "-ng."

In English, the sounds commonly represented by "l" and "r" (which are technically called **liquids**) can function either as consonants or as vowels. In some languages, the nasals also can function as vowels. For instance, in English, the liquids are consonants in the words "led" and "red," but have a vocalic (vowel) function in the second syllable of words like "diver" and "table." In addition, there exists in English a class of sounds that is not clearly either a vowel or a consonant. The sounds in this class are commonly referred to as **glides**. They are commonly represented by "y" and "w" in words like "yet" and "wet." They also include the ending sounds in words like "how," "boy," "buy," and "may." The changing vocalic elements that move from a fairly distinct vowel sound to a glide are commonly called **diphthongs**. Interestingly, when the transitional element comes at the beginning as in "yet" rather than "say," the term diphthong is not always applied. But glides also occur in words like "Hugh." Can you hear the "y" sound after the "H"? Try contrasting "Hugh" with "who." The word "who" has a simple vowel, but "Hugh" has a diphthong.

The liquids, glides, and other sounds like them are called **approximants** in view of the fact that the main articulators involved in the production of these sounds tend to come close together without completely closing off the passage of air. They are distinct from **fricatives** because the approximants are not mainly marked by friction as the air passes through. Examples of fricatives include the sounds commonly represented by the letters "f," "v," "th" as in "think" and "this," "s," "z," "sh" as in "shell" and "zh" as in "Zhivago," "ch" as in "church," "j" as in "just," and "h" as in "hot." (See a more complete description of the rich variety of sounds of the languages of the world at the website of the International Phonetic Alphabet, 1993–1996, retrieved January 28, 2006 from http://www2.arts.gla.ac.uk/IPA/fullchart.html.)

The Process of Differentiation Is Constructive and Analytical

In addition to introducing (or, possibly, reviewing) key terms and concepts concerning sounds and syllables, it is important to emphasize that, before the child can acquire even a single word, distinct syllables (or manual signs or other marks) must be noticed. How will the child tell the difference, for instance, between his or her name and other common words such as "mama," "dada," and "baba" if all these syllables sound alike? Because some of the syllables, for example, "mama" and "baba," are minimally distinct from each other, before recognizing such words the infant needs to distinguish the sound of "b" as contrasted with "m." The mystery is how a baby can notice such subtle distinctions at birth, or possibly before the baby is born.

Other species, such as cotton-top tamarin monkeys (Ramus, Hauser, Miller, Morris, & Mehler, 2000; Tincoff et al., 2005), dolphins (Kako, 1999), rats (Toro, Trobalon, & Sebastian-Galles, 2003), and certainly some birds such as the gray parrot (see Pepperberg & Gordon, 2005 and their references) and mynahs (D. K. Oller, 2000) may be able to discriminate some of the sounds and attributes of speech, but they do not seem to show special interest in them without intensive training by human instructors (D. K. Oller, 2000; Sebeok & Umiker-Sebeok, 1980; Tomasello, 2003; Tomasello & Call, 2004). Some birds, such as parrots and mynahs, can produce the sounds of speech, but, again, do not seem to do so naturally without the intensive assistance of a human trainer. Pepperberg and Gordon (2005) have suggested that a gray parrot can even understand abstract concepts such as numbers and the notion of zero. However, so far, no talking parrot has gone off into the jungle and taught all the other parrots to count and talk or to reason about abstract concepts.

To distinguish his or her own name from other words, the infant must evidently do some distinctively human work. Syllables (or other signs) of speech must be distinguished not only from other sounds but also from each other. To accomplish this work, it is essential for the child to begin to notice differences between syllables and their constituent sounds. The child must detect differences between linguistic forms to discover their associations with things, persons, and events. The mystery of how human infants accomplish this feat has resulted in a vast literature filled with many controversies. Among them is the controversy over how much of the development of speech and language is owed to the innate abilities of the child and how much of it is owed to the special assistance that the child gets from the **language community**?

Must We Choose Nature or Nurture? Or, Do They Cooperate?

Is the human being specially designed for speech and language as Noam Chomsky (1975, 2002) has argued? Chomsky wrote:

> some intellectual achievements, such as language learning, fall strictly within biologically determined cognitive capacity. For these tasks, we have "special design," so that cognitive structures of great complexity and interest develop fairly rapidly and with little if any conscious effort (1975, p. 27).

Is there an innate **language acquisition device** (LAD) or a specially designed language capacity or faculty, that only humans have in their **genome**? Chomsky (2002) has claimed that there is. He argues that human languages are like the heart, brain, or other organs that develop on a biological program. We don't learn to have a heart or a brain. Similarly, Chomsky says that we don't learn to have languages. They just naturally develop because of our genetic inheritance, or innate abilities.

But what role is played by experience? Others have insisted that a major role is played by learning (Dominey & Dodane, 2004; Skoyles, 1998) through the assistance of the language community. Even before birth, the human infant is exposed to a rich system of speech sounds produced by others. It seems that nature cooperates with nurture. When one of us was a child of about three (can you guess which one?), when assigned a task such as picking up toys, he or she would enlist help by saying, "Let's corroporate!" Interestingly, this creative combination of similar words suggests three aspects of the social processes that enter into normal speech and language development: cooperation, collaboration, and corroboration.

Without cooperative interaction language acquisition is hardly possible at all. To acquire a language we need to interact with people who know the language we are trying to learn. We must cooperate. Some tasks, however, are too difficult for us by ourselves. Like the infant walking in Figure 1–2, we need a collaborator. In doing so, the persons who cooperate and collaborate also corroborate (verify and confirm) each other's understanding and abilities. The doctor who assists the newborn in taking a few steps both assists the infant and verifies (demonstrates) the infant's ability to do this. Even more obviously when we agree on our understanding of linguistic forms and their meanings, we corroborate the shared forms and meanings of our language. We join, affirm, test, verify, and constantly renew our language. By learning a language of a community, we also become members of that community. All of this depends on certain kinds of social interactions governed by shared "rules or norms" as Piaget (1950, p. 163) described them.

For all of these reasons, Jerome Bruner (1983) argued that in addition to the innate **language faculty**, the underlying language capacity stressed by Chomsky, there must also be a **language acquisition support structure** (LASS). Bruner contended that "every LAD needs his LASS." In fact, no one, not even an adult, can learn any particular language without assistance from the community of language users that happen to speak the **target language**. Imagine the difficulty of someone trying to speak Cajun French, Russian, Mandarin, or pick any language you like, without ever having heard it before? How could anyone invent the syllables and words of Russian and relate them to their usual meanings? How would anyone be able to guess the word for "cake" in any language, or how to say "good-bye," say, in Mandarin?

In making his case for the LASS, Bruner followed others. The famous Russian psychologist Lev Vygotsky (1934/1962; 1930-1935/1978) argued that language development in certain respects must precede the development of speech. For instance, no child learns to produce his or her name without first coming to recognize it when produced by someone else. More importantly, every child depends on other language users to gain access to the syllables, words, phrases, clauses, and other forms of any given language. Vygotsky inspired his student, A. R. Luria, to study the relationship between overt speech and the control of behavior. In one of Luria's experiments (Luria & Yudovich, 1959), children of about two years were asked to push a button when a green light came on but not to push the button when the red light came on. Until the children were able to say the commands "Push!" and "Don't push!" out loud, they performed at chance levels. They pushed the button randomly irrespective of whether the green or red light was on. However, after they became able to issue the commands to themselves, they were able to perform the task very well. The experiment showed that there is a close relation between our ability to speak and our ability to control our own actions. In this way, as Vygotsky insisted, thought and language are intimately related.

Along this same line, Einstein (1941/1956) observed, "We might be inclined to attribute to the act of thinking complete independence from language if the individual formed or were able to form his concepts without the verbal guidance of his environment. Yet most likely the mental shape of an individual, growing up under such conditions, would be very poor. Thus we may conclude that the mental development of the individual and language are linked together" (p. 112). These are arguments to which we will return many times in this book.

Milestones of Development and the
Zone of Proximal Development

Perhaps Vygotsky's most important contribution to the study of early child development was his idea of the **zone of proximal development** (ZPD). Vygotsky argued that at every stage of development there are certain actions a child can accomplish without assistance. However, there are significantly more advanced actions that the child can accomplish only with the assistance of a more mature individual. Vygotsky summed up the idea of the ZPD, the next level up from the milestones already achieved, in saying that with a little help the child could become "a head taller than himself" (1930-1935/1978, p. 102)—as in Figure 1-4. In other words, the child would appear to be more mature with a little help from a more competent person than he or she could appear to be without the help. Could we expect the newborn infant shown marching like a soldier in Figure 1-2 to have done this without the doctor's assistance? Yet with the doctor's help,

Figure 1–4. A picture of a child who is a head taller than himself. Meet Luke Riley, age 18 months, used by permission.

the infant is able to do at birth, something that he or she will not be able to do without assistance for about a year or more after birth.

The following is the English translation of the somewhat more technical definition of the ZPD as given by Vygotsky:

> *the distance between the actual developmental level as determined by independent problem solving and the level of potential development as determined through problem solving under adult guidance or in collaboration with more capable peers* (his emphasis, 1930–1935/ 1978, p. 86).

Looking to the Common Ground: Where the Researchers Agree

In spite of the controversies that have raged over the details of the language acquisition process, there is one fact on which competing theories have tended almost universally to agree: all of them agree more or less that the development of speech and language abilities is constructive. The newborn does not come into the world with the full set of language skills already in place. These are built up over time, a little here and a little there, and sometimes in what may appear as fits and starts with abrupt advances followed by plateaus. Sometimes, the child may seem to have acquired a more advanced level of skill only to replace it later with what seems to be a less advanced one. For instance, a child between two and three years may correctly produce mature adult forms of certain irregular past-tense verbs, such as "went," "got," "fell," and "ran," but later the child will seem to backslide to forms like "goed" or "wented," "getted" or "gotted," "falled" or "felled," "runned" or "ranned," and so forth. However, as we will see later on, in normally developing children, even the apparent fits and starts of learning, including examples of what may seem to be **backsliding**, where the child seems to lose forms previously gained, all show the constructive nature of language acquisition and use.

Jean Piaget stressed the constructive nature of social and intellectual advances in child development through his famous stages. Here we will highlight just the four major levels that Piaget distinguished. The beginning stage of the child's conceptual development, according to Piaget, was the **sensorimotor stage**. It was supposed to cover the period roughly from birth to two years. Piaget stressed that normal development of the intellect had to begin with an interaction between the child and the environment through sensations and movements. Movements of the child give rise to sensations. At the next level, roughly from ages three to seven, Piaget saw the child advancing to what he called the **preoperational stage**. The child would begin to manipulate things and persons in the environment, for example, leading someone by the hand. At the third stage of development, roughly from ages eight to eleven, Piaget described what he called the **concrete operational stage** by which the child would learn to refer to and to physically manipulate objects, or move them around. Finally, at about age 12 according to Piaget, the child would advance to what he described as the **formal operational stage**. These would be distinguished from other operations mainly by their abstractness, in other words, their logical independence from particular concrete things, persons, or events. Also, formal operations of the kind we see in mathematics, such as addition, subtraction, multiplication, and division enable us to start with a particular **concept** such as the number 4, for instance, to which we can add 10 to get 14 or we can multiply 4 by 10 to get 40, and then, by reversing these processes, we can subtract 10 from 14 to get back to 4, or we can divide 40 by 10 and get back to 4 again. In formal operations, we have what Piaget called complete logical **reversibility**.

Consistency in Usage Is Necessary

While Piaget intended to describe development from an individual psychological point of view, like Vygotsky and others, Piaget also understood that the social guidance of a community of speakers is crucial to our acquisition of language. Piaget took the social aspect of development into account in what he called the **categorical imperative**. Piaget got this principle from the philosopher Immanuel Kant (1785/1964) who insisted that we must choose to be consistent in our thoughts in order to do any thinking at all. Piaget applied Kant's rule to the social actions of cooperation and collaboration. Piaget argued that the words, phrases, and higher structures that the child is acquiring must be consistently related to experience for the child to make sense of them. For instance, how could the child possibly discover his or her own name if that name were applied willy nilly by everyone around him or her to anything and everything? Or, how would the child discover the meanings of words such as "up" and "down," or any words at all if they were not applied with any consistency?

Piaget (1950) took the idea a step further. He noted that words and ideas (1) must have some meanings that are constant (consistency of icons), (2) they need to be applied consistently (consistency of indexes), and (3) the uses of words and ideas must be shared by others (consistency of symbols) for ordinary language acquisition and communication to be possible (see S. Oller, 2005). In fact, these are principles applied in judging whether or not a child has actually acquired a meaningful word. For instance, suppose a baby says something that mama thinks sounds like the word "mama"? Is it that word? Among the important questions to ask are: Does the form the child produces consistently resemble any form used by others, that is, does it sound like "mama"? Does the child apply that form in a way that seems to be consistent with the context or activities under-way, that is, does the child say "mama" when looking at her or when she is doing something the child is observing? And, is the form in question under-stood by others consistently to have a particular meaning, that is, do others besides mama, say, siblings, dad, and grandma, recognize the child's pro-duction to have that particular meaning?

Piaget argued that the requirement of consistency in our use of words and ideas is not merely a "social obligation" but that it is a logical prerequi-site "of operational thought" (p. 163). That is, unless words and concepts are consistently associated with things, persons, and concepts language and thought as we know them would be impossible. If the symbols, "1," "2," "3," "+," and "=" could be used to mean anything at all, how could we pos-sibly ever understand that "1 + 2 = 3" is a valid equation? If words could constantly change their meanings at a whim, how would anyone know the meaning of words like "one," "two," "three," "plus," and "equals"? Or, how would we understand the underlying concepts of such words as, for exam-ple, the ideas of unity, pairing, addition, and equality?

The need for words to have consistent associations with things, per-sons, and events in experience is an idea that has a long history. Saint Augustine in 401 AD wrote that infants begin to learn language by looking to things, events, and relations pointed out by others around them. Charles S. Peirce (1868) wrote, "The child learns to understand the language; that is to say, a connection between certain sounds and certain facts becomes established in his mind" (p. 202). Later, James (1907/1995), Dewey (1916), and Piaget would elaborate on the same idea. Wittgenstein (1933–1935/1958) observed that the life of signs is in their use (p. 4). Presently, among researchers, approaches that have gained many adherents in recent years are those known as **usage-based models**. Among their proponents, Michael Tomasello (2000) says, "In usage-based models . . . all things flow from the actual usage events in which people communicate linguisti-cally with one another" (p. 61). Langacker (1987) captured the essential elements in saying that "Putting together novel expressions is something that speakers do, not grammars. It is a problem solving activity that demands a constructive effort and occurs when linguistic convention is put to use in specific circumstances" (p. 65). Usage models put the empha-sis on use and users of language.

Typically, the proponents of usage-based models see the constructive aspects of language use and development as grounded in ordinary contexts of experience (Bybee, 2000, 2001; Clark, 1996; Clark & Wilkes-Gibbs 1986; Tomasello, 2000, 2003). They also see uses of linguistic forms as somewhat **normative** and conventional. For instance, we would not normally call a hawk an eagle, or say, "baba" for "mama." In its conventional uses, a word like "mama" is typically used to refer to someone's mother. Conventionally, that is, ordinarily, hawks are distinguished from eagles. Of course, new conventions can be proposed and existing conventions may change. However, if there were no consistency of usage whatever, there could be no languages, and without languages, thought, reasoning, and human communication as we know them would be impossible (Einstein, 1941; J. Oller, 2005). As a result, any satisfactory explanation of language acquisition is forced to rely to a considerable extent on the idea that many of the conventions of any given language must be relatively consistent and dependable. Otherwise that language could not be learned or known by anyone.

Doubt, Surprise, and Conflict as Motivators

Among the interesting findings of research on usage-based models of language acquisition is the discovery that language is a social phenomenon from start to finish. This fact was emphasized by Peirce, Vygotsky, Bruner, and others. Although Piaget tended to view the developing child from a psychological point of view as an individual, Piaget also took account of the fact that speech and language development are normative and social. An interesting part of that social aspect is contained in the process that Piaget called **disequilibration**—a characteristic of any social situation that becomes problematic because of doubt, surprise, or conflict. In problematic situations, the developing learner is often prodded by the problem itself to figure out a new way to think or act. For this reason, problematic situations push the child toward new ways of representing things and to new levels of learning. They prod the child to advance the zone of proximal development. An example from Travis Tomasello at 20 months was "Danny hit me tennis-racket!" recorded by her father Michael in a diary record of her advancing language skills (Tomasello, 1992). Her father wrote that he recorded this particular utterance "because this was a sentence on the cutting edge of her competence" (p. 32). It is evident from this example, and many others like it, that the zone of proximal development is moved ahead in large part by motivating elements of doubt, surprise, and conflict.

The social aspect of communication is crucial to many of the advances that must occur. Piaget wrote, "the child first seeks to avoid contradicting himself when he is in the presence of others" (p. 163). Peirce (1868, p. 202) explained the key idea with an example: "A child hears it said that the stove is hot. But it is not, he says." Now, suppose the child is not touching the hot stove yet but does the experiment of reaching out and touching it. Or, say the child touches the glowing cigarette lighter after being warned that it will hurt. As a result of such experiments, the child is apt to reconsider the way he or she supposed things were before the experiment. When this happens, the testimony of others takes on new meaning and the importance of the agreement (consistency) of words with facts also gains in importance. In this way, Peirce argued the child gets **self-awareness**. He or she comes to realize that different points of view are possible.

The need to recognize the distinct viewpoints of persons other than ourselves is impressed on us mainly because of conflicts that we have with others who do not always share our points of view. In fact, recent research by Dickinson and Givón (2000) demonstrates that our memories of the past, and especially of discourse commenting on the past, are closely linked to the persons who were involved and their attitudes. For example, assuming you have viewed the press conference involving Colin Powell and Kofi Annan that we referred to earlier in this chapter (see the link on the DVD-ROM to http://www.un.org/webcast/sg2004.html), what do you remember best about it? What images come to mind? What words and phrases? Do you remember the expressions on the faces of the two main speakers? Do you remember the accents of the speakers? The accent and demeanor of the female reporter? Was she an American or a Brit? What was Powell's reaction to her? Did he agree with the point of view she seemed to be expressing? And what about Annan?

Communication Is Complex

All the foregoing is probably more complex than you may have imagined it to be up to now. You probably never thought of the grammatical structures (nouns and verbs, agents, actions, and objects) underlying the simple acts of sucking, or walking. However, grammatical structures underlie all intentional acts. For instance, consider the Webcast of the United Nations press conference that took place a few days after the tsunami that occurred in the Indian Ocean on December 25, 2004 (see the link on the DVD-ROM http://www.un.org/webcast/sg2004.html retrieved on January 28, 2006). In the Webcast, United States Secretary of State Colin Powell and United Nations Secretary General, Kofi Annan are meeting with members of the press on the worldwide effort to respond to the unprecedented disaster claiming tens of thousands of lives.

Consider the complexity of the sign systems that are involved in this mature level of discourse. Notice that actions of looking, pointing, gesturing, facial expressions, and changing of turns are important to the comprehension of the discourse that is underway. It is easy to see that the initial remarks of the two main speakers at the press conference are vastly more complex than the actions underlying an infant's sucking of its thumb.

In the press conference, there are lengthy statements referring to past, present, and future events. There are two turns by Kofi Annan and Colin Powell in that order that we would call "speeches" or "statements." These longer turns in building the discourse are followed by interactive exchanges where members of the press raise questions that are addressed to one or the other of the two speakers. Notice that when a member of the press is recognized to speak, in other words, to ask a question or make a comment, the two main speakers (Powell and Annan) look toward that person.

These interactions show that among the main elements of the complex discourse are the persons who produce and understand it. We call these persons the **interlocutors**. Typically, there are at least two interlocutors: a *speaker* and a *listener*. We say that the speaker occupies the **first position** (and is the grammatical **first person**) of the discourse and the listener occupies the **second position** (and is the grammatical **second person**). These participants are active and may change positions. That is, a listener may become a speaker and vice versa. In addition, there may be many other interlocutors who overhear the discourse and who may interpret some or all of it, but who are not actively producers of any of it. As observers of the press conference, for example, we occupy a **third position** (or we play the role of grammatical **third persons**) as being in the same world where the tsunami and the press conference occurred, and yet we did not actively contribute to the shaping of the discourse in the press conference.

Looking back to the example, notice that when either Secretary Powell or Annan responds to a question, the tendency is to look back and forth between the person who asked the question and the larger audience. One questioner asked of Mr. Powell (beginning at 15 minutes and 55 seconds into the press conference and ending at 16:13): "Both the Secretary and yourself have emphasized the need to be in this for the long term, but isn't there a danger that once the limelight fades, once the interest goes away, that the commitment of certain countries, the powerful and rich countries, would dwindle, such as what happened in places such as Haiti, Afghanistan, and others?" Consider the number of distinct persons, countries, events, time frames, and changing states of affairs that are referred to in this one question. Among the referents that are either referred to indirectly or directly, there are the two persons standing at the front: Mr. Powell and Mr. Annan. There is the understanding that the questioner and those questioned are not only referring to each other but also to the tsunami of December 25, 2004 and to its victims. The questioner is also referring indirectly to the international response to the tsunami. There are the countries referred to loosely as "rich" and "powerful." These phrases probably include as referents, the United States and the United Kingdom. Perhaps also, Japan and the major European nations. There is a vague reference to the wars, strife, and other disasters in Afghanistan, Haiti, and "others," no doubt including Iraq and perhaps other countries of the Middle East. There is a reference to the international interest ("limelight") in the events associated with the tsunami at the time of the press conference. Also the speaker suggests that all of these elements referred to are in a changing dynamic relation over time that will probably have certain consequences.

Notice that some of the events referred to have already happened. The tsunami took place six days earlier. Many relief efforts are already underway at the time of speaking. Other events have not yet happened but are expected in the future by the questioner. For instance, interest in the tsunami victims has not yet faded according to her but possibly will in the future. She emphasizes the fact that she thinks this is likely by using a negative form of the question, ". . . isn't there a danger that . . . ?" She asserts in the way she asks her question that the interest in other international crises has faded in the past and also that the same thing could well happen in the future with respect to the tsunami that is already on the table for discussion. The whole press conference only lasted 19 minutes and 25 seconds, and the question took just 18 seconds.

In addition to the complexities of the linguistic forms used, consider the facial expressions, bodily movements, eye movements, and head turns. Notice that they are closely coordinated with the words, phrases, clauses, and higher structures of discourse that are being used by the interlocutors. We also want to point out the importance of turn-taking, how the role of producer (the first position) of the discourse shifts from one person to another and how the whole interaction seems almost to have a life of its own. Discourse is not the product of any one person. It is a team sport as is commonly observed. Discourse has a dynamic quality that involves the people who produce it as well as the events they are talking about and the context of their interaction.

Why We Start with Prebirth Fetal Activity

Although it would be possible to jump into the subject matter at the level of mature discourse, it is a lot easier to tackle the earliest sign systems of a baby in the womb than it is to handle the full complexity of adult discourse. For this reason, we start with the developing human embryo and follow the course of development from there forward. We are especially interested in the milestones that normal human infants will reach on a fairly regular schedule as they advance toward maturity. These milestones are important indicators of normal child development. When they appear on schedule, we can be confident that the child is advancing normally.

If they do not occur on the expected schedule, we may expect further difficulties in language and learning later on. The milestones along the way are indicators of normal or abnormal progress.

Although different normal children may advance at different rates, and although they may develop different skills in different ways, the milestones of development of greatest interest to child development specialists are those that have to occur in a natural logical sequence. For instance, if sucking has to occur for the child to receive nourishment, the sucking response must precede subsequent developments such as chewing and swallowing. Normally, chewing and swallowing will develop well before the acquisition of the first meaningful word, which will not occur until near or after the end of the child's first year of life outside the womb.

In fact, the most important milestones for the study of normal speech and language development are steps in a well-determined sequence. Each milestone is preceded by a surprisingly long and complex sequence of steps in development that make the achievement of that particular milestone possible. Typically, each milestone will also be followed by other developments which the milestone in question makes possible. The milestones of speech and language development are not exceptional. They depend on prior developments and lead to other later developments.

For instance, the sucking response cannot occur unless the neuromuscular systems that make it possible are already in place. Similarly, the normal (hearing) infant cannot notice distinct words represented in the syllables and rhythms of speech until the forms of speech are differentiated from other environmental sounds, for example, speech sounds must be distinguished from the scraping of a chair as it is moved on a hard surface, the screech of brakes, the sound of a siren or horn, the gurgling, sucking, and other noises that the infant may make. For a deaf infant, the movements of the body, hands, and face associated with **signed language** must be distinguished from other incidental movements, for example, walking around, picking things up, moving things around, and so forth. Among the distinguishing features of signed languages are its speed, its articulate changes, and its rhythms. They resemble speech more than any other kinds of movements. Infants can tell the difference.

When Development Goes Wrong

Understanding the milestones of normal speech and language development is essential to the study of communication disorders. It is also essential to the study of all the related diseases, injuries, and other causative factors that can produce disorders. How will we recognize the disorder if we do not know what the expected milestones of development are? How will the pediatricians, speech-language pathologists, special-education teachers, hearing specialists, and other practitioners correctly advise their patients or clients if they themselves do not know how development is expected to proceed? All too often parents have taken a doctor's advice to "just give the child some more time" to overcome his stuttering, or to start talking, or to take an interest in social relationships, or to start walking, or whatever, only to find out later on that they missed the opportunity to start a program of therapy or intervention that might have made a huge difference for the child. For reasons we have already noted, in the case of sign systems and their development, if early milestones are not achieved, later development may be threatened.

Not only is understanding normal speech and language development critical to knowing when and how to intervene and provide therapy as needed, but it is also crucial to our understanding of the nature and severity of the difficulties and disorders that may arise. Although some difficulties are minor with only localized and short-term effects, other problems are more serious and may have far-reaching global effects. For example, an articulatory difficulty such as lisping (substituting something like the "th" sound in "thumb" for the "s" sound in "sound") may be easy to correct in most cases and not very damaging to speech comprehension even if it is left uncorrected. Most adults know someone who is intelligent and highly capable in the business world who still has the remnants of a childhood lisp in the surface-forms of his or her speech. Other problems such as an infant's persistent failure to make eye contact, or the substantial loss of words that were previously learned but seem to disappear, or a sudden onset of unresponsiveness to social interactions, may be indicative of a more serious problem.

One of the reasons for studying normal speech and language development intensively is to be able to differentiate levels of severity within and across distinct difficulties and disorders that may arise. Even beyond that objective, the study of normal speech and language development can also contribute, at least indirectly, to the determination of causes of difficulties and disorders. To know if a treatment is producing improvement, we need to know how to recognize the improvement when we see it. How will this be possible without a good understanding of the normal milestones of speech and language development? Without a good understanding of normal development, we will be hard pressed to know when a given treatment for a difficulty or disorder is producing good results, having no effect, or possibly causing harm. Researchers along with educators, parents, and clinicians need a good understanding of normal speech and language development if they are to assess theories of what may cause difficulties and also what may make them better.

You Can Make a Difference

For anyone working in any area of child development or early education, and especially for those interested in communication difficulties and disorders, there are three main reasons to study normal speech and language development:

■ To be able to diagnose and recognize difficulties as well as to judge their severity.

■ To figure out how to intervene, where to focus attention in teaching or therapy.

■ To assess the effectiveness of treatments and sensibly evaluate theories of causation.

The study of normal speech and language disorders is especially important with respect to the discovery of the causes of disorders, especially severe disorders that presently remain unsolved mysteries. Do they have to remain that way? Can students starting out in an introductory course hope to make a difference or to help unravel some of the remaining mysteries? Interestingly, students at the introductory level in the study of normal speech and language disorders are roughly in the position of most parents who discover that their child has a difficulty.

Not many years ago, Augusto Odone and his wife Michaela, a couple of ordinary parents who were destined to become famous in a way that no parents would choose for themselves, discovered that one of their children was not progressing normally. Eventually their son, Lorenzo, was diagnosed with **adrenoleukodystrophy** (ALD), a rare childhood disorder that is linked to a defective gene. The disease attacks the **myelin** sheath that insulates the long fibers of the brain and spinal column (see the *Milestones Student DVD-ROM* for a link to the Myelin Project, 2002, retrieved January 28, 2006 from http://www.myelin.org/index.htm; also see information about the movie, *Lorenzo's Oil*, linked to the same site at http://www.myelin.org/themovie.htm). A major motion picture was made about the lives of these courageous individuals. It starred Nick Nolte as Augusto Odone and Susan Sarandon as Michaela.

In the film, as the disease progresses, Lorenzo loses one function after another. Augusto becomes hardened in his search for a cure. Michaela devotes herself to her wide-eyed son who loses the capacity to walk and talk. The loss of the power to breathe looms in his future. The Odones, however, in the film and in real life, refused to accept the medical **prognosis** that Lorenzo's situation was hopeless. Sarandon received an Oscar for her role as Michaela, and the truth of the matter is that the Odones made a huge difference. Without medical training, not knowing what they were up against, and contrary to all that they were told, the Odones refused to give up hope. They clashed with the doctors, the researchers, and even the support groups supposed to help people in their situation. The movie is appropriately titled, *Lorenzo's Oil*, with reference to the oil discovered by the Odones that slows (or halts) the deterioration in persons who already have the disease. It seems, in some cases, to indefinitely prevent persons who have the genetic disposition for the disease from becoming symptomatic.

Could someone reading this book have a similar impact? Consider the mystery of the fastest growing class of communication disorders at this present time. These are the **autism spectrum disorders** (ASDs). In the most severe instances, the affected individual either loses or never attains the ability to recognize other persons, or to acquire a language, and is apt to engage in stereotypical behaviors referred to as "hand-flapping" or "hand-waving." At the present time, the **diagnosis** of ASDs is 10 times more frequent than it was just 10 years ago. Is the diagnosis more common now because of changing levels of awareness or because the definition has been broadened? Or is something else causing what some are now calling an epidemic (for example, see the NBC series, Autism Speaks, retrieved January 281, 2006 from http://www.autismspeaks.org/founders.php)?

It is widely acknowledged that the number of individuals currently being diagnosed with autism spectrum disorders is much higher than it was in the past (see Muhle, Trentacoste, & Rapin, 2004). Prior to 1980 autism was occurring in about 1 person in 30,000. Now the Centers for Disease Control (2005; see http://www.cdc.gov/ncbddd/factsheets/asd.pdf visited on August 20, 2005) estimates that "between two and six of every 1,000 children born may have an ASD [autism spectrum disorder]." One proposal that is being followed closely in the research, concerns the possible impact of certain poisons, for example, mercury, that has been injected or otherwise introduced into the body. See the University of Calgary Faculty of Medicine (2002) "How Mercury Causes Brain Neuron Degeneration," retrieved January 28, 2006 from http://commons.ucalgary.ca/mercury/). The video at that website (and related research) shows that minute quantities of mercury (measured in parts per billion) can strip vital **proteins**, from the microscopic tubes that insulate nerve fibers. Because this insulation is critical to sensation, movement, and normal cognitive functioning, researcher are now asking if mercury poisoning in combination with certain genetic tendencies may be part of the reason for the rising incidence of autism spectrum disorders (see Bernard, Enayati, Redwood, Roger, & Binstock 2001; Bradstreet, Geier, Kartzinel, Adams, & Geier, 2003; J. Oller, November, 2004).

Summing Up and Looking Ahead

In this chapter we have introduced the purposes, methods, and some of the subject matter of the whole book. We have explained why we begin with the life of the baby before it is born. In Chapters 2 through 12, we will move on through the various milestones of sensory, cognitive, and linguistic development, especially language acquisition. We will consider literacy, reasoning, maturity, and aging. We will also cover second language learning and educational testing as they affect and are affected by normal speech use and language acquisition. We often refer to sign systems of Deaf cultures as linguistic systems that manifest many of the same aspects seen in speech and all the features that are common to the languages of the world. All along the way, our main concern is the development of speech and language, but we will also examine closely the iconic and indexical systems that must be developed to make it possible for speech and language systems to progress normally. In subsequent chapters, we will see that the three major sign systems (iconic, indexical, and symbolic) in various combinations make up all the rest of the signs that are of interest in our study.

STUDY AND DISCUSSION QUESTIONS

1. What are some of the key milestones of normal growth and especially of speech and language development that you learned about in this chapter?

2. In what way is a simple act like thumb-sucking grammatically structured? What distinct elements must it involve and how are these elements related to each other? Can you do a similar analysis for an action like walking around the wall of the womb, or what mothers sometimes describe as turning somersaults in the womb?

3. In what way do actions and experiences in the womb prepare the infant for life after birth?

4. Why does a problematic situation put the developing infant in a frame of mind where an advance in mental capabilities is called for? Can a doubt arise or have any impact if the child is not aware of it? How can an infant begin to appreciate the viewpoints of others if they never contrast with his or her own viewpoints?

5. Can you give some examples of iconic signs as distinct from indexical ones? Indexes as distinct from symbols?

6. What are the most important icons in the child's experience in the womb? At birth? Why are some icons more salient (more noticeable) than others? What factors cause the baby to single out certain icons above others? For instance, why would the baby notice its own hands sooner than most other objects? Why is the baby's mother or caregiver a salient entity? What role does movement, conflict, discomfort, hunger, and so forth, play in making these icons salient?

CHAPTER 2

Language Development Even Before Birth

 OBJECTIVES

By studying this chapter you will:

1. See evidence of consciousness, self-awareness, intelligence, memory, emotions, and dreaming in babies before they are born;

2. Learn about the integration of the major sensory-motor systems of signs that infants are beginning to develop even before birth;

3. Differentiate more completely the major sign systems: sensory, sensory-motor, and sensory-motor-linguistic;

4. Review arguments for and against emotional expressions in the womb (does the baby smile before birth? what does the baby's smile mean?);

5. Explore the development of the senses of touch (including balance), taste, smell, hearing, and sight in the baby before birth; and

6. Discover evidence that babies evidently begin to distinguish forms of their native language before they are born.

KEY TERMS

Here are some key terms and concepts that you can learn more about. See the Glossary for a definition of each one and watch for it in **bold print** in this chapter:

afferent nerves
amniocentesis
amniotic fluid
amplitude
anterior canals
attenuation
central nervous system
cephalocaudal
cognitive
decibel
efferent nerves
endogenous
exogenous
frequency
gestational age
handedness
hertz
horizontal canals

logarithm
mimetic
nonlinear
pitch
placental barrier
posterior canals
postnatal
prenatal
rapid eye movements (REM)
semicircular canals
sound pressure level (SPL)
stress-timed
syllable-timed
synthetic speech
translucent
umami
vestibular

It seems that milestones of infant development keep being pushed back farther and farther into the **prenatal** stages. Evidently there is life before birth. Consciousness, intelligence, and memory are certainly present before birth. Milestones that used to be associated with life after birth, the post-natal period, are increasingly being pushed back into the prenatal time in the womb. Milestones that are achieved earlier than previously believed include advances in (1) sensory systems, (2) sensory-motor systems, and (3) language. Although conception and birth themselves seem fixed relatively to each other, birth coming about 40 weeks after conception (give or take a few weeks), the major events from conception to birth keep being adjusted backward, increasingly toward conception (see Meltzoff, 1999). How old does the baby in Figure 2–1 look to you? Does it appear that the baby is standing up? Taking steps? See the moving video of this same infant, Video of a Fetus at 12 Weeks of Gestation on the *Milestones*

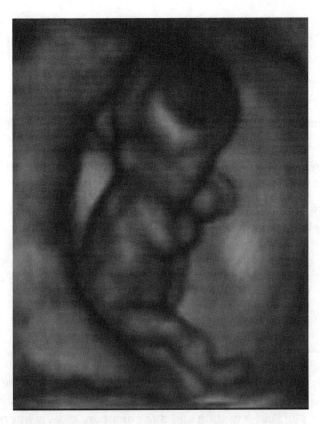

Figure 2–1. Baby in the womb at 12 weeks gestation— the first trimester. See *Video of a Fetus at 12 Weeks of Gestation* (Used by permission of Dr. Stuart Campbell at London's Create Health Clinic. Also see their website, http://www.createhealth.org/)

Student DVD-ROM (reproduced by permission from Dr. Stuart Campbell at Create Health Clinic in London). Is that possible at 12 weeks after conception? Let us consider some of the key milestones in terms of the three main sign systems of icons, indexes, and symbols.

Sensory Milestones

Looking toward normal speech and language development after birth, when it comes to sensory milestones, researchers and theoreticians have been mainly concerned with the baby's sensitivity to the sounds and rhythms of speech. However, all the senses seem to be tightly interrelated during prenatal development. Some of the key questions concerning the senses have included:

- When can the human baby first detect sounds? When can the baby first show sensitivity to loud noises or to voices? When can the baby distinguish mother's voice? Her language?

- What about light? What about bright sunlight, for example, when mom is sunbathing?

- Pressure? When is the baby first sensitive to touch? What can the baby feel?

- When does the baby's sense of taste develop? How can it be measured?

- How about the sense of smell? Is it possible for the baby to smell in the womb?

Keeping in mind the discussion in Chapter 1, these milestones all pertain to the child's ability to perceive qualities of icons through the senses.

Sensory-Motor Milestones

Interestingly, with our present technologies most of the sensory milestones achieved by prenatal babies can only be detected after the baby begins to move. As we will see, sensation and movement are closely interrelated, but they must logically be distinguished and they are known to involve distinct neural pathways. Sensations come to us primarily along what are called **afferent nerves**. These fibers send signals to the **central nervous system**, that is, the spinal cord and brain. Bodily movements (voluntary and involuntary), by contrast, must be initiated by distinct neurons or **efferent nerves**. These fibers carry signals from the central nervous system to the extremities. In spite of their differences, the afferent and efferent signals interact in important ways. If it were not for sensations, movements could not come under our control at all. There could be no voluntary movements in the complete absence of sensation. Also, without movement, it is difficult to differentiate sensations associated with different parts of the body. For instance, have you ever been lying so comfortably, about half asleep, that in order to tell where your right hand was you needed to move it? The sensory and motor systems are intimately interrelated.

During embryological development the brain and spinal cord function like a communication network on a large construction site. Until communication systems are in place, little construction is possible. With respect to sensory-motor development, studies of developing embryos and fetuses demonstrate that neural impulses within the developing organism can either originate inside the organism, in which case they are referred to as **endogenous**, or they can come through the senses to the central nervous system, in which case the signals are referred to as **exogenous**, meaning that they are generated from outside the organism. J. Z. Young (1978) suggested that, as the genome guides the details of the development of the chemistry and structure of an organism, the developing central nervous system is important to the development of the body and its sensory-motor functions. Damage to one side of the brain results in stunting of the opposing side of the body, that part of the body under the motor control of the damaged or underdeveloped portion. More recent work (see Penn & Shatz, 1999) has shown how signals generated from within the fetus interact with information coming from the senses to make possible the building of precise neural circuits. As a result, we must conclude that the development of sensory systems is activity dependent. For this reason, we do not talk about the development of independent sensory systems, but rather we deal with sensory-motor development. This is consistent with Piaget's terminology, although the development we are talking about here occurs prior to birth.

With respect to sensory-motor milestones here are some of the key questions that have been asked about early development. When can we expect to first see the baby do any of the following?

- Stretch, yawn, open its eyes, or squint.

- Kick, stand up, or make breathing movements.

- Make stepping movements.

- Make rhythmic movements in response to sounds.

■ Express or show sensitivity to human emotions, for instance, smile, cry, leap for joy.

Once again, looking back to the discussion in Chapter 1, we can see that these milestones are most closely related to indexical signs.

Linguistic/Symbolic/Cognitive Milestones

At the center of all theories of intellect, we find social interactions. At the center of those interactions we find linguistic abilities. However, Harvard professor Howard Gardner (1983, 1993) has argued that there are other kinds of abilities besides language. He has proposed seven additional kinds of intelligence including: (1) ability to reason with numbers (logico-mathematical intelligence); (2) the ability to understand scenes and use space (picture intelligence); (3) ability to move with grace and balance (bodily kinesthetic intelligence); (4) ability to understand and produce music (musical intelligence); (5) ability to get on with others (interpersonal intelligence); (6) ability to know and understand yourself (intrapersonal intelligence); and (7) being able to understand the world around you (naturalist intelligence).

However, verbal abilities remain front and center. Try, for instance, to imagine the meaning of a clause such as "the current population of the world" without relying on language. Or, try to think of the meaning, or imagine how you could figure out the meaning initially, of an equation such as "$E = mc^2$" without using any words. Try to think of the meaning of prime numbers without using any words or word meanings. Try to think of any number from 1 to 10,000,000 without using any words or word meanings. Or, try to imagine any abstract concept such as the day before yesterday, or 10 days from tomorrow, or a planet beyond Jupiter, and so forth. While overt speech may not be necessary to thinking, the meanings and concepts underlying words are so crucial to thinking that it is highly doubtful that any thought at all is possible except through such meanings and concepts. And yet, how can a child gain access to concepts and meanings without words? Is it necessary to acquire a language in order to acquire human intelligence?

Lev Vygotsky (1934/1962) was among the most influential thinkers of modern times to argue that thought critically depends on language. C. S. Peirce (1868) and Albert Einstein (1941) expressed essentially the same view. Peirce did not insist that there could be no thought without words, but he did argue that, without *some means of representation*, thought itself would be impossible. To understand the essence of his argument, just ask yourself how you might have a thought whose content could not be represented in any way whatever.

With respect to the prenatal period of development with respect to symbolic representations and meanings, here are some of the questions that have been considered:

- When does the first evidence of emotional reactions in the infant begin to appear?

- When does the baby begin to respond differentially to distinct voices? To tell mother's voice from the voice of others?

- When does the baby first tell the sounds and rhythms of its mother's language from other languages?

- When does the baby begin to show evidence of dreaming?

Again, recalling Chapter 1, the milestones referred to in these questions all are about symbols. It is, presumably, impossible to perform any of the actions without relying on abstract symbols to a considerable extent.

Life in the Womb

In the previous chapter we saw that a newborn can take a few steps standing up with the assistance of the doctor (Figure 1–2). Should it surprise us then to discover that a baby can stand upright and take steps in the womb during its first trimester of development? This is evidently possible and, in fact, common. (See the Video of a Fetus at 12 Weeks of Gestation on the *Milestones Student DVD-ROM* referred to above in relation to Figure 2–1, and see additional 3D and 4D ultrasound scans retrieved January 28, 2006 from http://www.createhealth.org/ January 21, 2006).

Until about the middle 1920s, when Peiper (1925) and Forbes and Forbes (1927) recorded evidence of fetal movements in response to loud noises, it was common for expectant mothers to be told that their babies would not be able to hear or see at birth. These ideas were mistaken but similar thinking persists to some extent even today. For example, among the most widely used textbooks for undergraduates majoring in communication disorders, special education, and related fields of study, it is still common to find statements suggesting that the smile of an infant may have little or nothing in common with the smile of an adult. The argument for this thinking goes back to ideas common in the middle of the 20th century. In his inaugural lecture at the University of Nijmegen in the Netherlands in 1947, the distinguished psychologist, Buytendijk (1947/2002) said:

> When a parrot says "good morning" . . . this is only acoustically similar to the same greeting by a human being. Just so the first smile of the

child might be only seemingly similar to the smile of the adult. This possibility needs serious consideration because adults too can show mimic expressions which do not really possess the expressive meaning that they seem to portray (p. 16).

Smiles during the time of Buytendijk's lecture were commonly explained as "gas pains," or something similar (Sullivan & Lewis, 2003).

Four-Dimensional Ultrasound Images

More recent technologies have made it possible for us to view the developing human baby during its life in the womb. No doubt future technologies will enrich the picture that is already emerging from four-dimensional ultrasound images, that is, three-dimensional moving pictures. Of course, the new technology can also produce flat two-dimensional images such as the one seen in Figure 2–1. It works by bouncing a very **high-frequency** sound wave off the object to be pictured. The echo that bounces from the object can be used to create an image of the object the sound beam is pointed at. By digitizing the processing, at very brief time intervals, of various parts of the echoing beam that is reflected back from the object, it is possible to focus a moving visual image of the object. With the present technology, it is possible to achieve very fine grained, well-focused images with less than 0.3 mm of error in the actual edges of the moving object (description of the process retrieved January 28, 2006 from http://www. gemedicalsystemseurope.com/euen/rad/us/technology/msudigit.html). The result is that we can see the moving baby in the womb. These images have forced major reassessments of many common, but false, claims about the milestones of early infancy, especially during the prenatal stages of development.

Many milestones that were supposed to be attained quite a while after birth have been shown to occur in normal infants during gestation. Even the term, *fetus*, is now being applied to an earlier stage of development of the baby in the womb. According to the *Oxford English Dictionary* (OED) the term *fetus* was applied from the 1300s until the middle 1800s to the stage of maturity seen just prior to birth. According to the same source, the OED, the term *embryo* was applied to the stages of development up through the fourth month. The key difference was that after the baby enters the fetal stage, all the extremities are evident and the baby looks like a human being. More recently, the period of fetal development is now considered to begin in the third month. It has been pushed back. We will see that probably quite a few additional backward adjustments are probably still needed. The developing infant does a lot of things earlier than previously supposed.

Prenatal Sensory-Motor Milestones

Although it is theoretically possible to measure some sensory responses apart from voluntary or other movements of the prenatal baby, current knowledge of sensation is generally associated with fetal movement. In fact, long before the development of computer-assisted ultrasound technologies, it was possible to detect the baby's heartbeat by about the third week. Now, with real time moving ultrasound pictures looking inside the womb voluntary movements that can be associated with sensations are detectable by about the 8th week (give or take a week) of **gestational age** (GA). Sometime between the 6th and 10th week GA the baby begins to move inside the womb. It can stretch, turn, and rotate its head. It can extend its arms and legs. The baby can touch its head, face, and mouth with its hands. The fetus can open and close its mouth and swallow at 10 weeks (Tajani & Ianniruberto, 1990). In the moving video associated with Figure 2–1, you can see a normal fetus at 12 weeks of age stretching its arms and legs and taking step-like movements. All this is taking place during a stage of development when it is difficult if not impossible for mom to distinguish the movements of the baby from her own digestive processes.

Touch and Balance

The sense of touch is developed sufficiently by the 8th week that the baby will move its hands and head to avoid a hair stroke to the cheek (Chamberlain, 1996, retrieved January 28, 2006 from http://www.birthpsychology. com/lifebefore/fetalsense.html). Later, in keeping with the **cephalocaudal** principle that development extends from the head downward and outward to the periphery, sensitivity to the stroke of a hair will extend to the genital area, the palms, and soles of the feet. As the DNA in the genome guides the details of the development of the organism, the brain and central nervous system lead the way in providing for normal sensory and sensory-motor development.

Closely associated with the sense of touch is the **vestibular** system, which involves the crucial **semicircular canals**. These develop in the inner ear in a delicately balanced relationship relative to three-dimensional space and the shape of the head. The semicircular canals, three of them on each side of the head, enable us to detect movements of the head to the left and right and up and down. These tiny connected bony pipes about 0.3 millimeters in diameter on the inside, (see Figure 2–2 where they are enlarged by about 100 times) are arranged at roughly 90 degree angles to each other so as to represent our orientation relative to the downward pull of the earth's gravity in three-dimensional space.

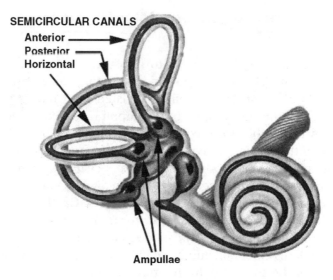

Figure 2–2. The semicircular canals of the inner ear (From http://paperairplane.mit.edu/16.423J/Space/SBE/neuro vestibular/NeuroVestibular/2_Physiology/PhysSub3.html. Reprinted by permission. Copyright © 2004 Massachusetts Institute of Technology).

The horizontal plane is represented in what are called the **horizontal canals**. They are not exactly horizontal, however. When the head is erect, these semicircles are tilted upward by about 30 degrees from the center of the ear. The center point where each of these semicircles comes together in this plane points straight toward the eye on the opposite side of the head (as shown in Figure 2-3, top). Relative to each other, these canals are at 90 degrees pointing toward the center of the head (Figure 2-3, bottom). The **anterior** (forward or front) **canals** are also at approximately 90 degree angles to each other in the vertical plane and pointed outward at roughly 45 degree angles from the center line of vision. The **posterior canals** (the ones pointing toward the back of the head in the vertical plane) project outward by approximately 45 degrees on either side of the head. This puts them at 90 degrees relative to each other in the horizontal plane (Figure 2-3, bottom). These canals are filled with a fluid that flows in one direction or the other within each canal enabling the brain to determine the orientation of the head relative to the center of gravity and to sense movements. From the range of movements of the fetus at 14 weeks GA, we can infer that the sense of touch, together with an internal representation of the body itself and its orientation is substantially in place (deVries, Visser, & Prechtl, 1985).

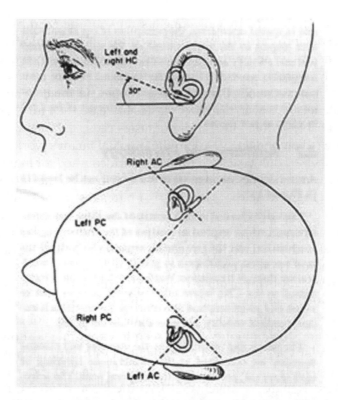

Figure 2–3. Orientation of the semicircular canals of the inner ear (From http://paperairplane.mit.edu/16.423J/Space/ SBE/neurovestibular/NeuroVestibular/2_Physiology/Phys Sub3.html. Reprinted by permission of Dr. Dava Newman. Copyright © 2004 Massachusetts Institute of Technology).

Taste and Smell

The sense of taste is greatly assisted by the sense of smell. This can be demonstrated by holding your nose and chewing alternately on a raw onion or an apple. Most of the tasted difference in this experiment will disappear showing that we rely mainly on smell to determine different tastes. We also depend somewhat on touch to determine texture. All of these sources combine to give us the sense of the flavors that we know. Tastes and smells during the baby's prenatal life result not only from the substances normally present in the **amniotic fluid** but also from other substances that may be swallowed, breathed, or absorbed by the prenatal baby's mother and that cross the barrier presented by the sack that encloses the developing fetus, that is, the **placenta**. Many chemicals, such as alcohol, caffeine, and medicines can cross over and end up in the amniotic fluid.

This can be determined by collecting a sample of the fluid by inserting a hollow needle into the placenta—a procedure called **amniocentesis**.

Evidence that the prenatal baby can taste from about the 14th week GA is mostly indirect. However, because the taste system is well formed by that point, it is assumed that the sense should be intact. There is some direct evidence, however, that sweet tastes increase the rate of swallowing in prenatal babies while bitter and sour tastes cause the rate of swallowing to decrease (Chamberlain, 1996). In the prenatal infant's world, the whole range of possible adult tastes are probably all accounted for in the amniotic fluid. These include the familiar tastes described in the terms (1) salt, (2) sour (as in citric acid), (3) sweet, (4) bitter (as in most medicines or strong coffee), and the taste called (5) **umami**. This last taste involves certain amino acids including glutamate, aspartate, and related compounds. It is associated with the flavor enhancer monosodium glutamate (also known as MSG). Umami is the primary flavor in soy sauce.

The prenatal infant is almost certainly exposed to all these possible tastes because the amniotic fluid contains them. The baby regularly breathes and swallows that fluid. Proof that substances like alcohol cross the placenta and enter the amniotic fluid is seen in experiments showing that a single ounce of vodka caused a complete halt in breathing movements in prenatal infants for between three minutes and half an hour (Fox, Steinbrecher, Pessel, Inglis, & Angel, 1978). As the alcohol wore off, breathing movements returned to normal.

The prenatal baby's sense of smell is also believed to be well established by about the 14th week GA as well. The nose is formed during weeks 11 to 15 GA. Researchers have demonstrated by analyzing samples of amniotic fluid that it contains an abundance of substances, about 120, that give off distinct odors (Schaal, Orgeur, & Rogan, 1995). It is also noteworthy that it takes many fewer molecules of a substance to produce a sensation of odor than it does to produce a sensation of taste. As a result, it is easy to see why the relatively few tastes that are possible are augmented by the many more smells that are noticeable.

We can infer, that if the prenatal baby can experience any tastes, he or she can probably smell a much greater variety of odors in the womb. The prenatal baby probably has many significant experiences involving the sense of smell. Additional empirical evidence comes from studies of fetal breathing and heart rate in response to specific substances ingested by the mother. Salvador and Koos (1989) found that the rate of breathing of prenatal infants was increased by intake of either caffeinated or decaffeinated coffee and both conditions resulted in a decrease in fetal heart rate. Additional indirect evidence that prenatal babies can smell is that newborns seem to know the odor of breastmilk even before they ever get a taste of it. The question is how the infants recognize the odor. Has learning occurred in the womb? Or, do the prenatal babies have innate knowledge of smells and tastes?

Hearing

With respect to speech and language development, researchers have been especially interested in the development of the sense of hearing during gestation. Of course, the sense of hearing may be augmented by touch and sensations of movement. This enhancement probably accounts for reports that babies at 14 weeks GA respond to a mother's cough or laughter by moving within seconds after the sound and movement occur. Research with ultrasound employing 400 fetuses showed responses to pure tones at 500 **hertz** by 16 weeks GA (Shahidullah & Hepper, 1992). The hertz unit is usually abbreviated Hz and it is a unit of frequency (or wavelength) indicating one cycle per second, as in a regular sound wave that repeats itself once per second. In a regular wave, the length of one cycle can be measured by drawing a straight line dissecting the wave through its middle and including one peak and one trough as shown in Figure 2–4. (See http:// www.keypress.com/sketchpad/javasketchpad/gallery/pages/sine_ waver.php visited January 23, 2006 for a moving illustration of sine waves.) A pure tone **pitch** of 500 Hz would repeat itself 500 times per second. The mature human ear is responsive to sounds within the range from 20 Hz to 20,000 Hz. Most of the information necessary to the perception of speech falls within the range from 100 Hz to 3000 Hz. It is surprising that the human infant at 16 weeks GA can detect any sounds at all in view of the fact that the ear is believed not to be fully constructed until about 24 weeks GA (Smotherman & Robinson, 1995). For the same reason, it should be unsurprising that frequencies outside the middle range are not yet detectible by the baby at 16 weeks GA.

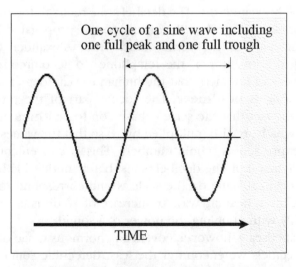

One cycle of a sine wave including one full peak and one full trough

TIME

Figure 2–4. Illustration of a sine wave.

Response of prenatal babies to pure tone sounds at different frequencies was studied under controlled conditions by Hepper and Shahidullah (1994). They presented sounds at 100, 250, 500, 1000, and 3000 Hz to human fetuses from 19 to 35 weeks GA. The sound was presented through an amplifier placed on the mother's abdomen. Interestingly, consistent with their earlier research showing responses in fetuses at 16 weeks GA, by 19 weeks GA all the babies were responsive to the 500 Hz tone. Later, the range of frequencies to which the babies responded expanded, first in the downward direction to 250 Hz, then to 100 Hz, and, only later upward to 1000 Hz and 3000 Hz. By 27 weeks GA, 96% of the babies could hear the 250 Hz and 500 Hz tones but none of them could yet hear tones at 1000 Hz or 3000 Hz. However, by weeks 33 to 35 GA all the babies could hear tones in the higher ranges and the loudness of the tones necessary to produce movement of the fetus was reduced.

Studies with babies born prematurely generally confirm these findings. However, after babies are born, their middle ears contain some amniotic fluid, which reduces hearing capacity until the fluid dissipates (Priner, Freeman, Perez, & Sohmer, 2003). This takes a few days or more after birth. This fact seemed to confirm the long-standing claim that the prenatal hearing experience is reduced because sounds have to go through mother's abdomen and through the amniotic fluid. This process of sound reduction is called **attenuation**. Researcher Anthony Decasper was quoted as saying that "the mother's voice would sound in utero . . . like Lauren Bacall speaking from behind a heavy curtain" (Palarito, 2004). It was also supposed that there should be greater attenuation at higher frequencies. For instance, the expected attenuation at 250 Hz would be less than the reduction at 2000 Hz (Hepper & Shahidullah, 1994).

The loudness, or **amplitude**, of sounds is most commonly measured in **decibels**, abbreviated "dB." The decibel scale refers to the relative power or **sound pressure level** (SPL) of any sound propagated through the air. The "-bel" part of the term comes from Alexander Graham Bell [1847–1922], the inventor of the telephone. To accommodate the huge range of degrees of loudness that the human ear can detect or withstand, the decibel scale is **nonlinear**. The "deci-" part of the term "deci-bel" comes from the fact that the scale is based on **logarithms** of numbers in the base 10, which are also multiplied by 10 so that the values on the scale are usually expressed as whole numbers. This is convenient because an increase or decrease of one decibel is just barely noticeable by the ear, so any leftover decimal value on the scale would correspond to an increase that the ear cannot hear anyway. An increase of 10 dB is usually judged to equate roughly with doubling the power of a sound.

The decibel scale, however, covers an enormous range of sound pressures. At 0 decibels we encounter the least detectible sound the ear can notice. Such a sound is just above total silence. The least detectible sound at 0 dB is about one trillion times less powerful than the sound of a jet engine up close, which registers on the scale at about 120 dB. This is the level of the loudest sound the human ear can handle without pain and immediate severe damage to our hearing. In fact, any sound above 90 dB (a noisy chainsaw) can damage our hearing if sustained over an hour or more.

For an infant in the womb, because of the relative thickness of the walls of the uterus, the tissues of the abdomen, and the density of the amniotic fluid, high-pitched sounds are attenuated (muffled and reduced in amplitude) more than low-pitched sounds. That is, sounds with longer wavelengths (lower frequencies) pass through the tissue and fluid better than the sounds of shorter wavelengths (higher frequencies). The loudness of sounds at 250 Hz would be reduced only by about 2 dB (a noticeable but very slight reduction). However at 2000 Hz the sound reaching the ear of the baby in the womb would be reduced by 26 dB (Hepper & Shahidullah, 1994). That is, the reduction at 2000 Hz would be like cutting the sound level by half, then again by half, and then almost by half a third time. The resulting power reduction at higher frequencies would be many times greater than the slight reduction at the lower frequencies.

For all these reasons, until recently it was widely believed that the sound reaching the human fetus would be much less intelligible than speech outside the womb. However, Smith, Gerhardt, Griffiths, Huang, and Abrams (2003) performed an interesting and relevant experiment with a pregnant sheep. They recorded sentences spoken outside the uterus of the ewe at intensities of 95 dB and 105 dB. They also recorded the same sentences from a microphone inside the animal's uterus through an underwater microphone and again from the inner ear of the unborn lamb inside the sheep's uterus. The three different sets of recorded sentences were scrambled and presented to 30 listeners in a random order. Listeners performed at about 99% for both the normal air recordings and the within-uterus recordings. The accuracy for the microphone made from the lamb's inner ear was 73% outside the womb and 41% inside. These results contradict the traditional claim that attenuation will greatly reduce the comprehension of speech as heard in the womb. However, there was significant attenuation for the fetal ear of the lamb. We can conclude that the sound of speech presented to a baby human in its mother's womb is highly intelligible. Although it is still unknown just how well the *human fetal ear* is able to process the speech sounds that reach it, Hepper and Shahidullah (1994) did find that babies in the womb become increasingly sensitive to sounds across the full range of frequencies between 19 and 35 weeks GA. The intensity of sound required to produce a response was reduced by about 20 to 30 dB from week 19 to week 35 GA. By the 35th week GA the babies were able to detect sounds that were only about 12.5% of the strength of the sounds needed to produce a reaction at 19 weeks GA, and the sensitivity had reached the full range of frequencies. All the foregoing results seem to weaken claims that the speech heard from within the womb is unclear or that it would be hard for anyone to understand. The reduction is measurable, but probably not sufficient to make speech unintelligible at normal levels of speaking (at about 60 dB).

Seeing

Four-dimensional (4D) ultrasound images show that babies can open their eyes by the 18th week in the womb. Until recently, researchers generally believed that the prenatal baby could not open its eyes until the 26th week GA. It was supposed that the baby's eyes were fused (stuck together) until then. However, with 4D ultrasound scanning babies have been observed opening and closing their eyes as early as the 18th week (see the BBC article retrieved January 28, 2006 from http://news.bbc.co.uk/2/hi/health/3846525.stm). Earlier, it had been maintained that the opening of the baby's eyes could not occur at all until after birth (see Chamberlain, 1996, retrieved January 28, 2006 from http://www.birthpsychology.com/life before/fetalsense.html).

There is also evidence that even before the eyes are ever opened the fetus shows sensitivity to bright light shined on the mother's abdomen. The infant's world in the womb is not always dark as might be supposed. To get an idea just how **translucent** body tissues are to bright light, try holding your fingers tightly closed over both eyes while looking directly toward the bright sun. Or, close both eyes and then, while facing a lamp or other source of light, alternately cover your eyes with your hands and then uncover them. Can you detect the changes in brightness? Similarly, the fetus in the womb is exposed to changes in brightness that are noticeable and account for the response from the infant that the pregnant mother experiences when first lying down on her back on the beach on a bright sunny day.

Symbols: Emotion, Memory, Imagination, and Language

Since the advent of ultrasound scanners in the late 1950s, researchers have been able to get an increasingly clear view of what goes on inside the womb. When ultrasound was coupled with high-speed digital processing, researchers could almost enter the womb to experience it as the infant does. It became possible not only to detect movements of the infant in response to sounds, but also to see evidence of infants expressing emotions, dreaming, and responding to the mother's voice and those of others around them.

For instance, with ultrasound images it is possible to see the fetus smiling by about the 12th week GA. (For instance, at 27 seconds into the recording retrieved from January 28, 2006 http://news.bbc.co.uk/2/hi/health/3846525.stm the infant smiles.) Theoreticians had sometimes argued that smiling is strictly **mimetic**, an imitative gesture learned by copying the smiles of other persons. It is hard to maintain that view when the smile appears on the face of a baby in the womb. Who is the baby imitating in there? On the other hand, if the smiling expression on the baby's face is caused by a gas pain, as doctors once commonly supposed, why don't gas pains cause smiling in adults?

The simpler theory is that the baby's smile in the womb has a meaning similar to smiling later on, showing that the baby is contented, happy, and secure. Gas? Probably not. At any rate, there are strong reasons to prefer simpler theories whenever they have not been strictly disproved. It is simpler to suppose that the infant's smile resembles an adult smile not only in its form but also in its meaning. In the end of his lecture on the first smile, Buytendijk (1947) reached the same conclusion about the baby's smile after birth. First, he considered all the arguments against supposing that the baby's smile might be caused by something other than a happy, secure, contented feeling. Then, he concluded the child's smile is "the awakening awareness of a felt security" (p. 24). What is more, if some theoretician wants to say that the smiles of the baby in the womb only accidentally resemble its later smiles (and those of others), then what about the other behaviors observed in the womb? Do stretching, yawning, leaping, hiccups, breathing movements, and so forth, only accidentally resemble actions that the infant will perform after birth? If so, there are many movements in the womb that just accidentally resemble, even duplicate, movements that will be performed after birth.

With the invention of new technologies for recording sounds and images inside the womb, it is as if a heavy dark curtain has been removed from the womb, and many false claims have been sharply refuted. For example, from 15 weeks GA to term (at 40 weeks GA), ultrasound images show that most infants have a preference for sucking the thumb of their right hand (Hepper, Shahidullah, & White, 1991). This suggests that the baby's **handedness** does not develop after birth as some had thought, but is either preprogrammed or else develops through motor activity in the womb. The notion that the fetus does not experience emotions is hard to maintain in the face of images of a baby smiling, or crying, or fighting the needle inserted into the womb to obtain a sample of amniotic fluid. All these are commonly observed with ultrasound images. Evidence that a prenatal infant can be traumatized by a needle stick during amniocentesis can be seen in wild fluctuations in the baby's heart rate and radical changes in breathing movements that may last for days (Chamberlain, 1996). All of these facts, together with the movements that the baby performs in the womb, suggest that the baby is able to represent the positions of its body parts, and to tell when things are going well and when they are not. If this is so, these movements must create memory traces in the baby's developing mind.

By 23 weeks GA the baby can be observed in deep sleep showing **rapid eye movements** (REM) similar to patterns observed throughout life when dreaming is occurring. Studies with premature babies born at 30 weeks GA show that essentially all their sleeping is of the REM (dream-related) kind (Birnholz, 1981). For many years, observers studying babies in REM-sleep described them as behaving like adults (Roffwarg, Muzio, & Dement 1966). If this is so, during deep sleep the baby must be imagining experience as if living through it somewhat as adults do in REM-sleep. Presumably, if the baby can perform intentional actions in the womb, the baby can imagine performing those actions in a dream. If leaping or kicking are possible at the 12th week GA, perhaps it is not unreasonable to suppose that imagined leaping and kicking are possible in dreams at week 23 GA and later.

Does the prenatal baby's imagination also present memories of mother's voice? Of music heard? Of stories read in the baby's hearing? To what extent is the mental development of the baby in the womb tuned to the social interactions going on between it and its mother and those with whom mother interacts? To what extent is it linguistic? Intriguing clues to the answers to these mysteries can be found in the current research with babies both before and very soon after their birth. For instance, Mastropieri and Turkewitz (1999) found that newborns were more apt to open their eyes in response to happy speech in the language of their mothers but did not respond to speech in a foreign language. They speculated that prenatal infants are learning the rhythms, stresses, and intonations of their native language even before birth. Rhythms of language have to do with the beat and flow of the syllables. Stress patterns have to do with the relative prominence of syllables, their loudness, length, and pitch. Syllables under stress are generally louder, longer, and higher in pitch. Intonation in English, for instance, has to do especially with the rise and fall of pitch and the tendency to differentiate the purpose of our utterances through these fluctuations. If we ask a question, for example, such as "What did you say?" the pitch usually rises throughout the utterance. In a comment such as, "Oh! That's what you said," the pitch on "Oh!" starts high and falls, and is more or less matched by the pitch over the whole next clause, "That's what you said."

With an experimental procedure judging infant interest by their sucking behavior, Moon, Cooper, and Fifer (1993) showed that two days after birth newborns have a preference for their native language. The researchers chose Spanish and English as the languages to study because they are quite distinct in their rhythms, sounds, and intonations. Spanish gives approximately equal time to each syllable, whereas English gives much greater time to syllables that are stressed. Compare the sounds and rhythms of the following sentences in <u>Spanish and English</u> (you can hear them on the DVD):

(1) Quiero decirte una cosa.

(2) I want to tell you something.

Although the two sentences have essentially the same meanings, they sound very different. The mothers of the babies in Moon et al. (1993) were speakers of either Spanish or English. By sucking on a special pacifier, the infants could prolong the playing of a recording in either Spanish or English. Infants responded more to the recordings of their native language as demonstrated in the length of play time. The researchers interpreted this result as showing that prenatal experience has resulted in some preparation for language learning prior to birth.

Other studies have confirmed and extended the finding that newborns prefer their mother's language. Nazzi, Bertoncini, and Mehler (1998) performed a series of experiments studying the ability of French newborns to discriminate between sentences in Japanese, English, Dutch, Spanish, and Italian. French is similar in its rhythmic aspect to Japanese, Spanish, and Italian. In all these languages, each syllable tends to be of approximately the same length. All these languages are dissimilar from English and Dutch where stressed syllables are much longer than unstressed ones. The researchers filtered out high-frequency information in the sentences leaving the essential information of rhythm, stress, and intonation. Infants could tell the difference between English and Japanese (languages with contrasting rhythms) but they could not distinguish English and Dutch (both of which are **stress-timed** languages with the same sort of rhythms). When infants heard different combinations of sentences from English, Dutch, Spanish, and Italian, they could tell the difference between English or Dutch sentences (stress-timed languages) contrasted with Spanish or Italian (**syllable-timed** languages). The results suggest that newborns rely heavily on rhythmic information to distinguish their native language from others.

Ramus and Mehler (1999) followed up this idea in a study with adult speakers of French. Using **synthetic speech** (speech created by a computer program), the researchers were able to recreate sentences in English and Japanese by preserving the sounds, rhythms, and intonations all together (condition 1), just preserving rhythm and intonation (condition 2), or only keeping intonation by itself (condition 3), or rhythm by itself (condition 4). Results supported the conclusion that rhythm all by itself is enough to enable French-speaking adults to tell the difference between a stress-timed language such as English and a syllable-timed language such as Japanese. These results confirm both prior research and theories predicting that rhythmic differences across languages must be the most salient elements in early infancy. Combined with research on the development of the prenatal hearing system, it is clear at least that normal prenatal babies are receiving rhythmic information from mother's heartbeat, the baby's own heartbeat, from mother's speech patterns, and from those of others speaking in mother's presence from about week 16 GA.

Summing Up and Looking Ahead

In this chapter we have focused most of our attention on the *prenatal* period. In Chapter 3 we will study the period from birth to the baby's sixth month in the **postnatal** period. We will also encounter evidence that the sensory-motor abilities of the normal infant are already well integrated at birth. We will also encounter and discuss experimental evidence discovered accidentally by a psychologist named Harry McGurk showing that visual and auditory perception, especially when it comes to speech, are more tightly integrated than anyone suspected. We will also see evidence that newborns seem to know in advance what shape the mouth must assume to produce a certain vowel sound, for example. We will also see evidence of a close interaction between intentional acts of movement, pointing, looking, and speaking that seem to direct the infant's acquisition of the speech forms of a particular language.

STUDY AND DISCUSSION QUESTIONS

1. If you are a mother (or a sensitive dad!), what kinds of emotional responses did your baby show, if any, during prenatal development? For instance, did your baby respond differently to happy conversations as contrasted with others? To loud noises? Speech? Music? Foods or drinks consumed?

2. If you happen to be the parent of more than one child, when could you first distinguish the personality traits of your children? Did they behave differently in the womb? Were the differences reflected later in life? If so, in what ways?

3. After reading this chapter, what are your thoughts on amniocentesis and other procedures that require inserting a needle into the placenta (or possibly the fetus)?

4. Do you think that the baby in the womb is capable of experiencing emotions? What evidence can you muster pro or con?

5. What are the arguments for or against the theory that the baby's first smile represents a contented security? What are some of the other possible explanations that have been proposed?

CHAPTER 3

Sign Systems at Birth

By studying this chapter you should:

1. Find evidence for the integration of the senses in the newborn child;

2. Learn about widely used methods of hearing tests applied in early infancy;

4. Become able to evaluate claims about what surprises the infant;

5. Get a basic understanding of the process of pragmatic mapping;

6. Become prepared to refute the myths that neonates cannot see and hear; and

7. Gain additional evidence on the nature versus nurture controversy.

━━━━━━━━━━━━━━━━━━━ **KEY TERMS** ━━━━━━━━━━━━━━━━━

Here are some key terms and concepts that you can learn more about. Each term is defined in the text and in the Glossary; watch for it in **bold print** in this chapter:

acronym	audiology
amodal	back-formation
articulation	biomechanical activity
auditory brainstem response	chameleon effect
audiologist	crossmodal transfer

deglutition (also glutition)
discriminate
discrimination
dynamic systems approach
electroencephalogram (EEG)
event-related potential
fixed vocal signals
frame-and-content
frequency of occurrence
hand-eye coordination
high-amplitude sucking (HAS)
illusion
innatist perspective
interactional synchrony
International Phonetic Alphabet (IPA)
intersubjectivity
intrinsic reinforcers
kinesics
mastication

McGurk effect
mnemonic
modality
neonate
nondistress vocalizations
operant
otoacoustic emissions
postnatal age
pragmatic mapping
protostructure
prototype
pupil dilation
rationalism
reference
self-synchrony
semantic features
synchronization
universal grammar
vowel space

Parents used to be told that newborn infants were unable to see or hear (Peiper, 1925). That idea was never completely accepted and we now have evidence showing that infants can both see and hear well at birth (Hepper & Shahidullah, 1994; Shahidullah & Hepper, 1992; Slater & Kirby, 1998). In Figure 3-1, you see a **neonate** that is about 40 weeks GA plus one-minute **postnatal age** (PA). Watch the video of this baby and ask yourself whether you think he can see and hear? What about this baby's responsiveness to touch? Do you see the startle response when he is lifted while holding on to the adult's fingers and his hands are suddenly (deliberately) released?

As seen in the video linked to Figure 3-1, during the first six minutes of the baby's postnatal life, pediatricians assess the baby's heart rate, breathing, muscle tone, reflexes (tested by the startle response), and skin color. The heart rate in a normal infant will be above 100 beats per minute, breathing will be regular, the baby will resist the stretching of its limbs and will pull them in toward the body after they are stretched out; the baby will show a clear startle response (including grimacing), and skin color will be pink rather than blue clear out to the fingers and toes. These five indicators are scored as recommended by Dr. Virginia Apgar (1953; see her original paper retrieved January 28, 2006 from http://apgar.net/virginia/Apgar_Paper.html) from 0 to 2 and then added up to create a 10-point scale. The infant's score is called the Apgar score after the doctor who recommended it. It is not an **acronym** from an abbreviated phrase. However, two **mnemonics** have been proposed. Butterfield (1962) recommended that pediatricians remember APGAR by thinking of the terms Appearance,

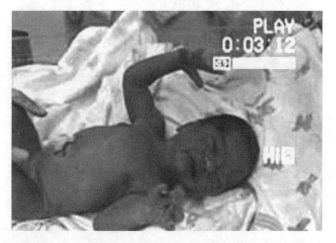

Figure 3–1. A newborn baby delivered at 9 pounds 22 inches by Cesarean (see and hear him at http://www.babycenter.com/general/pregnancy/newbornprep/8337.html). Reproduced by permission of the photographer, J. D. Lasica and the Baby-Center. Copyright © 1997–2005 J. D. Lasica.

Pulse, Grimace, Activity, and Respiration. This is a **back-formation** because the abbreviation and its terms were invented from Apgar's name, not the other way around. Another back-formation that has been used for the letters of Apgar's name is American Pediatric Gross Assessment Record (see http://dictionary.laborlawtalk.com/ for links to Apgar's original article and the criteria for the Apgar score retrieved January 28, 2006 from http://encyclopedia.laborlawtalk.com/Apgar_score). The Apgar score ranges from 0 to 10 and is now commonly applied to all newborns in the United States. Each of the five elements is scored 0 in the worst case, 1 if it is middling, and 2 if optimal. A total score of 7 or more is considered normal and below 3 as critically low.

It used to be common for pediatricians to tell first-time mothers that their neonates would have to gain quite a lot of experience before the babies would be able to see or hear anything, much less would they be able to distinguish mother's face or recognize her voice. It was not expected that neonates would show any special interest in speech for several months after birth. To see that this is not consistent with what we observe newborn infants doing, follow the link from Figure 3–2 (go to http://www.raisingdeafkids.org/hearingloss/testing/nhs.jsp, scroll down and click on

Figure 3–2. See newborns interacting with their mothers and hearing screenings of newborns at http://www.raisingdeaf kids.org/hearingloss/testing/nhs.jsp; or see Sound Beginnings on the *Milestones Student DVD-ROM*. The still picture and the video are both reproduced by permission of Deafness and Family Communication Center. Copyright © 2001–2004.

"Sound Beginnings"; visited January 29, 2006; also see the video Sound Beginnings on the *Milestones Student DVD-ROM*). At this website you can observe infants in close interaction with their mothers. The video also presents an explanation of two tests of hearing that are commonly applied to neonates. We will return to those tests in the section below on Hearing. In fact, until recent years, one of the common myths about early infancy was that the cooing, gooing, and babbling of human infants had little to do with the language they would acquire later on (Carroll, 1971; Grégoire, 1948; Jakobson, 1941, 1968; Velten, 1943; but to the contrary see D. K. Oller, 2000; D. K. Oller & Lynch, 1992).

In this chapter we examine relevant research evidence concerning what newborn infants can do. We are especially interested in the integration of the baby's senses and how they interact with the ability to perform deliberate movements and to hear, **discriminate**, and produce distinctive sounds. When it comes to language learning, the main problem the baby will solve in its first postnatal year, give or take two or three months, will involve a pairing of meaningful speech sounds with persons, objects, and events in the world. We begin to unravel some of the ways that the infant succeeds at this surprisingly difficult task. In studying the developing sign systems of early infancy, researchers have tried in various ways to learn how the baby sees, hears, and senses the world. To make inferences about what the baby may be thinking—about what the baby expects and does not expect, likes and does not like—parents listen to the baby and especially look to facial expressions. Researchers also look to these indicators and at the details of the movements of the mouth, eyes, head, and hands. Increasingly researchers are taking **dynamic systems approaches** (J. Oller, Chen, S. Oller, & Pan, 2005; Thelen & Smith, 1994). In development, sign systems of one kind commonly influence and interact with signs of a different kind. The interactions are dynamic and may be reflected in changes in heart rate, **pupil dilation**, the electrical potential of the skin, and such things as the rate of sucking behaviors. Surprises can often be detected by changes in systems that are not directly under the control of the infant, for instance, in heart rate and pupil dilation. However, movements that come under the baby's control are of special importance in the relevant research, for example, sucking, eye movements, and head turns.

Hearing from Birth

The study of the human sense of hearing known as **audiology**, is of special interest in normal speech and language development because the most common form of language that the normal baby begins to notice is speech—spoken words that can be heard. The baby also hears its own vocalizations and this is important to being able to tune and shape them in the direction of particular linguistic targets, that is, to make them more and more like the speech forms of the language the baby will eventually learn to speak. **Audiologists**, who study the sense of hearing in particular, have found ingenious ways to get information about hearing even in a newborn baby. For example, there are two ways to assess the quality of sounds the neonate can hear.

The most sensitive test involves what are called **otoacoustic emissions** (or an OAE test). For a clear and useful description of this test and an explanation of how it is performed, see Raising Deaf Kids (2005; retrieved January 28, 2006 from http://www.raisingdeafkids.org/hearingloss/testing/ nhs.jsp; also see <u>Sound Beginnings</u> on the *Milestones Student DVD-ROM*). In 1978, D. T. Kemp discovered that the inner ear emits echoes of the sounds presented to it. The ear not only detects sounds, but it also reproduces them. The sound emissions produced by the ear can be recorded. A miniaturized amplifier and microphone are embedded in a tiny ear plug that can be inserted in the baby's outer ear. This procedure is painless and can usually be performed while the baby is sleeping after feeding. Sounds are produced through the amplifier and the emissions coming back from the baby's inner ear are recorded. This test enables the early detection and treatment of hearing impairment. Because preverbal babies cannot be tested by presenting a sound and asking them to indicate if they can hear it, the discovery of otoacoustic emissions has helped health care providers to identify infants with hearing impairment much earlier than was possible beforehand (see Bess & Hall, 1992).

A second test for hearing impairment in newborns involves what is called the **auditory brainstem response** (ABR). This test emerged in the 1970s from research on the electrical waves generated by the brain and measurable in what is called an **electroencephalogram** (EEG). Like the OAE test, the ABR is painless and can be performed while the baby is asleep (see Weber, 1988). Three wires are taped to the baby's scalp. Clicking sounds are presented through miniature earphones to the baby. A little more than a tenth of a second after the presentation of the click but before a full second has elapsed, if the baby hears the sound, a change in electrical activity will be measurable at the scalp. These relatively sudden changes in electrical activity show that the sound has traveled from the ears and has registered in the brain. These changes in electrical activity are called auditory **event-related potentials** because they are indirectly related to sounds presented. By presenting sounds of different intensity, it is possible to measure the baby's threshold of hearing at different frequencies. The results of such procedures show that normal neonates can hear very well.

The Sound of Mom's Voice

Locke (1994, p. 441) had speculated that the sound of mother's voice in the womb provides the basis for the later linking of mom's voice with her face. If the infant in the womb becomes familiar with mother's voice along with her heartbeat, movements, smell, taste, and touch, after birth mom's voice should already be somewhat familiar. If this is so, the learning from the womb should carry over to experience after birth. However, we can logically distinguish at least three problems that the baby must solve to link mom's voice with her face:

- First, there is the problem of becoming familiar with mom's voice as distinct from other voices. We should keep in mind that this problem is really a linguistic one. How and when will the baby be able to tell the sound of mom's voice from the sound of other voices? How and when will the baby be able to distinguish different speech sounds in mother's speech, and how and when will the baby first be able to tell mom's language from other languages?
- Second, there is the problem of becoming familiar with mom's face. because the newborn has never seen any faces at all before its birth, how will it learn to recognize mom's face as distinct from others? When will this first become possible?
- Third, there is the problem of connecting mom's voice with mom's face. How is this possible and when does it occur?

The baby must map the familiar voice of its mother onto the person that will be discovered by the baby through its senses of sight, hearing, touch, taste, and smell very soon after its birth. We describe this process as **pragmatic mapping** (Badon, S. Oller, Yan, & J. Oller, 2005; Krashen, 1985; J. Oller, 1975; S. Oller, 2005). It is pragmatic because the baby must link the use of the sound of the voice of its mother with the moving face and body of its mother as shown in Figure 3-3. The process of pragmatic mapping, as we have argued elsewhere (Badon, J. Oller, & S. Oller, 2005; J. Oller, 2005; J. Oller et al., 2005) involves a dynamic association of (1) an abstract symbol (such as the voice of mom or an utterance or a word) with (2) a particular icon (such as a person, thing, event or relation pointed to by that voice or symbol) through (3) one or many indexes (actions) that dynamically connect the symbol with the icon.

The problem of Figure 3-3, as we will see in later chapters, is merely a simpler version of the problem of **reference** (Clark & Wilkes Gibbs, 1986; S. Oller, 2005), which involves linking a name with the person or thing named. Although it may seem simple to link a name with whatever is named, Naigles (2002) has argued that it is more difficult than merely discriminating voices and speech forms. The more general and more complex problem of linking words with their uses and with things, persons, events, and so forth is what we have called pragmatic mapping. Tomasello and Akhtar (2003) also argue that it is this richer and more complex linking of forms to meanings that is difficult for all language learners.

But first, let us concentrate on the simpler problem of linking mom's voice with her face. How does the human neonate accomplish this? In the

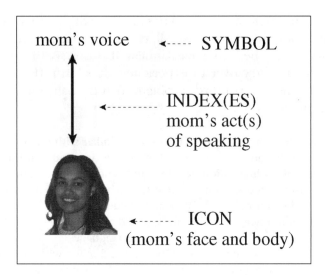

Figure 3–3. The three-part pragmatic mapping process that links mom's voice (a symbol of mom) through one or more actions of mom speaking (indexes that connect mom's voice through her acts of speaking) with mom's moving face (the icon of mom).

years that have elapsed since Locke (1994; also 2001) stated his hunch about the pairing of mom's voice with her face, research seems to have confirmed his prediction that the baby would apply knowledge of mom's voice gained from the womb to know her face. However, the association is more subtle and babies are better prepared to learn languages than almost anyone had anticipated. Let us consider first the how and when of the baby's **discrimination** of its mother's voice. How and when does the baby first tell the difference between its mother's voice and the voices of others? Does the baby also discriminate mom's speech and language?

Discriminating Mom's Voice, Speech, and Language

Kisilevsky et al. (2003) presented evidence that fetuses still in the womb at 38 weeks or more GA can tell their own mother's voice from that of a different adult female. This result also extends to the voice of the father as well. Belin, Fecteau, and Bédard (2004) wrote that "experiments measuring changes in heart rates in neonates during presentation of different voices demonstrate an ability to discriminate voices, and to recognize the voices of their mother and father" (DeCasper & Fifer, 1980; Ockleford, Vince, Layton, & Reader, 1988). Even unborn full-term fetuses can do this (Fifer, & Moon, 1994; Kisilevsky et al., 2003). During gestation the baby has been hearing distinct voices since sometime after the 16th week GA.

Should it surprise us that fetuses and neonates prefer mother's voice to the voice of a stranger? Perhaps not, but the neonate's special interest in human speech reaches beyond voice discrimination. As early as 1971 it was demonstrated that human neonates can tell the difference between syllables like [pa] and [ba] by the age of one month (Eimas et al., 1971). More recently, Dehaene-Lambertz (1998) has demonstrated that even premature babies born at 35 and 36 weeks GA can distinguish these and other syllables. What is more, neonates are particularly interested in the sounds of speech. Floccia, Christophe, and Bertoncini (1997) suggested that speech sounds can serve as **intrinsic reinforcers** (natural rewards) to newborn babies. They used **high-amplitude sucking** (HAS) as their measure of interest in a series of experiments. When speech sounds appeared randomly, whether the baby was sucking or not, the baby did not evidently link sucking behavior with the speech sounds. However, when speech sounds were presented in response to sucking but not to silence, the babies did more sucking. When the baby was presented with changing speech sounds, the sucking increased still further resulting in HAS. The researchers inferred that the co-occurrence of speech sounds with the infant-controlled sucking behavior is a natural reward causing the infant to suck more and harder. They inferred that they had produced **operant** learning in neonates. Presumably, this result is achieved partly because the infant is rewarded by being able to cause something to happen because of its own voluntary action. It is as if the infant thinks something like: "Aha! Look at this! I can cause interesting sounds to appear!" However, it seems also that speech sounds themselves have special interest to human neonates just because they are speech sounds. To see this it is useful to examine some additional evidence.

It had been shown as early as 1993 that two-day old neonates are able to tell the difference between languages such as Spanish and English (Moon, Cooper, & Fifer 1993). Babies whose mothers spoke either Spanish or English were presented recordings of female strangers speaking Spanish or English. The babies showed a significant preference for their mother's language. In a follow-up study, Nazzi, Bertoncini, and Mehler (1998) explored further how it is that neonates discriminate their native language. In particular they tested the theory that rhythmic properties are most important. First they filtered out the higher frequencies in the speech samples to focus attention on the rhythmic properties that are easily discerned in the lower frequency ranges. In their first experiment they presented English and Japanese to newborns whose mothers were speakers of French. With respect to timing, French is more like Japanese than English and the babies could tell the difference between both of the foreign languages. Next they tested French newborns with sentences in English and Dutch, which are both stress-timed languages. The babies could not tell the difference between English and Dutch. In their third experiment, different combinations of sentences from English, Dutch, Spanish, and Italian were presented to French newborns. The babies could tell English or Dutch sentences from Spanish or Italian, but they could not tell English from Dutch, nor Spanish from Italian. Evidently, rhythm is an important feature enabling newborns to discriminate between languages. Subsequently, Mastropieri and Turkewitz (1999) produced evidence that neonates differentiate happy speech in their native language from other emotional states but are not able to do this in an unfamiliar language.

If all the previous evidence were not enough to suggest that newborn human infants are especially well prepared and predisposed to acquire human languages, there is more. Because infants can learn any of the 6,000 plus languages of the world to which they may be exposed, it is clear that they are equipped, as Skoyles (1998) has speculated, to discriminate any of the sounds in any language. Chomsky (1965, 1972, 1975, 1980, 2002) has used this fact and others like it to argue that human infants have a special language acquisition capacity. He contends that we have an inborn ability, and a preprogrammed knowledge about the kinds of structures that are possible in the many languages of the world. All of those languages share certain structural properties which can be described in what Chomsky has called a **universal grammar**. He has supposed that certain aspects of that system of shared knowledge must be part of the human genome. Human babies, according to this thinking, are preprogrammed to acquire any language they might encounter. This idea stems from the philosophy known as **rationalism**, the idea that reason, ideas, and intelligence cannot be dispensed in explaining human experience and behavior. This is the essential basis of Chomsky's **innatist perspective**. It has been challenged, however, by those who question whether humans are really very different from any other species with respect to the language capacity.

We come again inevitably to the nature versus nurture controversy. Is the human baby's interest in mom's voice, speech, and language a result of a unique language acquisition capacity? Or is it the sort of interest that would be shared by other species very broadly. It has been demonstrated that other mammals, especially primates such as the cotton-top tamarin monkey, not only hear and distinguish sounds that humans distinguish, but the tamarin can also evidently tell the difference between utterances in Dutch and Japanese (Ramus, Hauser, Miller, Morris, & Mehler, 2000). Follow-up work by Tincoff, Hauser, Tsao, Spaepen, Ramus, and Mehler (2005) demonstrated that tamarins can also distinguish Polish (a **stress-timed** language) from Japanese (a **syllable-timed** language) but not English from Dutch (two stress-timed languages). Also, when the sentences are played backward, both the tamarin and the human neonates fail to tell the differences across languages. Evidently, the human neonate not only shares certain abilities with other species but shares some of the same inabilities as well.

Researchers have provided evidence that even rats, given a little train-ing, can also discriminate sentences across languages (Toro, Trobalon, & Sebastian Galles, 2003). But rats have difficulty when speech is played backward and also if multiple speakers are introduced (Toro, Trobalon, & Sebastian Galles, 2005). Toro et al. (2003) concluded, however, that rats, along with cotton-top tamarin monkeys, have "language discrimination abilities similar to those found in human infants" (p. 131). In addition to rats and tamarins, a long list of primates should be added here. The list would have to include the famous chimpanzees (Vicki, Sarah, Washoe, and Nim), the bonobo named Kanzi, and the gorillas named Koko and Michael. In addition to the primates, dolphins and birds also have the capacity to discriminate speech forms. What is more, not only mammals but also birds have significant linguistic abilities. This can be seen in talking parrots, talk-ing mynah birds, and especially the African grey parrot named Alex (Pep-perberg & Gordon, 2005).

The idea that neonates share many of their language abilities with birds and other mammals is consistent with the notion that speech and language are, from an evolutionary perspective, late-developing functions connected with such natural processes as chewing and swallowing, which are also commonly referred to as **mastication**, and **deglutition** (or **gluti-tion**) in the technical literature. MacNeilage and Davis (2000) proposed that the movements of the hinged jaw provide a natural frame for the development of the distinct syllables of speech. The emergent syllables, they contend, become differentiated and provide the content, in other words, the distinct surface-forms of speech and language. They reject Chomsky's idea that the human language capacity is unique to humans or that it involves special design. They argue that rhythmic opening and closing of the jaw while also producing intermittent sound with the voice will result in syllable-like, rhythmic output. The movements of the jaw pro-vide the frame for the syllable, and the content to fill up this frame is just whatever specific consonantal and vocalic sounds may emerge from this **biomechanical activity**. For this reason their theory has been called the **frame-and-content** theory. According to that theory, babbled speech, or speech of any kind, emerges from natural movements that are used in activ-ities such as chewing and swallowing. The theory is that the movements of the jaw provide a **protostructure** (an initial framework) for the invention of syllabic utterances. If the jaw is opened or closed during the production of voluntary vocalizations, the theory holds that the resulting sounds will tend to resemble syllables.

Some of the sensitivities of human infants to the speech forms of dif-ferent languages are also displayed by birds, rats, chinchillas, monkeys, chimps, and gorillas. This evidence seems to weigh in favor of the emer-gence and biomechanical theories of speech. Some who favor emergence theories have insisted that the sounds of speech are just more complicated versions of other vocalizations. MacNeilage and Davis (1995), for example, have argued for a continuum leading from "prelinguistic behaviors to early words" (p. 1199). However, the idea that infants just gradually work their way up from movements of the jaw to syllabic utterances of speech and then move on to language also faces some difficult challenges. Aldridge, Stillman, and Bower (2001), for example, have studied the response of neonates to vowel sounds. Before we look at their results, let us remember some aspects of vowels that must be distinguished if the neonates are going to discriminate these important elements of syllables. We should keep in mind that vowels are the most prominent elements of any syllable because they form its nucleus and the essential part of the rime. Deleting the vowel nucleus of an isolated syllable not only makes it unpronounce-able, but makes it no longer a syllable at all. The vocalic nucleus of the syllable is its indispensable defining element. It is the part of the syllable that carries the beat. Consonants that can be continuously produced on a breath of air can sometimes take on the role of a vowel nucleus, as in hissing sounds (sibilants) and nasals (mmmm, hmmmm), but a vocalic nucleus must be present for a syllable to get its defining beat (its moment on stage) in the stream of speech.

As we saw in Chapter 1, vowels are relatively continuous. By starting in the position for an "e" sound, as in "he," a sound designated as /i/ in the **International Phonetic Alphabet** (1993–1996; retrieved January 28, 2006 from http://www2.arts.gla.ac.uk/IPA/fullchart.html), for example, by simply lowering the jaw (that is, opening the mouth) we can move continuously through the range of vowel sounds from /i/ (as in "he") to /ɑ/ (as in "hot"). Or, by moving the tongue from the front of the mouth to the back while rounding our lips, while keeping our voice going, we can move continuously from /i/ to /u/. By unrounding the lips while saying /u/, we can move from the /u/ vowel to the back unrounded vowel of Mandarin /ɯ/ which does not occur at all in English. To hear what it sounds like go to the Power-Point presentation for Chapter 3 on the DVD and click on Figure 3–4. Starting in the /i/ position, while we keep our voice going, by just rounding our lips we can produce a vowel sound sometimes written as "ü," or as /y/ in the IPA system. This sound does not occur in English, but it is found in French, Mandarin, German, and many other languages.

As we have already noted, any normal human newborn can discriminate any and all these sounds and all those that fall in between. The neonate infant can do a great deal more than this, presumably, because it can also distinguish a great many consonants as well, not to mention tens of thousands of combinations of consonants and vowels forming different syllables. However, setting aside the consonants, Aldridge, Stillman, and Bower (2001) chose to concentrate on vowels because vowels are contin-

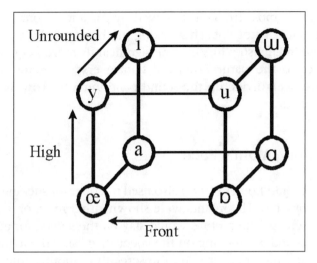

Figure 3–4. A diagram of the vowel space. See Aldridge, M. A., Stillman, R. D., & Bower, T. G. R. (2001). Newborn categorization of vowel-like sounds. *Developmental Science*, 4(2), 220–232. The diagram shown here is adapted from one on p. 221 and is used by permission. Copyright © 2001 Blackwell Publishing Limited.

uously variable as we have just seen. They proposed defining a **vowel space** in terms of three distinct features of the **articulation** of vowels: (1) the relative position of the jaw, high (relatively closed) versus low (relatively open); (2) the relative shape of the lips, rounded as in saying /u/ or unrounded as in saying /i/; and (3) the relative position of the tongue, toward the front of the mouth as in /i/ or toward the back as in /u/. With these features in mind, Aldridge, Stillman, and Bower (2001) defined the adult vowel space for the range of possible vowels as shown in Figure 3-4. However, they focused attention only on the top surface of the cube shown in Figure 3-4.

First they defined the corners of the space in terms of the sounds /i/, /y/, /u/, and /ɯ/. Then, having defined the corners of that surface, they created computer-generated vowels moving in 10 equal steps from corner to corner, along each edge, all the way around the surface. The question was how would the infants divide up this "one surface of the adult vowel space"? Would they show preference to some sounds over others? Results showed that infants sucked more and listened more often to vowels near or at the corners of the vowel space. What is more, the vowels could be ordered by preference. The most listened to vowel was /ɪ/ followed by /u/ then /y/ and finally /ɯ/. It just so happens that this order reflects the **frequency of occurrence** of these vowels in the languages of the world.

The vowel /i/ is most frequent followed by /u/ and so on. However, the infants were all born of English-speaking mothers and the vowels /i/ and /ɪ/ are found in English with /i/ being significantly more frequent than /u/. With respect to the nature/ nurture controversy, it seems that human neonates may well divide up the sound continuum for vowels very much the way adults do.

Discriminating Mom's Face

Walton, Bower, and Bower (1992) also used the operant sucking procedure in the study of faces. The infants were shown either mom or a stranger on a computer screen. The picture would stay on the screen for at least four-tenths of a second. By sucking on the specially designed pacifier the baby could cause the picture to stay on the screen for another four-tenths of a second. If the baby did not suck for a full second, the picture would change. They called this procedure "operant" because the baby determines when it will suck or not on the pacifier and this action controls what happens next. With this procedure, the researchers demonstrated that a newborn at only about 36 hours after birth is able to tell the difference between a picture of its mother as contrasted with that of a stranger that happens to look like its mom. The babies sucked more frequently and kept mom's picture on the screen significantly longer than the stranger's picture. The experimenters concluded that the babies can tell mom from a stranger. Earlier experiments had suggested this ability in newborns (Bushnell, Sai, & Mullin, 1989; Field, Cohen, Garcia, & Greenberg, 1984), but no one had demonstrated facial recognition at such an early age.

However, Walton and Bower (1993) took the work a step further. They showed newborns four distinct pictures of faces over a period of less than one minute. Then, using the same sort of operant sucking procedure used in the prior experiment, they showed the babies either a computer-generated composite (a kind of facial average) of the four familiar faces or they showed them a composite face based on four other faces that the newborns had never seen before. Newborns sucked more and kept the familiar composite on the screen longer than the unfamiliar one. The babies were evidently able to learn to discriminate different faces very rapidly. Slater and Kirby (1998) went so far as to suggest that newborns have an innate capacity to see faces not as mere composites but as whole faces (see also Slater & Quinn, 2001).

Do the babies already possess an innate knowledge of a **prototype** face when they are born? That is, do they have a built-in composite, a kind of average face in mind before they are born? Slater and Quinn (2001) suggest that perhaps they do. Although Slater and Quinn acknowledge that learning about faces may take place in the womb through the baby's touching of its own face and through the baby's ability to form different facial expressions, they cite research (Langlois et al., 1987; Langlois, Ritter, Roggman, & Vaughn, 1991; Langlois & Roggman, 1990; Slater, Bremner, Johnson, Hayes, & Brown, 2000; Slater, Mattock, Brown, & Bremner, 1991; Slater, Quinn, Hayes, & Brown, 2000) suggesting strongly that newborns prefer attractive faces, that is, ones that are symmetrical and conform to the presumed prototype face that the infant has in mind before birth. Or is it possible for infants to learn which faces are attractive almost immediately after its birth? Easterbrook, Kisilevsky, Hains, and Muir (1999) think that the newborns are just fast learners. However, Easterbook, Kisilevsky, Muir, and Laplante (1999) found that neonates can discriminate at birth between a scrambled image of a face and a picture of a whole face.

Connecting Mom's Voice with Mom's Face

In a series of experiments, Sai (2005) investigated how newborns almost immediately seem to know what mom looks like. Sai wanted to determine whether infants need to hear mom's voice in order to show a preference for her face over that of a stranger. To find out, from birth until the time of testing neonates were prevented from hearing mother's voice. In this case, neonates showed no preference for mother's face over that of a stranger. In another experiment, however, when the newborn infants were allowed to hear mother's voice and see mother's face from the time they were born and also just before testing, a strong preference for the mother's face was demonstrated. Sai concluded that prior experience with mom's voice followed by experience of the voice and face together is necessary for the infant to develop a preference for mom's face.

These results suggest that the pragmatic linking of mom's voice with mom's face requires learning. The results also suggest that, for the normal hearing neonate, the infant uses its prior knowledge of mom's voice to develop a preference for her face. The baby evidently uses its knowledge of mom's voice, gained while still in the womb, to first identify that same voice after birth, and then link it to the moving face that seems to be producing the voice. To support this proposed sequence of events, there is quite a lot of relevant research. Studies suggest that the infant's senses of sight, hearing, taste, touch, and smell are well-integrated before birth. Evidence for natural, unlearned transfer across **modalities**, for example, from touch to sight or from sight to hearing, are relevant to the basic problem of linking voices and speech forms first with persons and later with more abstract meanings. Also relevant are studies showing that neonates seem to know innately how sounds and facial expressions go together. These connections are important to every aspect of the infant's speech, language, and social development.

Crossmodal Transfer and Integration of the Senses

We can begin to appreciate the problem of **crossmodal transfer** (also known as *intermodal transfer*) by asking how a neonate, seeing a face for the first time, can imitate its expression (Reissland, 1988)? Though the infant cannot see its own face, Meltzoff and Moore (1977; also Meltzoff & Borton, 1979) demonstrated that human neonates can imitate certain facial gestures of others such as opening the mouth or sticking out the tongue. The research also shows (for example, see Kaye & Bower, 1994; Meltzoff & Borton, 1979; Sai, 2005; Streri & Gentaz, 2003; Walton & Bower, 1993; Walton, Bower, & Bower, 1992) that the neonate is able to perform rapid associations between signs that are very unlike each other. Crossmodal associations are possible between any of the senses but especially seeing, hearing, and touching. For instance, the neonate's association of mom's familiar voice with her unfamiliar moving face is crossmodal (Sai, 2005). Or, the infant can match an object in its right hand, but out of sight, with a visual image of that same object (Streri & Gentaz, 2003). However, Streri and Gentaz (2004) showed that crossmodal transfer from touch to seeing was limited to the right hand of the neonate. If the unfamiliar object was presented to the left hand of the neonate, it could not successfully identify the correct visual image of the same object. Evidently, what psychologists have long called hand-eye coordination is more complex than supposed and it also involves an innate component. Although Tatsumoto (1993) concluded that 6-week-old Japanese infants could not even discriminate different facial expressions, by 10 and 14 weeks they were able to imitate open mouth and tongue protrusion. He noted that the older infants outperformed the younger ones indicating a learning effect. Which crossmodal associations are innate (if any), and how are the connections made in cases where learning is involved? Can neonates imitate facial expressions of others? Are some facial expressions innate?

Or, here is another riddle: how can a baby who has never before seen a pacifier identify it by the feel of a pacifier in the mouth? See the shapes displayed in Figure 3–5. Kaye and Bower (1994) presented postnatal babies from 13 to 43 hours with a pair of distinctly shaped pacifiers like those seen in Figure 3–5. The babies were carefully prevented from seeing any of the pacifiers. Then, while the baby was sucking on one of the special pacifiers, they showed the baby a picture of either the pacifier in the mouth or a different one. Babies sucked more frequently and spent more time looking at the visual shape that matched the shape of the pacifier the baby was holding in its mouth. How does the baby match a visual image with a tactile one? Can the baby conceivably distinguish these shapes on the basis of its prenatal experience in sucking its own thumb, fingers, and toes (as suggested in private communication by our colleague Ruixia Yan)? Can it see

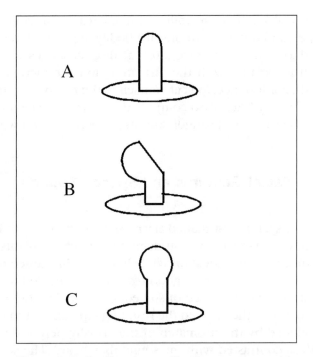

Figure 3–5. Pacifier shapes like these were used to demonstrate transfer from touch to vision in neonates. See Kaye, K. L., and Bower, T. G. R. (1994). Learning and intermodal transfer of information in newborns. The diagrams shown here are adapted from p. 287 and used by permission. Copyright ©1994 by the American Psychological Society.

these body parts in the womb? Or is the learning from the womb translated into the visual modality through some more abstract representation?

Kaye and Bower said the data suggested to them that "human newborns do not register the sensory impressions as such, but rather register abstract **amodal** or linguistic features specified by the sensory impressions" (p. 287). The abstract representations might be thought of as semantic concepts not associated with any particular language, and yet linguistic insofar as they are abstract and general. They went on to speculate that perhaps newborns "represent their world in some private language, complete with words and phrases" (p. 288). For example, such features as shape, volume, surface texture, and density of the felt object might be represented abstractly. Then, those same abstract **semantic features** could be associated with the same (or a similar) object represented in a different modality. That is, the seen object could be associated with the one being touched. Presumably in a two-dimensional visual image, the primary features to be noticed by the baby would be the shape of the surfaces of the object.

Next we will see that the ability of neonates to integrate the images, sounds, shapes, and other sensations of a bodily object with that object evidently extend to the ability to recognize the distinct shapes and movements of the mouth associated with the formation and production of different speech sounds. For instance, look at yourself in the mirror as you pronounce the syllables /ba/, /da/, /ga/. Also compare the lip and facial expressions that accompany different vowel sounds such as /i/ as contrasted with /u/ or /a/.

Facial Gestures and Speech Sounds

A now famous psychologist named Harry McGurk along with his research assistant, James MacDonald, was studying the effect on infants of presenting mom's voice from one location while her video image seemed to speak from a different location. For no good reason they decided to dub the syllable /ga/ onto the visual image of someone saying /ba/ (McGurk & MacDonald, 1976). When they played the resulting tape, they stumbled onto an **illusion** produced by the mismatch of the visually perceived movements of the mouth as contrasted with the sound they heard. The sound without the video was clearly /ba/, but when that syllable was coordinated with the lip and face movements associated with the actual production of the syllable /ga/, what the researchers perceived was neither /ba/ nor /ga/ but something in between. They heard /da/. You can check out the now famous **McGurk effect** (McGurk & MacDonald, 1976). Or, perhaps it should be called the "McGurk illusion." Refer to Figure 3–6 and both see and hear The Mcgurk Effect Demonstrated by Professor Arnt Maasø of the University of Oslo (photo and video retrieved January 28, 2006 at http://www.media. uio.no/personer/arntm/McGurk_english.html). Listen to the video as Professor Maasø speaker says /ga ga/ three times. You will find that you hear /da da/ or possibly some variation between /da/ and /ga/. Then look away from the video and listen again. The recorded sounds are /ba ba/ each time. The recorded sounds never include the syllables that we hear when we look at the video. On the visual part of the video, the speaker was filmed actually saying /ga ga/ and repeating this three times in a row. One of the things that this illusion taught psychologists is that voices and faces are much more closely integrated in our perceptions than was previously suspected. A few years after the McGurk effect was first demonstrated with adults, it was also shown with infants (Kuhl & Meltzoff, 1982). More recently, Lachs and Pisoni (2004) demonstrated that adults can match a heard voice to the face of a stranger. They cannot do this with static pictures, but with moving pictures the matching is much better than chance. However, as with infants, if the speech is played backward matching seems to be impossible.

Figure 3–6. The McGurk effect is demonstrated by Professor Arnt Maasø. This picture and the accompanying video linked on the *Milestones Student DVD-ROM* are both used by permission. See Professor Maasø's website at http://www.media.uio.no/personer/arntm/McGurk_english.html.

As you can easily imagine, researchers studying speech and language development in infants took a special interest in the McGurk effect because it showed a remarkably close integration of the senses of sight and hearing (Kuhl & Meltzoff, 1982; Patterson & Werker, 1999). Naturally, researchers wanted to know if the same effect could be found in neonates. Are the senses quite integrated at birth? Are they so integrated that the neonate already knows in advance that an /ɪ/ sound, for instance, should be produced by lips that are flat rather than rounded as in the production of an /u/? When the neonate hears /u/ does it expect to see rounded lips? Does the acoustic signal contain abstract information about the shape of the mouth or the movements that are needed to produce that sound? If it does contain such information, how much of that information is known in advance, innately programmed, and how much of it has to be learned after birth?

Kuhl and Meltzoff (1984) presented postnatal infants between 18 and 20 weeks with an auditory version of a sound and two faces one articulating the heard sound and the other a different sound. Infants preferred the face that matched the sound they were hearing. Later they presented two moving faces, one saying the heard sound and the other a different sound.

Babies preferred the match again. Walton and Bower (1993) replicated and extended these findings with 18 to 20 week old infants by showing that infants by 6 to 8 months of age preferred a possible face-voice pairing, for instance, the sound /y/ with facial expression for /y/ as contrasted with /y/ paired with a facial expression for the production of /i/. The latter would be impossible to produce. However, the infants tested had never heard the sound /y/ before because all of them were from English-speaking environments where that sound never occurs. Therefore, this result seemed to suggest that at least by 6 to 8 months of age infants already know a good deal about what lip shapes are possible even with novel sounds never before experienced. Again, relatively young infants showed what seemed to be prior knowledge of the association of speech sounds with visible shapes and movements of the mouth.

Just a few years later, in 1997, Rosenblum, Schmuckler, and Johnson (1997) reviewed the vast research on the McGurk effect and tested it in infants of just 5 months. Their infants performed so much like adults that they concluded that "the infants were visually influenced in the same way as English speaking adults are visually influenced" (p. 347). Subsequently, their results were replicated and extended first to infants at 4.5 months by Patterson and Werker (1999) and more recently to infants at only 2 months of age (Patterson & Werker, 2003). In their later work, the crossmodal transfer effect was stable and unaffected by gender. They concluded that "like the 4.5 month olds in past studies, the 2 month old infants tested in the current study showed evidence of matching vowel information in face and voice" (p. 191).

Synchronization, Entrainment, and Matching Rhythms

To communicate with each other, as we say in common speech, people have to get in touch with one another and they need to be on the same wavelength. They have to either be close to each other physically or they must somehow cross the space between them, as by telephone, radiowaves, or something that enables a connection. This is evidently true of mother and infant. They have to be together and they must have the opportunity to interact. To do this requires **synchronization** of their movements. The baby must attend to mom when mom is present, and vice versa. Psychologists, sociologists, and linguists (to mention only a few of the interested classes of researchers) have used a lot of different special terms to refer to the togetherness of human beings that is required for language acquisition to work. Jakobson (1968) wrote about the need for an **intersubjective** striving, as if mom and baby were necessarily seeking coordinated points of view so they could be with each other. Rommetveit (1979) used the term **intersubjectivity** by which he meant at least a partial sharing of perspective. More recently Trevarthen and Aitken (2001) have defined intersubjectivity as self-other consciousness. They see it playing a leading role in cultural learning and language. They argue for sensory motor coordination involving the neonate's capacity for imitation.

Chartrand and Bargh (1999) write of a **chameleon effect**, which they describe in terms of the tendency of interlocutors not only to coordinate their movements but to match them. We do this in many ways. We mimic each other's rhythms, postures, mannerisms, facial expressions, linguistic forms, and accents. If we observe someone else scratch their nose, we are apt also to scratch our own nose. We do it with strangers as well as familiar partners. The research shows that these coordinations increase the chances that interaction partners will like each other. Chartrand and Bargh (1999) also found evidence that highly empathic individuals are more apt to imitate others. John Locke (2001) called the emergence of coordinated conscious activity between mom and baby their "first communion."

We have already seen that baby and mom are together in an interactive way before the baby's birth. However, what happens at birth changes the former togetherness. In fact, every relevant source of information suggests that after birth, movements of mom and baby are required for them to mutually recognize each other. In order to pair the voice the baby learns in the womb with mom's face soon after birth, the baby must hear mom's voice and see her moving face *at the same time*. Sai (2005) demonstrated fairly conclusively that there must be a coordination of the rhythmic sounds of the voice with the observed movements of the face for the infant to make the connection. The infant has to hear the voice at the same time as seeing the moving face. In one of Sai's experiments, the neonates were deliberately prevented from seeing mom at any time while she was speaking until they could be tested for recognition of mom's face. In this case, the infants showed no evidence of preferring mom's face over that of a strange adult female. In fact, in the condition just described, the infants paid little attention to pictures of either mom or a stranger. However, when the infants had the opportunity to hear mom's familiar voice while observing her moving face as she spoke, all the babies were able to make the connection within a few minutes. Although it may be true that infants have an intrinsic interest in still pictures of faces (as demonstrated by Walton, Bower, & Bower, 1992; Walton & Bower, 1993), Sai's study shows that neonates appear to be more interested in moving faces that are accompanied by speech that the infant can hear. Brookes et al. (2001) also showed that by their third month infants can easily learn new face-voice pairs.

Evidently movement is important to capture attention. However, the dynamic coordination of sound and movement in one person, or the coordination of the movements across different persons, is crucial to language acquisition. How will the baby that happens to be exposed to French, or

Zulu, or Hottentot learn to form the sounds of that language without coordinating its movements with persons who are already speakers of that language? Body movement must come to be coordinated, and in sharing a common language they are. As early as 1966, Condon and Ogston had demonstrated through a frame-by-frame analysis of moving films that the body movements of interlocutors tend to fall into the same rhythms. Body movements of persons talking to each other tend to become coordinated. For people talking to each other (and paying attention), the body movements of all those involved are coordinated with the speech being produced. This special synchronization *between* different persons also occurs *within* one and the same person. That is, the body movements of a speaker tend to be closely coordinated with his or her own speech. Condon and Ogston called the synchronization of different actions within the same person **self-synchrony**. In the case where different persons synchronize their actions with each other, Condon and Ogston used the term **interactional synchrony**. The study of such synchronies is closely related to the study of significant bodily movements and gestures in general which Raymond L. Birdwhistell (1970) called **kinesics**.

The kind of synchrony that involves more than one person can be seen whenever a good storyteller interacts with an audience that is listening and understanding the story. For instance, William Labov (personal communication) told about a storyteller coming to the part where the speaker's throat is cut in a bar fight. The storyteller reported finding himself suddenly on the floor, looking up at the ceiling of the smoky bar. One of his friends bends over and says to him, "Don't move your head. Your throat's been cut!" According to Labov, when playing a tape of this story to different audiences, the people in the audience would hold their heads perfectly still for a few seconds at just this point. Their movements seemed to come under the control of the speaker's words. This would be an obvious example of interactional synchrony.

In fact, by slowing down the frames of films associated with ordinary conversational interactions, researchers can see much more finely grained coordinations between speech and body movements. Condon and Ogston (1967, pp. 225–229) suggested that the ordinary coordinations are so well synchronized that the movements of different persons engaged in the conversation seem like those of puppets being manipulated by the same puppeteer. There is considerable evidence that body movements tend not only to be closely coordinated with speech rhythms, but the coordination begins to emerge at a very early age.

For instance, we have already seen that by two months of age according to research by Patterson and Werker (2003) infants already expect certain speech sounds to be accompanied by certain facial expressions and movements. Also, Walton and Bower (1993) found that not only do postnatal babies by 6 to 8 months know the mouth shapes associated with different vowels in the language they are being exposed to on a daily basis, but the infants also evidently know in advance that certain combinations of mouth shape and vowel are impossible. For instance, the sound /y/ cannot be produced by a mouth shape for /i/. The lips must be rounded. If babies know this without having learned it, then how early does the baby synchronize its movements with the speech sounds of others?

Condon and Sander (1974) presented evidence that the body movements of neonates tend to fall into a rhythm that is closely coordinated with the rhythms in the speech of the adults they hear speaking when they are born. They recorded five hours of interaction between 16 normal neonates and speaking adults with sound-motion film or audio-videotape. They focused attention on segments where the baby was both alert and already moving during adult speech, or where the infant began to move in response to adult speech. About one hour of the five recorded hours was judged suitable for analysis. The authors concluded that the infant's were entraining on the adult speech. That is, the babies movements were closely coordinated with the rhythms of the adult speech. They inferred that this entrainment (or interactional synchrony) is evidence that neonates are especially tuned to the rhythms of their native language. To test the possibility that their analysis was merely wishful thinking, showing accidental correspondences between adult speech and movements of the infants, they compared movements of infants during silence with movements accompanied by overheard speech. Movements produced during silence could not be made to coincide with the rhythms of adult speech. They concluded that the neonates they studied were entraining on speech of adults. More importantly they claimed to be able to observe precise coordinations within 1/30th of a second. That is, at the speed of a single frame of video or film.

However, researchers coming after Condon and Sander (1974) have not always succeeded in replicating their evidence of precise entrainment in newborns (Dowd & Tronick, 1986). Nevertheless, there is abundant evidence that coordination of movements between infants and adults does occur and that it begins at a relatively early age. From the fourth week of postnatal life forward to the 24th Hsu and Fogel (2003) have found evidence that mothers coordinate their facial expressions and talk directed to their infants in response to vocalizations by the infant. Mothers are especially responsive to the vocalizations of their infants that do not indicate distress (in other words, to **nondistress vocalizations**). Jaffe, Beebe, Feldstein, Crown, and Jasnow (2001) demonstrated that postnatal babies by 4 months (16+ weeks) not only coordinate their actions with the speech of their mother, but that they also coordinate with strangers. Furthermore, the infant's degree of entrainment is a good measure of how well the infant will do 12 months later in terms of social and **cognitive** development. They studied 88 pairs of mothers and their infants as well as various pairings of infants and mothers with 30 strangers. They concluded that the degree of coordination at 4 months was a reasonably good predictor of later development. Similar coordinations and synchronies in infants from 2 to 5 months have been demonstrated in infants in France and India as well as the United States (Gratier, 2003).

Summing Up and Looking Ahead

It is clear from all the research to this point that from the 12th week GA the baby is active in building up and expanding its sensory and motor sign systems. The prenatal baby shows aversion to pain (as when stuck with a needle) and some of the representations the infant is able to construct seem to be either innate or triggered by prenatal experience. Clearly, the underlying sensory sign systems for hearing and balance, vision, touch and pain, as well as smell and taste must be largely innate. They are no doubt refined with experience, but the integration of the senses seems to have largely taken place before birth. What is more, the prenatal infant shows special interest in speech and language before birth. At birth the neonate shows very rapid learning of the pairing of its mother's voice with her moving face. There is even evidence that the infant may know in advance a good deal about what kinds of facial expressions can pair up with certain vowel sounds. There is no doubt that the neonate is a good learner from its first moments after birth. Sai (2005) showed that infants need to hear mom's voice while observing her moving face in order to form an impression of who she is, but that they seem almost immediately to discover that the familiar voice goes with mom's moving face as she speaks. However, it will be nearly 14 months before the infant is able to pair an arbitrary word with an object (Werker, Cohen, Lloyd, Casasola, & Stager, 1998). Our next objective is to examine some of the work the infant must do before becoming able to acquire its first meaningful word.

STUDY AND DISCUSSION QUESTIONS

1. What evidence is there that neonates have already integrated the senses of hearing and seeing? Touch and sight? What inferences would you make concerning the other senses?

2. Why would it be remarkable for a neonate to be able to recognize its mother's face without hearing her voice and seeing her face move at the same time? Can the infant know its mother's face without

hearing her voice and seeing mom's face move? What relevant research evidence can you cite?

3. What is the relevance of the McGurk illusion and how does it show the integration of hearing and seeing in the perception of sounds? Why would it be especially interesting if newborns showed this illusion?

4. What reasons can you think of for the fact that neonates can evidently discriminate their native languages from at least some other languages, but no neonates (nor any adults) can discriminate languages played backward?

5. If infants have prior knowledge of the "vowel space," or if they know in advance that certain mouth shapes are incompatible with certain vowels, how does this knowledge connect with the McGurk illusion and what bearing does it have on nature versus nurture controversies?

6. Consider the relation between learning voice-face pairs and learning word-object pairs? How are they similar and how are they different? Why is it that a neonate after only a few hours at most is already apt to know the pairing of its mother's voice and face but will require as many as 14 additional months to work out the pairing of an arbitrary word with an object?

7. If speech were emerging from biomechanical functions what about facial expressions such as smiling, grimacing, and so on? Could the notion of communion, intersubjectivity, or any kind of symbolic communication emerge from chewing or swallowing?

CHAPTER 4

Things, Persons, and Situations: Constructing Icons

━━━━━━━━━━━━━━━ OBJECTIVES ━━━━━━━━━━━━━━━

By studying this chapter you should:

1. See that the senses are well developed and integrated before birth;

2. Review evidence that infants express feelings and emotions without social training;

3. Better understand the building of iconic sign systems needed for speech and language;

4. Learn how infants discover the boundaries of objects (and persons);

5. Explore the process of abstracting sensory representations of bodily objects (and persons);

6. See why relations between bodily objects (and persons) cannot be discovered or noticed until they are represented in icons; and

7. Understand why active associations between abstract signs and particular things are crucial to cognitive growth and language acquisition.

KEY TERMS

Here are some terms and concepts that you will find in this chapter. These terms appear in **bold print** in the text and also are defined in the Glossary at the end of the book:

abstractive cycle
binaural hearing
bootstrapping
concept
conceptual
discriminated icon
discrimination
empiricist tradition
gustatory
hand-eye coordination
hypostasis
hypostatic icon
hypostatize
infant-directed speech
infrasemiotic system
innateness hypothesis
logical object
nondistress vocalizations

noun phrase
perceptual
phatic communion
pragmatic bootstrapping
pragmatic content
predicate
prescind
prescinded icon
prescission
prosodic bootstrapping
rationalist tradition
re-entry
semantic bootstrapping
semantic value
subject
syntactic bootstrapping
verb phrase

In this chapter, we consider the basic problems the infant must solve to identify significant entities, especially persons, in its experience in order to later associate these entities with abstract linguistic signs. We will see that the normal infant comes preprogrammed with integrated senses of seeing, hearing, touching, tasting, and smelling, and with the ability to express certain feelings in facial expressions and bodily movements. Still, much remains to be done for the baby to link its own voluntary actions with the bodily objects, especially the persons, that are constantly moving around and talking in the baby's experience.

There are essentially three distinct kinds of problems to be solved and three distinct streams of sign systems that need to be sorted out. Unsurprisingly, these are icons, indexes, and symbols. In this chapter, we look especially, although not exclusively, at the way the baby begins to take account of distinct icons in its experience. However, before tackling the problem of understanding icons, it will be useful to get in mind an overview of the three major sign systems that have to be worked out by the infant. Then, we will focus attention on the icons in this chapter. In Chapter 5 we focus mainly on indexes and in Chapter 6 on symbols. An important idea to keep in mind is that all the sign systems that the baby has to deal with must be built up as we noted in Chapter 1. The one thing that almost all researchers and theoreticians agree on is that the development of sign systems is constructive. In this chapter we focus attention on the lowest layers of signs, especially the icons or sensory signs that are required to begin to lay the foundations on which an amazing hierarchical system of additional sign systems will be grounded.

Three Kinds of Work and Theories About How It Is Done by the Infant

Three kinds of work can be distinguished and, unsurprisingly, three distinct emphases in theories are currently under discussion concerning how the infant accomplishes each kind of work:

> First, the infant must learn a good deal about bodily objects, especially other persons. What significant objects are there? The work to be done of this kind is essentially sensory in nature and grounded in perception and the signs required for it are icons. We concern ourselves mainly with this first kind of work in this chapter.

> Second, the infant must represent movements of bodily objects, especially the intentional gestures of persons that are involved

in the production of speech and linguistic signs. The signs required for this work are indexes that connect icons with each other. Clearly, the infant cannot notice or represent moving relations between objects (persons and other things) very well, until those objects themselves can be noticed and represented in the infant's experience. Ask yourself, how could I represent relations between things I cannot even perceive or notice? We will focus attention specifically on the kind of work needed to build up indexical sign systems in Chapter 5.

Third, the infant must gain control over the surface-forms of meaningful linguistic signs. This problem, although different for hearing and deaf infants, is solved by all infants that learn to express themselves in linguistic signs. The signs required to represent conventional symbols are conventional symbols. No other kind will do. Icons, like the letters on this page, can show the surface-forms of printed words and sequences of words, but for you to notice them or say them out loud, indexes are required. You have to perform certain actions to read or say the words. The indexes you produce can point to the icons of conventional symbols, and indexes can show some of the associations of symbols with objects, for instance. However, to represent the full range of possible associations of any given conventional symbol with all its meanings requires a whole elaborate system of other conventional symbols. It requires more than indexes (together with their associated icons) can deliver or represent by themselves. Symbolic meanings require the peculiar language capacity together with the ability to infer the intentions of others, and to associate purely conventional signs with both concrete and abstract meanings. We will focus attention on the symbolic kind of work the child has to perform in learning a particular form of speech and language in Chapter 6.

How does the infant perform each kind of work? How closely are they interrelated? Three distinct emphases in theoretical approaches have been proposed. They differ in where they place their emphasis. Those focusing attention on the linguistic work required for language acquisition to succeed, tend to prefer some version of the so-called **innateness hypothesis**. This is the idea advanced mainly by Chomsky, as noted in the previous chapter. He claims that language acquisition is mainly a process of tuning certain settings in the universal grammar, the knowledge that all human beings share concerning all possible languages (including the 6,900 plus languages of the world), to specify the grammar of the particular language, or languages, to which an infant happens to be exposed. Theoreticians drawn to the innateness hypothesis have stressed the complexity, abstractness, and generality of linguistic signs and have concluded that the human infant must be innately equipped to acquire any language at all (Chomsky, 1965, 1980, 1995, 2002; Fodor, 1980; Pinker, 1989, 2000; Stromswold, 2001).

Chomsky contrasts his innateness hypothesis with the **empiricist tradition**. The latter in one form or another is preferred by theoreticians who seek to explain language as an emergent phenomenon produced in relatively small steps by evolution/learning (Armstrong & Wilcox, 2005; MacNeilage & Davis, 2000, 2001; Tomasello, 2003). The empirical and materialistic approaches stress mechanical aspects of speech production, for instance, as associated with jaw movements (MacNeilage & Davis, 2000, 2001), whereas the **rationalist tradition** has stressed the underlying capacity needed for language acquisition to succeed (Prince & Smolensky, 1993/2004; Smolensky, 1996; Tesar & Smolensky, 1998). Theoreticians and researchers who look to the end of the sign spectrum where icons are linked to material bodies constrained by physics, anatomy, and mechanical forces tend to suppose that much, if not all, the complexity of language can be developed through simple principles of learning from the material world. They suppose that little, if anything, needs to be innate, or unique to humans, for language acquisition to occur. The linguists at the opposite end of the spectrum, by contrast, have tended to emphasize the remarkable abstractness of language and conventional symbols. Linguists have stressed the complexity of the grammatical relations and structures that must be acquired. The two extremes have tended to wage war against each other (for example, see Tomasello, 2003 arguing against the innateness hypothesis).

In between the extremes, however, there is another possibility. It takes both sides of the argument seriously but sees both of the competing theories as incomplete. In this chapter we discuss the common ground between the extremes. In particular, we place emphasis on the role of indexical relations that especially involve coordinated rhythms of articulated speech forms and gestures. Dating back to antiquity, theories of spoken languages and their acquisition have focused on the relation between utterance forms and the things, persons, and relations of experience (Augustine, 401 AD; Bloom, 1970; Clark & Clark, 1977; McNeill, 1970; Menyuk, 1969; Morgan & Demuth, 1996; Peirce, 1868; Sapir, 1921; Tomasello, 2001). More recently, the acquisition of the signed language systems of the Deaf have also become intensive objects of study (Armstrong & Wilcox, 2005; Bellugi, 1980; Masataka, 1992, 1996, 1998; Morford, 1996; Petitto, & Marentette, 1991; Wilcox & Wilcox, 1997; Stokoe, 1960). Studies of both spoken and signed languages have shown that coordinated rhythmic movements are especially helpful to the infant in discovering the boundaries of the surface-forms of speech and signing.

Coordinated Rhythms

As we saw in Chapter 2, the prenatal infant seems to be specially tuned to the rhythms of the womb and particularly to the speech that it hears while in the womb. Cutler (1994) suggested that speech rhythms may be crucial to the discovery of the boundaries of syllabic utterances. There is also evidence, as we will see in this and subsequent chapters, that coordinated movements are not only essential to the association of (1) the discovery of the boundaries and identities of bodily objects, but also to (2) the dynamic relations between bodily objects such as mom's moving face and the sound of her voice, and (3) to parsing and articulating the syllabic systems that constitute the surface-forms of language in speech or signed systems.

The experience of the womb cannot be entirely forgotten when the infant is born into the world outside the womb. The prenatal experiences and developing ideas are carried forward to be enriched and further developed by later experience. When the baby encounters a speaking person who sounds like the one the baby heard in the womb, this person is evidently more familiar and bears special meaning to the baby. The baby must think something like, "That voice is the one I have been hearing right along, and it seems to be connected with the moving face that I now see." One thing that seems relatively certain is that the infant's developing sign systems are constructed. They are not fully formed with all their details from the start, but they are built up in stages over time. The question for researchers is just how this process unfolds.

In this chapter, we explore the infant's voluntary vocalizations (one's not associated with distress) that point toward speech. Is the infant's use of voluntary vocalizations a unique linguistic function from before birth, or does it merely emerge from such biomechanical functions such as chewing and swallowing? Are the neonate's early voluntary vocalizations accidental phenomena or are they demonstrations of intentions? Could they possibly show that the human baby seeks to connect with others in what the anthropologist Malinowski (1923) called **phatic communion** (also recall Locke's title from 2001, "First communion")? By phatic communion, Malinowski intended to refer to the kind of communication that consists of affirming our relationships rather than providing any new information. Much of human communication seems to be of this kind (Watzlawick, Beavin, & Jackson, 1967). When we talk about the weather, about routine activities, in our exchanges of greetings even with strangers, or when we ask how someone is but really don't want to get a health report in response, we engage in interactions that seem almost empty of information. In many cases, it seems that we do little more than affirm to each other that we are creatures of the same sort. Can such an affirmation be encoded in the neonate's smile? Does the neonate already have a sufficient concept of itself at birth that it sees other human beings as like itself?

In the previous chapter, we saw that neonates have the capacity to link mother's voice with her face very soon after birth. The process evidently involves noticing the coordinated movements of mom's face as she talks with the sound of her voice as she speaks. We also saw that the neonate has some ability initially to mimic facial expressions of others, for example, opening the mouth, widening the eyes, and sticking out the tongue. The research also shows that moms (and caregivers) are very interested in the vocalizations of their infants (Hsu & Fogel, 2003). Moms know and respond not so much to the tone of the infant's nondistress vocalizations, but to the very fact that vocalizations occur and that they link the infant with mom. In the process, vocalizations and movements of both the baby and the caregiver come to be more and more interrelated.

Wilson (2001) has reviewed the literature showing that motor actions and perceptions of the movements of interlocutors come to be intensively coordinated. Gogate, Walker-Andrews, and Bahrick (2001) have argued that the dynamic changes associated with movement are critical to the comprehension and subsequent acquisition of words. Ordinary experience confirms and supports their hypothesis. We learn how to do some things by observing the actions of others, for example, how to thread a needle, and our perceptions of the actions of others can also be sharpened by learning to perform certain actions ourselves, for example, by learning to play a musical instrument we become better able to see the movements of another person playing the same instrument. Hecht, Vogt, and Prinz (2001) have demonstrated the reciprocal influence of gestures (motor signs) and sensory ones (**perceptual** signs). Not only do we learn how to perform movements by observing those movements as performed by others, but we can also become better perceivers of delicate or quick movements by learning to perform them ourselves.

Where Do Abstract Signs Begin?

We pick up the story roughly in the infant's second month but we must keep in mind that the infant's development at any particular age is a way station marking a history of development and, hopefully, looking forward to a future of additional enrichment. As we saw in the video linked to Figure 2-1, the smile of an infant in the womb looks a lot like the smile of an infant at 8 weeks as seen here in Figure 4-1. In fact, happy smiling at any age looks similar to smiling at any other age and this is so across very different cultures and at any age (Camras, 1992; Schmidt, Cohn, & Tian, 2003).

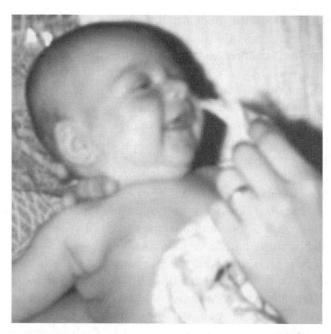

Figure 4–1. A baby at 8 weeks responds to touch. Reproduced by permission from: Sullivan, M. W., & Lewis, M. (2003). Emotional expressions of young infants and children: A practitioner's primer. *Infants and Young Children, 16*(2), p. 126. Copyright © 2003 Lippincott Williams & Wilkins, Inc.

According to the best available methods of analysis, the baby's smile before birth resembles the baby's smile after birth and throughout life. The smile at two months is better articulated than the smile in the womb. The smile of the more mature baby may have a particular external referent, for example, the smile of mom may elicit the baby's smile in return, but the basic meaning is probably the same. What has changed is that by the second month of life, the baby has become increasingly responsive to other persons and their actions. The basic pattern for smiling, however, seems to be largely independent of the particular culture, or context of experience (Schmidt, Cohn, & Tian, 2003). Increasingly, specialists have joined with parents in regarding facial expressions in early infancy as having meanings similar to the ones they have for adults. Compare the smile of the infant in Figure 4–1 with that of two young adults in Figure 4–2. Do the adult smiles seem to you to have different meanings or the same meaning as that seen in the smile of the 8-week-old infant?

Sullivan and Lewis (2003) observe that certain emotional expressions in infancy, including expressions of "interest, enjoyment, anger, pain, and disgust," are present between six and eight weeks. They are observed no matter what form of analysis is used and naïve observers can readily iden-

Figure 4–2. Young adults smile. Photographs used by permission of Ruthie *(left)* and Ashley *(right)*.

tify the different expressions and infer their meanings. The various facial expressions also seem to be culturally universal although there is more agreement (and more research) on the positive emotions (interest and enjoyment) than on the negative ones (anger, pain, and disgust). There is also likely to be more agreement on what a given facial display means if moving pictures are used rather than stills (see Moore & Calkins, 2004; also Sai, 2005 concerning infants). Adults, also, more readily notice the dynamic expressions on a moving and speaking face than expressions associated with still pictures (Detenber, Simons, & Bennett, 1997; Simons, Detenber, Reiss, & Shults, 2000). Also, Lachs and Pisoni (2004) showed that adults can match silent moving pictures of strangers with recordings of the voices of those strangers, but they cannot match voices of strangers to still pictures of the same strangers. There is something critical about the coordination of the rhythms of the speech sounds and the movements of the speakers. This seems to hold for the recognition of emotions, speakers, and voices. All of these findings suggest that it is the coordination of movements with sounds that help infants solve essential problems associated with language acquisition. Coordinated rhythms and movements are important to the process.

Figure 4-1 shows the most studied expression of emotion in infancy (or at any age), the smile from Sullivan and Lewis (2003, p. 126). They suggest that the expressions associated with movements of "the brow eye/cheek, and mouth regions of the face, are probably innate" (p. 126).

Cautioning against the claim of some researchers that we must be careful not to read too much into the expressions of early infancy, Sullivan and Lewis suppose that "early facial expressions have practical, signal value for caregivers and practitioners alike" (p. 120). Just as skin color, heart rate, and breathing are important indicators of the neonate's health as noted by pediatricians ever since Virginia Apgar (1953), emotional expressions are important indicators of the baby's internal states.

In the long tradition of the nature versus nurture controversy, however, some researchers have maintained that emotional expressions are not innate but must be learned (Ramey & Ramey, 1999). In fact, the theory that the facial expressions of neonates cannot be interpreted in the same way as similar adult expressions is a conclusion that only makes sense if we radically prefer the nurture explanation above the nature explanation. If infants have to learn emotional expressions from others, then it follows that the facial expressions of the neonate, not to mention those on the face of a fetus in the womb, must represent something other than the common emotions of adulthood. On the other hand, those who have favored the innateness hypothesis have held that emotional expressions of infancy are essentially the same as the similar emotional expressions of adulthood. Although the controversy is far from over, the results seem more and more to favor the notion that certain facial expressions are preprogrammed along with their positive and negative meanings. For instance, an expression of "disgust" as shown in Figure 4–3, is not evidently learned but is programmed to occur when the infant encounters a certain **gustatory** experience. The connection between the facial expression and the meaning seems to be preprogrammed. Quinine and other bitter tastes will also elicit a similar facial expression even in blind infants and neonates. Steiner (1979) found these expressions in all the populations studied. A range of emotional expressions indicating interest, enjoyment, anger, pain, and disgust, are seen in babies from birth or soon afterward.

The possibility that naturally suggests itself is that the underlying meanings of emotional expressions may provide a kind of foundational structure on which to build the more elaborate system of meanings that the baby will eventually achieve. This idea was first suggested by C. S. Peirce (1868). He argued that every emotional expression has its own intrinsic meaning and that it is essentially representational from the beginning. If he was correct, emotions are primitive innate symbols. These might be thought of as an **infrasemiotic system** containing certain unpolished building blocks for meaning. The emotion seen in Figure 4–3 at the very least seems to represent an evaluative feeling about the lemon juice. The infant is expressing its reaction toward the sour taste. If the facial expression of the infant more or less directly shows its evaluation, could it reasonably be interpreted to mean that the baby is really quite well pleased with

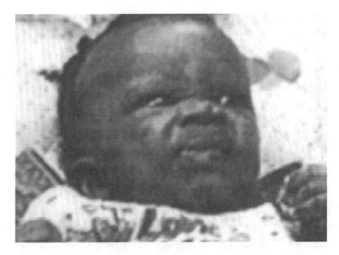

Figure 4–3. An infant at 4 months after tasting a sour lemon swab. Reproduced by permission from: Sullivan, M. W., & Lewis, M. (2003). Emotional expressions of young infants and children a practitioner's primer infants and young children. *Infants and Young Children*, *16*(2), p. 133. Copyright © 2003 Lippincott Williams & Wilkins, Inc.

the taste of lemon? Could it be that the expression really means something very different from what it would mean on the same person's face 20 years later? Or does the infant's expression mean pretty much what it means on the face of an adult?

We will argue, rather, that the facial expression is a natural symbol. It is indexically linked to (pragmatically mapped onto) the sour taste of the lemon, the iconic referent that is present only in the swab applied to the infant's tongue. To the extent that this analysis is correct and extends backward to the baby's experience in the womb, the emotional expressions of early infancy may provide at least part of the essential sign system for meanings that will be elaborated as the child acquires language. Before that can happen, however, additional work remains to be done.

The infant is born with the capacity to use its facial expressions and, evidently, knows in advance what they mean in terms of the particular feelings they express. The interesting part of the puzzle that still remains, and the part that we need to focus on in this chapter, concerns how the developing infant comes more and more to coordinate his or her actions, including facial expressions, with those of adult models. More particularly, we must consider the coordinated actions that are essential to the acquisition and use of a particular language.

Rhythm and Coordination Are Important

It is interesting that relevant research shows that the baby's earliest emotional reactions to vocalizations by others seem to be associated very early with the particular rhythms and sounds of its native language. Mastropieri and Turkewitz (1999) found that prenatal babies and neonates showed "differential responding" only to "emotional speech as spoken by speakers of their maternal language" (p. 204). There was no evidence that infants were able to differentiate emotions expressed in a foreign language. The question addressed here in this chapter is, how do human infants come to associate the distinctive surface-forms (sounds, syllables, and so on) of their native language first with innate emotions and later with the more complex structures and meanings of adult discourse? How does the infant go on later to identify particular elements of the stream of speech?

As Ferdinand de Saussure (1906/1959) pointed out a hundred years ago, in ordinary contexts of speech, linguistic utterances do not come pre-segmented into words, phrases, clauses, and so forth. Speech is a ribbon of relatively connected syllables that are run together without obvious boundaries (also Jusczyk, 1997). The problem of finding the boundaries in the stream of speech is not as easy to solve as it might appear to be to an adult. Adults hearing a foreign language for the first time can appreciate part of the infant's problem. Finding the boundaries of the surface-forms is part of the baby's problem. However, the baby must do a great deal more than this. The baby must also solve the problem of finding the boundaries of distinct objects, persons, events, and relations in the stream of experience. This also is a real problem that the newborn must solve and it is one that we cannot exactly re-experience as adults. However, we can imagine something about the infant's difficulty in finding the boundaries of objects, persons, events, and relations in experience by generalizing from the problem of finding word boundaries when we hear a foreign language for the first time. The boundaries seem obvious to a person who understands the language, but for the infant, they are not obvious at all. By generalizing from the language problem we can see that the infant must also face a similar problem when it comes to the stream of material experience that is presented to the senses.

How does the infant find the boundaries in its own stream of experience of the space-time world that will enable identification of persons, objects, events, relations, and meanings in general? Also, how does the infant find the boundaries in the stream of speech? A clue to how the infant does this is seen in the fact that although infants after the age of four months cannot identify emotions in speech presented in a foreign language (Mastropieri & Turkewitz, 1999), they can evidently distinguish between foreign speech addressed to an infant as contrasted with foreign speech addressed to an adult. Werker, Pegg, and Mcleod (1994) studied infants whose mothers spoke either English or Cantonese. They tested to see if these infants would show a preference for listening to **infant-directed speech** over adult-directed speech in both languages. In fact, both groups of infants showed a strong preference for infant-directed speech even in the foreign language. The clue that this suggests for the process of language learning is that infants are evidently sensitive at a very early age to what voice goes with what speaker and subsequently they come to pay close attention to speech that is addressed to themselves. We will return to this point in Chapter 5. Sai (2005) showed that neonates are able with very little experience to associate mom's voice with mom's face. This shows the neonate's basis for discovering the bodily content that goes with mom's voice. The problem is evidently solved by discovering that the voice of mom comes from a certain moving body. It is the one that is looking at and talking to the infant. This fact helps the infant solve the problem. Mom provides some help and the baby is able to move up in its zone of proximal development on that account. To recall Vygotsky's metaphor, even the tiniest newborn baby can stand a head taller than itself.

A Pragmatic Mapping Problem and Its Solution

In the previous chapter, we introduced the idea of pragmatic mapping. This is the process by which a given abstract sign (a symbol) comes to be associated through action (a dynamic index) with some particular bodily object (an icon). Our example in the previous chapter was the problem of associating mom's audible voice with her moving face as she speaks. For the infant, mom's distinctive voice is a kind of abstract symbol from its life in the womb, but the face of mom does not share that meaning. Mom's face is not particularly different from that of a stranger until the baby hears mom speaking and sees mom's face moving. The moving face as she speaks is a dynamic index connecting the audible voice (the symbol of mom) with a particular bodily object (the icon) that appears before the infant (see Figure 3–3). In fact, the movement is critical. It is, evidently (see Sai, 2005), the key factor that enables the baby to make the connection between the voice and the face. The movement is what demonstrates the coordinated association between mom's voice and mom's face.

In this chapter we must begin to sort out the cognitive operations that are necessary for this pragmatic sort of association to occur. The process of associating an abstract sign with a particular object is called *pragmatic* mapping. To review, this process is pragmatic because every association of this kind involves particular, concrete bodily objects (or persons), and can only occur in the present time of the person who is performing the mapping process and it must always, without exception, involve one or more particular persons acting in some particular context. In the previous chapter, an example of pragmatic mapping was the linking of mom's voice with mom's moving face by the neonate very early in its experience (see Figure 3–3). In this chapter, we have shown a more primitive example of a facial expression mapped onto a sour taste as seen in Figure 4–4. Such a mapping that is evidently innately preprogrammed and unlearned, we could say that the baby in Figure 4–3 (a particular individual baby) expresses its own reaction (a symbolic facial expression of that baby) toward the taste of the lemon juice on a particular swab that is presented by some experimenter to the infant. This presentation results in a particular experience of the infant associated with a certain kind of citrus fruit. The sour expression on the infant's face is a symbol mapped onto the taste of the lemon juice by the baby (as shown schematically in Figure 4–4).

In both instances, a certain symbolic element is associated with an impression that stands for a certain bodily object. The voice stands for mom (Figure 3–3). The sour facial expression of disgust (Figure 4–3) stands for the taste of the lemon juice (Figure 4–4). But consider how much more difficult it will be for the infant much later on, after about 10 months or more of additional experience, to associate the word "mama" with the person, mom (Figure 4–5). How can this later development take place? What ground work must be done first? Three kinds of work must first be done. For one, the infant must add to its existing sign system of content. For another, the infant must elaborate its system of speech forms. Then these

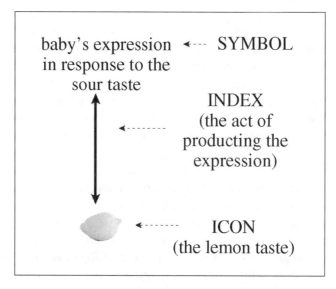

Figure 4–4. The pragmatic mapping of a facial expression onto an external stimulus.

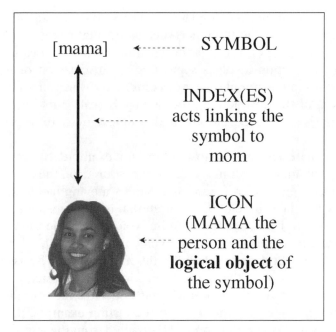

Figure 4–5. The pragmatic mapping of the word "mama" onto the person by that designation.

two streams must be connected through movements that actively link elements of the other two systems. We call this connection the pragmatic mapping process. Pragmatic mapping necessarily involves **abstraction** (J. Oller, 1996; S. Oller, 2005).

Abstraction

The process of taking content from a particular object (person, relation, or event) and associating it with an abstract sign is called *abstraction*. Abstraction is the process of carving out, parsing, or separating content from the stream of experience. It is the process of dividing up the stream of experience and associating the distinct parts, attributes, and relations with different abstract representations.

The process of abstraction begins with relatively simple associations that are largely preprogrammed. For instance, the mapping of a certain facial expression onto a certain taste such as the sour expression mapped onto the sour taste is relatively simple and evidently innately programmed (see Figure 4-4). Abstraction, however, will lead to more complex, more abstract, and more general associations such as the pragmatic mapping of mother's voice onto her moving face (Figure 3-3). Later still, it will lead to the mapping of a syllabic utterance such as [mama] onto the distinct person, MAMA, who responds to that designation as shown in Figure 4-5. The process of abstraction involves separating a particular bit of meaning or content from some material object or context in the stream of experience. This content of the abstractive process may be called its **logical object**. In the initial stages of development this object must be represented as an icon.

The neonate engages in abstraction, for example, by examining the bodily face of mother. Mom's face is the source of the content to be abstracted as suggested in Figure 3-3. Mom's moving face and her visual appearance are the source of the content that is to be abstracted. This content will come to be associated with her voice by seeing the moving face while hearing the familiar voice. The voice is a familiar abstract symbol of mom that the infant developed while still in the womb. The association of mom's moving face with that symbol constitutes an abstraction. The infant also performs such an abstraction when it associates the sour taste with its own special grimace in Figure 4-3. In the tasting example, the source of the content is the lemon, the content abstracted from the lemon is the sour taste, and the associated symbol is the infant's grimace.

Next, consider again the more difficult problem of solving the first word. As suggested by the arbitrary example in Figure 4-5, the source of the content in that case is the bodily mother of the infant. The content abstracted is all that the infant comes to know about her, and the symbol to be associated with this content is the word [mama]. Of course, the infant might make associations between different sources and symbols to start with (for example, a different first taste, person, or word), but the process of abstraction remains essentially the same. We will argue here that the process of abstraction involves three distinguishable aspects or phases. These must occur in sequence, one after the other. Also, we will argue here and in subsequent chapters that the process of abstraction must be applied to the stream of speech and to the stream of experience to build up the necessary sign systems for the acquisition of speech (or sign) and language.

Discrimination

The first phase of abstraction is **discrimination**. It involves telling the difference between sensations in hearing, seeing, touching, smelling, and tasting. The senses put the infant in contact with the stream of experience. Experience arises as the infant's body comes in contact with the material world. It must be presupposed that the infant has the capacity in advance, that is, innately, to differentiate distinct sensations of sound, sight, touch, taste, and smell. Psychologists universally use the term "discrimination" to refer to the differentiation of sensations of objects, events, persons, and relations in the world of experience. The process of discrimination is the basis for the construction of iconic representations that are differentiated from each other, for example, one taste is different from another, one face from another, one scene from another, and so on. Presumably the first icon that the infant begins to construct is a complex representation of its own body. The baby evidently does this construction (and a good deal more) before birth as shown by its ability to shape its own facial expressions to match those of someone else very soon after birth. The capacity to represent its own body (and face) must be innate because no infant yet has been born with a mirror in its hand so that it could have seen its own face while in the womb. Yet, newborn infants, according to the research from Meltzoff and Borton (1979) forward, are evidently able to match facial expressions of adults to an extent greater than chance, for example, sticking out the tongue, opening the mouth, and so on.

"Prescission"

Next, consider the second phase of abstraction which we call **prescission** (J. Oller, 1996). We will elaborate this phase of abstraction later on, but for the purpose of the present chapter we may note that it critically involves movement. The importance of movement to the discovery of the boundaries of words and objects is an idea that is suggested by other researchers (Ejiri & Masataka, 2001; Gogate, Walker-Andrews, & Bahrick, 2001). For instance, it is evident from Sai (2005) that the infant needs to be exposed to mom's moving face to associate her familiar voice with just that particular face. The movement distinguishes mom's face from other bodily things in the experience of the infant. We can say that the movement **prescinds** mother's face (separates it) from the rest of the scene and enables the association of mom's moving face with the changing sounds of mother's voice. In fact, it is the coordination of the two streams of sensations, auditory with visual, that presumably makes it possible for the infant to develop the correct association of mom's face with her voice.

Hypostasis

The third phase of abstraction is called **hypostasis**. This phase is the one that introduces an abstract symbol into the mix. It is distinctly symbolic because this phase involves a prior symbol (or abstraction) that generalizes across distinct and very different contexts of experience. The symbol must either be innate or constructed. An example of a symbol that is evidently innate is the infant's smile of contentment, or the infant's grimace at a sour taste. An example of a constructed symbol, evidently, would consist of the infant's knowledge of its mother's voice prior to its birth. All of these are abstract and general. They will be applied to the appropriate objects across a potentially infinite range of possible contexts of experience. For instance, the experience of the womb is no longer available to the infant, and yet, the sounds of mom's voice that were learned while in the womb general-ize to the sounds of that same voice outside the womb. As a result of the prior formation of a symbolic representation of that voice, that is, its prior familiarity, the infant is able to associate the new content of the moving face with the familiar sound of the voice from the womb. This mapping provides additional content with which to associate the sound of mom's voice. Once the association is established, the face alone will come to represent mom and cause the baby to think of mother's voice and the meanings (memories) associated with it. Similarly, the innate response to the sour taste of the lemon will easily and automatically generalize to addi-tional experiences that resemble the first experience with the sour taste of the lemon.

The symbol (for example, mom's voice) is enriched by content taken from experience by abstraction (for example, the look of her moving face as she speaks together with related dynamic sensations associated with feeding, changing, and so on). As additional content is associated with the sound of the voice, that content is re-entered into the stream of experience making the experience itself more intelligible than it was before. In an old and trite statement going back to Jean Jacques Rousseau and earlier, that the baby "learns to learn" is demonstrated and shown to be true.

We call the process of enriching the stream of experience the **re-entry** of content through abstract signs that are associated with whatever may be going on. Information, meaning, content is abstracted from experience and associated with the abstract signs. Then, the abstract signs are re-entered into the stream of experience making it more interpretable than it was before those signs were invested with particular content. The whole process is a cycle that can occur again and again as shown in Figure 4–6. Upon each occurrence of the cycle, however, new information is added into the developing system as it proceeds. The result is a kind of growth that accelerates over time as the baby learns to learn. The process of abstraction is not circular. In fact, a better analogy is a spiral as shown in Figure 4–7. The representational power and the meaning of the signs that are being invested with particular content by the process of abstraction grow in power, scope, and speed of processing over time.

In fact, each element of the abstractive cycle is itself a repeatable cycle. The first products of discrimination are mere sensations. However, as these come to be associated with bounded objects, the child's first coherent percepts are formed. This system of signs, that is whole percepts, as contrasted with mere features of them, are called **discriminated icons**. The first components of discriminated icons pertain to parts of the baby's

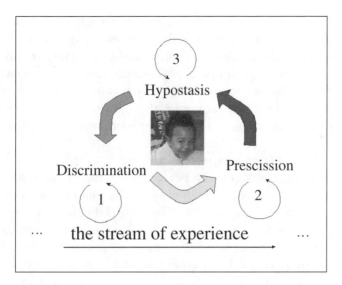

Figure 4–6. The cycle of abstraction shows how the baby learns to learn. Each phase is a cycle that forms part of the larger cycle enabling the infant to associate richer and richer content with the stream of experience.

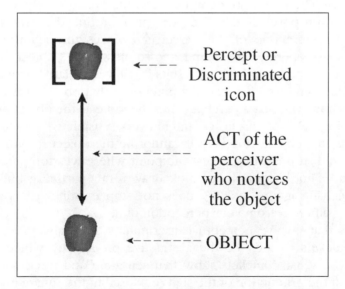

Figure 4–7. A diagram of the discriminated icon or percept of an object. The percept appears to be the object and seems to be where the object is, so it is taken to be the object for most purposes.

own body, the wall of the uterus, and the umbilical cord. The fact that the baby knows these things as distinct surfaces can be inferred from the way the fetus moves in the womb. These incoherent and incomplete components begin to take shape as the baby discriminates its own bodily surfaces by touch. Also the sounds presented to the infant in the womb provide discriminable stimuli but these are not yet coherent. They are only vaguely associated with the experience in the womb. All of these discriminated elements are only loosely connected to each other within the womb and through the amniotic fluid. However, the baby's own body, presumably, begins to form a coherent discriminable icon while the baby is still in the womb.

The percept itself incorporates its object as if the two were completely inseparable. The fact that a percept is not the same as the object can be demonstrated, however. We can remove the percept of an object from our consciousness by looking away from it, putting it down, or by otherwise ceasing to attend to it. However, the object is still there when we are not noticing it or representing it by any percept. So, the object must be distinct from the percept. The percept, in fact, is something produced by the perceiver and associated with the object through the act of perceiving that object. We can diagram the sort of relation a percept has to its object in Figure 4–7. Say, the object perceived is a shiny red apple. The percept of such a shiny red apple is abstracted from the apple by discrimination, but it must be projected right back where the apple is located if it is to count as a percept. The only distinction between the percept and its object, for all practical purposes, is that the percept is produced by the perceiver through an interaction of the perceiver's senses through the material forces of mass, energy, light, sound, and so on with the object that is perceived. If the representation that results is really associated with an object that is being perceived it is called a percept of that object. It is important to realize, however, that a percept is not the same as the object perceived. It just looks, feels, sounds, tastes, and in every sensible way resembles and represents that object. However, it cannot be the object itself or else the object would stop existing at just the point where we stop perceiving it. But this does not happen. If you look away from a particular building and stop perceiving it, the building does not stop existing. The building is something different from your perception of it.

Signs that involve perceptual discrimination are always enclosed in square brackets to indicate the abstractive process by which they are formed. The square brackets show that sensation and discrimination are involved in the production of the signs enclosed in the square brackets (as is the image of the apple in Figure 4–7). The double-headed arrow connecting the percept with its object shows their pragmatic relationship in the experience of the sign-user that produces the percept. There are really three indispensable distinct elements necessary to the formation of this and every higher coherent sign system that the baby will develop: for one, there is the logical object represented. For another, there is the abstraction that represents that logical object. In this case it is a percept (the mind's representation) of the object that is represented. For these two distinct elements to be connected with each other, an interaction must occur between them through the senses and the mind of the sign-user. That is, the sign-user must notice the object to represent it as an icon with certain surfaces, textures, and so on. Presumably the first object that an infant encounters in its experience is its own body.

Next comes prescission. Consider the way you represent a moving car on the street, for example. To know where the moving car will be after a brief lapse of time, the sign-user must imagine its line of motion along a particular trajectory. One of the elements necessary to this construction is the image of the car (or other object) that must be separated from where the car is now to place it where it will be in the future. Or to remember where the car was previously, the sign-user must take an image of the car as it now looks, sounds, and so on, and imagine it where it was before. The image that must be used in this construction involves a level of abstraction higher than discrimination. It requires separating an image of the object from that object and projecting it into a different location. This active separation of an object from its image, or an image from its object, is what is meant by prescission. The **prescinded icon** of an object, therefore, is constructed from its discriminated icon. For this reason, the discovery or construction of prescinded icons must come after the construction of discriminated icons. The result is an image of a percept of an object. It is easy to see, when we put the description of the prescinded icon in these terms, that it is more abstract than a mere percept of an object. The more abstract image must be abstracted, in other words, prescinded or taken away from, the percept. We must suppose that as soon as one or more discriminated icons are available to the infant, it is possible for the infant to move up to prescinded icons. For an illustration of the structure involved see Figure 4–8.

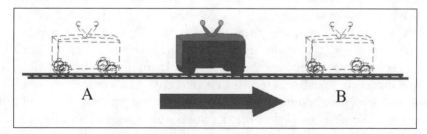

Figure 4–8. If we imagine a moving object where it was previously at position A, for instance, or where it will be later on at position B, we must use prescinded icons for each of these representations. A prescinded icon is at a higher level of abstraction than a discriminated icon because the prescinded icon is an imagined image of a percept of an object.

By moving its hands, that is, by prescinding its hands from one location to another over the surface of its body, or by moving its hands and feet against the walls of the uterus, or by feeling along the edge of a surface, the baby can integrate the many distinct discriminated icons into a more efficient system of prescinded icons. By moving, the baby discovers that the moving parts of its body are attached to a single body, as is the umbilical cord. By movement the baby gets a clearer notion of the space within which its body is contained. By movement, the baby prescinds an impression of its own body as distinct from the uterine wall. It prescinds its movable body parts as distinct from each other and from the body they are connected to. A prescinded icon necessarily is derived from a discriminated icon and must be constructed later for that reason. We have to notice an object before we can notice its movement from one location to another. We use the same sort of image to keep in mind a large object we move around it, for instance, such as a building or city. If we represent the percept of any object O as [O], the prescinded icon of that O may be represented as /[O]/ where the slashes show that the prescinded icon of an object is more abstract than the mere discriminated icon, that is, the percept of the same object.

Next, suppose that a conceptualization of the object can be removed entirely, or thought of independently, of its perceptual context. In this case the concept of the object would enable us to think of the object when it was not being perceived at all, that is, when it was not present in the context of our perceptions. Such a concept would require abstracting the content of the object so completely from its context(s) that the object would be regarded as if it were almost unchanging and completely separated from its contexts of experience. This sort of icon would involve the level of relatively complete abstraction from any real context of space and time, or the process called hypostasis. Such a sign is what we call a **hypostatic icon**. The hypostatic icon involves a level of abstraction above that of the prescinded icon. When any sign is **hypostatized**, its meaning is abstracted beyond any particular context(s) in which it may have occurred in the past. We can show all three levels of abstraction of hypostatic icon of an object, O, by enclosing the prescinded icon /[O]/, within curly braces, {/[O]/}. It is obvious that the hypostatic icon involves a step higher than the prescinded icon because the hypostatic icon, though grounded in the sort of image that is abstracted from a percept, is so completely removed from the perceptual context that the concept can be thought of without perceiving the object or its context. A hypostatic icon of an object is the sort of concept that can be conjured up in the absence of any particular context. We can think of it as an image that can be projected into empty space, an imaginary world, or anywhere and anytime we like. However, no one can reach a level higher than this sort of hypostatic abstraction because a concept cannot be any further separated from its object without losing touch with the object of which it is a concept. A concept of that sort would not be of much use. It would not be a concept of anything at all. Try to imagine an image that is not an image of anything in particular. Hypostatic icons are as abstract as icons can be, but they are extremely useful. They enable us to think of objects, persons, situations, and so on. With the help of symbols, we can even conjure up hypostatic icons of objects that we have never perceived at all, for example, unicorns and centaurs.

Can the Fetus in the Womb Form Hypostatic Icons?

The infant must come to the hypostatic level of abstraction as soon as it can think of objects that are not present. Is this level of abstraction achieved by a fetus still in the womb? Evidence that the fetus dreams suggests that it must rely on hypostatic icons in doing so. Presumably, the dreams are somewhat like the baby's waking experience in the womb. However, if the baby is able to dream of its own body, its own past actions and the like, the baby must have reached the higher level of abstraction known as hypostasis. It must have formed a hypostatic icon of itself within the womb which must also be represented abstractly for the baby to dream of itself and, presumably, its bodily experiences in the womb. Interestingly, it seems that the representations of the womb, however, are either forgotten in part or have to be relearned in the new world of perception that the infant finds him or herself in after birth.

At birth, the neonate is exposed to a whole new environment. About all that it takes with it from the womb is its own small naked body and whatever experience it can remember. Because memory is essentially dependent on signs, it is virtually certain that the baby's memory cannot contain anything for which the baby has no signs or representations. Therefore, the baby's experience cannot include much information about the outside world, and yet it also cannot be a blank slate. The evidence of dreaming along with other research evidence already presented shows that the newborn must have formed an idea of its own body. It also shows special interest in discovering the sources of the familiar voices it has been hearing while in the womb. The research shows that the neonate already discriminates the distinctive rhythms of the language of its mother.

As suggested by Figure 4-9, the neonate's development is like that of a growing spiral. At first, the relative distance separating a given sign from its object is very small. The spiral at its point of origin is very tight and the distance from one edge to another is almost zero. The distance across the spiral at any given point in time can be taken as a measure of the infant's attention span, memory, comprehension of experience, and so on. As the

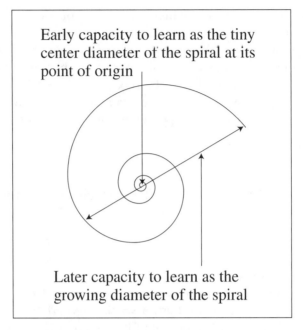

Figure 4–9. The hypothesized growth spiral resembling the shell of a snail and the shape of the cochlea in the inner ear.

infant learns to learn, all these capacities grow and they evidently do so exponentially as suggested by the growth spiral pictured in Figure 4-9.

The voice of mom, for example, is very closely associated with her face in the early experience of the neonate. Later, however, the distance from the sign to the object will become much greater. Compare the relative distance from mom's familiar voice to her, at first, unfamiliar face (for the newborn) as contrasted with the relative distance from the word "mama" to the bodily person, say, 12 to 15 months after the baby's birth. As the infant matures, signs become more abstract until they may be very remote and distant in space and in time from what they represent.

When fully abstract signs are acquired, they can represent imagined situations that never existed and even ones that are impossible, that never will exist (for example, a square circle, magic blue iron ideas, flying elephants with large leather feathers, and so on). As a result the abstractive distance of a sign to its logical objects (its content) can become so great as to be incomparably greater than any measurable distance in space and time. From here to infinity, or from now to eternity may be immeasurable distances, but adult sign systems seem to cross both distances with ease. Nevertheless, it is plain from the foregoing analysis that the infant must start in the present tense, the here and the now, just as many researchers and theoreticians have observed (Bruner, 1975; Macnamara, 1972; Pinker, 2000).

The Bootstrapping Problem and Its Pragmatic Solution

For many years there has been a great deal of discussion about how it is possible for a baby, or anyone for that matter, to come to understand what they do not, at first, understand at all? How can adults learn a foreign language? How can a baby learn its first language? The peculiar difficulty that these questions present has been discussed in a great variety of contexts.

The term "bootstrapping" has an interesting history associated with an imagined character named the Baron von Münchausen. He was invented by the humorist, Rudolf Erich Raspe [1737–1794]. On his many adventures, the unstoppable Baron was able to surmount obstacles by lifting himself out of a hole or over a mountain by pulling upward on his own bootstraps. Hence, the term "bootstrapping," which has been widely adopted into modern usage. In particular, it is applied as a back-formation to the process of "booting" up a computer. The start-up is considered a "bootstrapping" process because it is somewhat mysterious to the average user. Somehow the supply of electricity causes the system to start and the screen lights up, the programs load, and we are ready to go to work.

The question in learning theory, and in language acquisition theory, is how language learners, especially infants, are able to boot up the language learning process. How do they get started? At one extreme, some have argued that almost everything must be innate, hard-wired, and preprogrammed (cf. Chomsky, 1965, 1980, 1995, 2002; Chomsky & Fodor, 1980; Pylyshyn, 2002). At the other extreme, some have argued that almost nothing is innate and that essentially everything the infant learns must be constructed from experience (MacNeilage & Davis, 2000, 2001; Tomasello, 2003). The proposed solutions to the bootstrapping problem range at one extreme from the proposition that nearly all that the baby learns must have more or less been known in advance (cf. Chomsky, 1980; Fodor, 1980) to the proposition that the baby is able to construct any language system on the basis of at most a few simple principles involving such notions as association, reinforcement, and extinction (Skinner, 1957).

Some have proposed that the baby acquires the syntax of its native language(s) by knowing in advance some of the abstract meanings of linguistic signs. Pinker has argued that the infant only has to know the difference between "things" and "actions" to solve the basic syntactic structure of sentences which can be analyzed roughly as a combination of a **noun phrase** (NP) and a **verb phrase** (VP), or a **subject** with its **predicate**.

This proposal has been referred to as the **semantic bootstrapping** hypothesis (Pinker, 1984, 1987, 1989, 1994). Another group of theoreticians has proposed, essentially the opposite notion, that the infant has advance knowledge of syntax and is able to use this knowledge to solve for meaning. The latter proposal is called the **syntactic bootstrapping** hypothesis (Gleitman, 1990 ; Landau & Gleitman, 1985). More recently yet another theory, the idea of **prosodic bootstrapping**, has been proposed by Christophe, Nespor, Guasti, & Van Ooyen (2003). Their idea is that the rhythm of the surface-forms of a language provide cues as to its significant units of structure and syntax. Again, in this theory the emphasis is on solving the surface-forms of speech. They stress "prominence within phonological phrases" (p. 211).

In our view the first two of these proposals comingle two different kinds of meaning. Neither the semantic bootstrapping theory nor the syntactic bootstrapping theory distinguishes the kind of meaning that is fully abstract and general, which we term **semantic value**, from the kind of meaning that is fully concrete, particular, nonrepeatable, and unique, which we term **pragmatic content**. In our view, none of the three proposals takes adequate notice of the pragmatic kind of meaning. This is the sort of meaning we find in the ordinary stream experience that any normal living person who is awake encounters in the material world all the time. It consists of a stream of particular, unique, and nonrepeating perceptual experiences that are produced by the interaction of our senses with the material world as we move around in space and time. The pragmatic kind of meaning is connected to concrete bodily things situated in the world of experience that impinge on each other and interact through physical matter, force, and energy. In language use and ordinary discourse, the pragmatic kind of meaning is the sort that is directly or indirectly associated with referents consisting of persons, things, events, places, and relations between these.

Semantic meaning by contrast is abstract, general, and **conceptual** rather than **perceptual**. It is not tied to any particular material context or to any persons or even to any particular combination of words. However, to get access to semantic meaning, three things are evidently required: first, we must have some particular content to instantiate whatever abstract ideas we have the capacity to represent. That is, we must have some pragmatic content to initiate the underlying abstract concepts, in other words, to provide them with some content. To give them pragmatic (particular) meaning the abstract ideas associated at the conceptual level must become connected with some particular content.

To become connected in that way requires a particular kind of relation called reference. Such a relation must be established through an intelligent sign-user, that is, a person with the capacity to represent whatever content may be encountered. That particular content must be connected with a referring term or concept that represents it. We may say that the abstract concept, through a syntactic relation in time and space, comes to refer to certain perceptual content. For instance, the grimace of the neonate (which seems to be an innate symbol) is associated with the particular sour taste of lemon on a given occasion through the syntactic (indexical) relation that connects the grimace with the sour taste. The intelligent sign-user plays a critical role inasmuch as the grimace shows that the sign-user (the neonate) regards the sour taste as sour. For this to happen, we must presuppose that the infant has the capacity to experience the sour taste. That capacity must include the abstract semantic concept of a sour taste before any such taste is ever encountered by the infant.

The innateness hypothesis, therefore, comes into play because the abstract ideas (the concepts to be invested with perceptual content) themselves must pre-exist the particular content with which they become associated on particular occasions through acts of perception. The process of associating pragmatic meaning with such abstract concepts may be called **pragmatic bootstrapping**. That is, the formerly empty concept, a symbol without any content, or an idea that is not yet about anything in particular becomes associated with particular content through a syntactic relation linking the intelligent person with that content. Or, for an example that involves a little more learning than is required for the grimace at the sour taste, consider again the baby's discovery of the connection between mom's voice and her face. The neonate clearly does not know at birth what mom's face looks like. Sai (2005) demonstrated that infants who are kept from hearing mom's voice or otherwise sensing her, do not show a preference for her face over any other. Yet, the same babies will come to recognize mom's face easily upon experiencing face-to-face encounters where mom is talking to the baby.

Soon after this sort of experience begins, the infant has something like an "aha!" learning experience. The baby must think (in its own representational system) something like, "Oh! So this is the face of the person that goes with that familiar voice I have been hearing!" At any rate, by the 8th week of life outside the womb all the normal infants that have been studied have solved the problem of recognizing mom's face as distinct from other faces. Not only do infants by that time, or earlier, solve the problem of connecting the face with the voice, but they also soon start responding to speech directed to them with **nondistress vocalizations** of their own (Hsu, Fogel, & Messinger, 2001). That is, the baby responds with voluntary vocalizations that tend more and more to become speech-like. In fact, we can say that the infant's productions are tuned and shaped to the vocalizations of the language community into which the infant is being initiated. One of the critical keys to this initiation process is evidently the coordination of rhythms and movements.

Noticing Synchronized Movements

Sai (2005) demonstrated that the baby needs to experience mom's familiar voice along with mom's unfamiliar but moving face. We agree with Christophe et al. (2003) that prosodic features of speech provide important clues about what elements go with what referents, predicates, and so forth. But more importantly, the baby uses sensations of the pragmatic aspects of meaning to solve the surface-forms of speech or signing. The baby can perceive the familiar voice, for instance, and can locate it in space by virtue of the baby's **binaural hearing**. That is, because sound from mom's voice reaches the ear nearer to the sound sooner than it reaches the ear farther from the sound, the infant can judge which direction the sound is coming from. If mom turns the baby toward her face, the neonate can hear the sounds of the voice and can see the coordinated movements of the mouth and facial expressions at the same time. This coordination or synchrony of movements results in persuasive evidence to the infant that mom's voice is coming from that particular moving face, which must, therefore, be mom's face. The prosody, rhythm, and intonation of the voice, is important, but it is also pragmatically linked to the moving face, and the speech forms will eventually be connected with other elements of experience as well. It is the presence of mom's moving face, however, that enables the infant at just a few minutes after its birth to identify mom's face as the source of that familiar voice. What is more, the conclusion that the infant reaches while listening to the familiar voice and relating it to the, at first, unfamiliar face will later be supported by many additional experiences that confirm the baby's inference that mom's voice goes with this particular moving face. Therefore, this face is mom's face.

The infant confirms this conclusion by hearing the familiar voice while at the same time on many different occasions it is seeing, touching, smelling, and tasting the bodily presence that moves while the baby is intermittently hearing that familiar voice. The particular experiences with mom's bodily presence and the association of her face with her voice is confirmed many times over. It is facilitated at first by the prior experience that enables the neonate to distinguish mom's voice from others. The familiar linguistic rhythms and the sound of mom's voice, then, come to be coordinated with observed movements of mom's face and body. This is a prime example as demonstrated by Sai (2005) of what we have called pragmatic bootstrapping (J. Oller, 2005; J. Oller et al., 2005).

This start-up procedure for the language acquisition process involves investing existing abstract symbols with new particular content for the first time. It is a process of syntactically bringing the symbol constituted by the voice into coordinated association with the moving face. Similarly, the grimace of the neonate in response to the sour lemon taste involves the syntactic association of lemon taste with the grimace. If we suppose the infant is preprogrammed to grimace when presented with the sour taste for the first time, the particular experience of the sour taste nevertheless provides the symbol (the innate grimace) with its first particular content. Both of these examples show what we mean by pragmatic bootstrapping. They also show that the abstract concept (idea or symbol) pre-exists its instantiation in each case (as argued by Fodor, Chomsky, and others). However, that abstract concept could not have any particular content at all if it were never associated with any particular instances. The abstract general meanings (for example, enjoyment or disgust) have to be associated with particular experiences (for example, a comforting touch or the taste of a lemon) for their symbols (the smile of Figure 4-1 or the grimace of Figure 4-3) to come to have particular content.

The capacity to represent a sour taste would have little meaning to an infant that never happened to experience any sour tastes. An infant that never had any enjoyment or comfort would find little use for its own smile. Likewise the capacities to distinguish colors or sounds would have no use if they were never exercised with respect to particular colors and sounds in the real world. The capacity to recognize someone's voice would have no particular meaning if it were never associated with any particular bodily persons. Similarly, the capacity to associate complex abstract conventional signs of a language with complex states of affairs, sequences of events, and the like would also have little use if it were never pragmatically connected to the real world through perceptual experience.

The pragmatic bootstrapping theory, therefore, reaches beyond the syntactic and semantic hypotheses while at the same time incorporating elements from both. From the semantic bootstrapping idea the pragmatic solution incorporates the necessity for innate capacities including the prior existence of abstract ideas or concepts. From the syntactic bootstrapping hypothesis, the pragmatic solution incorporates the idea that a familiar element (for example, mom's familiar voice) can be brought into syntactic relation with an unfamiliar element (for example, mom's unfamiliar face) such that the familiar element syntactically linked to the unfamiliar one helps the infant to figure out the unfamiliar element. The syntactic relation enables the infant to discover meanings that would be inaccessible without that relation.

The pragmatic bootstrapping hypothesis also shows why both of the other proposals, in and of themselves, must come up short of any possible solution. There has to be an entry point to the complex and abstract world of conventional signs. The infant cannot process all the conventions at one time, and the infant cannot benefit from conventions that have not yet been discovered. For this reason, the first conventional sign, and essentially all referring expressions that point to particular objects in the real world, must be solved in the pragmatic way. That is, the infant must gain access to some particular content of the abstract sign to vest that sign with particular content. Before this happens, the sign is like an empty container. It is

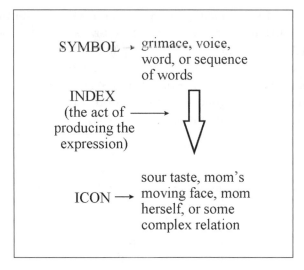

Figure 4–10. A summary and generalization of examples of pragmatic mapping relations involving icons, indexes, and symbols.

like a bank account with no money in it. It is like a pigeonhole with no pigeon. Conventional signs that are never used in the conventional ways would be completely useless.

But consider the examples of more or less abstract signs that we have already looked at in this chapter. Figure 4-10 sums up the pragmatic mapping process. An abstract symbol such as a sour face grimace is mapped through an act of perception by the infant (after some experimenter put a lemon swab in its mouth) onto the taste of the lemon. This sour face grimace, presumably, can occur in the womb. It is evidently a preprogrammed symbolic response to a sour taste, and it will generalize to a host of other things that have some similar repugnant meaning. Or, looking to the second element in Figure 4-10 on the right-hand side at the top, the familiar voice of mom, which already is associated with the womb and comfort, is pragmatically mapped onto mom's moving face through the act of mom's speaking (which the baby observes soon after birth). This mapping normally occurs a few minutes after birth, according to Sai (2005). It requires a close temporal association of mom's voice with her moving face. Or, looking to the upper right-hand side of Figure 4-10 for the next example, a word such as [mama], for instance, can be mapped through repeated associations onto the bodily person that the infant will learn to call and refer to by that sign. Interestingly, because of the vastly greater complexity of linguistic signs, as contrasted with less conventional symbols it should not surprise us that it takes a great deal more time for the infant to solve the first meaningful word and to become able to produce such a sign, one that can be understood by someone else, on its own. It takes about a year give or take a few months. And, finally, we suggest in Figure 4–10, in keeping with our own theory and research as well as the research findings of others, that the pragmatic mapping process must generalize to sequences of words and higher linguistic structures.

If any particular content or meaning for any fully abstract, general, or conventional symbol (or any concept whatever) is to be discovered, that discovery will have to involve a particular connection, a pragmatic mapping, of particular content onto that abstract symbol. There is simply no other way for a completely general abstraction to receive any particular content. Without such a particular pragmatic mapping, any abstract symbol, for example, word such as *mama*, for example, would remain without any particular content other than its own surface-form. For this reason, which we have elaborated on in other publications (see Badon, S. D. Oller, Yan & J. Oller, 2005; Oller, 1995, 2005; J. Oller et al., 2005; S. Oller, 2005), all the other kinds of bootstrapping that have been proposed and demonstrated in the literature, for example, syntactic, semantic, and prosodic, are utterly dependent on prior mappings of the pragmatic kind. For this reason, pragmatic mapping of symbols onto particular icons through indexical acts is the essential required solution to the bootstrapping problem.

Summing Up and Looking Ahead

Next, in Chapter 5, we ask how and when it is that the infant comes to recognize certain entities that move around. How does the baby know its mother, for instance, as the same person from one occasion to the next. More specifically, how does the baby come to know that its mom (or any particular bodily thing that moves) can only appear in one place at a time? How does the baby know that mom is the same person when she appears in different locations at different times? When and how does the baby come to know that an entity that disappears beyond the baby's own perceptual horizon (the baby's field of perception) is still out there? The solution to these problems are also crucial to the baby's becoming able to notice and differentiate particular syllabic utterances such as "mama," "dada," "no," and "bye-bye." Moreover, we will see that becoming able to notice events that involve motion, as distinct from each other, has to precede the infant's discovery that a certain syllabic sequence is repeated on different occasions. For this reason, the developments to be discussed in Chapter 5, concerning the baby's ability to handle motions, must come before those that are considered in Chapter 6, concerning the baby's handling of surface-forms of speech. And, in fact, they do. The baby must become able to recognize different instances of the same syllable before becoming able to produce any particular sequence in a repetitive babbling mode, for example, saying [babababa] and later [badaba], and so forth. To accomplish all this, the baby must develop systems of signs to represent movements. These are the foundational indexes which we focus on in the next chapter.

STUDY AND DISCUSSION QUESTIONS

1. When and how are babies able to develop a concept of their own bodies? What about the bodies of other human beings?

2. What role do the various senses play and how is a bodily image of the self informed by touch (pain and pleasure), taste, smell, hearing, and seeing?

3. What evidence is there that emotional expressions may be innate? In what ways can these expressions subsequently be influenced and shaped by learning?

4. Discuss the evidence for crossmodal perception. How can the infant learn to connect facial expressions and shapes with sounds of speech?

5. What evidence suggests that integration of the senses may be innate? How can we account for the fact that neonates can figure out the visual shape of an object held in the right hand but not in the left? How does this finding play into the nature/nurture controversy, if at all?

6. Discuss the different theories of bootstrapping and consider why it is essential to distinguish general concepts from particular percepts.

7. How can infants achieve higher levels of abstraction than the ones with which they begin?

8. What evidence is there that infants may possess certain abstract linguistic concepts, semantic notions, or categories from birth?

CHAPTER 5

Moving Things and Persons: Developing and Coordinating Indexes

OBJECTIVES

By studying this chapter you will:

1. Understand how talk directed to infants is easier to perceive and more interesting to them;

2. Learn more about the sound system that the infant must distinguish and differentiate;

3. See that the infants respond to actions and vocalizations which they imitate and replicate;

4. Understand how infants learn to represent persons, movements, and vocalizations;

5. See how abstraction enables construction of indexical signs;

6. Appreciate how the baby comes to know that its mom (or any singular entity) can only appear in one place at a time (excepting reflections) or that mom is still the same person when she appears in different locations at different times;

7. Discover how the normal infant, usually, by sometime between its third and sixth month, comes to know that an entity that disappears beyond the perceptual horizon is still there; and

8. Understand why indexes alone cannot fully show the distinct identities of persons.

KEY TERMS

Here are some key terms and concepts that you will find in this chapter. These terms appear in **bold print** in the text of this chapter and also are defined in the Glossary at the end of the book:

anecdotal

attentional gap

complementarity

concept of identity

conservation

discriminated index

discriminative index

Duchenne smiling

duration

experimental paradigm

formant

General Western American English

hypostatic index

identity of indiscernibles

inertial state

isomorphism

monotonic

motherese

nasalized

Ockham's razor

object permanence

panic tantrum

perfection (completeness)

prescinded index

reciprocity

sign cycle

social action

spectral properties

spectrogram

spectrograph

substance

synchronization

vegetative sounds

vocal imitation

In this chapter, we consider the processes by which the infant becomes able not only to coordinate its sign activities with the signs and social actions of others, but to represent movements efficiently through indexes. The ability of infants to coordinate their own actions and movements in response to movements of other objects and persons is essential to the development of indexes that are crucial to language acquisition.

In the previous chapter we saw that by the third month after birth, the normal infant is already able to differentiate the vowel space (refer to Figure 3–4) of its native language. By this time infants are actively engaged in defining key articulatory and auditory targets within that space that define and differentiate the vowels of their native language. They explore the space through the speech of others and through their own vowel-like cooing. We have already seen that infants at this stage can tell the difference, for instance, between the vowels /i/, /u/, and /a/ (Aldridge, Stillman, & Bower, 2001) and they seem to know what mouth shapes go with the production of different vowels (Kuhl & Meltzoff, 1982, 1984; MacKain, Studdert Kennedy, Spieker, & Stern, 1983; Walton & Bower, 1993). Also, the infant produces vocalizations that increasingly resemble the vowels they hear (Kuhl & Meltzoff, 1996). Even before three months of age the normal infant is intrinsically interested in speech directed to itself as contrasted with speech directed to others and the baby is becoming more and more competent at engaging mom or other adults in conversation-like exchanges. These exchanges are not only becoming more speech-like (Fogel & Hsu, 2003; Hsu & Fogel, 2003) but the infant and its communication partners are becoming more attuned to one another.

Infants not only begin to time the rhythms of their movements from birth (Condon & Sander, 1974) and to coordinate them with the rhythms of the speech of others, but normal infants will also imitate the actions (for example, tongue protrusion, lip rounding, and so on; Meltzoff & Moore, 1977, 1997) of others as well as the sounds that they make (for example, normal infants differentiate their own vowel-like cooing sounds; Kuhl & Meltzoff, 1996). What is more, as important as pitch and rhythms must be in helping infants divide up the stream of speech, Vouloumanos and Werker (2004) found that infants by as early as their second month prefer to listen to fully articulated speech rather than to synthetic analogues of speech retaining just the pitch and contour information. Even the youngest infants in their study (ranging in age from two to seven months) preferred to listen to fully differentiated speech.

Newborns Show Surprise and Take Defensive Actions

John Locke (1690) is among the most famous of philosophers of the past who is supposed to have argued (see Kaye & Bower, 1994) that infants come into the world with a brain that is essentially a blank sheet. His actual claim by our reading was that the infant's capacity for experience and memory is essentially an unwritten page. Locke never denied that human infants are different from stones and from other creatures that never learn to talk. He did not deny that infants have innate capacities that are different from the capacities of stones or even of other species. However, some have claimed that Locke's "blank slate" theory meant that infants have to learn everything from scratch. If this were so, infants would have to have quite a lot of experience in seeing, hearing, touching, smelling, and tasting to integrate their senses. They ought to have to discover from experience that a visible object is tangible. They should not know this before they are born. To the contrary, Bower, Broughton, and Moore (1970) demonstrated that newborns at less than a week, provided they are awake and sitting up, will take defensive action against an object approaching their faces. The eyes of the infant open wide suggesting surprise. Their heads go back suggesting avoidance of the oncoming object. And, their hands go up between the face and the object as if to ward off the impending collision. Although it used to be common to suppose that infants had to learn to see space as three-dimensional, and that they had to learn that visible objects are also tangible, the research of Bower and colleagues suggests that this is not so. The neonate evidently has built-in, innate integration of the senses.

In Chapter 3 we saw evidence that newborns can perform certain face and tongue movements in response to movements by an adult, for example, opening the mouth and protruding the tongue. In fact, in Chapter 2 we saw that babies in the womb can form certain facial expressions that resemble ones that they will use throughout their lives, for example, the smile, grimace, and so forth, and that fetuses seem to know a good deal about their own bodies. They can put their hand to their mouths, suck their fingers and toes, touch their faces, their heads, and the like. Also, research shows that fetuses take extreme evasive actions to avoid a needle stick in certain medical procedures (Birnholz, Stephens, & Faria, 1978). It is not surprising that older babies anticipate pain when presented with a needle in an inoculation procedure (Ramsay & Lewis, 1994). Also, heel lancing in newborns results in pain expressions and avoidance (Lindh, Wiklund, & Hakansson, 1999; Owens & Todt, 1985). For these reactions to occur at such a young age, the infants must be credited with some knowledge about their own bodies. While pulling away from a sharp needle might be attributed to a reflex, the widening of the eyes and movement of the hands to a defensive posture as an object approaches the baby's face cannot easily be explained in that way (Bower, Broughton, & Moore, 1970), much less can we explain the fetus striking the barrel of a needle that penetrates the womb with its fist (Birnholz, Stephens, & Faria, 1978).

If the fetus knows where its body parts are before it ever opens its eyes, and that a tangible object can be pushed away from its body, it would seem reasonable to suppose that the neonate must have a prior representation of its own body before it is born. In the womb the baby can feel the boundaries of its own body. Its own hands, feet, tongue, lips, head, and so forth come in contact with other surfaces and with each other. It is not too difficult to understand, therefore, how the fetus in the womb can perceive its own body, and the space in which it is contained. By the process of abstraction, the fetus should be able to provide specific content with which to invest the concept (the hypostatic icon) of its own body.

But, consider how much more difficult a task it is for the baby to notice distinct words, utterances, or vocalizations and how much more difficult still it will be to eventually associate those distinct forms with particular content. Werker and Tees (1999) described the process in terms of "breaking into" the continuous "stream of speech, pull[ing] apart and represent[ing] its units, and eventually map[ping] sound to meaning" (p. 510). But how can the infant discover the relevant meanings? What meanings precisely is the infant supposed to focus on at the beginning, say, before its first meaningful word? Evidently, the infant's world is chock full of potentially meaningful things, persons, events, relations, and so forth, so how does the infant ever discover what in particular someone else is talking about?

The problem faced by the infant is more difficult than the one faced by a foreign language learner. The infant not only has to discover where the boundaries of surface-forms of speech are, but must also sort out all the other experiences of the perceptual kind from all other sources as well. These are nontrivial problems that the infant faces on all accounts, and yet normal human infants universally solve both problems. According to the research infants evidently begin to solve both problems simultaneously by relying on the coordination, the synchrony, of various rhythms. The demonstrations by Sai (2005) show that infants see their mother's moving face moving in perfect cadence, an almost exact synchrony, with the familiar rhythms of mother's voice. Evidently, it is this rhythmic coordination that enables the solution to the problem of connecting the voice and the face. In what follows we argue that similar synchronies and variations on that same theme are essential to the infant's acquisition of any language system.

Isomorphisms, Synchrony, and Coordination of Movements

Neonates do a lot more than merely discriminate mom's moving face to associate it with her familiar voice. They begin to notice very early the distinct facial expressions of mom and others and they can imitate those expressions with some effort. If the adult opens her mouth, the neonate will, with some effort, more often than would be expected by chance, also open its mouth. The baby matches, at least in part, the other person's movements. To the extent that the movements are the same or result in the same facial expression, an **isomorphism** is achieved. The neonate is also engaging in a kind of intentional social coordination of its own movements in response to movements of the other person. The baby is engaging in coordinated **social action** by imitating the movements and facial expressions of the other person. In doing this, the baby is bringing its own rhythmic movements into a kind of **synchronization**, although it is a clumsy and imperfect synchrony at first, with the rhythmic actions of the other person.

Cutler (1994) has suggested that the rhythmic properties of speech enable infants to begin to segment the stream and to find the relevant boundaries of syllables, words, and phrases. A similar argument can be made for the segmentation of dynamic social interactions. How does the baby notice different facial expressions in order to imitate them? How are the distinct movements discriminated from the welter of different things going on? Interestingly, rhythms are defined by beats, like the beating of a drum, or the repetition of a syllable such as "babababa" where the number of syllables equals a certain number of beats. If we ask how the neonate notices the beats, the solution to that problem is similar to the solution to the problem of noticing changes in facial expressions. Sticking out the tongue starts with the mouth closed and then consists of the protruding tongue, and ends when the tongue is drawn back into the mouth. The opening of the mouth begins with the mouth closed, then consists of a sustained opening of the mouth for a brief time, followed by closure again. The protruding of the lower lip begins with the mouth closed, then the lip protruded, and then no longer protruding. Each of these actions is distinguished as a segment of time that is marked by a beginning, middle, and end. These phases combined constitute an event. In each case the event is different. If any one of these events is imitated by the infant, the infant's action is coordinated in time with the action of the adult. To accomplish this imitation, it is essential that the infant coordinate its bodily movements with those of the other person. The infant must achieve a kind of synchrony with the other person.

Another critical element of this kind of social interaction that theoreticians have commented on and that researchers have studied is the coordination of actions that is taking place. The infant and adult in imitative interactions are attending to each other. There is a kind of **reciprocity**, a mutual interest in each other that results in a kind of sharing of experience, or what some have called intersubjectivity. By this they mean that the baby and the adult are sharing the same subject matter. They are sharing a common experience. They are engaging each other in the same activity or game. In a single word, they are communicating. It is as if the infant were thinking something like "I see you seeing me" and "I see what you are doing" and "I can do it too because I am like you." Sometimes in early infancy the interaction takes the form of a voluntary vocalization (a nondistress vocalization) by the infant followed by a similar cooing vocalization by the adult that may be repeated by the infant through a series of multiple exchanges. We have all observed and participated in vocal interactions of this type with neonates. It is as if the neonate were saying by its vocalization, "I'm here, is there anyone out there?" and the adult is responding by saying "I'm out here, and I hear you. Do you hear me too?" In our own experience as adults, we suppose that much more is involved from the side of the father, grandfather, mother, or grandmother holding the newborn. The adult is thinking and possibly saying out loud something like, "Where have you been all my life and why do I love you so much seeing as how we have hardly ever met before?" And perhaps the infant is saying more too. Perhaps the infant is saying, "Oh good! There is someone out there. Let me just confirm that fact by cooing again." Once assured that in fact there is someone out there who is cooing back, the infant is apt to smile. The adult cannot keep from smiling back.

Among the evidence that supports this kind of analysis of what is going on as babies interact with their mothers or other caregivers is research showing that infants are considerably more interested from the earliest stages of their development in speech that is directed to themselves, or even to another infant, than to speech that is directed to an adult. It seems as though infants are intrinsically interested not only in where any given voice might be coming from, but sometime after the first month, the baby also seems to be able to tell the difference between speech directed to an infant or to another adult. As we noted earlier in Chapter 4, infant-directed speech is evidently more interesting to infants than speech directed to adults. For instance, Cooper, Abraham, Berman, and Staska (1997) demonstrated in one experiment that at one month after birth, even when infants do not know the voices of the persons speaking, they show a preference for recordings of speech directed to an infant as contrasted with speech directed to an adult. The authors conclude that there are distinct qualities associated with infant-directed speech that enable this preference to manifest itself. In another experiment with four-month-old infants the same researchers found that the four-month-olds had a marked preference for infant-directed speech.

What are those distinguishing qualities of infant-directed speech? It is, incidentally, often referred to as **motherese** or baby-talk, maternal speech, or parentese. Distinctive properties of motherese that have been studied include:

- the pitch (which tends to be higher and with exaggerated modulation in "motherese," or infant-directed speech),

- the rate of speech (slower than in adult-directed speech and with longer pauses),

- the length of syllables (longer),

- distinctness of vowels (exaggerated),

- proximity of the interlocutors (closer),

- accompanying gestures (more pronounced but also slower),

- emotional quality (positive and gentler in tone),

- and accompanying touch (which is less likely in adult-directed speech).

Kuhl et al. (1997) demonstrated that speech directed to infants by their mothers tends to involve a larger and more distinct vowel space. That is to say, in infant-directed speech the differences, for instance, between /i/, /u/, and /a/ will be exaggerated so that the vowels are made more distinct from each other. The mouth is opened more widely on /a/, the lips are more rounded on /u/, and the tension associated with the production of /i/ is increased in infant-directed speech. This kind of exaggerated articulation and facial expression is evidently a universal tendency of adults when addressing infants. Brand, Baldwin, and Ashburn (2002) showed that when mother's demonstrate novel objects to their infants (ages 6–8 months or 11–13 months) as contrasted with similar demonstrations to an adult partner they intensify their "interactiveness, enthusiasm, proximity to partner, range of motion, repetitiveness and simplicity" (p. 72). The researchers interpreted these results as indicating that mothers use these surface-form adjustments to assist infants in understanding the structure and meaning of such social interactions. Some of the main distinctive characteristics of motherese in spoken language systems have also been shown to carry over to signed languages of the deaf. For instance, Masataka (1992) showed that deaf mothers using Japanese Signed Language with their own infants used signs at a slower tempo, with more frequent repetition, and with exaggerated movements as contrasted with their signing when communicating with adult friends.

Moms and other caregivers also pay close attention to the vocalizations of infants and respond to them differentially. Hsu and Fogel (2003) studied 13 infant and mom pairs in face to face interactions from the second month roughly to the sixth month (weeks 4 to 24) of the infants. Their results suggested that nondistress vocalizations by the infant tended to be linked with maternal facial expressions and touching more than with mom's head movements. Reporting on the same 13 infant and mother pairs, Hsu, Fogel, and Messinger (2001) found that the number of infant nondistress vocalizations increased and the "speech-likeness" of those vocalizations increased when mom and the infant were looking at each other and smiling. The babies produced "more speech-like syllabic sounds when their mothers were smiling, when they were looking at their mothers' faces, and when the infants themselves were smiling" (p. 107). The rate of speech-like syllabic sounds "was highest during **Duchenne smiling** (cheek raise smiling)" (p. 107). The infants were more apt to produce speech-like sounds when they were smiling and looking at their mother smiling back at them.

Vocal Imitation

In the period from birth to six months the research shows that infants are not only especially interested in speech directed to themselves and to other infants, but that in their voluntary actions and vocalizations they increasingly tend to imitate the speech sounds that they hear. Kuhl and Meltzoff (1996) argue that infants start off with a universal capacity to produce voluntary vocalizations that are not language specific. However, as the infant progresses and develops, vocalizations become increasingly language specific. They contend that a key element in this process of change over time is **vocal imitation**. They studied the change in infant vocalizations from weeks 12 to 16 to 20 in response to the vowels /a/, /i/, and /u/ as produced by adults. The vowels were presented via videotape and the analysis of the baby's vocalizations was done with a computerized **spectrograph**. The spectrographic analysis enables measurement of the distance between the distinct resonant components, known as **formants**, of the vowels produced by the adults as compared with the vowel-like vocalizations of the infants.

Figure 5–1 shows the main formants (bands of sound energy) from about 20 Hz up to 4000 Hz in the vowel /i/ as in the word "heed" as

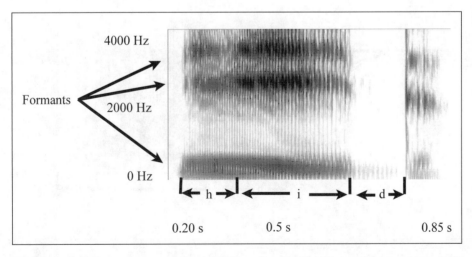

Figure 5–1. A spectrogram of the word "heed" as spoken by a 25-year-old male in General Western American English.

spoken in the most widely used variety of American English. We call it **General Western American English** (see Figure 5-2 below).

Usually the first three formants as seen in the bottom of Figure 5-1 are sufficient to identify the vowel. The **spectrogram** shows the frequency in hertz (Hz) on the vertical dimension and time in seconds on the horizontal. It can be seen that the entire word "heed" requires only about six-tenths of a second to produce, and that the vowel sound "ee," /i/, requires about half that time. The spectrogram shows that even after the /d/ is released, key formants can still be distinguished in the **spectral properties** of the preceding vowel. Similarly, we already see the vowel formants in the /h/ sound before the voicing associated with /i/ becomes evident in the picture.

Different vowels, of course, produce different spectral patterns. Compare Figure 5-2 showing the formant structure for /a/ as in the word "hod" as in "hod carrier" (where "hod" is a rare word in English used to refer to wet cement plaster before it is applied to a wall). According to Kuhl and Meltzoff (1996), between weeks 12 and 20, infant productions became more distinct and the vowel formants increasingly approximated those produced by adults. The analyses showed that infants hearing a particular vowel tended to produce vocalizations that resembled it. Evidently, the babies are able to represent the sounds they hear and use those sounds as models for their own productions. They imitate the sounds produced by the adults.

Patterson and Werker (2003) produced evidence that infants as young as two months of age already know something about the mouth shapes

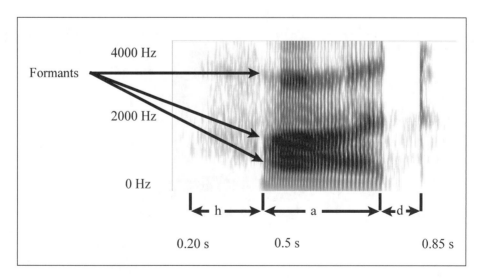

Figure 5–2. A spectrogram of the word "hod" as spoken by a 25-year-old male in General Western American English.

required to produce certain vocalic sounds. It had been shown earlier by Kuhl and Meltzoff (1982) and by Patterson and Werker (1999) that by 4.5 months infants know that an /u/ sound is distinct from an /i/ and can match them appropriately with lip shapes as well. In 2003, Patterson and Werker reported tests with 2 month old infants showing that they preferred lip shapes that matched the vowel they were hearing over ones that did not match, for example, /i/ cannot be produced with rounded lips, so the infants preferred to look at a widened flat lip facial expression when hearing that sound. More importantly, Aldridge, Stillman, and Bower (2001) found evidence that neonates of English-speaking moms seem to know without any experience of the sound /y/ (a high front rounded vowel of French as in "tu" and Mandarin that does not occur in English at all) that it requires rounding of the lips. The /y/ sound cannot be produced with the lips in the /i/ shape. How do the infants born to English-speaking moms know this? Aldridge and colleagues suggest that the association of lip shapes with vowel sounds may be innate. Or, if learning has produced this effect, it is difficult to see how that learning could have taken place.

On the other hand, there is no denying that infants are excellent learners from before birth. They seem naturally to associate new and unfamiliar stimuli with familiar representations. By three months of age, as Brookes, Slater, Quinn, Lewkowicz, Hayes, and Brown (2001) have demonstrated, infants can make new pairings of voices and faces. The researchers familiarized infants to novel voice face combinations (male face to female voice and vice versa). Later, when the infants were presented with a familiar voice and a familiar face that had not previously been combined as contrasted with a pairing that had been presented previously, infants studied the novel pairing. This result suggests that infants can easily learn arbitrary voice face associations. Therefore, human infants are not only endowed with certain innate capabilities by virtue of their being human, but among their remarkable capacities is the ability to notice and remember arbitrary associations. That is, human infants are good and fast learners.

The Infant Coordinates with Adult Rhythms and Imitates Forms

Normally, around the third postnatal month, the infant makes a significant transition from vocalic sounds to more syllabic vocalizations. Vocalic cooing sounds of infancy are voluntary vocalizations distinct from **vegetative sounds** (burps, grunts, gurgles, raspberries, and so on). Vocalic sounds tend to be relatively **monotonic** (the same pitch throughout), shorter (about 500 ms, or half a second; Masataka, 1995) and more **nasalized**, whereas syllabic vocalizations are longer in **duration** (about 870 ms; Masataka, 1995), less nasalized, and more varied in pitch (Bloom, Russell, &

Wassenberg, 1987; Ejiri & Masataka, 2001; Masataka, 1995). At about the third month the normal infant makes a significant transition from vocalic cooing to more distinctly syllabic vocalizations. At this transitional point, the infant begins to produce vocalizations that increasingly fit the consonant-vowel (CV) structure that is not only universal to child language development but also to all the languages of the world (Pan, 2005; Pan & Snyder, 2003, 2004, 2005; Prince & Smolensky, 1993/2004). Even before this transition from cooing to more syllable-like vocalizations takes place, as early as the ninth week, normal babies will commonly extend their index finger after cooing in what appears to be a pointing gesture (Fogel & Hannan, 1985; Masataka, 1995). The research shows that adults are more apt to regard these syllable-like vocalizations as conversational acts. As a result, when the infant produces more syllabic vocalizations, adults are more apt to try to engage them in conversation-like (turn-taking) exchanges (Bloom & Lo, 1990; Masataka, 1995; Masataka & Bloom, 1994).

Additionally, research by Meltzoff and his colleagues has demonstrated that infants from birth not only engage in rhythmic turn-taking exchanges with adults, but they also shape their actions to imitate those of the adults. Meltzoff (1999) concludes that "parent infant games are often reciprocally imitative in nature" (p. 256). That is, when the infant does something, an adult partner is apt to replicate the action and to invite the infant to repeat its action. Meltzoff agrees with Bruner (1983) and Stern (1985) that this "kind of turn-taking forms a sort of 'rhythmic dance' between mother and child" but he speculates that "reciprocal imitative games provide the infant with special information about how it is like another person and how another is 'like me'" (p. 256).

The fact that neonates will imitate tongue protrusion or other facial gestures (Meltzoff & Moore, 1977, 1997; Tatsumoto, 1993) supports the notion that the form and not merely the timing of exchanges is important from a very early age from the infant's point of view. In an experimental context, Meltzoff (1990) presented infants with a pair of adult experimenters sitting across from the infant in plain view. One experimenter did everything the infant did. The other at the same time imitated the behavior of a different infant. Both were doing things that an infant does, but only one was doing the same things as the infant being tested. The infant looked more and smiled more at the adult doing what the infant was doing. The results showed that infants directed more visual attention and smiled more at the person who was imitating them. They preferred an adult who was playing a matching game. If we take into consideration that within their first two to three weeks infants can imitate tongue protrusion, mouth opening, lip protrusion, and simple finger movements according to 24 research studies reviewed by Meltzoff and Moore (1997), we are led to suppose that in making the transition from cooing to more syllable-like sounds, three-month-old infants are being influenced by the syllables commonly produced by the adults in the infant's community.

Fleshing Out and Connecting the Signs
Needed to Develop Language

As we have seen in previous chapters, the infant must fill out and integrate three distinct kinds of sign systems. These consist of (1) icons, (2) indexes, and (3) symbols. The most basic symbols, emotional expressions, seem to be connected to objects at first by innate built-in systems that are preprogrammed (for example, the taste of lemon produces a grimace). However, symbols consisting of voluntary vocalizations and voluntary movements must be incorporated into the infant's repertoire by experience with the particular conventional associations that vest those symbols with particular meanings. In the normal infant's third month it is generally conceded that the baby has *not yet learned any conventional linguistic signs* (for example, Ejiri & Masataka, 2001). However, the pointing gesture suggests that the baby is on the verge of acquiring referential signs. What is more, pragmatic mappings of voices to faces, which occurs within minutes or at most an hour or two after birth, seem to suggest that even the neonate is capable of building primitive referential associations that consist of unique and arbitrary symbolic associations of voluntary vocalizations with particular bodily objects, for instance, mom's voice with mom's face. That is, the neonate is already capable of discovering a new conventional association of a voice (as a distinct symbol) through an indexical coordination (a series of coordinated actions) with a new icon never before perceived (mom's face).

There are also many other indications that the baby is intensely interested in the surface-forms of conventional signs, especially linguistic ones, and in the persons who produce them even before birth. In this chapter we delve further into the indexical processes by which these associations are worked out by normal infants. We suppose that advances are critically dependent on the cyclic process of abstraction (J. Oller, 1996; J. Oller et al., 2005; J. Oller & Rascón, 1999; S. Oller, 2005). We have given the basic elements of that process in Chapter 4. To see how the infant works out the **concept of identity** of bodily objects that move around, appear, disappear from the infant's perceptual field, and later reappear multiple times, it is necessary to examine more closely the relations between icons, indexes, and symbols. It turns out that icons are the least abstract of these three most basic sign systems and that they must be discovered first. Indexes can only be constructed after at least some icons have already been represented by the infant. What is more, indexes are crucial to working out the identities of persons and to distinguishing and recognizing conventional linguistic signs.

The Concept of Identity

In a series of experiments, Bower (1971) showed that human infants by two weeks after birth expect a visible object to be tangible. This shows some fairly advanced knowledge about relations across sensory modalities. It also shows that the infant has prior knowledge (presumably innate knowledge) that a visible object has some mass, density, and inertial momentum. They seem to understand something about folk physics. At the same time, infants before about 12 weeks after birth demonstrate in a variety of ways that they do not know that a moving object is the same object when it stops moving. They also do not know that an individual object (or person) can only appear in one place at a time. Infants do not understand identities the way adults do. Still, they know some things about objects, evidently from birth, that Piaget thought they ought to have to learn much later. The discovery of these facts, along with other similar discoveries was so unsettling that Meltzoff (1999) says it resulted first in the "gradual weakening, and finally the collapse of, classical Piagetian theory (Piaget, 1952, 1954, 1962)." To see why this happened, it is useful to review some of the relevant findings in detail.

Among the first of the surprises that challenged Piaget's theory was the fact that neonates evidently already know from birth that visible objects are tangible and that things have enduring qualities. According to Piaget, this was not expected. He believed that infants had to learn to associate sight with touch by seeing and touching. He also thought that infants required a good deal of experience to discover that solid objects do not cease existing when they pass from view. He referred to this problem as one of **object permanence**. He saw it as a special case of what he called **conservation**, the tendency for solid objects and to a lesser extent for liquids to maintain their mass, volume, and the like. Piaget noted that infants before about three months of age will seem to search for an object that is covered by an adult's hand in plain view of the infant. If the infant is attending to the object when it is concealed by the adult, the infant will seem to look in other locations as if the object might reappear somewhere else. It seems that the infant is unable to take account of the obvious fact (at least obvious to the adult) that the object is still where it was before it was hidden by the adult. From this observation, and others like it, Piaget inferred that infants do not know that solid objects have durability, or what he called "object permanence."

But Bower's studies with neonates from birth to two weeks showed that they make defensive movements when a visible object seems to be on a collision course with the baby's face. Provided the infant is awake it will perform defensive movements to avoid the impact of an object moving toward its face. Infants younger than two weeks probably have not been hit in the face by moving objects (other than their own flailing hands perhaps), but they show evidence that they know that visible objects should also be tangible. Their expectations concerning the solidity of a visible moving object are much more like those of an adult than Piaget's theory suggested they ought to be. The baby seems to know that the visible object has properties like solidity (that is, it can be touched), mass (it has weight), and momentum (if moving at me it may hurt me).

Bower found that infants of 16 to 24 weeks show intense surprise when they reach for a visible object that turns out to be an illusory image. When their hand reaches the place where the object appears to be, the infants universally show astonishment in their facial expression and accompanying vocalizations. By 20 days postnatal (less than one month of age), infants also evidently expect an object that is briefly screened by another object that moves between the infant and the first object to still be there when the screen is removed. Bower found that infants at only 20 days show marked surprise when an object that has been occluded for 1.5 seconds is no longer present when the screen is removed. Evidently, infants know that the occluded object should still be behind the screen. Contrary to the Piagetian theory, these infants seem already to know that visible objects have some durability. Although very young infants seem to forget the object if the occlusion persists, say, for 15 seconds, all the evidence combined suggests normal human infants know at birth that visible objects are solid, that they have some durability, and that they are tangible. Objects in the world of the infant are more like those in the adult world with respect to solidity and durability than Piaget's theory predicted.

However, in studying the infant's expectations concerning bodily objects (including persons), Bower discovered that infants make certain distinctions that adults do not make and that infants before about week 16 seem to overlook certain relations that are so obvious to adults that we take them completely for granted. By 8 weeks, normal infants can easily track a slow moving object by moving their head and eyes as needed, but, surprisingly, if the object stops in its path of motion, the infant looks at the stationary object and then continues to follow the former path of motion as if the object that has stopped in plain view is a totally different object. Bower demonstrated this phenomenon in an interesting series of experiments. In one **experimental paradigm**, illustrated in Figure 5–3, infants at 8 weeks of age would watch an object move in a complete circle in full view, but when the object stopped moving in plain view of the infant, the infant would seem to search ahead along the line of motion as if looking for the moving object. As shown in Figure 5–3, all positions on the path were visible to the infant. Nevertheless, when the moving object stopped, the infant would look ahead along the circular path as if searching for the formerly moving object. Why? It seems that the baby does not yet know that the moving object is the same one that has just stopped. For this reason Bower supposed that the problem is one of identity. The baby indicates that it can see the object that has stopped by pausing to look at it briefly, but then looks ahead along the path of movement as if searching for the moving object. Bower concluded that the difference between the world as represented by the infant before its 16th week, and the world as repre-

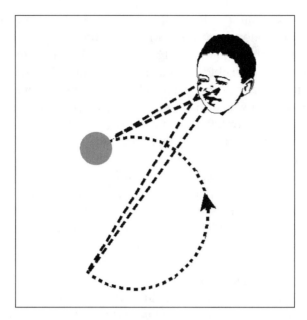

Figure 5–3. The infant seems to search for a moving object along its former path of motion even though the object has stopped moving in plain view. See Bower, T. G. R. (1971). The object in the world of the infant. *Scientific American, 225*(4), 30–38. The diagram shown here is adapted from p. 34 by permission. Copyright © 1971 by Scientific American, Inc.

sented by an adult, is not so much a problem of conservation or object permanence as Piaget supposed, but is more a question of object identity.

To follow up on this surprising finding, Bower (1971) devised a series of additional experiments with moving objects. The results tended to show in a variety of ways that infants before about 16 weeks of age do not know that the moving object that stops its motion is the same object as the one that was moving before. Bower supposed, therefore, that the world as represented by the infant before 16 weeks of age seems to contain a much greater number of objects than the adult world. Bower inferred from several studies that infants simply do not know two things that are obvious to adults: for one, the infants before about 16 weeks do not know that the same object can appear in different states, for example, stationary versus moving. But, if this is so, a second aspect of adult knowledge must also be missing from the infant's representations. If the infant (before about 16 weeks) supposes that objects that seem different in their appearances must be different objects, then, infants at this stage of development should not be surprised if an object turned up in several places at once. If objects that seem different in any way are naïvely taken to be completely different objects, then, how would the infant differentiate the case of one object that moves around from several similar objects appearing in different locations at the same time?

The difficulty faced by the infant can be made obvious. It can be diagramed, as shown in Figure 5-4. Imagine that the columns in Figure 5-4 are objects (any similar objects would do, for example, like similar-looking horses or cattle in a corral). Suppose they appear in different places, say, place *a, b,* and so forth at the same time. By contrast, imagine that the cups on the rows are ones that are being moved around (like cattle in a corral, say) so that at time *1*, cup *a* is in place *1*, but at time *2*, it is in a different place, and so on for all the cups, for all the places, and for all the different moments in time. The problem faced by anyone wanting to tell which objects are the same and which ones are different only seems easy to solve from the point of view of someone who has already solved the problem.

Adults have solved it so well that it does not seem to be a problem anymore. But now and then, it comes up in a form that makes the problem obvious. Consider the difficulty we have in singling out a person or following someone in a huge crowd. In a movie about a thief in a museum, the police are befuddled when the museum is suddenly populated by several men dressed alike, going in different directions. Which one is the thief? Whom should they follow? Or the difficulty can be seen in trying to keep track of a particular card as it is reinserted face down into an entire deck of cards. Yet another demonstration is the so-called "shell game" where a

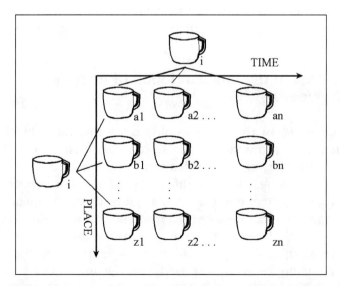

Figure 5–4. The same object seems the same at different times, and similar objects seem the same in different places, so, indexes alone cannot fully differentiate distinct identities.

pea is placed under one of three similar looking shells and the shells are shuffled rapidly. The problem is to say which shell has the pea under it after the shuffling stops. Perfectly normal human infants before the age of about 16 weeks have not yet solved the problem in question for the simpler case of a single object that moves around. The object seems the same but the places are different. How is the infant to know for sure that the object has not also changed its identity along with its location?

Bower inferred from infant behaviors with moving versus stationary objects that for infants between about 8 and 16 weeks, the world must seem to contain many more distinct objects than are actually in it. He described the infant's world as "grossly overpopulated" where "an object becomes a different object as soon as it moves to a new location. In this world, every object is unique" (1971, pp. 37-38). Looking to Figure 5-4, from the adult point of view, several cups perceived, say, on different shelves (for example, cups *a*, *b*, and *z*, in Figure 5-4) at the same time must be taken to be different objects. The infant before 16 weeks would agree. However, for an adult, any given cup, say *a* or *b* or *z*, that might be moved around to different locations would still be the same cup. But here the infant before 16 weeks would not agree. The infant would regard the same object appearing in different locations as if it were several different objects. For the infant at that age, there would be as many different objects as there are locations and movements between those locations even if one and the same object were moved around. For instance, if cup *a* were moved from position *1*, to position *2*, and to *n* different positions, the baby before 16 weeks would tend to regard all these as different objects. In fact, the situation is evidently even a little more severe. The infant would also regard each instance of movement as involving yet another object.

A Crucial Test of the Infant's Notion of Identity Before 20 Weeks

Bower wondered how the infant would react if the same object appeared in multiple places at the same time. He supposed that if the infant before about 16 weeks does not know that a moving object is the same object when it stops moving, then, the infant should also not expect any given object to appear only in one place at any given time. The infant before 16 weeks of age should not be surprised if a familiar object, say, mom, should turn up in several places at the same time. If the infant regards the situations shown on the columns and the rows of Figure 5-4 as the same, then the infant could not be much surprised if a single individual should turn up in several places simultaneously. This event should be no more surprising than several different objects turning up in different places at the same time.

To test the latter hunch, Bower devised an experiment involving the baby's mother. We now know from various studies that a baby can distinguish its mother's voice before birth. Also, from Sai (2005) we know that a neonate can associate its mother's face with the familiar voice of mom very soon after birth. Bower (1971) inferred that if normal infants until about 16 weeks see moving objects as distinct from their stationary counterparts, even when the objects are the same, these infants should not be surprised by seeing multiple images of mom in different locations at the same time. By using an arrangement of mirrors, Bower was able to present infants (before 20 weeks of age) with three simultaneous images of mother, or of mom with two strangers. Infants before week 20 differentiated mom from the strangers, but were not at all surprised by mom when she appeared in three places at once. They cooed and smiled at each of the three images of mom.

The obvious conclusion was that the infants before 20 weeks knew their mother's identity in the sense of recognizing her as distinct from other persons, but they did not know that mother must be a single individual who can only appear in one place at one time. Infants 20 weeks or older, however, were surprised when mom appeared in three places at once. In Bower's words they "became upset at the sight of more than one mother" (1971, p. 38). Infants at 20 weeks or older showed disturbed surprise at mom appearing in three places at once. Evidently, the older children had learned something that the younger infants did not yet know about mother's identity. All the children recognized their mom and distinguished her from the strangers, but the more mature infants seemed to know that mom should only appear in one place at any given time.

Bower's research not only tells us something significant about the sign system that young infants are developing, but it also shows that the concept of identity itself is more complicated and subtle than it might seem to mature language users. Mathematicians have known for a very long time that the number 1 is unique and different from all other numbers in quite a few respects. The number 1 is the universal multiplier and divisor not only of itself ($1 \times 1 = 1$; and $1/1 = 1$), but any number, n, can be divided by or multiplied by 1 as many times as we like and it will always produce the same n that we started with. Similarly any number divided by itself, n/n, will produce 1 which assures us that 1 is a factor of every number. It is also the case that the only divisor of any number such that n divided by that divisor is n is 1. It follows that 1 raised to any power, $1^1, 1^2, 1^3, \ldots$ will always be equal to 1, and any root of 1, written as $1^{-1}, 1^{-2}, 1^{-3}, \ldots$ likewise must always give 1 as its only result.

However, the notion of identity when it is applied to real objects, or to persons, involves more than just unity in the sense of the number 1. An identity in ordinary experience, such as the identity of an infant's mother, involves a special kind of individuality. There is just one individual with the identity in question. The identity involves uniqueness of **substance**. No other existing bodily person is the mother of the infant in question. It also involves completeness, wholeness, or what grammarians call **perfection**. The mother in question is the whole mother of the infant, and not merely part of the infant's mother. Identity in the required sense also involves **complementarity**. For any given object out of all the possible objects that may exist, for any given object that may be selected, it either is or is not the mother of the infant in question. The whole universe of existing bodies can be divided into two nonoverlapping sets: one set contains the infant's mother and the other set contains everything that is not the infant's mother.

Recognizing Objects

What precisely are the requirements that must be met for any given bodily object to be recognized as the same object on different occasions? Why is it that the infant seems to know at birth that a visible object should be tangible and yet the infant does not know that the same object cannot appear in more than one place at one time? Why does the infant at a very early age (20 days, less than one month) expect an object occluded by a screen to still be where it was before when the screen is removed? Yet the same infant, does not know that a moving object is still the same object when it stops moving. The infant also does not realize yet that a stationary object remains the same object when it begins to move. Why should these things be so? To answer these questions, we must to some extent discover the world as the infant represents it. We must enter the world of the infant from the infant's point of view. To do this we need to be able to infer what representations, what signs the infant is using at any given time and just how these signs are being applied.

To solve the mysteries that Bower uncovered (and that others have confirmed), the theory of abstraction introduced in Chapter 4 was invented (J. Oller, 1996; J. Oller et al., 2005). An important step in understanding how infants vest their systems of signs with meanings is to see that some signs are necessary to the discovery of others. For instance, a movement can only be noticed by the infant if something moves relative to something else within the perceptual field of that infant. To notice any movements of any kind, it follows that the infant must represent objects that move. To represent any objects whatever, of course, the infant needs icons. Therefore, icons, as signs that can be used to represent things other than themselves, have to be produced before any indexes can be distinguished. That is, for movements, which must be shown in indexes connecting locations or as relations between distinct objects located in space and time to be created the infant must first produce some icons. Movement is so dependent on something that moves, that movement without an object to move simply cannot occur. Movement cannot exist without moving objects. Therefore, the representation of objects through icons must underlie the representation of distinct movements. In fact, a moving icon, relative to other icons, is a prerequisite to the noticing of any movement whatsoever.

Bower (1971) observed that "place and vision are separately coded in the visual system" (p. 38). In fact, it can be shown by strict logical reasoning that neither places nor movements can be noticed at all by any of the senses apart from icons that enable the determination (noticing and fixing) of places and paths of motion relative to the infant observer. Without an icon of a refrigerator of a certain relative size and shape, how would it be possible to identify a location for such an object in a kitchen? How could we recognize the footprint of the refrigerator on the tile if we had no icon of the refrigerator? How could we know whether or not the refrigerator could fit in a given space if we had no idea of the size and shape of the object? Or suppose we knew nothing at all about the size or shape of an object, where would we look for it and how would we notice its movements if there were any?

Similarly, to determine any particular location requires reference to relations between situated objects (located icons). If all the objects (all the icons) were entirely removed from any scene, and if the scene itself were not situated relative to other objects, there would be no meaning left for the term "location" at all. What would a scene be if it had absolutely nothing in it and could not be found? What would a location be if there were no way whatever to identify it? It follows, therefore, by strict logic that iconic representations (absolutely) must be presupposed if any indexical ones are to exist. Similarly, indexical relations are absolutely critical to any pragmatic mapping of any symbol onto any icon. Even with innate symbols such as the grimace as a response to the sour taste of a lemon (see Figure 4-3), the infant has to taste the lemon (actively). That is, an indexical relation has to be established before the symbol (the grimace) can be associated with the sour taste (the icon of the lemon). The indexical association is essential to vesting the grimace with the content that consists of the taste of the lemon.

At least one index, therefore, must precede (or be involved in) the first application of any abstract symbol. If no sour taste is ever encountered, for example, the infant will never be able to show the application of the grimace to such a taste. Or, to take another example, before the neonate can associate mom's voice with her bodily presence, it is essential for the baby to represent mom's moving face. The neonate must notice that mom's face (an icon) is actively through its movements (indexically) connected with the sound of her voice (which is a symbol of the infant's prior experience with mom while the baby was in the womb). This can only be done through indexical associations of the movements of mom's face with the production of her voice. Otherwise, the infant could not, as Sai (2005) showed experimentally (by temporarily depriving certain neonates from seeing mom's moving face while hearing her voice), discover that mom's voice (a kind of symbol of mom from the womb) goes with her particular face (an icon of mom after birth).

The Sign Cycle

Thus we discover a **sign cycle** from icon to index to symbol as shown in Figure 5–5. The relation between the major sign systems from icon to index to symbol is a cycle like the cycle of abstraction (as shown in Figure 4–6). It is important to admit, however, that the symbolic capacity (for example, the capacity to associate a conventional sign with an arbitrarily selected object) must be presupposed. The capacity must exist independently of and prior to its use and its subsequent maturation (see Meltzoff & Moore, 1998). It would make no sense to try to get an amoeba, a tree, a stone, to notice the association between a particular name and person, for instance. The language capacity in particular must be presupposed as a distinguishing innate attribute of the human infant (per Chomsky, 1975).

Although the content of the symbol, and the capacity to comprehend or produce such a symbol, does utterly depend on an association of icons through indexes, both the symbol and the content to be associated with it must pre-exist their association. It is true that the use of the grimace to express the sour taste of the lemon depends on an indexical encounter

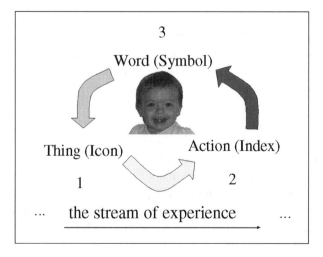

Figure 5–5. The sign cycle from icon to index to symbol.

with the juice of the lemon. The infant has to taste the sour juice. Also, the discovery of the body that goes with mom's voice requires one or more indexical encounters with mom's moving face while hearing her voice. The infant has to hear the voice while observing the moving face. But it is important to realize that the infant's capacity to produce a grimace in response to a sour taste must exist independently, before the infant ever tastes the first bit of lemon juice. Similarly, mom's voice exists before the infant ever hears it not to mention associating it with mom's moving face after birth which also could not occur if mom's voice and face did not both exist.

Returning to Bower's discovery, why is it, then, that infants after about 8 weeks but prior to about 16 weeks of age regard the same object as if it were a different one when it moves or stops moving?

A first step in solving this mystery is to notice the logical distinctness of icons and indexes. To represent an index, any noticeable movement (or any spatial relation between objects), requires at least three icons, as shown in Figure 5-6. First, there must be an observer of the movement. That would be the infant in Figure 5-6. Second, there must be a moving object (possibly the observer). That would be the ball moving in a circular path in Figure 5-6. Third, there must be a space within which the movement

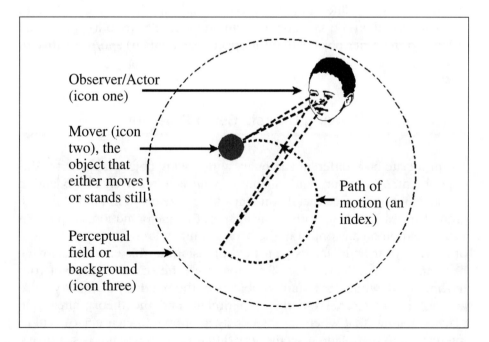

Figure 5–6. Three distinct objects in the path of motion paradigm. (The diagram shown here is adapted from Bower, T. G. R. (1971). The object in the world of the infant. *Scientific American, 225*[4], p. 34, with permission. Copyright © 1971 by Scientific American.)

occurs. In Figure 5-6 the field of perception, or background, is the area or scene within which the observer is located. It is marked in the figure by the larger roughly bounded circle that includes the observer and the moving object. If we consider the case carefully, we can see that there can never be fewer than three objects (icons) in any relation that involves the perception or observation of movement. There is the icon of the observer (the situated body of the observer), the icon of the moving object (it might be the observer in some cases), and there is the icon of the larger scene (the place where the movement occurs relative to other objects, or the ground).

But suppose, as the theory of abstraction requires, the neonate cannot, at first, discriminate more than one object at a time. That is, suppose the neonate has to start in defining icons one at a time by discriminating their boundaries. In that case, a moving object would seem very different from a stationary one even if the two objects were one and the same. But this is not merely what the theory of abstraction predicts, the outcome also appears as the result obtained in several of Bower's experiments with young infants (1971; also Bower, Broughton, & Moore, 1970; Bower & Paterson, 1973). Although neonates are attracted from birth to bounded objects that move and talk, for example, to faces, they cannot at first easily track an object that moves across the field of vision. This ability is not seen until about the second week or so. By that time, however, any object in motion must seem different relative to the space in which it moves (and to the observer) than the same object standing still relative to its space (and relative to the other objects that the space may contain) and/or relative to the observer.

Moving Objects Seem Different

To appreciate how different stationary and moving objects appear, try this experiment. Move your hand in front of your face relatively slowly and in a steady motion. Notice that if you focus your gaze on your hand, the background appears as a blur moving away from the line of motion. Next, focus your attention on any object in the background and repeat the experiment of moving your hand across your field of vision. In this case, the moving hand appears as a blurry line of motion, with the size and shape of your moving hand, while the bounded objects in the relatively stationary background remain clear. From this experiment, and the theory already in place, it follows that when an object (say, as shown in Figure 5-6) is moving relative to the infant, it seems very different from when it is stationary. The object does not seem the same when it is moving as when it is stationary anymore than an object situated in different locations against different backgrounds looks the same relative to those distinct spatial locations.

Here is another experiment. Try moving an object around, say on a desktop. Notice how the background relative to the different positions appears as the object is moved from one location to another. If the infant regards objects that seem different as different objects, it follows that the infant should regard the same object in different locations as if it were a different object in each location. Similarly, an object that stops its motion should seem to be a different object than the one that was formerly moving, and vice versa. The stationary one appears different from the one that was moving, and when the moving object stops, it seems different (relative to its background) than the moving one did.

Also, the actions of the infant in observing a stationary object as contrasted with the same object when it moves are different. Just as the same object appears different against a different background in different locations, because of the change in the background and the direction of movements necessary for the infant to perceive and represent a moving object, the moving object must seem different from the same object when it is stationary. If this were not so, the movement itself could not be noticed. But infants begin noticing movements from a very young age. Evidently they can notice movements before they are born. However, to know that a moving object is still the same object when it comes to rest in the field of the infant's perception, or that a stationary object is still the same when it begins to move is a much more difficult inference than it appears to be from the adult perspective.

The Identity of Indiscernibles

In the theory of abstraction, we suppose that the infant operates by a simple rule: *if icons seem different, they must be different*. If an icon, on the other hand, *does not change it will be regarded as an individual entity, that is, as one and the same object, an identity*. The infant evidently uses the basic definition of identity that was summed up by Leibniz (1714/1953): Leibniz referred to it as the **identity of indiscernibles**. In effect, that principle says, if no difference can be discerned (that is, if no discrimination is possible), the object in question is an identity (a single individual). Leibniz's principle resembles another old philosophical saw that cuts through a lot of nonsense. It resembles the rule known as **Ockham's razor** (Ockham, 1320/1957). The Earl of Ockham [1285–1349 AD] probably did not originate the rule, but he popularized it in medieval times. His rule was that entities should not be multiplied beyond necessity. In other words, simpler theories should be preferred over more complex ones. Apparently, infants respect this idea exactly as far as things appear to be the same. However, when things change in any way, infants are apt to suppose that the changes are significant. As a result, infants posit new objects freely.

If a difference is noticed, Leibniz's principle demands that the objects in question must not be regarded as the same. The difference seems to demand, without violating Ockham's rule, that the infant is dealing with a whole new object.

Consider how different a stationary object and the same object in motion must appear to the infant. To notice the stationary object, the infant does not need to move much, but to notice and fix his or her gaze on a moving object to track its line of motion, the infant must move his or her eyes (and possibly his or her head and body as well) as the object moves. The infant's movement (of eyes and head) must correspond to (and replicate on a smaller scale) the movements of the moving object. Therefore, any object that begins to move or comes to rest, though it may be the very same object in all its states of movement and rest, must seem different to the child not only in terms of the background against which the object is discriminated, but also in terms of the movements that the infant must perform to maintain focus on the object in any of its states. Each persistent state of any object, whether a moving one or a stationary one, can be thought of as an **inertial state**. If the object is stationary, its inertial state defines a place or location in space and time relative to the location of the infant and the ground. If the inertial state is one of motion, it defines a path or line of motion as the object moves. In the cases of interest here, in other words, in early infancy, the object must move slowly enough for the infant to track it. A quick movement might be noticed by the infant but cannot be tracked.

Icons at Rest and in Motion

The infant must begin its process of abstraction with whatever object the infant can discriminate it its field of perception. An object that moves too quickly cannot be noticed by the infant at first. The initial inertial state of an object that the infant can represent in a discriminated icon must be the kind where the object appears to be motionless relative to the observer. Later, however, the infant will be able by fixing on a relatively slowly moving object, to track the object in its path of motion. For a young infant to do this, the object must move at a relatively constant rate and it must do so slowly enough so the infant can follow the moving object with eye gaze and/or head turning. When the infant becomes able to do this, the inertial state of the moving object seems different from the inertial state of the same object when it is stationary for all the reasons already noted above. However, the moving object also maintains its boundaries, shape, color, and so on, although as it moves it is prescinded (actually and logically it is separated) from its background.

In a slow-moving inertial state, nevertheless, the boundaries of the objects in the background, remain in place while the boundaries of the moving object go with the object that moves. To follow a moving object with our eyes, or hands, or in any other way, we must move our eyes, our hands, the camera, microphone, or whatever. The infant must learn to do this. It takes about two weeks before the neonate acquires sufficient tracking skill to follow an object that moves across the field of view. To voluntarily reach out and touch or grasp even a stationary object will require considerably longer. To reach and grasp a moving object is a much more difficult task somewhat akin to catching a ball on the fly. However, most infants eventually learn to do all these things. The question is how? Or in different words, what steps must the infant work through to come to understand that an object at a certain location that begins to move is the same one that formerly was stationary? What steps must the infant follow to know that a moving object that comes to a stop is the same one that was moving beforehand? First, the infant must notice the objects (this requires the creation of the signs we call discriminated icons). Next, the infant must learn to track moving objects. This requires the creation of what may be called prescinded icons. Third, the infant must think of the object when it is no longer present where it was before. In other words the infant must be able to think of the moving object that has stopped moving and is now stationary, or of the stationary object that has now begun to move and is no longer in the location where it was before. That is, the infant must next develop the hypostatic icon (an abstract concept of an object that is not present in the infant's field of perception). Summing up these first three steps of abstraction, we find the creation of the following kinds of sign systems in the order specified:

1. Discriminated icons are percepts of bodily objects or bounded spaces. These are the sorts of icons associated with logical objects that maintain a particular position relative to the infant long enough for the infant to discover the boundaries of the object (body) in question. A discriminated icon is a sign that is positioned where its object is when it is being perceived. It is the percept of a bounded object, that is, one with edges, surfaces, or boundaries, for example, a bottle, a bed, or a room. There are as many discriminated icons as there are percepts.

2. Prescinded icons are percepts of moving objects. This kind of icon is separating itself from its background. However, because it is a percept, it must remain within the infant's field of perception. A prescinded icon is a sign that is

associated with a moving object. The object is displacing itself from its surroundings. A prescinded icon is the percept of an object that is separating itself from its former location, that is, a moving object. It consists of the bounded object that is represented as a discriminated icon plus the line of motion that the object is following.

3. Hypostatic icons are abstract concepts of logical objects. This kind of icon is the sort that applies to a logical object that is no longer where it was before in the field of perception. It has already prescinded itself from its former inertial state. It has either moved from where it was before, or it has stopped moving along some line of motion. The hypostatic icon consists of a prescinded icon plus a memory of the former state of its object (location or line of motion).

It can be seen that all three kinds of icons constructed by the infant become vested with particular material (bodily) content by being associated with relatively bounded bodily objects. The signs the infant applies become associated with objects through the senses and the actions of the infant. Notice that the infant at birth (and no doubt before birth) can begin to perform the acts of discrimination. As soon as voluntary movements are possible, the infant can begin to form signs associated with prescission, and as soon as the infant begins to remember its former sensations and actions, hypostasis, and dreaming, become possible. Presumably, all these things begin before birth.

In life after birth, the infant continues to explore the world outside the womb forming many discriminated icons that represent bodily objects. The most important of these discriminated icons are those associated with other persons. All the while the infant continues to develop voluntary control of its own movements. By about the second week, it can track another moving object and the formation of prescinded icons begins to flourish. Similarly, during all this time, the infant is also building memories. These memories reach back before the infant's birth, but are constantly being enriched with new experiences in the baby's life after birth. As memories are established, it becomes possible for the infant by about its third week to briefly recall an object that has disappeared from view. For instance, as Bower (1971) showed, by 20 days, the normal human infant is surprised if an object obscured by a moving screen is not still present after a lapse of 1.5 seconds or less. For at least that long, the infant is able to remember the object. However, within a few more weeks, the infant will be able to keep the hypostatic icon of an object in mind much longer. By about the eighth week, and probably before the twelfth week, the infant will be able to think of an object that has either moved to a new location, been screened from view, or was formerly progressing along a certain path. That is, the infant will have formed hypostatic icons. Once all the foregoing steps have been accomplished, the infant will be able to think of an object that is not present, and it will become possible to conduct a deliberate search in the former inertial state (a location or path) of the object the infant is looking for. At this point, the infant is ready for another significant advance.

Developing More Advanced Signs: Indexes Incorporating Icons

After the infant has developed the hypostatic icon, so that it is possible to think of an object that is no longer present in the same inertial state where it was noticed before, the infant will be able to conduct a search through what may be called a **discriminative index**. The discriminative index is a deliberate act on the part of the infant. In performing such an act, the infant first thinks of the object it wants to look for and then searches the location or path where the object was formerly noticed. To search such an inertial location, either a place or a path of motion that an object formerly occupied, the infant must add a discriminative movement of its own to a hypostatic icon of the object that the infant is looking for. The discriminative index, then, will consist of the same sort of perceptual act that formerly led to a percept of the object (a discriminated icon). However, to know what sort of percept to look for, the infant must have a concept of the object and its former inertial state in mind before conducting the search. Otherwise, the infant would not know what it is searching for. To hunt for a screwdriver in a drawer, for instance, even an adult must keep in mind what sort of object is being hunted for. Thus, the discriminative index has three essential parts: first, the infant must represent the thing to be searched for. This requires a hypostatic icon, a concept of the object to be looked for. That concept must be associated by memory with the location or path along which the object was previously noticed. Second, the infant must perform an appropriate act of looking, reaching, or otherwise attending to the location where the object searched for was previously noticed. Third, if the search fails, the infant will find the empty location where the object formerly appeared. It the search succeeds the infant will find a percept of the object (a discriminated icon) and the discriminative index will become a fully **discriminated index**. That is, the infant will locate the object searched for.

The systematic structure underlying the discriminated index, one that succeeds in locating its object, is as shown in Figure 5-7. To conduct any search for an object, the infant must have in mind the object searched for.

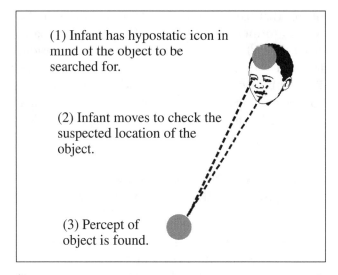

(1) Infant has hypostatic icon in mind of the object to be searched for.

(2) Infant moves to check the suspected location of the object.

(3) Percept of object is found.

Figure 5–7. The key structure of a discriminated index required for a successful search for an object. (The diagram shown here is adapted from Bower, T. G. R. [1971]. The object in the world of the infant. *Scientific American, 225*[4], p. 34, with permission. Copyright © 1971 by Scientific American.)

This requires an abstract concept to represent the object searched for. Such a sign is the hypostatic icon. If the search for that object succeeds, the concept will be connected through an indexical act to a percept of the object. In case the search does not succeed, the index will merely point to the percept of a location, and the discriminated icon that is searched for will not be found there. We can infer from several of Bower's experiments that normal infants have commonly achieved the level of discriminated indexes by about their eighth week. For example, in one of his studies, Bower (1971) had the infant sitting up, looking toward a car on a track as seen in Figure 5-8. The car was remotely controlled by the experimenter. It had flashing lights to attract and hold the infant's attention. It remained in position A for 10 seconds, then moved slowly to the infant's right through path B until coming to position C. It stayed there for 10 seconds then returned along path D to position A. After 10 cycles the car did not stop at A but went on to E where it stopped for 10 seconds. Bower predicted that the infant would look back to position C from where the car had consistently appeared previously after moving.

In fact, the results of this experiment and subsequent ones (for example, Bower & Paterson, 1973) with moving objects showed that infants less than 16 weeks of age tend to search all the former inertial states (that is, the locations and paths) of the object, that is, A, B, C, and D. The infant could plainly see the object at position E and would look at it and then still search the other locations as if looking for additional objects. Infants before

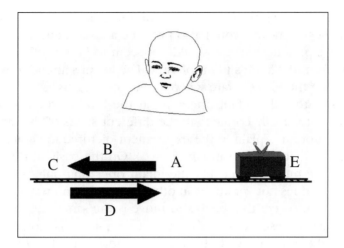

Figure 5–8. How many objects does the infant perceive as the car moves repeatedly from A through B to C then back through D to A? On trial 11 it goes along path D and stops at E. See Bower, T. G. R. (1971). The object in the world of the infant. *Scientific American, 225*(4), 30–38. This diagram is adapted from p. 36 by permission. Copyright © 1971 by Scientific American, Inc.

about week 16 did not recognize the object that stopped was the same one that was formerly moving. Evidently, infants before week 16 noticed that the car in motion looks quite different as it moves along the track from the stationary object that stops anywhere along the path of movement.

Try this experiment again. Focus on an object moving across your field of vision, say your own hand, and you will notice that the background blurs out. The stationary objects in the background seems to move away in lines parallel to the line of motion of the object you are focused on. If you move the object in the other direction, the blurred out portion of the background again looks different. The blurred lines of stationary objects in the background move away from the moving hand in the opposite direction. Next focus on an object in the background and repeat the experiment of moving your hand through your field of vision. You will notice that the boundaries of the background object(s) on which you have fixed your gaze remain clear in this case but the moving hand is blurred as it prescinds itself from the other objects.

Next, suppose that it takes the infant a few moments to shift attention from a moving object to the same one when it stops moving, or to shift from a stationary object to the same object when it begins to move. If this were so, the infant would have a small **attentional gap** caused by the time it takes to begin to notice the movement (or its cessation) and the time it takes to shift attention to the now moving (or stationary) object. This attentional gap along with the difference in the appearance of a moving object (or stationary one) as contrasted with the same object when it comes to rest (or begins to move) would also produce a discontinuity between the perceptual experiences. They would not seem to be smoothly connected as they do from the adult's point of view. The infant's attention would still be focused on the former state when a new one begins.

Evidence that the infant operating at the level of the discriminative index does not actually connect all the different states of the same object as it moves around is plain in the experiment pictured in Figure 5–8 (also in the experiment pictured in Figure 5–6). On the basis of the theory of abstraction we must predict that the infant operating only with discriminated indexes does not yet know, in other words, has no way to represent, the fact that an object that begins to move is the same one that formerly was stationary. To discover that the two different-looking icons are actually connected, the infant needs to be able to compare the object in motion to the former stationary one, and vice versa. To make such a comparison, it is logically necessary to keep the moving (or stationary) object in mind while also remembering the former object that was stationary.

To connect the different inertial states of the same object, the infant needs to form what may be called a **prescinded index**. That is, the infant needs to prescind (separate) its attention from one location and move it to another while keeping the result of the former search in mind. If we simply imagine the infant moving its attention across all five different inertial states pictured in Figure 5–8, that is, A, B, C, D, and E, we get a notion of what the prescinded index is. It begins with a discriminated index that moves with the moving object. The discriminated index itself is prescinded from the former inertial state of the object so as to stay attached to the percept of that object as the object begins to move. This requires some coordination on the part of the infant. The infant must move its eyes, and possibly its head and hands, in synchrony (though on a smaller scale) with the motion of the moving object. That is, the infant must prescind the discriminated index from one location and move it to others as the object of perception moves. The prescinded index, more than any sign system discussed up to this point, makes it clear why the coordination of movements is so important to the infant's ability to acquire the dynamic (moving) signs of language whether it is spoken or manually signed. For the infant to follow a movement and correctly represent the object that moves, the infant must articulate its own movements in coordination with the movements of the object that it is tracking.

The prescinded index is necessary if the infant is to become able to connect each of the distinct states of the same object as it moves within the infant's field of perception. The formation of the prescinded index is spurred on by the contrasts between discriminative and discriminated indexes. The infant discovers the difference between discriminative indexes on the one hand, where a search of several former locations fails to produce the objects searched for, and a discriminated index where the search of a given location succeeds in locating a percept of an object. The contrast between these two classes of results prods the infant to wonder why the object appears in one place but not the others. As the infant moves more quickly between the various inertial states that the object has previously occupied, the normal infant is bound to discover the prescinded index. The development of this level of sign systems requires a tighter coordination between the infant's movements and those of moving objects within the infant's perceptual experience. The lapse, for instance, between the time that an object begins to move and the time the infant begins to track the movement must be reduced for the infant to advance from the discriminated index to the prescinded index.

To precipitate the discovery that all the different inertial states of the same object, say, in the experiment pictured in Figure 5–8, are in fact states of just one object, several things need to happen. All of them are assured more or less simultaneously with the discovery of the first prescinded index. Based on Bower's research we may suppose that this advance occurs in normal infants sometime roughly between the 16th and 20th weeks after birth. One of the precipitating factors is that the infant notices that the hypostatic icons (percepts) resulting from the movements of a single object are all so similar that only their backgrounds distinguish them. As soon as the backgrounds are ignored, all the different hypostatic icons (percepts) of the same object appear to be not only identical, but continuously connected over time. To discover this, however, the infant must coordinate its own movements fairly closely with those of the moving object. Once this occurs, the distinct percepts (hypostatic icons) of the object in question merge into a single continuum connecting the various inertial states of the object into a single history. This event marks the beginnings of narrative, story-like connections in the experience of the infant. The notion of what an entity is, also changes. The infant advances and the complexity of the former world is reduced to a simpler more connected world.

The formerly distinct percepts of an object when it was stationary in contrast with the same object when it moved to a new location, or the percept in the new location in contrast to the percept in the old location, can no longer be distinguished. The principle of the identity of indiscernibles does its work. It causes the infant to suppose that all the formerly distinct objects are actually one and the same object. Another factor that helps to precipitate this development and the formation of the prescinded index is that the infant is gaining in skill at tracking objects as they move in the infant's perceptual field. As a result, the attentional gap that formerly separated the various inertial states of an object such as the one pictured in Figure 5–8, is being reduced almost to nothing. The lapse, and the consequent abruptness of the appearance of the moving object, is smoothed. Finally, and perhaps most importantly, there is a logical pressure on the infant to suppose that an object that begins to move is the same as the identical-seeming object that was formerly stationary. This logical pressure arises because as soon as the one appears the other disappears. No matter how many searches the infant performs in paths A, B, C, and D, for instance, if the object is at E, then the other searches will all come up empty. To notice this dependency relation, the infant only needs the prescinded index. When the first such index becomes available, a major problem is solved and a great simplification is achieved by reducing the number of objects to be attended to and represented. Evidently, most normal human infants reach prescinded indexes sometime after their third month and before their sixth month.

Consider next how the infant can represent an object that disappears from the perceptual field altogether. The object goes over the horizon, around an edge, through a door, or simply disappears in the distance like a house that is left behind. To represent the object that disappears beyond the edge of the infant's perceptual horizon, a prescinded index comes up short. How will the child keep in mind the fact that the object is still out there somewhere? Though not in any of its former locations within the infant's field of perception, it is still out there in some unknown location but along a certain line of motion. To represent such a fully abstract line of motion, that is, to connect the prescinded index across distinct locations that are not now present in perception, a **hypostatic index** is needed. An index of this kind is required to represent the fact that an object which disappears entirely from the infant's field of perception is still out there and apt to reappear. The hypostatic index can be thought of as the indefinite continuation of a line that connects to an object that is no longer perceivable but that was known to have exited from the field of perception in a certain direction, or to have been screened off from perception.

An adult example of a hypostatic index is found in the sort of experience we have when we see, hear, and feel the whoosh of a passing truck on the highway (or we may pass the truck). Soon it may pass over the horizon, say, ahead of (or behind us). However, with a hypostatic index, we know in what direction it disappeared and we have the idea that it is still out there somewhere in that direction. We generalize from the perceptual field that we are presently in to ones that we know are out there but that we cannot yet perceive. Let us consider next how the infant can develop the hypostatic index.

As soon as the infant has developed the first prescinded index, it is possible to track an object within the field of perception and to notice its movements, but when the object is removed beyond the infant's field of perception, say, mom leaves the room, the prescinded index can no longer be used to reattach itself (in the infant's present field of perception) to a percept (discriminated icon) of mom. To know that mom still exists when the baby is not perceiving her requires a higher sign system. It requires the sort of index that not only connects the various icons of mom when she is present, and that not only represents her when she is not present, but that also points to her in the sense of knowing she still exists somewhere else even when the baby is not perceiving her.

The hypostatic index, therefore, links up prescinded indexes that have pointed to mom and generalizes to other perceptual fields where the infant has experienced mom previously. The hypostatic index not only consolidates the present with the past, but enables a more certain anticipation of the future. The hypostatic index connects the places and times within the infant's perceptual field and extends to other places and times by pointing to some substantial object, say, mom, that is no longer present within the infant's perceptual field. We know that this stage of development commonly occurs between the infant's fourth and sixth months (give or take a few weeks).

Evidence for the stage of development marked by the hypostatic index is essentially **anecdotal**, that is, it comes from reported experiences. However, it is ubiquitous in the experience of parents. Until the infant develops to the level of the prescinded index it is hardly possible for the infant to be much disturbed when mom leaves the room and disappears from the infant's perceptual field. The baby may be disturbed by an interruption of feeding, or rocking, or something of that sort, but to notice that the object of the baby's attention is no longer present a prescinded index is needed. What is more, until the development of the hypostatic index occurs, the infant operating with prescinded indexes only is apt to experience a marked anxiety when mom (or the infant's primary caregiver) leaves the room. Before the infant has developed the prescinded index, the disappearance of objects is so commonplace in the infant's world that it cannot be very disturbing. But after the prescinded index is developed, the disappearance of the infant's main caregiver is apt to cause severe anxiety. The theory predicts what may be called a **panic tantrum** in normal infants at the level of the prescinded index that can be expected to occur repeatedly when mom disappears from the field of perception. Presumably this sort of infant tantrum expresses the sort of feeling that a parent feels when their child playing on the beach seems to have disappeared. The infant operating at the level of the prescinded index must feel as if mom has more or less fallen off the face of the earth.

However, this sort of anxiety reaction will soon disappear, according to the theory of abstraction, because the normal infant at the level of the prescinded index is on the verge of discovering the hypostatic index. As soon as the latter sign system is achieved, the infant will know that when mom disappears she is still out there somewhere. When the hypostatic index is achieved, therefore, we may predict that the phase of panic tantrums precipitated by mom leaving the room will suddenly disappear. They will stop occurring as soon as the child has a way of realizing that mom is still out there and that she has not been lost from the infant's world.

Summing up the development of indexes we have noted the following:

1. Discriminative indexes are necessary for searches to be conducted and successful searches result in discriminated indexes. Each such index begins with a hypostatic con of the object searched for and, if successful, ends in an action that leads to a percept (a discriminated icon) of the object searched for. Infants normally achieve this level by about their eighth week after birth (give or take a couple of weeks).

2. Prescinded indexes are necessary for an infant to discover that an object that moves around within the field of perception is still the same object. Each prescinded index contains at least one discriminated index (with the percept of an object attached to it) plus one or more discriminative indexes (which connect with empty places or paths where the object was previously located). Infants normally achieve this level by about their 16th to 20th weeks.

3. Hypostatic indexes are necessary for the infant to generalize from the prescinded index in the present perceptual field to other perceptual fields. The hypostatic index consists of a prescinded index in the present perceptual field pointing toward the discriminated object that has disappeared from the present perceptual field. Infants normally achieve this sign level by about their fifth or sixth month. The hypostatic index is different from other indexes because it links a prescinded index of an object in the present perceptual field with a hypostatic icon of that same object beyond the limits of the present perceptual field.

Summing Up and Looking Ahead

From all the foregoing, we see that the infant's developing sign system of meanings (the material content of experience) consists largely of percepts or icons of bodily objects. Even the icons form a layered system of richly integrated signs. At a somewhat higher level of abstraction, a series of layered indexical signs are formed relying heavily on the resources provided by iconic signs. At a still higher remove, another layered system of sign systems consists of the socially significant gestures, actions, and speech of other human beings. These social actions (Bruner, 1975; Hsu, Fogel, & Messinger, 2001; Masataka, 1995; Sacks, Schegloff, & Jefferson, 1974) constitute the essential basis for linguistic symbols. These higher signs involve speech or signing from the earliest experience of the baby. They have, as we saw in previous chapters, begun to influence the baby even before birth. Later on, these linguistic sign systems will incorporate the printed (or written) forms of words. For parents who read to their children in early infancy, printed linguistic signs can be, and sometimes are, associated with speech forms from about the time the infant can sit up. For instance, the baby in Figure 6–1 (at the very beginning of the next chapter) began by her fourth month to hold a book and examine the pictures and printed forms in it. In Chapter 10, as surprising as it may seem, we will encounter evidence that normal babies can read at least from about 9 months (even before they can say the words out loud). In Chapter 6 we discuss in greater detail the stages leading up to true speech-like babble. More specifically, we consider the infant's discrimination, prescinding, and hypostatizing of the surface-forms of speech and language. Interestingly, this kind of babbling is important for both hearing and nonhearing infants. Deaf infants who are exposed to manual signs babble with their mouths and with their hands.

STUDY AND DISCUSSION QUESTIONS

1. Consider some of the different ways that infants bring their own bodily movements into synchrony with the movements of adults? How do the ideas of reciprocity, intersubjectivity, the chameleon effect, and the McGurk effect come into play?

2. How does the demonstration of surprise that a visible object is not tangible show that the infant expected to be able to touch the object? What else could it show, if anything? What other evidence can be mustered to show the integration of the senses in the infant?

3. What theories can you come up with to explain the seemingly universal ways in which doting grandparents, parents, and total strangers choose to use when speaking to an infant? What do you think accounts for the changes in pitch, rhythm, exaggeration of vowel contrasts, lengthening of syllables, slower speech, and so on? Why is it that many if not all cultures seem to make similar modifications? Is this something learned? How?

4. What is the best explanation you can give for the distinct formants of any given vowel? For example, in the word *heed* can you guess (or figure out) which resonant cavities are producing the formants you

can see in the spectrogram? What arguments can you offer to sustain your hunches? How could these ideas be tested?

5. Discuss the difference between the identity problem as construed by Bower and the conservation problem as developed by Piaget. Why and how do objects that move around present a special problem to infants? Where do some of these same problems, or similar ones, come up in adult experience?

6. Why would infants naturally tend to prefer simpler representations over more complicated ones? How does Leibniz's principle of the identity of indiscernibles reduce complexities? What about Ockham's razor? When is it necessary to multiply entities? In other words, under what circumstances is it desirable to use two different words, phrases, or representations rather than one?

7. Exactly how does an object look different when it is moving relative to other objects as contrasted with the same object at rest relative to other objects and its background? How does the point of fixation of the observer figure in, in other words, whether the observer is looking at the moving object in the foreground or some other stationary object in the background?

8. What icons must be involved in the formation of a discriminated index? What sorts of distinct discriminated and/or discriminative indexes must be involved to correctly work out the solution to the problems posed in the experiment of Figure 5–8? And, finally, why is a hypostatic index necessarily more abstract than a prescinded index?

CHAPTER 6

Integrating Icons and Indexes with Surface-Forms of Speech and Language

By studying this chapter you will:

1. Learn how the infant moves from vowel-like vocalizations to syllabic babbling;

2. Understand why repetitive syllabic babble is a major milestone moving toward language;

3. Explore the referential meaning from the earliest stages through syllabic babbling;

4. See the infant as a theoretician working out logical problems in acquiring speech forms;

5. Consider again the controversy over innate capacities versus environmental influences;

6. Understand the logical positions of discourse in relation to first, second, and third person in grammar; and

7. Differentiate the pragmatic forces of meaning as proposed by J. L. Austin.

KEY TERMS

Here are some terms and concepts that you can learn more about in this chapter; also see the Glossary for definitions of them:

acoustic phonetics
acquiescence response bias
approval motive
articulatory phonetics
auditory (perceptual) phonetics
canonical babbling
concordance
discriminated symbol
discursive act
Einstein's gulf
error term
exclusive-we
expansion stage
gender
high saliency
hypostatic symbol
illocutionary force
inclusive-we
inter-rater reliability
latching
locutionary force
mother tongue
multimodal sensory impression
number

perceptual field
perlocutionary force
phonation
pragmatic forces
prescinded symbol
preverbal systems of signs
primary reference
protophone
quasivowel
response set
risk factor
satisficing
secondary reference
self-flattery
sensitivity
significance
specificity
speech act
tertiary reference
token
unreliability
validity
vocative
volitional control

The so-called **preverbal systems of signs** (icons and indexes) will be integrated with speech forms by the baby as it develops over the next seven or eight months (give or take a couple of months). During that time, the baby will acquire the first meaningful words of its native language. There are two essential layers of signs that need to be integrated through indexes: on the one hand, there are the icons that represent the material world of bodily objects as they move around in space and time. On the other hand, there are the conventional signs of language. These conventional signs are shown in speech for hearing infants and signed language for deaf infants and they also have written forms that can be used both by hearing and deaf infants.

Linguistic signs are distinguished mainly by the fact that they are related to their meanings by conventions. That is, they are merely arbitrarily associated with their objects, for example, an infant's name, say, Abigail, becomes the infant's name only because her parents gave her that name when she was born. She did not come with the name stamped on her and she does not know her name at birth. There is nothing about her bodily appearance that would require for her name to be Abigail. Because the name is conventional, the little girl in Figure 6–1, or any baby, must discover the meaning of the name. Not only must the baby discover the content of experience through icons associated with objects and indexes associated with movements of objects, but the infant must also parse the surface-forms of speech (or deaf signing), and somehow associate those

Figure 6–1. A baby at 10 months studying and "reading" a book. Used by permission of Dr. Liang Chen and Dr. Ning Pan, this is their daughter Abigail, also see Aleka in Figure 10–1.

surface-forms with their meanings. All of these developments are dependent on indexical associations, but also on the fairly extreme generalizations of abstract and arbitrary linguistic conventions.

The conventions to be discovered are themselves general, abstract, and arbitrary and can only be represented by symbols that have all these qualities too. How can we point to nothing at all? Or how can we point to all the instances of given kind, for example, all stars? Does the term not include the ones that have already burned out? Ones not yet evident? Ones only imagined? How could all these stars be pointed out? To recall the bootstrapping problem discussed in Chapter 4, when we come to understand the nature of fully abstract linguistic signs, we see that the bootstrapping problem is very real. The Baron who supposedly lifted himself by his shoelaces might be a fantasy, but the acquisition of languages is such a common occurrence that its reality cannot be denied. The problem to be solved is real. How can the infant discover general, abstract, and arbitrary conventions when these cannot adequately be pointed out through any conceivable indexes (recall the problem of Figure 5–4)? No indexes are fast enough, nor general enough, nor abstract enough to reach out and connect with all the instances that a conventional symbol applies to. There is no way to point out all the applications of any symbol to the child. Nor is there any way to point out all the ways that a symbol cannot be applied according to its conventional uses. You just can't point out to the child that a bird is not a *star*, neither is a wall socket a star, or a bit of lint, or a shirt, or a gas line, or a hurricane, and so forth. We cannot point out all the things that are not stars. Yet children come to know all this. How do they do it? Similar observations lead theoreticians to suppose that the infant must possess the symbols, in a real sense, in advance (cf. Chomsky, 1965, 1980, 2002; Fodor, 1980; Pylyshyn, 2002). This is a strong argument on the side of the innateness hypothesis of Chomsky and company. Nevertheless, there are some aspects of conventional signs that can at least be illustrated through exemplary uses, through pragmatic maps of experience.

Reviewing the Indexes and Moving on to Linguistic Symbols

The baby must come to know when a sequence of syllables produced by others is repeated. The baby must come to recognize certain surface-forms of speech (or signed language) prior to being able to associate those distinct forms with distinct meanings. According to the theory of abstraction, before the baby can recognize a repeated syllable in someone else's speech, even its own name, it must evidently do a good deal of groundwork. Hearing babies must first learn to discriminate, then to prescind (and thus produce), and only later to hypostatize the particular social acts that constitute meaningful forms of speech. Or, if the baby happens to be deaf or born to deaf parents, the baby still has to do much the same groundwork before beginning to acquire the surface-forms of a signed language that correspond to the syllables of speech. In Figure 6–1 we see a baby of 4.5 months engaged in what looks like reading. We introduce this picture here to point out several things: first, that as the baby moves from icons to indexes to linguistic signs, the baby's activities become increasingly social. The book is provided by a community of sign-users who speak a particular language. It represents a social connection and could not be created by the baby. It is provided by a community of sign-users. The signs that it contains, especially the printed words that it contains, could not be invented by the baby. They too come from the social acts of others. Even the baby's behavior of looking intently at the signs in the book is modeled first by others. The baby is imitating behaviors observed in others (mom and dad, especially, in the case shown). A conclusion to be drawn from all these observations is that the signs of language whether spoken, written, manually gestured (as in a signed language), printed in a book or on a road sign, a building, or wherever, are all produced by a community of sign-users. The baby does not produce them but receives them from the community.

In Chapter 5 we worked forward from about the third month after birth until about the fifth month, give or take a few weeks. In that chapter we explored the development of the indexes needed to search for an object in the field of perception. Unsuccessful searches end with just a discriminative index pointing to a possible location of the object searched for. The object represented by a hypostatic icon (the memory of the searched for object) informs the infant concerning what he or she is looking for, but cannot find in the location searched. A successful search, by contrast, ends with a percept of the object searched for and enables the formation of a complete discriminated index. Later the infant will prescind the discriminated index from the various inertial states of an object that moves around and the infant will coordinate its own movements with those of the object to discover that it is the same in all these different states. For this to occur, the prescinded index is required. That is, the infant must prescind (remove) the pointing index from the former inertial state to keep up with the present movement of the object. If the object stops, the infant must prescind the pointing index from the former moving state and now point to the stationary state of the object. These acts require the formation of what is called the prescinded index.

Finally, we saw that the infant will later achieve the highest possible index where the object disappears from the field of perception and yet is represented by a hypostatic index that continues to point to the line of movement that carried the object away from the perceiver. The hypostatic index is necessary to keep the object in mind after it has disappeared from view. All these developments take place in normal infants roughly between months three and five and logically must be completed prior to the recognition of any repeated linguistic symbol. We have already seen in prior chapters that neonates can discriminate distinct syllables. Even monkeys, rodents, and birds can do this. But human infants by about their third month do at least two things that other species do not do: for one, as Masataka (1995, 2003) showed they begin to extend their index finger as if pointing, or experimenting with the pointing gesture, and they move from vocalic to more syllabic sounds in their voluntary vocal productions.

The Repetition/Recognition Problem

Imitative gestures of pointing and shaping the vocal apparatus to imitate someone else are presumably possible without conscious recognition by the infant, that certain sounds and gestures are commonly being repeated by others. Of course, gestures and sounds that are commonly repeated must become more familiar to the infant. But how can the infant represent the *repetition* of a word? What does it take for the infant to think something like, "Aha! I've heard that sequence before! This is a syllable or sequence of syllables that I recognize!" In fact, it is clear that the infant cannot represent the *repetition* of a fleeting event, like a spoken word or a repeated gesture, without the benefit of a hypostatic index. There has to be some representation of the prior event that is not present for that one (or a series of them) to be compared to the present event so that the infant can know that they are similar or the same in some way. To compare a present event with a past event that is no longer perceivable, the infant requires at least a hypostatic index.

In this chapter we consider how the infant moves forward and upward in the sign hierarchy from the hypostatic index to the first recognized surface-forms of language. That is, the infant comes to recognize certain syllabic sequences as distinct, discrete, repeated entities in the stream of speech. In the theory of abstraction, these new and more abstract signs are called **discriminated symbols**. In many cases, the first sequence recognized by the infant is likely to be the infant's own name. At this stage, if the baby's name is "Abbey," for instance, the syllables [ǽbi], will stand out (perceptually) as different from syllable sequences that have a similar shape, for example, [máma], [bába], [dáda], and so on.

Some weeks later, after the infant begins to show evidence of achieving the *discriminated symbol*, that is, recognizing the surface-forms of certain syllables or sequences as repeated entities, the infant will begin to vocalize repeatedly certain distinct syllables of speech at will. These vocalizations might be accidents in some cases, but more often are imitative acts. Also, they soon become deliberate repeated acts and form the building blocks of the surface-forms of more complex speech. This chapter deals with the various stages and the distinct streams of development leading from the discriminated symbol to the **prescinded symbol**. The infant shows this achievement by producing recognizable syllabic sequences at will. Later still, the infant will come to associate a prescinded symbol with a particular meaning and the first **hypostatic symbol** will come into the child's repertoire of signs. Let us see how these developments can occur and what kinds of work the infant must do to begin to crack the code of the surface-forms of a particular language.

The Developmental Basis for Linguistic Symbols

It is easy to show logically that the hypostatic index is essential to the development of the ability to recognize distinct syllabic sequences. To compare one sequence with another, it is essential for the infant to compare occurrences that take place at different times. But syllabic sequences are brief and fleeting. The average syllable requires something less than half a second to produce. Then it is gone. The same is true for the production of a distinctive movement or hand-shape in manual signed language. With speech forms or the manual gestures that constitute the signs of a signed language system, to associate any pair of repeated forms requires a hypostatic index at a bare minimum. Sign gestures and speech sounds are fleeting images. They are within the field of the infant's perception only for a few hundred milliseconds at most. To associate any pair of such occurrences, or a whole string of them, requires a hypostatic index linking two or more of the discriminated syllabic sequences constituted by, say, a series of repetitions of the name [ǽbi], where "Abbey" requires only a few hundred milliseconds to say (or sign) on each occasion. Each production is gone from the infant's field of perception within the time it takes to produce.

How will the infant keep the surface linguistic form in mind in order to recognize a repeat occurrence? Clearly, it cannot be done at all without three critical elements:

1. For one, the infant must have repeated access to the surface linguistic form. because the infant cannot produce that form on its own, the whole series of forms must be supplied by someone else. Thus, for the infant to have the slightest hope of achieving its first meaningful word, the surface-forms of that word (or conventional manual sign) have to be supplied by the linguistic community into which the infant has been born.

2. For another, the infant must also have already developed the capacity to represent events across distinct perceptual fields. To do this the infant requires the capacity to produce a hypostatic index linking different occurrences of the syllabic (or signed) form in question. Otherwise, the infant would be unable to recognize any pair of occurrences of the same form. The foregoing requirements must be met to provide the necessary foundation for the first discriminated syllabic sequence, where the infant will be able to think something like, "Aha! This syllabic utterance that sounds like [ǽbi], I've heard that one before!"

3. In addition to both of those requirements, the infant must also learn to differentiate the syllables (or manual signs) that constitute the word. Otherwise, [æbi] will not sound different from [dada], [mama], [baba], and so forth. That is to say, in addition to speech forms provided by the language community, plus hypostatic indexes, the infant also needs to learn to differentiate syllabic sequences.

Clearly, all the foregoing discriminative work must be done before the infant is able to develop its first discriminated symbol. It will normally consist of a syllable or syllabic sequence (or in the case of deaf infants with signing parents, a linguistic sign presented manually). It is also possible for printed words to be very early discriminated symbols in a child's repertoire (see the references to Aleka Titzer in Chapter 10). Consider the signs that are necessary to the discovery of the first discriminated symbol as diagramed in Figure 6–2. The idea that the symbol to be discriminated is often repeated in the infant's experience is suggested by the subscripts n, $n + 1$, and so forth. We must suppose that the first notice of the discriminated symbol as such can only take place after the infant has heard the syllabic sequence or observed the manual sign many times. Relevant research on the social interactions of infants and adults during language acquisition shows that factors that influence how quickly the first syllabic sequences are discriminated include (1) how much functional diversity is present in the speech directed to the infant (Pan, Rowe, Singer, & Snow, 2005), (2) especially the lexical diversity of the input, and (3) mother's educational background and literacy. Although Pan et al. (2005) argue that the amount of talk directed to the infant does not seem to be a factor in linguistic growth, there is independent evidence that the frequency of repetition of forms presented to the child is a factor in acquisition (Cameron-Faulkner, Lieven, & Tomasello 2003; Ellis, 2002; Tomasello, 2003; Zamuner, Gerken, & Hammond, 2005). All else being equal, the higher the frequency and saliency of inputs to the child the earlier those inputs are likely to be acquired.

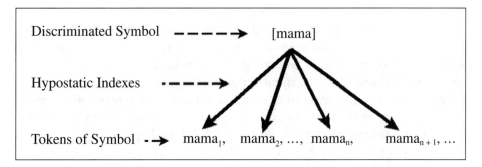

Figure 6–2. A diagram of an arbitrary example of a discriminated symbol, in this case, the surface-forms of the word "mama."

For all these reasons, functionality, diversity of uses, frequency of occurrence, saliency, and importance from the child's point of view, in many cases the first discriminated symbol will be the syllabic sound (or manual sign) for the infant's name. Or, it will be some other commonly repeated syllabic sequence that is frequent, significant, salient, and so on. For instance, the infant may come to recognize a form like "bye-bye" accompanied by the waving gesture, "hmmaa" accompanied with a kiss, or something similar. It will usually have a high frequency of occurrence, that is, be an often repeated surface-form. It does not have to be a noun, but, most commonly, it is likely to be some kind of naming word, a vocative, or an activity-related word that is appropriate to a commonly occurring event sequence. For example, "bye-bye" is a sequence embedded in a familiar activity where everyone waves bye-bye and kisses are exchanged with the baby, and then some of the folks get in the car and leave. In some cases **high saliency** might make up for a lack of frequency. For instance, a word like "hot" might be acquired suddenly because of its association with an unpleasant experience, for example, touching a hot stove, stepping on a burning ember, or something of that sort.

The discovery of the first discriminated symbol can be expected to occur soon after the baby reaches the stage of the hypostatic index. In normal infants this development is apt to take place sometime between the fourth and fifth month (give or take two or three weeks). The discriminated symbol, however, cannot, for reasons already noted, develop before the level of the hypostatic index has been achieved. In Figure 6-2, as is shown, multiple hypostatic indexes are required to form a single discriminated symbol. The infant must keep in mind one or more surface-forms that have occurred, flown by, and that are no longer evident, in order to recognize the next one that comes along. In the diagram of Figure 6-2, we indicate the first, second, and *n* later occurrences of the surface-form, the syllable sequence [mama] in the example chosen, and then we show subsequent occurrences as *n + 1, n + 2,* and so forth.

If the surface-form in question happens to be the baby's name, or the name of someone else, one partial evidence that the baby is able to discriminate that particular symbol, is that the baby will turn to attend to someone who produces a **token** of that familiar form. This is especially indicative if it occurs on the mention of the baby's name. In Figure 6–2, the tokens of the syllable sequence [mama] are the separate pronunciations of that sequence in distinct surface-forms shown at the bottom of the diagram. These tokens must be noticed by the infant. Logically each one that is noticed is pointed to by a hypostatic index that connects it with the more abstract discriminated symbol. With a signing infant, the analog event will be for the child to show special interest in some high-frequency sign gesture. The special interest in the familiar syllable sequence, or manual gesture, shows that the baby has probably attained the discriminated symbol. At this stage, however, the infant has not yet mapped the surface-form onto any particular referent or activity. However, an important step in that direction has been taken.

The Prescinded Symbol

When the infant begins to vocally (and/or manually, in the case of deaf infants) produce the first distinct syllables and sequences of them (or the first recognizable surface-forms of manual signs), we may say that the infant has achieved the level of the *prescinded symbol*. Following a long-standing tradition in linguistics of representing the phonetic forms of linguistic symbols as enclosed with square brackets, like these, "[," "]," we represent a discriminated linguistic symbol (or any other kind of discriminated sign) by enclosing it in square brackets. The point of this notational convention is to show that what appears between the brackets is a token or surface-form that is perceivable in some way, for example, look back to the percept of an apple in Figure 4–7. In that case the square brackets enclose a discriminated icon. To show the process of prescission, we follow another linguistic convention and enclose the prescinded sign in forward slashes, like these "/," "/." Any prescinded sign may be shown in this way. The idea here is to note the fact that the learner/sign-user at this level has gained motor control over the production of the form in question. With a prescinded icon, the baby must imagine a percept of an object where none is present. This requires mental action on the part of the infant. With a prescinded index the baby must separate the index that points to the inertial state of an object from that state to move it to another state of the same object (or to a different object in order to represent several different objects). With the prescinded symbol, the child demonstrates motor control over the syllable by producing it, for example, by saying /ma/ or /mama/, or by replicating a signed language gesture, hand-shape, or sequence of these.

It is important to note that the surface-form produced as a prescinded symbol not only has an abstract form as represented by its surface-form as produced by the child, but this symbol is recognizable as a syllabic sequence of sounds that can be discriminated by someone else. For instance, if the baby begins to babble the syllable /ma/ or /mama/, the sequence must be recognizable by adults as a distinct syllabic utterance that resembles the familiar sequence in the target language. At this stage of development, however, typically, the infant does not yet know the meaning of the babbled sequence.

The stage of the prescinded symbol is culminated and distinctly marked by what has been called **canonical babbling** (D. K. Oller, 1980; D. K. Oller, Eilers, & Basinger, 2001; D. K. Oller, Eilers, Neal, & Schwartz, 1999; D. K. Oller & Lynch 1992; Stark, 1980). This kind of babble is characterized by speech-like repetitive sequences, /mamama/, /bababa/, /dadada/, and so on. This development normally precedes by several months the discovery of the first intelligible meaningful word by the infant. In the meantime, before the first "word" appears in the child's speech (at about 12 to 15 months of age), a good deal of groundwork must first be accomplished. In this chapter we review three distinguishable streams of development leading up to canonical babble and going on to the child's so-called "first word."

Three Distinct Streams of Development

As suggested by Figure 6–3, what is happening as the child advances from the prescinded symbol to the hypostatic symbol is that three distinct and yet interacting streams of development are coming together very rapidly. The first stream has led to (1) icons differentiating material objects and persons (as we have seen in preceding chapters, especially Chapter 4); then to (2) indexes that connect the icons more completely with each other and with the perceiver (as we have seen in the immediately preceding chapter, Chapter 5); and then these two streams of development converge with (3) the somewhat independently developing stream of differentiated symbols. In this chapter, we pay special attention to the third stream. We are particularly concerned with the syllables (surface-forms) of speech, but analogous developments are known to occur in the acquisition of signed languages of the deaf by deaf children and also by hearing children with deaf parents who sign (Petitto & Marentette, 1991; also see Ejiri & Masataka, 2001).

All three of the distinguishable streams of development are being discussed extensively in the relevant research literature. Because we are mainly concerned with speech and language development in this book, we begin by examining that stream of development first. It is also useful to keep in mind that the three distinguishable streams are integrated to some extent

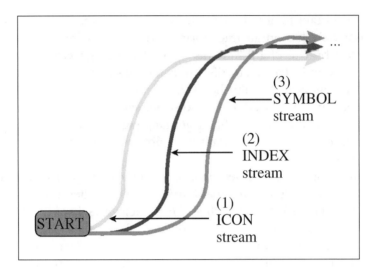

Figure 6–3. A schematic view of the three streams of sign development as they converge toward the discovery of the first meaningful word.

from the infant's experience before birth and certainly from birth forward through the process of pragmatic mapping (stream 3; cf. Figures 3-2, 4-1, 4-3, 4-4). As the infant matures, the sign systems characteristic of each stream of activity are increasingly articulated and the three streams are being more and more articulately interconnected as the infant progresses toward the first meaningful words. When that milestone is achieved, in other words, when the infant uses its first meaningful word, the crucial problem of integrating icons and indexes with linguistic symbols is soon solved sufficiently well that the child will turn attention to relations between linguistic symbols, that is, to syntax (as we will see in greater detail in Chapter 8).

The primary task in this chapter is to see how the infant achieves the integration of the three main developing streams of sign systems as suggested by Figure 6-3; these systems are converging as the child progresses toward the first word. To arrive at that higher level, the iconic signs have to be sufficiently developed to enable the development of the indexical ones, and the indexes, similarly, have to be developed sufficiently to sustain the development of linguistic symbols. For these reasons, in this chapter we need to examine the stages of development that are progressing more or less in parallel in all three streams. Also, we are interested in how the streams come to be increasingly well integrated. We will see in this chapter how the development of canonical babbling is taking place concurrently with the development of certain referential (meaningful) aspects of linguistic forms. In particular, we see how indexical acts of the infant are pragmatically mapping vocalizations onto bodily persons and then onto external objects and scenes through meaningful gestures.

In babble, the infant is mainly working out the surface-forms of speech (the symbol stream in Figure 6–3). At the same time, the infant is working out a problem of a deeper sort, namely, the problem of pragmatically mapping of those surface-forms onto material content displayed mainly in icons (the first stream in Figure 6–3). To accomplish the linking of linguistic surface-forms with their particular referents and meanings, it turns out that indexes (the middle stream of Figure 6–3) are crucial. These may be expressed as finger extension, rhythmic hand movements, mutual gaze patterns (looking to see what someone else is looking at), pointing, handling, and moving objects. All these indexical actions help the child to find out the intentions of others and, eventually, the meanings of their words. The problems to be solved are formidable ones from the infant's vantage point, but all normal infants solve them within about 12 to 15 months after birth. How does the infant do all this?

Infant Phonation

To distinguish voluntary vocalizations that are somewhat speech-like from other vocalizations of infancy, D. K. Oller (1980, 1995; D. K. Oller & Lynch, 1992) proposed the term **phonation**. The purpose of this term was to distinguish its vocal products, called **protophones**, from two other common kinds of infant vocalization that are not considered to be speech-like. The first are *vegetative* sounds such as burps, grunts, coughs, and sneezes. A second class of sounds that are not considered as any part of the inventory leading to speech are **fixed vocal signals** such as cries, laughter, groans, and the like. Although many species exhibit vegetative and fixed vocal signals, only humans produce protophones. In doing so, D. K. Oller has observed that there is an "international consensus" on four stages of protophone development in infancy (Elbers, 1982; Holmgren, Lindblom, Aurelius, Jalling, & Zetterstrom, 1986; Koopmans, van Beinum & van der Stelt, 1986; D. K. Oller, 1980; Stark, 1980; Zlatin, 1975). An important point to notice is that the protophones build from stage to stage and eventually culminate in canonical babbling which normally precedes the onset of meaningful speech. Perhaps the most important distinguishing characteristic of protophones is that they are voluntary vocalizations. They are acts that the infant performs at will.

Stage 1: Quasivowels

The first stage in the development of protophones is completed during the infants first two months of life. During that time, the research of Aldridge, Stillman, & Bower (2003) shows that the infant can already distinguish the key elements of the adult vowel system, /i/, /u/, and /a/, but it will take some time before these discriminated sounds can be recognizably produced. For this reason, because symbol development of the linguistic kind is known to proceed from the womb forward, the symbol line of Figure 6–3 extends all the way back to the starting point. However, the first stage of voluntary protophones produced by the infant seem to be tending in the direction of adult vowels. This is why that phase of protophone development is referred to as the **quasivowel** stage. The quasivowel protophones are like vowels but without any deliberate shaping of the articulators. Quasivowels sound like vowels except with the mouth in a relaxed posture. That is, these protophones are produced without the shaping of the lips, jaw, or tongue that will later distinguish different vowels.

Quasivowels are vowel-like because they involve what linguists call *voicing*. In their production, the voice is used in the same way that it will later function in the production of more developed vowel sounds. Therefore, we could say that the infant is taking a first step toward speech sounds and syllable formation. Also, the infant's actions in producing quasivowels provide additional inputs for discrimination. To the extent that quasivowels are extended over time, they also provide a present-time on-line basis for exploring the relationship between the sound being produced (that the hearing infant can hear) and the way the body of the infant, especially the vocal tract, feels during the production. As a result, by producing protophones, the infant gains access to inputs necessary to begin building its own phonological mapping of the vocal movements and the sounds they enable the infant to produce.

Stage II: Primitive Articulation Stage

By *articulation* what is meant is the shaping of the vocal tract through movements of the tongue, jaw, and lips. According to the international consensus on the development of infant phonation, between months two and three, the normal infant will begin to differentially shape the articulators. In doing this, the former quasivowels now become more vowel-like because of the infant's voluntary shaping of one or more articulators. The articulatory movements that produce contrasts in the vowels of the languages of the world include moving the tongue forward or backward in the mouth, opening or closing the jaw, and rounding or flattening the lips. Some of the results of these articulatory movements are summed up in the diagram of the vowel space seen in Figure 3–3. Of course, most infants will never produce all those distinctions because few languages contain all those vowel sounds. However, during months two and three, the normal infant will begin to shape the articulators so as to distinguish different vowels.

We know from the research of Meltzoff & Moore (1977, 1997; also Tatsumoto, 1993) that neonates imitate facial gestures such as eye blinks, opening of the mouth, sticking out the tongue, and lip protrusion. These actions suggest that infants are not only attentive to the articulatory movements and facial expressions of adults, but that the infants intend to and do imitate them. Kuhl and Meltzoff (1996) found that infants at 12, 16, and 20 weeks are able to produce vocalic sounds that resemble the vowels they are hearing at the same time. Also, they showed both by transcriptions and by spectrographic analyses that infant vocalic sounds become more differentiated between weeks 12 and 20.

Stage III. The Expansion Stage

Somewhere between months three and six (give or take a month), infants will continue to expand their repertoire of articulatory movements and will move to fully vowel–like sounds. During the **expansion stage**, the protophones produced begin to show the rich and varied *resonance* properties of adult vowel sounds. By manipulating the shape of the vocal tract through movements of the articulators the infant is able to produce contrasting vowels that resemble those produced by adults. Also, by initiating the articulation of distinct vowels starting from a closed mouth position, the infant is also able to produce the first syllabic structures of the universal consonant-vowel (CV) shape. This results in what D. K. Oller, Eilers, Neal, & Schwartz (1999) term "marginal babbling." To move from this marginal kind of babbling to the real thing, the infant only needs to speed up the transition from the consonant-like sound to the vowel-like one. When that happens a well-formed syllable is the inevitable result.

Stage IV. Canonical Babbling

Usually by about the sixth month and rarely after the tenth month, the infant reaches the stage known as *canonical babbling*. The infant begins to produce well formed syllables that adults will readily recognize as speech-like forms. In fact, research by Papoušek (1994) shows that parents begin early on to try to recruit the canonical forms, such as [mama], and to get the infant to use them as words, for instance, to refer to the infant's mother. A canonical form such as [baba] may be pressed into service as a word to refer to the baby's bottle, or to signify leave-taking ("bye-bye"), and so forth.

Because of the cumulative nature of sign development, failure to achieve any particular milestone of development may be indicative of risk for additional difficulties later on. This inference follows from the constructive nature of the sign hierarchy. If certain building blocks are not in place on schedule, the whole hierarchy of sign systems can be delayed in development. Canonical babbling is a particularly important milestone because it is evidently a necessary stepping stone toward essentially all aspects of subsequent speech and language development. Vocabulary growth, for example, not to mention all the later developments that depend on it, will almost certainly be delayed if canonical babbling is delayed. For all these reasons, a failure to achieve the milestone of canonical babbling, therefore, is highly likely to be associated with subsequent delays in language and learning. Failure to perform canonical babbling more or less on schedule would be judged a significant **risk factor**. On this account, some researchers (for example, see D. K. Oller, Eilers, & Basinger, 2001) have been especially interested in studying the trustworthiness, that is, the **validity**, of judgments about the achievement of canonical babbling.

The Validity Question

The research shows that not only expert researchers (D. K. Oller, Eilers, & Basinger, 2001), but also untrained parents are very good at knowing whether or not their infants have reached the stage of canonical babbling. As soon as the parents are provided with a description of the kind of babbling the researchers are asking about, parents or other caregivers can say with considerable accuracy whether or not their child has achieved canonical babbling. In binary (two-way) judgments, for example, where the child either has or has not achieved canonical babbling, researchers distinguish two aspects of judgment accuracy. There are exactly four possible outcomes as shown in Table 6–1. As the table shows, there are two possible kinds of correct judgments and two possible error judgments.

The underlying question involves the general problem of validity. Does the measure proposed really measure what it is supposed to measure? This problem, at its basis, boils down to the foundational question of whether

Table 6–1 Possible Outcomes for a Binary Judgment Concerning the Canonical Babbling Milestone

	The Parent Reports Correctly	The Parent Reports Incorrectly
Canonical babbling has not been achieved and the child is at risk	True Positive Judgment of the risk factor	False Positive Judgment of the risk factor
Canonical babbling has been achieved and the child is not at risk	True Negative Judgment of the risk factor	False Negative Judgment of the risk factor

or not a certain proposition that claims to be a statement of fact is true or not (Badon, S. Oller, Yan, & J. Oller, 2005; Borsboom, Mellenbergh, & van Heerden, 2004). If the parent says the child is or is not doing canonical babbling, is the parent's judgment correct? The validity question, and more particularly, the sort of binary judgment at stake in this instance (that is, in the case of canonical babbling) is *the* essential basis for any scalar judgment or measurement of any kind (J. Oller & Chen, in press). All judgments about the identity, traits, and qualities of any object or person, or any state of affairs whatever, depend at their basis on the same kind of binary judgment, for example, in this case as made by the parent who is asked to say whether or not the infant has achieved the stage of canonical babble. So this case is worth looking at closely. The concepts introduced here will come up again when we deal with language in relation to educational tests (Chapter 11) and they are relevant to every kind of educational measurement, every diagnosis of disorders, every medical assessment of disease, and any kind of scientific measurement whatever.

In Table 6-1, the percentage of true positive judgments constitutes what researchers call the **sensitivity** of the measure, test, or judgment. That is, to what extent does the procedure identify true positive cases, that is, infants who are judged to be at risk, in this case, because they have *not* yet achieved the stage of canonical babbling. If multiple judgments are made, the number of true positive judgments divided by the total number of positive judgments (the two cells in the top row of Table 6-1) will give the estimated sensitivity of the judgments at stake. The percentage of true positive judgments out of all the positive judgments made gives the likelihood of a correct true positive judgment being made with the measure at hand. This is the meaning of sensitivity. In the case at hand, the question is, how likely is it that a parent will make a correct judgment that the infant is at risk for not having achieved the level of canonical babbling if the infant in fact has not done so?

By contrast, the percentage of true negative judgments constitutes what researchers call the **specificity** of the measure, test, or judgment. That is, to what extent does the procedure identify persons who have achieved the milestone in question and who are not at risk (or who do not have the condition, disease, or whatever). If multiple judgments are made, the number of true negative judgments divided by the total number of negative judgments (the two cells in the bottom row of Table 6-1) will give the estimated specificity of the judgments at stake. The percentage of true negative judgements out of all the negative ones gives the best estimate of the likelihood that correct true negative judgments will be made with the procedure. This is the meaning of specificity. In the case at hand, how likely is it that the parent will make a correct judgment that the infant is not at risk, in other words, has achieved the level of canonical babbling, if the infant in fact has done so?

The first column of Table 6-1 shows correct judgments of both the positive (sensitivity) and negative (specificity) kinds. This combined pair of cells gives the overall **concordance** of the two sets of judgments with what is known in some other way about the infant's development. That is, how much do the parents agree with true judgments of the status of the infants? If the true judgments can be known, the concordance of any other judgment with those true judgments is a measure of their validity, that is the extent to which the judgments tell us what they are supposed to tell us. The agreement between any given pair of judges, say a parent and an expert evaluator, is a measure of what is called **inter-rater reliability**, that is, the tendency for different judges to agree with each other.

The second column of Table 6-1 shows the corresponding error judgments, false positives and false negatives. The combination of these two components is a measure (or estimate) of the **error term** or what may be called the **unreliability** of the proposed measure. In a false positive, for example, the parent would say the child is at risk, that is, has not achieved canonical babbling when in fact the child has already arrived at that milestone. In a false negative case, the parent would say that the child is not at risk when in fact the infant has not yet achieved the milestone and is at risk.

Potential Sources of Error

There are many potential sources of errors in the kinds of judgments that concern milestones of achievement. In surveys, interviews, questionnaires, and screening procedures of all kinds, parents, doctors, or anyone, may give wrong answers for a great variety of reasons. They might not understand exactly what they are being asked, and, for this reason, give a wrong answer. Or they might just overestimate or underestimate based on faulty memory or inadequate evidence. Or instead of examining or thinking about the relevant evidence the respondent might give what he or she thinks is the most desirable answer.

The tendency to give a response that the respondent thinks is desired by someone else has been discussed in a variety of contexts in the measurement literature. For instance, if the respondent thinks that a certain response will make herself (or himself) look better in the eyes of someone else, **self-flattery** (Biemer & Lyberg, 2003; J. Oller & Perkins, 1978a, 1978b) may be the source of the error.

If the response is merely an attempt to provide what the experimenter may be looking for, as noted by D. K. Oller, Eilers, & Basinger, (2001), the source of the error may be what has been called **acquiescence response bias** (see Lehman, Krosnick, West, & Li, 1992). In an extensive review of survey literature, Krosnick (1999) has documented a tendency for respondents sometimes to give a response to get off the hook so to speak. Kros-nick calls this source of errors **satisficing** to suggest the notion that the respondent is merely trying to produce a response that will suffice to satisfy the questioner, hence, to "satisfice."

If the respondent is merely trying appear socially acceptable in the eyes of the interviewer, the source of the error may be owed to the widely studied **approval motive** (Crowne & Marlowe, 1964; Biemer & Lyberg, 2003). Yet another source of error, also alluded to by D. K. Oller, Eilers, & Basinger, (2001), is the tendency to stick with a response once it has been given even when contrary evidence appears. For instance, some parents might take "a resistant posture against changing their stories in response to directed questions" (p. 57). In any case, the tendency to be consistent with what was said or done beforehand is a potential source of errors. It has been referred to as **response set** meaning a tendency to give the same response multiple times just because it was given before (Oller & Perkins, 1978a, 1978b; Biemer & Lyberg, 2003). There are other sources of errors besides these, but these give a glimpse of the many different ways that errors can arise.

The underlying question in all kinds of measurement is whether a given judgment or measure is valid, in other words, true. In communication in general, disagreements and failures to communicate are like the errors in measurement. They are relatively easy to come by and relatively easy to account for. Except for biases, that is errors that arise consistently because of some predictable tendency or other, errors can be attributed to chance. In the final analysis, there are so many different ways to account for errors that failures to agree are relatively unremarkable. Errors can occur by chance, or because of a plethora of possible distractions, breakdowns, dif-ficulties, and so on. On the other hand, agreement is so much less likely than disagreement, when it occurs, it is a great deal less likely that the agreement can be attributed to accident, chance, or error. For this reason, agreements across persons, measures, or judges are usually a great deal more informative from an experimental or measurement perspective than are errors.

Parents and Experts Usually Agree on Achievement of Canonical Babbling

In the case of parental judgments of whether or not the infant has reached the stage of canonical babbling, the researchers (D. K. Oller, Eilers, & Basinger, 2001) asked whether the parents' judgments would agree with those of experts. In fact, on the basis of a general theory of signs, it can be logically demonstrated in a series of rigorous proofs that all measurement judgments ultimately must be tested for their validity against some criterion of agreement (J. Oller & Chen, in press). Although disagreements between different judges are relatively easy to obtain and not difficult to explain, agreements between judges, on the other hand, are more informative. Unless the judges really have some shared knowledge, their agreement in any complex conversational exchange would be a kind of unexplainable accident. The kind of agreement that depends on abstract conventional signs and their applications is so unlikely to occur by chance that these kinds of agreement must have some other explanation. For instance, if judges agree on when infants achieve the stage of canonical babbling, then we must attribute some validity to their judgments. Such agreement probably means that the parents and experts both are competent judges of what canonical babbling is. It is extremely unlikely that such agreement could be owed to error or to chance.

D. K. Oller, Eilers, & Basinger, (2001) report three separate studies on this question. With groups of 57, 56, and 100 parent-child pairs in the three studies, respectively, they found that relatively untrained parents from a diversity of ethnic and socioeconomic levels agree with experts in a high percentage of cases whether or not their infant has achieved the canonical babbling milestone. The measured levels of overall concordance on the achievement of the babbling milestone was 86% for the first study, 93% for the second, and 97% for the third group. The groups of parents studied included a wide range of socioeconomic levels. In the first study, most of the 57 participating families were classed as "very low socioeconomic level" (Eilers et al., 1993) and the infants in that study were all born prematurely. In the second and third studies, the 56 and 100 families, respectively, were of mixed levels. Infants in the three samples covered a range of ages beginning at 4 months and with an average of 8.2 months for the first study, 9 months for study two, and 5.5 months for study three.

Participants voluntarily met with an interviewer who asked the parent (or primary caretaker) a series of questions about the infant. The interviewer asked about the infant's vocalizations and provided examples as deemed necessary of both precanonical and canonical vocalizations. Later on the same day of the interview, the infants themselves were recorded in a laboratory setting. The tape-recording session took about half an hour while the infant played with quiet toys and interacted either with a caretaker or a researcher, while another trained and qualified individual observed and made a judgment about whether or not the infant had achieved the stage of canonical babbling. The laboratory judgment, then, was used as a standard against which to assess the judgment from parents. The researchers pointed out, however, that laboratory judgment might in some cases fail to observe an instance of canonical babbling in the half-hour session even if the child had already achieved that stage of development. The infant just might not perform at the highest level of his or her capability during that particular half-hour.

Nevertheless, in the three studies at issue, the sensitivity of parental judgments about whether infants were at risk (for not having achieved the canonical babbling milestone) was 100%, 88%, and 98% in the respective studies. Specificity was 77%, 95%, and 96%, respectively. We are led to conclude that parental judgments of the canonical babbling milestone have high inter-rater reliability and substantial validity. Overall in all three studies, parents agreed with the expert researchers 93% of the time. Untrained parents and experts alike are able to judge the relative speech-likeness of phonations produced by infants. They are not only able to distinguish syllabic utterances of infants from vocalizations of the vegetative and fixed signal kinds, but they are also able to make the much more subtle distinction between syllabic, canonical babbling, and the other stages of phonation that precede it. Because canonical babbling is a good predictor of later cognitive, social, and linguistic developments, Eilers et al. (1993) concluded that the milestone of canonical babbling may be a suitable screening device for the early identification of children at risk for learning difficulties and communication disorders.

Integrating Vocalizations with Referential Content

In addition to the stream of development by which infants sort out the syllables of speech, there are two other streams of development that are progressing simultaneously and to some extent in parallel (as suggested above by Figure 6–3). One stream of signs consists of iconic representations. We focused on that stream in Chapter 4. Another stream consists mainly of indexes that connect and relate distinct icons. We focused on that stream in Chapter 5. Here, in Chapter 6, we must consider the integration of all three strands as suggested in Figure 6–3. The fact that three distinct streams must be integrated is important to understand. Even specialists who deal with language arts, literacy, special education, or communication disorders are apt to underestimate the importance of this integration because much of the work normally occurs well before the child arrives at kindergarten. What is more, much of the work that the infant does in developing iconic and indexical signs is less observable to adults and teachers than the developments that pertain to the surface-forms of speech and language. The development of speech is easier to observe because it is ultimately an intentional social activity (as noted by Vygotsky, 1934/1962, 1930–1935/1978).

For all the foregoing reasons, it is easy even for specialists to underestimate the importance and the difficulty of the integration that is required. As the infant is breaking into the linguistic process, the differentiation and parsing of the surface-forms of speech (or manual signing in Deaf cultures) is going on concurrently with the differentiation and parsing of the material world of experience. From the viewpoint of almost any observer of the infant, these distinct streams of sign development are so intermingled that it is difficult to distinguish them at all. Yet, theoretical analysis justifies the distinctions. The surface-forms of speech (or manual signing) are fundamentally different from the persons, things, events, sequences of events, fantasies, and so on, to which they are used to refer. Likewise, the material content of experience is so distinct from the surface-forms of speech that Albert Einstein argued that they exist on the opposite sides of a logically uncrossable gulf.

Einstein described the adult's natural blindness to the distinctness of our impressions of the material world and the linguistic signs we use to represent that world, in this way:

> . . . we have the habit of combining certain concepts and conceptual relations (propositions) so definitely with certain sense experiences that we do not become conscious of the gulf—logically unbridgeable—which separates the world of sensory experiences from the world of concepts and propositions (1944, p. 289).

Is it any wonder, then, that adults have trouble seeing how it is that the human infant connects icons of material experience with linguistic signs? We call the gulf that separates sensory impressions, leading to the formation of icons, from the abstract ideas represented in surface-forms of linguistic symbols, **Einstein's gulf**, as shown in Figure 6–4. As we examine several competing theories, we will discover that the main elements that have been neglected or entirely left out of the picture in some theories are the connecting indexical signs that link icons (sensory impressions) with

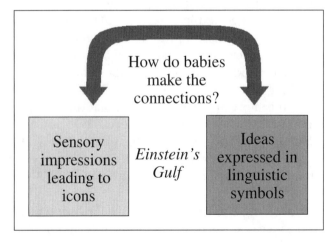

Figure 6–4. A schematic representation of the problem presented by Einstein's Gulf.

linguistic signs (symbols). The principal problem of language acquisition is how the gulf can be crossed at all. Obviously it is crossed by every child that acquires a language. The question is how? We have argued that indexical signs are necessary to jump start pragmatic bootstrapping. These are the signs that enable the initial pragmatic mapping of sensory impressions onto abstract symbols, especially the symbols of speech (or manual signing).

Competing Theories

Several competing theories have been proposed and, interestingly, they tend to emphasize one or another element in the diagram of Figure 6–4. If we look to the linguistic structures they turn out to be formidably complex. The infant has to:

- Identify them as distinct from other objects, events, relations, and so on (by discrimination);

- Divide them up into units, associate them with different producers, and replicate them (by prescission); and then

- Discover their meanings by associating them with other bodily objects in the infant's experience in addition to persons (by hypostasis).

If all this linguistic and cognitive complexity is considered, the theoretician is apt to prefer a rationalist approach along the lines of Chomsky. A natural outcome of such a rationalist approach, emphasizing the complexity and abstractness of the language capacity, is the sort of innateness hypothesis that Chomsky and his followers have tended to settle on.

If, on the other hand, the theoretician looks to the material world (on the left side of the diagram in Figure 6–4), an empirical approach is certain to emerge. If the emphasis is placed on the material itself and its concrete structures, these may be supposed to be the source of the abstract systems found in the languages of the world. Theoreticians preferring to emphasize the material side of Einstein's gulf, therefore, may try to find ways to build up linguistic structures of great complexity from anatomical structures and their mechanical movements (for example, see MacNeilage & Davis, 1995, 2000, 2001).

Regardless which of the two radical extremes theoreticians might lean toward, there must be some middle ground. For instance, Chomsky and colleagues (Chomsky, 1965, 1980, 1995, 2002) have tended to suppose that experience in the world merely serves as a triggering device to start the language acquisition process. Fodor (1980) limited the triggering effect to one of merely fixing (determining or marking) the content to be referred to by particular abstract concepts that the infant must already possess. According to Chomsky and Fodor, in the proceedings of the 1980 debate between Chomsky and Piaget (cf. Piatelli-Palmarini, 1980), the infant must have all the concepts in advance, before language acquisition begins. Their argument limits the role of learning from the environment to merely "fixing" the content of the concepts the infant already possesses. On the contrary, opponents of the innateness hypothesis invariably stress the role of learning (Tomasello, 2003), the social experience of the child (Bruner, 1975), and the significant effects of the environment into which the child is born (Locke, 1994).

To some extent all the competing approaches must admit that there is some common ground between the extreme abstractness of linguistic concepts and the concreteness of the material world of experience. Still everyone seems, often without acknowledging it at all, to be troubled by the necessary crossing of Einstein's gulf. If the common ground is emphasized (namely, the middle parts of Figures 6–3 and 6–4) elements from the competing theories may be incorporated and consolidated. Almost all theoreticians will admit that human infants have certain unique (innate) capacities enabling the acquisition of language, and they will also admit that experience has a role to play. Otherwise, if experience played no role at all, a child might be as likely to start speaking any one of the more than 6,000 languages of the world (see Gordon, 2005) as the one (or ones) to which the child happens to be exposed. For instance, why should deaf children born into Deaf cultures learn manual signs while hearing children in the same context learn both manual signed language and spoken languages (Petitto & Marentette, 1991)? By contrast, hearing children learn the language, or languages, to which they are exposed. Children do not just learn any old language out of all the languages that exist. The evidence suggests that experience plays a role. Every theoretician admits these facts but is nevertheless apt to emphasize one side of the nature versus nurture argument more or less than the other depending on the theory preferred.

Clearly, innate capacity plays a role. No one has yet succeeded in getting baby parrots, chimps, gorillas, or any other species to do what human infants do in babbling (D. K. Oller, 2000; Sebeok & Umiker-Sebeok, 1980). Also, no one seems to have succeeded teaching other species to consider the abstract intentions of humans. Yet human babies seem to do so without special teaching, and they seem to know that languages are important even before birth. Human infants clearly are different from other species in having an innate propensity for language acquisition, for abstract thought, and for representation. Because human infants perform so differently from other species, and because human infants seem to take the intentions of others into consideration from a very early age, many theoreticians have made the infants themselves out to be theoreticians (for example, Baron-Cohen, Tager-Flusberg, & Cohen, 1993; Gopnik, Capps, & Meltzoff, in press; Meltzoff, 1999). The babies are regarded as little researchers testing hypotheses about language and how it may work.

Many variations on these themes are possible. Our own preference, as we have indicated in Chapter 4, is summed up in the theory of pragmatic bootstrapping. All theories of bootstrapping acknowledge the middle ground between certain elements that have to be connected with each other in language acquisition. All of them appeal either overtly or covertly to indexes. That is, some theories, notably the theory of pragmatic bootstrapping, acknowledge the crucial role of indexes explicitly. Other theories, for instance, the theories of syntactic bootstrapping (Landau & Gleitman, 1985; Naigles, 1990), semantic bootstrapping (Pinker, 1989), and prosodic bootstrapping (Nazzi & Ramus, 2003) also depend on indexical links of one or another kind. Syntactic bootstrapping requires indexical links between different syntactic structures to be used as a scaffolding for the discovery of new meanings. Semantic bootstrapping requires indexes linking surface-forms of syntax (also phonology and the lexicon) with abstract concepts (per Chomsky's innateness hypothesis). Prosodic bootstrapping requires sophisticated indexes to track rhythms and make use of them. Pragmatic bootstrapping stresses connections between icons (sensory impressions) on one side of Einstein's gulf and symbols (linguistic forms, including syllables) on the other side through indexes. In the theory of pragmatic mapping, as we have seen in earlier chapters (especially Figures 3–3, 4–4, and 4–5), indexes play a crucial role, but they are not the only elements. Icons and symbols are also important, and the symbols must be available in advance just as has been argued by Chomsky (1980) and Fodor (1980).

Connecting the Streams and Building Referential Meanings

We will return to the controversies concerning the competing theories of how the infant crosses Einstein's gulf in Chapter 8 but here we intend to begin to unravel the mystery of how the infant connects iconic sign systems through indexical signs with linguistic symbols. To initiate the required series of increasingly abstract operations, leading up to the first meaningful referential symbols, the baby must first begin to coordinate its own voluntary movements and vocalizations with those of the language community into which it is born. In order to do this, the infant must attend to the coordinated speech and other movements of more mature models in its life space. The infant begins by taking a special interest in those entities that make the vocal noises we call speech, or for deaf infants, the rhythmic movements of a signed language.

Stage 1: Primary Reference (the First Person or Speaker)

The hearing newborn, as we have seen in earlier chapters, takes special interest in the persons that it has heard speaking while in the womb. Soon after its birth, the baby connects one or more bodily persons with familiar voices by observing the articulatory movements of speakers while hearing the sounds and rhythms of their speech. These connections form, according to the theory of pragmatic mapping and more particularly of pragmatic bootstrapping (Badon, S. Oller, Yan, & J. Oller, 2005; J. Oller, 2005; J. Oller et al., 2005), form the first primitive stage of referential meaning. From the infant's point of view, the speaker becomes the first referent of the act of speaking. This level is what is meant by the term **primary reference**. The infant thinks something like this: "Aha! That person is speaking." The person that is the source of the speaking is also a primary pragmatic referent of that act. Vygotsky (1930-1935/1978) observed that social signs and "all of the higher functions originate as actual relations between human individuals" (p. 57). From the naïve perspective of the infant, the speech of the person who speaks calls attention to that person. While watching and hearing a speaker produce speech, the coordination of the vocal sounds with the moving body, especially the face of the speaker, enables the baby to connect the sound of the voice with the person producing the speech (see Figure 3–3). Similarly, a deaf infant in observing the production of signed language is able to associate the rhythm of movements of the sign system with the person producing those signs (per Petitto & Marentette, 1991). Such experience enables the baby (whether hearing or deaf) to begin to initiate a primitive but meaningful linguistic sign system. In Chapter 4 we proposed calling such a primitive system, an "infrasemiotic" system. Presumably any such system must be extremely limited at first only being applied in the present tense. They provide a basis for the formation of memories, but are barely grounded in memories to start with. In proposing this stage of referential development in infancy, we realize that we are expanding the very definition of what *reference* is, but the expansion appears to be completely consistent with what infants are observed to do. Look again at the video of mothers interacting with their infants and consider the intensity of the reciprocal interest displayed there (see http://www.raisingdeafkids.org/hearingloss/testing/nhs.jsp visited on September 10, 2005).

According to a general theory of signs (J. Oller et al., 2005; S. D. Oller, 2005), the definition of reference requires this expansion. There simply are no instances of speaking where there is no speaker. Therefore, speaking is an act that always attaches (through an index) to a material and bodily speaker. The same holds for manual signing, writing, thinking, or any form of representation that depends on and results in the production of distinct signs (even if they are just imagined). Although it is sometimes argued that the initial speech-like vocalizations of early infancy are without any content (see, for instance, Bloom, Russell, & Wassenberg, 1987), if any vocalization is attached to a bodily person (say, its producer) or if it is evidently directed at some other bodily person (for example, its listener or audience), it is not entirely without content.

As we saw in Chapter 3, the neonate pragmatically maps the voice it hears onto the moving face of the producer to achieve the first referent of linguistic interactions. As a result we can say that the producer becomes a primitive referent of the vocalizations, and the distinctive voice of that person. The association constitutes a primitive referential relation between the voice and the face (as shown in Figure 3–3).

All three of the basic sign systems can be seen in the most basic pragmatic mapping relation. There is the dynamic bodily icon of the speaker that is constantly changing as the speaker moves while talking. This changing icon provides material (bodily) content that is associated with the voice of the speaker. The familiar voice, then, comes to signify (and thus to refer to) that moving person. The voice with its rhythms and speech sounds emanating from the bodily person come to signify that bodily entity. What connects the voice with the body, however, is the sign system of coordinated, synchronized movement. That is, the rhythms of the voice are exactly like the rhythms of the moving articulators of the speaker. There is an isomorphism in these rhythms. Although the speech sounds are heard whereas the bodily movements of the speaker are seen and possibly felt by the baby, the sequence and cadence of the heard rhythms and the seen movements are isomorphic. Therefore, the baby cannot resist the inference that the speech emanating from the speaker is being produced by that person. For this reason, the baby takes the sound of the voice and the speech being produced as evidence that the voice is coming from the speaker and the voice comes to signify the person speaking.

We have suggested that this mapping process is a crucial step in beginning to build a symbolic linguistic system. The evident movements of the speaking person, say, mom, are closely coordinated with the familiar voice. So the child thinks something like this: "That body is making those noises and that voice is familiar." The salient experience of the voice is connected with the bounded moving body. What is more, the rhythms of the speech are matched by coincidental rhythms of the body. The child is probably not inclined to wonder if this matching could be accidental. To do that would require a much more complicated theory than the assumption that the isomorphism shows that the moving face is producing the sounds. The child is too smart for that. Rather the child is inclined to think that the coordination shows for a certainty that the voice is coming from the moving body and that the moving body is producing the voice. It would seem, therefore, that the baby's first significant referent for any voice other than its own voice is probably the familiar voice associated with the bodily appearance of this face that moves in perfect cadence with the rhythms of that particular familiar voice.

Solving the Primary Referent of a Discursive Act

We can infer that the bounded body of the speaker provides the material content for the primary referent of an act of speaking, signing, or any **discursive act**. The bodily speaker can be discriminated from the rest of the infant's perceptual experience because the body of the speaker stays intact as it moves around. As mother comes in and out of the infant's **perceptual field**, her rhythmic **speech acts** are timed so as to be coincident with her movements. The speech acts are also bounded. Sometimes she is present but not speaking. At other times she is not present but the infant can still hear her speaking. Sometimes mother is both present in the infant's perceptual field and speaking at the same time, and at still other times mother is neither present nor speaking within the hearing of the infant. These four simple logical pairings can be treated as distinct logically possible situations giving evidence of greater or lesser degree of connection between the voice and the face.

There Are Four Logically Possible Degrees of Association

We can analyze the four possibilities as follows:

1. Mom's voice cannot be heard and mom's face cannot be seen (or sensed otherwise).

2. Mom's voice cannot be heard but mom's face can be seen (or sensed otherwise).

3. Mom's voice can be heard but mom's face (or body) cannot be seen (or sensed otherwise).

4. Mom's voice can be heard and mom's moving face can be seen (or sensed otherwise).

We can see in describing the possibilities in this way (expanding on Bower, 1997) that the four logical possibilities produce a scale starting from no evident relation at all between the voice and the face in situation 1, and ranging to a relatively perfect coordination of the voice with the face in situation 4. The four possibilities can be arranged from lesser to greater evidence of relationship as shown in the formula: $1 < 2 < 3 < 4$ where the symbol "<" is read as "is less than." Or, if we look at the relation in the other direction, $4 > 3 > 2 > 1$, we may say that 4 shows greater relationship than 3 and so forth.

From possibility 1 by itself, the infant could not learn that mom's voice is connected to her face because the infant could not even learn that mom has a voice, nor that she has a face. In situations of the kind described in (1) the infant can neither perceive mom's voice nor her face so how could the infant discover from such situations that these entities are related?

From that kind of experience, the relation could not be discovered at all. Situation 2 is not a real possibility for the infant in the womb because the fetus in the womb cannot perceive its mother's face at all. But after its birth, situation 2 becomes a real possibility and will arise quite often. Sai (2005) showed that neonates prevented from hearing mom's voice while seeing her moving face, that is, infants exposed to situation 2, do not associate mom's voice with her face at all.

Next consider situation 3. This is the sort of relation that prevails in the womb. The infant hears mom's voice intermittently bounded by silence and sometimes the infant hears other voices besides mom's. However, mom's voice is heard a lot while the infant is in the womb. So a certain familiarity with the voice derives from situation 3 while the baby is still in the womb. After birth, situation 4 is commonly realized. The infant often hears mom's voice while at the same time seeing her face, feeling her touch, and so forth (see the video associated with Figure 2-1). When that happens, the research (especially see Sai, 2005) shows that the pragmatic relation between the face and the voice is established very quickly.

Next, consider the way the four possible relations play out after the infant succeeds in making the pragmatic mapping of the voice to the face. This mapping according to Sai (2005) critically requires experience that conforms to logical possibility number 4. But once that possibility is realized in the infant's experience, it becomes possible, because of the often repeated pragmatic association of the face with the voice, for the infant to infer from situation 3, where it can hear the voice but not see the face, that the face is out there. This inference requires a generalization from the voice that is present in the perceptual field of the infant (say, it can hear the voice) to the face that is outside the infant's perceptual field (say, the baby cannot see the face). However, because the voice is associated with the face (say, is an abstract general symbol of the face) when the voice is heard the face can be called to mind and the baby will look for it.

Next consider situation 2 in the case when the face is seen (or otherwise perceived) but the voice is not heard. Will the infant be able to think of the voice? Presumably, the answer to this question must be yes, but only after a considerable amount of experience with the pragmatic linkage of the voice and face has occurred. However, it remains an open question how long it will take for the infant to make this generalization. Finally, suppose that neither mom's voice nor her face is available within the perceptual field of the infant. When will the infant be able to think of either the familiar voice or the face that is associated with it? The answers to these questions are not trivial and they are related to a host of other questions that have to do with the acquisition of abstract linguistic signs. At first bodily objects must be coordinated in some way with linguistic signs. Evidently the first inkling of such a coordination is in the baby's increasing familiarity with its mother's voice and linguistic rhythms. This happens in the womb. If we look back to the growth spiral of Figure 4-9, the baby's initial familiarity with mom's voice would be represented by the innermost turn of the spiral.

Next, after the baby is born, it can associate the familiar voice with the bodily person whose face moves while producing the voice. When this occurs a primitive referential relation is established insofar as the voice refers to the face that produces it (as seen in Figure 3–2). When this occurs, the infant will infer the presence of the face (and its attached body) when it hears the voice. By looking in the direction from which a voice is heard, the infant shows its inferential knowledge (generalization) that voices are connected with the bodies that produce them. This logical conclusion establishes the first logical position of all discursive acts. It provides the basis for the first person of grammar, or the producer of any given speech act.

Linguistic Signs Originate with the Community of Sign-Users

Although it might be argued that the infant could discover the first position (the primary referent) of discourse, or begin to define it, by its own voluntary acts of vocalizing, the distinctly linguistic aspects of speech and its rhythms are supplied from outside the infant. They are supplied by the community of language users that provide access to the baby's native language community or **mother tongue**. From such inferential connections by the infant (linking a voice to a producer of that voice), the basis for more abstract acts of reference, is established. The foundation of the infra-semiotic systems is laid. The human infant achieves stage 1 of primitive referential development very soon after its birth. This stage is roughly contemporaneous with the first stage of infant phonation. Its main outcome is that the infant takes account of the fact that some bodily persons in the postnatal world are also speakers.

Stage 2: Secondary Reference (the Second Person or Consumer)

If speech or signs are attached to at least one bodily referent, for example, the person producing the surface-forms of the signs, and if these signs are understood as being directed to another person, they must also (logically speaking) be associated with a **secondary reference** which is the listener/recipient or consumer. By about their first month and certainly before the second month, infants are able to differentiate the sort of speech that is commonly directed at themselves (or another infant) from the sort that is directed at adults. It seems that the infant either knows beforehand or learns very soon after birth that it can, to some extent, control the actions of others by its actions. For instance, Fogel and Hsu (2003; also see Hsu, Fogel, & Cooper, 2000) provided evidence that the voluntary vocalizations of the normal infant tend more and more to be coordinated with social actions of the baby's mother. We may infer that this socialization of the infant will generalize over time to other adults in the language community but especially to other caregivers. Kenny, Mohr, and Levesque (2001) have proposed that the social relations of dyads such as we see in mother-infant pairs can be analyzed into three distinct components:

1. The first person's effect as an agent or initiator of action;

2. the second person's ability and willingness to be a partner to the first, that is, to act as a second person; and

3. the "relationship effect," that is, the dynamic product of the interaction that could not exist without the two partners joining with each other.

In discursive relations we discover that there are really three distinct logical positions. First, there is the position of the producer of the voluntary vocalization (the discourse or conversation or other interaction). Second, there is the position of the receiver, consumer, or audience of the voluntary vocalization. The second person is the one addressed or spoken to. And finally, there is logically a third position which is occupied by the vocalization itself. That is, the relation between the first and second persons (or logical positions of discourse) is established by the vocalizations that connect the first two positions. Because these vocalizations have to be transmitted from one position to the other across an intervening space, the vocalizations necessarily occupy a third position that is larger than the first two positions. It must, in fact, include those other two positions. Figure 6–5 shows the hypothesized relation between the three logical positions of discourse.

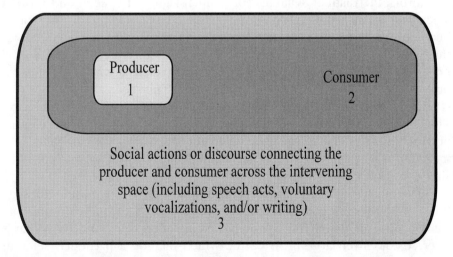

Figure 6–5. The logical positions of discourse: (1) the producer or first person; (2) the consumer or second person, and (3) the discourse itself and the whole rest of the world.

The third position contains all the rest of the world. It contains the physical waveforms produced by the speaker/vocalizer. It contains the bodies of both the first person and the second person. In fact, logically if they did not share space in that third position they could not interact at all. Therefore, the third position must be one that is common to both the first person and the second person of the communication dyad. However, it takes a good deal of work and a highly abstract linguistic capacity for the human infant to take account of the third position of discourse.

Stage 3. Linguistic or Tertiary Reference (the Third Person and the Third Logical Position)

We have already begun to deal with the third logical position. When that logical position in any symbolic form comes into play, the symbol has what may be called linguistic or **tertiary reference**. This logical position in the experience of the infant comes into view in the developments of phonation leading from prenatal experience all the way up to canonical babbling. The syllables of speech, or the distinct movements of manual signing, constitute the detectable forms of linguistic symbols. These are the surface-forms of speech and signing. They are invariably in the third logical position of discourse. The speaker occupies a different logical position from the listener, and these two logically different positions of discourse could not be connected at all if there were not a larger material context constituting a third logical position containing both of the other two. This is shown in Figure 6–5. If it were not for this third logical position of discourse, what is normally recognized as the process of linguistic, or tertiary reference, could not arise at all. If it were not for distinct discriminated surface-forms, the distinct syllables (or manual signs) of speech and written language systems, could not be noticed, much less could the distinct forms become associated with any **tertiary referent**. Any referent that occupies the third logical position of discourse is a tertiary referent. The first logical position is necessarily occupied by the primary referent who is the speaker or producer of the surface-forms of discourse. The second logical position is necessarily occupied by the listener or consumer of the linguistic forms. The tertiary referent may be the speaker, or the listener, but it necessarily occupies a different logical position in the discourse. We can think of a meaningful act of tertiary reference as involving all three logical positions shown in Figure 6–5.

The resulting structure involves the surface-form of a meaningful symbol that is not only connected to its producer, and to one or more consumers, but that also signifies (is about) some other thing or activity that is referred to, its tertiary **significance** which may be a particular referent (for example, the name of some person or thing), or an activity to which the surface-form is appropriate (for example, waving bye-bye), or an act such as kissing (accompanied by a voluntary utterance such as "hmmaa"). In Figure 6–6 this three-part relation is diagramed. In the example, we suppose that the producer presents a linguistic surface-form for the benefit of the consumer who understands (as does the producer) that the form in question refers to or signifies the thing pointed out. In the picture shown the example involves the first person presenting a symbol that refers to a certain pet, and the child looks to the pet that is called or referred to. Let us consider how this process of referring or signifying a tertiary referent can work.

The Zero Order Step on the Way to Tertiary Reference

The key to all referential relations is that one thing, a symbol, must successfully point to or suggest another, something other than the symbol itself. For such a relation to be possible, there must be symbols and they must be connected to things other than themselves. For example, if infants are ever to acquire the notion that certain vocalizations point to or signify other things besides those sounds or gestures, the infant has to notice those vocalizations or referring gestures. Therefore, noticeable surface-forms of symbols are prerequisite to any referential relations of the linguistic kind, either in speech or manual signed languages. Therefore, it is prerequisite to any referential relations whatever that the referring vocalizations or signals themselves must be noticed. Hearing and even deaf babies undoubtedly achieve this prerequisite knowledge in the womb.

We could call this a zero order step because the fetus cannot avoid it and it is absolutely prerequisite if symbols are ever to be acquired. Hearing

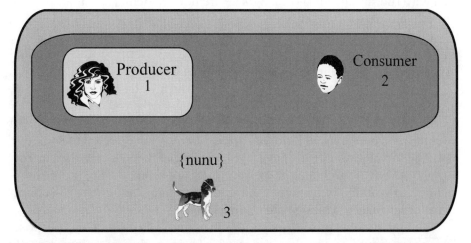

Figure 6–6. In this diagram, suppose that the adult produces the word *Nunu* to refer to or call or otherwise signify the dog and the child directs attention from the producer to the object referred to.

infants can certainly detect mother's voice, and the voices of others in the neighborhood of the womb, before they are born. Deaf or hearing fetuses born to a signing mother, presumably, can detect the rhythmic syllabic gestures of mom (assuming she is a signer), as distinct from other bodily movements. Manual signed language uses movements that are faster, more rhythmical, and more repetitive than other bodily movements. Other non-linguistic movements (e.g., standing, sitting, walking, turning, and so forth), are less rapid, less rhythmic, and less repetitive than the articulated syllables of speech or the manual gestures of any signed language. Thus the "voices" of either speaking or signing adults are provided to the normal fetus by the speech community before the baby is born. For this reason, the noticing of the surface-forms of speech and/or signed language in the womb may be considered a zero order (ground level) step toward the development of referential signs. Normal infants get this knowledge before birth.

The First Order of Reference

Among the very first **multimodal** sensory experiences of the neonate is hearing mom's voice while seeing her moving face up close. This experience as Sai (2005) showed, leads very early to the notion that a certain bodily object, another person, like the infant, is making certain vocal sounds. What is more, the voice is familiar from experience in the womb. The voice comes to refer to the person that is speaking or signing. That is, the infant perceives that the vocal noises or manual gestures are distinct from other movements by being rapid, rhythmic, and repetitive and the infant seems to know that these movements are also intentional. That is, the infant seems to know intuitively (innately) that the observed movements associated with the surface-forms of language are not accidental, but that they are caused, and that a certain bodily person (namely the speaker) is causing those movements. Thus, the first order of reference is established along with the first logical position of discourse. This step requires postnatal experience by the child as Sai (2005) demonstrated.

We know that the infant is able before birth to distinguish the rapid, rhythmic, and repetitive surface-forms of language (symbols) from other movements or noises. If so, probably the neonate is also able to distinguish intentional acts of a social kind that are deliberate and directed to someone else. The infant must already have a glimmering of the idea that the surface-forms of the symbols being perceived really are symbolic. So, the infant is inclined to wonder first where the rapid, rhythmic, and repetitive surface-forms of language (symbols) are coming from.

The infant must pose a question: What are these distinct and purposeful noises about? At the first order of reference, that question is partly answered. The infant discovers that every speech or sign event has a bodily producer at the other end of it. The vocal noises are coming from and being deliberately produced by that other person. This discovery provides the seed for another question: Why is this person producing these rapid, rhythmic, and repetitive articulations and sounds? At birth, the infant is presumably unable to notice the many individual features of speech or signing that are being produced. They are too rapid and too numerous to sort out entirely and all at once. But the infant can distinguish rhythms and sounds very early.

Also, according to research by Meltzoff and Moore (1977, 1997), the fact that the neonate will adjust its own mouth or face to match the shape of an adult's mouth or facial expression, for example, by opening the mouth, protruding the tongue, and so on, shows that the infant knows that the facial expressions and mouth shapes come under **volitional control**. The infant proves this by imitating those expressions. What is more, according to the literature on babbling, the infant by about the second month will already be able to imitate certain vowel shapes (Kuhl & Meltzoff, 1996). At about the same time the infant between about 9 and 12 weeks shows that it can distinguish speech directed to an infant from speech directed to an adult. When this occurs the infant has moved up another level to another order of reference. The infant now incorporates the second position of discourse as part of it vocal sign systems. Let us consider how this is possible for such a young infant.

The Second Order of Reference

By about the second week of its postnatal experience (Bower, 1971) we know that the infant can tell when a moving object is on a collision course with the baby's face and will take defensive actions, for example, raising the hands, moving the head back, and so on. It is also evident that from a very early age, perhaps from birth, the infant is differentially responsive to joint eye contact with another person. Therefore, as soon as the first order of reference is achieved and speakers are identified as distinct sources of speech (or signing), the infant is ready to move on to the second order of reference. That is, the infant is ready to consider where the speech (or signing) is directed. As soon as the infant notices differences between the eye movements, gaze patterns, gestures, facial expressions, and tone of voice of adults addressing the infant from an adult addressing another adult, the possibility of beginning to differentiate the second logical position of discourse arises. The infant moves to a second order of reference. The infant shows by the defensive movements it makes in response to a moving object that it is able to detect directions of motion and their trajectories toward or away from the infant. Therefore, it is no great problem for the infant, as soon as it gains control of head movements, to tell when a speaker is addressing the infant as contrasted with anyone else. Thus, the second logical position of discourse comes into view by about weeks 9 to

12. By the time this level is achieved the signs of discourse (surface-forms of speech or signing) become associated with at least two referents: the speaker on the one hand, and the person(s) addressed on the other.

Judging from the infant's line of sight (so-called "gaze" patterns) and other attentional behaviors, the producers of speech are of special interest very early on. Talkers who also look at the infant and engage in mutual "gaze" patterns are most apt to elicit an increased rate of vocalization (Bloom, Russell, & Wassenberg, 1987). Unsurprisingly, the infant begins by attending to speakers rather than listeners. But, as soon as the speech or signing of the speaker is connected with its producer, it becomes possible for the infant to also take account of whom the producer is attending to. From the beginning, the infant shows special interest in speakers that happen to be holding, looking at, and face-to-face with the infant. Even in their first month, infants show evidence of preferring speech directed to an infant over speech directed to an adult (Cooper, Abraham, Berman, & Staska, 1997). By the fourth month, infants generally show an even more marked preference for speech addressed to an infant over speech addressed to an adult (Cooper & Aslin, 1994; Hayashi, Tamekawa, & Kiritani, 2001; Werker & McLeod, 1989; Werker, Pegg, & Mcleod, 1994).

Early on, infants can even differentiate infant-directed speech from adult-directed speech across distinct languages. For instance, Werker, Pegg, and Mcleod (1994) found that infants who had been exposed only to English, at 4.5 and 9 months, respectively, showed preference for infant-directed speech in Cantonese over adult-directed speech in Cantonese. This is remarkable because the infants from an English-speaking environment are detecting subtle differences in the speech forms of infant-directed speech in a markedly different foreign language. Cantonese sounds very different from English (hear samples of Cantonese Versus English on the DVD). From their sixth month deaf infants can distinguish infant-directed from adult-directed signed language forms. Masataka (1996, 1998) reported results showing that not only do 6 month old deaf infants prefer infant-directed Japanese Signed Language, but 6 month old hearing infants *also* prefer infant-directed signing to adult-directed signing. Masataka concluded that infants can detect the characteristic qualities of motherese without specific experience in the modality in which those forms are constructed, whether spoken or signed.

It is clear that adults, especially parents, structure their vocalizations in speaking to infants quite differently than they do when addressing other adults (D. K. Oller, Eilers, & Basinger, 2001). Adults seem to tune their interactions to the perceived level of the infant. If the infant produces a nasalized vocalization, the adult (or an older sibling) is apt to imitate it. If the infant smiles, the adult is apt to smile in return. In fact, it is very difficult for a parent (or almost any attentive adult) not to return the smile of the infant. The parent's response to the smiling infant as D. K. Oller, Eilers, and

Basinger (2001, p. 50) point out, occurs so fast as to seem automatic (innate, intuitive, and beyond conscious control) but just slow enough (within two to three hundred milliseconds) to allow for the baby's smile to register consciously in the mind of the adult.

As the infant advances toward increasingly articulate vocalizations, adults also adjust their interactional patterns to the perceived level of the infant. It seems that parents are naturally inclined to the Vygotskyan recommendation (Vygotsky, 1934/1962, 1930-1935/1978) that interactions should be aimed at the infant's zone of proximal development (see Chapter 1). Bloom and Lo (1990) found evidence that adults show preference for infants as conversational partners who produce more speech-like (more adult-like) vocalizations. Infants producing more syllabic vocalizations were rated as more pleasant, friendly, fun, likable, and cuddly. Masataka and Bloom (1994) found that adults are also more apt to engage in turn-taking episodes with infants producing more speech-like vocalizations. Key elements in differentiating speech-like sounds is their longer duration and lesser nasality as compared to less speech-like vocalic sounds which tend to be shorter in duration and more nasal.

Infants likewise are susceptible to adult influence. Masataka (1995) found that when an adult partner engaged a three-month-old infant in a give-and-take conversation-like exchange, the infant tended to produce a higher proportion of more speech-like syllabic sounds. In the meantime, the proportion of nasal vocalizations, for example, sounds that are sometimes made by the infant with the mouth partially or fully closed, tended to decrease during "conversational" interactions with an adult. This and other evidence shows that infants naturally begin to take the second position of discourse into consideration from an early age, but not quite so early as they take the first person into consideration. The first person (logical position 1 show in Figures 6-5 and 6-6) is associated with a particular stream of discourse, as Sai (2005) demonstrated, within the first few minutes of life. It evidently takes about 8 to12 weeks before the infant begins to show clear evidence that it is taking the second person (logical position 2 in Figures 6-5 and 6-6) into consideration. The main evidence that the second position is being differentiated comes from studies showing the infant's preference for infant-directed speech. It takes quite a bit longer still, about three or four months, as we will see, for the infant to become able to take the third logical position into account.

The Third Order of Reference

Interestingly, by about the third month, at about the same time infants have begun to easily handle second order reference, in other words, to tell who is talking to whom, they also are using their pointing finger in a way that begins to resemble the adult pointing gesture. Fogel and Hannan (1985) with 28 three-month-old infants, found that well over half of them (64%) extended their index finger at least once in a two-minute interaction with mom, while some extended their index finger as many as 6 times. Masataka (1995) lengthened the time frame with 14 infants. He videotaped face-to-face interactions of infants and mothers over an 18-minute segment. He also found that infants at this age are already using their index finger in what appears to be a pointing gesture while they are engaging in face-to-face interactions with their mothers. Masataka was concerned to discover whether the pointing tended to occur more frequently in the context of syllabic phonations than in the context of presyllabic phonations by the infant. In fact, the gesture occurred most frequently after a syllabic cooing. That is, the pointing was most often associated with a voluntary vocalization that had a distinct syllabic quality. Masataka concluded that the extension of the index finger by the infants was not a response to a model gesture, nor was it caused by the speech of someone else. It was just naturally part of the infant's effort to interact with mom. He said, "the pointing action was inadvertently conditioned as infant vocal activity was contingently stimulated" (p. 256). He cited McNeill (1985) who "proposed that gesture and speech can be conceived as an integrated whole" and that "linguistic production and gestural production develop together at a very early stage" (Masataka, 1995, p. 256).

Another interesting feature of the pointing gesture at three months is that it seems also to coincide with the transition point between the primitive articulation stage and the expansion stage where the infant moves from articulating somewhat distinct vowel-like sounds to the production of the first well-formed syllables of the CV kind. What Masataka (1995) was able to show was that the pointing gesture was more apt to occur just after the production of a syllable-like phonation of the infant than after a more primitive presyllabic phonation. He observed that "the age of three months marks a threshold between the earliest, nasalized sounds of short duration and little pitch contour and the longer, pre-babbling vocalizations which have higher pitch, simple consonant-vowel combinations and more pitch contours" (p. 248). In addition, the research also suggests that handbanging is an important rhythmic precursor of the development of canonical babbling which most commonly takes place a few months after the pointing gesture emerges (Eilers et al., 1993; Ejiri, 1998). The question remains whether the pointing gesture and the hand-banging are merely surface manifestations of the same underlying system of rhythms that are needed for syllabic speech, or whether one or the other are causally related. They seem to arise at about the same time on the schedule of infant development.

Research with manual babbling by deaf infants (Petitto & Marentette, 1991; Ejiri & Masataka, 2001), however, suggests that the motor rhythms must be achieved before canonical babbling will be possible. Masataka (2001) notes that rhythmic hand movements precede the development of canonical babbling both in hearing and deaf infants (also see Petitto, Holowka, Sergio, & Ostry, 2001). We should add that the extension of the index finger in hearing infants also seems to precede the development of canonical babbling by about three months. This result is exactly what the theory of abstraction, and the logical sign cycle, require. Iconic representations have to be developed before indexical signs can be differentiated and these have to appear before the first symbols can be discovered by the infant (see Figure 5-5). At the same time, the evidence concerning the pointing gesture shows a precocious interest by very young infants in what may be termed referring acts. As we have already seen, by about their third month of postnatal experience infants have easily achieved the first two orders of reference. The extension of the index finger suggests that they are already beginning to be aware of where adults are looking and what they are attending to. They are on the verge of discovering the first tertiary referents. As soon as this development occurs, the infant is on the verge of discovering that the rapid, rhythmic, and repetitive articulations of speech (or sign) have tertiary referring significance. That is, some syllabic sounds not only point from a speaker (first order reference) to a listener (second order reference), but they have additional referential significance in pointing to something else (third order reference). The logical relation between icon, index, and symbol, is summed up in Figure 6-7, which also shows all three positions of discourse.

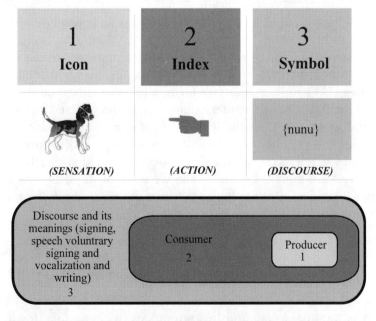

Figure 6–7. The logical relation between icon, index, and symbol as well as the logical positions of discourse. Notice that all these relations are at play when the child solves the problem of tertiary reference, for example, discovering that {nunu} signifies a certain dog.

As soon as the infant begins to distinguish the first two logical positions in a conversation-like interaction, the possibility of responding differentially to a discriminated symbol arises. When that occurs by about 4.5 months, the infant will not only begin to take account of where someone's speaking (or signing) is directed, that is, to whom it is directed, but the infant will also begin to notice that some surface-forms are often repeated. For instance, the infant's name, or a syllabic sequence like *bye-bye*, or words such as *mama, Nunu, no*, and so on, will recur frequently. After the construction of the hypostatic index, it will become possible for the infant to recognize distinct occurrences of repeated utterances on different occasions. When this occurs, the infant achieves the level of the discriminated symbol. Subsequently, the infant will prescind some of these discriminated symbols, and will gain motor control over some of them. At this stage, we see the development of canonical babbling which occurs normally between months 6 and 9, give or take a month. Sometime after the prescinded symbols begin to appear, the infant will discover the first hypostatic symbol, that is, a syllable structure that comes to be associated with a particular meaning or significance. At this point the stage of tertiary reference is achieved. This advance does not usually occur until about month 7 to 10, give or take a month.

Among the most common third order referential relations to be discovered by the infant will be the infant's own name. Often, the name is used in a **vocative** way, to call the child's attention. Another commonly acquired early referring form is the bye-bye wave possibly together with recognition of the corresponding symbol, for example, the linguistic expression *bye-bye*. In order to produce a token of a hypostatic symbol and also use it as a predicate, say, to apply the name "Nunu" to the dog that is called by that name, or to say "bye-bye" on an appropriate occasion, the infant must do more than merely associate the form with its meaning. The infant must also produce a surface-form, a token or instance of the word that is recognizable to other interlocutors. To be recognized as a word, the token produced must (1) resemble the word closely enough to be recognized by someone else; (2) be applied on a appropriate occasion; and (3) must subsequently generalize to other similar occasions and applications. When these criteria are met, in ordinary talk, we say that the baby has acquired his or her first word. Ordinarily this advance occurs at about the end of the infant's first postnatal year, give or take 2 or 3 months.

The Infant Uses All Three Positions of Discourse

As soon as the infant distinguishes utterances by its mother, for instance, from its own voluntary vocalizations, the three positions of discourse are already at least "backgrounded." There are the two positions of the two persons who are interacting in a cooing conversation, say. There is the person who starts the interaction (first person) and there is the person who is addressed by the first vocalization. Then, there is a response of the second person to the first where the second person produces a vocalization and the first person now responds. And so on it goes with each interlocutor changing positions with the other acting at one end of a turn as a producer and at the other end of the same turn as a consumer of the next vocalization. Meantime, as the vocalizations are exchanged and the turns are connected, or **latched** (per Sacks, Schegloff, & Jefferson, 1974), a discourse begins to unfold. It also takes on a status of its own. Once it is created by the interlocutors, others may interpret what is going on in general terms.

The research shows that the goodness of fit of the interpretations of what is going on, for example, what surface-forms are being produced and how they are intended by the interlocutors, depends to a great extent on how much the forms produced resemble conventional forms of speech (Hsu, Fogel, & Cooper, 2000; D. K. Oller, 1986; D. K. Oller & Lynch, 1992). As soon as the observer's position, or that of the larger world, is added to the communication dyad, it follows from strict logic (as noted by Peirce, 1868), that there need not be any logical positions greater than the third position. Because all the people who might observe or later get access to any discourse must be in the world where that discourse is located, it follows that the three positions of discourse form a logically complete system. There cannot be any discourse without some initiator, there cannot be a listener/consumer of discourse without a second position, and these cannot be connected at all except through a common or shared world in space and time. Thus, all three positions are required in the very first voluntary social interactions an infant may enter into through its own voluntary vocalizations. The first person is required for the interaction to count as any kind of voluntary interaction. There can be no response to that discourse (much less any comprehension of it) if there is no one to notice (or understand) it. So the second person is also a required position. Even if the second position were occupied by the same person who produced the discourse, if the discourse has any external realization, for example, as a vocalization or in a written form, or both, the discourse also has a separate existence of its own. If the vocalizations can be judged to be voluntary or intentional, this interpretation requires an observer who has access to the general signs employed. As a result, the third position is implicit in every social action that involves intentionally produced conversation-like interaction. There is the producer, the consumer, and there is the world in which the discourse is produced (Figures 6–5, 6–6, and 6–7).

If conventional signs are used, they can be understood by anyone who knows the conventions, in other words, the language in question. It seems as if one of the questions that comes to the mind of the infant concerns whether the other person is talking to the infant. We are reminded here of the famous line from Robert de Niro in *Taxi Driver* where he says, "You talkin' to me?" He repeats this question belligerently several times. De Niro would not evidently have posed the question if nothing had been said to him. The line from the movie serves to show that the second logical position entails the first. That is, the second position logically includes the first as a defining feature (as shown in Figure 6-5). If there were no first person, there could not be any second. By the same token, the third position logically requires both the first and the second. The second position becomes second to the first and the third becomes third only in its relation to the first and the second. Or putting the case differently, the third position, the one that is occupied by the discourse itself, logically must include the first two positions (again, as shown in Figures 6-5 and 6-6).

The Three Logical Positions Are Complete

Beyond the third position which connects the first person to his or her vocalizations (or writings) and those same signs to any second person or group, there is only the third position occupied by the signs themselves. These may be perceived by anyone who may come along and hear the recordings, or see the writings, and so on. But there is no fourth position that is outside and not logically contained in the third. As a result the system of discourse positions is logically complete with only three positions. The three positions consist of (1) the one occupied by the producer, (2) the one held by the consumer(s), and (3) the one held by the discourse itself, including anyone else who might ever gain access to that discourse by overhearing it, reading a transcript of it, hearing a replay of a recording of it, or whatever.

For this reason, most languages of the world distinguish only three "persons" in their grammatical systems (the speaker, the listener, and anyone else). For instance, in English we distinguish "I" or "we" (first person) from "you" (second person) and from "he," "she," and "it" or "they" (third person plural). In English we distinguish the **number** (singular or plural) of referents in the first and third positions, and the **gender** (male, female, or neuter) in the third position only. In some languages, additional grammatical distinctions are made. For instance, it may be necessary to distinguish instances where the speaker includes himself and/or some or all the audience in the first position when it takes plural referents. In some languages, for instance, there are different forms of "we." There is a so-called **inclusive** "we" meaning "all of us," and a so-called **exclusive** "we" meaning "we two, three, or four excluding you, him, or her" and so on. But all languages seem to make use of at least the required three logical positions of discourse.

Speech Act Theory and Pragmatic Forces

Interestingly, the philosopher J. L. Austin (1955) distinguished just exactly the three positions of discourse spelled out in Figures 6-5, 6-6, and 6-7 in his trichotomy of the **pragmatic forces** common to speech acts. By a pragmatic force, Austin meant to refer to the way a speech act is generally understood, intended to be understood, and/or acted upon. The **locutionary force** of any speech act is its general meaning as would be understood more or less by any interpreter (the third logical position). It is the general semantic meaning put into this particular context of discourse. Parents, it seems, are very much inclined to coo back to the infant (see D. K. Oller, Eilers, & Basinger, 2001). We might ask why this is so. It seem almost to be universally so. The locutionary force on the side of the infant seems to be something like, "Here I am!" which gets an almost obligatory affirmative parental response something like, "There you are! And here I am with you!"

The **illocutionary force** from the adult side, say a father, mother, or grandparent cooing back to the infant, presumably means a little more than, "I see you there." The meaning intended by the speaker (the first logical position), or its illocutionary force, seems also to include something like the obligatory tag, "And I absolutely just can't help loving you!" It is as if the parent (or grandparent) is saying something very specific to the occasion and particularly addressed to just this particular infant. The parent is expressing a pragmatic meaning intended to be understood by the infant as expressing love, affection, the promise of security, and so on, and the hope is that the infant will take the exchange as having this intended meaning. The illocutionary force, as Austin put it, consists of the intended meaning that will hopefully be understood by a particular interlocutor.

At the same time there is an invitation from the producer of the surface-form that suggests an action on the part of the consumer. This recommended action is the **perlocutionary force** of the speech act that may or may not be accepted and acted upon by the hearer. In the case of the cooing conversation, if the second person coos back, presumably, the perlocutionary force is acted upon as the second person steps into the first logical position and provides a basis for a continuation of the conversation. The cooing of the one person causes, or at least is the occasion for, the cooing of the other person. And so it goes back and forth for as many turns as the conversation may consist of. In the terms of Sacks et al. (1974), we could say that the cooing of the infant calls for a cooing action of the parent. When that action occurs the infant has a turn and another cooing event is called for by the infant. As these exchanges occur, the infant is at one moment the initiator and at the next the recipient. The positions (social roles) of speaker and listener are exchanged somewhat in the way that a pair of individuals playing catch must throw the ball back and forth. The cooing vocalizations are the demonstrations of the exchange.

The Three Logical Positions and Phonetics

It should also be noted that the three logical positions of discourse also differentiate the distinct phonetic aspects of the surface-forms of speech. From the producer's point of view, the first logical position, the surface-forms of speech must be articulated. Studies of speech sounds from the viewpoint of the first logical position of discourse, that of the producer, fall under the scope of **articulatory phonetics** (Ladefoged, 2001). By contrast, we may study speech sounds and the stream of speech from the vantage point of their perceivers or consumers, the second logical position. The study of speech sounds from the viewpoint of their perceptual impressions, in the second logical position of discourse, is known as **auditory** or **perceptual phonetics**. Sometimes the articulatory and auditory approaches to phonetics are combined (Johnson, 1997). This is natural because conversations commonly involve at least two persons, or two logical positions. Finally, it is possible to study speech sounds in terms of their own physical properties as measured somewhat independently of their articulation or perception. That is, they may be studied from the vantage point of the third logical position. The process or result of studying speech sounds from an objective purely physical point of view is referred to as **acoustic phonetics** (Fant, 1970; Fry, 1976; Ladefoged, 1996). It is also possible to combine articulatory and acoustic approaches (Ball & Müller, 2005), although, usually, articulatory approaches are basic as we should expect. Logically, articulation occupies the first position.

That is, the logical entailments of the three positions (as shown in Figure 6–5) still hold here. There could be no study of auditory phonetics if there were no articulations, so the second position requires the prior existence of the first. Likewise, there could be no study of the acoustic properties of speech if the speech were not both articulated and audible. Therefore, the third position still logically includes and necessitates the prior existence of the other two positions. Position 3 entails 2 and both of them entail 1. Without position 1 there is no way to define position 2, and without both 1 and 2, there is no way to define position 3. As a result all three positions must be presupposed.

Each branch of phonetics is somewhat distinct from the others just as each position of discourse is distinct from the other two. For instance, from the articulatory point of view, an "r" sound (as in words like "bird," "red," and "car") can be produced in General Western American English (its most widespread American variety) by either raising the tip of the tongue or by raising the blade of the tongue.

The qualities of these two distinct articulations cannot be discriminated perceptually or acoustically but they differ sharply in terms of their articulation. From the receiver/consumer's point of view (the second logical position) phoneticians sometimes speak and write about the impressions created by particular articulatory movements and acoustic signals. The research shows that certain aspects of sounds can best be evaluated perceptually rather than in terms of articulation or acoustics. For instance, perceptual judgments are often essential to tell whether or not a particular stream of speech is accented or not. Perceptual judgments are best in determining the smoothness of sound transitions and the extent to which sounds produced by an infant resemble the syllables of adult speech (D. K. Oller & Lynch, 1992).

Certain other features of sounds can best be judged with the help of devices that directly measure aspects of the physical waveform of the speech signal (from the third logical position). For instance, recorded speech sounds can be analyzed in terms of their distinct physical properties. Some properties such as *amplitude*, *duration*, and *spectral properties* of the stream of speech can best be judged in terms of acoustic qualities of the signal itself. Of course, the articulatory, auditory, and acoustic properties of the stream of speech are closely related, but they are logically distinct in precisely the manner that the three logical positions of discourse are distinct.

Summing Up and Looking Ahead

In this chapter we have examined the differentiation of syllabic forms (the surface-forms of speech) leading to canonical babbling. We have also explored the foundations of referential meanings and have seen how the processes of infant phonation and reference develop from birth forward. We have seen that the infant's notion of reference first takes account of the first logical position of discourse, that of the speaker. Second, the infant takes account of the listener position, the second logical position of discourse. Both of these developments must occur before the infant can take account of the third logical position of discourse where tertiary reference becomes possible. It is with respect to the third position, as we saw in Figure 6-6, that symbols can come to *refer* in the more traditional sense of *reference*.

Infants deal with the logical positions in exactly the required logical order: 1, 2, then 3. This sequence is not an option. It is logically guaranteed by the logical structure of discourse latchings as described in Figures 6-5, 6-6, and 6-7. When the surface-forms of words come to be distinguished (discriminated symbols) and then begin to come under the motor control of the child (prescinded symbols), the attainment of the first meaningful word becomes a logical possibility. The fact that the third position of discourse is distinct from the other two positions can be shown in a variety of ways. One proof that it is a distinct position can be found in the fact that discourse has a separate existence of its own. Anyone who overhears a discourse or conversation and who knows the language in question can understand it just to the extent that the words are used according to their normal conventions. Or, the discourse can be written or recorded and gains an existence in its own right in addition to the existence of the speaker and consumer. The existence of the third logical position of discourse enables putting discourse on a computer, film, or tape, and the subsequent processing of the discourse by any observer. In Chapter 7, we move on to consider in greater detail what is traditionally referred to as the first word stage of child language and development.

STUDY AND DISCUSSION QUESTIONS

1. What do you think is the reason that infants at about three months of age are observed to begin extending the index finger at about the same time that the baby also moves to more syllable-like vocalizations? If it is not a mere coincidence, what other facts can you muster to show that these events are (or may be) closely related? Recall comments about the development of the prescinded index, hand-banging, and other developments that are occurring at or about the same time.

2. Why is a hypostatic index required for the infant to compare a present event with a past event that is no longer perceivable? How about a discriminated symbol? Could the infant gain control over a syllable sequence accidentally by just producing voice while opening and closing its mouth? Could it recognize the syllables it produces in this way without hypostatic indexes? Without discriminated symbols? Would accidental productions qualify as canonical babbling (prescinded symbols)? Why or why not?

3. Review the stages leading up to canonical babbling. Have you observed these stages in your own child or a younger sibling? Can you describe the stage the infant you have in mind is working through at the moment or the last time you observed the infant?

4. Why is canonical babbling relatively easy for parents to identify even though they may have no training at all in phonetics, linguistics, or psychology? Consider why parents and other interlocutors of the baby are apt to regard the canonical babbling stage of development as especially indicative of the child's moving on toward speech and language. What are some of the articulatory, auditory, and acoustic properties of canonical babbling that make it appear more speech-like than preceding stages of development?

5. What are some of the factors that make survey data less reliable than we might hope?

6. Why do the languages of the world generally distinguish only three persons in their grammatical systems? Are these distinctions related in any way to Austin's pragmatic forces? What about the three logical positions of discourse and their relation to the three distinct branches of phonetics? Are there other trichotomies that are related to these that you can think of? Are the terms, icon, index, and symbol related directly or indirectly to these distinctions? If so, how?

7. Would acoustic phonetics be a possible field of study if spoken discourse did not have a real existence? Why so or why not? Should we expect to find analogs for the spectral properties of speech in the manually signed languages of the Deaf? If so, what sorts of characteristics would you expect to find in signed languages that would correspond to and mirror similar properties in speech? Recall the research findings of Petitto and Marentette (1991; also see Ejiri 1998; Ejiri & Masataka, 2001).

CHAPTER 7

From Canonical Babbling to the "First Word"

By studying this chapter you will:

1. Learn how the infant moves from syllabic sequences, for example, [bababa] to the "first word";

2. Differentiate the words the child can understand by about month 7 from the child's own production of a recognizable "first word" which appears about 5 to 8 months later;

3. See how babble persists alongside the child's first productive meaningful words;

4. Understand why the receptive repertoires run ahead of and exceed productive repertoires;

5. See how the child differentiates the symbol from its referent(s); and

6. See why the child shifts from acquiring new words to figuring out how to combine them.

Here are some terms and concepts that you may learn more about in this chapter (these are also listed in the Glossary):

adinity

animate beings

appropriateness requirement

argument

argument structure

convention of use

conventionality requirement
diagnostic
discrete
dyad
free will
intelligence
linear
monad
polyad
predicate-argument structure
predication
presymbolic forms

productive vocabulary
receptive vocabulary
recognizability requirement
reversion hypothesis
sign hierarchy
silent period
suffix
surface-form requirement
triad
variegated babbling
volition
zero order predicate

In this chapter, we examine the advances the child must make in order to move from the onset of canonical babbling to the first word. The research shows that normal infants will begin to show what is taken to be recognition of their own names (the first discriminated symbol for many babies) as early as 4.5 months of age. In a few more weeks, after month 5 but usually by about month 7 the prescinded symbols of canonical babble will begin to show up. Shortly after that, by about months 7 to 10, the normal child will begin to show evidence that one or more words have been associated with their intended referents or their situational significance. After all this has occurred, an additional 3 to 5 months will usually be required before the child takes the additional step of not only understanding a few words but also producing the first word with meaning. Why does it take such a long time after the first symbol is discriminated at about 4.5 months to produce the first meaningful word at about 12 to 15 months? The answer to this question has to do with the intermediate sign systems that the child must develop in order to reach the production of the first meaningful word. These are the focus of this chapter.

Requirements to Be Met by the First Meaningful Word(s)

The production of the first meaningful word is marked by three distinctive characteristics. All three are social or communicative requirements. All involve what theoreticians have called intersubjectivity at a higher level than earlier forms the child has achieved:

- First, the word must have a sufficient resemblance to an adult form, or sufficient support from the context (for example, a novel form invented by the child may be used repeatedly until others catch on to the meaning), so that someone else will recognize the word. This is the **recognizability** or **surface-form requirement**. This is an iconic requirement because at its basis it asks whether the syllable(s) produced by the child sufficiently resemble(s) some word to be recognizable as that particular word and not some other. Because it is a problem of resemblance or similarity, it is an iconic requirement. The latter stage is achieved when the infant's word or utterance is understood by someone else.

- Second, the word must be appropriate to the context in a way that cannot be explained away as an accidental association. This is the **appropriateness requirement**. When it is met, it shows that the indexical association of the symbol with the context in which it is applied is comprehensible to other interlocutors. This is a pragmatic mapping requirement. Because it requires the child's word to be connected to a con text in a meaningful way, it is an indexical requirement.

■ Third, the word must recur on later occasions in similar contexts showing that the child has generalized the meaning of the word in an appropriate way. This is the **conventionality requirement**. It is a symbolic requirement. When this requirement is met, it shows that the child is applying the symbol according to a general **convention of use**, that is, the child is using the word in a rule-governed, regular, meaningful way. This shows the child has generalized the conventional use of the sign across distinct contexts in an appropriate way. Because this third requirement involves the conventional use of the sign, it is necessarily a symbolic requirement.

According to the theory of abstraction, the reason that it takes the child as long as it does to move from the first recognizable syllabic sequence to the production of its first meaningful word is that there are several intervening steps that must be taken before the first word can be produced. In the preceding chapter we discussed in some detail the progress of the infant up to the level of canonical babbling, that is, the prescinded symbol, and then the hypostatic symbol. In this chapter we map out the sequence of events that must take place leading from the prescinded symbol to the "first word" that the child produces in a recognizable surface-form. To map out that sequence some additional intermediate steps must be sorted out.

Working Backward from the Goal

As we saw in the prior chapter, the first word stage of development involves an intentional act of tertiary reference plus an intentional production of a surface-form to represent the symbol for that act of reference. For instance, the infant may say "mama" to refer to mother. Or, the infant may say "baba" ("bye-bye"), for example, to mark events of leave-taking. Or, the child may use a word like "ha" to refer to the stove or a glowing coal or flame as the source of a salient experience.

Setting aside hypothetical possibilities, consider a real example. When Brenden was 13 months old, at approximately the age shown in Figure 7–1, his first intelligible word involved his new shoes. The word was an emphatic syllable [ʒus], "Zhus!" while he squatted down and pointed to his shoes. He was talking to his paternal grandfather. All the requirements for

Figure 7–1. Brenden at 13 months in his new sandals.

a meaningful word were met. The word was recognizable as the English word *shoes*. It was appropriately connected to the context. Brenden was, in fact, pointing to and talking about his shoes. Finally, the word was subsequently generalized to other contexts. Later he would use this word again, many times, in reference to not only his own shoes but those of others.

Here is what happened on the day when he first used the word, *shoes*. Brenden had just had an unfortunate experience with his brand new sandals. He was especially excited about these particular sandals because they were miniature replicas of a pair owned by his grandfather. When Brenden's sandals were taken out of the box, after Brenden had his shoes on, his grandfather took him to the shoe closet, where Brenden loved to spend time taking all the shoes out of the shelves. As soon as grandpop had put the matching sandals on his own feet, he and Brenden did a little jig showing off their shoes to Brenden's grandmother, Mimi. Brenden grinned and danced with his grandfather. Everyone had a good time laughing and dancing. Then Pop went back to work in the living room leaving Brenden with Mimi in the back part of the house. About when Pop resumed his work on the laptop there was a sound of a small boy falling on a hard floor with a thump. This sound was followed, after a very brief interval from the sound of the thump, by a substantial bout of hurt crying by the same little boy. The crying gradually gave way to the sound of comforting words from

Mimi who reported to Pop in a louder voice from the other room that Brenden was going to be okay and that he had just bumped his head.

A few moments later, Brenden toddled into view in the hallway with a pout on his face. He promptly squatted down, pointed to his shoes with his right hand, and said [ʒus], "Zhus!" It seemed plain that he was a little disappointed in the shoes. They weren't all they were cracked up to be, and evidently they were the cause of the fall. Mimi explained that he had tripped on the carpet with his new sandals and had fallen on the hardwood floor in the adjoining hall.

This example shows all the elements of a meaningful word. In addition to the word itself, "Zhus!," its producer (the first person) and its hearer (the second person), there is something else that is intentionally referred to, pointed out, and signified by the symbol. That is, in the third logical position we don't just find a recognizable instance of the word "shoes" but we also find a pair of shoes with the producer of the word standing in them, pointing to them, and looking to the listener for a sympathetic reaction. All three requirements for a meaningful word are met. The vocalization is recognizable, appropriate, and conventional.

Analyzing the Objective to Be Achieved

Such a meaningful act involves **predication** of the symbol, the word *shoes* presented by (1) Brenden to (2) his grandfather about (3) his shoes. There are logically three slots to be filled in the predicate structure. We can describe the three positions in a simple formula:

The predication, *P*, is used by *(1)* addressed to *(2)* and is about *(3)*.

P stands for the predication of a surface-form of some meaningful linguistic symbol. It may be a word or phrase and the numbers 1, 2, and 3 in the blanks stand for the particular referents to be filled in. The referents themselves may be persons, things, or whatever may be pointed out by person 1 to person 2 through *P*, the predication. The structure can be thought of as an assertion (a statement of fact), or a comment on a situation. In the case of Brenden's use of the word, *shoes*, the predication seems to be a statement about his having bumped his head and that the shoes were somehow to blame for it. It is an act of reference, a statement of belief, and an act of phatic communion. He wanted some sympathy to compensate for the pain that had befallen him. He was producing a predication constituting an explanation. It was a complaint against the shoes. First words are invariably what we will call **zero order predicates**. They are so closely associated with their meanings that the word and the meaning seem to be the same thing. That is, the discursive act (predication) is so involved with and about the material world and what is going on in it that the discourse is hardly separated at all from what it is about. Therefore, it is termed a zero order predicate.

Such conventional predications, however, are always associated with bodily persons in the world of experience, in other words, to other elements that are associated with the predication. Linguists and psychologists have commonly followed logicians in referring to those other distinct elements as **arguments**. They are commonly thought of as fillers in certain slots as if the predicate system were like a grappling hook that can attach one or several objects to itself. In the example of the word "Zhus!" as uttered by Brenden, there are three essential arguments although the first two of them are more or less taken for granted. There is (1) the producer, (2) the consumer, and (3) the shoes that are commented on in relation to recent events. All of these are arguments.

What Is an Argument?

What theoreticians have traditionally meant by the term "argument" has varied a great deal so we will be very explicit about how we and others use this term. Tomasello (1992, p. 212), for example, discusses Nelson's (1985, p. 210) analogy of bricks and mortar where the arguments are bricks that are put together with predicates which are the mortar of linguistic predicate-argument structures. This is a good analogy and we would only add to it that combinations of arguments with predicates can also become higher level building blocks.

For instance, an argument in a linguistic structure may consist of a single referring term, for example, *he*, in a sentence like "*he* lives there" or the argument may consist of a whole sentence describing the person referred to, for example, "*the man I am talking about* lives there," or a whole string of clauses may be combined to refer to a given argument, as in, "*the man that I told you about when we were talking at the gymnasium yesterday after we worked out* lives there."

Three Senses of the Term Argument

By the term *argument* we mean the sort of material object, force, or relation that is able to stick up for itself. In doing so, arguments in the most basic sense become arguments in all the common ways that the term is used. There are three valid senses of the term *argument* and all of them apply to the term as we intend to use it in everything that follows.

1. First, an *argument* can be a material bodily object like a wall, table, or the body of another person that will resist your bodily momentum if you happen to run into it. Brenden's shoes qualify as an argument in this sense

for the predicate "Zhus!" This first sense of the word *argument* is the *iconic meaning* of the term. It represents the content of the term as expressed in an icon. The content of the argument directly referred to in the case of Brenden's first word consists of the shoes themselves. The shoes are the main iconic argument pointed to by his act of predication.

2. Second, the term *argument* can mean the kind of quarrel that happens when two objects or opposing forces run into each other. For example, when Brenden tripped and fell, he bumped his head on the floor. We could say that the floor stuck up for itself in a way that resisted the pressure of Brenden's head. The two bodily objects, Brenden's body and the floor, had a quarrel that was evidently caused by his tripping on his new shoes. The floor prevailed. Here we find *the indexical meaning* of the term *argument*. The indexical meaning of argument involves the active interplay of bodily forces over time. The indexical aspect of the argument involves the tripping and falling and the head of the falling subject (Brenden) striking the hard wooden floor.

3. A third meaning of the term *argument* is *symbolic* (or logical). An argument in this sense can be any representation from which valid inferences can reasonably be drawn. Brenden's utterance is also an argument in this sense. He was evidently not too happy about the shoes. From this we might infer that he thinks the shoes caused him to fall down and get hurt. If we draw any such inference, we are treating his use of the word, "Zhus!" as an argument in its third, symbolic sense. If his using the word "shoes" makes us think of feet, clothing, walking, the shoes in the closet that he likes to play with, the shoes of someone else that are like Brenden's shoes, other experiences with shoes, or with tripping on a pair of shoes, and so on, we are also reasoning in terms of the associations of abstract symbols and, again, all the inferential connections that we make of this abstract kind are based in symbols.

When we use the term *argument* in its relation to a meaningful act of predication, which involves saying anything about or appropriate to anything whether an event, state of affairs, or action, we always intend to include all three senses of the term as we have just explained them in the three numbered paragraphs just preceding this one.

Next, we can diagram the sort of relation between Brenden's predication and its three main arguments as shown in Figure 7–2. The first argument of the predicate /ʒus/ is Brenden (its producer). The second argument is Pop (its consumer). The third argument consists of Brenden's new sandals.

The sort of relation depicted in Figure 7–2 is sometimes called an **argument structure** in the linguistic literature (Goldberg, 2003) or a **predicate-argument structure**, but we prefer to think of such relations as dynamic systems (Badon, S. Oller, Yan, & J. Oller, 2005; J. Oller, 2005; J. Oller & Giardetti, 1999; S. Oller, 2005; Thelen & Smith, 1994). Whereas

Figure 7–2. A diagram of the three main arguments associated with the predicate-argument structure of Brenden's first meaningful word.

structures are commonly thought of as static entities consisting of parts joined together in fixed relations like a solid bridge, a building, a table, or a chair that doesn't initiate any movements on its own, a dynamic system is the sort of entity that involves abstract relations between material components that can move or be moved. As a result they interact and can change or influence each other. For instance, Brenden's feet were in the shoes and connected to his legs and body when he fell and bumped his head on the floor. The boy and the shoes entered into a dynamic changing tensional relation with the carpet and the adjoining hardwood floor. His interactions with the other persons around him at the time were influenced by the changing dynamics of his experience, and his actions influenced the other persons too.

Because discourse is dynamic, as we have just illustrated, we prefer a dynamic systems approach rather than one that deals in classes or static structures (see Thelen & Smith, 1994). The logician Peirce (1933), argued that *systems* are higher and more inclusive than *classes*. Although classes (sets or categories) are grounded in the relation of similarity, that is not the only kind of relation that things, persons, and events enter into in experience. Dynamic systems of relations, by contrast, are completely general. Systems, of course, incorporate classes built up by the similarity relation as well as identities that involve complete similarity or sameness, but systems also extend to include all other relations as well. In fact, the concept of identity itself does not make much sense apart from a history of a bounded bodily object extended over time and space. Therefore, the notion of identity itself requires a systems approach rather than a mere categorical approach based on the relation of similarity (or its limit, sameness). The notion of sameness only makes sense when the representations being compared are associated with a history that is extended over space and time. How can we say, for instance, that something is the same as something else, or that two representations pertain to the same thing, if there is no basis for comparison? Sameness, or identity, requires an extended history for the idea itself to be generated as an abstract property of any object or body.

Systems involve movement, change over time, interacting forces, purposes, intentions, and volition. Classes, which are grounded in similarities, mainly consist of collections based on hypostatic icons. These are very useful for the definition and description of fixed structures like bodies, buildings, bones, tables, chairs, walls, and so on. However, all human discourse, all social interactions, and all linguistic exchanges of any kind involve dynamic **animate beings** who not only move around but who also exhibit the properties of **intelligence** and **free will** (or **volition**). A car can move, of course, but it is not an animal. The car is animate (moves), ordinarily, only when it is being driven by a person who manipulates the car by harnessing other forces.

The Important Role of Volition (Willful Action) in Discourse

An intelligent animal is different from an inanimate thing by choosing when and how to move. A human being may choose to pick up the laptop and move it to another location, or not. An intelligent person can not only move, but usually can do so intentionally, when and as he or she wants to move. With respect to the production of meaningful signs in speech and manual systems, mature language users can use signs so easily and effortlessly that it is actually common among theoreticians to take the bodily interlocutors of discourse more or less completely for granted. In fact, ordinarily, when linguists, psychologists and other researchers talk about language acquisition, it is common to take for granted the first two positions (the producer and the consumer of Figure 7–2) while attention is directed to where the first and second person are attending, that is, to the third logical position. Often attention is directed to the linguistic form itself. This is because theoreticians tend to see things from the adult perspective. From that perspective we think of reference as only involving the linguistic symbol, /ʒus/ in our example, and its tertiary argument, that is, whatever is talked, written, or signed about, namely, the shoes in question.

However, from a more complete theoretical perspective, to understand how the child takes account of the tertiary referent (for example, the shoes in Brenden's case), it is crucial to realize that to deal with that third argument in the predicate system, as is suggested in Figure 7–2, the child must have already learned to connect acts of speaking or signing with the first two logical positions. The child must know that he (or she) can get the attention of the other person by speaking. Also, the child must have already learned that certain surface-forms, for example, the word *shoes*, are connected with certain objects, events, or activities, for example, putting on a pair of shoes, walking in the new shoes, dancing in the new shoes, tripping on the new shoes.

Considering the Dynamics of the Sequence

The first two referential connections are actually made long before the infant comes close to becoming able to distinguish particular referents in the third position through the production of a conventional symbol. The first referential connection with the bodily producer of syllabic speech occurs shortly after birth. This has been shown to occur by Sai (2005) through the linking of mom's voice with her moving face a few minutes after birth. The second logical position is not well established until about eight or nine weeks later when the infant begins to show that it has differentiated speech addressed to infants from speech addressed to adults. The third logical position does not really begin to come into view until after the infant begins first to discriminate linguistic symbols (to tell them apart) by about 4.5 months, then to prescind them, by about month 6 or 7, then to understand the meaning of some of the forms by about months 7 to 9, and finally to produce and apply one of the surface-forms in an appropriate way by about month 12 to 15. The determination of a referent in the third logical position by speaking or signing a word normally requires a full year, plus one or several months. Next let us consider in a little more detail the steps the child must take to move from the prescinded symbol (the level of canonical babbling) to the production of his or her first comprehensible word.

The Discriminated Symbol

The first inkling that the infant is beginning to take special notice of particular syllabic sequences, for instance, the infant's own name, is that the baby will respond to the familiar syllables distinctively, for instance, by looking in the direction of the person who produces the familiar syllabic sequence. This first inkling of the distinctive significance of syllables marks the development of the *discriminated symbol*. When this occurs at around the infant's fourth or fifth month, the baby shows its recognition of the syllable(s) in question by looking to the person who produces the symbol.

This event is marked by the baby responding to its own name by about age 4.5 months (Werker & Tees, 1999). When the name is used as a vocative form, to call the baby's attention, the baby is apt to look to the person who produced the name. In a sense, the baby at this stage "knows its name." At least, it recognizes the syllables, the surface-forms, that are involved as distinctive, different from other syllables. The baby knows the surface-form of the name. However, several additional steps must be taken before the baby will produce its first syllable(s) with the intention of commenting on or pointing out something else.

A month or two after the normal infant shows that it has attained the discriminated symbol, the first prescinded symbols will begin to appear. This usually happens sometime after the baby's month 5. That is, the baby will probably start producing canonical babble, between months 6 and 10. In the meantime, the baby continues to discriminate additional symbols (syllabic sequences) and gradually to expand the repertoire of prescinded symbols. Very soon after the child reaches the stage of the first prescinded canonical syllables (after the child produces its first babbled syllables), the child will make an additional discovery. It will arrive at the stage of the hypostatic symbol. That is, the infant will discover that certain distinct syllabic sequences are associated with different individuals, objects, or events. When this occurs the infant will not only respond to his or her own name as a discriminated symbol, but will look to another person, object, or event when it is referred to. We diagramed the achievement of the hypostatic symbol as shown in Figure 6–6. The difference between the achievement of the hypostatic symbol at about 7 to 9 months and the later achievement of the so-called "first word" as shown in Figure 7–2, is that the child is merely a consumer of the meaningful symbol in Figure 6–6 but also has to become its producer in 7–2. Both theoretically and in practice it is evident that merely comprehending a word produced by someone else is considerably easier than having to think of the meaning of the word, then think of the word, and then also to produce a surface-form of that word. The hypostatic symbol is easier to achieve than the first zero order predicate because the hypostatic symbol requires fewer steps to be taken by the child. If all else is held equal, there is less work involved in understanding a meaningful word produced by someone else than there is in thinking of the meaning and producing the word ourselves. Still the symbols that the child will later seek to reproduce must first be discriminated.

The Prescinded Symbol

A good deal of attention was given to the prescinded symbol in the just prior chapter. There we saw that normal infants typically begin to produce recognizable repetitive syllabic utterances (or manual signs in the case of deaf infants) sometime after month 5. Typically the prescinded symbols (that is, canonical babbling) begins by around months 6 or 7 and almost always by month 10. Again, if we think about the processes involved in achieving the level of prescinded symbols, it is clear that the level of discriminated symbols has to come first. In fact, the evidence shows that it does. The child begins to show evidence of noticing distinct syllables, for example, its name, by about 4.5 months on the average, but the child does not produce its first repetitive syllabic babbling until a month or several months later than this. In fact, Brenden O. began repetitive babbling during the latter part of month 5 and was holding forth with extended repetitive babbling by month 6.

The Hypostatic Symbol

The hypostatic symbol made a dramatic appearance in Brenden O's case when he was 6 months and 23 days old, at a family gathering with multiple people seated at the dining room table. Here is what everyone present observed on that day. Brenden was seated in his mother's lap at one end of the table. His grandfather got his attention, "Hey Brenden!" and then asked him, "Where's Ruthie?" Brenden turned and looked at Ruthie on his left and then back to Pop. Then, his grandfather asked, "Where's Nana (his maternal grandmother)?" Brenden turned to his right and looked at Nana and then back to Pop again, as if to ask, "Satisfied yet?" But, of course, Pop was not yet satisfied. He systematically went through all the people seated at the table and Brenden gave the appropriate response by looking from the questioner to the person referred to. He did this, flawlessly, for seven of the individuals seated around the table. As the person was named Brenden would look at that person and then back to his grandfather at the opposite end of the table. Finally, Pop asked, "Where's mommy?" Brenden had to turn his head almost 180 degrees and to look up to see her and then turn around to look back as if to say, "There's my mommy, don't you know who these people are?"

He obviously knew the names of all the people. That is to say, he had solved the hypostatic symbols for each person. Still, it would be almost exactly 6 more months before he would produce his first recognizable meaningful word as recounted earlier (see Figure 7–2). What this clearly demonstrates is that infants at the stage of babbling have already developed a significant repertoire, an expanding inventory, of what language teachers, literacy specialists, speech-language pathologists, and others commonly refer to as **receptive vocabulary**. We would describe the words that the infant can understand (but not yet produce) as *hypostatic symbols*.

Lower Order Sign Systems Persist Alongside
More Advanced Ones

The fact that the repertoire of *receptive vocabulary* exists and exceeds what the child can produce is evident from the examples of comprehension provided by Brenden O. at 6 months and 23 days. That is, the receptive inventory will contain words the child understands long before any of them can be produced intentionally by the child as meaningful predications, in other words, as zero order predicates such as the word used to refer to the shoes 6 months later by Brenden O. That is to say, the child may know the name of some person or object, provided the word is produced by someone else, but the child cannot yet produce that word on his or her own. Thus, the receptive repertoire exceeds the repertoire of what language teachers, speech-language pathologists, and others commonly refer to as the **productive vocabulary**. In fact, the words that the infant associates with a conventional meaning may advance to a substantial number before the infant expresses the first intelligible word out loud. For instance, it is quite certain that by the time Brenden (at 6 months and 23 days) was able to demonstrate knowledge of the names of all the persons seated at the dinner table, he almost certainly already understood other words referring to things, events, activities, and so on. However, children at the level of the hypostatic symbol still have a lot of work ahead of them before they will be ready to produce the first conventional predication on their own.

Before the first recognizable spoken or signed word is produced by the infant, canonical babbling will give way to **variegated babbling** (D. K. Oller & Lynch, 1992) where the infant mixes different syllables in a string, for example, [babama], [dabaga], and with an increasing variety of intonational patterns that are better and better controlled by the infant. Normal infants during this phase of development will often engage in fairly long "speeches" that sound like something the infant has heard other speakers do. It may seem that the babbler, for instance, is advising the dog to stay in the yard, or offering advice to a younger sibling about how to behave, or explaining something to an adult. A greater variety of vocalic elements also appear during the phase of variegated babble (roughly between 7 and 12 months). It is also useful to note that variegated babbling of the kind just described will persist long after the child has begun to produce intelligible words. That is, the child will often revert to babbling as a kind of vocal play or imitative behavior.

As the child produces more and more speech-like sequences, the babbled sequences (prescinded symbols) also come to resemble the target language increasingly (Koopmans-van Bienum, & Van der Stelt, 1986; Locke, 1983; MacNeilage & Davis, 1995, 2000, 2001; D. K. Oller, Eilers, & Basinger, 2001; Takei, 2001). For this reason, some have argued that babbling just naturally develops into speech where the first words are constructed out of babbled forms. Others have argued that there are or may be substantial discontinuities such that the babbled forms produced by the infant are quite unlike the first words they will acquire and produce later on (Carroll, 1960; Grégoire, 1948; Jakobson, 1941, 1968; Oxley et al., 2000; Velten, 1943; Vihman, Macken, Miller, Simmons, & Miller, 1985; Werker & Tees, 1999).

Apparent Discontinuities

Werker and Tees (1999) argue for two discontinuities (nonlinear and nongradual advances). One of the supposed discontinuous developments, involves what they believe is a decline between early infancy and adulthood in the ability to distinguish different sounds of speech. Werker and Tees note that before their seventh postnatal month, infants are able to discriminate contrasts in sounds and syllables that do not occur at all in their native language(s) (Aslin et al., 1981; Polka & Werker, 1994; Werker, Gilbert, Humphrey, & Tees, 1981; Werker & Tees 1984). However, sometime later this capacity is either lost or diminished. For instance, adults have trouble discriminating sounds that do not account for any significant differences in words in their native language. Japanese speakers, for example, find the /i/ and /r/ contrast hard to notice at all (Best & McRoberts, 2003; Strange & Jenkins 1978). This evidently has to do with the fact that this contrast is not used to differentiate words in Japanese. English-speakers have similar troubles with certain vowels and consonants that do not occur in English, for example, the /I/ and /y/ contrast that occurs in French and Mandarin but not in English, or the /u/ and /ɯ/ contrast that occurs in Mandarin but not in English, and so forth. Arabic speakers find the /p/ and /b/ contrast difficult in English because it does not exist in Arabic.

Werker and Tees (1999) cite their own work and that of others showing that "adults may need short familiarization periods even to discriminate acoustically quite salient non native distinctions" (p. 515). What happens between infancy and adulthood? Are some of the abilities that infants possess before 7 months of age "pruned" or trimmed out of their sensorymotor sign systems so that they can be more efficient learners and users of their native language? Perhaps so. At least this is one of the hypotheses under consideration (Werker & Tees, 1999).

Another discontinuity proposed by Werker and Tees has to do with the transition from babbling to what they describe as "constructing a lexicon based on full referential understanding" (1999, p. 515). They speculate that new demands on attentional resources may arise at this transition point because of the need to discover how syllables are associated with external referents. Or, they suggest, "the limits may come from the very act of building a new representation. Although further work is needed to understand this new process, we are confident that there is a discontinuity at this point in development that requires explanation" (p. 515).

The Hierarchy of Sign Systems

The theory of abstraction suggests that from the earliest memories in the womb, the baby has been developing meaningful representations, sign systems. The systems are arranged in a kind of spiral growth pattern (see Figure 4-9) that yields layer upon layer of new sign systems arranged in what may be called a **sign hierarchy**. This hierarchy has a necessary point of origin in the experiences of the infant. According to the theory, sign advances take place in phases or stages that produce systems of signs that are re-entered into the stream of experience in such a way as to enrich it. In fact, each new layer of signs provides a scaffolding for the next layer. Many signs may be added to any layer before advancing to the next level upward. Or, in some cases, children may seem to advance fairly rapidly through multiple layers. A general principle of the hierarchy is that lower levels are accessible from any higher level, but the reverse is not possible. A child cannot just reach up to any higher level at will. The necessary growth, development, and cognitive work must be accomplished to advance upward through the hierarchy. However, a child who is at the two or three word stage may carry on a conversation with a younger sibling in variegated babbling that reflects a much lower level of sign use than the older child is capable of producing.

Development may add many signs to any given level before the child advances to the next level upward in the hierarchy. In cases of disabilities, advances may be delayed or, in extreme cases, may not occur at all. The first layer of signs systems that the neonate produces consists of discriminated icons. The next layer, which depends on the prior development of discriminated icons will consist of prescinded icons. After that the infant comes to hypostatic icons. Then the infant moves up to discriminated indexes, followed by prescinded indexes, and then hypostatic indexes. Soon after that, the infant will advance to the discriminated symbol, then, the prescinded symbol, and after that the hypostatic symbol. The next sign system after the development of the hypostatic symbol (for example, the level Brenden O. had reached by his seventh month) is the *zero order predicate*, or the "first" word. Brenden's first word was "Zhus!" as noted earlier in this chapter. Table 7-1 gives a summary showing the first 10 levels of the sign hierarchy and the rough estimates of the ages when these levels are typically attained and then surpassed. In the first column the description of the kind of signs that are produced at that level appears. In the second

Table 7–1. The Sign Hierarchy as Predicted by the Theory of Abstraction up to the First Meaningful Word

Description of Level of Signs Produced	Range of Ages for Attainment	What Any Given Sign at This Level Can Represent
(1) Discriminated icons	week 12 prenatal to week 3 postnatal	A relatively stationary object; infant shows special interest in studying the bodily object (a percept of the object is a discriminated icon of that object)
(2) Prescinded icons	2 to 4 weeks	A moving object; infant tracks the slowly moving object as it separates itself from its background, or as the infant moves away from the object (a prescinded icon is an intermediate idea more abstract than a percept of an object but less abstract than a concept of the same object)
(3) Hypostatic icons	3 to 8 weeks	An object when it is not present; infant can think of the object when no percept is available (concept)
(4) Discriminated indexes	6 to 20 weeks	An index with a hypostatic icon at one end used to search a location at the other end for the object that the hypostatic icon represents
(5) Prescinded indexes	16 to 24 weeks	A moving object that stops moving is recognized as the same object and the infant shows surprise if the same object (e.g., mom) appears in multiple places at once (e.g., with mirrors)
(6) Hypostatic indexes	20 to 36 weeks	An object or person that moves beyond the horizon of perception is known to still be out there; infant does not show much surprise when it disappears from or reappears in the field of perception
(7) Discriminated symbols	3 to 6 months	Surface-forms of the target language are distinguished from each other by their shapes or spectral properties
(8) Prescinded symbols	5 to 10 months	Rhythmic, repeated, and rapid syllabic forms of the target language are "babbled" in speech or sign (this is the stage of "canonical babbling")
(9) Hypostatic symbols	6 to 12 months	A person, an object, a familiar action (also called *receptive vocabulary*, e.g., baby knows its name, those of other family members, understands bye-bye, and familiar actions like pick me up, put me down, etc.)
(10) Zero order predicates	10 to 18 months	A person, object, familiar action (also called the "first word stage," consists of *productive vocabulary*, for instance, "mama," "bye-bye," "no," etc.)

column we give the rough age limits for the normal attainment of the level in question. In the third column we give a nontechnical description of the kind of sign systems characteristic of the level in question.

Are There Silent Periods?

It seems likely, and sometimes evident, that as the infant is experiencing rapid growth in one sign system, there may appear to be a quiescent phase in another. That is, while the child is doing a lot of work on one aspect of the sign hierarchy, another may seem to be neglected or temporarily put on hold. Such examples of possible discontinuous development, as the infant advances from sign system to sign system, are sometimes referred to as a **silent period**. This does not mean, however, that the language acquisition process has gone dormant. In fact, some theoreticians have speculated that perhaps a silent period, or a period of what appears to be inactivity on the part of the language learner, may be necessary for essential cognitive work to be completed before the next overt advance can occur.

For example, the speculation that this is apt to occur can be traced to Jakobson (1941, 1968) who proposed that there is a major and nearly complete discontinuity between babbling and speech. He argued that the sounds produced prior to the first meaningful words have no relation at all to those used once an infant begins to attempt to produce words. That is, Jakobson argued that the repertoire of babbled syllables was entirely distinct from the sounds that would be produced in the child's first productive words. He underlined this claim in arguing that one vocal production system was actually being replaced by another. Jakobson even suggested that there is commonly a period of silence between the babbling period and the onset of true word production in many children. Other researchers have made similar proposals with respect to second language acquisition (Asher, 1969, 2003; Krashen, 1985, 1991; Krashen & Terrell, 1983). On the other hand, the notion of discontinuity between babbling and the first word has not met with universal acceptance (D. K. Oller, Eilers, & Basinger, 2001). Those who oppose the idea of discontinuities do so from a variety of different points of view, but generally share the notion that changes in child development are usually gradual and do not show major jumps or sudden leaps.

Coexisting Sign Systems at Different Levels

Regardless how the controversy over continuity comes out, there is strong evidence that the signs of lower levels persist alongside more advanced systems that are "under construction." As a result, for instance, when the infant at the stage of canonical babbling, he or she will often revert to presyllabic phonations, for example, blowing raspberries, cooing and gooing, and so on. In fact, even children who have already acquired their first words will commonly produce preverbal phonations during playtime activities (Oxley, Daniloff, Pirolli, & Roussel, 2000). Similarly, a child that has already achieved the one-word stage of productive speech or signing is occasionally apt to produce what appears to be a stream of meaningless canonical and or variegated babbling. Or, to take a more extreme example, most adults can easily imitate the babbling of an infant without difficulty and doting grandparents, are notoriously susceptible of engaging a babbling infant in babbled conversational exchanges. That is, the adults can easily revert to the level of the prescinded symbol.

By contrast, it is *not* the case that the infant can imitate everything that a mature adult can do in producing discourse forms. An infant at the babbling stage, obviously, cannot read or write the words on this page. The tendency for sign-users in general to be able to revert to systems of signs that are less advanced than the highest level they have already achieved is both predicted by the theory of abstraction (Oller & Rascón, 1999) and explained. The relevant principle has been referred to as the **reversion hypothesis**. It states quite simply that a sign-user/learner can often fall back to a level of sign systems that may be one or several levels prior to the one under development. However, the same learner cannot leap ahead to a sign system at a higher level for which the necessary supporting subsystems have not yet been developed.

As a result, it turns out that the most advanced level of signs that an individual has achieved is necessarily **diagnostic**. That is, it shows whether the individual in question, relative to expected milestones, is within or outside the normal range. Because an infant cannot jump from the discriminated icon, for instance, to the prescinded symbol, that is, from just beginning to notice the boundaries of bodily objects to canonical babbling, it follows that any child that has achieved the level of canonical babbling must also have achieved all the levels below that one. It also follows that a child that achieves any given milestone ahead of schedule can be expected, in most instances, to progress more rapidly to still higher levels, and that a child that is delayed outside the expected range is at risk of further difficulties.

However, progress in the normal infant's sign systems as he or she progresses from birth to canonical babbling on to the first word and beyond does not appear to be either **linear** or **discrete**. That is, the advances made by the sign-user are not necessarily one individual unit, or a single sign at a time. Sometimes one step may advance an entire repertoire of signs almost over night. Although it is true that some advances seem to progress discretely, one-by-one, step-by-step, every now and then the child seems to make a jump almost straight upward. For instance, as the child gradually seems to be expanding some repertoire of signs, all of a sudden there may be a nonlinear (exponential) advance where the child moves fairly suddenly into a whole new realm of signs. The child advances upward to a whole new level of greater representational power. For instance, when the infant roughly between weeks 16 and 20 discovers that a moving object that stops is still the same object, and that mom can normally only appear in one place at any given time, a quantum advance is achieved. This sort of "aha" experience where some whole new way of thinking is achieved, a nonlinear advance occurs.

If biological systems were strictly subject to logic, which they are not, we should predict that the infant should always retain access to all the lower levels of the sign hierarchy, but not to any of the higher levels. On the contrary, according to the research, some of the systems that are necessary to the development of the sign hierarchy not only fall into disuse as the infant advances, but are eventually removed from the hierarchy by something like a pruning process. For instance, although most adults can easily imitate canonical babbling so long as it employs the syllables of a language they happen to have learned, few adults (if any) can produce anything like the variety of phonations that infants between, say, 3 and 6 months can both discriminate and produce.

Moving on up to the First Word

Within the theory of abstraction, the first meaningful word produced by the child is referred to as a zero order predicate. It is called a *predicate* because the symbol is used, applied, or we could say *predicated*, with reference to something. It is called a predicate at a *zero order* because the predicate is so closely identified with its argument(s), that the predicate itself tends to be taken for granted. It is as if the predicate had no separate status at all, or, as if the argument were the same thing as the predicate. Later on, as predicates and arguments are more sharply distinguished at higher levels of abstraction we will see that higher order predicates, ones that appear in sequences of two or more words, can show relations, states, or actions involving one, two, three, or more arguments. As the child advances, not only will the different arguments be distinguished more sharply, but distinct words will be used to refer to them. For instance, the word "barks" in "the dog barks," has "the dog" as its one argument; the predicate "scratched" in "the cat scratched the dog" has "the cat" and "the dog" as its arguments; the predicate "gives" in "Mary gives Bill the book" has "Mary," "Bill," and "the book" as its arguments. Just as "Chica" in "Chica barks" is a zero order predicate referring to "Chica," "barks" is a higher predicate taking "Chica" (a zero order predicate) as its one argument.

Adinity

We say that a predicate with only one explicit argument, as in "Chica barks" has an **adinity** of one. It has only one argument. A predicate like "scratched" in "Felix scratched Chica" has an adinity of two. That is, "scratched" takes two explicit arguments, "Chica" and "Felix." The predicate "gives" in "Mary gives Bill the book" has three arguments and therefore an adinity of three. "Mary," "Bill," and "the book" are its three arguments. And so forth. The adinity of a predicate is the number of arguments that it takes. A zero order predicate has an adinity of zero because the argument is regarded as the predicate and the predicate as if it is the argument. Zero order predicates provide the necessary basis, however, for the development of higher order predicates.

The term "adinity" comes from C. S. Peirce. For its basis, he had in mind the terms **monad**, a structure, system, or relation involving only one element (an idea from Leibniz, 1714/1953); **dyad**, a relation involving two distinct elements; **triad**, a relation or system involving three elements; and so forth. All systems higher than the monad are referred to as **polyads**. By using the **suffix**, *-ad*, Peirce made up the term *adinity*. This term is useful because it tells us something very basic about the complexity of the relation(s) contained within the predicates that the child must learn. As soon as we begin to analyze predicates closely, we discover that their adinity is a key factor in the order in which the predicates will be acquired. Predicates of the zero order must be acquired before any predicates of higher adinities.

The Zero Order Predicate as a Basic Building Block

Figure 7-2 shows the underlying system of a zero order predicate. It is like a percept (discriminated icon), as shown in Figure 4-7. That is, both the zero order predicate and the percept involve an almost inseparable association between the abstract sign on the one hand and its logical object on the other. In both cases, the object causes the sign-user to think of the sign and the sign causes the sign-user to think of the argument that the sign stands for (that is, its object). With the discriminated icon, the association is almost complete. It is difficult for the infant to learn that objects exist independently of our perception of them. With the zero order predicate, however, the problem is more abstract but it is a little easier to solve because words are distinct from objects. Still, at the appearance of the first words, the child has not yet learned to distinguish the predicate from its argument. Because this problem has not yet been solved when first words begin to appear, we call predicates at this level, zero order predicates. The fact is that predicates at this level are almost welded to the contexts in which they occur. This idea has been stressed by many observers from a variety of viewpoints.

For instance, Tomasello (1992, p. 42) called these "first words" **presymbolic forms**. The list for his daughter Travis included words like *mma*, a preliminary sound to kissing, or as an accompanying gesture and sound; *tickle*, when she wanted to play the tickle game with mom; *rockin* as part of the activity of rocking, to point to the chair, or even when she didn't want to rock; *play-play*, when playing the piano or referring to it; *Ni-Ni*, as in "nighty-night" to refer to bedtime, sleeping, or the like; *Mi* to call her dad ("Mike") or mom; and so forth. Tomasello (1992) explains that "I now believe that the issue of whether they referred to objects or actions (or both) is not an issue because they did not refer, in the strict sense of that term, at all . . . they did not symbolically represent either the object or the activity . . . but were themselves a part of the object-related activity." Also, he notes, "Some of these presymbolic forms were only used for activities, that is, they were never used to name objects" (p. 43).

We agree entirely with Tomasello's point that the forms in question are invariably attached to particular kinds of entities, especially persons, engaging in particular kinds of activities. On the other hand, the fact that they are genuine predicates with generalized meanings, we believe, cannot be denied. How else is it possible to explain the fact that *mma*, to take the least word-like example of the whole list given by Tomasello, is used not only to accompany the act of kissing but in anticipation of it when no kissing is actually taking place? Or, how else is it possible to explain the generalization of *play-play* from engaging in the activity of banging on the keys of the piano to a pointing gesture calling attention to the piano when no one is playing it? Although zero order predicates are at first embedded in ongoing activities that involve particular entities (persons and things) that engage in those activities, for example, mama plays the piano and Travis plays the piano, and so on, to manifest the meanings (and whatever arguments) that may be associated with *play-play*, the fact that such forms generalize in their applicability to any new contexts at all shows them to be symbolic and predicative in all the required senses.

These forms also involve reference at all three of the levels we described earlier: first, to the producer of the form; second, to the person or persons that may be addressed by the speaker; and third, to the activity and any other entities with which the form in question is conventionally associated. The very fact that the only association of the form with a context is by convention shows it to be a symbolic association. It is not merely iconic and may not be iconic at all. The word *mma* does involve the sort of lip formation involved in kissing, but *play-play* has little association with banging the keys on the piano, except, perhaps, the repeated banging movements of a small child being reflected in the repetition of the word. By contrast, *Ni-Ni*, as a symbol for bedtime activity or sleeping, has no iconic relation to the action involved. Neither do these forms have any natural or necessary indexical association with the activities in which they may be embedded. Kissing is certainly possible without saying *mma*. Similarly, the baby can be put to bed without saying the words, *Night night!* The piano can be played without saying the words *play-play* and so forth. We go through these details to point out that the only basis for the association of these forms (or any others like them) with the activities in question are conventional associations. A speaker of Japanese, or Hottentot, or any other language does not have to use any of the particular forms in question for any of the particular activities in question. The same holds across different varieties/dialects of English, or across different families of users within the same variety/dialect of English. There is only a conventional association between any other forms in question and the activities in question. Therefore, they are intrinsically and necessarily symbolic in the only respect that counts. The predicates themselves can only be discovered by their conventions of use.

However, the key fact remains that as long as the argument is not distinguished from its zero order predicate, and vice versa, so long as the zero order predicate is regarded as the argument, the argument does not count as a separate entity because *it* is regarded as the predicate and vice versa. That is, the argument and predicate are so closely identified that the two are more or less regarded as one activity/entity. It is as if there were no separate argument, or no separate predicate, only the joined predicate-argument system. For this reason we call predicates at this level zero order predicates. They clearly are symbolic, however, because of their conventional generalizability, their recognizability as distinct forms, and their replicability by other persons.

Summing Up and Looking Ahead

In this chapter we have considered the child's development from canonical babbling that takes place sometime between months 5 and 10, on up to the development of the first productive words which usually appear about month 12 to 15. When symbols are associated with tertiary meanings, they become hypostatic symbols, also known as receptive vocabulary. However, the first word stage is not recognized as such until the child produces one or more words with the clear intention of communicating some tertiary meaning to someone else. When this occurs the child moves up to the level of the zero order predicate and initiates what has commonly been called the first word, and the productive vocabulary. At this point, the lexical development of the child advances to a significantly higher level and the child is initiated as a speaker of a particular language. In some cultures, this event marks the shift from regarding the child as an "it" to regarding the child as "he," or "she" (Fromkin & Rodman, 1998). Through his or her own deliberate actions the child becomes a member of a language community. However, as we noted in this chapter, this advance does not bring an end to the babbling stage, nor does the productive vocabulary, consisting of overt, deliberately produced zero order predicates, replace the receptive vocabulary. These coexist alongside the zero order predicates (the productive lexicon). Similarly, the child will still occasionally lapse into babble (the repertoire of prescinded symbols), and even pre-babble phonations (levels of presyllabic vocalizations).

In the next chapter we will see how the child's next series of developments initiates a new interest in syntax. The next series of problems to be addressed involves distinguishing syntactic details in symbolic relations. These syntactic developments will be increasingly incorporated into the continued growth of the repertoires of signs already on hand. In the next chapter we see how the child advances to two and three word constructions. What is more, we will see how this development enables the child to distinguish arguments from the predicates that signify them.

▬▬▬ STUDY AND DISCUSSION QUESTIONS ▬▬▬

1. Why does it take such a long time after the first symbol is discriminated at about 4.5 months to produce the first meaningful word at about 12 to 15 months?

2. What are the criteria that must be met for the first productive word? Why does a babbled /mamama/ not necessarily count as a reference to the person the child will someday call "mama"? What additional elements must be present and why?

3. Why is it that the first two arguments associated with a zero order predicate, for example, in the "Zhus!" example, tend to be taken for granted? Clue: Would the conversation be possible without those two arguments? Also, why do we not mention the person spoken to when giving an urgent command, for example, a warning such as, "Watch out!" Why don't we commonly say the sort of thing that is sometimes found in stylized dialogues of unrealistic dramas: "I say, oh Brutus, son of Caesar born during the earthquake that destroyed the southern half of Athenia's garden, take care for there is a speeding horse and chariot bearing down upon your backside!"

4. Discuss how all three of the usual senses of the term "argument" can be applied to any one of the arguments entering into Brenden O's zero order predicate applied to the unfortunate incident with his new shoes.

5. Why is it reasonable to expect receptive vocabulary to exceed productive vocabulary? Should this expectation carry forward throughout the lifespan? Does it generalize to other sign repertoires? Does it apply to babbling? Will it apply later on to discourse in general?

6. What is the possible role of one or many silent periods in the development of new levels within the sign hierarchy? What implications, if any, do such phenomena have for the problem of continuous (gradual) advances versus sudden leaps and discontinuities among coexisting sign systems at distinct levels? What arguments or facts, if any, can be given pro or con for the existence of discontinuities?

7. What is the reversion hypothesis and how does it relate to the notion that the highest level of signs a child has achieved is diagnostic of that child's social and intellectual development?

8. In Tomasello's examples of what he called "presymbolic forms" what arguments or facts can you offer to show that these forms are not separated in the mind of the child from the activities in which they are embedded? Can you think of any ways that the child might be able, later on, to notice the distinctness of the surface-forms embedded in the interactions described? What new evidence would need to become available to the child?

CHAPTER 8

Moving on to Syntax

By studying this chapter you will:

1. Appreciate the fact that general predicates, lexical items with generalized significance, are necessarily at a limit of semantic generality, in other words, they cannot become more general (in principle) than they already are because they are completely general;

2. Learn how the vocabulary explosion (the lexical growth spurt) that occurs at around 18 to 20 months sets the child up for a series of syntactic advances;

3. See how predicates become more fully differentiated from their arguments at around the time of the child's rapid growth in vocabulary during the one-word stage;

4. Understand the difference between zero order predicates (ones not fully distinguished from their arguments) and first order predicates which are sharply distinguished from their arguments;

5. Understand how second order predicates, ones that modify those of the first order, which in turn modify those of the zero order, are constrained relative to the viewpoint of the child;

6. Find out how children advance from second order predicates to predicates of the third and higher orders; and

7. Understand why there is a limit of diminishing returns where acquisition of new syntactic relations levels off, usually, somewhere between years 4 and 7.

KEY TERMS

Here are some terms and concepts that you may learn more about in this chapter (these are also defined in the Glossary):

bound morpheme
comprehensiveness
deixis
ego-centric particulars
endogenous syntactic development
exogenous syntactic development
first order predicate
fossilization
free morpheme
fundamental frequency
grammatical gender
grammatical number
grammatical person
hallucination
holophrasis
holophrastic construction
intuitions of the ideal native speaker
lateral development
mistaken representations (errors)
morpheme
morphological marker
morphology

naïve realism
nominal
noun phrases
pivot grammar
plural morpheme
plurality
possessive marker
powers of representation
primary stress
relevance
second order predicate
secondary stress
semantic limit of generality
shifters
syntactic function
syntactic limit of diminishing returns
third order predicate
verb phrases
verbal modifier
vertical development
vocabulary spurt

Figure 8–1. A bodily thing, such as the dog on the left side of this diagram, exists on the opposite side of Einstein's Gulf from a word like "dog" that may be used to refer to the dog. The entities are not like each other very much. The word is not a dog and the dog is not a word.

From the adult perspective it is not difficult to see that a word used as a predicate, that is, a symbol for something else, is very different from its argument(s). As shown in Figure 8-1 the word "dog," for instance, is not itself a dog, just as the dog is not a word. They are different kinds of objects. Similarly, a two-word sequence of predicates that someone might produce, such as, "Nunu barks," is certainly not the same act as the barking of the dog. Also, it is not the dog itself. The barking is something the dog does. An adult can easily see the difference between the dog, its name, and its barking. However, even adults have difficulty seeing the significance (or meaning) of a word as something other than the word itself. We can hardly think of the meaning of any word without thinking of the word itself. For instance, if we see a dog, we are apt to think of the concept underlying the word "dog." Similarly, if we think of that concept, say, when we don't have any particular kind of dog in mind, we still tend to think of the word "dog" to invoke or call the concept (its meaning or significance) to mind.

Names as Predicates and Named Things as Arguments

Names make us think of whatever is named. When we hear the name of a person, we are apt to think of that person. For instance, a name like "Hillary Clinton" is apt to call to mind a certain bodily person. But what does "Harcourt Brace" call to mind? Books? A place? If so, where is the place called Harcourt Brace? Is there just one place? When we think about these issues we discover that the meaning of any predicate is not the same as any bodily object or any physical location. Predicates and their meanings are also distinct. A publisher, such as Harcourt Brace, or better, Plural Publishing, is an abstract idea, but it may also involve many different locations, events, books, authors, staff members, editors, readers, teachers, and students. It may also involve many different ideas, a philosophy of how books should be written, edited, and presented. But the meaning of a name like "Plural Publishing" is certainly not just a place anymore than the meaning of any name is just a body.

In the same way that the word "fox," for instance, is not the same as the fox crossing the road in front of our car, the abstract meaning of a predicate or sequence of predicates is also very different from any object, person, event, or whatever that sequence may be used to point out or refer to, or otherwise signify. For instance, the fox itself may be pointed out, or we may refer to the crossing of the road by the fox, or the road that was crossed by the fox, or the place on the road that the fox crossed it, or the car that ran off the road because of the fox that crossed there, and so on. The words are different from their meanings. But words and sequences of words are commonly associated with material things in our experience through their abstract meanings.

Those material things, bodily persons, and other entities that can be referred to by words, are called *arguments*. The words that refer to them, on the other hand, are called *predicates*. In the most common and ordinary uses of language, and certainly in the one-word stage of child language development, we find that the first predicates tend to refer to arguments that are noticeable, important, and salient from the child's perspective. That is, the child tends to refer to persons, things, events, or relations that achieve saliency in the child's experience, for example, "mama," "hot," "no," "bye-bye," "Nunu" (the name of the pet), and so on. The child tends to pay close attention and to form lasting memories and associations between predicates that signify or involve salient arguments, or frequently repeated activities related to salient arguments, for instance, calling the dog, putting baby to bed, knocking down the blocks, playing peek-a-boo, and so forth. Tomasello (1992, pp. 41–43) calls these kinds of first words "presymbolic" because they are so completely embedded and inextricably associated with arguments involved in activities.

In some languages, English, for instance, these first, zero order predicates appear to be predominantly **nominals** (Slobin, 2004). That is, they resemble nouns or names of things. In English, a first word like "mama" or "Nunu" would be expected, but words like "hot," "no," "bye-bye," or "up" (meaning "pick me up"), or "down" (meaning "put me down") would seem to be exceptional. In other languages, Mandarin (Chinese), for instance, the first words appear to include about equal numbers or even more words that seem to be verbs than words that can be identified as nouns (Chen, 2005). That is, they commonly seem to show salient actions involving familiar objects, for instance, the Chinese equivalent of "up," or "down," would be more common while a first word like "mama" would be a little less so. But it would be a mistake to suppose that the first words can disregard arguments entirely. This cannot happen because there are no actions that do not involve actors or moving things.

Regardless which grammatical classes the first words of any child in any language may *seem to belong to from the adult perspective*, those first words are *zero order predicates* that are attached to particular *arguments* that consist of salient objects, persons, or events involved in frequent activities that have **relevance** in the experience of the child. The relevance is determined by the fact that the arguments in question are significantly related to the child. For instance, "up" may signify that the Chinese-speaking child wants to be picked up by mom. "Mama" may mean the very same thing from the English-speaking child's point of view. However, the research shows that either form may occur as an early word in either language. Another important aspect of first words is that they tend to be predicates that are associated with events of high-frequency. That is, the events tend to be repeated over and over again on a regular cyclic basis. Every morning, mom picks up the baby and throughout the day does so repeatedly, especially at mealtimes. The picking up event has a high-frequency of occurrence. Associated with this common event are words that are also often repeated in the same context.

Thus, zero order predicates acquired by children all over the world, tend to have the properties of *saliency*, *frequency*, and *relevance*. However, the fact that a low frequency word like "hot" may come into the repertoire of first, or very early, words, shows that saliency (for example, the memory produced by a painful experience) may compensate for the low frequency of some words. Nonetheless, the most important abstract characteristic of the first meaningful words that children acquire (that is, their first zero order predicates) is relevancy. Arguments that have no relevance to the experience of the child, are not going to be associated with any zero order predicates.

Uses Are Important

As has commonly been emphasized, the abstract meanings of words are derived from their uses (Tomasello, 2003; Wittgenstein, 1953, 1958). As a result, even as adults there is a tendency for us to think that the things, persons, and situations that we refer to with words really are the meanings of the words we use. This cannot, however, be strictly true because word meanings are abstract and the things, persons, relations, and so on, that we point out or refer to are mainly concrete. In this chapter we examine the difference between predicates that serve as symbols to stand for abstract meanings on the one hand and to refer, sometimes but not always, to concrete arguments that are things, persons, and relations between them. We also consider how children advance from zero order predicates to more complex predicate systems at what we call first, second, third, and higher orders.

From the child's point of view the natural separation between any argument and any predicate is not at first very obvious. In terms of ideas advanced in previous chapters, however, we can say that the key elements of the zero order predicates that form the first entries in the child's productive lexicon exist on opposite sides of Einstein's gulf as shown in Figure 8–2. Take a word like "shoes," for example, as applied to the material articles of clothing that a child wears on his or her feet. The shoes are concrete. The child can touch and handle them. The word, "shoes," on the other hand, is abstract. It cannot be handled. A token of it, that is, its surface-form, can be heard or spoken, written or read, but the spoken word is not like the object, or a written word, that sticks around. The surface-form of the spoken word can be articulated on particular occasions, but as soon as any one surface-form is produced, it is very quickly gone. The production of the word takes about one third to one half a second if we say it slowly. Then, it is over. The utterance of that word is history. However, the conventional meaning of the word is available for application, presumably, whenever the need may arise even when its surface-form is not being produced by anyone. The meaning of the word "shoes" is available at any time even when the word is not being spoken, written, read, or otherwise signed in any particular language.

As a result, an interesting philosophical question comes to light. Does the word stop existing when its surface-form is not being produced or

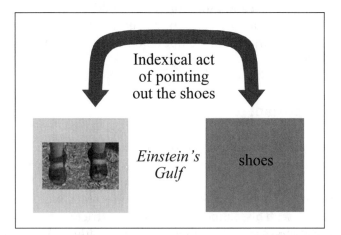

Figure 8–2. Another look at the three main elements of a zero order predicate relative to Einstein's gulf. On the material side of the gulf is the icon of the main argument, the actual shoes, and on the other side is the surface-form of the predicate, the word "shoes." In the middle is the indexical bridge that connects the two sides of the gulf with each other.

noticed by anyone? Does its meaning evaporate if its surface-form stops being noticed? Where does the meaning go? Actually, the meaning of a word is not necessarily something that can be visualized at all. For instance, what is the meaning of "the"? And even with words for which we can think of a concrete object of some sort, for example, "shoes," "dog," "cat," "mama," and so on, we still have the problem of deciding just what sort of object to think of. For instance, if the word is "dog" what sort of dog should we think of? We might think of a Collie, or a Great Dane, or a Husky, or a Chihuahua, or no particular dog at all. Yet the abstract meaning of words seems always to be available, once it has been acquired. The more commonly the word is used, the more readily it will be available (Tomasello, 2002). Still, the utterance of a word, say, "the" or "dog" or "shoes," usually takes less than a half a second. The articulation of even a multisyllabic word usually lasts only for a second or less and then it is gone. The abstract meaning or concept, however, for example, of what the word "shoes" or "syllable" mean, on the other hand, by contrast with the material objects of activities to which or in which either of these words might be applied as predicates, is valid for any pair of shoes or any syllable. The word "shoes" does not just apply to the ones on any particular child's feet. The word "syllable" can apply to any syllable. We can say that the abstract concept that is associated with any predicate, for instance, the meaning associated with the word "shoes," seems to be something eternal and quite independent of what may be happening in the material world at any given place or time. The abstract meaning does not require a place or time to occupy. What is more, the abstract meaning of "shoes," the concept of footwear, is actually much broader than can be represented by any particular pair of shoes. For example, there are lots of different kinds of shoes: sandals, loafers, tennis shoes, high-heeled shoes, cowboy boots, and so on. Similarly, the word will eventually generalize to shoes that are quite unlike the ones on the child's feet, for example, to shoes for horses, brakes on a car, and so forth.

As a result of thinking about the abstract meaning, the form, and the concrete referents of the sort of zero order predicate, for example, "Zhus!" as produced by Brenden, we come to realize that the picture is more complex than Einstein suggested. Figure 8-2, incorporating the zero order predicate "shoes," as actually produced by Brenden, cannot show the full complexity of the picture either. It shows the three main elements of the zero order predicate but it does not show that each of those elements is associated with at least three other components. For instance, on the side of the concrete referents of Brenden's speech act, there are at least three distinct bodily referents (as shown in Figures 6-5, 6-6, and 6-7. There is the first person (Brenden), the second person (the person to whom the utterance is addressed), and there are the shoes (in the logical third position that all of us also occupy). There are also three distinct levels of symbols. There is the discriminated symbol noticed by the second person (the person addressed in the speech act). There is the prescinded symbol produced by the first person (Brenden). And there is also the hypostatic symbol, "shoes," which is associated with three distinct levels of significance. First, it points out Brenden's shoes. Second, it records Brenden's complaint that the shoes caused him to fall. And, third, it shows that he knows and his listener knows as all speakers of English do, that these particular things are called "shoes." Much more could be said along this line. The speech act shows that Brenden has acquired the conventional rule that things of this kind, that are used as footwear, can be called "shoes."

It turns out that the zero order predicate involves three distinct components each of which consists of at least three other components. Such systems are at least triadic in complexity. That is, they have at least three components. However, the child operating at the stage of the "first word," that is, the level of the zero order predicate cannot yet call attention to all the distinct elements. In fact, the child cannot sharply distinguish the predicate from its argument. He can only use the predicate to call attention to the argument. The child can associate the predicate with its argument, in other words, the word "shoes" with the shoes on his feet, and vice versa, but the difference between the word and the object may be taken for granted, but the child at this stage cannot add a separate predicate to show that he thinks the shoes caused him to trip. We may infer that he thinks this, that the shoes caused him to fall, but he cannot point this out explicitly without making some additional distinctions. The child also needs additional linguistic resources to be able to make sharper distinctions. To do so the child not only needs additional zero order predicates, that is, words for other arguments, but also additional predicates that modify the zero order predicates. The child needs to move up to predicates about those zero order predicates. To do this will require the development of genuine two-word sequences. These will be sequences of at least two distinct words with different meanings. Such two-word sequences are different from singular **holophrastic constructions** of what may appear to be two or three words in a sequence to an observing adult but that are not regarded as more than one word (that is, they are treated as a single zero order predicate) by the child. However, when the child reaches the level of zero order predicates, there is a certain natural barrier that forces the child to begin to pay attention to the syntax that connects sequences of two or more distinct and higher level predicates.

The Semantic Limit of Generality

When the child comes to the level of the zero order predicate, a certain **semantic limit of generality** is achieved. We can appreciate this limit if we ask the question, when is the name of the dog not appropriate as a means by which to refer to the dog? The answer is, never. The name of the dog is always appropriate as a way to refer to that dog. The predicate is applicable to its arguments in all their contexts. Or, to take another example, when is the word "hot" not appropriate to apply to hot things? Or when is "bye-bye" not an appropriate way to describe a leave-taking experience where people or other entities, for example, trains, planes, or cars, are departing from the infant? Or when would the term "shoes," say, not apply to a pair of shoes? Because every zero order predicate that the child acquires falls at the upper limit of semantic generality in the ways just described, it is not surprising that the attention of the infant soon turns from the discovery of such general abstract meanings of words to the determination of how such general predicates are differentiated from each other and from higher order predicates.

As soon as there is a sufficient supply of meaningful "first words" (zero order predicates) in the child's productive repertoire, and as the receptive repertoire of new candidates (hypostatic symbols) grows increasingly, the child soon has more than enough zero order predicates to begin to make some additional distinctions between them and to begin to notice relations between them. That is, the child can begin to regard the zero order predicates as entities that enter into higher sign relations. The child turns attention from the fundamental semantic question concerning what any given predicate signifies, to the question of how the general predicates that have already been discovered get connected with other predicates. That is, the child turns his or her attention from the meanings of predicates, that is, their *semantic values*, to their combinatory properties, in other words, their *syntax*.

At the level of the zero order predicate, it is as if the argument is the predicate and vice versa. MAMA, the person, is known as "mama," a predicate referring to that argument. Also, "mama" the predicate is so closely associated with its argument, MAMA, the person, that the predicate is virtually identified with its argument, that is, MAMA = "mama." As a result, at the beginning of what is loosely called the "first word" stage, even if a child seems to produce a sequence of words, the theory of abstraction shows that, at the level of the zero order predicate, it is as if there is only one predicate, just one word. The technical term for what may appear to be two or three words as produced by the child, but where the child sees the whole sequence as a single zero order predicate, is **holophrasis** (Bates, 1976; McNeill, 1970; Tomasello, 1992). For instance, at around 13 months, a certain child, ML, produced the expression /onfawe/ which was a holophrastic version of "Don't go far away."

What ML meant by his rendition was, something like, "Open the door." However, before letting him go out into the front yard to play, his mother always told him, "Don't go far away." His way of getting her to let him go outside, was to repeat what she always said, as best he could. Was he producing three distinct words? No. At least, judging by the fact that he only applied this predicate to that one situation, he was not distinguishing the component parts. The surface-forms of his zero order predicate, [ŏfawe] were distinct syllables, but not distinct predicates. There was only one predicate in the surface-form from his point of view. What is more, he didn't really have that predicate in mind. His thought concerned getting out that door. The predicate was just a means to that end. His attention was on getting outside. Or, here is another example from the same child later on. When he was thirsty, he would say [ŏfɪs]. This form was evidently derived from the surface-form of the question, "Are you thirsty?" It had a singular meaning. Water, or give me a drink. (Hear <u>Examples of Holophrasis</u> on the DVD.)

As soon as the limit of semantic generality is reached in the zero order predicates (the child's first words), attention must invariably turn to syntax if the child is to progress further and not remain at the one-word stage of development. Normal children all expand their sign systems from the first word forward to the discovery of syntactic relations. The infant by the achievement of the zero order predicates has already discovered the sorts of symbols that are as general as any symbols can be. So, the child has come, at this stage, to a kind of semantic ceiling on the process of generalization. There simply are no symbols that can be any more general than symbols that are completely generalized (or that can be completely generalized). As a result, the infant soon expands from just acquiring new zero order predicates to figuring out new combinations of them.

Going to Work on Syntax

This does not mean that the child stops paying attention to meanings, but rather that the child also begins to pay attention to parsing, separating, and recombining the forms (the predicates) that are used to express those meanings. A first step will be to discover that any given argument, that is, whether it is a thing (a car), person (the child's mama), or a salient event or activity (such as might be represented in "hot," or "bye-bye"), can be referred to by more than one predicate. Similarly, the same predicate can apply to other arguments. For instance, a toy car the child can hold in his or her hand may be referred to as "a car," and the toy car the child can sit in is a "car," and the car that mommy drives is a "car," and so forth. The same predicate can be attached to lots of different arguments and contexts. The match flame is hot, but so is the burner on the stove, mom's coffee, Mr. Smith's cigar, Aunt Tina's cigarette, and so forth. On the other hand, multiple predicates can also be associated with the same argument. The dog has a certain name, say, "Chica," but is also called a "dog," and is said to "bark," "sit," and so forth. There are lots of predicates associated with the same argument. The cigarette is not only "hot," it is also "nasty," "stinky," and so on. The stove is not just "hot" it is also a "stove," "off," "on," and so forth.

Differentiating the Predicate from Its Argument(s)

The difference between any predicate and its argument(s), does not begin to be accessible to the child until about the time of what has been called the **vocabulary spurt** (Fernald, Swingley, & Pinto, 2001; Jusczyk, 1997; Werker & Tees, 1999). This is the rapid growth in the number of words the child controls in his or her productive lexical repertoire. The inventory of zero order predicates seems to expand very rapidly by about 18 to 20 months. When this occurs the child seems to experience a sudden growth in the number of words in his or her productive lexicon. Up until about the time when this growth spurt begins, the first meaningful words (zero order predicates) are associated with their meanings somewhat in the way a percept (a discriminated icon) is associated with its object. It is almost as though the sign and its object are inseparable. Wherever the object turns up in the experience of the infant, the percept is there, and when the percept appears it is always attached to its object. Wherever the percept is found, the object is right there too. The situation is similar with the zero order predicates. Whenever one of them turns up in the child's early uses of his or her first words, an argument for that predicate is also present.

Naïve Realism

If, at any stage, the infant supposes that the object and the percept are identical, an extreme form of **naïve realism** results. According to such a view, things really are however they seem to be. If things seem different, they must be different. If they do not seem different, they must be the same. (Recall Ockham's rule and the Leibnizian principle of the identity of indiscernibles.) The research literature shows that infants really are naïve realists to a high degree and they only gradually become less naïve with each advance in their **powers of representation**. As they mature, they encounter situations where the rules of the naïve realist do not work very well. For the percept and its object, for instance, the rules work fairly well. Whenever the object is perceived it is associated with its percept, and vice versa. If the object is thrown overboard and sinks in the ocean, the percept sinks too. They seem to be the same thing, so what is the harm in supposing they are the same? There is very little, if any, conflict produced by this assumption.

But, of course, the association of percept with its object is not complete. It is not perfect in the grammatical sense of the word "perfect." The percept is not exactly the same thing as the object and the object is not exactly the same thing as the percepts to which the object gives rise in any number of perceivers on any number of occasions. We can perceive our car 50 times in an hour but this does not produce 50 different cars. If it did we could manufacture cars, houses, cities, or whatever we like. However, the chair we are sitting in is not multiplied by the number of times that we pay attention to it. Neither is the desk in front of us, or the room it happens to be in multiplied by the number of times we may perceive either of these logical objects. This is obvious to adults because we can understand that a multitude of different percepts of the same object can be produced by just one person. Also different perceivers necessarily produce a greater multitude of percepts of the very same object. Adults can easily see that perceivers do not ordinarily produce the object perceived. The universe would be suddenly cluttered and filled to overflowing if the process of perception could produce a new object for every percept. Theoretically an infinite series of distinct new objects would be appearing all the time for every perceiver. Clearly, that is not the way perception works. It does not produce new objects, just new representations of objects. Objects are different from representations of them.

Illusions and Hallucinations

Illusions in our perceptions are not really as uncommon as they may seem to be. Consider Figure 8–3. By staring at the dark donut in the middle for, say, about 30 seconds, and then looking away to a white part of the page, or to a white wall, you will see a lighter donut illusion. Or, by looking at the lower half of the same figure, notice that the two lines appear to be different lengths with line A appearing to be longer than line B. In fact, the two line segments are of equal length if perpendicular lines are drawn from the ends of segments A and B as shown in the lower part of the figure in line segments C and D. Illusions of both these sorts are common and yet normally go unnoticed. Still, our perceptions do not usually deceive us. In fact, even in the length "illusion" of Figure 8–3, the fact is that the longer appearing line, A, actually is longer than B if the angular ends ">" pointed inward in one case and outward in the other are taken into consideration.

Relatively rare exceptions, where perceptions do deceive, or may deceive the perceiver, are **hallucinations**. Even these can sometimes be detected for what they are by the person affected. That is, even the person having the hallucination(s) may discover that what seems to be real is not. In the case of hallucinations, what the perceiver thinks he or she is perceiving is actually only imagined. Hallucinations are like experiencing vivid dreams when we are awake. The film titled *A Beautiful Mind*, directed by Ron Howard and featuring Russell Crowe as Princeton genius Dr. John Nash depicted the true story of a person whose vivid hallucinations formed a narrative structure. In real life it seemed plausible to himself (John Nash) and sometimes to others as well, in his experience (read the story as told by Nasar, 2001). Somewhat similar hallucinations, though usually not form-

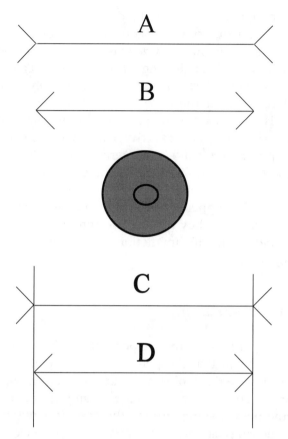

Figure 8–3. Exemplary illusions. Does A seem longer than B? Either can be superimposed on B or D. Stare at the donut in the middle for 30 seconds, then stare at a white place on the page and see a lighter illusory donut.

ing a coherent story line, may be caused by drugs, by disease, by extreme exhaustion, or by combinations of such factors. However, such hallucinations are relatively rare, and when they occur in any one person (someone on drugs, say) they are rarely, if ever, shared by anyone else. In the film, John Nash is shown asking someone else to verify his perceptions so that he can tell the real ones from the hallucinatory ones.

In fact, the extreme rarity of any possible coincidence where two people, much less three or more, have the same hallucination at the same time, is a sound argument for the conclusion that the world we perceive when we are awake is very probably real and that our perceptions are not deceiving us. It also leads us to suppose that any agreement among different observers on what is going on in the world at any given time is probably not an accidental coincidence, but is rather caused by the fact that the senses of most people can be trusted almost all the time. In other words, when we agree with others on a sequence of events that we have all observed, for example, the motorcycle crash that happens right in front of us, we are probably not hallucinating, or in error, or dreaming, and so on. When we are awake and alert, our senses do not usually deceive us. When several of us agree on something that is happening or has just happened, this agreement is probably not the result of a group hallucination. When the police and various ambulances arrive, we have every reason to suppose that the perceptions are valid. Our agreement with the many other witnesses at the scene of the accident, along with later recollections that are shared with others, is probably caused by something that really is happening or has actually happened. At any rate, if it were always impossible to determine the facts as they actually are through perception, it would also be impossible to identify any fictions, errors (including illusions and hallucinations), or lies.

Representing Versus Being

When we say that perceivers produce percepts of objects, we suppose that the objects are real and that the percepts are really like the objects that they represent. However, any object, unlike a perceiver, does not produce percepts of perceivers, nor even of itself. The lamp sitting on the desk does not perceive the people sitting around the desk. It is not aware of any of us or of itself. The lamp can be represented by its perceivers, but the lamp does not represent the perceivers on whom it sheds its light. Also, the perceptions of the lamp are shaped by the lamp, but the lamp is not usually changed much by our perceptions of it. If we happen to knock it off the desk when groping in the dark, the bump and the crashing of the lamp on the hard floor may change the lamp, but whatever changes occur are not because of our perceptions, but because of physical forces acting on the lamp. We knocked the lamp off the desk onto the floor. The point is that there is a huge difference between *representing* something and *being* something. To be a lamp is not the same as perceiving one, and perceiving a lamp is not the same as producing one. All of these differences, and there are many more that could be pointed out, have to do with the fact that a representation is an abstraction, while the lamp is a concrete thing. Representation is not the same as being, and being represented to be a lamp is not the same as being a lamp.

The Role of Ordinary Truth

The differences between representation and being represented are the heart of what differentiates ordinary true representations as distinct from fictional representations, **mistaken representations** (errors), and intentional lies. A true representation, in the most ordinary sense of the word "true," is one where the predicate applied is appropriate to its argument. For instance, if Brenden calls a pair of shoes, "Zhus!" his statement has the ordinary property of "truth" in the required sense. That is, the word "shoes" is conventionally associated with footwear of the sort just pointed out by the 13-month-old child. If we think of a pair of shoes where there aren't any shoes, but we are not claiming that there are any shoes there, our imagined pair of shoes is a fiction. If we think Brenden, say, is talking about his shoes when he is referring to a glass of juice, we commit an error. If we claim that something is a fact when we know it is not, we lie.

Working out the differences between these several possibilities, however, requires more than figuring out semantic values and syntactic relations. To sort out the differences between representations that are true as contrasted with fictions, errors, and lies requires the solution of a series of fundamental problems in the pragmatics of language and representational acts. It will require quite a lot of syntactic development and several more years of work before the child is able fully to make sense of the profound differences between facts, fictions, errors, and lies. We will come to that series of problems in Chapter 9.

In the meantime, we need to keep in mind the fundamental differences between the two sides of Einstein's gulf as suggested in Figures 8–1 and 8–2, for instance. On the one side there are concrete objects, bodily persons, their actions, and observed relations between all these. These concrete bodily things and their relations in the material (physical) world of space and time provide the substance of what we are calling arguments. On the other side of the gulf, there are abstract ideas, concepts, and meanings that are accessed through predicates that are at first used to refer to and comment on arguments.

Predicates That Have Arguments Become Arguments

The abstractness of the zero order predicate makes it difficult to regard it as a potential argument in its own right. That is, at the point of the discovery that things, persons, events, and certain relations have predicates to signify them, the child is not very apt to notice or think of the difference between the predicate and its argument, nor of the fact that the whole relation can be regarded as an entity in its own right. That is, the relation between a symbol and its object, such as the one diagrammed in Figure 8–2, can be regarded as an entity and may itself become an argument for a higher predicate, for example, the shoes can become the argument for a higher predicate, such as "Brenden's shoes," "Pop's shoes," or "shoes hurt," and so on.

The predicate "hot," for instance, may cause the child to think of or notice the hot stove, the lighted cigarette, the burning coal, the flaming match, or whatever. In the uses of this first word or any other, the child tends to associate the word so closely with the properties and attributes of its particular arguments (say, a thing, person, relation, or experience) that the word itself is not noticed as a separate entity. The flare of the match may cause the child to think of the predicate, "Hot!" And that predicate is apt to cause the child to think of the flare of the match. The predicate is almost as closely associated with its argument as a percept is with its object.

It is useful to keep in mind that the relation between an object and all its different percepts is somewhat the same as the relation of an argument to its predicates. Consider first the solution to the problem of realizing that the discriminated icon (the percept) is distinct from its object. Although the normal infant solves this problem between months 4 and 5, it is more difficult than it may seem at first from the adult perspective. The baby has to come to the realization that an object no longer being perceived, or thought of, is still there; that there are objects that are not perceived, or being thought of; and that things are not always as they seem to be or as we think they are. One way to show that an object and its percept (the discriminated icon of that object) are different entities is to direct our attention away from whatever object is being perceived, for example, the lamp on the table, the keys in the purse, or the door in the corner of the room. If we do this, we notice that the percept of the object ceases to be available to our senses, say, when we are not looking at it or touching it, but when we redirect our attention to the object again, the object is still there.

Something very much like the discrimination of the percept from its object must also be done with the zero order predicate to distinguish the predicate from its argument. The child has to notice the predicate as something independent from what it is about, its argument. The child does not have to discover that the predicate is abstract. This is guaranteed by the nature of the conventional symbol and its application. To see just how abstract the first word can be, consider the following example. In a segment of the public video (the *Mind Series*), Jill DeVilliers tells of the first word of her son, Peter. It was the name for his dog. Not long after he worked that out, he is reported to have used the same word, "Nunu," the name of his dog on three new occasions in a brief period of time (over a couple of days). He used it to refer to two cored olives on a plate of salad that evidently reminded him of Nunu's cold wet, black nose. He used the same predicate to comment on a pair of soft furry slippers his mom tried on at a department store. And, he also used it to refer to another four-legged animal standing out in a field. Evidently, Peter was thinking of Nunu, a dog like the one in Figure 8–4, on each of the several occasions of the use of the predicate. When he thought of the predicate he thought of the dog, and vice versa. Still there can be no doubt that Peter was using an abstract predicate, the name of his dog, in some creative ways to apply to a considerable variety of contexts and meanings. According to the story, he did this all in a very short time after his first use of the word.

Figure 8–4. This is not Nunu, but it is a dog like him.

In fact, any zero order predicate that the child acquires presents new possibilities for further learning that were not evident before. That is, a word like, "mama," say, or "hot," once it is produced and the significance and social impact of the production is observed by the infant, becomes a source of new possibilities. For instance, mama can go bye-bye, mama can feed, bathe, and put the baby to bed, mama can pick up the baby, and so forth. Similarly, "hot" is a predicate that can combine with different arguments. For instance, the stove can be hot, the match can be hot, the food can be hot, and so on. What is more, each predicate, as it is attached to various arguments, can be discriminated as a separate entity in its own right.

Treating a Zero Order Predicate as an Object

As the associations of zero order predicates with their arguments are secured, the distinct meanings of first order predicates that take zero order predicate-argument relations as their components can come into view. For instance, the infant can discriminate the new predicate of predicates in a sequence such as "mama up," where the predicate "up" is new, or "Brutus bark," where the predicate "bark" is new, by simply noticing the new predicate as distinct from the part of the sequence that has already been deciphered earlier. Say the child already understands the predicate "mama" as a zero order predicate referring to mom, or suppose the child already understands the zero order predicate "Brutus" as the name of the dog. At this stage of development, about the time of what is called the "vocabulary spurt" the child will begin to notice (i.e. discriminate), produce (prescind), and differentiate (hypostatize) the surface-forms and meanings of **first order predicates**, in other words, higher predicates applied to zero order predicates.

For example, suppose "up" signifies the act of being picked up by someone, say, mama. Or suppose the predicate "barks" comes to be associated with the action of a certain dog. If the predicates that refer to these arguments (mama and say, Nunu) have already been acquired as zero order predicates, it becomes possible for the child to notice the higher predicates in "Nunu barks" and "mama up." From an adult perspective, we might say that the child works from the known nominal (for example, "mama" or "Nunu") upward to the new **verbal modifier** (for example, "up" or "barks"). However, the child can about as easily work in the other direction from what appears to be a verb or modifier of a noun back to what appears to be the nominal form. For instance, if the word "hot" has already been understood and acquired as a zero order predicate, it can be distinguished from "stove" in the sequence "stove hot" or "hot stove" where the meaning is understood to be something like, "The stove is hot." Similarly, if "hmaa" has been associated with the act of kissing, "hmaa mama" or "mama hmaa" can come to mean something like, "I kiss mama," or "Mama, kisses me" or "Mama! Kiss me!" And so forth.

The Two-Word Stage

At the point of the discovery of first order predicates, the child reaches what is commonly referred to as the "two-word" stage of development. This stage is not the same as a holophrastic production that may look like two or three distinct words, for instance, a holophrastic production that looks like the three word sequence "don't go far away," may be just one word from the child's point of view. At the genuine two-word stage, the child demonstrates that a given predicate is distinct from the argument it signifies and the argument is distinct from the predicate that may be used to signify it. These facts are demonstrated in part when the child associates multiple arguments with the same predicate, and conversely, when the child associates multiple predicates with the same argument. However, the discrimination of the predicate from its arguments is fully accomplished at the genuine two-word stage of development. As soon as the child begins to produce genuine two-word sequences, where one word signifies an argument and another some state, or action of that argument, or a relation of that argument with some other argument, the child has achieved the genuine two-word stage.

At about the time of the vocabulary spurt, the child will discover that more than one predicate can refer to the same argument, and that more than one argument can go with a single predicate. It is inevitable, therefore, at the genuine two-word stage of development that the distinct predicates themselves can be singled out for attention in their own right. The zero order predicates the child already knows take arguments that have been discriminated, prescinded, and hypostatized. It remains only for the child to perform essentially the same operations of abstraction on the new predicates of predicates (first order predicates) that are attached to those zero order predicates. That is, soon after the child knows that the dog may be referred to as "dog" as well as by its name, say, "Snaps," "Chester," "Chica," "Brutus," "Nero," or whatever, any predicate associated with one of these becomes available to be singled out for attention in its own right.

The new predicate, in a two-word sequence, for instance, can be regarded as a symbol first to be discriminated from other such entities, then, to be prescinded from the familiar parts of the sequence, and separately produced, and finally to be hypostatized with respect to whatever significance it may acquire. At that point, the child can differentiate discriminated first order predicates, prescinded first order predicates, and hypostatic first order predicates. Let us consider each of these in its turn keeping in mind that the child may fairly rapidly, sometimes seemingly all at once, run through all three steps with a given sign. The sign systems to be worked out are summed up in Figure 8–5.

On the one hand there is the argument, Brutus, that is represented by its zero order predicate (a referring use of the name "Brutus"). On the other hand there is the action that Brutus performs, the barking. If Brutus were barking at a cat named Felix, we could add Felix to the picture and the first order predicate, "barks" would have Brutus as its agent cause and Felix as its recipient (patient) object. However, to keep it simple, let us just think about Brutus and the barking. In this simple case, as in more complicated ones involving all higher order predicates, the relation into which one or several arguments happen to enter provides the basis for the child's discovery of the meaning of the new predicate in question.

In Figure 8–5, the learning problem depicted from the child's point of view is to figure out the surface-form of the predicate "barks." The child must discriminate it, then, produce it, that is, prescind it, and finally understand and intend its meaning. That is, the predicate must be hypostatized with respect to the action of the dog. For example, the child will become able to say with the usual conventional meaning that "Brutus barks!" Notice that the relation expressed in the first order predicate (and all higher order predicates) in true statements attaches itself to its argument or arguments. That is, the barking of the dog, Brutus, does not occur without the action of Brutus. This absolute dependency relation holds for all predicate relations that any argument or sequence of arguments may actually enter into. Without any dancer, there cannot be any dancing. If a cup shatters into a thousand pieces when it is dropped on a concrete floor,

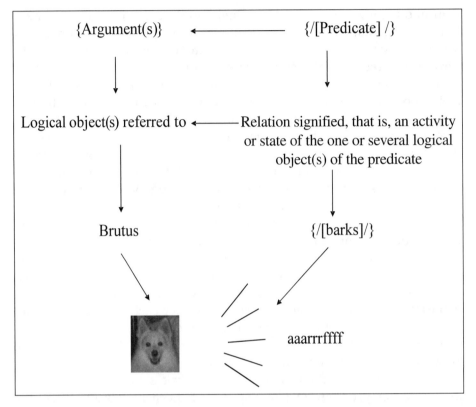

Figure 8–5. The sign systems underlying the series of discriminated, prescinded, and hypostatized first order predicates (e.g., "barks" in this example). Suppose the dog's name is "Brutus" and that the child already knows this word and can produce it, but does not yet know the word "bark." In the example, "barks," can be discriminated, prescinded, and hypostatized, as a first order predicate to be associated with the action of Brutus.

the shattering is so closely associated with the cup and the floor that without them, the shattering could not have any reality or existence. The same holds for a 100 car pileup on the freeway. Without the freeway and the 100 cars, the pileup (as described) could not occur at all.

In the same way, zero order, first order, and all higher order predicates are absolutely dependent for their meaning on the relations, expressed as actions and states, that their arguments enter into. Without Brutus, to return to our simple example in Figure 8-5, Brutus's barking would not exist. For this reason, to discover the meaning of any first order predicate, such as the barking of Brutus, the child needs first to develop the zero order predicate that enables him or her to represent Brutus as a zero order predicate, in other words, as an argument. Without arguments to build upon, there cannot be any higher order predicates.

The Discriminated First Order Predicate

The discriminated first order predicate can be any word together with one or more zero order predicates that is noticed as distinct from those other predicates whose meanings have already been worked out. A discriminated first order predicate is a predicate marked as distinct from one or more arguments (namely, zero order predicates) for which zero order predicates have already been acquired. During the vocabulary spurt, the child notices that the dog can be referred to in more than one way. It is a "dog," and it is also "Nunu." Mother is called "mama" and also by her name, say, "Stacy" or "Mary Anne" or "Linda," or whatever. Daddy is called "dada" and also "John," or "Steve, or "Ronnell," or whatever. Grandmother is called "Nana," "Mimi," or "Grandma," or whatever. When these contrasting pragmatic mappings come to be noticed as distinct from each other the child is on the verge of discovering that there are predicates for states and actions of arguments as well as relations between arguments.

We see the emergence of the discriminated first order predicate sometime after the so-called vocabulary spurt at about months 18 to 20 for most normal children. However, we may suppose that this development can occur earlier or later by a few weeks or more. We know that the child has achieved the level of the discriminated first order predicate when, for instance, a predicate in a sequence of at least two distinct predicates is singled out for attention. For instance, if the child distinguishes "Mimi's house" from "Mama's house" by using either the predicate "Mimi" or "Mama" to indicate one rather than the other, the child shows in doing this that he or she is already comprehending the gist of a sequence of two distinct zero order predicates. In these kinds of sequences, one of the predicates is used as a comment or modifier of the other. In "Mama's house," the predicate "house" is attached pragmatically to a particular domicile (a certain house) which is modified by the predicate "Mama" indicating that this is where Mama lives rather than Mimi and so forth. Or, the child may understand a sequence like "Chica barks" and be able to meaningfully produce the word "bark" on an appropriate occasion. When these kinds of advances occur, the child is on the verge of producing meaningful two-word sequences. The sign systems at this level can be diagramed as in Figure 8-5. The child at this stage of development will show comprehension but not necessarily produce the first order predicate in question.

The Prescinded First Order Predicate

Logically, the discrimination of any first order predicate, for example, [barks] in Figure 8-5, and its incorporation into the receptive repertoire, must precede its overt use by the child as prescinded first order predicate, /barks/, in the productive repertoire of the child. However, because of the acceleration that is occurring in the rate of learning, the discriminated first order predicate may be prescinded soon after it is first discriminated. The stage of prescinded first order predicates, however, will be marked by an increasing tendency for the child to generalize a given predicate to signify different arguments, and by the child's use of more than one predicate to signify different aspects of the same argument. This level of sign systems is usually achieved by about the end of the vocabulary growth spurt, for example, by month 20 give or take a few weeks. The child may produce the predicate to indicate a relation with a lower order predicate, but as a one-word utterance, for example, "Bark!" meaning "the dog is barking," or "just barked." Or the child may say "Mimi!" meaning "Mimi's house" rather than "Mama's house," or the reverse. That is, with the prescinded predicate, the child produces a predicate showing that he or she has understood a relation incorporating one or more previously acquired zero order predicates. The prescinded predicate is produced in relation to an argument that is taken into consideration, but not necessarily overtly signified.

The Hypostatic First Order Predicate

The development of the hypostatic first order predicate is marked by the fact that a distinct two-word sequence is produced where the meanings of two predicates are understood and the intention of the child in using them is to show the relation of the argument to the predicate. For instance, the child may intend to point out that a certain hat that belongs to a certain person, for example, "Pop hat" meaning "This is pop's hat." Or the child may intend to refer to the barking that is an action of the dog. "Brutus bark." Or the child may refer to a state of some object or person, for example, "Mama bye-bye" meaning that Mama is gone or leaving, or whatever may be the case. In all these cases, the predicate that is hypostatized is also distinguished from the zero order predicate(s) with which it is associated. For instance, the hat, in "Pop hat" is signified not merely by a zero order predicate, "hat," but by a predicate used to comment on or modify another argument, Pop, through a different zero order predicate, "Pop." The meaning is something like, "this hat belongs to Pop." If the child also builds other two-word sequences on appropriate occasions such as "Pop shoes" meaning "those are Pop's shoes," "Mimi shoes" meaning "those shoes are Mimi's," and so forth, we can be quite certain that the child has achieved the level of hypostatic first order predicates. In "Brutus barks," the barking is referred to and associated with Brutus. In "Mama bye-bye," the leaving is referred to and associated with Mama.

Even one instance of a genuine two-word sequence, if it is intended and understood correctly in the manner described by Figure 8–5, shows that the child has achieved the level of the hypostatic first order predicate. That is, the child is using a first order predicate incorporating one or more zero order predicates as its components. The higher predicate subsumes and signifies a particular relation, action, or state of at least one zero order predicate (its argument). All of these instances of "two word sequences" can be diagramed as shown in Figure 8–5. As the figure shows, the hypostatic first order predicate is merely a predicate that is associated with one or more lower zero order predicates designating one or more arguments that the first order predicate subsumes. Such a hypostatic first order predicate cannot fully be demonstrated as a hypostatic instance until the lower zero order predicate(s) and the higher first order predicate are manifested as distinct surface-forms in the child's speech. In the case of a compound sequence of two zero order predicates, for example, "Mimi" and "house" the higher, first order predicate is shown in the sequential order and in the stress pattern.

For instance, Brenden says, "MIMI house!" where the modifier "Mimi" is produced under **primary stress** while the zero order predicate that is modified is produced under **secondary stress**. That is, the first zero order predicate is marked as a first order (higher) predicate by the fact that it is stressed. Stress is shown in higher amplitude (that is, it is louder), higher pitch (that is, the **fundamental frequency** of the voice is higher involving shorter wavelengths), and longer duration (that is, the syllables in question are longer). The advance to the first order predicate cannot happen until the genuine two-word level is achieved. Normally this occurs sometime around month 24, give or take a few weeks. The development of the hypostatic first order predicate involves figuring out what state, action, or relation is to be understood as being signified by the first order predicate. For instance, the child needs to realize that "bark" signifies an action performed by the dog, that "up" is an action of Mama, that "hat" is an object that Pop wears, and so on. As soon as first order predicates begin to appear in the surface-forms the child uses, that is, as soon as first order predicates are used as comments on zero order predicates, the relations between words and objects, or persons, or events, can be treated as abstracted objects in their own right. (Hear <u>Illustrations of Stress</u> on the DVD.)

Meaningful Questions About Words Emerge

When the conventional uses of words are hypostatized to the level of predicates of predicates, or genuine first order predicates, the possibility of asking questions about words emerges. The child may point to an object and ask for its name. The possibility of seeking help in finding out what predicate is appropriate to refer to a given argument (or complex of arguments) comes into view. That is, it occurs to the child to point to an object to ask the equivalent of a question requesting an additional predicate. For instance, Brenden says, "Pop hat!" and gets confirmation from Pop. "You're right, Brenden!" Then he says, "Pop shoes!" and gets additional confirmation. Next, he points to the guitar on the stand near the desk as if to say, "What's that?" and he gets from Pop, "That's Pop's GUITAR!" where the word "guitar" is singled out for attention by prominent stress. Commonly, adults will also supply a separate production of the new predicate bounded by silence. For instance, Pop may say, "Guitar!" and try to elicit the word from Brenden. By the time the child is working at the level of first order predicates, zero order predicates can be added to the system with surprising speed.

Because Brenden has just indicated that he knows that bounded objects have distinct zero order predicates to refer to them, when an object is pointed to for which Brenden does not yet know the zero order predicate, there is an implicit question. The meaning of his implicit question is what is that thing, relation, or event called? At this point, the zero order predicate is clearly being treated and regarded as an entity in its own right. To regard a zero order predicate in this way, the child must first hypostatize one or more first order predicate argument relations in genuine two word sequences. When that occurs, the child is also on the verge of becoming able to understand yes/no questions. He or she is prepared to consider options proposed by someone else, for example, do you want milk or juice? Would you like to go with mommy or stay at Mimi's house? When the child is able to express meaningful preferences in response to such questions, there is no doubt that the stage of the hypostatic first order predicate has been achieved and somewhat exceeded. These developments usually occur sometime after month 24 give or take a couple of months. Another conclusive indication that the child has achieved the level of the hypostatic first order predicate is any genuine combination of two words where one is used to modify or comment on the other, for example, Chica and her barking, or to show the relation between them, for instance, Pop and the hat, Mimi and the house, and so on.

Because hypostatic first order predicates take zero order predicates as their arguments it is reasonable to see the zero order predicate as a kind of pivot point while the higher predicates to be associated with such a pivot represent an open class of items that are added to a pivot point. For instance, as seen in Figure 8-5, the hypostatic first order predicate (for example, "barks" in "Brutus barks") subsumes Brutus as a component part. The barking is an action performed by Brutus. Braine (1963) proposed the term **pivot-grammar** to suggest that certain predicates, we would say "zero order predicates" serve as anchor points or pivot points where additional predicates can be attached. However, we prefer to recognize the fact that the child at the genuine two-word stage is beginning to differentiate arguments and predicates very much in the manner in which they are differentiated by adults. As a result it is advantageous to use the adult terms to refer to the systems of signs that the child is developing as soon as the distinct categories begin to emerge, that is, at the one and two-word stages.

As soon as the child begins to produce sequences that consist of at least two distinct predicates, each of which is appropriately associated with its respective meaning, we can legitimately claim not only that the child is at the "two-word" stage but that the basis for differentiation of nominals and verbals is also present at this stage. We know this because to qualify as a two-word sequence there must be a predicate relation between the elements at the surface, and one of these elements must be regarded as a comment on the other. That is, it may show that a certain argument is in a particular relation with another (for example, "Pop's hat" shows that the hat belongs to Pop), or that a certain argument is performing a noticeable action (for example, "Brutus bark"), that someone should perform a certain action (for example, "Mimi up" meaning Mimi pick me up), or that a certain argument is in a particular state of being (for example, "Foot hurt" meaning my foot is hurting). What is more, for any given two-word sequence to qualify as consisting of two different words, the words have to independently meet the requirements laid down earlier for the first word stage of development.

That is, for any given sequence to qualify as a hypostatic first order predicate (as applied by the child), it is essential that it meet all three of the requirements laid down at the beginning of Chapter 7 for the first word. The predicate relation that is understood (recognized by someone else) as intended by the child must be contextually appropriate (that is, it has to meet the appropriateness requirement) at the time that it is produced and it must conform to the generalizability requirement (that the conventional use extend to other similar occasions). It is not necessary for the child to use the very same form across all contexts, but to be certain that the level of the first order hypostatic predicate has been achieved, it is essential that the child demonstrate generalization of the predicate relation in question, for instance, by saying appropriately not only "Pop hat," but also "Dada car," "Mimi house," "Foot hurt," "Thomas fall," "Chica bark," and so on. If the child builds up these kinds of sign systems in appropriate contexts and generalizes them to new contexts there can be no reasonable doubt that he or she has acquired systems at the level of the hypostatic first order predicate.

Second Order Predicates

Next the child will move up to a higher level that relates the predicate-argument relations already signified in hypostatic first order predicates more explicitly to the child's point of view. The distinctive trait of second order predicates is that they express **deixis** (pronounced "dike-sis"). This word comes from a Greek root, *deik-*, meaning to show or demonstrate, to point out. Deictic or second order predicates, however, do not merely point out relations between objects, persons, events, and so on, but they also take account of and express to some extent the speaker's point of view relative to the viewpoints of others. In child language development, the incorporation of second order predicates is marked by the fact that they appropriately and differentially incorporate the child's perspective into surface-forms. Consider the distinction between "I" and the person addressed in a statement like "I walk mall, Dada" by a child of 26 months. When such a report is appropriate and true, in other words, grandmother confirms that the child did spend much of the day walking the mall, not only does the child incorporate more than one argument within the scope of the predicate "walk," but one of the arguments, designated correctly by the pronoun "I" shows that the speaker is on the verge of taking his own viewpoint into consideration. He seems already to know that "I" is a form that refers to himself while "Dada" refers to his father.

The use of both terms in the same surface system suggests that the child is at least beginning to refer to the person addressed and to distinguish at the surface, at least, the two points of view in the reported action, that is, the child's point of view, and his daddy's in "I walk mall, Dada." However, it takes quite a long time after the surface-forms begin to emerge in the child's speech for the child to sharply differentiate all the meanings and referential (deictic) relations that are involved from the adult perspective. For example, it takes the child about 3 years or more to sharply and consistently differentiate the subjective personal pronouns "I" and "you" as well as the objective ones "you" and "me." For instance, Brenden said things like "I walk mall" at about 26 months, well before the "I" and "you" deictic problem was fully solved. At 30 months, long after producing and differentiating the surface-forms of the main subjective and objective personal pronouns, Brenden would still occasionally say things like, "I pick you up," while reaching up to his father with an obvious request meaning, "You pick me up."

Edward Sapir (1921) called referring terms such as the pronoun "I" **shifters**. Sapir referred to all such terms as *shifters* because they have entirely different arguments associated with them when they are used by different persons. When I say "I," I mean to refer to myself, when you say "I" it means you. Because the meanings of these pronouns are determined by who happens to be speaking at a given moment, Sapir called them *shifters*. Bertrand Russell (1948) called them **ego-centric particulars**. Russell called them *ego-centric* because we must know who is doing the talking, and who is being addressed, to know who the terms refer to. Similar difficulties are associated with words like "here" and "now." They are applicable to any time or place whatever, provided the viewpoint person happens to be thought of as being in that place and at that time. Words like "then" and "there," "this" and "that" share in these interesting properties of being definable (and usable) only relative to some speaker's point of view.

For this very reason, deictic forms are notoriously hard for children to sort out. How is the child to tell who is "I" and who is "you"? Children at the three-word stage are apt to say, "I help you," while showing by their actions that they want you to help them. The problem of who the words refer to is intensified by the fact that they constantly change their meanings. The problem during its initial phases breaks down to one of correctly mapping the predicate in question onto its argument relative to the viewpoint of a particular speaker and/or person spoken to. Similarly, differentiating "this" and "that," "these" and "those," "this one," and "the other one," as well as "here" from "there," "now" from "then" also critically involve deixis. The question is how are the various referring terms (the surface-forms) to be associated with the various available (or possibly missing) arguments. For instance, in "Where's the gorilla?" as asked on a trip to the zoo, the key argument referred to may not be present.

It is not hard to see that the difficulties associated with figuring out deictic terms, for example, where "here" is, and when "now" is, spill over into problems associated with figuring out the meaning of *tense* (past, present, and future) and *aspect markers* (having to do with whether an event is thought of as in progress or completed). The present time, for instance, can only be determined relative to someone's point of view. All time is present to the persons who happen to be experiencing whatever is going on at that time. All places are present from the viewpoint of the persons who happen to be in those places. However, when Brenden says, for instance, "Chica is barking," the time of the barking is expressed at the surface relative to the time of speaking. As a result, it is clear that tense marking is a deictic problem. Aspect too is a matter of how events are thought of from some point of view. Are we in the middle of the event? If so, it is ongoing (imperfect). Or, are we standing somewhere outside it after it has been completed? If the latter, it is complete (perfect). What is more, all deictic connections constitute pragmatic mapping problems for the child. who is learning a language. They involve at least the complexity of what we are calling second order predicates. That is, the meanings of the predicates in question can only be figured out by taking into account the point of view of one or more particular persons, usually the speaker and the person spoken to, and commonly, at least three points of view become involved (see Figures 6–4 and following).

With second order predicates, what will develop into an expanded range of distinct **noun phrases**, for example, phrases that have nominals as their focal elements, such as "I" as contrasted with "you," "this" as contrasted with "that," "here" as distinct from "there," begin to come into the child's repertoire as discriminated and prescinded signs. However, the full range of their meanings have not yet been worked out by the child. The surface-forms that will develop into expanded **verb phrases**, for example, "is barking," "barks" as contrasted with "bark" or "barked," and so forth, begin to appear in the surface-forms produced by the child. These developments can be expected to emerge by about the end of year three or later. At the next level up, the different surface-forms contained in verb phrases that contrast with respect to tense, aspect, and modality will begin to be differentiated with respect to their meanings as well.

Third Order Predicates

Up to this point, in this chapter, we have concentrated on what may be called **exogenous syntactic developments**. That is, zero order predicates are subsumed within higher first order predicates which in their turn are subsumed under second order predicates. The result seems to be linear growth in the number of distinct words in any string that the child may produce. The child goes from one word, to two words, to three words or more. The growth is outward, upward, and additive. It involves additional layers of distinct signs. For instance, the surface-form "bark" is added to another word, say, "Chica," or "dog." Or the word "Pop" is added as a modifier to the word "hat." The word "Mimi" is added as comment or modifier of the word "house" to distinguish Mimi's house from Mama's house, and so on. Deictic forms such as "I" as contrasted with "you"; "this" as distinct from "that," are also added to the child's repertoire and appear as additional distinct words in surface-forms.

In all these examples the growth of the surface syntax involves joining relatively distinct, discrete, and different predicates to each other. However, with the development of third order predicates another kind of development emerges where words or phrases seem to expand from within. It can be called **endogenous syntactic development**. Such development involves the association of any third order or general predicate with one or many second order predicates. For instance, a noun phrase involving a second order predicate such as "this" conjoined to the word "train" to distinguish the train engine of interest, "this train," from some other or others, may be expanded by adding a **morphological marker** to distinguish one train from two or more others. For instance, the child will first discriminate, then prescind, and later hypostatize the "-s" on "train" to produce "trains" intending to mark **plurality**. At about the same time, the demonstratives "this" and "that" will be distinguished from "these" and "those." The fact that the **plural morpheme** is a higher order predicate in English (and in other languages too) is evident, in English, in the way it must be copied from the demonstrative to the head noun in a phrase like "these trains" where the plural morpheme appears in two places, that is, the "-s" on "trains" and the change in the demonstrative from "this" to "these."

If we ask, what factors cause or require these change in surface-forms, the only valid answer is that they are conventional requirements of the particular target language. For instance, in Chinese, plurality is not marked in the surface-forms of either nouns or verbs the way it often is in English. But what exactly causes the change in English from singular to plural? How is the marking determined? Surely it is not just a whim of the speaker or else we could use singulars any place we like. The answer is obvious. The determination of whether we use the form "dog" or "dogs," for instance, is made by whether there is only one or more than one dog to be referred to. The basic element in the plural marker has to do with number and it is determined by counting arguments in some way. This is essentially a pragmatic problem that involves deixis.

These endogenous developments within existing lexical and syntactic forms involve something like what Tomasello (1992, p. 23) called "assembly instructions." That is, the child begins to work out the internal **morphology** of words and their relations to higher syntactic structures. To avoid positing morphological advances when the child is merely repeating forms uttered by someone else, Tomasello argues for the conservative rule that the new forms should only count as grammatical advances after the child uses those forms to distinguish different contexts and situations, for example, to show the difference between singular and plural. The trick is to distinguish actual advances in the internal structures and meanings of distinct predicates and their parts (that is, their morphology), from mere repetitive holophrastic utterances. Tomasello (1992) suggests that the key is to determine whether or not the child uses any particular surface-form "contrastively," that is, whether its presence or absence affects the meaning of the utterance for the child" (p. 39).

Linguists generally refer to these endogenous syntactic developments as morphological because they often involve the addition of a **bound morpheme** to a distinct word or **free morpheme**. The development of these kinds of forms is endogenous, or within a given lexical category because the bound morpheme cannot occur without being attached to some other form. In the case of regular plural marking, however, such an addition is still a third order predicate because the meaning of the new morpheme is attached to more than one predicate at the second order. For instance, words like "words," "children," "women," and "men" are all marked as plural, and yet, only the first word in this list is regular. A **morpheme**, in general, can be defined as any distinct surface-form that has either a distinct semantic or pragmatic significance, or a distinct **syntactic function**. In the case of the *plural morpheme* the rich complexity and interrelatedness of syntax, phonology, morphology, and the lexicon begins to come into view. For instance, at about the same time that the plural marking begins to appear in nominal phrases, the child will also begin to mark verbs for **grammatical number** as well. For instance, in English we distinguish the number of discrete and countable arguments that may be associated with a verb. We say, "the dog barks" but "the dogs bark." During their third year normal children begin to make these distinctions at the surface and fully differentiated third order and higher predicates will also begin to emerge soon after.

With respect to morphological development, in a classic study, Roger Brown (1973) studied 14 morphemes in particular. Among them were the following: (1) the present progressive ("-ing" on progressive verbs, for example, "Chica bark*ing*"); (2) spatial prepositions, "in" ("*in* car"); (3) "on" ("*on* table"); (4) the regular plural "trains"; (5) irregular past tense markers "*fell*," "*did*," "*went*," and so on; (6) possessives ("Mimi*'s* house"; "Pop*'s* hat"); (7) full copula ("we *are* here," "Thomas *is* there"); (8) determiners ("*a* train"; "*the* train"); (9) regular past tense ("I walk*ed* mall"); (10) third person regular present tense ("Thomas run*s*"); (11) third person irregular present tense ("he *does* it," "Simon *says*"), (12) uncontractible auxiliary ("*Are* they here?"), (13) contractible copula ("he*'s* here"); and the (14) contractible auxiliary ("he*'s* gone already" meaning either "he *is* gone" or "he *has* gone"). The order in which these morphemes tend to be acquired is as they are written here.

The Syntactic Limit of Diminishing Returns

To a high degree different relations tend to be marked at the surface by different orders of predicates. For instance, referring (including naming) relations are marked first by zero order predicates, but later on, as the child matures into an adult, they may be marked at the surface in countless different ways. The pet formerly called "Nunu" can be called "that big shaggy dog," "the brown one that we had when we lived on Fairfield," "the dog that used to chase old Mr. MacGregor's rabbit," and so on. In the beginning stages of language development, referring relations are incorporated into first order predicates that express what can be termed relations between relations. At the level of second order predicates the child begins to differentiate points of view more sharply in surface-forms, and by the time the child has incorporated third order predicates, the power of the developing sign systems reaches astronomical proportions. There are vastly too many combinations to list them all and the number of combinable forms ascends into the thousands. As soon as the child advances to relations between relations between relations, the power of the language the child is developing necessarily (and normally) reaches a point where the pragmatic relations of interest in experience can be adequately expressed with the resources already on hand. At that point, the child reaches what has been termed the **syntactic limit of diminishing returns**.

That is, the child comes to a point in syntactic/morphological development where all the major syntactic features of the language have been acquired and there is little or no reason to produce more complex syntactic combinations than those that are already available with the sign systems the child already has on hand. The child comes to a natural limit of diminishing returns. Little or nothing at all would be gained by adding more syntactic complexity, so, the child's attention turns to other matters. In particular, the main problems to be dealt with as the child comes to a relatively mature level of syntax sometime usually between ages 4 and 7, are problems that are increasingly focused on pragmatic issues concerned with imagination, errors, and deliberate misrepresentations. The questions of interest to the child increasingly involve evaluations of the way things are, have been, might be in the future, and so forth.

Vigil and J. Oller (1976), borrowing a term from Selinker (1972), proposed a basis for the step-like advances seen in the syntactic development of infants learning their first language (L1) and also for similar developments in second language (L2) learners acquiring another language beyond their L1. That hypothesis aimed to explain why some L2 learners tend to plateau, to level off with a limited repertoire of words and especially syntactic and phonological systems. This process in the L2 literature was termed **fossilization**. The idea proposed was that fossilization tends to occur at the level where all the communication needs of the L2 learner are being satisfied. That is, when the learner reaches the place where all the communication demands are being met, the learner has no remaining incentive to advance further. For instance, as soon as a lecturer at the college level, say, a Pakistani teaching mathematics, who can say everything he or she wants to say in English (an L2 for the teacher) so that what is said seems to be understood by the students, has little reason to advance further in English. Why bother to advance to the level of passing, for instance, as a native speaker of the L2? What is the need? However, a professional spy, say someone who is working in the pharmaceutical industry, or for a cosmetics company, or for the Russian KGB or the American CIA, may have higher communication demands. The spy may work harder at trying to eradicate every trace of a foreign accent. A gas station attendant or hair dresser, by contrast with the spy, may have lesser communication demands and can be expected to plateau at a lower level of proficiency in the L2.

Interestingly, the principle underlying fossilization in L2 learners, also helps to explain why normal L1 learners do not usually level off and fossilize at any of the lower sign levels along the way. They progress up through the various levels of sign systems in the hierarchy until they achieve what Chomsky (1965) referred to as the **intuitions of the ideal native speaker**. They tend to keep going until they are indistinguishable from the run of the mill adult native speakers of whatever L1 they happen to be acquiring. When Chomsky chose the term "ideal" native speaker, although he was severely criticized for this choice of words, he did not evidently mean "perfect" or "flawless," but he meant rather something more like "the theoretically typical or average" native speaker. To the extent that there is such a communal target of language proficiency that is achieved by normal adults, L1 learners who reach it (or approximate it) must theoretically come to a limit of diminishing returns for their efforts to acquire the syntax of their L1. This limit will be attained as soon as the child is able to express essentially all the meanings that the child has need of expressing to other language users in the L1 community. As soon as the child is able to get his or her meaning across to others without any significant loss of whatever the child is trying to accomplish, the learning of syntactic complexities will come to the limit of diminishing returns. It is not a definite boundary, but it is nonetheless real although it is not a fixed point. It is widely agreed by child language specialists that most normal children achieve syntactic maturity in their L1, or very nearly all the syntax they will ever acquire, roughly between the ages of 4 and 7 years, give or take a year or two.

Summing Up and Looking Ahead

After the child reaches the stage of the zero order predicate, syntactic advances provide for richer and more complex predicate combinations. The essential problem is how are the predicates of the target language connected with their argument(s) and with each other. There are three evident kinds of advances that occur:

> ■ For one, many additional hypostatic predicates will be added to the child's receptive and productive repertoires. This kind of expansion within systems may be considered a kind of **lateral development**. It results in a continuing increase in the breadth of the child's vocabulary. If we think in terms of the ideas that the child can express and understand, the growth involves both *comprehension* and **comprehensiveness**. That is, the child becomes able to refer to a greater variety of arguments with a greater variety of predicates. The child's vocabulary is increasing in its comprehensiveness. It applies to a greater variety of possible referents. An example of this sort of lateral growth would be the addition of many more zero order predicates. For instance, after the child can use words like "mama," "hot," "bye-bye" and the like, hundreds of additional words of this sort will also be added to the child's

repertoires. But higher predicates will also grow in number once they are established, so lateral growth combines with the next two kinds of growth to produce an exponential increase in the child's power to understand and represent meanings through the developing linguistic signs. Learning produces an increasing power to learn more.

■ Another kind of learning occurs as the predicates in the repertoires are enriched by being modified by higher order predicates. In other words, lower order predicates enter into relations of a higher order that are indicated in predicates of predicates. This kind of growth in the child's syntactic capabilities can be considered a kind of **vertical development** both upward and outward. The expansion that this kind of vertical growth allows is not only additive, but also multiplicative. For instance, when predicates that modify other predicates are incorporated in two, three, and higher word sequences, the number of possible combinations grows exponentially. For instance, if the child has a vocabulary, say, of 10 zero order predicates and adds just one predicate that can modify each of these, the higher predicate increases the repertoire not by 1 but by 10. If 10 higher order predicates of predicates were added to modify those 100 combinations, the result would be 1,000 new possible combinations. As the length of sequences that the child can manage increases the number of combinations rises increasingly rapidly until the number of combinations the child can understand and produce, by about age 7, becomes so vast that linguists commonly refer to it, for practical purposes, as infinite (Chomsky, 1957, 1965; Pinker, 1994).

■ A third kind of growth occurs within the predicate systems that the child has already acquired. That is, increasingly subtle subsystems are incorporated within existing sign systems. For instance, in learning English, the child will distinguish *plural* and **possessive markers** on nouns. Subsystems of pronouns of various sorts will be acquired and marked for **grammatical person**, **grammatical number**, and **grammatical gender**. In English, the child will begin to differentiate person, number, tense, and aspect, in verbs. As these systems within systems are added to the child's repertoire, many additional subtleties of predicate to predicate and predicate to argument relations will be differentiated. These kinds of developments of systems within systems can be considered a kind of intensive vertical growth. Linguists typically refer to these kinds of developments as morphological (Brown, 1973) but they involve crucial pragmatic distinctions as well. For instance, to distinguish "the dog barks" from "the dogs bark," requires noticing whether one or more than one dog is barking. The question from a child's point of view involves noticing the relations between predicates relative to each other and relative to their arguments.

After the child reaches the limit of diminishing returns sometime between years 4 and 7, attention shifts away from syntactic development to what are essentially pragmatic problems. The child shifts the focus from the relatively unprofitable expansion that is still possible in the syntax of the language to its relatively richer and practically more valuable pragmatic aspects. What kinds of statements and linguistic behaviors are appropriate to different situations? What assertions are true? What is the difference between fact and fiction, between imagination and reality, between correct representations and errors, between innocent mistakes and deliberate misrepresentations? The child's attention, as we will see in Chapter 9, turns to pragmatics.

STUDY AND DISCUSSION QUESTIONS

1. Why is it, according to the theory of abstraction, that the child's attention turns to syntax soon after the so-called "vocabulary spurt"?

2. In what ways are bodily objects distinct from the words that may be used to refer to or signify those objects?

3. What are some of the crucial properties of the normal child's typical "first words"? Why do those particular properties have the impact that they do on the acquisition of the words that commonly keep popping up as "first words"?

4. What is the difference between what may be called the "token" or "surface-form" of a word, or any linguistic sign, and the word itself? Why isn't the word completely identical with its surface-forms or tokens?

5. How can we tell the difference between holophrasis in the speech forms of a child and the two-word stage of development?

6. What are some of the main differences between being and being represented?

7. What arguments pro or con can you think of concerning the idea that children are beginning to move toward adult grammars or norms

from their first words? Recall the arguments pertaining to the interpretation of emotions? Are there parallels here? Is it reasonable to suppose that a child differentiates the basis for verbs and nouns at the two-word stage? Why or why not?

8. Consider the role of deixis in second order predicates. What demonstrations show that deixis is problematic from the young child's point of view?

9. What is the difference between exogenous syntactic developments and endogenous ones?

10. Does fossilization play a role in normal L1 acquisition? What about the boundaries that separate babbling from the level of the first words? Do the child's first words differ significantly phonologically and otherwise from forms that will enter the linguistic repertoires a year or so later? What, if any, are the salient differences?

CHAPTER 9

Essential Pragmatic Problems Are Solved by Children

By studying this chapter you will:

1. Review the difference between semantic and pragmatic meaning and see why all meanings must be grounded in reference of the pragmatic sort;

2. Consider distinct pragmatic functions of language such as requesting, asserting, denying, questioning, exclaiming, describing, complaining, and so forth;

3. See the formal differences between facts as contrasted with fictions, errors, and lies;

4. Understand why the content and representational systems for producing fictions, errors, and lies must be abstracted from prior representations of facts;

5. Understand how and why children progress in their comprehension from facts to fictions, fictions to errors, and from errors to lies in exactly this order;

6. Get to know the Gricean maxims and some of their implications for communication and child language development; and

7. Understand the limit of abstraction that is encountered at any normal level of adult maturity.

KEY TERMS

Here are some terms and concepts that you may learn more about in this chapter (these are also defined in the Glossary):

behaviorism

connectedness

determinacy

exemplar

general limit of abstraction

generalizability

Grice's maxims

inferential implication

maxim of manner

maxim of quality

maxim of quantity

maxim of relevance

nonprimary language

past morpheme

presupposition

semantic association

sincerity maxim

theory of markedness

true narrative representation

truth maxim

In this chapter the primary focus is on pragmatic growth. After the child somewhere between the ages of 4 and 8 reaches the limit of diminishing returns with respect to syntactic growth, attention turns increasingly to questions concerning the pragmatic consequences of different representations. Children at this age not only become more interested in working out what people mean by what they say, but also in understanding social relationships. Children devote considerable attention and energy to what others say and what they mean by what they say. By this time children distinguish more sharply between pretense and reality. They are able to talk about whether a given representation is true or not of certain facts. They are becoming increasingly able to discuss the meanings of words, to talk about the intentions of others, and to consider whether or not certain representations are true or false, appropriate or inappropriate, good or bad. By about age 7 or 8, children are able to distinguish an innocent error from a deliberate lie. In this chapter we consider the underpinnings of these developments.

From Syntax to Inferences Grounded in Pragmatics

In the preceding chapter, we made the case that simple building blocks consisting of predicate-argument systems can be used to develop much more complex representational systems. The case is summarized nicely by Tomasello (1992):

> Much of the subsequent grammatical development of children may be seen as the acquisition of more and more adult-like ways for marking argument slots . . . and for filling these slots with ever more complex linguistic material such as noun phrases, complement clauses, and even entire sentences. . . . In the current view, none of these require anything other than the basic cognitive processes involved in the learning and development of verb argument structures (pp. 28–29).

As the child solves the syntax toward a limit of diminishing returns, attention turns more and more to pragmatic questions concerning the ideas and intentions of other persons, and concerning the abstract meanings of the forms of discourse. What inferences can be drawn from those forms? In figuring out surface-forms used by someone else, the child must first determine what the forms themselves are. How are they different from each other? This question addresses the fundamentals of phonology, morphology, lexicon, and syntax. Also, what do the forms mean? This is the fundamental question of semantics. It is dealt with every time a word is added to the child's receptive or productive lexicon. It is also dealt with as the child proceeds to the formation of the first, second, and third order predicate-argument systems. Secondarily, the child is also concerned with what the surface-forms are about in particular. With what persons are they associated? Who is talking, writing, or signing to whom? And what about? There is the question of what facts are being referred to, if any, and how are those facts regarded? Are they good or bad? Do they make us happy or sad? The last several questions are mainly about pragmatic meanings.

As soon as the child begins to see how zero order predicates can combine with higher order predicates, the problem of meaning is greatly enriched by the complexities introduced through syntactic combinations of predicate-argument systems. What begins to emerge is a rich repertoire of first, second, and higher order predicates. By the time the child begins to approach the syntactic limit of diminishing returns where the benefits of adding new syntactic complexities begin to fall off rapidly, it naturally follows that the child will come more and more to attend to questions concerning pragmatics. This is not to say that lexical acquisition stops when the child moves from the simplest syntax of zero order predicates to higher predicates, but rather to say that when the fundamental problem of the zero order predicate is solved, the child can begin to attend to the way predicates of that level combine to form predicate systems of higher levels. In fact, vocabulary acquisition continues throughout the lifespan. However, once the syntax of the target language is worked out to a degree of complexity where the child is able to express essentially all the meanings that the child needs or wants to express, there is less and less incentive to continue to build more complex syntactic systems. Later, the child will invariably come to a syntactic limit of diminishing returns, as we saw in the previous chapter. At that limit, attention will turn more and more to pragmatic issues at the same time as the child is still advancing in lexical knowledge. During that phase of development, the child will raise the bar and begin to consider issues that pertain to increasingly complex and more abstract questions of pragmatics.

When the child is able not only to play the "language games" but also to "play and win" (that is, to comprehend and to be comprehended by others) then attention to surface-forms as such comes to a natural limit. As soon as the child discovers, imitates, and is able to produce the conventional surface-forms of any bit of discourse, the child is ready to move on to other concerns. Recall the requirements development psychologists and cognitive linguists have applied to identifying first words as contrasted with babbling. The form used has to be distinct and recognizable. The first word must sound, or in the case of manual signing it must look, different from babbled forms. The word has to be applied in a conventional way. And, it has to generalize to other contexts. It is not enough for the child to call the dog *Nunu* on just one occasion, but the word has to be used in similar ways across occasions and in different contexts to which it is appropriate. Once all these concerns have been met, what else is there?

It turns out that there is the vast world of pragmatic concerns where the child finds him or herself at risk because of factors that need to be represented correctly to achieve desired goals and to avoid harm while doing so. The problem is not merely what do words mean, in other words, what are the conventions of their use, but when they are used meaningfully how do they actually relate to the facts of experience?

The Role of Truth

For many years, roughly from 1933 until about the middle 1970s, it was unpopular for American linguists to even speak of meaning, much less of truth. These ideas were left to philosophers. The meaning-shyness of the whole period was partly owed to the emphasis of people like J. B. Watson (1925), Leonard Bloomfield (1933), and B. F. Skinner (1957, 1971/2002) on the material side of experience. All these individuals argued that attention should be paid to the observable behavior of organisms. For this reason they are called *behaviorists* and their method of thinking and research, **behaviorism**.

Skinner (1957, 1971) went so far as to argue that concepts such as mind and meaning, and even freedom and dignity, needed to be rethought in terms of a nonindividualistic, material, and behavioral perspective. He argued that freedom of the will and moral responsibility are old ideas that need to be replaced with more modern, less individualistic concepts. We could say that theories of behaviorism have emphasized the material realm of the senses more than the abstract realm of the mind. For a good long while it was taboo to speak of meaning in theories of learning and especially in American linguistics. Some of the more radical claims of behaviorism were challenged in a celebrated review by Noam Chomsky (1959) of Skinner's book *Verbal Behavior*. A year earlier, in a less well-known review, the philosopher Charles W. Morris (1958), if possible, had written an even more critical complaint against Skinner titled: "Words without meaning: A review of Skinner's *Verbal Behavior*."

Still, it was not until about the 1960s that anything more than a handful of psychologists, philosophers, and linguists began to argue for the reinstatement of the study of the meanings of words. In 1975 the Berkeley philosopher H. P. Grice took another giant step and indirectly, at least, reintroduced the concept of truth along with meaning into what was destined to become mainstream thinking. Grice argued that ordinary conversation, and by implication, communication in general depends on following, more or less, four basic rules or what he called **maxims**. Because Grice was the first author to put these rules into words in just the way he did, they are called **Grice's maxims** or the "Gricean Maxims." There are four of them:

1. There is what is known as the **maxim of quantity**: this
   is the notion that what we say should be as informative as
   necessary but not more so. In other words, we should not

exceed the limit of diminishing returns in the syntactic complexity of what we say.

2. There is the **maxim of quality**: that we should not say anything we know to be false or anything concerning which we have insufficient knowledge of its truth or falsehood. This one might have been called the **truth maxim** but that term was avoided by Grice. A widely cited contemporary philosopher, Davidson (1996), wrote a substantial argument saying why he thinks it is a futile exercise to even try to define truth. Perhaps the same sentiment is involved in the fact that instead of the truth maxim, the quality maxim is often called the **sincerity maxim**. But being sincere at least means aiming to tell the truth or at least trying not to assert or imply anything that is known to be false, that is, known not to be true.

3. There is also the **maxim of relevance**: Whatever is said should be relevant, that is, related to the issue(s) under consideration in the present conversation.

4. There is the **maxim of manner**: that we should avoid being obscure, ambiguous (deliberately incorporating expressions that can be taken in more than one way), wordy, or beating around the bush.

It is interesting, and worth noting, that children in acquiring languages are bound to follow Grice's rules fairly closely, without ever knowing them. In fact, Dale and Reiter (1995) have argued from a computational perspective that Grice's rules are implicit in the systems that we call referring terms (zero order predicates and complications of them). That is, the way referring phrases and predicate-argument systems are built up virtually demands that the Gricean maxims will be more or less adhered to. For example, the quantity maxim is entailed, and logically required as an outcome, by the limit of diminishing returns on the use and acquisition of syntax. The whole argument can be summed up in a single rhetorical question, in other words, one that has an obvious answer: Why, for instance, would a child or any language user build up syntactic structures that are more complex than the ones required to express the child's intended meaning fully and in a satisfactory way? The answer is that children don't normally make their communications more complex than needed. At least they do not do so intentionally, and, in general, language users are not rewarded for being overly complicated. As a rule, children just don't make things more complex than needed.

Next, take the sincerity or truth maxim. If we ask what kind of representational systems are defined by all the requirements that have been placed on the child's first word, we will discover that they are essentially the same as the requirements that must be met if an assertion of any given predicate is to be judged *true* of any given argument or context of situation. In fact, it can be strictly proved by exact and rigorous logic that in acquiring their first meaningful words, that is, the first zero order predicates, children are absolutely dependent on uses of those forms in contexts where they are applied in appropriate ways according to their usual conventions. For instance, for Peter DeVilliers to learn the name of the dog NUNU (let the capital letters stand for the physical dog rather than the name of that dog), the word *Nunu* (where the lower case italicized letters stand for the name rather than the dog), it was essential for other interlocutors to use that name in appropriate ways as applied to that particular dog. Imagine the difficulty Peter would have faced if any and all syllable sequences were randomly applied to the dog NUNU, and the word, *Nunu*, had been applied to all possible objects, events, and relations imaginable. How would Peter ever have discovered the dog's name? Or, worse still, how would any language user discover the dog's name? Or worse yet again, how could the dog have a name, or how could any language whatever exist? The answers to all these questions are negative. They wouldn't, couldn't, and therefore don't. As a result, Grice's truth maxim is a logical requirement. It is a prerequisite to the existence of any languages, and therefore to their meaningful use and/or acquisition.

Why have theoreticians shied away from the term "truth," preferring an expression like "not false" instead (as Grice did)? Ordinarily, philosophers, linguists, and other theoreticians might be reluctant to call the most ordinary uses of referring terms, or zero order predicates, "true" because these uses seem to reduce "truth" itself to such a mundane and trivial level. However, the name of a dog, as applied in acts referring to that dog, is as true as the use of any predicate can ever be. This follows from the fact that a name, say, *Nunu*, as applied to the dog, NUNU, has no other purpose in relation to the dog than to signify or refer to that dog. So, if the name is used to call the dog, to refer to the dog, or to represent qualities of the dog, or when someone is playing with the dog, to ask about the dog, to complain about the dog, or in any activity that in any way involves the dog, the name fulfills its whole reason for being. The name of the dog has no uses, as a predicate applied to that particular argument, that would be more appropriate or truer than the kinds of uses just described. Therefore, it turns out that children are utterly dependent on true uses of zero order predicates in relation to the arguments of those predicates (which may consist of activities, for example, saying "bye-bye" while waving good-bye or saying "hmaa" while kissing someone) to begin to unpack their meanings.

If it were not for **exemplars** of the surface-forms of any target language being used in relation to suitable ongoing activities relevant to the experience of the child, it would be impossible, for reasons already made clear with respect to Peter and NUNU, for anyone to be able to acquire any language. This constraint also holds for the acquisition of any **nonprimary language** as well (see Chapter 10). As a result, it is clear that Grice's relevance maxim is a requirement contained in his truth maxim. The truth maxim absolutely guarantees the relevance maxim. A predicate cannot be truly applied at all, to anything, unless it is somehow relevant in its application.

Finally, there is the manner maxim. Logically speaking it is clear that this maxim merely sums up what has already been said or implied by earlier maxims. It adds nothing new. Consider the fact that being obscure, ambiguous, wordy, or beating around the bush, is to violate the quantity maxim, and the relevance maxim. What is more, if the truth (sincerity) maxim is adhered to, that is if the conversationalist does not say anything false, and does not say more than is necessary, how would it be possible to beat around the bush or to be obscure or ambiguous? Any of the latter alternatives would involve saying more than what is necessary. As a result, the manner maxim is redundant and as we have seen the other three are natural outcomes of ordinary language acquisition. They merely summarize conditions that must be met, more or less, if there are to be any language systems at all.

Succinctly put, the truth maxim guarantees the remaining three Gricean maxims. The truth maxim requires (1) representing things so that others can understand us; (2) representing things truthfully to the best of our knowledge; and (3) representing things that are relevant. Although it is true that these maxims are valid summaries of certain aspects of how languages are used and even acquired, as we will see in what follows, Grice's rules by themselves would fail to account for the kinds of representational acts that a normal eight-year-old can perform. To account for the full range of language abilities that adults are able to develop, we must look well beyond the Gricean maxims.

The Special Place of True Narrative Representations

In addition to the fact that the naïve infant absolutely must rely on true uses of relatively simple predicates in acquiring his or her first words, it is also obvious that children rely on true uses of predicates that are connected to and relevant to the infant's own experience. For instance, in learning the word "Nunu," Peter DeVilliers was motivated by his interest in the dog NUNU and by the recurrent experience involving both the dog and the word. True uses of the word in relation to the dog have a couple of other interesting logical properties in addition to their mundane variety of truth. They are also necessarily part of the unfolding experience of the child as it develops over time. The uses in question form part of the child's own developing story. As a result the language uses that enable the child to figure out the first meaningful words are invariably part of the unfolding story that constitutes the child's experience over time. That is, the first words, the zero order predicates, are always parts of a narrative-like sequence of events. For instance, say, the child's first word happens to be the name of the dog. This was the case for the second author of this book.

How did it come about that he happened to discover the meaning of the word, *Chester*? Almost every evening without fail, his father would put the dog out. Later, dad would go to the door and call the dog to bring him in the house, and later put him in the garage overnight. The repeated activities involved an object of great interest to the child. It involved the dog, CHESTER. It also involved a word that was repeated many times in the hearing of the child, the word, *Chester*. The events involving the calling of the dog, putting the dog in the garage, bringing him in the house, putting him in the car, getting him out of the car, looking for him when he was lost, feeding the dog, and so on, were not only salient but also frequent events. Some of these events could occur several times on the same day and some were repeated every day. Each of these events had a high level of predictability. Each event was part of a familiar narrative-like story that the child was familiar with already. This kind of familiarity, when added to frequency of occurrence, saliency, and relevance of the word to be acquired provides an optimal setting for learning. It meets all of Grice's requirements.

It also defines certain necessary conditions without which normal language acquisition cannot occur at all. For language acquisition to proceed at all, it is essential for the child to have access to true representations that are fitted into a meaningful narrative-like sequence of experience. That is, the child has to have access to activities of the sort that involve the use of signs to be acquired and the signs have to be appropriately applied in those contexts. Without exposure to such data, the child could not acquire any zero order predicates whatever. The child requires access to true uses of conventional signs to discover those conventions. However, true uses of the required kind only occur in association with narrative-like event sequences. Therefore, language acquisition requires exposure to what we have called **true narrative representations** (TNRs; see J. Oller et al., 2005). These are narratives, or narrative-like representations of someone's actual experience, that are true (as far as they go) to the experience represented. They must consist at least of a sequence of perceptions at their basis and they may be linked with linguistic predicates as in a true story or a faithful report of a sequence of events. The logical form of such sign systems involves three elements that are systematically and dynamically interrelated. These elements include:

1. The surface-form of the representation itself, for example, the surface-form of a predicate;

2. An accessible icon or percept of any arguments which any predicates in the surface-form may refer or which they may signify; and

3. A noticeable action or complex sequence of actions associating and connecting the representation with the logical object(s) represented.

These elements are familiar. For instance, all three elements can be seen in Figure 3-3 and in Figures 4-4, 4-5, and 4-7. However, for the purposes of this chapter, it will be useful to abbreviate the three elements of any TNR by using S for the sign or predication, π, for the pragmatic actions and inferences that connect it with its logical object(s) or argument(s), and O for the object(s) as shown in Figure 9-1.

The figure summarizes the action of Brenden taking an adult by the hand and leading him or her to the table where Thomas the train engine and his train engine friends, Edward, Gordon, Percy, and so on, are set up with their tracks, tenders (coal cars), and other paraphernalia. Brenden's common approach, from about age 26 months was to take the adult by the hand and say, "Pay ___, pay!" where the blank could be filled with any referring term, for example, Ruthie, Mimi, Nana, Pop, Dada, and so on, and the word "pay" was understood to mean "Let's play trains" or "Let's play ___" where Brenden would clarify his plan by leading the adult to the appropriate location getting them to sit down, in a chair, on the floor, or whatever, and then by proceeding to play. Often, Brenden would lead the adult to his little train table at Mimi's house and proceed to hand over one of the engines, disconnect some tracks, put the cars together, and so on.

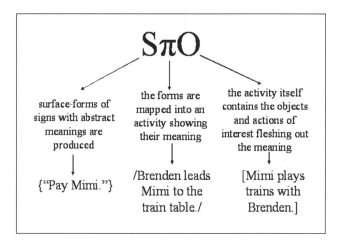

Figure 9–1. The abstract structure underlying activity-based, ordinary true and appropriate conventional linguistic representations.

Or, he might get the adult to sit on the floor and he would bring his colors and a book and proceed to scribble great works of art. Notice that in all these cases, the surface-forms of words used in the activities were embedded in the activity as Tomasello (1992) emphasized in reference to what he called "presymbolic" uses.

Using our notational system, as seen in Figure 9–1, we can sum up the formal structure underlying any TNR system of signs as consisting of at least a triad: SπO. The S may be a single predicate like "hmmaa" as a sign embedded in the act of kissing someone; the O may be the act of one person making a kissing gesture, or, say, mom or dad kissing the baby, or dad kissing mom; and the π may be the act of uttering the S in conjunction with the activity designated by O. However, to have a well-formed, complete, TNR, it is essential that all three elements be present in the system. When they are all present the discovery of the conventional meaning of S is possible even by an infant who does not yet know the S in question. In fact, without such associations it is obvious that the infant has no way whatever of discovering the convention in question. Even if the child were smart enough to guess the convention without any appropriate data, to test the inferred convention, for instance, "I think *hmmaa* is about kissing," the child would have to produce or otherwise discover exemplars of other persons performing acts of kissing in conjunction with uttering the word *hmmaa*.

Surprisingly, TNRs are the only kind of representations that have the property of **determinacy**. That is, TNRs enable the child to find out the conventional meanings of words that are unknown to the child beforehand. For instance, to find out the meaning of an abstract S it can be strictly proved that TNRs are required to enable the meaning to be bootstrapped, indexically tied, to appropriate referents consisting of persons, things, events, and activities. Also, TNRs provide the only source of access to the **connectedness** of actual events of experience. There are causal, temporal, spatial, and other kinds of connections. Generally the connections are represented in some way in perception, in thought, and in discourse. To know the connections between a cause and its effects, for instance, both must be represented. To represent both, it turns out that a TNR is required. For instance, to know that striking a ball with a bat causes it to fly through the air and break a windshield on someone's car, the sequence of events must be represented in the way a narrative unfolds. Also, to be able to generalize the meaning of any S to new appropriate occasions, it is essential to have access to at least one or more appropriate uses of that S. It turns out that every such use is a TNR and that only TNRs have the required logical property of **generalizability**. That is, TNRs can be generalized to all similar situations exactly to the extent of the similarity across the situations. For instance, a child may notice that a dog's cold wet nose can be compared to the color and texture of hollow black olives laid side by side in a plate of salad.

There is no way to manifest a conventional use of a sign except by using the sign in just that conventional way (or describing the use in other conventional signs in a way that shows or manifests the convention). One way or another, the child must get access to the conventional uses of signs to acquire any language or language variety. To do so requires the production of one or more TNRs. In fact, in this respect, the acquisition of any nonprimary language, that is, a second language or a foreign language, abbreviated as "L2," is not different. While the acquisition of any L2 by an adult, say, is different in many respects from primary language acquisition by a child, abbreviated as "L1" acquisition, both L1 and L2 acquisition require access to **exemplars** of the surface-forms of the target language being applied according to the conventions of the target language in known contexts of experience. If these exemplars are missing, language acquisition simply cannot take place.

From True Representations of Facts to Imagined Fictions

Children acquiring their L1 will typically begin to understand their first words (hypostatic symbols) at around the time they begin canonical babbling. For instance, when a baby at only 9 months shows complete comprehension of multiple printed words (see the demonstration for Aleka at http://www.infantlearning.com/videoclips.html visited January 29, 2006; also see Aleka and Other Early Readers on the *Milestones Student DVD-ROM*) the baby is clearly operating with true narrative representations. That is, the surface-form of the printed word is being mapped correctly, appropriately, and truthfully (in the most mundane sense of the word) onto the appropriate body parts as can be seen in the video. When Aleka's dad shows and says the printed word "teeth," Aleka gestures vigorously and repeatedly with her pointing finger to her mouth. She babbles, it seems, [adada]. When the word on the card says "foot" she grabs one of her feet, and so forth. At around the time of the first birthday, within a few weeks or months (plus or minus), the normal child will go on to initiate and produce his or her first zero order predicates. These predicates also, to the extent that they are recognizable, appropriate to the immediate context, and generalized across different occasions and similar contexts, are invariably TNRs. That is to say, the first meaningful words applied by the child will be applied in the course of activities unfolding over time (narrative-like experiences) to which those words are appropriate and true in the most mundane sense of the word. This is all that is meant by the term TNR.

It will take about another year, or somewhat longer, before the normal child will be able to handle imagined fictions. Let us consider why it has to take longer for the child to come to be able to represent imagined fictions. The underlying structure of a fictional representation, as contrasted with a

TNR, involves relaxing the requirement that the logical object, O, of the sign, S, be real. It only has to be imagined. For instance, suppose that a certain object has been moved from its former location. Say, we take a toy train engine, or a doll, or some object of interest, out of a cabinet, and put it in a drawer. How will the young child who observes this action be able to represent the former location of the object in the cabinet? It is no longer there, so that representation is not now a TNR representing a present factual state of affairs, but requires the use of the imagination (and memory) to recall the object where it was located earlier. Now it is in the closed drawer where we just put it and the cupboard where it was located before is empty of that object. To represent the object as it used to be, when it was in the cupboard, the child must imagine the referent. A TNR representation of where the object now is would require something like "Train drawer," meaning "The train is in the drawer" (if we translate the meaning into adult English).

But how will the child represent the situation of the train formerly in the cupboard? A statement like, "Train drawer" could be verified by looking into the drawer. But to represent the train in the cabinet, where it was before it was moved, would require a similar sequence of predicates, for example, "Train cabinet." Although it is true that the train was in the cabinet a short while ago, to verify this statement we (the child too) will have to consult recent memory. If we look in the cabinet now, we will not find the train in question there because it has been moved. In the statement "Train cabinet" the train must be imagined to be in the cabinet. As a result to understand any statement about the past, or the future, some part of the logical object to be represented must be imagined. In the case at hand, a primary referent, the train, which is the focal object of the predication, "Train cabinet," must be imagined. We have a structure that involves a fiction. That is, the train is not now in the cabinet but has been in the cabinet in the past. To understand the meaning of the assertion about the train that is now in the drawer, we have to imagine it in the cabinet. The general systematic structure of any representation involving a fictional element (no matter how complex the structure may be) involves imagining some aspect of the logical object, O that is represented in the sign, S. We can represent such a structure simply as $S\pi\underline{O}$ where the underlining shows that the object, or some aspect of it, must be imagined. That is, the train that is now in the drawer must be imagined to be in the cabinet.

We must predict that the representation of any fictional case, $S\pi\underline{O}$, as contrasted with the simpler TNR, $S\pi O$, will require more cognitive work. If all else is kept equal, a fictional structure is what linguists call a more marked structure according to the **theory of markedness** (Bailey, 1973, 1996) than a factual TNR. Simply put, marking is added to an existing sign and makes it more complex. In our notational system (see J. Oller, 2005; J. Oller et al., 2005) the underlining of the $\underline{O}$ in any fictional representation is an added "mark." It is intended simply to show that the O in this case is not contained in the factual context as would be the case for the less marked TNR, but rather the O must be imagined by the interpreter/producer of the fictional representation. The child cannot now discover the train in the cabinet, for instance, because in fact it is now in the drawer. Therefore, because fictions are more complex, children first learn TNRs which are the unmarked instances. Our theory predicts that acquisition of fictional structures must take longer, and in fact, it does.

Carpenter, Call, and Tomasello (2002) discussed several variations of an experimental paradigm similar to the one described above in studies of normally developing young children. Two experimenters, E1 and E2, are present with the child when a certain object is placed in a certain location, say in a cabinet, in view of all three parties. Then the door to the cabinet is closed and E2 leaves the room. Next, E1 invites the child to help him or her play a trick on E2 by moving the object from say, the cabinet to the drawer (or the reverse). They move the object to the drawer and close it. When E2 comes back into the room and says that he or she is looking for the concealed object, the question is whether the child thinks E2 will look for the object where E2 last saw it before leaving the room, in the cabinet (its former location), or if the child will expect E2 to look for the object where it is now, in the drawer. In fact, normally developing children prior to the age of 35 months, give or take a few months, tended to look to the present location rather than the one that E2 had last experienced. These normally developing children seemed to expect E2 to look to the new location of the object, which E1 and the child know about but E2 does not yet know about, rather than for E2 to look to the location where the object was when E2 left the room. Normal children before about age 3 tend to default to the present known location of the object. Carpenter et al., attributed this finding to what they called "the pull of the real" (p. 393ff). We would call it a tendency to default to TNRs over fictions.

In other words, the child, before about age 3, relies on the factual situation as represented in a simple TNR. In our terms, the child resorts to the unmarked SπO construction rather than the more marked and abstract SπO̅ fiction that the other person should be expected to have in mind. Only about a third of the children prior to age 3 evidently took the fictional possibility into consideration and looked to the cabinet. Unmarked referential constructions, TNRs, precede and form the basis for the more marked fictional ones. Although a TNR involves a relatively complete act of reference to an object through its percept, a fictional representation requires the imagination of the O. But how can the child imagine something prior to representing it? It follows that the act of imagining a certain object is dependent to a very high degree on prior perceptions of that same object.

The sign-user who interprets (or constructs) the fiction must imagine the O because that O is not present to be perceptually consulted as it would be in any TNR. Worse yet, what if the S is of unknown content? S cannot help the sign-user to determine the content of the fictional O. The formal structure of a fiction, therefore, provides a poor basis for enabling the child to decipher unknown words and provides another demonstration of the fact that pragmatic bootstrapping is necessary. To figure out the meanings of any unknown predicates the child must at some point and in some way ground those predicates in TNRs. Other researchers, for example, Putnam (1975) and Barsalou (2005) have reached much the same conclusion. Barsalou notes that any description whatever of a category will never by itself "be sufficient to fix the category's reference" (p. 27). That is, if we want to know just exactly which train is in the drawer, was in the drawer, or will later be in the drawer, we need to get access to the train itself.

Because any fiction of the form SπO requires additional work to enable the conjuring of an imaginary O, it follows that ordinary successful acts of reference, SπO, must be acquired before any fictions. It should also be noted that the only guide for conjuring any fiction has to be found in whatever Ss it may contain. Thus, fictions cannot provide the basis for discovering the meanings of unknown Ss (see J. Oller, 2005). It follows, all else being equal, that it should be easier to learn concepts, procedures, and the like as instantiated in ordinary truthful descriptions, reports, and stories than in fictions. This is because fictional discursive structures require their producers and interpreters to conjure some of the objects, events, and situations, by imagining them rather than perceiving them.

Fictional narratives, all else being equal, will be more difficult to process in language acquisition and in discourse processing in general than TNRs. In theory, the more marked form involves additional structure and thus requires more cognitive work to construct or to comprehend. For instance, the word *marked* consists of the verb *mark* plus the **past morpheme** *ed*. When we add the *ness* to the form *marked*, as in *markedness*, the resulting representation is more marked still. Applying the theory of markedness to fictional structures as contrasted with ordinary TNRs, or any appropriate acts of reference, it follows that TNRs, if all else is held equal, will be easier to process. For example, consider the difference between understanding a reference to an actual horse, say, when a real horse is being pointed out as contrasted with the cognitive work needed to conjure a fictional unicorn. Perception can help us to understand the remark about the present horse, but to deal with an imaginary unicorn, we need to conjure a horse with something like a goat's horn in its forehead. The O of any fictional SπO triad requires one or more steps of abstraction than are required in the case of any unmarked referential SπO triad. Ordinarily, of course, fictions are not taken to be true, so they do not result in any error. Also they are not intended to deceive anyone so they are not lies. When the child in the Carpenter et al. paradigm expects E2 to look in the cabinet where the train was before E2 left the room, the child correctly understands a fictional possibility. The child makes no error. If E2 actually believed that the train was in the former location, from which it has been moved, an error would be committed.

Moving on from Fictions to Representing Errors and Lies

In fact, whenever a fiction is mistaken for an unmarked TNR, the outcome is an error. It turns out that the formal structure of an error is even more marked than that of a fiction. Suppose, for instance, we think we see a certain friend approaching but it turns out to be someone else. We might think, "Here comes Nancye," but it turns out to be JUDITH. The S, *Nancye*, is associated with the wrong O, JUDITH, not NANCYE, and the O that is represented, NANCYE, is not the O at hand, which in fact is JUDITH. As a result, two elements of the basic formal triad, the S and the O, are fictionalized and filled out incorrectly. To represent the underlying systematic structure of any such error, we may write $\underline{S}\pi\underline{\cancel{O}}$. In this notation, the underlining shows the fictionalization of the S and the O, and the strike through shows that the S and O are mistaken. That is, in the example at hand, for the S we should have *Judith* and not *Nancye* and for the O we should have JUDITH and not NANCYE. Keeping in mind that the Ss are not the Os that they represent, it follows that errors are considerably more marked than fictions. In fact, every error involves the fictionalization of two elements, the S and the O. Each error also requires the replacement of both the S and the O to produce a TNR, for example, "Here comes Judith."

It follows that the ability to represent an error, provided all else is held equal, involves more work than is involved in representing a mere fiction. We must predict then, all else being equal, that errors of the form $\underline{S}\pi\underline{\cancel{O}}$ must be harder to comprehend than fictions, $S\pi\underline{O}$, or unmarked referential structures, $S\pi O$. These predictions can be read directly from the formal structures of the sign systems in question irrespective of any particular content or context. In normal child language development, we must predict that the child will need additional time to move from representing fictions as distinct from TNRs to representing errors, as distinct from TNRs and fictions. Of course, fictions are different from errors because fictions are not asserted as true. For instance, if we imagine an old-fashioned typewriter on the table in front of us this is not the same as supposing that we are in fact perceiving an old-fashioned typewriter on the table in front of us. Errors, by contrast with merely imagined fictions, are mistaken for TNRs. Errors conforming to the structure $\underline{S}\pi\underline{\cancel{O}}$ also, as we have already seen, are more complex Ss than are fictions which conform to the simpler structure, $S\pi\underline{O}$. In a fictional case, when an object is imagined where it was formerly but no longer is located, we do not suppose that the imagined object is real. We know it is imagined. Errors are different.

In an error some object X is confused with some other object Y. This is not the same as merely imagining X or imagining Y. Errors are therefore more complicated than fictions. Deliberate lies, however, are more complicated still. Errors are not intended to deceive the person who commits the error. Lies on the other hand are, by their very nature, intended to deceive. They also involve an additional error that the producer deliberately introduces and that the interpreter is invited by the producer to accept as a TNR. The additional problem in a lie involves the π mapping. This mapping is intentionally corrupted to get the consumer of the lie to mistake it for a TNR. Suppose for instance that a certain person, A, claims A has never met some other person B. However, it turns out that A and B have been lovers, or intimately involved on multiple occasions. The underlying systematic structure of any such lie can be shown as $\underline{S}\cancel{\pi}\underline{O}$. Here, as before, the underlining means that the element in question is fictionalized, and the strikeout means that the form in question is also in error. The difference, however, between an error and a lie is that in the intentional construction of a lie, the π mapping is deliberately fictionalized and also falsified. What is more, if the lie is to work at all as it is intended to work, it has to resemble a TNR.

Again it must be predicted that, all else being equal, it will be more difficult for children to learn to understand and produce lies than to understand and to represent errors. It is interesting that neither of these systematic structures can be understood at all unless it is compared against the contrasting TNR structure. To know that it is a lie that A is not the lover of B, we must discover the TNR that A is the lover of B. Similarly, if someone makes the error of supposing that NANCYE is approaching when in fact it is JUDITH, to discover the error fully it is essential to find out that the person approaching is, in fact, JUDITH. It follows that correct understanding of errors should not appear in the discourse of normal children until some time after fictions are correctly represented. Also, errors should be correctly represented and understood before lies.

These predictions have actually been borne out in an interesting study. Berthoud-Papandropoulou and Kilcher (2003) studied 60 children between the ages of 3 and 8. They were individually presented with the following scenario: A puppet called Mr. John carries a matchbox on stage and the experimenter asks, "What's in there?" Another puppet, Mary, says, "Matches." But when Mr. John opens the box there is a pencil inside. The formal construction of the error, $\underline{S}\pi\underline{O}$, involves an S (*matches*) that is not true of the O at hand, which should be referred to as a *pencil*, and the O, the PENCIL in the box, is not what was represented to be there, MATCHES.

To test understanding of Mary's error, a third puppet, Pierre is introduced. The question is, when he comes on stage, what will Pierre say is in the box? In their study, by age 4, about 35% of the children could predict and express Pierre's expected error correctly, 42% could do so by age 5, and 91% by age 6. At age 3 fewer than 10% of the children could express

Pierre's expected error. To test when children would become able to represent lying as distinct from an unintentional error, they asked the 60 children a further question: "When Mary said there were matches in the box, was she lying?" Up to age 6 the children generally took lying to mean holding any false belief (a mere error). After age 6, most of the children appealed to mental states (knowing, not knowing). In doing this, they were able to differentiate intentional misrepresentation $\cancel{S\cancel{\pi}\cancel{O}}$ from mistaken belief, $\cancel{S}\pi\cancel{O}$. Only one of the children, before age 6, could explain why Mary was not lying. The fact that children before age 6 generally failed at this task confirms the necessary prediction that comprehension of lies must come after the comprehension of errors.

Summing up the various experimental results just reviewed, consider the order of acquisition as predicted from the various representational systems involved. In fact, TNRs with the structure SπO, should be acquired first and they are at about 12 months, give or take two or three months. This development, as predicted, precedes the development of fictional representations, Sπ<u>O</u>, by about two years. Children do not seem to be able to understand or produce fictional representations until about age 3 (give or take a couple of months). Similarly, the representation of errors with the structure $\cancel{S}\pi\cancel{O}$ follows the representation of fictions by two or three more years, somewhere around age 4 to 6 (give or take a few months). The comprehension and ability to represent lies, with the structure, $\cancel{S\cancel{\pi}\cancel{O}}$, is not achieved until about two or three years after errors are handled, between ages 6 and 8.

From the formal properties of ordinary unmarked SπO sign systems as contrasted with fictions, errors, and lies certain other deductions follow. For one, ordinary referential triads are situated in the space–time episodes of actual experience. Because of this it is possible to use them as scaffolds to help the child figure out the meanings of other signs that are not yet known through what others have called syntactic and semantic bootstrapping. From the analysis we learn that the meanings of any Ss to be learned must be displayed in some manner through π mappings of Ss onto Os through social actions that reveal the conventional uses of the Ss (Halliday, 1978). It follows that fictional representations, errors, and lies (or any bits of uninterpretable nonsense) provide a poor basis for the teaching or learning of languages. Learners need access to appropriate (true) uses of the conventional Ss of a language to discover what those conventional uses are. There is simply no other way for the conventions to be found out. True and appropriate uses are essential.

The Adult Level of Mature Reasoning

It is not necessary, however, to be a rocket scientist to achieve linguistic maturity. One of the most amazing things observed by foreign language students is the fact that any normal child can accomplish the business of language acquisition. When the L2 student travels to a country where the target language that he or she has been struggling to acquire is spoken by little children, it never ceases to amaze. All language students are impressed. If we just turn that idea around and look at it from the other side we should realize just how impressive any human being is in having acquired an L1. What is more, these skills are typically achieved well before the language user is 20 years old. In fact, normal individuals master their first words by about the end of the first year of life. By age 3 they are able to distinguish play and pretense from ordinary talk about the real world, and sometime between 4 and 6 the normal child can discern errors and distinguish them from true representations. Sometime after age 6 the child becomes able to understand the difference between an error and a deliberate misrepresentation and sometime before 20 the normal individual can draw mature inferences about representations of various sorts.

For instance, the mature language user is able to differentiate many social and pragmatic functions of language forms in discourse. For instance, the mature user can differentiate a host of language functions:

- Assertions, for example, *That's an ashtray!*

- Questions, for example, *Is that an ashtray?*

- Requests, for example, *Bring me that ashtray.*

- Denials, for example, *That's not an ashtray.*

- And so on.

The mature user will know, for instance, that an assertion like, "It's getting cold in here," may actually imply that the speaker would like for the listener to close the window, turn up the heat, get her a sweater, or something of that sort. In fact, any surface-form may have almost any function. A statement may be used to pose a question. For instance, "She wouldn't do that!" meaning, "Would she?" Or, a question may be used to make a statement, "Would your mom have done that?," for example, may mean that she definitely would not (or would) have done whatever is in question. And so on. But mature language users are able to draw the right inferences, in other words, to understand the intentions of the speaker in many instances.

Drawing Inferences from Representations

What is more, from the sounds, intonations, and the words, phrases, and clauses of discourse, the child becomes able to infer many meanings that are not necessarily expressed in the surface-forms. These additional meanings come from inferences which are grounded in pragmatic perceptions that lead to fully general **semantic associations**. The fully general semantic sort of associations are inferences that apply across times and places. Although they originate in the real world they cross over into imagination and even apply to representations that point to unimaginable things, for example, a perfectly square circle. To illustrate what is meant by semantic associations, consider that the word *brick* ordinarily applies to an object that is heavy, oblong, used in building, and so forth. However, when we use the word *brick* we do not always mention what the brick is made of, the fact that it has a certain shape, size, weight, density, and so on. Instead we rely on the ability of our interlocutors to infer these generalized semantic attributes. These inferred meanings that are associated with discourse are essential if we are to make any sense of what is said. For instance, if someone asks us to close a certain door, we must suppose that the door is open at the time of the request. If the only door around happens to already be closed, we have trouble making sense of the request. This kind of inference, that the door must be open if we have been asked to close it, is called a **presupposition** because it applies to a state of affairs before the facts at hand. The door must be open before we can reasonably be asked to close it, so we presuppose that the door is open in interpreting the request to close it. A presupposition is the sort of inference that is prerequisite to our comprehension of a request or statement or any representation. If someone issues a warning or a threat, the act implies that whatever we are warned against doing, or whatever consequences may be threatened if we do whatever we are not supposed to do, must have some chance of occurring in the future. For instance, *Look out for that car!* implies the possibility of our being struck by the car. But it would be a strange statement if there were no car in the vicinity. For inferences that apply after the fact the term **inferential implication** is useful. Any warning implies some kind of impending danger or undesirable consequence to follow. In fact, there are uncountably many inferences associated with any meaningful abstract symbol and presuppositions, implications, and other general semantic associations can come into some interesting conflicts.

The different kinds of inferences grounded in experience of the real world through pragmatic perceptions of that world, elaborate the cycle of abstraction in an interesting way. As seen in Figure 9–2, perceptions lead to our ideas about what is going on in present experience. Perceptions, of course, are built up through acts of discrimination. From those same perceptions, memories are formed by prescission. By change over time, the present becomes the past and leads us to have both memory of what has come before and expectations about what will come after the present experience. Hypostatic generalization of symbols, however, enables us to draw inferences that apply not only to past, present, and future experience, but that also cross over to imagined experience and to our interpretations of signs in all their uses. Hypostasis of fully abstract symbols enables us to draw inferences to fantastic and even impossible worlds that can, however,

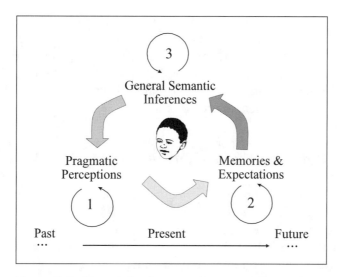

Figure 9–2. The relation between the stream of experience and inferences pertaining to the present, past, and future. Pragmatic (discriminated) perceptions lead to memories and expectations. As the present changes (is prescinded by memory and imagination into the past and future), general semantic inferences are enabled by (hypostatic) signs.

be represented in words, for example, we have difficulty imagining a perfectly square circle, but we can talk about such a fantastic idea even if it is beyond our imagination. We can talk about loud paint, a rational square root for the number 2, a perfectly even number pi, and so on.

Take an example next showing how inferences can come into conflict with each other. For example, suppose a judge in handing down a sentence says, *You are to be hanged at dawn. Let this be a warning to you!* Consider some of the inferences we might reasonably draw from this statement. Being hanged at dawn carries with it the implication that the person who is hanged, some presupposed prisoner, will be dead shortly afterward. Being warned by contrast carries the implication of an opportunity to repeat some offense. But persons cannot usually repeat any offenses of any kind after they have been hanged. It also carries the presupposition that the person being sentenced has been convicted of some crime. The judge's statement carries the semantic association that the prisoner is being sentenced to death. The fact that the sentence is a form of the death penalty carries the presupposition that the offense was a serious crime, a capital offense. To warrant hanging as a punishment the crime must have been severe. We infer that the judge is an elected or appointed official in a judicial system. And so on and so forth. In fact, the inferences that can be drawn from any meaningful use of conventional signs in discourse are unlimited in number and extent. The power of inference evidently derives from the fact that things, persons, and relations in experience are actually connected in space and time. As a result, when we generalize to fictions and even impossible fantasies some of the same restrictions are still inferred. Otherwise, there would be no way to know how to interpret the fiction, or to conjure up any meaning for the fantasy.

Ordinary Referring Expressions in Appropriate (True) Uses

It is interesting that ordinary referring expressions, say, in talking about *the neighbor's dog*, or *Brenden's baby sister* usually occur in association with appropriate facts. At least, this will be true of much ordinary discourse about actual experience. However, with fictional representations some aspect of the object(s) referred to or signified is (are) not real, for example, as it cannot be real in reference to a perfectly round square. As a result it should not surprise us to discover that if all else is held equal, fictional representations are harder to process than ordinary appropriate true uses of the same linguistic forms. The reason is that the sign-user has to imagine the fiction, and it some cases this will be impossible, whereas a report of actual events is supported by perception and by memory. True representations may be supported by present events that are now accessible. For instance, it is easier for a child (or anyone for that matter) to figure out the use of a phrase such as *the neighbor's dog* or *Brenden's baby sister* if these terms are applied appropriately in relation to actual experiences than if they are applied randomly to anything or everything. Or, what if the learner does not already know the conventional meanings of these forms and is asked merely to imagine their referents?

How will this be possible for us, for instance, if the referring expressions are presented in a language we do not know? If we already know the language, we have some hope of success in coming up with the right sort of imagined fictions. But what if we don't know the language at all? Suppose the description of whatever is to be imagined is given in Igbo or Mandarin? If we don't know the language of the described fictions, we cannot use the symbols to infer anything about what we are asked to imagine. Consider the difficulty of conjuring up the meaning of *the neighbor's dog*, for instance, if the referring expression is presented to you in some language that you do not know, say, Navajo or Chinese. So fictions are not very helpful either to babies learning their first language or to adult second language learners either. The meanings of fictional representations cannot be determined by pointing out the imaginary objects to which they refer. To imagine those objects, in fact, we rely on prior comprehension of the fictional representation.

So how are fictions understood? Evidently, to understand fictions, we assume that some of the normal connections that exist in the real world must also hold in the imagined world of the fiction. Similarly, to comprehend false beliefs (that is, errors), it is necessary for us to take account of connections in the real world. For instance, if the salt shaker on the table at a certain restaurant does not contain salt, but, say, contains sugar, how will we find out? We depend on the connections between things that normally hold in the real world. Salt is salty and sugar is sweet. We can shake some of the white stuff out into our hand and taste it. If it tastes salty, we may assume it is salt, if it is sweet we may take it to be sugar. Of course, there are other white and grainy substances besides salt and sugar, for example, white sand, but sand will not melt in your mouth or dissolve in water, so, again, the connectedness of things in the world will enable us to test our inferences about what is in the salt shaker.

We also have no valid reason, normally, to expect that anyone would put sand in a salt shaker and put it on a table at a restaurant. Pranksters might put sugar in a salt shaker, but restaurant owners would usually discourage this practice. So, it follows that in most cases, our expectations about the intentions of others, and about their connections with the world of our experience will turn out to be valid. In those cases where these expectations are not met, it becomes difficult for us to make sense of the fiction, or to figure out where we made an error, or to assign meaning to what turns out to be a lie. For all these reasons, children require access to ordinary true uses of conventional forms of language to learn their meanings.

Intentions Are Inferred

Tomasello (2001) sums up a series of experiments with children at about 24 months of age. He demonstrates that by this age, and possibly as early as 16 months, normal children are already able to take advantage of connections between persons, things, and actions in the world to correctly infer the intentions of an adult interlocutor. For instance, children at this age are already able to understand when an adult is searching for a novel object, referred to by a novel term, even when the object is concealed from the child. Likewise, the child as early as 18 months (Meltzoff, 1995), and certainly by 24 months, is already able to draw correct inferences about intended actions even when those actions fail to achieve their objective (Tomasello, 2001). Mature individuals, however, sometime after age 12 and usually by age 20 reach a remarkably advanced level of abstraction. In fact, they come to a **general limit of abstraction**. This limit is not about the syntactic or pragmatic complexity of thoughts or representations. There is no absolute limit on the syntactic and pragmatic complexities that can be achieved. There is only a limit of diminishing returns for the effort required to construct representations of increasing complexity.

However, there is a general limit of abstraction. As Peirce (1861) put it, "A thought of a thought may differ from the thought itself; but they must both belong to the same abstraction" (1982, p. 84). Although uncountably many inferences of increasing syntactic and pragmatic complexity can be drawn at the highest attainable level of abstraction concerning any given representation, no matter how many times the operation of representing a given abstract representation may be repeated, all the representations that we can produce to represent a given representation remain at the same level of abstraction. Here is a simple illustration of the general limit of abstraction. Consider how many different times and in how many different places the word *the* appears on this page. Imagine how many times that word would be uttered aloud if someone were to read this page out loud. Yet no matter which representation we may pick as a representation of the word *the*, and no matter how many times that word may appear or be represented, it never becomes anything other than a representation of that word. In the same way, we may represent a thought, by thinking it, or by representing it in some other way, by writing it down, reading it after writing it down, and so on. However, the thought of a thought, or the writing down of the thought of a thought, or the saying out loud of the thought that is written down, and so on, never becomes anything more abstract than the thought that we started out with.

In the same way, although we may have many thoughts of the same thought, or memories of a memory, or representations of a representation, there is no way that the thought of a thought can be anything other than a thought, or the memory of a memory other than a memory, or the representation of a representation cannot be other than the representation of a representation. So, when the child becomes a mature adult and comes to the point where normal speech and language development enables us to represent any other representation we can come up with, our representational ability has reached what appears to be an absolute limit of abstraction. Suppose, for instance, that a certain third-grader thinks, *Some day I will be in the eighth grade*. Later, say in the eighth grade, the same person remembers having been in the third grade and having thought, *Some day I will be in the eighth grade*. Later still, say in high school, the same person remembers having remembered the thought, *Some day I will be in the eighth grade*. And, of course, there may be a host of other representations of the original thought, *Some day I will be in the eighth grade*, but are they any more abstract than the representation of that representation? The answer is, no. Representing a representation yields the same sort of product as it starts with: the representation of a representation. So, there is a limit of abstractness that cannot be exceeded.

Summing Up and Looking Ahead

In this chapter we have seen that semantic meanings are general and abstract while pragmatic meanings are particular and concrete. The general and abstract semantic meaning of a term such as *mama* is very different from the particular referents it may take on when associated with different particulars. For instance, Mary Anne and Bill may both have mamas, but the mothers in question don't have to be the same person. The difference between semantic and pragmatic aspects of meaning is essentially the same as that between an actual particular object (person or event) and an abstract general concept. For the same reason that we must distinguish particular objects from general concepts, it is also necessary to distinguish the intentions of a particular person from intentions in general. Even if two people have the same intentions, the intentions themselves are nevertheless different because of being associated with different individuals. For instance, if Sam and Bill both intend to marry Susan, their intentions may be the same as far as abstract representations go, but the intentions may not achieve the same pragmatic effect.

Inferring intentions is essential to knowing when a given bit of discourse is an assertion, request, denial, question, or whatever. In this chapter we differentiated factual representations from fictions, errors, and lies and showed why language learning depends on factual representations. We also saw why, all else being equal, children progress in their understanding from facts to fictions, fictions to errors, and from errors to lies. We showed how the Gricean maxims can be simplified and derived from constraints on child language development and how adult level inferences can achieve any degree of complexity and yet cannot go beyond a certain level of abstraction. In the following chapter we consider the question of how children acquire the ability to read and write and how literacy affects their mental development in general. Is it possible for a child, for instance, to read words before the child is able to produce those words in speech? In the next chapter we will present a surprising answer to this question.

STUDY AND DISCUSSION QUESTIONS

1. Why does the development of syntax level off sometime between ages 4 and 8?

2. What does it mean for a child to play a "language game" and win?

3. Why did some American psychologists and linguists shy away from the notion that words have meanings and that human beings have

intentions and make arbitrary choices? What arguments can you offer pro or con on these issues?

4. What are the Gricean maxims and how do they relate to language use and language acquisition? Why do you suppose that Grice in 1975 reintroduced the problem of truth and sincerity when these ideas had so long been banned from polite academic discussions?

5. In what way do exemplars of true uses of linguistic signs differ from fictional uses of the same signs? Why is it that appropriate conventional uses cannot be easily discovered by a child learning a first language or by anyone learning a second language from purely fictional representations?

6. Discuss the experimental evidence showing that true (factual) representations are understood and used by children before imaginary (fictional) ones, and that the latter tend to appear a year or two before errors are sharply distinguished, and the discernment of deliberate deceptions (lies) usually takes about 6 years plus one or two more. Why do you suppose children are not usually allowed to contradict adult testimony in court cases unless they are at least 6 years or older?

7. What are some of the ways that social misunderstandings may arise because of the conflicts of inferences drawn from linguistic signs? Recall the case of the hanging judge.

8. When we realize that representations can be represented in other representations we come to another limit beyond which an increase in abstraction is impossible. Besides the thought of a thought, Peirce's example, can you think of other representations of representations that show this same limit? Is the picture of a picture more abstract than the first picture? The copy of a copy of a copy of a copy? Why or why not? Supposing the copy of a copy may have a lesser quality, is this a difference in the degree of abstractness involved? What about a digital copy sent to a hundred or 10 million different readers who copy the copy to their friends?

CHAPTER 10

Literacy

After studying this chapter you should:

1. See that a normal child can understand and read printed words before being able to say the words out loud;

2. Understand the reasoning behind the letter-to-sound approaches to literacy;

3. See why some theoreticians and practitioners believe phonological awareness is crucial to getting ready to read;

4. Know the difference between surface-form and content-based approaches to literacy;

5. Understand why narrative structure is basic to experience, conversation, and discourse;

6. See why experience and conversation unfold in a linear sequence over time;

7. Understand how literacy enhances representational abilities; and

8. See how readers and listeners make sense of text, discourse, and conversation.

KEY TERMS

Here are some terms and concepts that you may learn more about in this chapter (these are also defined in the Glossary):

affix
algorithm
alphabetic/phonemic principle
blend (in phonics)
bottom-up
chronological order
cognitive momentum
comprehensibility
consciousness
content-based approaches
correlation
decoding
dyslexia
emergent literacy
episodic memory
episodic organization
expectancy
flashback
flashforward
ideographic orthography
kinesthetic
lemma
linguistic neighbor
linguistic neighborhood
literacy
loanword
logographic orthography
meaning-oriented

meshing
narrative structure
numeracy
oracy
orthographic
orthography
phoneme
phonics
phonographic neighbor
phonological awareness
prefix
priming
probe words
pseudowords (nonce words)
quasi-alphabetic
reading aloud
reading comprehension
reading readiness
semantic conceptualization
semantic memory
silent reading
surface-oriented approach
syllabary
top-down
transitive relation
unity of coherence
whole-language approach
whole-word approach

When a baby at only nine months comprehends printed words (see Aleka at http://www.infantlearning.com/videoclips.html visited January 23, 2006) a lot of claims about reading are drawn into question. In the video, Aleka and Other Early Readers (on the *Milestones Student DVD-ROM*), you can see Aleka as shown in Figure 10-1, read each word in turn before her dad says the word. When Aleka's dad shows the printed word "foot," Aleka grasps her right foot with her right hand and moves it around vigorously. After that he says the word *foot* out loud. The same procedure is followed with each of the words. When he presents the printed word "teeth," she gestures vigorously and repeatedly with her pointing finger to her mouth, lips, gums, and teeth. She babbles, /ʔaʔdada/ when her dad does not respond to her first vigorous gesture to her mouth. In the short video, this is the only time that Aleka utters any syllables. When the word on the card says "pointing" she makes a pointing gesture with both hands, but extending the right hand further than the left. She also shows comprehension of the printed words "hand," "head," and "ear." Aleka shows comprehension of the meanings associated with the surface-forms of the printed words. In this chapter we consider what reading is, how normal individuals learn to read and write, and how becoming literate affects linguistic and other abilities.

Figure 10–1. Aleka reads the word *foot* at 9 months although she does not yet say the word. See the relevant video clips at http://www.infantlearning.com/videoclips.html (visited January 29, 2006; also see Aleka and Other Early Readers). Used by permission of Dr. Robert C. Titzer.

Reading by Phonics

In the United States, especially, after the impact of the "science of linguistics," it has been widely believed that learning to read involves learning how to convert printed words to speech. Whether or not the idea originated with the linguist Leonard Bloomfield, he certainly helped to promote it. He supposed that the essential manifestation of language is speech and he advocated the formula that

reading = conversion of printed forms into speech

Bloomfield (1933, 1961) argued that letters and sequences of letters have to be "sounded out" through explicit associations of letters with **phonemes**. Saussure (1906/1959), Sapir (1921, 1933/1949) and Bloomfield (1933) defined phonemes either as abstract systems of sounds based on their oppositions and contrasts to each other (Saussure and Sapir) or as classes based on their phonetic properties (by Bloomfield). As phonemes are strung together in rapid sequence, Bloomfield supposed that the sounds would be **blended** together and the person saying those sounds aloud would discover the words by "sounding them out." According to Bloomfield reading means **reading aloud**, that is, converting printed forms into speech. This idea provided the basis for what would later be known as the **phonics** approaches to the teaching of reading. Somewhat later still, all such surface-oriented approaches to any kind of discourse processing would commonly be referred to as **bottom-up** approaches. These are now commonly contrasted with **meaning-oriented** approaches that are sometimes referred to as **top-down**.

Phonics approaches teach letter-to-sounds relations grounded in the **alphabetic principle**. If that principle were strictly followed, each letter of any alphabetic writing system would correspond to one and only one phoneme. We need to keep in mind the fact that a single phonemic class may be realized by different phonetic surface-forms (sounds), for example, /t/ can be realized as a flap of the tongue in *better*, as the aspirated initial consonant of *Tom*, as the unaspirated consonant after the sibilant of *stick*, and so forth. With that in mind, each letter of a strict alphabet represents a whole class or system of sounds (multiple sounds) rather than a single phonetically distinct segment. For this reason the "alphabetic" principle is also often referred to as the **phonemic principle** of writing.

In actual practice, however, English uses the least phonemic writing system of all the languages that use alphabetic writing. We get some idea of the misfit when we consider that the most widely spoken variety of American English has about 46 phonemes but there are only 26 letters in our alphabet. It is also worth keeping in mind that some of the most widely used languages of the world, for example, Chinese, do not rely on the phonemic principle for their writing systems. In the 10 most widely spoken primary languages of the world according to the most recent edition of the *Ethnologue* (Gordon, 2005) which lists 6,912 distinct languages (see Table 10-1), Spanish, Portuguese, German, Russian, and English are the only ones that use writing systems that aim to be more or less phonemic. Of all these writing systems, the English **orthography** is the least phonemic.

The rest of the 10 most commonly spoken languages use nonalphabetic systems of writing. That is, instead of using letters or symbols to represent classes of individual phonemes (distinct sound segments), they may use symbols of their writing system to represent abstract concepts as in an **ideographic orthography**. Or, they may use written symbols to represent whole words as in the **logographic orthography** of Chinese, for instance. Or, they may use symbols that represent syllables as is done in Bengali, Hindi, and Japanese. A writing system that represents syllables rather than phonemes, concepts, or words is called a **syllabary**. Incidentally, Japanese uses an ideographic system borrowed from Chinese in addition to its syllabary. As a result some of the world's most important languages, ones associated with large numbers of speakers, do not use an alphabetic writing system.

Combinations of the different approaches to writing are possible but most languages choose one or another focus for their writing systems from just three choices: they concentrate on (1) phonemes (alphabetic), (2) syllables (syllabic), (3) or concepts/words (with some combination of ideographic

Table 10–1 The 10 most widely spoken languages of the world according to the 2005 *Ethnologue* at (http://www.ethnologue.com/ visited August 9, 2005).

1.	Mandarin Chinese	885,000,000
2.	Spanish	332,000,000
3.	English	322,000,000
4.	Bengali	189,000,000
5.	Hindi	182,000,000
6.	Portuguese	170,000,000
7.	Russian	170,000,000
8.	Japanese	125,000,000
9.	German	98,000,000
10.	Wu Chinese	77,000,000

and logographic writing). Japanese is exceptional in using three distinct writing systems. However, two of the systems used for Japanese are syllabaries and the remaining one is logographic based on Chinese ideographs. Japanese uses two syllabic scripts, called "hiragana" and "katakana," and thousands of Chinese characters, called "kanji" (Halpern, 2001). The hiragana script is used mainly for writing native Japanese morphological markers and a relatively few whole words of Japanese. Katakana is used for **loanwords** from other languages and for words that need to be sounded out, and kanji is used for almost all the rest of the lexicon of Japanese. Thus, the ideographs of Chinese can be adapted as a logographic (word writing) system, evidently, for any language. For instance, the symbol for "man," "person," or "human being" from Chinese, as seen in Figure 10–2, could be used to represent the same meaning in any language of the world.

In a strict alphabetic/phonemic writing system, theoretically each letter should represent a different phoneme and each phoneme should be represented by just one and only one letter. There would be a one-to-one relation in such an orthography between letters and sounds. But, English is very far from this. In English orthography each phoneme is represented on the average in about 13.7 different ways (Crystal, 1987, p. 213). Also, because sound-to-letter relations in any language make reference to oppositional classes of sounds (see the example with /t/ above) that are highly abstract, the relations between sounds and letters are not simple. They are particularly complicated in English orthography. As a result, a phonics

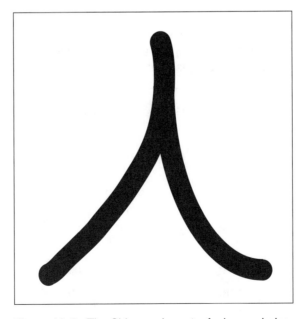

Figure 10–2. The Chinese character for human being.

approach to reading requires learners to be at a fairly advanced stage of development before reading instruction can begin. As a result the idea of **reading readiness** has been promoted by proponents of the phonics-based approaches. For the phonics approaches to the teaching of reading to be comprehensible to children, it is generally assumed that children should be between 5 and 7 years. Before that time, many have argued, children have not yet advanced to a sufficient level of cognitive development and representational ability to begin to understand phonics-based teaching (Al-Otaiba & Fuchs, 2002; Fuchs & Fuchs, 2005; Fuchs et al., 2001, 2002). The difficulty is to understand the abstract relations of letters-to-sounds and when English happens to be the target language for literacy development, the child faces the added complexities of the English orthography.

The phonics philosophy accounts well for phoneme-to-letter relations just to the extent that a writing system conforms to the alphabetic principle. But as we have already seen, English does not conform very well to that principle and the orthographies applied by hundreds of millions of people in the world do not use an alphabet at all, for instance, Chinese (see Pan, 2004; Pan & Chen, in press), Bengali, Hindi, and Japanese. How do people learn to read in those languages? What about deaf children who learn to read in a language they cannot speak? How do they learn to read if they do not speak the language they are reading? Are deaf children able to benefit from phonics?

As we have seen in the video of Aleka, she does not read the words out loud at all. In fact, her dad does not say the words until after Aleka has shown that she understands the meaning of each printed form. Aleka, in fact, does not say anything except for the babbled /ʔaʔdada/. This only happens once. Dad is not looking at her when she does her first vigorous gesture pointing to her mouth in response to the printed word "teeth." Her babbling in this particular case may or may not be an attempt to say the word *teeth*, but it appears to be merely a vocalization affirming that she knows the meaning in question. Her dad does not say any of the words until after Aleka shows in each case that she understands the meaning of the printed form in question. We will consider each of these problems for the phonics philosophy as we proceed through this chapter.

The Argument for Nonsense

Bloomfield (1933) did not deny that words, phrases, sentences, and higher discursive forms have meaning, but he did argue that meaning was too complicated a subject for linguistic analysis. He preferred to concentrate on the sounds emerging from the mouth of the speaker and impinging on the ear of the hearer. Bloomfield identified language closely with speech subordinating all the other manifestations of language including writing, verbal thought, manual signs, and combinations of these to speech. He even went as far as to argue that any attention to meaning in the early stages of teaching a child to read would be a distraction (Bloomfield, 1933, Bloomfield & Barnhart, 1961). He placed emphasis on the surface-forms of print and speech. He said that we would only make the task "more difficult . . . by asking the child to attend to the meaning of what he reads" (1961, p. 36). In the early stages, Bloomfield advocated teaching the child to read pronounceable nonsense words with no referential content at all. His method was an extreme **surface-oriented approach** to literacy. If **nonce forms**, also called **pseudowords** or nonsense words, are used in the early stages **reading comprehension** takes on a strange meaning. It becomes merely a matter of converting print to meaningless spoken forms. In that way, according to Bloomfield (1961), the child will not be distracted by meaning but can concentrate only on letter-to-sound relations. Bloomfield supposed that using meaningful words, or telling a story, or anything of that nature, would just draw the child's attention away from the crucial sound to-letter correspondences. As a result, the phonics approaches to literacy set aside the deeper aspects of the reading process. It has little or nothing to say about morphology, lexicon, syntax, semantics, or pragmatics. It does not deal with meaning or comprehension except as a by-product of converting text to speech.

Bloomfield's insistence on using nonsense in the initial stages in the teaching of reading is still applied widely both in teaching and especially in the testing of letter-sound skills and phonological awareness (Byrne & Fielding-Barnsley, 1989, 1993, 1995; Torgesen et al., 2001; Wagner & Torgesen, 1987). In more recent years, (Ball & Blachman, 1988; Rivers & Lombardino, 1998) many researchers have commonly used pseudowords to teach and or test phonological associations. Commonly, tasks used to teach and to test phonological awareness require the learner to sound out words or nonsense forms with minimal or no attention to meaning. Later proponents of Bloomfield's method would use a variety of terms to describe it. They would call it alternately:

- a phonetic approach,

- a phonemic approach,

- an alphabetic approach,

- a linguistic approach, and

- a scientific approach.

However, no single descriptive term has been used more commonly than "phonics." Today, it remains the most widely advocated and most commonly applied method for the teaching of reading in the world (Ball & Blachman,

1991; Bradley & Bryant, 1983; Byrne & Fielding-Barnsley, 1989, 1993, 1995; Tangel & Blachman, 1992; Torgesen, Wagner, & Roshette, 1994a, 1994b; Williams, 1980). As a method of reading instruction it is most prevalent in the schools of the United States and English-speaking countries.

The main tenets of the phonics approach to the teaching of reading can be summed up in a few sentences:

- Reading is **decoding** printed symbols, **orthographic** representations, to speech.

- Children must be taught the phonemic values of letters, that "b" stands for the sound at the beginning of the word "bat," and so forth.

- Reading only incidentally involves meaning, so it is okay to use nonsense.

- **Phonological awareness**, knowledge about the sounds that letters represent, is essential.

Developing Phonological Awareness

Commonly, to develop phonological awareness (see Calfee & Norman, 1998) tasks such as the following are used. The child (or adult, for that matter) may be asked to:

- Identify rhyming or nonrhyming words, for example, to know that *tame* rhymes with *came* but not with *time*;

- Say what is the first sound of the words *pit*, *pack*, and *pine*;

- Count the sounds in a word, or move, delete, or add a sound, for example,

  - how many sounds are there in each of the following words, *hat*, *six*, *kick*, and so on;

  - what word do you get if you move the "t" sound of *tap* to the end of the word, (where the expected answer is *apt*);

  - what do you get if you delete the "h" sound from *hat* (where the expected answer is *at*);

  - what happens if you put an "r" sound after the "t" sound in the word *stuck* (where the expected answer is *struck*).

Calfee and Norman (1998) also note that the tasks commonly used to teach and/or test phonological awareness are excessively hard for very young children and too hard for some adults. Also instilling phonological awareness does not necessarily result in reading comprehension.

A common comment of teachers and other professionals (especially speech-language pathologists), the vast majority of whom advocate phonics and decoding skills in their own teaching and therapies, is that the child can sometimes sound out (that is, decode) words, one by one, but cannot understand the meaning of whatever is read. In a survey of 150 licensed and practicing speech-language pathologists, Nelson, Damico, and Oller (2002) found that 86% of the respondents (all of them holding a masters degree or higher) claimed that knowledge of sound-letter correspondences is crucial to learning to read, but many of these same practitioners simultaneously expressed puzzlement that training in phonics/phonological awareness does not lead to reading comprehension for about 20% of the children taught by such methods.

Calfee and Norman (1998) summed up the problem by saying that building phonological/orthographic knowledge does not lead "to fluent decoding of connected text, nor to the capacity to comprehend and compose" (p. 258). In fact, there are widespread reading failures, especially among English-speaking children taught by phonics. About one child in five does not become a fluent reader by that method. This fact has led Lyon (1995; also Lyon, Shaywitz, & Shaywitz, 2003; Shaywitz et al., 1999) to infer that about 20% (one in five) of American children must have a learning disablement, which they identify as **dyslexia** in the majority of cases. They believe that this disablement has a genetic basis causing a certain kind of brain dysfunction. Dyslexic persons are believed to read with effort and slowly (Lefly & Pennington, 1991; S. Shaywitz, 2003) because their brains are functioning in an abnormal way. Succinctly put, the slowness and effortfulness is believed to "result from a deficit in the phonological component of language" (Lyon, Shaywitz & Shaywitz, 2003, p. 1). The same authors describe the problem as involving the "region" of the brain that they believe is "pivotal in mapping the visual percept of the print onto the phonologic structures of the language system" (p. 3).

Doesn't this sound like a definition of the phonics approach to reading? Is it merely a coincidence that the diagnosis of dyslexia matches the prescribed solution for it? Is it also just a coincidence that the rate of reading failure in children who are predominantly taught to read through some variant of phonics is almost identical to the estimated incidence of so-called reading/learning disability? Can it be true that the 20% of all children taught by phonics are victims of genetically caused brain deficits? If we ask what causes the genetic problem leading to the hypothesized brain deficits of dyslexia, the proponents of the phonics method and phonological awareness training, reply that the causes of the brain deficits themselves are unknown genetic factors. The recommended remedy? Provide additional phonics instruction and phonological awareness training (Lyon,

1995; Shaywitz et al., 1999; and also see their references). In fact, in spite of the evidence that 20% of school-going children cannot become good readers by that method, there remains widespread support for it as the best solution for reading disabilities, especially dyslexia (Berninger, 2001; Clay, 1990; Felton & Pepper, 1995; Lyon, 2001; Rosenshine, 1986; Shaywitz et al., 1999; Stanovich, 1987, 1988, 1992). The question that has not been asked by the proponents of the phonics approaches is why the phonics approach ought to work after the child is diagnosed with dyslexia when it didn't work before.

Some have suggested that phonics approaches may be focusing too narrowly on letter-to-phoneme correspondences. Perhaps sequences of letters corresponding to a larger unit of structure, for instance, the syllable should be taken into consideration. More particularly, one idea that has been proposed places emphasis on the rimes of syllables, for example, "-ite" of *kite* and *invite*, the "-ost" of *cost* and *lost*, and so on. This shift was first recommended by Stanback (1992), though as early as 1973, Ainsworth had already taken certain rimes into consideration as separate elements. By two different methods, Stanback estimated 42 to 52 distinct phonemes but there are a considerably larger number of syllables and syllable rimes. To pay attention to rimes would require teachers of phonics to teach a larger number of rules, but according to Stanback, might reduce the percentage of reading failures.

In a sample of 17,602 of the most frequent words of English, Stanback (1992) found 824 different letter sequences representing distinct rimes. Of these 824 rimes, 616 were sufficient to build up almost all the 43,041 syllables in the whole data sample. Of the 616 most common rimes, 436 were regular and consistent in their orthographic representation, for example, words like "red" and "can." Only 86 were really exceptional, for example, such as words like "through" and "doubt." Based on these findings, Stanback proposed that perhaps more emphasis should be placed on the teaching of letter sequences representing particular rimes in early reading instruction. Following this idea in studies with children and adults, Treiman, Mullennix, Bijeljacbabic, and Richmondwelty (1995) showed that the rimes of syllables not only tend to be more consistently represented in spellings but also in the read aloud pronunciations of those spellings by readers. Readers tend to make fewer errors when reading rimes that are consistently represented in spellings, for example, "-ack," "-ick," "-uck" than ones that are inconsistently represented, for instance, "-ead," "-ede," "-eed," "-ied," "-eid." Kessler and Trieman (2001) showed that rimes are also the most consistent parts of monosyllabic words of English. The implication is that rimes ought to be easier to learn than single letter-to-phoneme relations. Although not directly testing the idea about rimes, White (2005) has shown that second-graders are able to read about 83% of novel nonce words correctly by *analogy* with known words where rimes are the key basis for their correct judgments.

An obvious obstacle to the success of phonics is that the writing system of English is only **quasi-alphabetic**. In a strict alphabetic system, if General American English has, say, 46 distinct phonemes, there should be exactly 46 letters in our writing system. But, this is not the case. English is represented in an alphabet of 26 letters, and each letter is estimated to represent on the average at least 6 different phonemes and each phoneme can be represented in 13.7 distinct sequences of letters (Crystal, 1987, p. 213). So, undoubtedly part of the reason that a phonics approach to English instruction does not work perfectly well is because the orthography of English does not conform to the *alphabetic principle*. That is, English does not spell each phoneme with one and only one distinct letter. There is also research showing that languages such as Albanian, unlike English, for instance, which conform very closely to the alphabetic principle of writing are easier to work with by applying the phonics approach (Hoxhallari, van Daal, & Ellis, 2004).

Another problem with phonics as a starting point for the teaching of reading, and a problem that is universal to all phonics approaches in all languages, is that it requires the child to attend to the letters of print while recalling their relations with abstract surface-forms of speech, phonemes. Teaching by phonics, regardless of how well or badly any language conforms to the alphabetic principle, necessarily involves abstract linguistic analysis. The teacher/clinician might point out that the letter sequence "c k," also commonly represents the sound /k/ as in the word *kick*. Or, in the case of an emphasis on rimes, the teacher might point out that the sequence "-ick" represents the rimes in *kick, tick, click*, and so forth. This approach is surface-oriented because it directs attention to the visual shapes of letters and to the auditory and **kinesthetic** impressions made by the class of sounds they represent in the English orthography. Even if the teacher/clinician calls attention to the initial consonant "k-" for example, in the word *kick* following with the rime "-ick" and then blends the two parts together by pronouncing the whole word, the approach is still focused on surface-forms abstracted away from their meanings and uses. The meanings, intentions, and the sense of the words taught in this way tend to be lost. With pseudoword teaching, for example, *fick, ick, jick, yick,* and *zick*, there is no possibility of discovering any meaning because there is no meaning to be discovered. Even if lists of actual words are used, as long as they are not related to meaningful events, for example, as in a game, an activity, or a story, the association of the letters and sounds of those words remains focused on surface-forms. Even if the motor impressions (kinesthetic aspects) are drawn into play by writing out or printing a letter or by locating it in a string of letters in a text, or by typing a letter on a keyboard, surface-forms are still the main focus of attention.

As a result, such methods of teaching fall short of ordinary meaningful uses of language. They also fall short of what we normally do when we understand written material. We don't just convert letters into sounds. The reason we don't do that is that sounds and syllables by themselves have no determinate meanings. What, for instance, does the sound /k/ or the sound /æk/ mean? Although we can produce the nonce spoken form, *kack* (a pseudoword) by blending *k-* with *-ack*, what is a nonce form like this good for? In fact, even the sounds of meaningful words like *dog, cat, jump*, and *run*, do not have any necessary relation to the meanings of the words they form, and their uses in spelling those words can only be reasonably understood by associating the sounds through their uses with the meanings of the words. Ordinary language does not use isolated sounds or meaningless syllables. In fact, most ordinary uses of language do not involve pseudowords or nonce forms. As a result, some teachers, researchers, and others have argued that any emphasis on surface-forms should be subordinated to content, to meaning.

Meaning-Based Approaches as an Alternative

Smith (1988a, 1988b, 1997) argued that readers with excellent comprehension commonly do not translate written forms to oral ones at all. He has argued that competent readers seem to read right through the written forms directly to the meaning without translating the printed forms into the surface-forms of speech at all. This idea is consistent with the fact that most reading comprehension does not require that we read aloud. Research also shows that competent readers can read faster silently and with superior comprehension (McCallum, Sharp, Bell, & George, 2004). In support of Smith's claim see the video clip of 9-month-old Aleka as she reads (http://www.infantlearning.com/videoclips.html visited January 29, 2006; also see <u>Aleka and Other Early Readers</u> on the *Milestones Student DVD-ROM*). Aleka begins with **silent reading**. When Aleka's dad shows and says the printed word "teeth," Aleka gestures vigorously and repeatedly with her pointing finger between her lips while touching her teeth and gums. When the word on the card says "foot" she grabs one of her feet, and moves it around with her hand. And so forth for "ear," "head," and "hand." Evidently, Aleka at 9 months knows the meanings and can recognize the printed words before she has become able to produce their surface-forms in speech.

There is something else to notice in the dynamic demonstration provided by Aleka and her dad. She is operating with true and appropriate representations. She is performing the process of pragmatic mapping. She takes the surface-forms of the print and maps them onto appropriate meanings. The surface-forms of the printed words are being mapped correctly and appropriately (that is, truthfully in the most mundane sense of the word "true") onto appropriate actions and objects as can be seen in the video. When she demonstrates the pointing gesture, she does not produce it exactly in the adult way, but it is clear that she has in mind the right sort of gesture. Her ability to associate abstract linguistic symbols with their meanings clearly precedes her being able to produce all the surface-forms in speech. This capacity is exactly as predicted by the theory of abstraction, but contrary to the Bloomfieldian "scientific theory" of linguistics and the phonics approaches to reading. As soon as the child is able to associate a linguistic symbol with an argument (for example, someone's name with the person named) or with a particular action of one or more arguments (for example, Aleka's pointing gesture or someone else's), the child is capable of associating any abstract symbol that she can notice and discriminate, including a printed one, with a meaning or context in just the same way. It is clear, incidentally, from Aleka's production of the form /ʔaʔdada/ that Aleka has already reached and surpassed the level of the prescinded symbol (that is, the level of canonical and variegated babbling). However, she reads the words for meaning not only before producing them out loud, but also her access to meaning precedes the expected time of "reading readiness" by about 4 or 5 years.

Advantages of Meaning-Based Approaches

For all the reasons given above in Chapter 4 showing why conventional signs are necessarily dependent on pragmatic bootstrapping, that is, if all else is held equal, meaningful **content-based approaches** are bound to be superior to surface-oriented approaches. Let us review the main reasons why this must be so: first, the kinds of relations that hold between abstract graphological symbols, which must include not only letters but also marks of punctuation, spacing, capitalization, changes in font sizes and types for emphasis, and so on, and their meanings are not really different in kind from the relations that hold between the surface-forms of speech, verbal thought, or signing and the meanings associated with these different surface-forms. The meaning relations that the various surface-forms encode and represent remain essentially the same across distinct modalities of processing. We can see this by considering a few examples of a single message that can be presented either in print or in some other medium. For instance, consider the message that "Delta Airlines Flight 175 from New York Kennedy to Atlanta will depart at 3 PM from Gate 29E instead of Gate 30C."

Do the referents or the relations between any of the arguments change if the message is spoken over a loudspeaker as opposed to being written on a computer monitor? Would any of the meanings change if it were repeated by one passenger to another after hearing it over the loudspeaker or reading it from a monitor? Would any of the meaning relations change if the message were written down on a sheet of paper or routed to a printer from a computer? What if the message is remembered after the fact and the surface-forms of the representation that was formerly heard over a loudspeaker or read from a computer monitor are now merely imagined by the person rushing from Gate 29 in Concourse E to Gate 30 in Concourse C. Would it matter if the message were spoken over a telephone line or whispered in someone's ear or shouted across a crowded room?

Assuming only that the message is true and correctly understood, the meaning relations within it do not change when it is converted from a written to a spoken form, or from spoken to written, or from either of those to a merely remembered message represented in verbal or some other form of thought and action, say, by the traveler who moves from Gate 29E to Gate 30C to make it on time to Delta 175. Or, to take a simpler example, would Aleka's understanding of the printed word "foot" be any different if it were associated with the spoken word *foot*? Would the hypostatic value, the semantic meaning, of the term change by changing the modality of its surface-form, for example, spoken, read, written, and so forth?

In view of the fact that the answers to all the foregoing questions are evidently negative, we should expect the factors that make pragmatic bootstrapping (also known as pragmatic mapping) more fundamental than either syntactic or semantic bootstrapping, will also apply to make content-based approaches to the teaching of literacy superior to those focusing more or less exclusively on surface-forms of speech and writing. In fact, it must be predicted, based on the theories presented earlier in this book, that any approach to literacy that begins with nonsense forms and tries to teach letter-to-sound correspondences based on those forms will be a great deal more difficult than an approach that relates relatively simple surface-forms to visible, tangible, audible, and otherwise sensible arguments. For instance, should we suppose that Aleka's dad would have had more success in teaching her that the printed words she learned if he had first taught her to sound out the letters "f" "t" "oo," and so forth? Or, if he had started with the rimes of syllables, for example, "-and," "-ead," "-oint," "-oot," and so on?

If we ask why not, the answer is evident: letter-to-sound relations are excessively abstract and linguistically analytical by comparison to the relation between the word "foot" printed on a visible card, say, and Aleka's foot. Her foot is concrete, particular, attached to her body, tangible, visible, audible at times when it smacks into something else, and easily noticeable to Aleka. Her foot has been an object of interest since before she was born. The card dad is holding up with the printed word "foot" on it is also visible, tangible, and audible when he moves it around. The whole pragmatic mapping relation between the printed word in each case and the object or action signified is a lot easier to take account of than some abstract, linguistic, analytical letter-to-sound relation. In fact, the ideas underlying phonemic oppositions in a language, not to mention the various phonetic realizations for any given phoneme, are a challenge for college-level students to acquire. What is more, in linguistics the concept of the phoneme as a category or system of analysis (not to mention the syllable, see Pan, 2005), has been controversial and problematic since it was first introduced and it remains controversial today (Chomsky & Halle, 1968; Goldsmith, 1990; Gussmann, 2002).

The question we have to ask ourselves as educators, teachers, therapists, parents, or what-have-you, is whether we want to enable children to become literate, or whether we want to teach them the theory of phonemes and the alphabetic principle of writing. As already noted, the alphabetic principle is far from being the only basis for writing systems. The most ubiquitous exception which makes the phonics approach to literacy inapplicable for a huge part of the world's population is Chinese which uses a logographic and ideographic system. Chinese writing does not directly show the pronunciation of its symbols as is done in alphabetic systems. Chinese can be represented alphabetically in what is called the Pi-Ying system, but the traditional standard writing system of Chinese is not alphabetic at all. Other writing systems, as we have noted, may represent syllables, or use some mix of syllabic, logographic, and alphabetic writing systems. Modern English incidentally also uses some logographs such as "&" for "and," and "@" for "at," "$" for "dollar," and "¢" for "cents." Some symbols, such as the "$" sign can also have an ideographic function as a representation of wealth, or lots of money. English comes up far short of a phonemic writing system where each letter/symbol has just one phonemic value. In English writing a single letter may have multiple phonemic values, for example, the letter "c" can represent the sound /k/ as in "can," or /s/ as in "citation" or "France," or /z/ as in "Czar." Similarly, the same sound, for example, /z/ can be represented as "s" in "represent," or "z" in "zoo," or "x" in "Xerox." Some singular sounds are represented in two letters such as the /θ/ of "think," the /ð/ of "this," and the /f/ of "enough." Some dual sound sequences such as the /ks/ of "sox" are represented in just one letter. Some letters are retained in written words that do not in fact represent any phoneme at all such as the "p" of "psychology," or "pneumonia," or the "b" of "doubt" and "subtle." Some phonemes that are present in spoken forms, for example, the "t" of "Nancy" or the "p" of "Chomsky" have no corresponding letters to represent them.

The letters representing vowels are even less reliable than the ones representing consonants. For instance, "o" can represent /a/ as in "modern" and "phonics" or it can stand for the /o/ and /ɔ/ in the first two syllables of "notorious." The sequence "ou" can represent /æu/ in "sound," the /u/ in "through," and the /ə/ in "tough," and the /ɔ/ in "trough," and so forth. As a result, the number of words that can be deciphered strictly by applying standard rules of decoding, the kind that can be taught in a phonics classroom, are relatively few. Names are nearly impossible to sound out in many cases, and in fact even in materials written for children the percentage of words that can be reliably sounded out by relying on the alphabetic/phonemic principle is often less than proponents of the phonics approaches say is essential.

More importantly, the percentage of words that can be decoded by applying the rules of phonics may not make any difference to reading comprehension at all. Jenkins, Peyton, Sanders, and Vadasy (2004) were able to find stories for beginning readers where less than 11% of the words in the texts could be decoded by relying on phonics, and they were also able to find beginning readers where more than 80% of the words were decodable. However, when they compared a group of 40 children who studied the less decodable stories against a matched group of 39 children who studied the more decodable stories, the two groups of children showed no differences. Having access to more or less decodable stories made no difference. By contrast, in many different experimental comparisons of a wide variety of different participants in various contexts, where the factor varied is the accessibility of meaning, the contrasts are substantial, highly significant, and pervasive (see J. Oller et al., 2005). It can be inferred that decodability of texts, where all else is held equal, has little or no impact while greater access to meaning has a substantial effect that tends to grow over time.

Readers Can Also Rely on Analogy and Higher Levels of Grammar

Decoding from letters to phonemes according to the alphabetic principle is not the only way that successful readers figure out the highly irregular orthography, in other words, the spelling system, of English. In fact, it is impossible to rely on phonics exclusively in reading English words because in a running text that is not deliberately salted with decodable words (that is, if the test is not artificially constructed to include a high percentage of decodable words) less than 20% of the words encountered will be spelled phonetically.

To figure out irregular, less decodable forms, however, readers and learners alike can appeal to pragmatic information as Aleka does in the video referred to at the beginning of this chapter. Aleka knows what her foot is, and she is able to associate the printed form of the word "foot," a whole lexical item, with her foot. She does not stop to sound out the word by first recognizing the letter "f" and associating it with the phoneme /f/, then remembering that "oo" is one of those irregular letter sequences that stands for the sound /ʊ/, then noticing the letter "t" and associating it with the phoneme /t/, and finally blending all these together to produce the surface-form [fʊt]. In fact, Aleka does not produce the word in speech at all. She does not read the word out loud, but demonstrates by her gesturing that she knows its meaning nonetheless. She demonstrates reading comprehension.

Mature adult readers can evidently do what Aleka does and a good deal more. Consider for example, how you are able to figure out the words in the following title used by Andrews and Starrett (1998). Especially consider the part of the title that comes after the colon:

> "Rule and analogy mechanisms in reading nonwoody: Hough ou peapel rede gnew wirds?"

How did you know what the second part of the title, the part after the colon, says? How do people read new words? That's a good question and it is partly answered in the demonstration that is deliberately and cleverly embedded in the title. Ordinarily, in reading with comprehension, several factors come into play:

- The pragmatically inferred meanings help us to figure out the written text. For instance, we know from the first part of the Andrews and Scarrett title "Rule and analogy mechanisms in reading nonwoody" that the article is about how people figure out nonwoody. This is a high-level pragmatic inference that is grounded in knowing what others are talking, writing, reading, or thinking about.

- In addition to pragmatic information mature readers can rely on the general semantic meanings associated with lexical items, phrases, and higher structures of thought and language. For instance, in the context of discourse about reading and literacy, there is a strong semantic basis for the pragmatic **expectancy** that whatever surface-forms may come up, they are likely to be about concepts having to do with literacy.

- There are also syntactic elements that come into play in reading and discourse processing in general. When we come to the colon after the word "nonwoody" in the title, we expect not only for the continuation to make sense, but to express a thought related to the topic already up for discussion or consideration. As soon as we recognize any single part of the strange sequence after the colon, say, we figure out the word "rede" and make it out to be *read* spelled in an unusual way, if we take this word as a verb, we may expect a noun phrase to follow it. Reading requires an object suitable to be read, and we may expect it to be preceded by a noun phrase referring to the sort of argument (a subject for the verb *read*) that is capable of reading. This same sort of interaction can be shown for any item in the sequence. If "hough" is recognized as *how* we expect a modal such as *do*, *may*, *can* or the like to follow it. As a result, the deciphering of any single form in the sequence, because the sequence is a coherent and meaningful whole, helps us to figure out the rest.

■ Finally, we should notice that phonological elements also come into play. After all, every one of the words in the unfamiliar part of the sequence has some letters or letter sequences that are more or less familiar by analogy with other words. For instance, "peapel" looks like *pea* and like *Papel*. The word "hough" looks like and can rhyme with *bough*, "du" looks like and rhymes with *you*, and so forth. Also, every word in the unfamiliar part, "Hough du peapel rede gnew wirds" has one or more letters that are used with their usual phonetic value, for example, "h" in "hough," "d" in "dou," and so on.

Therefore, summing up, the mature reader can figure out unfamiliar or new words by relying on referential (pragmatic) meanings, on knowledge of other words, on concepts that generalize from particular words or referents, on syntactic and semantic relations between all the foregoing, and on phonetic/phonological values associated with letters and letter sequences. But which if any of these is crucial and essential? Could Aleka, for instance, rely on the phonetic values of letters? Evidently not, because she does not yet produce most of the words she is reading and the names of individual letters are still out of her reach. Could she rely on sounding out the words? Evidently not, because she does not use the alphabetic connection between letters and sounds to figure out the words. She goes from the surface-form of the word to its meaning.

Aleka relies on the pragmatic connection between the distinct word shapes she recognizes and the things or actions that they are associated with. Just as we saw in earlier chapters (in Figures 3-3 and 4-5), Aleka, see Figure 10-3, pragmatically maps the word form, which was unfamiliar to start with, onto an object or activity that is more familiar to her. For instance, she associates the word "foot" with her own right foot by grabbing it and moving it around with her right hand. Aleka not only engages in the language game of figuring out the meaning associated with the abstract linguistic symbol printed on the card her dad is holding up, but she shows that she has mastered the game by performing an action demonstrating the pragmatic mapping relation. Referring back to Wittgenstein's claim about children learning to play "language games," this is a game that Aleka can not only play but also win. In understanding how children succeed at becoming literate we need to understand the game as the child

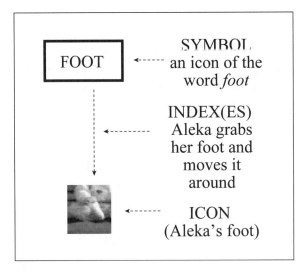

Figure 10–3. The pragmatic mapping process underlying Aleka's reading at 9 months. Also see http://www.infantlearning.com/robert.html; and see *Aleka and Other Early Readers* on the Milestones Student DVD-ROM.

sees it and also to understand how it is that the child is able to succeed when she plays the game. Failures are relatively easy to explain. It is successes, however, that require close scrutiny so that we can see how the pieces of the puzzle all fit together. Clearly, the pragmatic mapping of forms to meanings is crucial.

The Role of Analogy

If the mature reader encounters a new word, all the above factors can come into play. Ordinarily, a mature reader does not read just one word at a time. Occasionally, however, when we come to a strange word that we do not know, we may pause to think about just that particular word. Andrews and Scarrett (1998) stress that we read a new word in part by analogy with other words that we already know and that resemble the new word. For instance, when we meet a word like "Australopithecus" we might think of words with similar shapes. These other words may help us figure out the sound and the meaning of the new one. For instance, we may think of words like "Australia" and "Austria" and "pithy," "Ithaca," and "us." Words that resemble some target word either in shape, sound, or meaning are called its **linguistic neighbors** and the theoretical domain that they occupy are called the **linguistic neighborhood** (Peereman & Content, 1997). Words that resemble a target word in terms of their shape, that is, the letters they contain and the order in which those letters appear, are called orthographic neighbors. Ones that resemble the target word in sound are called phonological neighbors and ones that share some abstract meaning are termed semantic neighbors. Words that share both phonological and orthographic properties (but no others) are called **phonographic neighbors**, examples would be "trough" and "cough." Peereman and Content (1997) found that pseudowords are easier to read if they have a larger number of neighbors. According to their findings, a target pseudoword, for example, "hough" will be harder to read as *how* than "gnew" is to read as *new* because "hough" has only one good neighbor in the word *bough* (and various bad neighbors in *tough, trough, enough, through,* and *though*) while "gnew" has many good neighbors including *blew, crew, dew, few, hew, jew, knew, Lew, pew,* and *threw* (and few bad ones such as *sew*).

Commonly, resemblances of shape, sound, and meaning are partially overlapping, so that the neighbors of a given target may be related in shape (orthographically), sound (phonologically), and meaning (semantically/pragmatically). For instance, if we look to the roots underlying the words "Australopithecus," "Australia," and "Austria," historically, we find that the word "australis" in Latin means "southern" and it turns out that "Australopithecus" was the skeleton of an ape found in southern Africa, Australia is fairly far down in the southern hemisphere, and even Austria, a German-speaking country, is south of the main German-speaking population of Europe. The reader may note, however, that to point out these meaning resemblances, we have to appeal to relations between logical objects involving pragmatic references (countries, the skeletal remains of an ape, and the standardized global map of the earth). The "-pithecus" part of "Australopithecus" comes from the Greek word "pithekos" meaning "ape." The form "-pithecus" orthographically (by spelling) and phonologically (by sound) resembles "pithy," "Ithica," and "us," but the latter forms do not share any meaning with "-pithecus."

The spelling system of English on a letter-by-letter basis is not transparent to beginning readers or to researchers. Estimates vary of the percentage of words that can be deciphered by rules that convert letters or letter sequences to sounds, or vice versa. Hanna, Hanna, Hodges, and Rudorf (1966) studied 17,000 words from an English dictionary. They were able to devise a program that would spell (from phonemes to letters) about 50% of the 17,000 words correctly. To accomplish this they used 308 rules and set aside 88 exceptional words. Later readers of their work would ask whether the glass is half full or half empty. Did they show that phonics is apt to succeed in enabling children to figure out about 50% of the words they encounter or that they will fail to do so with about 50% of the words?

Ainsworth (1973) worked in the opposite direction from letters to sounds (text to speech). His study was one of the first and most cited attempts to synthesize speech from text. He used 159 rules translating letters, letter sequences, spaces between words, and punctuation marks into breath groups, then into phonemic symbols, and then into surface-forms of pronounceable speech. He used three texts of about 1,000 words each for his research. One passage was from a text about phonetics, one was from a novel, and the other from a newspaper article about a political issue. In addition to his 159 rules for translating letters and letter sequences into phonemes, he worked out an **algorithm**, an embedded system of additional rules, for defining breath groups on the basis of certain punctuation marks or conjunctions. If the sequence was too long for his program, he just inserted a breath group boundary after a certain number of characters. He also developed a system to assign stress to syllables of individual words. His program was a good deal more complex than what can easily be taught to first-graders.

In the end, he produced spoken versions of each of his texts and presented them to three adult listeners. The task set for the listeners was to write down each breath group. The written texts were then scored as the percentage of words written down that were actually in the original texts. Results ranged from 50% to 90%. It is interesting to note that the **comprehensibility** of Ainsworth's passages probably benefitted from the fact that he used connected texts. In a connected text, as we saw earlier in connection with the title, "hough ou peapel rede gnew wirds?" interpreters benefit from knowledge of what the text is about. If Ainsworth had used isolated words, the research shows that the comprehension scores would not have been as high. Also, it should be noted that neither Ainsworth (1973) nor Hanna et al. (1966) relied exclusively on letter-to-sound correspondences. They also applied:

- Knowledge of morphology including the difference between **affixes** (including those that come in front of word roots, that is, **prefixes**, and those that come after, in other words, *suffixes*) and the **lemmas**, that is, the roots or stems of words,

- Lexical information showing exceptional words as special cases,

- Inferences about breath group boundaries based on punctuation,

- Inferences about sentence syntax based on conjunctions, and

- An arbitrary cutoff for long sequences.

In spite of all these additional sources of information and guesses, the attempts by expert linguists and systems engineers to construct text-to-speech or speech-to-text programs have only been able to achieve about a 66% level of accuracy.

In fact, the results achieved by Hanna et al. (1966) and by Ainsworth (1973) in the earliest computer-based studies of English orthography are consistent with those of much more recent text-to-speech programs. Damper, Marchand, Adamson, & Gustafson (1999) followed-up by Marchand and Damper (2000) found that the most sophisticated programs available with thousands of rules, huge lexicons, and high-speed computers consistently produce text-to-speech conversions at only about 66% accuracy. If we compare this to the near 100% accuracy of any normal mature adult reader, the discrepancy requires explanation. Evidently, the normal mature reader does not rely only on the phonetic/phonemic relations that hold between letters, sequences of letters for rimes, or combinations of these with punctuation marks, large lists of exceptional words, distinctions between affixes and word stems, and rules for stress placement. Something more must be involved.

Whole Words, Phrases, Sentences, and Whole-Language Approaches

Readers not only recognize letter sequences, but they also use the spaces between words, marks of punctuation, indentations, capitalization, and other symbols. Also, in addition to words the mature reader relies on phrase groups, sentences, and higher units. A skilled reader not only sees the print on the page, but also thinks of the sequence of events that a novel, for instance, is about. Readers often say they get into the story. From these facts about reading the **whole-language approaches** to literacy were conceived. Whole words, of course, are involved in whole-language approaches but reading is not just about identifying individual words by a long shot. For this reason the so-called **whole-word approaches** come up short. Although, the mature reader can benefit from relations between familiar words as easily, or more easily, than between letter sequences and phonemes, or even the rimes of syllables, a great deal of additional meaning and structure can also come into play. For instance, a strange new word such as "Australopithecus," may benefit from its resemblances to other whole words such as "Australia," and "Austria." However, the fact that the word appears in a book on archeology may be even more helpful in figuring out the meaning.

Higher levels involving combinations of words also come into play in whole-language and especially in content-based approaches. Phrasal structures and breath groups tend to be marked by commas, periods, and other signs. Sentences tend to begin with capital letters. These facts already rise above the level of the individual letter-to-phoneme correspondences that are emphasized in phonics approaches and yet these relations contribute to the meaning of a text. More importantly, as soon as the reader has a notion concerning what a text is about, that is, who wrote it, who it concerns, what purposes it may serve, who and what may be referred to in the text, and the like, the reader is able to take advantage of high-level semantic/pragmatic information in forming correct interpretations, memories, and expectations about the text as a whole.

Many practitioners and theoreticians alike have realized that the ability to recognize letter-to-sound relations is not all there is to the language games that we call reading and writing. In addition to whole words, literate persons learn to deal with phrases, sentences, conversations, and stories, all of which may be embedded within each other and within other structures. Mature readers also use elements other than sounds, such as syllables, rimes, rhythms, breath groups, intonational patterns, and the like, as the research on phonics approaches has also discovered (Lyon, Shaywitz, & Shaywitz, 2003). Mature readers not only relate written texts to spoken forms but also to highly abstract meanings, to contexts of experience, to other forms of discourse such as conversations, debates, news reports, instructions about how to put things together, insurance policies, traffic tickets, road signs, product guarantees, and countless other functions. Literacy extends to our interactions with computers, with recording and playback mechanisms, cell phones, and other communication devices and technologies. It extends not only to the way we deal with books, dictionaries, and encyclopedias, but also to movies, videos, and games.

As many theoreticians and researchers have argued, literacy like speech, is an emergent ability that develops over time (Hall, 1987). As a result, **emergent literacy** can be shaped by all kinds of experiences. Also, as we learn from the video of Aleka Titzer at 9 months, experience can be shaped so as to cause literacy to emerge a good deal earlier than some of the experts have supposed possible. For instance, the meanings of printed words can be understood even before those words appear in the speech forms of the reader. Also, research with emergent literacy suggests that when preschool children read or are read to by their parents, attention to print, even in an alphabetic language, is not necessarily associated with an advance in alphabetic knowledge (Justice, Skibbe, Canning, & Lankford, 2005). Evidently, even preschoolers naturally concern themselves with meaning and with the sense of text rather than with sound-to-phoneme relations. Research also shows that directing learner attention to meaning is a more effective approach to reading instruction (than phonics) even when working with children who have experienced difficulty in learning to read (Badon, J. Oller, & S. Oller, 2005; Badon, S. Oller, & J. Oller, 2005).

Phonology Does Come into Play in Every Writing System

In English as in all the languages of the world regardless of their writing systems, the sounds and the symbols of writing are pragmatically associated with each other. Ability to read and write must reflect the conventional associations of writing with spoken words. These associations are conventional because there is nothing in any particular letter or written symbol that would force us to use it to represent any particular phoneme, syllable, rime, word, or meaning. The associations are conventional, and therefore they must be learned. In this much, the phonics approach to reading is certainly correct from a logical perspective as far as it goes. It is true that letter-to-sound relations, for instance, play a role in literacy in English just as Shankweiler, Lundquist, Dreyer, and Dickinson (1996) have found. At all ages, literate persons rely to some extent on sound-to-letter relations in dealing with English orthography.

Even in a quasi-alphabetic system of writing, such as we have in English, there is a persistent **correlation** between knowledge of printed forms and their association with forms of speech. That is, the better people are at reading, the more likely they are to be able to convert printed forms to speech. Should this surprise us? Hardly, because conventional meanings of signs can only be discovered through exemplars of the conventions. This requires associating meanings with forms. Therefore, there must be a correlation between knowledge of print and speech forms. However, there is no evidence in favor of the view that children require access to pseudowords or nonsense to acquire the conventional uses of words or the sound values of letters. In Chapter 4 with reference to the pragmatic bootstrapping argument we showed that children require access to the forms and their meanings. Babbling might seem to be counter evidence, but infant babble is always associated with the speaker and shows primary reference at a minimum from the beginning. Later it incorporates deliberate attention to the listener, secondary reference, and eventually moves on to tertiary reference, that is, meanings beyond speaker and hearer. There is no stage, however, where babble is exclusively about the surface-forms of speech. It appears always to involve people interacting through voluntary vocalizations.

What is more, written symbols are related to sounds even in nonalphabetic languages (Pan, 2004; Pan & Chen, in press). There are associations between written symbols and the phonological (or manual) forms of speech (or manual signs) in all languages. This must include languages that use ideographic or logographic symbols and syllabaries as well as languages that use alphabetic writing systems. This follows because the ability to translate between printed forms and speech forms is a necessary aspect of ordinary literacy in any language regardless of the type of orthography the language may use.

Phonetic/Phonological Correspondences Are Not the Whole Story

The phonics approaches to explaining the processes of reading and writing, and of becoming literate, however, are both superficial and incomplete (Goodman, 1967, 1972, 1993, 1996; Goodman, Goodman, & Flores, 1979;

S. Oller, 2005; Pan, 2004; Pan & Chen, in press; Rattanavich, Walker, & J. Oller, 1992; Smith, 1988a, 1988b). They are superficial because they place essentially all their emphasis on surface-forms. Although most literate persons can read aloud, mature readers are also able to read faster without saying the words aloud. And even some readers at the early stages of becoming literate, for example, Aleka in the video at the beginning of this chapter, can make sense of printed forms of words before being able to say the words in question. If Aleka can do this, should it surprise us that mature readers can also take advantage of entire sequences of letters, for example, in representing the rimes of syllables, or whole words, phrases, or perhaps larger units? Mature readers can use word and letter sequence analogies and take advantage of morphology, phrasing, and syntax to help figure out breath groups and syntactic constructions in general. Mature readers also take advantage of high-level knowledge of meaning. This fact is seen in a great variety of studies of native speakers of English and in nonprimary language users as well (cf., J. Oller & Jonz, 1994; J. Oller et al., 2005).

Throughout the process of language acquisition and certainly in the most effective approaches to early reading, learners rely on the connections between persons, events, and actions in experience. These connections make their experience meaningful. They give it the structure of a story that unfolds over time. We call this **narrative structure** or, **episodic organization**. It affects all sequences of events, stories that report those events, conversations, activities, reports of activities, and so forth. All else being equal, the sequential organization of events and actions applies even to parts of words, to their sounds, letters, or their prefixes, suffixes, and so forth. It tends to apply to words in a phrase, phrases in a sentence, and sentences in any longer text. Narrative reports of a sequence of events tend to be told in **chronological order**. That is, a sequence of events will tend to appear in the narrative in the same order that it seems to occur in experience. For instance, if someone has an accident and then goes to the hospital, the sequence of events tends to be reported in the same order that the events occurred. The events can, of course, be reported in any order we like, but we tend to use a chronological order for reporting.

If we ask why the chronological order of events tends to be preferred in a narrative, we discover that chronology of events is only one aspect of the episodic organization of discourse. Episodic organization of discourse can also be based on spatial, causal, and other **transitive relations**. When we talk about the picture to the left of the fireplace and the window to the left of the picture, the order of the spatial relations is the order in which we think of (A) the fireplace, (B) the picture, and (C) the window. There is a sequence in our talk from A to B to C. If we think of moving our eyes from right to left, we mention the objects in the order A to B to C. On the other hand, if we think of scanning the scene from left to right we are apt to mention the same objects in the order C, B, A. The spatial relation, and the way we act on it gives episodic organization to our discourse. The same system of episodic organization appears in dealing with the spatial relations between the first, second, third, and successive floors of a building, right on up to the top of it. Why do we mention them in the order we do? If we are moving from the bottom upward, the order from bottom to top is likely. However, the opposite would be true for reporting events concerning, say, folks trying to exit from the top floor of a burning building. We would tend to report the sequence starting at the top and working down. Similarly, in a causal relation where a certain event A causes B which leads then to C, to D, and so on, causal relations also provide a basis for episodic organization as seen in written texts (and in narratives). Again, the sequence in the discourse tends to reflect the sequence of events.

It is evident, then, that episodic organization is more general than mere chronological ordering. It is involved in the order of steps, for instance, in solving an algebraic equation. The order in which operations are performed may be important to the solution of the problem. However, the sequence of steps is mainly a question of algebra and only secondarily is it expressed in a certain chronology in discourse. The order of sentences in the report, however, will reflect the order of the steps taken in solving the problem. So we see that episodic organization in discourse can be based on any transitive relation. If A stands in a certain relation to B which stands in that same relation to C, then A must also have the relation in question to C. This is what is meant by a transitive relation, and any such relation will tend to lead to the episodic organization of discourse. Countless transitive relations are possible including chronological ones, causal ones, spatial ones, relations of being greater than (or less than), to the left of, to the right of, above, below, before, after, and so forth. Any one (or any combination of these) can contribute to the production of episodic organization in any given text. In surface-form, however, episodic organization must be reflected in a chronological ordering, or some other marking, of those forms. If event C, for instance, is mentioned ahead of A in telling a story of an event sequence leading from A to B to C, it will be necessary to say something like, "So let's start with C, but keep in mind that before C, B happened, and B was caused by A." This report is more complex than just saying, "So A led from B to C."

Syntactic, Semantic, and Pragmatic Factors All Come into Play

In general, all else being equal, any surface-form (word, phrase, sentence, or whatever) in a connected context, for example, a narrative, activity, or conversation, that fits the sense of the whole dynamic structure of the context will be easier to process than one that does not fit. For example, if we read,

(1) The boy was bucked off by the ____ .

It will be easier to anticipate, to process, and to recall the word *pony* or *horse* in such a context, than a word like *barn* or *car* (Frederiksen, 1975). Why is this? The difference, has little to do with surface-forms as such, but rather it has to do with syntactic, semantic, and pragmatic expectancies that are created by the internal dynamics of the unfolding textual narrative or story. If we think about it, *barn* or *car* are possible terms that could appear in the sequence presented in sentence (1) from a syntactic point of view and neither is much easier or harder from a phonological or lexical point of view than, say, *pony*, or *horse*. However, the latter words are easier to process because they are semantically and pragmatically more predictable. The syntax sets us up to expect an agent rather than a location. It isn't that we don't expect a location at all, but just that we have a greater expectation for an agent (something that bucked off the boy) than for a location (a place where the boy got bucked off).

Or, consider the fact that expectancies can help us at the level of nonsense forms of the sort that were recommended by Bloomfield and his followers. For instance, a sequence of nonce forms like:

(2) nox em glerf onmo keb

is more difficult to read aloud fluently or to reproduce from memory (Osgood, 1949) than

(3) The nox ems glerfed the onmo kebs.

Why is this? Again, it has to do with expectancies. The **cognitive momentum** that is created by syntax assists the mature reader in processing (3) while (2) seems like a disjointed list of pseudowords. Oddly, it is the longer sequence that is easier to say and to recall while we might ordinarily expect the shorter one to be easier. The explanation is clear. Conformity to syntactic expectations makes the pseudowords easier to produce and to recall. We know more about sequences that incorporate the syntax and morphology of English and are thus better able to produce and recall sequences of forms (all else being equal) with the syntactic and morphological markers present rather than omitted.

Similar principles apply when it comes to the processing of phrases of a sentence. Next, consider examples (4) and (5):

(4) We, unprecedented author support, as in the past and our
     record turn around time of an aggressive marketing
     program high quality publications our legacy will continue
     to maintain.

(5) As in the past, we will continue to maintain our legacy of high quality publications, unprecedented author support, an aggressive marketing program, and our record turn around time.

Isn't (5) easier to read fluently and to understand than (4)? All we did in creating example (4) was to change the order of key phrases in (5). Everything else remains equal across the two examples, and yet, (5) is a lot easier to make sense of. The fact is that the order and arrangement of phrases is important. The same holds for ideas in a text. We expect them to flow in forward motion from beginning to end. This is nicely illustrated in an example from Graesser, Millis, & Zwaan (1997):

(6) A mushy, brown peach is lifted from the garbage and placed on the table to turn pink. It turns pink, it gets firm, it is carried in a shopping sack to the grocer's, put on a shelf, removed and crated, returned to the tree with pink blossoms. In this world time flows backward (from Lightman, 1993, p. 102).

Graesser et al. (1997) observe that "without seeing the last sentence, the event sequence is 'incoherent' because there are no obvious causal connections" (p. 168). Or, expressing the case more completely, we believe, the mature reader does not expect time to flow backward and is surprised to be told that it does. On the contrary, the mature reader expects time to flow from the future, through the present, and into the past rather than the reverse. Or, alternatively, we may think of the present becoming the past while the future becomes the present. Regardless how we think of it, experience and what some have called "time's arrow" seems to have a certain, evidently irreversible, direction to it. In experience, at least, time only seems to go one way (see http://www.philphys.nl/conferenceslouvain.html visited on October 9, 2005) and even in the processing of what seem to be very brief individual events temporal sequence is still a factor (van der Meer, Kruger, & Nuthmann, 2005).

Conversations, dramatic re-enactments, and both of these as incorporated in narratives, films, plays, and novels also show important chronological elements. For instance, consider the following conversations:

(7) Conversation 1 between speakers A and B.

    a. A: Hey man! How was the trip to Berlin?

    b. B: Great! Good conference. Met some people. Sunny most of the week. I've been thinkin' about that racquetball game.

    c. A: Well, I've got to put it off for a while. I'm going in for back surgery on Wednesday morning.

(8) Conversation 2

    a. A: Sunny most of the week.

    b. B: Great! Good conference. Met some people.

    c. A: I'm going in for back surgery on Wednesday morning.

    d. B: Hey man! How was the trip to Berlin?

    e. A: I've been thinkin' about that racquetball game.

Although both conversations involve the same surface-forms, the sentences in (8) make a lot less sense than the ones in (7). Why is this?

The difference is that the exchanges in (7) are connected to each other through what Sacks, Schegloff, and Jefferson (1974) called latchings. In fact, the latchings involve inferences that reflect episodic organization of the chronological sort. The turns of the speakers in a conversation occur in a certain order. They are typically marked by pauses, intonations, and the like that show beginnings and endings. Even when these marks are left out of the written form, for the most part mature readers can imagine them for (7) but not for (8). How do we do this and what is the difference? Each turn in (7), but not in (8), is followed by a response that takes the former turn into account. The connections are reflected in the argument structures and shared referents from one turn to the next. In (7a) speaker A refers to a trip, and B in (7b) describes the results of the trip and then changes the topic. In (7c) A comments on the racquetball game, which we infer was agreed to earlier, and A explains why it will need to be postponed. A then brings up a new topic. The latchings in question show the episodic organization according to chronological and causal relations in ordinary experience. If the conversation is based on true representations, we may suppose that B has recently traveled to Berlin and returned to the point of origin, that A and B had planned to play racquetball, that A is going to have surgery, and that the racquetball game will have to be put off. The difference between conversation and narrative, or other forms of discourse is profound, but like narratives, conversations are also subject to constraints from episodic organization, in other words, from abstract transitive relations.

Chronological Order in Narrative, Conversation, and Actions

Relevant research and theory shows that all cultures and languages operate with the expectation that narrative structures tend to flow in a certain direction from the relatively well determined past, into the dynamic and changing present, which looks toward the uncertain future. This is not merely a western European point of view as some have attempted to argue (for example, Clarke, 1982: Clarke, Losoff, & Rood, 1982). It is a universal necessity of the nature of human experience. There are no cultures where the natural birth of an individual, for example, comes after the individual's parents have grown old and died, nor are there any cultures where the aging process leads from old age to infancy rather than in the reverse direction. Grandparents do not become parents and then children in that order. The opposite is true and the transitive temporal relation (all else being equal) of A coming before B which comes before C guarantees that A will come before C in all cultures and languages.

Figure 10–4 is a diagram of the way narrative dynamics normally work. At the left-hand side of the diagram we represent the past relative to any ordinary observer. The middle part of the diagram represents the changing present, and the right-hand third of the diagram represents the relatively unknown future. The ellipses on either side of the diagram show that there is no necessary starting point for the past nor any necessary ending point for the future. The top part of the diagram shows how representations flow into the material world of ordinary experience which is represented in the bottom part of the diagram. You will notice that at just the point where the present meets the past, an indefinite moment in any case, the realm of representations joins up with and is welded to the realm of material events. That is, once representations are formed and become memories, they are as much joined to the unalterable past as any other actions are. As for the future, it is known to us only through representations of an inferential kind. We have expectations about the future, but no memory. With the present where actions are occurring, we have consciousness and memories are in the process of being formed. With the past, we have both representations in the form of memories and these seem to have been welded together with what was formerly a perception of the present but now is just a memory in the past.

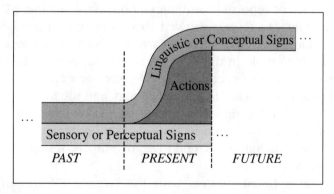

Figure 10–4. The pragmatic mapping process distributed over time.

We cannot recover the words we have already uttered (though sometimes we would like to). We cannot change any of our past actions. We may be able to change directions in our car, to back up and take another road, but we cannot change the facts of our actions once they have already been performed. This includes the sorts of actions involved in producing and interpreting representations. The only place where we can act is in the present and all that we know about the future, as the diagram suggests is based on expectancies that are formed and known in representations. Our perceptual experience ends right at the edge where the present meets the future. Past experience of any observer, by contrast with the future of the same observer, is known because the observer has lived through the past when it was still present. So memories of the past, in just this way, are very different from anticipations of the future. However, the only place where actions can be taken is in the middle of the diagram which represents the present.

Certain Predictions Follow

On the basis of the relations depicted in the diagram of Figure 10-4, all else being equal, it is possible to predict that texts conforming to ordinary chronological arrangements ought to be easier to process, that is, for speakers and writers to produce, and for listeners and readers to interpret, and for either or both of them to recall and/or reproduce than texts that violate chronological order. In fact, the relevant research bears out this prediction in a great many ways (cf. J. Oller et al., 2005). The normal expectation that events in experience, conversations, and therefore in narratives and reports of experience, should unfold in a temporal order according to ordinary causal relations is manifested in countless ways in ordinary discourse and in writing. What is more, these manifestations of the ordinary unfolding of event sequences are evidently quite independent of cultural background, language of reporting, and interactions between these factors.

For example, Lin (1989) showed that Chinese and English-speakers tend to report a sequence of events in a wordless film in the same order in which the events unfold in the film. In the film known as *The Pear Story* (Chafe, 1980), a series of events occurs. We see, for example, a boy load a box of pears on his bicycle. He has an accident and the pears are all spilled on the ground. Both Chinese and English-speakers tend to relate the sequence of events in the film in the same chronological order. Chinese and English-speaking bilinguals tend to report the event sequence similarly in both languages.

By the same token, studies with the so-called "frog stories" have produced a similar result across the languages that have been studied. See Figure 10-5 for a couple of pictures from the wordless *Frog! Where Are You?* book. In using that book, Chen (2005) found, among other things,

Figure 10–5. A sequence of pictures (reading top to bottom) from the middle of the story, *Frog, Where Are You?* by Mercer Mayer (1967). Used by permission. Copyright © 1967 W. W. Norton & Company, Inc.

that Mandarin speakers at all ages, like speakers of the other languages that have been studied, also tend to report the events in the order in which they appear in the wordless picture book. There are interesting differences within sentences and in the way motion events are conceptualized, but the event sequence, or the series of changes in states of affairs, tends to be treated chronologically.

The Frog Story Narratives

Although it was not the purpose of research with the "Frog Story" to verify that episodic organization is universal, the research done nevertheless supports this conclusion. Episodic organization with a temporal chronology as its default starting point is evidently universal. The fact that languages tend to respect such a chronology is not surprising. Because all experience in every culture must of necessity unfold over time because of the nature of the material world, the human body, and how our senses work, it should not surprise us that narratives, reports of activities, and even fictions, errors, and lies tend to be constructed so as to account for temporal relations in ordinary experience.

On the other hand, perhaps it should surprise us, that phonics approaches to literacy and reading instruction do not take much notice of the kinds of expectancy that are based on temporal relations in experience. If we ask why a chronological report is more likely than any other order that might be associated with a series of events in experience, in an activity, or in a conversation, the answer is not difficult to find. From the point of view of the theory of pragmatic mapping, if each event in a series, E1, E2, E3, and so forth, is assigned a distinct symbol, say, S1, S2, S3, and so on, to represent it, the logically simplest order in which to present the sequence of symbols in representing the sequence of events is in the same order in which the events occurred in the first place. Putting the whole argument simply, the simplest representation of any sequence of events represented in any sequence of symbols will be the chronological one. If E1 is mapped onto S1, E2 onto S2, and so forth, both the producer of the sequence of symbols and any interpreter can easily recover the sequence of events. Similarly, the sequence of events will help in constructing the sequence of symbols. Any other mapping arrangement, for example, S1 to E3, S2 to E1, S3 to E2, say, will require special marking of the symbols so that the original order of the events can be recovered. For instance, it will be necessary of the interpreter to know that E3 did not actually occur first in the sequence, and so on for any event reported out of order. Because of the need to specially mark the symbols reporting events out of sequence, no matter what nonchronological order may be proposed, it will always be more complex than the chronological one. For this reason, all speakers in all languages tend to prefer the default chronological order in reporting narratives, conversations, activities, and the like. Even fictional stories and films are easier to understand and to recall when event sequences are presented in a chronological order.

Violations Are More Difficult to Process

Ohtsuka and Brewer (1992) found that texts violating ordinary chronological order either by **flashbacks** or with **flashforwards** were more difficult to understand. A flashback would be the sort of case where, in the case of the text about the mushy brown peach, if after seeing it mashed on the grocery store floor that we saw the same peach in a nice firm shape hanging on the branch of a peach tree, being picked, placed in a box, shipped to the grocery store, and then placed on a shelf. A flashforward in the same sequence of events would be to see the peach hanging on the branch of the tree and then to skip over the picking of the peach, its transportation to the store, its being placed on the shelf, and to leap ahead to its being smashed on the floor of the grocery store. Ohtsuka and Brewer found that flashforwards in narratives were so disruptive that they reduced comprehension scores to chance levels. Similarly, all kinds of scrambling of the orderly arrangements in any text will, all else being kept equal, ordinarily make it harder to process, to understand, and to recall.

Becoming Literate Is Cognitive Empowerment

Learning to read and write provides us with tools that increase our power to represent things. More particularly literacy enables us to represent ideas, to explore them, and to develop them more thoroughly than we could without being literate. With respect to episodic organization in text and discourse, several paradigms of research have demonstrated that literacy enhances our listening comprehension and speaking abilities, or what has been called **oracy**. This idea has been suggested by Gernsbacher, Varner, & Faust (1990) who have said that "performance in language comprehension tasks should correlate with performance in other comprehension tasks" (p. 12).

Literacy is less obviously related to our ability to comprehend mathematical problems or what has been called **numeracy** (Capps & Pickreign, 1993; Kolstad, Briggs & Whalen, 1996; Schell, 1982; Schwartz, 1988). Could you solve the following math problem if you could not read it? Could you solve it at all without relying on your language capacity and your ability to draw inferences?

> Bill has $10 in his pocket. He spends half of it for candy at the movies and it costs him $4.50 to get into the theater. He lost a quarter that fell from his pocket while he was watching the film. When he heads for home, how much money does Bill still have in his pocket?

Literacy enhances all our discourse processing skills, our memory, our inference making abilities, and our reasoning (for example, see Gernsbacher et al., 1990). Literacy provides a toolbox of resources that harness and enrich our representational capacities and make us more capable thinkers and better communicators in general. Among the early research showing the profound relation between literacy and listening comprehension is a study by Sticht (1972). He wondered if an oral representation of an instruction manual for mechanics could be made more intelligible if he presented the instructions orally. What he found was a strong correlation between the ability to understand the written manual and an oral presentation of it. On the whole, native speakers of English who had trouble understanding the written instructions had trouble understanding the oral reading of the manual when it was provided to them on tape. Those individuals who could understand the written instructions also excelled at understanding the oral ones. At about the same time, multiple studies of nonprimary language acquisition were showing the same result. Although the ability to understand speech in a particular language is certainly not perfectly correlated with the ability to understand written forms of the same language, there is a significant and substantial correlation between these abilities (Hofstetter, Sticht, Hofstetter, 1999; Sticht, 1972, 1978, 1988, 1995; Sticht, Hofstetter, & Hofstetter, 1996). What the research shows (for example, J. Oller, 1976; J. Oller, Kim, Choe, & Hernandez-Jarvis, 2001; J. Oller & Perkins, 1978b) is that literacy and oracy are interrelated. A language user who improves in one tends also to improve in the other.

Literacy empowers us as thinkers. The research shows that as we advance in our abilities to represent and to understand representations, our cognitive abilities are enhanced. Literacy further develops our capacity to:

- Acquire knowledge about how things work, for example, how the parts of a new piece of equipment go together, or who ordered the laptop,

- Plan a course of action, for example, to remember what to buy at the grocery or hardware store,

- Make sense of a conversation, for instance, to know that Austria is on the southeastern border of Germany,

- Figure out what a set of instructions means, for example, to know how to load new software,

- Know what someone else is talking about, for example, understanding a term like "bootstrapping,"

- Make sense of discourse of any kind, and

- Draw appropriate inferences from experience, discourse, and text.

The same kinds of pragmatic reasoning and inference apply to our understanding of representations in general and to our understanding in particular of written texts and of spoken discourse. As a result, as we improve in ability to understand written texts, we are virtually certain to improve in our ability to understand spoken discourse forms as well. This is entirely obvious when learning a second dialect or language, for instance. Before we understand the target language we will not understand the written texts of that language or its spoken discourse. However, as we acquire spoken words in the language we are better able to understand those same words when they are written down, and vice versa. The same is true in our native language. Consider a word like "Australopithecus Africanus." Before we saw these words written down they would have been harder for us to understand in the stream of speech or in writing. Once we learn that they refer to a certain species of ape and so forth, we can make shorter work of processing the sequence and we can integrate it into any text or spoken discourse more easily.

The Unity of Coherence

Literacy improves our ability to make associations leading to what C. S. Peirce (1903/1934) called the **unity of coherence**. The unity of coherence is the sort of interpretation of a representation that not only makes sense, but it fits so well that we quit looking for any other interpretation of that representation until or unless some bit of information comes up that does not fit into the picture as we have already understood things. Ordinarily, the experience of a normal individual is coherent. The same holds for our understanding of ordinary representations including conversations, news reports, written texts, and all kinds of discourse.

When you wake up in the morning and find yourself in the same room where you remember falling asleep the night before, and where you usually wake up, you do not suddenly go into a panic and ask yourself, "Oh my! Where am I?" The evidence that surrounds you on all sides conforms to the interpretation that you are, say, at home in your own bed, in your own house, at a certain address, on a certain street, in a certain town, in a given state, and country on good old planet Earth, at a particular time, and so forth. This interpretation fits all the relevant facts so well that it leads to what Peirce called, "the unity of coherence." An analogy for this kind of coherence is the way things sometimes fit together, like your upper and lower teeth when the bite is well adjusted. In Glenberg's terminology, they fit together. They **mesh**.

Discourse in context is commonly like ordinary experience. Much of the time it achieves the unity of coherence. We often, usually in fact, come to an interpretation that fits, meshes, with all the facts. For instance, if suppose someone calls you on the phone in the morning to ask if you sent that important Email last night concerning the book you are co-authoring. That person, reminds us of a meeting later in the day that both of us, and several other persons are supposed to attend. In conversations like this, we have little reason to doubt the facts, the reports, or our own understanding of these things. We do not stop to wonder long about whether we or they are actually just dreaming, mistaken about the facts, don't know who we are talking to, or what we are talking about, and so forth.

It is true, of course, that some doubtful philosopher might say that you don't really know where you are, or who you are, but to make sense of this sort of argument, the philosopher will have to go to a lot of trouble to explain that you might be mistaken, you might be having a vivid dream about waking up in your bed at home, that you and he could be on Mars in some space travel experiment, or you could really be in prison at this very moment having a vivid dream where the person you think you are talking to on the phone is a figment of your imagination, or you may have fallen into evil hands and some crafty individuals may have devised an elaborate scheme to deceive you by setting up a place in a remote desert of Nevada that just looks like your house, and so on and so forth. But, after the philosopher poses these ideas, suppose you get up and go into the bathroom and brush your teeth. Your toothbrush is in the drawer where it usually is. The toothpaste you bought at Walgreens is there. It tastes the same as it did the day before when you brushed your teeth. And so on.

For all these facts to achieve so much unity without being as they seem to be would become more and more difficult to such a degree that it becomes less and less likely that your belief that you are at your own house and that you slept the night in your own bed is probably correct. When we achieve this sort of unity of coherence, where every bit of evidence available to us supports the understanding we are inclined to reach, we suppose that our interpretation of things is correct. And most of the time it is.

In fact, every kind of representational evidence that can be mustered commonly comes into play sooner or later in our ordinary experience and is useful in enabling us to achieve the unity of coherence about who we are, where we are, and what is going on around us, what someone just said, what this or that written text means, what the news means, what is happening in a conversation, a movie, or a novel, and so forth.

Distinct Kinds of Conceptualization and Memory

With respect to literacy and the processing of written texts in particular, two sources of inference from memory have commonly been distinguished. These have often been referred to as **episodic memory** and **semantic memory** (Tulving, 1972). Episodic memory is the sort that enables us to recall a sequence of events. What has been called semantic memory, by contrast, has to do with what Glenberg (1997) has termed "permanent links or associations." Sims and Gray (2004) explain that episodic memory is the sort we have for the birth of a our first child or our first new car. Semantic memory by contrast concerns such isolated things as how many states there are in the United States or whether Georgia is in the south. However, episodic organization, as we have already seen, reaches across time. It reaches from the past, which we know about from memory, through the present which we know though our own **consciousness**, to the future about which we have certain expectancies and anticipations. As a result episodic organization is not restricted to memories. It also applies to our consciousness of the present, and to our anticipations and expectations for the future. However, the term "episodic memory" reminds us that memories of events tend to be connected with each other in the order in which they occurred. In episodic organization, distinct events A, B, C, D, and so on, are temporally, spatially, causally, or otherwise connected in some order that enables us to connect A with B and B with C and so on in a certain order in the way we represent them conceptually in imaginations, in actions, or in words. The episodic connections between A with B and B with C, however, require some lapse of time as in acting, moving, or scanning, for example, referring to A before mentioning B, and so on. Episodes and episodic organization involve time.

What has been called "semantic memory," which is more accurately termed **semantic conceptualization**, by contrast, does not seem to require much or perhaps any time at all. Glenberg (1997) referred to semantic memories as "permanent." They appear as if they were instantaneous or prior associations between concepts. For example, our knowledge of the usual shape, size, weight, density, texture, and so on, of a brick, or a pillow, balloon, or any familiar thing that we have previously conceptualized seems to be available to us all at once whenever we think of it. For instance, consider the meanings you would associate with the following sentence if you alternately put the words *balloon*, *pillow*, or *brick* in the blank:

(8) Bill playfully threw the _____ at Susan.

We are less apt to question Bill's motives with the balloon than with the pillow, but by the time we get to the brick, we begin to doubt whether or not Bill is being playful. In fact, the inference of the danger associated with the throwing of a brick, as contrasted with a balloon or a pillow, comes from the nature of the objects referred to. Balloons and pillows are generally soft and harmless while bricks are hard and potentially harmful. What is more, by the same sort of inferential processes, we suppose that Bill, knowing the difference between bricks and pillows, either has playful or harmful intentions. We tend to hold Bill responsible for the danger to Susan if he throws a brick at her. His motive in throwing the brick is tainted by our semantic conceptualization of what a brick is and the damage that it can do when it is thrown. It is difficult for us to see such an act as playful while throwing a pillow or a balloon at Susan seems harmless enough to be a playful act.

Meshing, Priming, and Probes

The idea of playing seems compatible with throwing a balloon, pillow, beanbag, or anything soft at someone, but it comes into conflict with the conceptual properties associated with something like a brick, or a chair, or a bicycle, or anything dense, hard, heavy, with well defined surfaces and edges. To use Glenberg's term, playing does not "mesh" with a person throwing a brick at someone else, but it does mesh with a person throwing a balloon. To use a different example, we can push an apple with a stick, but we cannot push an apple with a thread (Glenberg & Robertson, 1999, 2000; Kaschak & Glenberg, 2000). In Glenberg's use, meshing is the sort of thing that occurs when gears fit together well in dynamic harmony. The opposite of meshing might be termed clashing, repulsion, or just a failure to connect or to harmonize. Incompatible meanings seem to repel each other and do not mesh. Other meanings are attracted to each other like chemical elements that fit together and form bonds. But notice that with semantic conceptualizations, or any abstract symbolic representation, there are so many possible meanings that could be mentioned that we can never exhaust them. We cannot list all of them. We have not mentioned that bricks are inert, inanimate objects, small enough to be picked up in one hand, used in building, and so forth. Oddly, on the other hand, we seem to know all these facts and a great many more as soon as we have the semantic conceptualization of the sort of brick that someone might pick up. We have all this information available suddenly, all at once.

As a result, what has been called episodic thinking or experience seems very different from what has been called semantic conceptualization. With episodic understanding distinct events seem to appear one after another. They come on stage as distinct things and unfold, develop, or emerge over time. By contrast, semantic conceptualizations, or in fact any symbolic representation, seems to be already complete as soon as it comes to mind and all its countless associations seem to be more or less suddenly available, all at once. Experimental evidence of the power of semantic conceptualizations to shape and guide our interpretations of texts and discourse are abundant in the vast research literature of psychology and related fields. One such evidence is that in sentence (9) the perception, production, and recall of words like *balloon, pillow,* and *beanbag* will be facilitated by their compatibility with the notion that Bill is playing with Susan, while words like *brick, chair,* and *bicycle* will be more difficult to process. Such effects are called **priming** and can be demonstrated in a great many ways.

One way is to present a series of sentences similar to (9) with either a semantically primed word appearing in the blank, or an incompatible word appearing there. Later, subjects may be asked to say whether or not the word they heard in that blank was say, *brick,* an alternative that is incompatible with the word *play,* or was say, *pillow.* The words that participants are asked to recall in such a paradigm are called **probe words** (or just "probes"). Because of the semantic priming effect, if all else is held equal, normal listener/readers will tend to perceive, produce, and recall compatible probes better than incompatible ones. That is, in Glenberg's terms they will prefer probes that "mesh" with the whole context over probes that are not consistent with the context. We can say that, just as water seeks its own level, reader/listeners tend to seek out the unity of coherence.

There are many variations in the literature on this theme, but all of them show that reading, writing, conversations, and discourse processing in general normally involve subtle processes of inference at the very highest levels of the representational hierarchy. In short, reading is much more than just converting letters to sounds. It commonly involves all the representational resources that are applied by human beings in seeking the unity of coherence. Literacy involves making sense of discourse and representations. In this respect it is just another manifestation of the human language capacity.

Summing Up and Looking Ahead

In this chapter we have seen how a normal child can understand and read printed words before being able to say the words out loud. We have reviewed phonics and whole-language approaches to building literacy and have seen why narrative structure is basic to experience, conversational interaction, and to all forms of discourse. We see why events and episodes of experience tend to be reported in their chronological order and why conversations must unfold more or less in a linear sequence over time. We have seen evidence that literacy enhances representational abilities and that readers and listeners tend toward the unity of coherence in making sense of text, discourse, and conversation. In the following chapter we consider the problems associated with the great diversity of languages and dialects in the world. We will see there that just as literacy enhances oral language knowledge, skills, and abilities, acquiring another language/dialect, provided the learner advances to a sufficiently high level of proficiency in the target language, also enhances cognitive and linguistic abilities in general.

STUDY AND DISCUSSION QUESTIONS

1. When and how does it become possible for a child to convert printed words to speech? By contrast, about when can the normal child first demonstrate comprehension of spoken words? What

explains the separation between these events and why should we expect that children are able to start reading words about 4 to 5 years before they achieve what used to be called the age of "reading readiness"?

2. In addition to alphabetic writing, what other kinds of writing systems are there? Is it essential to be able to sound out words in order to read them? If not, why not? What evidence can you offer to support your argument one way or the other?

3. What are the main arguments of the phonics approach in favor of using nonsense to learn to read? In what ways does the research support or not support these recommendations? For instance, does it generally make things more difficult for us to remember, to perceive, or to comprehend words if we know their meanings? Think of the case of foreign language learning? Is it easier to recall words in the language of which you have no idea of the meaning? If so, why so? If not, why not?

4. What are some of the methods used to teach phonological awareness? How well do they work according to their proponents? What explanations can you offer for the observed outcomes in teaching phonological awareness? Is there are relation to dyslexia? Does phonological awareness training cure most dyslexia? Does it remove the tedium, effortfulness, or slowness of reading by sounding out words?

5. Consider the role of analogy and inference in reading comprehension and literacy. What is the difference between semantic and episodic memory? How do these concepts relate to the ordinary organization of experience and inferences drawn from it?

6. What is the unity of coherence and how is it commonly achieved by interlocutors? How do you know when you have achieved it?

7. What is Glenberg's idea of "meshing" and how does it relate to the "connectedness" of discourse? Consider causal, temporal, and spatial relations? Which of these are more tightly integrated and how do they relate to chronology in narratives or reports of event sequences?

CHAPTER 11

The Role of Nonprimary Languages and Dialects

After studying this chapter you should:

1. See why language/dialect differences are important to communication everywhere;

2. Better appreciate the vast but uncertain number of languages and dialects in the world;

3. Be able to explain and identify characteristics of good testing and assessment procedures;

4. Realize why language/dialect differences are not the same as deficits or disorders;

5. Understand how nonprimary language/dialects are normally acquired;

6. Know the difference between tests aimed at intelligence, achievement, aptitude, personality, and so on, and why all of them depend on language/dialect skills; and

7. Know how acquiring a new language/dialect can enhance representational abilities.

KEY TERMS

Here are some terms and concepts that you may learn more about in this chapter (these are also defined in the Glossary):

achievement test
African American Vernacular English
alveolar
aptitude test
attitude measurement
bodily kinesthetic intelligence
code-switching
common writing system criterion
competency test
contrastive analysis
criterion-referenced test
diglossia
final position
foreign language setting
genderlect
General American English
general intelligence
graduation test
immersion program
innate intelligence
intelligence test
intelligibility criterion
interpersonal intelligence
interpretability (practicality)
interval scale
intrapersonal intelligence
journal assessment
language/dialect deficit
language/dialect difference
logical mathematical intelligence

medial position
minimal pair contrast
multiple intelligences
musical intelligence
mutual intelligibility criterion
national boundary criterion
nominal scale
nonverbal (nonlinguistic) intelligence
norm-referenced test
ordinal scale
performance testing
personality inventory
polyglot
portfolio assessment
qualitative assessment
quantitative assessment
ratio scale
regional dialect
second language setting
social dialect
spatial intelligence
standardized test
submersion program
task-based language teaching/testing
    strategy
total physical response (TPR) strategy
velar
verbal fluency
verbal (linguistic) intelligence
vocabulary fluency

What happens when the language/dialect at school, work, and on the road is not the one spoken at home? What happens to children who come to school speaking some language/dialect that is not the main language/dialect used by the school community? What happens to workers and travelers for whom the language/dialect they need to use is not their native language/dialect? Children of minority language/dialect backgrounds not only face all the usual challenges of normal schooling, learning to read, write, do arithmetic, and to socialize with adults and other children, but they have the additional challenge of doing all this in a language/dialect they have not yet learned. Adults who work and live where the language/dialect is not their primary language, face problems similar to those of children in the schools, but the cost of miscommunications may, sometimes be greater, even a matter of life and death as it is, for instance, in today's global international travel by air (see Badon, S. Oller, Yan, & J. Oller, 2005).

Minority language/dialect users have to accomplish all the usual tasks in a language that may be as unfamiliar to them as Chinese is to an English-speaker. Or, even if the individual speaks a dialect of English, the main dialect of the school may sound as strange as Jamaican English, say, does to most Californians. In this chapter we will see that misunderstandings associated with **language/dialect differences** are widespread, commonly underestimated, and increasingly vital to the well-being of individuals throughout the world. We also consider how much it is possible to compensate for language/dialect differences at school and in the workplace through nonverbal, or so-called **performance**, tasks and tests. Can language/dialect differences be neutralized in nonverbal tasks? Is it possible to get the instructions to nonverbal tasks across without recourse to any particular language/dialect? Can unbiased judgments be made about abnormalities, disorders, and giftedness, say, on the basis of nonverbal tasks? In other words, how can we avoid confusing mere language/dialect differences with **language/dialect deficits**?

The Importance of Language/Dialect Differences

On March 27, 1977, the worst air traffic accident in the history of aviation, at least up to now, occurred at Tenerife Airport in the Canary Islands. Two fully loaded Boeing 747s collided killing 563 passengers. The Dutch KLM 747 was taking off while a Pan Am 747 was crossing the runway. Like 70% of the near-misses and fatal accidents reported in international aviation (see Ritter, 1996; Tajima, 2004), this one too was caused by a misunderstanding of language. The pilots and air traffic controllers were speaking to each other in a common language, English, but it was not the native language of any of the key speakers.

In a study published in 1996 by Boeing Aircraft, concerning 28,000 written reports of incidents and near-misses occurring between 1982 and 1991, 70% of all these problems and 11% of the fatalities could be attributed to language/dialect problems. Writing for and about the International Civil Aviation Organization (ICAO), Day (2005) said, "The most vulnerable link in our . . . airspace system is information transfer between air traffic controllers and pilots" (p. 1). Because the lives of international travelers, not to mention commerce and the transportation of goods, depend on successful communication between pilots and air traffic controllers, the ICAO has established more stringent English language standards to be complied with by March 5, 2008 (Day, 2004, 2005; Mathews, 2001, 2003, 2004; Mell, 2004). In international aviation, near native skill in English is required because of the life and death issues at stake (Mitsutomi & O'Brien, 2004).

The fact that English is the default language, of international aviation, of course, is not because it is a better language but because English is the most widely spoken nonprimary (second) language. At Tenerife Airport, the difficulty arose because crucial statements were not understood as intended. In the end the interpretations did not agree with the facts. The errors cost a lot of people their lives. A critical linguistic problem came up when an air traffic controller issued certain climb out and heading instructions to the KLM captain. The captain repeated the instructions and said, "We are now at takeoff." He meant that he was accelerating to takeoff speed. The controller understood the statement, "We are now at takeoff," to mean that the pilot was waiting at the end of the runway for clearance. The lives lost that day came to depend on whether the phrase *at takeoff* meant "ready and waiting to take off" or "already taking off."

Not only is the example relevant to all travelers who fly in or out of international airports, but it is relevant to all communications that depend on shared language/dialect uses. It is also more obvious with respect to international aviation than in many other applications of language that understanding representations and getting the facts right is critical. The stakes are life and death and the problems faced affect all flights, all travelers, and all the people on the ground coming and going from international airports every day. All international travelers are dependent on the intelligibility of the languages/dialects used in international airports by pilots and air traffic controllers every time they travel. However, air travel is not the only industry where agreement on the meanings and uses of linguistic representations matters.

Using intelligible language/dialect forms is essential to teaching, learning, and assessment in classrooms and educational contexts everywhere. The importance of making sense of linguistic forms may be less evident in schools than it is in international airports, but language/dialect use and comprehension is probably the most important work that goes on in any school at any time. Also, just as 70% of the reported mishaps and near-mishaps in international aviation critically involve the use of one or more language/dialects, the vast majority of difficulties in teaching and testing are also dependent on using and understanding a common language/dialect. Increasingly, teachers and learners throughout the world, and especially here in the United States, are faced with situations where they do not necessarily share a common language/dialect. The problems that arise because of the mismatches are on the rise.

The Growing Multitude of Languages at School

Today, in urban centers around the world, from Los Angeles to Bangkok, from Buenos Aires to Toronto, and from Singapore to Nairobi, everywhere we look, the number of languages and dialects to be dealt with in schools and in the workplace has exploded from a handful at most to dozens or even hundreds of languages. During the last three decades researchers have discovered that the surprisingly large number of distinct languages of the world is even greater than previously believed.

What Counts as a Language and What Counts as a Dialect?

What makes two languages different languages as opposed to being different dialects (varieties) of the same language? Three criteria have been applied in distinguishing languages and their dialects. However, it should be kept in mind that everyone speaks one or more dialects of some language. For a given dialect to count as a separate language, according to Max Weinreich (1953), it just needs to acquire its own army and navy. But with the idea in mind that everyone everywhere speaks a "dialect" and that no dialect is intrinsically better than any other, let us see how the practical distinctions are commonly made between languages and dialects.

The main criterion for telling the difference between languages is whether or not the users of the potentially different systems can understand each other or not. That is, can the speakers who use system A understand the speakers of B and vice versa. If A and B meet this **mutual intelligibility criterion**, they are commonly judged to be dialects of the same language (Karam, 1979). For example, speakers of American English readily understand speakers of British English, for the most part, so we would say that these two varieties of English are in fact dialects or varieties of the same language. However, French, Italian, Spanish, Portuguese, and Romania are all varieties of Latin, but speakers of French, for instance, do not readily understand speakers of Spanish and vice versa. Therefore, we would say that French and Spanish are different languages even though they are both derived from Latin. One of the reasons we do not consider French to be a dialect of Latin is because the modern languages derived from Latin, including French, Spanish, Portuguese, Italian, and Romanian, for the most part, are not mutually intelligible.

Although mutual intelligibility is important to practical distinctions between languages, it is not the only basis for distinguishing languages. Some languages are mutually intelligible and yet are still considered to be different languages because of national boundaries. For instance, Swedish and Norwegian are considered different languages but Swedes and Norwegians can usually understand each other. Spanish is considered a different language from Italian and yet these systems are somewhat mutually intelligible. In these cases the **national boundary criterion** overrides their mutual intelligibility. Also, mutual intelligibility is not an on-or-off issue. It varies by degrees and with a lot of dynamic unevenness. In some cases, A can be understood by speakers of B, but speakers of B have a hard time understanding A. If a third related system C, for instance, is added into the picture the dynamics may be more complex still. Speakers of A may understand B and B may understand C, but A and C may not understand each other. Or, speakers of A may be understood by both B and C, though B and C cannot understand each other well, and A may understand neither B nor C. For instance, speakers of Portuguese understand more of Spanish and Italian, typically, than Spanish or Italian speakers understand of Portuguese.

According to the mutual intelligibility criterion, dialects (or varieties) of a given language are merely different forms of the same underlying language system. However, even if we combine the mutual intelligibility criterion with the national boundary criterion, we will not be able to account fully for the common distinctions that are made between languages and dialects of a language. In addition to those criteria we must add that sharing, or not sharing, a common writing system is a third criterion that also comes into play. Because the same standardized Chinese writing system, for example, is used throughout China, in spite of the fact that there are several major dialects of Chinese, including Mandarin, Wu, Cantonese, Hunanese, Min, Hakka, and Gan (Gordon, 2005), that are *not* mutually intelligible in their spoken form, all these are Chinese. In another notable case, Urdu (of Pakistan and Northern India) and Hindi (common to much of India), though essentially the same in their spoken forms, use different writing systems and are considered different languages rather than dialects of the same language. So, the **common writing system criterion** is also a third factor sometimes used in differentiating languages and dialects of languages. However, it is not decisive by itself. Japanese and Chinese have many characters in common in their writing but are regarded as different languages because of national boundaries and because they are not mutually intelligible.

If we ask how do people tell which dialect is which, the answer is that even the experts run into difficulty. The more intensively and minutely the question is examined the more difficult the problem appears to be. Viewed in historical perspective, over the long haul, factors that tend to produce or be associated with language/dialect differences include geographical boundaries like rivers, mountains, and oceans. These factors tend to produce **regional dialects** (Bloomfield, 1933; Kurath & McDavid, 1961). Factors known to contribute to diversity also include differences in gender, ethnicity, and social status. These kinds of factors tend to produce what have been termed **genderlects** (Tannen, 1986) or **social dialects** (Labov, 1994). However, no combinations of factors is certain to produce language/dialect differences nor are there any known factors that are certain to reduce or eliminate them. On the other hand, factors that tend to be commonly associated with the homogenization of language/dialects, that is, the reduction of differences, are greater mobility, commerce, and transportation.

One inevitable conclusion is that the number of dialects, that is, the varieties of any given language, can never be fully known. One reason is that languages and all their varieties are constantly subject to change. The need to achieve communication forces changes in the surface-forms of language. As people seek ways to understand and to be understood, the surface-forms of their speech and all the manifestations of language are constantly subject to tuning, retuning, shaping and reshaping. When communication succeeds, people tend to use the same facial expressions, the same gestures, and the same forms of speech as those around them are using (Wilson, 2001). By contrast, when communication does not succeed, conflicts and upheavals are more likely. As a result, when different systems come into contact, they are almost certain to change (Weinreich, 1953; Labov, 1994).

Differences between varieties can arise in all the same ways that differences between mutually unintelligible languages arise: the differences can be in the sounds, rhythms, intonations, and absolutely any aspect of surface-form; they can be in the words used to represent a given concept, in the syntactic structures used to express a given meaning, in the way concepts are parsed up and packaged in different surface-forms (Slobin, 1996, 2003, 2004; and Strömqvist & Verhoeven, 2004). So what is it that causes a mere dialect or variety of a language, say, Danish or Portuguese, to come to be recognized as a separate language rather than a mere dialect or variety? The best answer we know is still Weinreich's: the Danes and the Portuguese have armies and navies. The fact is that everyone who speaks any language at all must speak a dialect/variety of that language. There are no accentless, unmarked, strictly "vanilla" varieties of any language. All languages and all their dialects are flavored. However, it is inevitable that some language/dialects have larger numbers of speakers and greater political power in the world.

Code-switching is the ability that many language users employ when they change their dialect or language to suit the purpose or demands of the moment (Poplack, 1980). Reasons for code-switching are varied. Usually it takes place in multilingual settings where different individuals or groups use different languages or dialects. For instance, the child of an Uzbek mother and an American father may speak Uzbek with mom, English with dad, and Russian at school. Mom speaks Uzbek to the child and her parents. The babysitter, however, speaks Russian to the child and to the parents of the child. Mom speaks English with her husband and his parents, and so on. Other factors that may influence code-switching include the context of the interaction. Is it in a court room, for example, addressing a judge, or in a less formal context, for example, conversing with a friend. Sometimes the language/dialect that is preferred for a given context is determined by how the language/dialect is viewed by people in the culture in question. When one language or dialect tends to be used for casual conversations and another tends to be generally used in more formal settings, for instance, the preferred term is **diglossia** (Ferguson, 1959, 1991; Hudson, 1991). It is possible also for users, including children, to mix language/dialects in a great variety of ways. When the changes are not predictable or systematic the term commonly applied is **code-mixing** (Nicoladis & Genesee, 1998).

How Many Languages Are There?

In the 1970s and 1980s, linguistics books commonly reported that there were about 3,000 to 5,000 distinct languages in the world (Fromkin & Rodman, 1973, 1998). In the year 2005, the most comprehensive listing of the world's languages, the *Ethnologue* (see http://www.ethnologue.com visited August 10, 2005) records 6,912 distinct languages. The number, of course, is subject to change as some languages are dying out, others are merging or splitting. Over time, the cataloguing of the recently discovered and especially the lesser known languages and dialects can be expected to change. One important thing to keep in mind is that the number of languages in the world is vast. Another important fact to keep in mind is that languages and dialects are constantly changing. Populations are shifting and the communications systems used by different people are constantly influencing each other. The uses of words are changing and new forms are also being invented all the time. For instance, the former distinctions between *will* and *shall*, *lay* and *lie*, and even *bring* and *take* in some varieties have almost been lost in today's English. Also new ways of saying things are being invented all the time. Consider words like *dis* and *bling*, and forms are being traded between different languages and different varieties of the same language.

If a really skilled language learner can hardly expect to master more than two, three, or maybe four or five languages, what are we to make of problems facing teachers, clinicians, and others who may be called on to deal with classes and caseloads that involve 10 or even 20 distinct languages? Roman Jakobson used to joke of himself with his thick Russian accent that he spoke "Raaassian in saaaventeen laaangvages!" (personal communication to J. Oller, summer, 1969). However, even a gifted **polyglot** like Jakobson could not hope to speak and understand 50 languages, much less 100, or 1,000. So what are teachers and others to do about the problems facing minority language/dialect children in the schools?

In the United States, and increasingly throughout the world, the problems faced by minority language/dialect users are increasingly prevalent because of greater worldwide population mobility. There are more people and they are moving from country to country and from city to city more than ever before. Ortiz and Yates (1983) predicted what has come to pass: the number of speakers of minority languages in the United States has surpassed the number of persons who share the majority language (English). In fact, this trend can be seen worldwide (Ortiz, 1997). Because of increased worldwide travel and commerce, people are also more dependent today than ever before on technologies and communication. Central to all these demands is the need for people to be able to understand one another, to speak a common language/dialect. As the population continues to grow and move, communication problems become increasingly evident. World travelers, teachers, clinicians, health providers, doctors, lawyers, and anyone who deals with people is certain to face a growing number of difficulties because of differences in the languages and dialects of the world.

Telling the Difference Between Language/Dialects and Learning Disorders/Disabilities

In countries like the United States, the United Kingdom, Canada, Australia, and New Zealand, where English is by far the most common language in use, it is easy to form the impression that "foreign language" means one of two or three, or maybe a dozen languages. Educated persons are apt to think of the particular languages that were offered in the curriculum at the schools they happened to attend. The most common foreign languages taught in the United States, for instance, are still Spanish, French, and German. Colleges and universities are apt to offer a richer curriculum extending the options to Russian, Japanese, Mandarin (Chinese), and perhaps one or several of a few dozen other languages, but no universities offer foreign language instruction in, say, 10% of the languages of the world. So, the tendency of educators, policy makers, and the rest of us everywhere, is to underestimate the problems associated with language/dialect differences. They must be greater than we can easily imagine.

The language/dialect differences themselves are problematic. It is difficult for anyone to function in a social situation where everyone else speaks one or more languages different from the one(s) you happen to know. The reader can get an idea of just how difficult this really can be only by being in such a setting. A glimmering of the difficulty can be obtained by trying to watch television without subtitles when the sound is turned off. Or, by trying to understand a film in a language you do not know, say, Mandarin, or Japanese, or Norwegian. However, it is evidently difficult for anyone not in the situation to understand how frightening the situation is for minority language children at school. A dialect issue may not present quite as severe a problem as completely unintelligible language differences, but anyone who has struggled to understand a really thick foreign accent in any language, for example, Dennis Weaver's Spanish, or Clint Eastwood's Russian, or any unfamiliar dialect, will be able to appreciate something of the difficulty faced by children of minority language/dialect backgrounds in classrooms.

Confusing Differences with Disorders

Besides the language/dialect differences themselves, other problems are commonly created, unintentionally, by teachers, testers, social workers, clinicians, and others who do not take into account what the minority language/dialect child is up against. Perhaps the most widespread problem involves the confusion of language/dialect differences with language/dialect deficits, that is, with disorders, mental retardation, and learning disability. Montgomery (1999, p. 78) has commented that "in the United States, speakers who use accents and nonstandard dialects of English do not [necessarily] have communication disorders, yet they are often regarded by the public as though they do. Furthermore, members of the speech language and hearing professions who use accented or dialect inflected speech patterns are within this group, and often face some of the same types of discrimination."

In 1968, Lloyd Dunn, the principal author of the *Peabody Picture Vocabulary Tests*, described the disproportionate numbers of language/dialect minorities in classes for the mentally retarded as "morally and educationally wrong" (p. 5). He estimated that 60 to 80% of the children in about 10,500 classrooms for the educable mentally retarded (at that time) were there for the wrong reasons. He singled out various language/dialect minorities including "Afro-Americans, American Indians, Mexicans, and

Puerto Rican Americans" (p. 6). Dunn was writing almost four decades ago and everyone would hope that the situation would have changed by now.

However, in 1983, based on national norms, Ortiz and Yates showed that Spanish speaking children in Texas were 300% overrepresented in classes for the educable mentally retarded. Similarly, Damico, J. Oller, and Storey (1983) showed that standard procedures for referring children to special education classes commonly mistake minority language/dialect learners for children with some kind of learning disability or disorder. Serna, Forness, and Nielsen (1998; also see Chamberlain, 2005; Hosp & Reschly, 2004) noted that the situation has hardly changed since Dunn first issued his complaints against overrepresentation of language/dialect minorities in special education classes. The overrepresentation persists and with the influx of large numbers of additional language/dialect minorities into American schools and urban centers worldwide, if anything, the situation is almost certainly going to get worse before it gets better.

Language/Dialect Minorities Overrepresented in LD Categories

For the last four decades, no serious researcher has denied that language/dialect minorities are overrepresented in LD classes and caseloads and are commonly underrepresented in classes for the gifted and talented. However, different explanations have been proposed for the inequities. Chamberlain (2005) argues that "general education" teachers may tend to refer more language/dialect minority children than they should. Others have stressed the ways that children's abilities are assessed, tested, or evaluated (Ortiz, 1997). Still others, notably Hosp and Reschly (2004) have proposed that low school achievement itself may explain the fact that language/dialect minorities are overrepresented in LD case loads. To us this seems circular. It seems to try to offer the problematic outcome as its own cause.

If we ask what school achievement depends on, the answer is clear. It depends more on language/dialect proficiency than on any other single factor. Do the children know the words, understand the phrases, know what the teacher and others are talking about? Almost a century ago, Alfred Binet (1911), the father of the modern IQ testing movement wrote the following:

> One of the clearest signs of awakening intelligence among young children is their understanding of spoken language. For a long time our speech has affected him only by the intonation of the voice. The first step toward acquiring a language is its comprehension. We understand the thought of others expressed in speech before we are able to

express our own. Consequently, the first test is given to show that the child understands the meaning of ordinary words (p. 186).

But what if the child speaks a different language/dialect than the teacher does? How will the teacher assess the child's knowledge, skills, and abilities?

Different Kinds of Tests Mainly Assess Language/Dialect Proficiency

If we ask how teachers, parents, or other adults typically evaluate any give child or group of children, the child's proficiency in one or more languages/dialects is still the obvious answer. Although there are many different kinds of tests that have been developed for different purposes all school tests depend largely on language abilities. For instance, **achievement tests** are supposed to assess knowledge, skills, and abilities already acquired. These are commonly specially focused on a particular kind of knowledge such as reading, writing, or arithmetic. Achievement tests may be focused on even more specialized subject areas such as geometry, algebra, accounting, business law, educational statistics, and so forth. Some achievement tests are used to place students in special programs according to their assessed knowledge, for instance, as in advanced placement tests for a college foreign language class, or to see whether a student should take a lower mathematics class or move on to advanced algebra or calculus. Another use for certain general achievements tests is as so-called **competency tests** or in some cases **graduation tests**. Sometimes specialized achievement tests are used as the basis for advancement from one course level to another in a specialized program of study. There are also **aptitude tests** that try to assess how easily a person can acquire new knowledge, skills and abilities, for example, aptitude for math, a career in marketing, or for learning a foreign language, and so forth.

Among the most widely used tests of aptitude, which are distinguished mainly by their use to forecast future performances, for example, how well children would do in schools, were the so-called **intelligence tests**. These are also known as IQ tests where the letters are an abbreviation for "intelligence quotient." The ability to think things through or to see a solution to a problem had already been defined as **general intelligence** by Charles Spearman (1904). This general mental capacity, however, was differentiated in testing recruits for World War I into two supposedly different varieties of ability: **verbal intelligence** and **nonverbal intelligence**. The term verbal intelligence really meant knowledge of one's primary language and nonverbal intelligence was a term invented to account for the kinds of tests first developed for application with individuals who did not speak or understand English, the primary language of the American and British recruiters for World War I. In more recent years, various kinds of intelligence, commonly referred to as **multiple intelligences**, have been proposed by Howard Gardner (1983) as we noted in Chapter 2. In addition to verbal intelligence, Gardner has argued for logico-mathematical intelligence, picture intelligence, bodily kinesthetic intelligence, musical intelligence, interpersonal intelligence, intrapersonal intelligence, and even naturalist intelligence (ability to understand the natural world). Another variety sometimes proposed is **spatial intelligence**, the ability to understand and use relations between bodily things in a spatial context.

It is worth noting that by far the most common tasks used in psychological, social, and mental tests are ones that crucially involve language. In assessing whether or not a child's development is progressing on schedule, teachers and others are apt to ask questions such as: How well does the child express ideas in speech and language? How well does the child understand the speech and writings of others? How well does the child read in the language/dialect used at school? Here is a list of some of the many tasks that have been used in tests since the time of Binet to assess reading readiness, school achievement (competency), innate intelligence, verbal ability, aptitude, personality, reading achievement, mathematical skill, reading comprehension, and vocabulary. Variations have been widely used by classroom teachers. Some tasks are also commonly used to assess proficiency in a foreign language. As you read through them, ask yourself how you would do on each task if you were presented with the instructions for it in a foreign language or in a language/dialect you do not understand well. Which ones could you do without difficulty? What about the rest? What are the differences between them? Try to imagine how the instructions for the task might be demonstrated without words:

1. *Solving a puzzle.* Among the least verbal of tasks are jigsaw puzzles that could be solved by considering iconic shapes and finding the places for them in a cut-out, as seen in Figure 11–1. Verbal instructions for an iconic task of this sort could be kept to a minimum by demonstrating how to solve the puzzle. A slightly more complicated version would be the kind of maze that requires tracing a solution through passages and avoiding barriers as shown in Figure 11–2. Of course the solution does not have to be simple.

2. *Carrying out commands.* The test-taker or person being assessed may be asked to do things like: *Point to your nose*; *lift your left hand*; *show me your right hand and touch your left ear at the same time*; and so forth. These kinds of commands can be arranged so that they become increasingly complex. They have been used to assess

Figure 11–1. A seven-piece jigsaw puzzle with two pieces missing.

"The exit? Sure...take a right, then left, left again...no, wait...a *right*, then...no, wait..."

Figure 11–2. Mazes do not have to be simple or even solvable, but they rely on indexes. We must connect the starting point with the exit (if we can find it). What is wanted is a line with two ends, an index. The instructions, however, for this and other puzzles often require words, symbols. Reproduced by permission of Bruce Beattie and Copley News Service.

language/dialect comprehension, foreign language proficiency, intellectual ability in young children, and so forth. A variation of this task involves the use of objects, cut-outs, or figures that have to be arranged in a particular way, for example, *Take the red block out of the bucket and put it in the drawer*, and so forth. Countless variations of greater complexity are possible and many have been used in teaching and testing foreign language comprehension. Tasks of this sort were used by Piaget and later developmental psychologists in a great variety of tasks assessing the language and cognitive abilities of young children (for example, see Bower, 1974; Piaget, 1970; Tomasello, 2003).

3. *Naming presented objects.* In this sort of task objects may be common household things like a knife, fork, or spoon, or they may consist of toys, tools, or other objects. Such naming tasks are commonly applied in assessing first language/dialect proficiency, foreign language proficiency in young learners, and the severity of loss in aphasia or certain forms or dementia. A modified version of this task has been applied with pictures or drawings as in the Peabody Picture Vocabulary Test and in many related tests to measure of what is called "receptive vocabulary."

4. *Producing as many words as possible in three minutes.* Tasks of this sort are oddly called "verbal fluency" or "vocabulary fluency" measures (Wesseling & Reitsma, 2001), although they involve an unusual kind of fluency. Ordinarily fluent speech does not consist of naming everything you can see or think of in a short space of time. These kinds of tasks have been widely applied in studies of language acquisition, literacy, and as measures of vocabulary knowledge.

5. *Saying how a folded paper will look after a pattern is cut out and it is unfolded.* The task is formidable mainly in its requirements on linguistic production but it also challenges the ability to represent images iconically and to imagine their transformations. Consider how difficult it would be in a nonprimary language.

6. *Judging the relative length of two lines, two weights, or two quantities.* In these tasks which Binet applied to the assessment of certain kinds of thinking, we see the seeds for tasks that would later be developed and applied by Piaget and his followers to study the child's ability to think

about quantities, for example, to know that a quantity of water poured from a short fat tube into a long skinny one is still the same quantity. The interesting thing about these kinds of tasks is just how hard it would be without a lot of explanation in some language/dialect to understand what the child, or anyone else, is being asked to judge. Imagine doing the task in a foreign language. How would you know for certain you were being asked to judge the quantity of water and not the length of the tubes? Or, the length of the tubes and not the width? How can such a task be scored with any certainty if the test-taker has not understood the instructions? These kinds of tasks would lead, nevertheless, to the famous conservation tasks that would be developed later on by Piaget and his followers.

7. *Arranging objects in a series.* Another task used by Binet to assess the child's intelligence involved arranging a series of objects according to their size or weight, or some combination of attributes. Many developmental toys for children have been created with this idea in mind. It is certainly related to the ability of children to deal with transitive relations of all kinds, with sequences of numbers, and with greater or lesser amounts or quantities of a substance. This kind of item would lead to the creation of the nonverbal tasks known as "progressive matrices" developed by Raven (Raven & Court, 1938–1983). See Figure 11–3. Other variations on the so-called nonverbal test theme included tests of complex relations (Cattell &

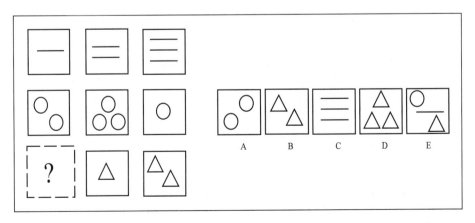

Figure 11–3. A matrix type item of the sort common to so-called nonverbal IQ tests patterned after Raven and Court (1938–1983).

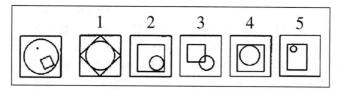

Figure 11–4. Here is a Cattell-type item. Can you figure out what you are supposed to do to solve it?

Cattell, 1933–1973). Some of these would be a little more complicated to explain. In Figure 11-4 the problem is to find a figure on the right where the dot can be put in the same relation to the circle and the square that it has in the figure on the left. These tasks are still regarded as nonverbal in today's tests, but try to imagine the instructions that would make clear what the test-taker is supposed to do with a given ordinal series or a relational problem of the sorts shown in Figures 11-3 and 11-4.

8. *Repetition of numbers.* This task is a variant of elicited imitation or can be done as a dictation task where the numbers must be written down. Try doing it in a language you do not know and you will see just how challenging it can be and the extent to which it involves language proficiency.

9. *Naming coins, denominations, or amounts of money.* This task can be limited to small change, say, a penny, nickel, dime, quarter, for a small child, or may be extended to larger denominations. With more advanced test-takers the task may require the test-taker to say how much money is present in a given combination of coins and bills.

10. *Answering questions about known facts.* For instance, a young child might be asked, Are you a boy or a girl? What color is the sky when the sun is shining brightly? This sort of task is commonly used in testing the language abilities, alias "verbal intelligence" of young children. Similar tasks are also applied to assess foreign language comprehension in some contexts, even with adults.

11. *Elicited imitation.* Items of this sort consist of an orally presented stream of speech, for example, a statement, question, or other intelligible sequence, say, of about 5 to 15 words. The task set the person being tested is to repeat what is said. It sounds easy, but try repeating the examples

on the DVD in <u>Mandarin, Spanish, and/or in an Acadian dialect of Creole/Cajun English</u>. This sort of task has commonly been used to assess foreign language proficiency and knowledge of one or another dialect of a language.

12. *Telling what is going on in a photograph.* This sort of task is commonly used in foreign language testing. Variations on the theme, where the picture is deliberately obscured or stylized, or made to look like a blot of ink, have also been used in various forms of psychological and personality assessment tests, for example, the Rorschach inkblot test.

13. *Giving the present day of the week and the date, in other words, day, month, year.* This sort of task is commonly used to see if a person with a head injury or who has been knocked unconscious is fully aware of what is going on. It was used by Binet with young children to assess their intellect. It is sometimes used as a teaching or testing exercise in foreign language classes.

14. *Taking dictation.* In a dictation task, the problem set the test-taker or person being assessed is to write down exactly the words that are heard. Usually bursts of 5 to 15 words or so are presented between pauses. The test-taker is supposed to write the words down during the pauses. Often this sort of task is presented via a prior recording and may or may not be accompanied by interfering noise. (This task is commonly used in foreign language classrooms. It has also been used to assess the intelligibility of text-to-speech readers for the Deaf. It is also commonly applied to assess the intelligibility of one language/dialect to speakers of another.)

15. *Copying a bit of written text.* This task is like dictation or elicited imitation and can be made more or less difficult depending on the length of text presented and the time span over which it is made available. Originally, the task was used by Binet and others to see if a child could write recognizable letters, or sequences of letters, after being able to see them. Such tasks have been applied in a variety of ways to test vocabulary, reading comprehension, and verbal memory. As far as we know, these tasks have not been applied much as foreign language tests but they certainly require proficiency in the language used.

16. *Reciting a known series.* For example the test-taker may be asked to recite the alphabet, days of the week, months of the year, and so forth. This sort of task is commonly used with young children but makes an interesting problem for foreign language learners.

17. *Reading aloud (or silently) and recalling points of information.* These kinds of tasks have been used mainly as measures of what has been called "reading comprehension" but Binet first applied them as measures of what he called intelligence.

18. *Defining words or concepts.* This task has been used as a measure of verbal intelligence, and especially of vocabulary knowledge. It is surprisingly difficult in our first language even with familiar words such as *stick, stone, egg, dog,* and so forth. It can be made more difficult with abstract concepts such as *charity, justice,* and *goodness.* Such tasks are commonly used in primary language, language arts contexts, but rarely in a foreign language. The task is too difficult even for most advanced foreign language classes. Another variation applied by Binet and in verbal tests of intelligence involved opposites or related pairs of words, for example, what the difference is between *hot* and *cold*; explain the difference between *pleasure* and *happiness, wisdom* and *knowledge,* and so forth. These kinds of items can be made challenging to adults and have also been used in measures of personality. For instance, this sort of item underlies the kind of forced choice used in certain **personality inventories** where test-takers are asked whether they would rather be, for instance, an *introvert* or an *extrovert.* On one inventory, to go unnamed, participants were asked whether they would rather be *mean, stupid,* or *ugly.* Imagine making and explaining these kinds of choices in a nonprimary language.

19. *Making change with money.* Binet used this task to assess intellectual ability in older children. It has been used as an advanced exercise/test in foreign language classes, and sometimes as a device to assess which language a bilingual or multilingual person regards as his or her primary system. Rarely can multilinguals make change comfortably in more than one language.

20. *Using three words to make a sentence or putting words in order.* This task as applied by Binet involved taking

words like *cat, dog*, and *tree* and constructing a sentence like, say, *The dog chased the cat and it ran up a tree.* Many variations on this theme have been applied in assessing syntactic knowledge, reading ability, and nonprimary language skills.

21. *Answering questions about physical or social problems.* This sort of task was a kind of elicited oral essay. For example, the test-taker might be asked, for example, what should you do when you miss a bus, or why should a person be judged more by actions than by words. These kinds of items have been used to assess everything from verbal intelligence to social knowledge and personality.

22. *Saying what is wrong in a strange sentence.* Examples applied by Binet included sentences like: *You are to be hanged at dawn: Let this be a warning to you!* Or, *In a train wreck, the cars at the back are usually damaged the most.* Or, *Whenever two people quarrel there is usually a yellow dog standing nearby.* These tasks critically involve the ability of the test-taker to draw inferences about the presuppositions and implications of conventional signs in a particular language/dialect. To our knowledge they have not been widely applied for anything other than intelligence testing. However, the tasks present challenging problems that would be difficult for foreign language learners or most users of nonprimary languages.

In all the foregoing tasks with the possible exception of jigsaw puzzles and mazes, the test-taker is largely dependent on proficiency in a particular language/dialect (Oller, Kim, & Choe, 2000a, 2000b). Some testers argued that the instructions to so-called "nonverbal" tasks such as those illustrated in items 6 and 7 can be understood through pantomime, that is, without words (Jensen, 1980). However, it has been shown conclusively (Oller, Kim, & Choe, 2001) that this is not possible for the kinds of relational problems posed by Cattell as shown in Figure 11–4. In the sort of task pictured there, no amount of gesturing from one element to another will ensure that the learner understands that the dot in the example at the left has to be placed in a similar relation to the circle and the square in one of the alternatives at the right. In fact, for any task that is above the complexity of a simple jigsaw or maze, words are not only essential to make the instructions clear but the underlying concepts of words are necessary for testers to agree on the correct answers and for test-takers to agree on the correct answers.

For the foregoing reasons, it is not surprising that the ability to solve complex nonverbal problems is dependent on the development of language skills. Research with subjects becoming bilingual shows that the correlation between first language proficiency and nonverbal scores is stronger than the correlation of nonprimary language ability and the same nonverbal scores. The reason, evidently, is that test-takers rely on reasoning with the concepts gained through acquiring their first language. The same abstract concepts, relations, and ideas are less accessible through the nonprimary language, so tests of proficiency in that language do not correlate so strongly with nonverbal test scores (Oller, Kim, & Choe, 2000a, 2000b; Oller, Kim, Choe, & Hernandez-Jarvis, 2001). The research shows, however, that nonverbal test scores are typically correlated significantly and with moderate strength with first language proficiency. The conclusion to be drawn is that both verbal and nonverbal tasks draw on the test-taker's first language knowledge.

The Language/Dialect Factor

If we take the time to analyze what each of the tasks listed above requires the child or test-taker to do, it is evident that the main requirement for successful performance on all or nearly all the kinds of tasks described above is proficiency in the language/dialect of the testing. In the United States, the language/dialect that is likely to be used for most assessment, testing, or evaluation will be the most widely spoken variety of American English. This is the language/dialect typically spoken by television and news anchors, by broadcasters in general, and by most of the American population in the western half of the country; see Figure 11–5. It might be called General Western American English because it dominates in the west, but it is also widely spoken in major population centers in the eastern part of the country as well, and in both the north and the south.

Many distinct minority dialects are spoken by classroom teachers, but are less likely to be used in standardized testing and rarely in written materials. Because of its wide use in the western and northern states, the most widely spoken dialect of English in the United States is commonly referred to as **General American English** (for example, Peter Ladefoged uses this term on his website http://hctv.humnet.ucla.edu/departments/linguistics/VowelsandConsonants/vowels/chapter3/amengvowels.html visited on January 27, 2006; also see Ladefoged, 1996, 2001). However, because the homogenization of American English seems to have taken place mainly west of the Mississippi River, and after the American Civil War, the term General Western American English can also be applied. It is worth noting that General American English is common especially in urban centers in the northern states, and throughout the southern states as well, where it exists alongside other dialects.

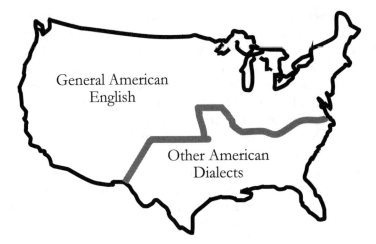

Figure 11–5. The extent of General Western American English.

It Is About the Language/Dialect of the Tests and Assessment Procedures

So what is the explanation for the disproportionate representation of language/dialect minorities in LD classes and caseloads in schools? Let us consider two ways this question has been asked by researchers. We want to show that each of the research questions can be rephrased so that it plainly shows that language/dialect proficiency is probably the main factor in the disproportionate representation at issue. Also, we offer a statement of the problem that provides its solution:

1. *One way the question has been put*: Is the disproportionate representation of language/dialect minorities in LD classes and caseloads in schools possibly because minority language/dialect users are naturally low achievers?

   A better way to ask the same question: Or, does not knowing and not understanding the language/dialect of the school produce low achievement?

2. *Another way the question has been put*: Is the disproportionate representation because general education teachers, that is, the folks who are not trained in special education or communication disorders, tend mistakenly (because they are not trained) to refer (that is, recommend placement

in special education or therapy for the disordered)
disproportionate numbers of children of language/dialect
minority backgrounds?

A better way to ask the same question: Or, do all
individuals without exception have greater difficulty
understanding and communicating with someone else
in a language/dialect that the other person does not
know well?

3. *A simpler way to put the question*: Are the tests used in
assessing the children presented in a language/dialect that
the minority language/dialect children understand well
or at all?

A conclusive way to answer the question: Actually, the
testing, evaluation, assessment, and placement of children
in classes for the mentally retarded, learning disabled, and
so on, is done almost exclusively in a language/dialect that
the language/dialect minority child does not know well
or at all.

If we think through the three competing explanations that have been
offered, we see again the three positions of discourse with responsibility
assigned differently to each one. In the first proposal the responsibility is
assigned to the child (as producer of the problem). In the second proposal
the responsibility for the problem is assigned to the teacher (as the consumer of the child's attempts to communicate). In the third instance, the
problem is more correctly assigned to the language/dialect differences that
make communication harder between speakers of General American English (the dominant language/dialect by far) and speakers of minority lan-
guage/dialects.

However, all the competing proposals point to the essential need to
be able to understand what is going on in the classroom. The children need
to know what they are expected to do in taking the tests, in doing classroom exercises, in reading the textbooks, watching the videos, working on
the computer, and so forth. Children who have difficulty understanding the
language/dialect of the teacher, tester, clinician, or therapist, are bound, on
the whole, to show up as low achievers. General education teachers, of
course, will also tend to refer these children for further evaluation and possible placement in special education or therapy. If the testing, evaluation,
interviewing, and assessment, is taking place in a language/dialect that the
child does not understand well or at all, we come to the bottom of
the problem.

The Language/Dialect Proficiency Factor in Testing and Placement

In a thoughtful review of the literature, Ortiz (1997) concluded that tests are the primary explanation for the overrepresentation of language/dialect minority students in LD classes/caseloads and their underrepresentation in classes for the gifted and talented. She found that "the intelligence, achievement, and language tests used to assess Hispanic students referred because of suspected learning disabilities were essentially the same as those used to assess their Anglo peers" (p. 325). Ortiz also found that English language tests and procedures are often applied with minority language/dialect backgrounds including children of Asian, **African American Vernacular English**, and other minority language varieties. Similarly, Jitendra and Rohena Diaz (1996) observed that "assessment procedures used to diagnose communication disorders" have "virtually ignored the linguistically diverse nature" (p. 42) of students from minority language/dialect backgrounds. Tests in the majority language/dialect, General Western American English, have been widely used to diagnose LD candidates and, inadvertently to create the disproportionate representation of minority language/dialect users in classes for LD and to exclude them (presumably without intending to do so) from classes for the gifted and talented (Buros Institute of Mental Measurement, 1938–2005; Chamberlain & Medeiros-Landurand, 1991; Hamayan & Damico, 1991; Hayes-Brown, 1984; Mercer, 1973; 1984; J. Oller, 1997; J. Oller, Kim, & Choe, 2001; Rivera & Simich, 1981). In fact, tests in the majority language/dialect predominate in all kinds of testing of individuals from minority language/dialect backgrounds. Intelligence, personality, achievement, and skill testing, as well as, **attitude measurement**, filling out of questionnaires of all kinds, conducting of interviews, materials sent home for parents to read, and so on are commonly presented in a language/dialect that the child does not yet know or understand well, if at all.

Validity in Testing, Assessment, and Evaluation Is Crucial

The overrepresentation of minority language/dialect speakers in LD classes and caseloads is associated with the language/dialect factor as it affects the assessment, testing, and placement process. With that in mind, in this section we need to look to the tests. Particularly, what are the procedures, assessments, observations, activities, or tasks that are used to evaluate language/dialect abilities? The most critical question is whether or not the procedures used are giving a true picture of what they are supposed to measure, assess, or evaluate.

The extent to which a test measures what it is supposed to measure is termed its *validity*. Borsboom, Mellenbergh, and van Heerden (2004) say that a measurement procedure (test, or whatever) has validity if scores on the procedure vary as the attribute being measured varies. By their definition the *reliability* of a test, the extent to which the variance is consistent across occasions of measurement, is subsumed under validity. Another characteristic of procedures that is commonly proposed as essential to validity is that the applications and uses of the procedures should be practical, helpful to people rather than harmful, and that the results should be as useful, fair, and interpretable as possible. For example, if a given approach to language/dialect assessment and testing results in a higher success rate in schools, a lower dropout rate, or fewer communication breakdowns it would be judged to have greater validity. Or, in international aviation, if a language/dialect testing program for pilots and air traffic controllers can be shown to have reduced fatalities and related incidents at international airports, the testing approach would be judged to have greater validity.

In agreement with Borsboom et al., Badon et al. have also argued on independent grounds that validity is the same construct as ordinary truth. However, Badon et al. have also agreed with the arguments of Messick (1989) that validity is ultimately associated with the **practicality** of tests, how useful they are, and also with their **interpretability**, how easy they are to understand. No matter how good a test may be for one purpose, if it is misinterpreted or used for some purpose for which it is not appropriate, the test will not be valid. Or, no matter how valid the test might be otherwise, if its application and results cannot be understood by the people who use that test, it cannot have validity in the required sense. For these reasons, the interpretability of measurement and assessment procedures is critical to their validity. The research also shows that to whatever extent educators and psychologists, teachers, clinicians, diagnosticians, administrators, speech-language pathologists, or others, have trouble understanding the nature of tests and assessment procedures the more likely they are to misuse them (Anastasi & Urbina, 1996; Buros, 1970; Buros Institute of Mental Measurement, 1938–2005; Uebersax, 1988, 1992).

To assess whether individuals at a school or in any other context, say, international pilots and air traffic controllers, can understand each other when speaking English, we need to test them in English. If they have to be able to manage multiple accents, dialects, and different varieties of English in a variety of situations, then these factors need to be reflected in the tests. Many different varieties of validity have been proposed having to do with the practical, theoretical, or experimental interpretation of tests. If the test transparently appears to be a test of whatever it is supposed to be a test of, it is said to have *face validity*. This description of validity obviously involves interpretability. If the test involves the sort of content (for example, say, being able to carry on a conversation with an English-speaking teacher, or understanding English transmissions from an air traffic controller) that would normally be involved in whatever the test is supposed to measure, it is said to have *content validity*.

If the test is reasonably associated with the factor(s), or theoretical constructs (attributes, traits, or abilities), that it is supposed to measure, it is said to have *construct validity*. To show construct validity requires a theoretical understanding and analysis of whatever the skills, attributes, or capacities the test is supposed to measure. If a school testing program, or a whole battery of procedures, say, is supposed to be assessing normal language development for third-graders, for instance, to have construct validity, it should take into account the language requirements usually placed on third-graders. In fact, every language test for children or adults must be justified in terms of the kinds of milestones and capacities that are dealt with in this book. Valid language testing and assessment procedures must take account of milestones of development, the acquisition of literacy, the variety of ways development manifests itself, differences in language/dialects, and the interactions between all these.

In addition, there are two closely related kinds of *concurrent validity*. They have to do with the statistical correlations between different tests and measurement procedures. To the extent that tests that are aimed at measuring the same constructs are correlated with each other they are said to have *convergent validity*. The other kind of concurrent validity is complementary and not quite the opposite. To the extent that a test does not correlate with tests that are supposed to measure unrelated factors, the test is said to have *divergent validity*. All of these different kinds of validity, however, boil down to whether or not, and if so, the extent to which, any given test is giving true, appropriate, and useful information about whatever it is supposed to measure.

How to Achieve Valid Measurements, Assessments, and Judgments

All aspects of measurement, assessment, diagnosis of disorders, or any kind of observation always come back to the question of validity. In the search for valid approaches to the assessment and measurement of language/dialect knowledge, skills, and abilities, much has been learned but many controversies and questions remain. Among the questions that have been raised are the following:

- Is it necessary to use normative concepts and to distinguish between what is normal or typical and what is abnormal or atypical?

- Is it possible in particular to replace **norm-referenced tests** with what have been called **criterion-referenced tests** or "can do" tasks?

- ■ Because normative approaches essentially involve **quantitative assessment**, some have wondered to what extent can we do away with both normative and quantitative procedures by using what are called **qualitative assessments**?

- ■ To what extent is it possible to replace all quantitative approaches, especially all **standardized tests**, in other words, ones that involve certain prescribed procedures for administration, scoring, and interpretation of scores, with qualitative assessment procedures?

Let us take these questions one at a time.

Normal Versus Abnormal

Language/dialect assessment procedures that have been widely used in the research literature are commonly calibrated with reference to the normal milestones of sensory, sensory-motor, and linguistic systems of development. We have used the word *normal* in the title of our book. What does it really mean? Is it necessary? Is it a valid concept? It is sometimes argued that normative concepts, and normative tests, especially standardized tests, need to be replaced by something else. Often times in school tests, observational assessment procedures, screening devices, interviews, or activities of one kind or another are used to screen children who may be considered at risk. Terms such as *disorder, delay, impairment, abnormality,* and *disability* are commonly applied. Like *disease, injury, damage, error,* and so on, these terms have negative connotations. No one wants to hear them applied to themselves, their child, or anyone they care about. Some have argued or implied that the difficulties arise for some children because comparisons are being made against norms, or because children are being compared with each other, or groups are being compared with other groups, and so forth. Wouldn't it be possible, and desirable to avoid all such comparisons?

In an effort to do so, some have argued that it should be possible to define criteria for screening, assessment, evaluation, testing, and measurement that are fully independent, or as independent as possible, from normative comparisons. The kinds of procedures that seek to provide independent nonnormative criteria for assessment are often called "criterion-referenced" procedures (Anastasi & Urbina, 1996; Bond, 1996). For instance, what have been called "can-do" tasks, are sometimes referred to as criterion-based. A typical can-do task in the language/dialect area would be to be able to order a meal at a restaurant, to follow the plot line in a film or novel, to understand the point of a joke or illustration, and so forth. A variation on the same theme involves teaching and/or testing for mastery

(Valette, 1967; also see the bibliography at http://www.agsnet.com/assess ments/bibliography/wrmt.asp concerning the Woodcock Reading Mastery Test and others, visited on October 22, 2005) where the tasks to be performed supposedly define success. As in all criterion-referenced tests, students are said to compete only with themselves.

Another alternative to norm-referenced assessment that has been proposed is essentially to replace quantitative approaches with qualitative approaches to assessment (for example, see Tetnowski & Franklin, 2003). Instead of standardized tests or other procedures teachers can rely on collections of student works, writings, projects, and the like that are collected in portfolios. The sample of work may also include tape-recorded conversation or video, one or more journals kept by the student recording experiences, work accomplished, progress made, and so forth. It may include essays, letters, summaries of conversations, interviews, reports on trips, a list of books read, written book reports, and so on, all compiled by the student/learner. Commonly, a **journal assessment** may be included as part of the larger, usually unspecified and open-ended, **portfolio assessment**.

The portfolio might also include interactive comments from a teacher/ clinician on the journals, projects, or what-have-you. It might include letters or correspondence with pen pals. It might include, in some situations, records of conversations and interviews between the student and teacher, or parents, pediatricians, or others associated with the person being assessed or evaluated.

It is evident that, except for limits on time, energy, and resources, the breadth and depth afforded by qualitative procedures in schools and in all aspects of language/dialect assessment and testing can be expanded in countless ways. Qualitative procedures, it is true, offer a wealth of ways to expand beyond traditional norm-referenced tests. They also offer teachers and clinicians ways to guide the student/learner into approaches to assessment and learning that empower the student/learner and provide greater opportunities for self-control, initiative, cooperative learning, and so forth. Qualitative devices are commonly used in grade promotions, grade placement, in college admissions, placement, and in employment contexts. For instance, letters of recommendation, job interviews, on the job testing/ training, and the like are widely used and are all more qualitative procedures than quantitative. As a result it is reasonable to explore the extent to which quantitative comparisons of all sorts might be replaced with qualitative procedures of assessment (see Sanders & Horn, 1995).

Qualitative Assessments Are Necessary

It has been demonstrated that all quantitative measurements must be based on **qualitative assessments**. A qualitative assessment is the kind that says whether or not a given quality, attribute, process, performance, or whatever, is present or not present. For instance, has the individual in question achieved a particular milestone of development? Has the child achieved the stage of canonical babbling? Does the child discriminate his or her own name and orient toward the person who says the child's name? Does the child show comprehension of the names of other persons in his or her life space? To answer these questions validly we must make valid qualitative judgments.

If we go further to ask how much of a given quality or combination of qualities or attributes is present (or absent), or if we ask in how many cases or instances the trait in question was manifested, we come to **quantitative measurement**. J. Oller and Chen (in press) have shown that all valid quantitative measurements must necessarily be grounded in qualitative judgments. The argument is based partly in the work of S. S. Stevens (1968) who distinguished the most widely used kinds of quantitative scales. His terms are the ones we find in standard statistical packages including Statistical Package for the Social Sciences (SPSS, see http://www.spss.com/ visited October 22, 2005) and the "statistical analysis system" that has become better known by its trade name "SAS" (see http://www.sas.com/ visited October 22, 2005).

According to Stevens, quantitative scales begin with **nominal scales** where the question is, does the case (person, or whatever we are measuring or assessing) have a certain attribute, or belong to a particular class or category, or not? For instance, is the child at the stage of canonical babbling yet? A nominal scale always involves a categorical, on-or-off, 0 or 1, type of judgment. If we examine any categorical or nominal judgment, we discover that it must necessarily be a qualitative judgment. Furthermore, it comes out that all quantitative judgments or any kind are grounded in this kind of holistic quantitative, 0 or 1, on-or-off, judgment.

At a more abstract level of measurement, we can ask how much of a given attribute is present, or how many times has it been manifested or observed in a given period of time, or in how many different ways has the attribute been manifested, and so forth. When the qualitative question is validly amplified in this way, the result is an **ordinal scale**. Over and above the ordinal type of judgment it is possible to impose a particular unit of measurement such as inches, yards, miles, seconds, minutes, days, words, phrases, and so forth. If the unit of measurement validly involves a comparison against a standard unit or interval, the scale is said to be an **interval scale**. However, it can be seen that any interval scale involves all the requirements of nominal scales, plus those of ordinal scales, plus a comparison with some standard interval. When comparisons between units and quantities validly enable differentiation of ordinal relations into ratios, for example, where a quantity may be judged to be half (or twice) the size of some reference quantity, we come to **ratio scales**.

Many other variations on kinds of scales are possible, but there are no valid quantitative judgments that are not grounded in valid qualitative judgments. Even in judgments that only involve letters, words, numbers, or other abstract symbols, for example, we must at least be able to tell what the surface-forms of the symbols are, and this means making valid qualitative judgments. For all the foregoing reasons, the basic question in assessment, measurement, and judgment of any kind comes back to whether or not (or to what degree) the assessment, measurement, or judgment is true.

Language/Dialect Difference Does Not Equal Learning Disorder/Disability

With respect to testing language/dialect minority children in schools, it is one thing to assess how well the child can understand a certain dialect of American English, but it is a very different matter to ask if the child is developing normally with respect to his or her first language/dialect if the latter happens not to be the language/dialect of the school. To answer either of these questions, however, requires reference to the normal ways in which any given language/dialect is used by the people who happen to speak and use that language/dialect. The idea of a norm-less language is impossible to imagine. It could not have any conventions or regularities of use. A language/dialect without any norms at all would be one that people could neither learn nor communicate in. The only way that English-speakers understand each other is by conforming sufficiently well to the norms of English use. If they were to use German, Russian, or Navajo norms, English-speakers would not understand them. To say that a particular word is normally, usually, or conventionally pronounced or spelled in a particular way, or that it has a certain range of meanings, or that it is used in a certain range of contexts, and so on, is to appeal to norms of use at every step. To say that a child normally reaches the milestone of canonical babbling by about 7 months after birth, or that a child who is still not speaking as the age of 7 years is delayed relative to the expected milestones for a 7-year-old, requires appeal to normative observations.

In educational, psychological, and social testing, it is not the appeal to normative uses (as in standardized normative tests) where educators have typically gone wrong, but as we have seen it is easy to misinterpret tests that greatly depend on proficiency in a certain language/dialect as measures of innate intelligence, achievement, personality, or something else. If a child whose native language is Igbo, happens not to speak Chinese (or any one of 6,912 other languages of the world), or speaks Chinese poorly, we should not conclude that the child is mentally retarded on this account. We can, however, if the test in Chinese is valid conclude that the child speaks Chinese poorly or not at all, whatever may be the case. No harm will be done in saying that a child does not speak English well (or at all) provided our assessment is a valid measure of English proficiency. In fact, such a test may help us realize the need to provide every opportunity for the child to learn English. Where things have gone seriously wrong, however, is in treating language/dialect assessment procedures as if they were suited to tell us directly about a person's intellect, innate intelligence, or capacity to learn (Chamberlain, 2005; Jitendra & Rohena-Diaz, 1996; J. Oller, 1997; J. Oller, Kim, & Choe, 2001; Ortiz, 1997).

If the question concerns proficiency in a particular dialect of English, it is perfectly reasonable to test children on tasks that require the use of that dialect of English. But using tests that are greatly dependent on proficiency in a particular variety of English, to say whether or not a minority language/dialect child is intellectually delayed, retarded, learning disabled, and the like does not make good sense. The child should be tested in his or her strongest language/dialect. If screening for disorders is done in a language/dialect that many of the language/dialect minority children cannot understand well, many normal individuals are certain to be mistaken for individuals with learning disabilities, disorders, mental retardation, and so forth. By such a method gifted children will also be overlooked and many normal children will end up in classes for the mentally retarded. The research and analysis of available evidence shows that this is exactly what has been happening and still is happening even now (Chamberlain, 2005).

Most Educational, Psychological, and Mental Tests *Are* Language/Dialect Tests

To correct this situation, the first step is to recognize that most of the tests being applied are mainly tests of English language proficiency for the minority language/dialect children, and often not very good tests at that because they may be far too difficult. A second step is to find ways to do preliminary screening for normal versus delayed language development in the child's primary language/dialect. This is not necessarily easy, but it needs to be done. It may require finding some bilingual individual in the child's language community who can serve as a go-between and interpreter. Then interviews should be conducted with the child and parents of the child with the assistance of the interpreter as needed to assess the major milestones that the normal child at the age in questions would be expected to have achieved. If development seems to be delayed in the first language, then further and more intensive assessment would be recommended. However, if development is normal in the first language, there is no reason to suppose that the child will *not* be able to acquire the new language/dialect of the school. Mainstreaming would probably be recommended. However, even in cases of significant disorders, learning disabilities, and the like, with appropriate nonprimary language instruction many LD individuals can be expected to acquire the nonprimary language/dialect system up to the limits of their intellectual and social capacity.

However, regardless whether the minority language/dialect user is ultimately found to be normal or delayed in his or her primary language, the next step is still to provide effective instruction in the nonprimary language. Therefore, next let us consider the question of just how nonprimary language/dialect acquisition can be facilitated. The research shows that some methods work a great deal better than others (J. Oller, 1993; Richard-Amato, 2003; Savignon, 1997) and also that the same kinds of factors that make language acquisition easier for normal learners, taking into account their sensory, motor, cognitive, and social limitations, will also make things easier for LD children.

Nonprimary Language Instruction/Acquisition

When it comes to nonprimary language instruction there are two major types that are typically distinguished by teachers and researchers. On the one hand, there is the traditional **foreign language setting** where elementary, middle, high school, or college students typically meet from two to five times a week for an hour or so of instruction in the target language. In nearly all these cases, the target language is not spoken in the larger community outside the classroom. To get in touch with people who use the foreign language for regular purposes of daily life and ordinary communication the student would have to participate in a study abroad program, to travel to the country, or marry someone who happens to speak the language, or go to some effort to view films in the language and the like.

By contrast, there are contexts of learning where the target language is used in the larger community both in and out of the classroom or school. These situations are often referred to as **second language settings**. Examples would include English for foreign students who are studying at American or British universities, for instance. It would also include the kinds of study that might take place in Quebec, Canada where the English-speaker is acquiring French and where French is commonly spoken by people in the surrounding community, say in Quebec City. Or, if a French-speaker is studying English in Ottawa, there will also be many opportunities to hear English spoken in the community outside the classroom. English in India is often a second language acquired at school, but it is widely used in many contexts in the workplace and in communities throughout the country where it may be the only common language among people who speak any one of 500 other native languages not to mention languages from other countries.

Typically, if all else is the same, so-called second language contexts have the advantage over foreign language teaching because the second language context provides greater access to the essential ingredient for language acquisition. That ingredient is access to pragmatic mappings of the surface-forms of the target language onto known contexts of experience. As we saw in respect to first language acquisition, the critical step in language acquisition is mapping previously unknown surface-forms onto their intended referents. While there are numerous instructional programs that are used in nonprimary language teaching, methods tend to emphasize either the surface-forms of the target language, as is done in phonics approaches to the teaching of literacy, or they tend to emphasize content, in whole-language approaches to reading and writing.

Why Not Focus Attention Mainly on Form?

Teaching methods that focus on surface-forms are common. Students who have taken a foreign language often comment that they "learned more about English while taking Spanish (or French, or German, and so forth) than in any English class." The comment also shows that in many foreign language classes the teaching may have more to do with grammar than with becoming a speaker of the foreign language. It shows also the common emphasis on the surface-forms of the target language as contrasted with those of English. In addition to teaching foreign language students about the phonetic qualities, the phonology, lexicon, and syntax of the foreign language, form-focused courses also usually provide students some exposure to the culture, foods, architectures, history, and literatures of the foreign language. Form-focused courses, however, rarely attempt to enable students to communicate through conversation. More commonly exercises are built around reading, writing, or otherwise manipulating words, phrases, and exemplary sentences or texts in the target language.

Methods and approaches to nonprimary language instruction that place a high premium on surface-forms tend to require students to do contrastive drills on the isolated sounds and syllables of the target language as distinct from those in the student/learner's native language. For instance, the vowels and consonants differ across languages and combine in different ways. The rhythms and intonations are distinct. English and Chinese, for example, are stress-timed while Spanish, Italian, and Japanese are syllable-timed languages. These contrasts can be illustrated with examples focusing on surface-form contrasts in just the sound of a pair of sentences such as, *It was William that kissed Susan* and *Era Guillermo quien besó a Susana*. The contrasts are striking to someone who knows both languages but are not as easy to appreciate for folks who do not know one or both languages. Focusing on surface-forms often leads to isolated sentences that illustrate grammatical or syntactic patterns. Paradigms of verbs and their various conjugations are common. Interestingly, it is still possible from such exercises, to get the idea that speakers of French, for instance, "are strictly systematical beings who . . . say the most disconnected things only for the sake of being able to use all the persons in the tense which for the time being happens to be the subject for conversation while they carefully postpone the use of the subjunctive until next year" (Jespersen, 1904, p. 17). But, of course, no one uses language in the way it is likely to be portrayed in many foreign language books and lessons.

There are other more intensive foreign language programs, however, where the goal is to enable students to communicate in the target language. In most programs with communication as their main goal, the focus tends to shift to content. In contrast to foreign language programs, second language programs tend to pay more attention to content, and even if the main focus in the classroom *is* on surface-forms, as it is in some cases, the surrounding community affords more opportunities to use the target language for communication. Unlike the foreign language student, the second language student often has to use the target language to communicate about ordinary activities and their content. For instance, the second language student will not only speak the target language in the classroom, but will also use it to register for classes, to talk to instructors, to use public transportation, to buy groceries, to order meals, and so forth.

Although surface-forms are important in nonprimary language acquisition, just as they are in acquiring literacy, in ordinary conversation, reading, and writing, surface-forms are subordinated to content. We would be unlikely to talk to a waiter at a restaurant about the fonts used, or the words, phrases, and sentences on the menu. We would be more likely to talk about the food, its preparation, and the waiter's recommendations concerning what is good to eat at the place in question. There is an invented story that illustrates the issues at stake and the contrast between programs that stress form over meaning and the reverse. A nonnative speaker of English, Hamid, polishes his skills until he is certain he has mastered all the aspects of the surface-forms required to order a meal at a restaurant. He practices the sounds, the words, the phrases, their morphology, and so forth. He gets the accent and rhythms down until he sounds like a native. Then, Hamid goes into an establishment and gets the attention of a waiter. He calls the person over and orders a meal: he says, "I'd like the eggs benedict but with bearnaise sauce, please, not the traditional hollandaise. Thank you, and unsweetened iced tea to drink."

The waiter just looks at Hamid, shrugs, and raises his palms as if to say, "Sorry, I can't understand you." He repeats himself. Gets the same reaction. Tries a slightly different phraseology. Still the same answer. Hamid is puzzled. He asks himself: Was it the phonology that tripped me up? Did

I use the wrong word? Some syntactic nuance? The rhythm maybe? My intonation? Stress patterns? What was the problem? It occurs to Hamid that maybe the waiter doesn't speak English, so he asks: "You do speak English, don't you?"

The waiter says, "It's the only language I know."

Still eager to get to the bottom of the problem, Hamid presses on. "Tell me," he says, "was it my accent or did I get the syntax messed up? Why couldn't you understand what I said."

The other person shrugs and says, "This is a hardware store."

The upshot of the story is that perfectly learned surface-forms will still fail if they are not appropriately connected with content. The successful language user must take account of the great variety of contexts of communication and the many different kinds of content found in those different contexts. In nonprimary language teaching, the teaching of literacy, and in speech therapy it is common for teacher/clinicians to focus attention on contrasts between surface-forms. For instance, the nonprimary language teacher is apt to point out the contrasts between the sounds, words, phrases, and so on, of the target language and the native language that may be shared by the learners. Among the sounds, words, and phrases that are often difficult for nonprimary language learners are those that are similar to, but not the same as, sounds, words, and phrases in the target language. Like siblings or twins that resemble each other closely, similar surface-forms in the same or different languages are difficult to tell apart.

For example, native speakers of English are apt to confuse the word *mnemonic* with *pneumonic*. These words look and sound more alike than many others. They have some letters, phonemes, and syllables in common, but they are "false neighbors." Although both have so-called "silent" letters to start with, the "m" of *mnemonic* and the "p" of *pneumonic*, and though the first phoneme in both words is /n/, they have different vowels in their first syllables, /i/ and /u/, respectively. The remaining two syllables are identical. Or, to take a different example, for the beginning reader, letters like "p," "d," "q," and "b" look a lot alike. Or, to take still another example, consider the similarities of the English words *can*, *man*, *fan*, *Dan*, *ran*, and *Jan*. Until their different initial consonants are distinguished they are more difficult to tell apart than words that look and sound less alike, for example, *Jen*, *cat*, *lock*, and so forth. However, educators and therapists are often encouraged to use such lists of similar surface-forms in teaching and intervention. For instance, in the McGraw-Hill SRA, *Pig Can Jig* series, see Figure 11–6, words that rhyme such as *can*, *man*, *fan*, *Dan*, *ran*, and so on, are deliberately presented together on the theory that their similarities will help children learn sound-letter correspondences. However, a pitfall is that student/clients are apt to confuse the similar forms. In fact, the research evidence shows that **contrastive analysis** of this sort, and **minimal pair contrasts** presented without sufficient meaningful context, often lead to

Figure 11–6. Phonics-oriented books like many of those produced by McGraw-Hill Science Research Associates including the one shown here present similar sounding and similar looking words together to illustrate rules of phonics (see http://www.sraonline. com/index.php/home/curriculumsolutions/reading/basicreading/ components/810 visited January 29, 2006). Reproduced by permission. Copyright © 2003 SRA/McGraw-Hill.

confusion of the similar forms. It is better to present similar forms in different contexts where subtle differences in form are made salient and significant by obvious differences in content.

To motivate the distinctions between similar and yet subtly different sounds (or letters) and combinations of them in any language we need to call in meanings. But for the student/learner who is struggling to make out the surface-form distinctions the meanings may not yet be easily accessible. As a result, so-called contrastive teaching may produce more confusion than anything else. The problem is that different letters (sounds) or combinations of letters and sounds that are maximally similar (almost but not quite the same) are the ones most likely to be confused by student/learners (Brown, 1994; Osgood, 1949). The speech-language pathologist or therapist is apt to point out that /s/ and /θ/, for instance, have different points of articulation and sound different. But suppose the child is having trouble distinguishing both the point of articulation and the sound. Will minimal pairs like *think* and *sink*, *thigh* and *sigh*, *thick* and *sick*, and so on, help solve the problem?

In addition to the surface contrasts and the sensory distinctions that people who make the contrasts can see, hear, and feel, it is also important to bring meaning into the picture. The relevant research shows that different content applications can help a great deal to enable learners to make sense of subtle surface-form contrasts. An example from a true incident of first language learning will illustrate the point. On a blustery cold Albuquerque evening a certain three-year-old was zipped up into his jacket and buckled in the backseat after a trip to the mall in search of a coat for dad. Earlier that evening the family had made a quick stop for food and the little boy's coke was placed between the seats between his mom and dad. After they got underway on a busy street near the Winrock Mall, the little boy said, "I want my [koʔ]."

His father answered, "You have your coat on."

The boy protests, "No! I want my [koʔ]!" Mom understands that he wants the root beer between the seats, the coke that is beyond his reach, and not his coat which he is, in fact, wearing. Dad, being a linguist, sees an opportunity for a lesson and points out the difference in the sound of [kot] and [kok] by exaggerating the contrast. The little boy easily repeats the exaggerated contrast and a few days later when the story is told to a friend of dad's who is a speech-language pathologist and one of dad's doctoral students, the three-year-old provides the contrasting words with exaggerated final consonants for the punchline, "Yeah! [kok], daggy." Within two more weeks the same child generalizes the contrast between the **velar** [k] and [g] with **alveolar** [t] and [d] in the **medial position** in words as well as in **final position**. The generalization is extended, for instance, to the word [dægi] (for *daddy*) by changing it to [dædi]. The desire to get the coke that was out of reach, served as a motivating factor to distinguish the word *coke* from *coat*.

The difference is one of pragmatic mapping. Which referent are we talking about? Because the referents are very different, the distinction between the surface-forms of words is motivated by the difference in the pragmatic content in the situation. Another thing to notice about this case is that the learning takes place in real time in a dynamic communication setting. The example comes from first language acquisition, but the principles at issue generalize to nonprimary language acquisition, to literacy, and to many aspects of speech-language therapies.

Pragmatic Requirements for Communication

Programs and methods of study and instruction that enable student/learners to become effective communicators in the target language typically do three main things:

1. They require and enable student/learners to map surface-forms of the target language onto meanings in ordinary (common) contexts of experience.

2. They engage student/learners in purposeful and meaningful communication activities in the target language.

3. They eventually require and enable the student/learner to perform the communication activities in the target language under normal time constraints.

These three aspects of communication-oriented language teaching (see Krashen, 1991; J. Oller, 1993; Richard-Amato, 2003; Savignon, 1997; Stevick, 1997) have also been applied as constraints on valid testing, assessment, and evaluation of language proficiencies and related skills (Badon, et al., 2005; J. Oller, 1979; Hamayan & Damico, 1990; Simich-Dudgeon, 1992).

As illustrated in Chapters 2 through 10, the pragmatic mapping process is the means by which surface-forms are associated with their meanings. In content-based (communication-oriented) approaches to non-primary language instruction, there must be some content to talk, read, or write about. There needs to be someone to interact with. There must be access to ordinary appropriate uses of the target language. The content can be provided through an activity such as sharing a meal, taking a trip, buying groceries, playing a game, engaging in a drama or play, telling a story, and so on, but access to conventional uses of the target language is essential. In addition, the effective communicator needs to be required to comprehend and produce target language forms under normal time constraints.

At the beginning states of nonprimary language acquisition, communication-oriented approaches do not present nonsensical pseudowords or other meaningless surface-forms. Rather, they present surface-forms connected to meaningful content through pragmatic mapping relations that are relatively easy for learners to discover and understand.

For instance, in what has been called the **total physical response (TPR) strategy**, developed and advocated by Asher (1969; also see Richard-Amato, 2003; J. Oller, 1993). The idea was built around observations of first language acquisition. Asher noted that much of the language directed to young children consists of commands or directives (for example, *wave bye-bye, come here, hand me that*, and so forth). His claims about the early language of children are surprisingly consistent with recent research showing the importance of verbs of motion and how they are used by young children and their interlocutors (Chen, 2005; Slobin, 1996, 2004; Tomasello, 1992). It is relatively easy to adapt commands to nonprimary language teaching. For example, in any language the instructor can start off with simple commands and illustrate the carrying out of those commands in the target language. These can involve movements like standing up, sitting down, standing up and turning around, and then sitting down again. At first blush, the idea may sound too simple, but commands can be expanded to more complex constructions about who did what to whom, who told whom to do what, and so forth. Questions can and complex syntax can be brought in fairly naturally: *Did so-and-so stand up? What did Susan do after Bill stood up?* and, in fact, all kinds of constructions and functions of language can be built up starting from simple commands.

Although Asher argued that the TPR strategy mirrors primary language development in critical ways, children are, of course, exposed to a great deal more than commands and motion verbs. They also hear and observe lots of questions, and statements about themselves, their environment, their activities, daily routines, and so forth. Put a child in the arms of any grandparent and consider the complexity of the language addressed to the infant: *Aren't you the cutest baby ever. You are so sweet. Look at those eyes, they are so pretty. Have you got a smile for me? Yes, you do. Look at that smile!* and so on and so forth. Of course, Asher also realized that acquiring a language involves more than just commands, but one of the important facts he demonstrated was that commands, if they are carried out, are memorable. In one study (see Asher, 2003) students still remembered 95% of the commands in the target language that they had learned to carry out three years earlier. Evidently the memorability of the target language forms is caused in part by the physical involvement of learners in activities that they regard as a kind of game. Also, they are engaged in pragmatically mapping the surface-forms of those commands onto meanings that they themselves are demonstrating. So, the connections are memorable for that reason.

In fact, the whole TPR strategy is merely one of a much larger category of **task-based language teaching/testing strategies** that meet the three pragmatic requirements highlighted above. Those other methods and approaches all have one feature in common with TPR: all of them involve some activity in which the student is engaged that requires the use and comprehension of the target language under normal time constraints. The activity can range from on the job training for an airplane mechanic, to familiar everyday activities like a trip to the grocery store or going out to lunch. It can also involve such things as viewing a scene in a full-length motion picture and then learning to take a part in a re-enactment. The key to all pragmatically valid task-based instruction is that it must take place in a context that provides a meaningful framework for the use of the target language. The task itself naturally provides a content-rich scaffolding of accessible meanings that enable the learner to make sense of the surface-forms of the target language.

Rodrigues and White (1983) reported on a study where learners participated in a "grocery shopping experience." In this task, the students made their list of items, planned what they would purchase, and then actually went to the grocery store and obtained the items on the list. A variation on this theme proposed by Richard-Amato (2003) is to gather the ingredients for a recipe from the refrigerator, the cabinets, and so forth in a kitchen and then put the items together describing the process in the target language. A vidcotapc of one of Rachel Ray's 30-minute meals would provide an excellent resource for such a task-based lesson (see Chen & J. Oller, 2005). The key to task-based instruction is that the surface-forms of the target language are not taught in isolation from their meanings, but in close and meaningful association with their meanings. As a result, the pragmatic requirements of purposeful language use under normal time limits are met and the new surface-forms are encountered in a rich context where many of the referents are readily apparent.

Another whole class of approaches to content-based nonprimary language instruction consist of the what are commonly called **immersion programs**. These tend to be task-based for the most part and commonly use elements of TPR in particular. However, in most immersion programs the primary focus is on the subject matter to be taught whereas the target language is merely a means for presenting the content. The term "immersion" comes from the idea of bathing students in the nonprimary target language. Instead of teaching Chinese in English, as is commonly done in foreign language classes where most of the talk is often not even in the target language, in an immersion program the content of all classroom activities whether they involve getting out a book and turning to page 15, or doing math, science, or literature, reading, and so on, takes place in the target language. In the immersion programs the nonprimary target language becomes the language of the classroom. It has been observed that immersion programs resemble the simple *mainstreaming* of the nonprimary language learners. However, in the typical case of mainstreaming, where a child is placed in a class with 25 to 30 children who speak a language that the child does not know, Cummins has suggested that the proper descriptive term would be to call that sort of approach a **submersion program** (Cummins, 1981; Rossell, 2000).

The difference is that in immersion programs all the children in the classroom are facing the same sort of learning problems. There is a more or less level playing field. In the submersion case, the nonprimary language learner is apt to feel isolated, alone, and at a disadvantage. The submersion case may resemble, for the short term, the situation that an LD child may encounter in the mainstream classroom. Of course, there are countless variations on the immersion theme. Provided the programs are sufficiently intensive and extended over time, after three to five years, children in immersion programs do as well in subject matter tests as their monolingual counterparts. The children in immersion programs normally become competent communicators in the target language. It has been complained that because many of their peers are speakers of the same primary language that immersion programs produce children with "accents" tending toward the common primary language, this minor disadvantage does not apply universally while the advantages of immersion programs are robust and do benefit all the children. Even children diagnosed with LD benefit from immersion programs and are able to acquire a nonprimary language (Bruck, Lambert, & Tucker, 1977; Rossell, 2000).

Benefits of Primary and Nonprimary Language/Dialect Acquisition

Language tests, and all other kinds of tests that depend mainly on language proficiency, show more than anything else how proficient an individual is in the language of the test. It is interesting and well supported in the research literature that the vast majority of educational and psychological tests are dominated by a single general factor of first language proficiency. This factor has often been identified with **innate intelligence**, for example, by Jensen (1969, 1974, 1980, 1995), Herrnstein (1973; Herrnstein & Murray, 1994) and others, but the research evidence shows that proficiency in any particular language must be acquired. Children are not born speaking French, Igbo, or Wu. Normal human beings are born with the capacity to acquire any language (cf. Chomsky, 1965) and the proficiency attained in any given one, or ones, will be affected by access (exposure) to that language in addition to native ability.

Jensen (1980) and others have argued that about 80% of what he calls "intelligence" is determined by genetics. He argues his case mainly on the basis of studies of identical versus fraternal twins versus siblings versus unrelated individuals reared in the same community. The fact that children who are more closely related genetically will have more similar test scores leads Jensen and others to suppose that whatever the tests may be measuring must be largely determined by genetic capacities. Jensen, Herrnstein, and others have argued that environment and upbringing play a much smaller and less significant role in the abilities displayed in all kinds of educational, psychological, and mental tests. In 1984, Jensen followed Gordon (1980) and even argued that low verbal scores in English, for certain minority language groups, can be interpreted as showing that 'the educational disadvantage of bilingualism may be largely the result of lower verbal aptitude per se than of a bilingual background' (p. 535). Strangely, Jensen supposes that becoming "bilingual" is somehow causally related to having a low IQ to start with.

We do not dispute that the human language capacity must be innate. If this were not so, other species would presumably do better than they do when taught human language by human beings. Also, other species would be able to learn languages without human teaching. They would, presumably, teach human language to their offspring and to other species as humans do. So, there is no question about the fact that much of the human language capacity must be innate, but is 80% of the capacity innately determined or perhaps less than that? Equally importantly, is the human language capacity helped or hindered by acquiring two or more language dialects? Contrary to Jensen's claims, our understanding of the relevant research literature leads us to conclude that becoming multilingual leads to certain cognitive and social advantages that the monolingual person cannot attain, all else being equal. For instance, the monolingual person can never have the experience of "thinking in another language" or of understanding the quite different ways that speakers of different languages divide a series of events and package them into different surface-forms.

Slobin (1996, 2004; also see Chen, 2005) has used the phrase "thinking for speaking" (or writing, or signing, presumably) to describe the different ways the world and its event sequences are parsed up and represented in the different surface-forms of distinct languages. For instance, an English-speaker can say, *The bottle floated into the cave*, but if Spanish-speakers say, *La botella flotó en la cueva*, the conception of the event(s) described does not involve passing from the open sea, say, into the cave, but simply being inside the cave throughout the floating. Similarly, if the Spanish-speaker says, *La botella flotó a la cueva*, it means "toward the cave" and not across the mouth and into the cave. Linguists and others are hard pressed to say why it is that speakers of one language tend to conceptualize and represent events in one way while speakers of a different language do so in a different way. What is virtually certain, however, is that learning more than one language/dialect expands our minds and gives us a better basis for understanding other people who often see things differently than we ourselves do. The most careful and relevant research shows that individuals who acquire more than a single language/dialect, if all else is held equal, have a significant advantage in certain kinds of tasks that require linguistic and conceptual flexibility (Cummins, 1984). Provided only that language acquisition proceeds to a fairly advanced level, above what is common in foreign language classes that focus on surface-forms, the research shows that learning an additional language is beneficial (J. Oller, 1997; Hakuta, 1986).

Summing Up and Looking Ahead

Normative language/dialect assessments are necessary in schools. They are essential if we are to identify children who need special services for disorders. They are essential in differentiating normal from abnormal linguistic, cognitive, and social development. They are also crucial for the purpose of providing appropriate and effective language/dialect acquisition opportu-

nities for the many children who have not learned the main language/
dialect of the school as their native system. One of the keys to providing
appropriate services is to provide appropriate assessments for minority
language/dialect children. Children should be assessed in all the language/
dialect systems that they know and judgments about disabilities and disorders need to be grounded in procedures applied to the child's strongest
(primary) language system. Educators and other test users need to be
aware of the research evidence showing that the language/dialect factor
not only dominates all complex educational, psychological, and mental
tests, but is also the largest single factor underlying so-called "nonverbal"
or "performance" tests as well. This is why a plurality of testing methods
are needed. Portfolios and intensive qualitative assessments are useful.

We also need to ask how a child performs in relation to peers, that is,
how that child is progressing relative to known milestones in his or her
primary language. For students being educated in a language/dialect that is
not their primary language/dialect system, it is imperative to assess them
in their strongest language system. In the next chapter we conclude the
book by looking ahead beyond maturity to the inevitable loss of representational abilities in advanced old age. This is inescapable because of cumulative
damage due to diseases, poisons, and physical injuries that must inevitably
lead to death. We will see that in certain respects the order of loss of certain representational abilities mirrors the milestones of development.

STUDY AND DISCUSSION QUESTIONS

1. Why is communication more difficult when the interlocutors do not
   speak the same language/dialect? Have you had the experience of
   trying to talk to someone who does not understand your primary
   language/dialect at all? If so, what other methods did you use to try
   to make yourself understood, and what did the other person do to
   try to be understood? Based on that experience, to what extent do
   you suppose the instructions for nonverbal tasks or performance
   tests can be made perfectly clear without any use of language?

2. What are some of the ways that language/dialect differences are apt
   to interfere with successful communication in a high-stakes industry
   such as international aviation? To what extent can similar problems
   arise in education?

3. What factors are taken into consideration in determining how many
   languages there are in the world? Why is it that every expert in the
   world agrees that the number can never be finally settled, and the
   number of distinct dialects of different languages is even more
   difficult to determine?

4. Which of the various tasks used to assess intellectual development (IQ) or related mental constructs are free of dependence on language/dialect proficiency?

5. What do you think causes the disproportionate representation of language/dialect minority children in classes for the mentally retarded, learning disabled, communication disordered, and so forth?

6. What are the essential elements of a valid test? Can qualitative assessments do all the work that is currently done by normative tests? Why so, or why not?

7. What pragmatic elements of communication are overlooked or neglected in approaches to literacy and foreign language instruction that focus on surface-forms? What's wrong with just showing contrasts between surface-forms?

8. What are some of the content-based approaches to foreign or second language instruction? How and why do they work and what are the benefits they offer to those who become fairly advanced bilinguals?

CHAPTER 12

Development in Relation to Disorders and Dissolution

 **OBJECTIVES**

By studying this chapter you will:

1. Review some of the major milestones of development already discussed in prior chapters;

2. See how the achievement of milestones can be delayed by genetic errors, physical injuries, diseases, and poisons that can have cumulative and cascading effects over time;

3. Become familiar with certain common disorders associated with aging;

4. Learn about the impact of certain poisons that are commonly introduced into the body;

5. Review ways to enhance language development and to prevent, halt, or delay the loss of knowledge, skills, and abilities; and

6. Find out about some of the professions that deal with normal speech and language development as well as difficulties and disorders of communication.

KEY TERMS

Here are some terms and concepts that you can learn more about in this chapter (these are also defined in the Glossary):

Alzheimer's disease
amyotrophic lateral sclerosis
aphasia
arcuate fasciculus
attention deficit/hyperactivity disorder
  (ADD/ADHD)
autoimmune disease
autopsy
blood brain barrier
bradykinesia
Broca's aphasia
carcinogen
cascading effect model of risk
chelation
cleft palate
codon
comorbid
craniofacial anomalies
dementia
dementia pugilistica
dental amalgam
dissolution
DNA
domino model of risk
dopamine
Down syndrome
ethyl mercury
etiology
gender bias
genetic code
genetic disorders
genotoxic
hemoglobin
homeostasis
immune system
immunity
lesion

Lewy-body disease
lexical taxonomy
longevity
Lou Gehrig's disease
Merthiolate
metabolism
methamphetamine
methyl mercury
mirror image hypothesis
mortality
multiple sclerosis
neurodegenerative
neurotoxin
null hypothesis
Parkinson's disease
pervasive developmental disorders
plaque
psychiatric disorders
quarantine
recommended therapy
RNA
senescence
sickle cell anemia
speech-language pathology
Swiss cheese model of risk
symptomology
thimerosal
thiomersal
toxicity
toxin
trauma
traumatic brain injury
tubulin
vascular system
Wernicke's aphasia
xenobiotic

Like every good story (as we saw in Chapter 10), this one too is motivated by conflict. As we saw in the theories of Vygotsky, Piaget, and others from Chapter 1 forward, advances in representational systems appear to be motivated by surprise, conflict, and disequilibrium. Now in the final chapter, we note that the whole story of milestones is motivated by risk. At every step, developmental delays can be understood as possible indicators of risk for difficulties, disorders, and disabilities. For this reason, in discussing progress from one milestone to the next, we have always had in mind the processes associated with errors, missteps, and cumulative damage to bodily systems. In addition to showing how key milestones are achieved, we have also demonstrated some of the ways parents, teachers, and other interlocutors can help children advance through the milestones while avoiding risks along the way. By studying the research base we not only learn how we can all become better and more effective parents, teachers, and communicators, but what we can do to increase the **longevity** of cognitive, linguistic, and social skills. All the previous chapters show that the study of the development of normal speech and language across the lifespan is essential to the discovery, definition, diagnosis, and treatment of communication difficulties, disorders, and disabilities. Because of the cumulative effects of damage to the organism, the **dissolution** of communication abilities becomes increasingly likely with aging. This process is known as **senescence**. Some difficulties are certain to lead in some cases to what are commonly called language disorders, learning disabilities, and/or learning disorders. In some of our own work, we have preferred to use the abbreviation "LD" to account for all these and to generalize to communication disorders (Badon, S. Oller, & J. Oller, 2005). However, in our judgment, there is no completely satisfactory term for all the things that can go wrong. The facts are complicated by interactions between different adverse factors and by cascading effects across the lifespan. For all these reasons, this last chapter not only highlights major milestones leading up to maturity and senescence but it focuses particularly on risks from genetic errors, diseases, **toxins**, and injuries.

Highlighting Key Milestones of Development

Even prior to birth, with four-dimensional ultrasound video (see the video from Dr. Stuart Campbell of London's Create Health Clinic associated with Figure 2–1 in Chapter 2 on the DVD), it is possible to observe the development of the baby in the womb. Behavioral milestones during gestation are becoming better defined as a result. At present, key milestones include limb movements, thumb-sucking, fetal breathing, smiling, stepping, leaping, and voluntary acts such as rubbing the eyes or scratching an itch.

Immediately after birth, among the most important and obvious indicators in the Apgar scale of well-being for a newborn infant is a strong cry (see the Apgar test of the Lasica baby associated with Figure 3-1 on the DVD). Just as a lusty cry within a minute after birth is considered a sign of well-being, voluntary vocalizations (or phonations), as contrasted with *vegetative* sounds such as burps, grunts, coughs, and sneezes, are among the most important indicators of normal development expected in the life of the newborn during the first week or so. Within this period we should also expect to see evidence of postnatal smiling. Although some have questioned whether the baby's earliest smiles are signs of well-being, contentment, and happiness, it is true that early smiling appears to be universal in normal infants across all cultures and that it is regarded by naïve observers in all cultures as a social sign of well-being. Smiling and laughing are both regarded as important social milestones. Recall the response of mothers to

their own newborns (see the video, Sound Beginnings associated with Figure 3-2 on the *Milestones Student DVD-ROM*). Not only is smiling a significant milestone to which other persons react, it is evidently a social act that has an almost universal impact on adults who interact with babies. As noted by D. K. Oller, Eilers, and Basinger (2001, p. 50) when the infant smiles, it is almost impossible for an adult interacting with that infant not to smile back. The response is almost completely automatic and it is obviously social (see the discussion in Chapter 4 associated with Figure 4-1). A little later on, the normal baby will laugh in a social situation. In the Navajo culture of North America a special ceremony is celebrated for the first noticed social laugh (Kavasch & Baar, 1999). See the photograph of Macy by Bob Rothman, 2004 in Figure 12-1.

After analyzing in detail the standard objections to reading too much into the infant's smile, psychologist Buytendijk (1947/2002) quoted the poet Frederik van Eden who wrote:

> Then he smiled, the first of his life
> And thus he came to us from a far still land
>
> He sent us to hold this sign of love
> He who smiled himself—
> No longer alone by himself

Whether the first smile means to the infant just what it means to an adult may be debatable, but there is no doubt that the first smile of the infant is commonly understood as a sign of well-being. In the video on the DVD, Sound Beginnings, associated with Figure 3-2, notice that when the infant smiles the interacting mother is smiling too. It is difficult even for a casual observer not to smile when looking at these pictures. Try the experiment and see. The smile appears to be a spontaneous gesture by the infant, and

Figure 12–1. This is Macy at her "first laugh" ceremony. The photograph by Bob Rothman is reproduced here by permission of the photographer and author, from *Focus: News from the Harvard Medical, Dental, and Public Health Schools.* Copyright © 2004 Ellen Rothman. See the full article by Ellen Rothman, M.D., at http://webweekly.hms.harvard.edu/archive/2004/12_13/student_scene.html.

it seems to reach out and connect with other persons. On the other side of the ledger, prolonged failure to engage other persons, say, within the first few days and weeks of life, should be taken as a sign of risk. We should expect to see smiling, voluntary vocalizations, response to eye contact, and other milestones early in the neonate's development.

It should also be noted that parents are likely to be the first to notice and to identify developmental difficulties in their own children. Probably the reason that parents tend to be the first to notice such problems, as is the case with autism (Ohta et al., 1987), is that they tend to spend more time with their child than anyone else does. With disorders in the autism spectrum, parents commonly identify the problem well before it is confirmed and diagnosed by professionals (Filipek et al., 2000).

Within the first four to six months, a normally developing infant will move from highly nasalized vocalic phonations to less nasalized vowels followed by the first recognizable CV sequences at around the third or fourth month. By about the middle of the fourth month, give or take a few weeks, the infant should show the achievement of the first discriminated symbol. Usually this will be displayed as an orientation response where, for instance, the baby will turn to look at the person who says the baby's name. The recognition of the infant's name is quite far from the achievement of the first meaningful word, but it is a step in that direction showing that the baby distinguishes the surface-form of a spoken word. At about this time, infants also become increasingly responsive to social interactions including pretend conversations and games like peekaboo (Montague & Walker-Andrews, 2001; Hodapp, Goldfield, & Boyatzis, 1984).

By the fifth to tenth month, as noted in Chapter 6, we can expect to see speech-like repetitions of CV sequences, for example, /bababa/, /dadada/, and the like. This phase of canonical babbling gives way to variegated babble with distinct CV sequences, /badaga/, uttered in relatively rapid and rhythmic speech-like syllabic bursts. Intonational contours that are characteristic of distinct social functions of speech, such as making an assertion, asking a question, producing an exclamation of approval or disapproval, and so forth should begin to appear at about this time as well. During this period of development the child will expand the repertoire of discriminated symbols, sequences that are distinguished by the infant, and prescinded symbols, syllable sequences that are produced by the infant, and also will begin to develop hypostatic symbols, words that the infant does not yet produce but already associates with distinct persons, events, and the like. Multiple examples of hypostatic symbols are displayed by Aleka Titzer in the DVD associated with Figure 10–1 at 9 months of age.

If any of the foregoing developments is excessively delayed, or simply does not occur, these facts should be taken as indicators of risk. The child should be evaluated for possible learning difficulties. The research shows that canonical babbling is a particularly useful reference point because parents with very little instruction are able to say whether or not their child has achieved this stage of development (D. K. Oller, Eilers, Neal, & Schwartz, 1999). The research, furthermore, shows that children who achieve canonical babbling earlier will remain ahead throughout the rest of their development (Rvachew, Slawinski, Williams, & Green, 1999). It follows that children who are delayed are at risk of additional delays later on.

Within about five to seven months after the onset of canonical babbling, the infant can be expected to produce his or her first meaningful word (a zero order predicate). This word will be identifiable by its surface-form and will be applied in such a way that at least some of the other persons in the child's life space will perceive the appropriateness of the word to the context in which it is used. What is more the word will generalize appropriately to new contexts of experience. Within roughly the following six months to a year the child will differentiate the predicate from its argument(s), and will enter the genuine two-word stage of development. By now the child is about two years old, give or take a few months. After first order predicates are differentiated from their arguments, the child will begin to move on to first order predicates that can take two or more arguments. At this stage, the normal child will be able to express an interest in a future action in a different location, for example, "Go outside" meaning something like let's take the wagon outside and play out there.

By about the third year, give or take a few months, the normal child begins to incorporate second order (deictic) predicates. These are relations that not only refer to one or more arguments, for example, persons, things, locations, and the like, but that also distinguish the positions of discourse occupied by speaker, hearer, and others. That is, by this stage the pronominal distinctions between the speaker (*I*) as contrasted with the listener (*you*) begin to appear. By the fourth year the child will normally begin also to master third order predicates which incorporate more subtle aspects of viewpoint, for example, tense (past versus future), aspect (progressive versus perfective), and modality. Within a few months of the fourth birthday, the normal child will come to a vague limit of diminishing returns in syntax and will begin to pay more attention to the ways in which representations relate to the facts of experience. As soon as second order predicates are beginning to come into the child's repertoire, simple narrative-like sequences will begin to emerge but it will be some time, a year or two later (by about age 5 or 6), before the child can report a coherent narrative sequence of events.

As the child's attention turns more and more from the mastery of syntax to the subtleties of pragmatics, by about age four or five (give or take a year), the normal child will become able to distinguish pretending from nonplay activities, for example, pretending to take a trip from actually going on a trip. Not until a year or two later will the child be able to sharply distinguish pretense from belief, and one or two additional years beyond that will be required to distinguish innocent errors from deliberate lies (roughly between ages 6 and 8). Subsequent development will lead to maturity somewhere between 12 and 20 where uncountably many inferences can be drawn from symbols and especially from transitive relations. The most common transitive relations are the kind seen in narratives, for instance, where a certain event tends to be reported ahead of another because it occurred before that other event. But discourse inferences can be drawn from any kind of transitive relations, such as causal, temporal, or spatial ones. The more the sign hierarchy advances, the greater is the tendency for the sign-user to make inferences that are grounded in the abstract signs of discourse. Amazingly subtle elements of surface-form, of intonation, choice of words, posture, facial expression, and prior experience with the interlocutor, are known to interact in discourse processing (see references in J. Oller et al., 2005).

Classifying, Diagnosing, and Differentiating Disorders

All along the path of development, things can also go wrong. In fact, as we have noted, one of the main reasons for studying milestones of normal speech and language development is to enable early and accurate identification of risks. The various classes of difficulties and disorders that affect communication can be distinguished and classified in a variety of ways.

In the first place, (1) difficulties are noticed and classified by their **symptomology**, that is, by the way they affect the appearance, behavior, and/or abilities. Symptoms can be roughly divided into those mainly affecting (a) cognition and mental abilities, (b) feelings, moods, and behavior, and (c) the body in terms of (i) sensation, (ii) movement, and (iii) neurophysiology. In the second place, (2) difficulties can be classified with respect to **recommended therapy**, that is, whatever is commonly done to prevent, lessen, halt, or possibly cure the problem. Treatments are typically undertaken by different professional groups and may involve approaches addressing bodily functions of the individual affected by the difficulty. Treatments may include (a) medicines aimed at improving body chemistry and/or removal of toxins, (b) dietary regimens with a similar purpose, (c) physical or speech therapies aimed at improving aspects of behavior including range of motion, swallowing, articulation, gesturing, and so forth. In some cases the goal is merely to keep the condition from getting worse. In the third place, difficulties may be classified (3) by their supposed **etiology**, that is, by their suspected or known causes. In fact, all the major systems of classification look ultimately to the diagnosis and description of the disease, disorder, or difficulty itself in terms of what causes it.

Physical, Emotional (Social and Behavioral), and Mental Development

In speech and language development it is not surprising that things can go wrong. In fact, when something goes wrong at one level it can often affect subsequent developments as suggested in Figure 12-2. This model may be called the **domino model of risk** or the **cascading effects model of risk**. The earlier a difficulty appears, the more likely it is to have long range consequences. A subtle problem in hearing, for example, can evidently affect communication and learning across a wide spectrum (for example, see Rigo, Arehole, & Hayes, 1998). It is as if the toppling of one domino causes a cascading effect. Genetic errors also may produce physical problems in development. Physical problems in the development of the body can influence emotional development. Emotional problems can affect behavior and cognition. Mental and behavioral difficulties can similarly slow down communication and social development.

For all these reasons, it should hardly surprise us that things can go wrong in complex representational systems at any level and at any stage of development. On the contrary, what should surprise us is that communication commonly succeeds. Ordinarily our perceptions do not deceive us. We often understand the communications of others as they are intended. We get to the lunch meeting. We arrive at the right place on the right day and

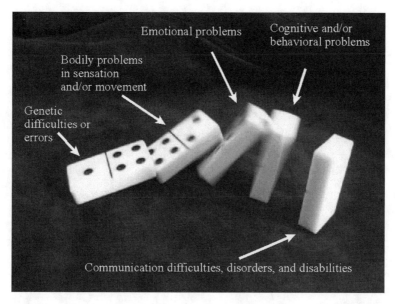

Figure 12–2. The domino, or cascading effect, model of risk factors in communication disorders.

at the right time. The airplane departs as expected and arrives at its destination as intended. If communication did not commonly succeed, we would not be able to discover errors. We would not be able to identify diseases, disorders, and difficulties of communication. Language acquisition usually proceeds without fail so that the individual becomes an effective native speaker of one or more languages. Typical individuals all over the world are able to acquire whatever language or languages, in some cases, two or more, to which they happen to be exposed. Evidently, all normal individuals can also become literate and it is possible to do so at an early age.

There are also multiple layers of built-in protections against genetic errors, bodily malfunctions, toxins, diseases, and breakdowns in social relations and communication. In fact, James Reason (2001) has proposed a model of these protections which he has dubbed the **"Swiss Cheese" model of human risk**. Figure 12-3 adapts his model to the achievement of the milestones of normal speech and language development as they relate to communication difficulties, disorders, and disabilities. Protections against risk factors, as the figure shows, exist at many levels. Only a few of the known systems of protection against risk factors are suggested in Figure 12-3. There are protections against genetic errors. The body also has built-in protections against a great variety of toxins that are filtered out and excreted or **quarantined**. There is an elaborate and complex immune system for fighting viruses, bacteria, and foreign organisms. There are also social, educational, and legal systems to provide for the care, upbringing,

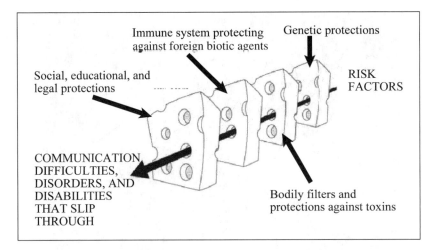

Figure 12–3. An adaptation of Reason's "Swiss cheese" model of risks from: Reason, J. (2000). Human error: Models and management, *British Medical Journal, 320*(7237), p. 769. Adapted by permission. Copyright © 2000, *British Medical Journal.*

and education of human beings so as to try to minimize risks of communication difficulties, disorders, and disabilities.

Nevertheless, as our adaptation of the Swiss cheese model shows in Figure 12-3, things can still go wrong, and risk factors can slip through wherever vulnerabilities coincide, that is, where the holes in the Swiss cheese line up. In fact, as the domino model of Figure 12-2 suggests, diseases, disorders, and difficulties can have far reaching consequences across the lifespan. The accumulation of damage over time leads to the eventual dissolution of communication abilities. Difficulties can begin before birth with **genetic disorders**. More than 6,000 such disorders are known (Eldadah, Grifo, & Dietz 1995) and many of them can cause difficulties that directly or indirectly affect speech and language development. Among the best known genetic disorders affecting speech, language, and social development are physical deformities including **cleft palate** and other deformities of the head and face known as **craniofacial anomalies**. Because these genetic problems may affect social development and behavior, they may in turn have effects on mental growth and development. Problems at the genetic level may also include **Down syndrome** and **sickle cell anemia**. Both of these are known to be caused by errors in the genome. Down syndrome is commonly known to affect communication abilities while sickle cell anemia is rarely connected with communication disorders at all. Down syndrome is associated with mental retardation and abnormal physical characteristics that can be detected in the developing fetus. Sickle cell anemia, on the other hand, though present from conception is not usually detected until sometime after birth (Platt et al., 1994; Serjeant, 2005).

These and other genetic factors have far-reaching effects on **metabolism**, **homeostasis**, **immunity** to disease, and ability to expel or quarantine toxins.

The interaction of genetic factors with other factors leading to difficulties, diseases, and disorders is evident in many ways. For instance, deaf parents are more apt to have a deaf child than nondeaf parents and there are many genes involved (Steel & Bussoli, 1999; also see Cargill, Famula, Strain, & Murphy, 2004 for their genetic research with deaf Dalmatians). Parents who stutter are more apt to have children who stutter than parents with no history of stuttering (Yairi, Ambrose, & Cox, 1996). In general, persons born to parents or relatives of persons with any kind of difficulties or disorders of speech and language are more likely to be diagnosed with the same or related difficulties themselves. It is also commonly noted that males are more often affected than females by the most common communication disorders including stuttering, dyslexia, autism, attention deficit/hyperactivity, and a large variety of behavioral and social problems. For instance, in the case of the autism spectrum, males are about four times more likely than females to be diagnosed. Clearly, there is a preponderance of males and thus a significant **gender bias**. These trends show that genetic make-up plays a role in many communication difficulties and disorders. Some have suggested that the preponderance of males in certain categories of disorders may have to do with the difference in the way males and females are treated by others and thus learn to behave (Anderson, 1997). But however large a role social learning may play, gender bias is still so obvious and extreme in the case of autism and many other communication disorders that we must suppose that genetic differences between males and females must play a significant role.

Cascading Effects Can Emerge

Across the life span unexpected effects can emerge. For instance, a genetic problem such as the one resulting in sickle cell anemia not only affects development but commonly also results in developmental delays and premature death. In sickle cell anemia, the shape of the red blood cells is deformed in a way that interferes with circulation especially at the level of the smallest capillaries. A colleague at the University of New Mexico School of Medicine reported an incident where a student transcribing a tape-recorded medical report wrote "sick as hell anemia" when the doctor dictating the report had said "sickle cell anemia" (Dr. Jack Omdahl, personal communication, about June 14, 2004). The anecdote may be amusing, but unfortunately the mistaken transcription is, in fact, a valid description of the disease. The problems created by this genetic disease result from poor circulation of the blood owing to the sickle shape of red blood cells. Symptoms can include delayed development, chronic fatigue, rapid heart rate, severe pain in the joints, jaundice, fever, and pain in the bones (http://www.nlm.nih.gov/medlineplus/ency/article/000527.htm visited October 24, 2005). When a person is this sick, social skills and development will be affected. The commonly fatal disease adversely affects every aspect of social and mental life. It is caused by a single error in a sequence of approximately 600 genetic **codons**, the genetic words that specify the sequence of amino acids that make up the protein known as **hemoglobin**. The result of this error is to distort the normally round shape of red blood cells and cause them to clog the smallest blood vessels.

Because genetic development affects every other aspect of the organism, it is inevitable that severe genetic disorders, by affecting the overall health of the individual, will also spill over into social experience (per the model suggested by Figure 12–2). As a result, the mental growth and communication abilities of the individual can be affected by almost any and all serious genetic disorders. Of course, in addition to genetic difficulties, disease, physical injuries, and toxic insults can damage the human being at any stage of development across the life span. In cases where multiple disorders or diseases are present we can say that one disease is **comorbid** with others. For example, language delays/disorders are often comorbid with sickle cell anemia.

Disorders Linked to Toxins

The most controversial and best studied neurotoxin known to affect neurological development and normal functioning of communication abilities is mercury in any of its forms. Only plutonium is more toxic for human beings than mercury. There have been two major incidents of relatively widespread mercury poisoning. One occurred in Minamata, Japan in the 1950s and the other in Iraq in 1971 (Kirby, 2005). In Japan the poisoning was traced to contaminated fish and in Iraq to seed grain from Mexico. The grain was not supposed to be directly consumed, but planted. It was treated with methyl mercury. The sacks were marked with the skull-and-cross-bones to indicate that it would be poisonous to eat it, but starving Iraqis consumed it by the thousands though the grain was intended exclusively for planting. From these and other incidents it has become widely known that as little as one part per million of mercury (per body weight) can be fatal. The Environmental Protection Agency (EPA), the Federal Drug Administration (FDA), and the Centers for Disease Control (CDC) all have concluded that in amounts greater than 0.4 parts per billion mercury is unsafe (see Kirby, 2005, p. 49). In fact, this is the highest threshold regarded as safe by any of the protection agencies and the EPA estimates the safe limit at less than 0.1 part per billion. Some studies suggest that the threshold should be, in fact, lower still (see Kirby 2005, p. 50).

Beginning with studies published in 1973 (according to a search on January 16, 2006), the Web of Science lists 3,370 studies of the toxicity of mercury in various forms including **dental amalgam** and **thimerosal**. Dental amalgam is the material currently used for approximately 92% of tooth restorations and thimerosal is a preservative that has been commonly used to preserve multiple-use vials of vaccine. Both of these substances are approximately 50% mercury by weight. Recent studies show that the mercury gas rising from a single filling with dental amalgam (see the video Smoking Teeth prepared by the International Association of Oral Medicine and Toxicology, on the DVD), or a single inoculation containing thimerosal (see Kirby, 2005), exceeds the estimated safe limits of the EPA many times over. There are also hundreds of studies among the published reports showing that minute quantities of mercury cause neurological damage. Mercury is a potent neurotoxin. Mercury in any form is known to cause genetic mutations (Shenker, Pankoski, Zekavat, & Shapiro, 2002), in other words, it is **genotoxic**. Neurological damage, depending on the dose, ranges from mild impairment to death. Recent work by Hornig, Chian, and Lipkin (2004; also see follow-up by Humphrey, Cole, Pendergrass, & Kiningham, 2005) shows that genetic make-up is a highly significant factor in an organism's ability to eliminate mercury. As a result, some individuals are harmed more than others by the same quantity of mercury.

About two-thirds of body mercury found in human beings is from dental amalgam used in tooth restorations (Lorscheider, Vimy, & Summers, 1995). Additional body burden is known to come from thimerosal (Bradstreet, Geier, Kartzinel, Adams, & Geier, 2003), and other sources. Unfortunately, the effects of such toxins and their interactions are cumulative and long-term. Because dental amalgam and thimerosal account for the vast majority of mercury burden in human beings, it is useful to consider them in a little more detail. Also, it is important to keep in mind that neurotoxins affect normal speech and language development. For parents, and those involved in fields that deal with child development, a closer look at the research on mercury in dental amalgam and vaccines will be both interesting and useful.

Dental Amalgam

Amounts of mercury released as gas from dental filling material (see the video titled Smoking Teeth on the DVD associated with this chapter) greatly exceed estimated safe limits. Nevertheless, the American Dental Association (2003), which owns the patent on amalgam and makes a profit from its being used in tooth restorations, continues to hold that mercury in dental fillings is safe. They refer to the fillings as "silver" though the mercury content outweighs the silver by 1.4 to 1 (see http://www.ibiblio.org/amalgam/amalgamtext.html visited on January 16, 2006). Still the ADA says on their website in 2006:

> Dental amalgam (silver filling) is considered a safe, affordable and durable material . . . Dental amalgam has been studied and reviewed extensively, and has established a record of safety and effectiveness (see http://www.ada.org/prof/resources/positions/statements/amalgam.asp visited on January 16, 2006; also see the Federal Drug Administration, 2002 for a similar statement).

Peer-reviewed empirical research by contrast shows that the mercury content of dental amalgam is linked with neurotoxic effects in a wide variety of **neurodegenerative** conditions and diseases (see Mutter, Naumann, Walach, & Daschner 2005). Research shows that the mercury used in dental fillings strips nerve fibers of their insulating material, **tubulin**, in particular, and damages the cells with which it comes in contact. See the video on the DVD linked to Figure 12–4 that shows just how the nerve fibrils of

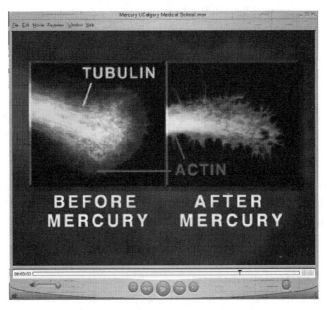

Figure 12–4. See How Mercury Damages Nerve Fibrils on the Milestones Student DVD-ROM. Reproduced from http://movies.commons.ucalgary.ca/mercury. This picture and video are used by permission of the University of Calgary Medical School, Dr. Fritz L. Lorscheider, and Dr. Naweed Syed.

a snail are affected in real time by minute quantities of mercury. Similar quantities of other toxic metals such as lead, aluminum, cadmium, nickel, and manganese (Leong, Syed, & Lorscheider, 2001). do not produce such damage (http://movies.commons.ucalgary.ca/mercury/ retrieved January 16, 2006; also see How Mercury Damages Nerve Fibrils on the *Milestones Student DVD-ROM*).

Thimerosal

Turning next to the preservative thimerosal (also known as **thiomersal**, in British English), which was introduced into certain vaccines and other products in the 1930s by Eli Lilly and Company, again we find that the main ingredient by weight is mercury, in this case ethyl mercury. This preservative is also known by its commercial name, **Merthiolate**, and was commonly used as a topical disinfectant. It has been used to prevent bacterial growth in multidose vials of widely used vaccines. Recently, it has been banned from many of them but is still included in others. Thimerosal is a chemical foreign to living cells, therefore, a **xenobiotic**. For an even-handed account of how this neurotoxin was introduced in vaccines see Kirby (2005). Although proponents of mercury in vaccines have argued that ethyl mercury is less harmful than the more common **methyl mercury** found in the environment, for example, in tuna fish, careful research (Havarinasab, Lambertsson, Qvarnstrom, & Hultman, 2004) reveals that ethyl mercury easily crosses the **blood brain barrier** (Havarinasab, Haggqvist, Bjorn, Pollard, & Hultman 2005) where its damaging effects accumulate. In addition to damaging nerves, ethyl mercury (thimerosal), like methyl mercury (with one more carbon atom) suppresses the immune system. In "genetically susceptible mice" it has a secondary effect of causing self-immunity. In this way, ethyl mercury may be more harmful to genetically susceptible individuals than methyl mercury (see Havarinasab & Hultman, 2005, for a review).

Autism Spectrum Disorders

Among neurodevelopmental disorders that are affected by toxic effects of mercury and other environmental factors, none is more devastating than autism. Figure 12–5 shows Eric Gallup at age 10. His father, Ray Gallup, Founder of the Autism Autoimmunity Project (TAAP), estimates the cost of caring for an individual with severe autism at between $50,000 to $100,000 per year (see http://www.taap.info retrieved January 29, 2006). If the individual in question is institutionalized when he or she becomes an adult, as Eric was because of violent outbursts beyond his or his parents'

Figure 12–5. Eric Gallup from http://www.avn.org.au/Children%27s%20Gallery/eric.htm (retrieved January 29, 2006). Reproduced by permission of Ray Gallup.

control, the cost rises significantly. At age 17 Eric became increasingly violent and is 21 at the time of this writing. His father explains:

> In 2002, Eric started to develop aggressions . . . he would bite, head butt, kick, scratch and pull hair. . . . in February 2003, Eric broke my left index finger with his teeth almost amputating it . . . Eric grew to be 6'2" tall and I am 5'10" so he was a handful. . . . When Eric had an aggression, we would have to go behind our bedroom or bathroom doors and lock them so Eric couldn't hurt us (retrieved January 29, 2006 at http://www.avn.org.au/Children%27s%20Gallery/eric.htm and quoted by permission of Raymond Gallup).

Because autism affects social relations, it has been classed with **psychiatric disorders** and is placed at the center of **pervasive developmental disorders** which also include at the margins of the category, **attention deficit disorder/attention deficit hyperactivity disorder** (ADD/ADHD; see Breggin, 1998). Increasingly, evidence suggests that autism has biochemical causes and that neurotoxins such as mercury are certainly involved in many cases if not primary causal agents. Before 1943, no one had described or heard of autism. In 1980, the incidence was estimated at fewer than 1 case in 10,000. The CDC now estimates that the incidence of autism spectrum disorders is 1 in 166 and still rising (http://www.cdc.gov/ ncbddd/autism/asd_common.htm visited on January 27, 2006). This represents an increase of about 60-fold. It seems unlikely that such a rapid and marked growth could be explained as a result of genetics. Some have suggested that criteria for identification have been broadened. However, the central characteristics of severe autism have hardly changed at all since the disorder was first described by Kanner (1943) and Asperger (1944, 1979). Strengthening the suspicion that autism and various other neurodegenerative conditions are linked to toxins such as mercury is evidence that **chelation**, that is, the removal, of toxins from the body, is being shown to dramatically lessen the symptoms of those disorders for individuals undergoing treatment (see the website of Dr. Amy Holmes and references linked there retrieved January 28, 2006 from http://www.healing arts.org/children/holmes.htm).

Dissolution with Aging as the Mirror of Development

In the 1920s, A. R. Luria (see Cole & Cole, 1979) was among the first to speculate that the dissolution of communication abilities and skills tends to occur in the reverse order of their acquisition. This notion can be called the **mirror image hypothesis**. Roman Jakobson (1968) also subscribed to this idea. Although Lev Vygotsky (1934/1978) did not, as far as we know, advocate the mirror image hypothesis, he recommended the study of "defectology" (his term for communication and other disorders). He saw the study of disorders as a way to better understand normal development.

In any case, dissolution does seem to occur in the reverse order of development with respect to some aspects of development. However, the mirror image hypothesis is clearly overstated. Many milestones do not disappear from the sign-user's repertoire in the reverse order of their acquisition. However, it is generally true that words that seem hardest to retrieve from long-term memory tend to be ones that have been recently acquired. Thus, the loss of vocabulary seems to be roughly in the opposite order of acquisition (Light & Burke, 1988). Also words lost early tend to be ones of low frequency. A caricature summing up the problem is the absent-minded professor who extends his hand to introduce himself, then, stammers, "I'm uh, I'm uh, I'm uh . . . terrible with names." The joke partly reflects reality because proper names are an ever expanding category, but only in extreme cases of memory loss, or **dementia**, is the individual apt to fail to retrieve his or her own name.

Alzheimer's and Other Neurodegenerative Diseases

A person with advanced **Alzheimer's disease** (AD) can in some cases become unable to recall his or her own name. For a discussion of clinical symptoms see Müller and Guendouzi (2005). In modern times the latter disease has become so well known and is so common that it is often referred to as "old-timer's disease." Also, AD is sufficiently rare in younger individuals as to lead specialists to believe that aging, in combination with genetic tendencies, really is the largest factor in this most common form of dementia (Manning, 2004; Kave, 2005). AD accounts for about two-thirds of diagnosed cases of dementia in persons over 65 (Geldmacher, 2003). Sailor, Antoine, Diaz, Kuslansky, and Kluger (2004) showed that individuals with AD are less likely than age-matched controls without AD to recall atypical, low frequency, words from a given **lexical taxonomy**. In the taxonomy of "furniture," for example, words like "table," "chair," "desk," and "couch" were more apt to come up than less frequent words like "credenza," "buffet," or "hutch," but AD patients were less likely than age-matched controls to think of the less frequent exemplars in any given category. The authors suggested that AD patients operate at a slower speed of processing. Some authors have also speculated that the slowing of the processing speed is, in fact, what produces the memory loss.

Although a recent study by Lemke and Zimprich (2005) found a significant correlation (0.61) between loss of memory and loss of processing speed over a four-year period in 474 persons between the ages of 59 to 65, the authors concluded that loss of processing speed cannot be the only factor causing memory loss. In fact, based on the evidence the authors present, it is equally likely that the memory loss is producing the reduction in processing speed. The question of what causes AD and other forms of dementia is, surprisingly, still an open question. Manning (2004) notes that "age is the most important risk factor" but that other potential causal factors include genetic propensities, being female, and suffering from depression. In view of the fact that not every person of advanced years experiences the deterioration associated with AD, it certainly cannot be entirely explained by aging. If aging were the sole cause, then all people beyond a certain age would get AD, but they do not.

Peng (2003) points out that it is uncertain whether AD may be caused by degeneration of blood vessels, the **vascular systems**, that supply the brain or whether the degeneration of neurons leads to the problems in blood supply. Learning the causes of AD, and differentiating AD from other consequences of aging, will almost certainly help us in understanding and treating other dementias as well. It is known that the ability to attend to multiple objects, events, or streams of experience simultaneously decreases with age (Hasher & Zacks, 1979). Though other factors are certainly involved in AD in addition to aging, consider the fact that between ages 59 and 65 only about 3% of the population will be affected by AD while at age 85 and beyond over 50% are affected. Genetic components are known to be present in about 50% of the cases (Manning, 2004) and there is mounting evidence that genetic factors interact with environmental factors (Plassman & Breitner, 1996). One of the neurotoxins that has been associated with AD, unsurprisingly, is the mercury in dental amalgam (Enestrom & Hultman, 1995; McGrother, Dugmore, Phillips, Raymond, Garrick, & Baird 1999; Mutter, Naumann, Walach, & Daschner, 2005; Prochazkova, Sterzl, Kucerova, Bartova, & Stejskal, 2004).

Broca's and Wernicke's Aphasias

Degenerative diseases, disorders, and difficulties are more apt to affect older people because of their cumulative effects. **Traumatic brain injuries**, for example, may happen at any age and can cause the same losses in speech and language that seem to have more gradual onset in dementias. However, the longer a person lives, the more likely he or she is to be affected by the sort of damage that can result in **aphasia**, a loss of speech or language capacity. Aphasia can be caused by **trauma**, that is, by a blow to the head, or a sudden stop causing internal bruising of the brain. Aphasia can also be caused by anything that damages the brain sufficiently, for example, by disease, toxicity, and by any factor leading to clogging or bursting of blood vessels in the brain. The two best known types of aphasia are those that affect either speech fluency leaving much of the comprehension and sense-making more or less intact, known as **Broca's aphasia**, or the reverse in which the person affected may retain fluency but lose the sense-making capacity, in which case the condition is **Wernicke's aphasia**.

In 1861 through an **autopsy** of a patient that had died of syphilis, Paul Broca identified a brain region damaged by a syphilitic **lesion** (an area of damage caused by the disease), in what is consequently now known as "Broca's area" (Broca, 1861). The patient had lost the capacity to produce fluent speech, the condition now known in a variety of forms as Broca's aphasia (see Figure 12–6). The kind of aphasia that affects comprehension and sense-making but tends to leave fluency and surface-forms intact is known as **Wernicke's aphasia**. The latter kind was defined in 1874, 13 years after the Broca type aphasia, by Karl Wernicke (1874). As it turns out, Broca's and Wernicke's areas of the brain are connected by a bundle of fibers known as the **arcuate fasciculus**. Since the discovery of the involvement of these brain areas in speech and language production, many other disorders have been studied and have helped us to better understand normal speech and language functions.

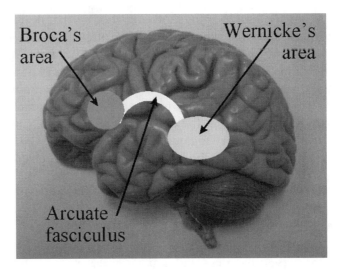

Figure 12–6. The approximate locations of Broca's and Wernicke's areas as connected by the bundle of fibers (beneath the surface of the cortex) known as the arcuate fasciculus.

Mortality, Senescence, and Communication Disorders

Although certain occupations, for example, soldiering, boxing, driving race cars, and the like, are more apt to result in traumatic brain injuries, aphasias caused by trauma, also tend to be more common in older people. If we ask why, the answer is obvious. The older we get the more likely it is that some significant injury will occur. It is not that injuries necessarily occur more often in old age, though this too may be true, but because injuries accumulate over time, longevity itself provides more chances for injuries to show their effects.

Mortality itself is evidently a consequence of the cumulation of various kinds of risk and damage factors. There are genetic errors, there is biochemical damage due to toxins, there are physical injuries, and diseases. What is called aging, or *senescence*, is plausibly explained as cumulative damage to the dynamic systems that make up the organism (Gavrilova & Gavrilova, 2001, 2004). All the damaging factors together, and in various combinations, not only tend to produce death ultimately and universally, but they also guarantee the ultimate dissolution of communication abilities in the end. Even external factors that affect the organism also tend to be cumulative over time. For instance, potentially harmful chemicals in agriculture, food preservation, pest control, consumable goods, and in industrial products and wastes, not only end up in the soil, water, and the air we breathe, but they also accumulate in individuals. However, toxins may have much more dramatic effects in early stages of development than they do later in life in spite of the fact that toxins must eventually lead to cumulative damaging effects in aging as well. The greater impact of toxins during early stages of development is explained in two ways: for one, the organism's defenses are less developed early on, and, for another, the quantity of a toxin relative to the size of the body is vastly greater for a developing embryo or infant than for an adult.

For all the foregoing reasons, it is certain that many of the degenerative conditions discovered in the 20th century are being caused, or worsened by cumulative effects of toxins. Many formerly rare or previously unknown degenerative diseases have become increasingly common since the middle of the 20th century. Alzheimer's disease (AD) was defined in 1907 by Alois Alzheimer [1864–1915]. It is now estimated to affect about four million individuals in the United States alone and 50% of those more than 85 years of age (retrieved January 28, 2006 from http://www.alz.org/AboutAD/WhatIsAD.asp). The next most common disease of aging is **Parkinson's disease** (PD). It was first described diagnosed in 1817 by James Parkinson in *An Essay on the Shaking Palsy*, but the key factor of **dopamine**, the neurotransmitter involved in directing muscle activity, was not verified until 1961 by Oleh Hornykiewicz, who wrote his own account of this discovery in 1992. Today PD is estimated to affect about 1.5 to 2% of the population over 60. This disease manifests with trembling in the extremities when they are at rest and the rigidity of certain muscles producing slowed movement described by the technical term **bradykinesia** derived from Greek roots meaning "slow" (*brady*) plus "movement" (*kinesia*).

Another disease associated with aging along with PD and AD is **Lewy-body disease**. Lewy-bodies are abnormal clumps of proteins that develop inside nerve cells. The hallmark symptoms are hallucinations and illusions of various sorts. They can be visual or auditory and may involve well formed or fleeting images or sounds. The person affected may think that some person or animal has just passed by when, in fact, none is present. Sometimes the illusions are so well formed that the affected person will hold a conversation, for instance, with someone who is not present. Such well-formed hallucinations also occur in about 9 to 22% of cases of PD (Fénelon, Mahieux, Huon, & Ziégler, 2000). Lewy-body disease as distinct from PD, however, can only be definitely diagnosed by autopsy. Interestingly, about 15 to 30% of persons diagnosed with AD also have Lewy-body disease, and of persons diagnosed with Lewy-body disease, 60 to 90% are also diagnosed with AD (http://ci.columbia.edu/c1182/web/sect_5/c1182_s5_2.html retrieved January 28, 2006). Similarly, about 25% of PD patients can be expected to show the hallucinatory symptoms characteristic of Lewy-body disease (Fénelon et al., 2000), although in PD some portion of the hallucinations that occur are thought to be caused by the medications used to treat it. In a careful study of 216 PD patients, Fénelon et al. (2000) found that 39.8%, somewhat higher than the 25% expected, showed hallucinatory symptoms. The possibility that prescribed medications will produce toxic effects is always a factor to be kept in mind.

Although all the foregoing diseases and disorders are more common in older persons, they can, atypically, occur in younger individuals. For instance, among well-known celebrities who have campaigned for legislation and funding of research on PD is Michael J. Fox. In his case, the PD may have been caused by exposure to certain chemical toxins to which he and others may have been exposed (Vingerhoets, Snow, Tetrud, Langston, Schulzer, & Calne 1994; Wood, 1997). The substance believed to have caused his PD is a known by-product of **methamphetamine**, a stimulant. Methamphetamine, unfortunately, also contains hidden components known to be extremely neurotoxic (Nicklas, Youngster, Kindt, & Heikkila, 1987; Sweeney, 2005). PD can also be caused by repeated traumatic injuries to the brain as seen in boxers such as Mohammed Ali. This kind is called **dementia pugilistica**. It can be caused by a single severe head injury, or by an accumulation of many smaller injuries over time. But damage from injuries and from toxins are also associated with other neurodegenerative diseases including AD (see Traumatic Brain Injury, 2005) so singular causes are not necessarily to be expected in sorting out the dementias.

Autoimmune Disorders

In addition to the neurodegenerative and vascular degenerative problems already mentioned, there are many others that tend to become more common with aging or that may be induced by toxins, or even prescribed medications. Although difficulties accumulate with advancing age, almost any sort of problem can occur at any age. Among them are many that affect the **immune system** by which the body defends itself against invading foreign objects, organisms, viruses, and toxins. When things go wrong with the immune system it can attack the body that it normally defends. Diseases producing this undesirable effect are called **autoimmune diseases**. Among the more common disorders of this kind is **multiple sclerosis** (MS). In this particular autoimmune disease the immune system attacks the proteins that insulate nerve fibers. Without their insulation the nerves cannot function and muscle control deteriorates. MS today is believed to affect about 400,000 people in the United States alone. The first recorded case is believed to have occurred in the 1400s but the disease was not clearly described and identified until 1868 by Jean Martin Charcot. In MS, scar tissue referred to as **plaques**, form in nerve tissues. These plaques were first discovered in 1925 by E. D. Adrian. He also showed that nerves stripped of their myelin cannot transmit electrochemical impulses (see National Multiple Sclerosis Society, 2003). The prevalence of MS in the 20th century, however, has greatly increased until it is now believed to affect about one person in 700. Its causes are still considered unknown, although some of the contributing factors must include toxins that destroy or interfere with the production of proteins involved in insulating nerve fibers. Among the most damaging neurotoxins known to have this effect is mercury, and elevated levels of mercury have been found in persons with MS (Mauch et al., 1995; Siblerud, 1992; Siblerud & Kienholz, 1994).

Another autoimmune disease that involves the destruction of insulating proteins is **Lou Gehrig's disease**, also known as **amyotrophic lateral sclerosis** (ALS). Today this disease is believed to affect about 20,000 to 30,000 people in the United States and to be increasing in the United States alone at a rate of about 5,000 persons per year. ALS was not known until 1869 when it was discovered by the same neurologist who identified MS, Jean Martin Charcot. ALS destroys the power of movement until the patient is unable to breathe. There are a number of studies linking this disease with toxins including mercury poisoning, although the effects appear to be modulated by genetic and other factors (Adams, Ziegler, & Lin 1983; Barber, 1978; Kasarski, Haley, & Gunnerson, 1993; Khare, Ehmann, Kasarskis, & Markesbery, 1990; Pamphlett & Png, 1998; Pamphlett & Waley, 1996; Su, Wakabayashi, Kakita, Ikuta, & Takahashi 1998; Wicklund, 2005).

Carcinogens

Carcinogens are agents known to produce cancers (Ferguson, 1999; http://ntp.niehs.nih.gov/ntp/roc/toc11.html visited on July 11, 2005). Ferguson (2002) claims that 40% of known cancers may be caused by carcinogens that are found in food. According to Ames and Gold (1998) more than "a thousand chemicals have been reported in roasted coffee" and "more than half of those tested . . . are rodent carcinogens" (p. 205). However, they do not recommend that everyone should stop drinking coffee because human beings, they contend, are very different from rodents and rarely consume carcinogens in the quantities that have been shown to produce cancers in rodents. The vast majority of carcinogens that negatively affect sensation, movement, cognition, and communication (Rusyniak, Furbee, & Pascuzzi, 2005) are found in natural forms (Ames & Gold, 1998). They write,

> . . . humans, like other animals, are extremely well protected by many general defense enzymes, most of which are inducible (that is, whenever a defense enzyme is in use, more of it is made). because the defense enzymes are equally effective against natural and synthetic chemicals one does not expect, nor does one find, a general difference between synthetic and natural chemicals in ability to cause cancer in high dose rodent tests (p. 205).

Vested Interests and Interpretations of the Research

There is an old adage sometimes attributed to Mark Twain that "figures don't lie but liars do figure" (see Huff & Geis, 1993); see Figure 12–7. Although we admit there are different ways to interpret data, Robert F. Kennedy, Jr. (senior attorney for the Natural Resources Defense Council and chief prosecuting attorney for Riverkeeper as well as president of Waterkeeper Alliance) argued recently that "mercury in childhood vaccines may have caused autism in thousands of kids." He also claims that the government "rushed to conceal the data and to prevent parents from suing drug companies for their role in the epidemic" (http://www.common-dreams.org/views05/0616 31.htm visited July 11, 2005). He says that Eli Lilly, the developer of thimerosal, "knew from the start that its product could cause damage and even death in both animals and humans. In 1930, the company tested thimerosal by administering it to 22 patients with terminal meningitis, all of whom died within weeks of being injected, a fact Lilly didn't bother to report in its study declaring thimerosal safe." For documentation of these claims by a dispassionate journalist, see Kirby (2005).

Although the Federal Drug Administration recommended a ban on thimerosal in 1982, in 1991 the Centers for Disease Control announced that it would continue to be used in various vaccines including those for

Figure 12–7. Are the vested interests trying to keep information from the public? This cartoon is from p. 9 of *How to Lie with Statistics* by Darrell Huff illustrated by Irving Geis. Copyright © 1954 and renewed © 1982 by Darrell Huff and Irving Geis. Used by permission of W. W. Norton & Company, Inc.

hepatitis B (for newborns), *Haemophilus influenzae B*, and diphtheria tetanus pertussis used for two-month-old babies. The widely recommended flu vaccine of 2005 and 2006 contained thimerosal. The World Health Organization continues to say that thimerosal is safe, but it promises to keep the possibility that it is linked to neurological disorders "under review." To all the foregoing arguments about the role of thimerosal in particular in developmental disorders, Verstraeten (2004), a researcher formerly associated with the CDC and now with a large pharmaceutical company in Europe, issued an interesting disclaimer about the association between thimerosal and neurodevelopmental disorders. He wrote, that

> ... an association can neither be found nor refuted. ... The CDC screening study of thimerosal containing vaccines was perceived at first as a positive study that found an association between thimerosal and some neurodevelopmental outcomes. . . . Because the findings of the first phase were not replicated in the second phase, the perception of the study changed from a positive to a neutral study . . . the investigators could neither confirm nor exclude an association, and therefore more study is required (p. 932).

Parker, Schwartz, Todd, and Pickering (2004) also concluded that no association can be found in the research between thimerosal and autism.

However, there is something fundamentally odd about claiming to demonstrate a **null hypothesis** that has already been rejected on the basis of multiple positive results. In scientific research we can often disprove a null hypothesis but by performing any number of empirical studies we can never prove a null hypothesis, that is, in the case of thimerosal the general claim that no association has been or will ever be found with neurological disorders and diseases. Supposing that no relation will ever be found between neurodevelopmental disorders and a known neurotoxin like mercury is like claiming that gold will never be discovered in California. It was found there long ago and no number of subsequent failures to find gold in California, could possibly prove that no gold exists in California. A null hypothesis can never be proved, by any number of negative empirical results. What is remarkable about the particular null hypothesis that is supported by Parker et al., the CDC, the FDA, and other federal agencies, is that this one has already been disproved many times over by the demonstration of positive associations between mercury and neurodegenerative disorders (see Bradstreet, Geier, Kartzinel, Adams, & Geier, 2003; Geier & Geier, 2004, 2005a, 2005b; Mutter et al., 2005).

Kirby (2005) has published a follow-up study of Verstraeten's original data by Mark and David Geier. The reanalysis of the raw data shows (see Kirby, 2005, p. 408) a positive association between injections containing thimerosal, in contrasted to thimerosal-free vaccines of the same kind, and the incidence of neurological disorders. Also, Kirby cites memos and E-mails recovered through the Freedom of Information Act that seem to suggest that some individuals at the CDC knew that thimerosal in vaccines was positively linked with nerurodevelopmental disorders in their database, but that they tried to keep this information from the public. At any rate, the research evidence showing mercury to be a potent neurotoxin is not controversial. Everyone admits that it is extremely neurotoxic even in relatively minute quantities.

Hygienic Alternatives and the Professions

What can parents and others do to help ensure longevity and good health with respect to normal speech and language development and maintenance? The obvious alternatives include eating a healthy diet rich in nutrients and as free as reasonably possible of known toxins. Rest and exercise are also important. In vaccinating our children, we should use vaccines that are known to be free of mercury (thimerosal). No reasonable parent or grandparent would unnecessarily expose a child to a known neurotoxin such as ethyl mercury. In fact, it is interesting that some of the persons who have argued for the safety of shots containing nearly 50% ethyl mercury have wisely refused to allow their own children and grandchildren to be inoculated with vaccines containing thimerosal (see Kirby, 2005, for examples).

Similarly, in dealing with our dentists, we should require restorations free of mercury. If existing fillings containing mercury are to be removed, the procedure should guard against inhaling vapors or swallowing residues (see Smoking Teeth video on the DVD. There are suitable alternatives to dental amalgam made of polymers and porcelain. Also, we should continue to follow the ongoing research studies that are accumulating. Access to information concerning safe alternatives is far less likely to be harmful than to be helpful. We should learn all we can about hygienic alternatives to foster normal development and to prevent, halt, or at least delay dissolution.

Language and Genetics

It is inevitable that our story begins and ends with language as its central component. As human beings, throughout all of our experience, we are especially interested in and dependent on language. It defines us and differentiates us from other species. As we learn more and more not only about normal speech and language development, but also about the genetic basis for our unique human capacities, we see evidence everywhere that the whole biosphere is fundamentally dependent on the complex systems of representation found in the **genetic code**. The latter language-like system involves at least three distinct yet interrelated systems of representation consisting of long molecules of **DNA**, **RNA**, and proteins (J. D. Watson, 1968/1998). The genes are read from DNA, transcribed into RNA, and eventually translated into proteins, such as tubulin, myelin, and hemoglobin, along with thousands of others. As we learn more and more about the remarkable immune system, we see that it to is a multilayered system of representations.

In a complex developing organism, cells have to communicate with each other. It used to be debated whether the conversations between cells were dull and boring or complex and interesting (Champe & Harvey, 2005). It is now known that they are not only interesting but crucial to our survival and especially to the normal functioning of our immune system (Watkins & Salter, 2005). Cells have to be identified as belonging to the organism or as potential foreign invaders. For the immune system to work, potentially lethal invaders have to be either quarantined or expelled. For this to happen, they must first be identified. In cases where potentially lethal invaders cannot be quarantined or expelled, they must be attacked and destroyed. Cells that belong to the organism, in contrast, need to be nurtured and supported. If they are damaged, they need to be repaired; if repair is not possible, they need to be disassembled, or expelled. Among the sciences that study the development and maintenance of organisms, those that focus on the ways in which communication systems function can only rise in importance in the future. Not only are these sciences critical to understanding normal speech and language development, but they are also crucial to understanding the logical basis of genetics, embryology, and immunology.

For all the foregoing reasons, the professions that deal with childrearing, the education of children and adults, the teaching of languages, and all aspects of the systems that enable successful communication are particularly valuable to us all. Teachers who work with literacy skills, special education, communication disorders, and all the medical professions that deal with language-based systems are likely to benefit and also contribute to new knowledge on the subject matter of this introduction. All of us owe a debt of thanks to those who devote their lives to the study of communication systems. Also, as is becoming increasingly evident, no system under study is more important to us socially and intellectual than our language capacity. The development of language, literacy, and related systems of knowledge and skills across the human life span is miraculously complex. For good reason, therefore, we study milestones of development to postpone the seemingly inevitable dissolution owed to cumulative damage from physical, chemical (toxic), and biological injuries. As we look to the roots of the interacting systems, at their very basis, we come to language systems again in genetics. The linguistic metaphor seems to be crucial to our understanding of genes, proteins, and their functions. From beginning to end, it is evident that life crucially depends on language-like representational systems.

Among the professions that seek to enhance human experience, to increase longevity, and to minimize the difficulties that may be encountered along the way are education, nursing, medicine, and the fields specially known as **speech-language pathology** (American Speech-Language-Hearing Association, 2006) and *audiology* (American Academy of Audiology, 2006). To learn more about these professions, see http://www.asha.org/default.htm concerning speech-language pathology and audiology; also see http://www.audiology.org/ concerning audiology and see http://www.interdys.org/ concerning literacy and the International Dyslexia Association and follow the links found at these sites. (All these sites are linked on the *Milestones Student DVD-ROM* and were visited on January 21, 2006.) Some teachers will specialize not only in development but also in the disabilities that can occur along the way. We expect that many users of this book will enter one of these helping professions.

With the hope that increased understanding will lead to greater enjoyment of the benefits of language and communication for us all, and in the interest of enhancing and extending these abilities throughout the life span, we close with the invitation of Robert Browning (1864, lines 1–6):

> Grow old along with me!
> The best is yet to be,
> The last of life, for which the first was made.
>
> Our times are in His hand
> Who saith "A whole I planned,
> Youth shows but half; trust God: see all, nor be afraid!"

Summing Up and Looking Beyond This Book

This chapter has reviewed some of the key milestones examined in previous chapters. It has also looked ahead to the dissolution of normal speech and language knowledge, skills, and abilities in senescence. We have suggested throughout the book ways that parents, teachers, and other communicators can help infants, children, and other adults advance through the milestones of normal speech and language development. We have highlighted both the milestones and relevant research across the life span. Our primary focus has been on the systems and processes of normal speech and language development but in the sequel (a companion introduction to communication disorders, J. Oller, Badon, & S. Oller, in press), we discuss in greater detail the full range of difficulties, disorders, and disabilities that interfere with and ultimately result in the dissolution of communication capacities.

In this book we have seen that the study of the normal processes of speech, sign, and language development is at least a corequisite to the study of communication disorders, special education, and related developmental sciences. More specifically we believe that the foundation for understanding breakdowns, difficulties, and disorders of communication, especially, of natural human language systems, must be grounded in study of the normal milestones that are commonly achieved on schedule. To understand how processes of communication break down, it is essential to understand how they often succeed. Children usually develop to maturity and succeed in acquiring the full complexities of the human language systems to which they are exposed. Commonly, communication succeeds.

Based on the reactions of our own students who have worked through this book with us, and as shown in their collective writings, their scores on the test questions associated with this material (as documented in the Teacher's Manual on the *Milestones Teacher's DVD-ROM*), it is our belief and expectation that students and teachers of *Milestones* will not only understand well what we have written, but that they will join with us and our colleagues worldwide in applying, further developing, and extending the relevant paradigms of research, study, and practice.

▬▬ STUDY AND DISCUSSION QUESTIONS ▬▬

1. Why is it essential to know what normal speech and language development is like to identify communication disorders?

2. In what ways are phonological, lexical, syntactic, morphological, and pragmatic milestones distinct from each other? Is there continuous development from syllables to meaningful words? Meaningful words to syntactically complex strings of words? In what ways are the developments that we observe continuous, and in what ways do the various higher levels depend on completely new information that is not available at the prior level of structure?

3. What are some of the ways that disorders of communication can be identified, differentiated, and classified?

4. Keeping in mind the constructive nature of sign systems, why should we expect therapy tuned to a particular level of development to

be more effective than an intervention or treatment that is less well-fitted to the individual's prior achievements? Recall Vygotsky's idea concerning the zone of proximal development.

5. Discuss the Swiss cheese and domino models of risk factors as seen in human speech and language development across the life span. How do these models relate to the problems posed by neurotoxic effects of mercury in dental amalgam and in inoculations? Combining the two models, consider why cumulative effects and interactions between, for instance, genetics and toxins are difficult to pin down.

6. What is the "mirror image" theory of the dissolution of human mental abilities in senescence? What are some obvious ways that this theory fails? In what ways does it succeed in explaining observed phenomena?

7. What causal factors are involved in producing mortality? How do they relate to common disorders of communication? How is it possible for disorders of senescence to appear at relatively young ages? Consider, for instance, dementia pugilistica and Parkinsonism.

8. What are some of the ways that the development of linguistic and other representational abilities in children can be enhanced? Similarly, how can the longevity of communication abilities be extended?

References

Adams C. R., Ziegler, D. K., & Lin, J. T. (1983). Mercury intoxication simulating amyotrophic lateral sclerosis. *Journal of the American Medical Association*, *250*(5), 642-643.

Ainsworth, W. A. (1973). System for converting English text into speech. *IEEE Transactions on Audio and Electroacoustics*, *21*(3), 288-290.

Al-Otaiba, S., & Fuchs, D. (2002). Characteristics of children who are unresponsive to early literacy intervention—A review of the literature. *Remedial and Special Education*, *23*(5), 300-316.

Aldridge, M. A., Stillman, R. D., & Bower, T. G. R. (2001). Newborn categorization of vowel-like sounds. *Developmental Science*, *4*(2), 220-232.

Alzheimer, A. (1907). Über eine eigenartige Erkrankung der Hirnrinde. *Allgemeine Zeitschrift für Psychiatrie*, *64*, 146-148.

American Academy of Audiology. (2005). How's your hearing? Ask an audiologist. Retrieved January 28, 2006 from http://www.audiology.org/.

American Dental Association. (2003). ADA Statement on Dental Amalgam. Revised January 8, 2002. Retrieved January 28, 2006 from http://www.ada.org/prof/resources/positions/statements/amalgam.asp.

American Psychiatric Association. (1980). *Diagnostic and statistical manual of mental disorders* (3rd ed.). Washington, DC: Author.

American Psychiatric Association. (1987). *Diagnostic and statistical manual of mental disorders*. (3rd ed. rev.). Washington, DC: Author.

American Psychiatric Association. (1994). *Diagnostic and statistical manual of mental disorders* (4th ed.). Washington, DC: Author.

American Speech-Language-Hearing Association. (2005). Speech, language, & swallowing. Retrieved January 28, 2006 from http://www.asha.org/public/speech/.

Ames, B. N., & Gold, L. S. (1998). The causes and prevention of cancer: The role of environment. *Biotherapy*, *11*(2-3), 205-220.

Anastasi, A., & Urbina, S. (1996). *Psychological testing*. Englewood Cliffs: NJ: Prentice Hall.

Anderson, K. G. (1997). Gender bias and special education referrals. *Annals of Dyslexia*, *47*, 151-162.

Andrews, S. & Scarratt, D. R. (1998). Rule and analogy mechanisms in reading words: Hough dou peapel rede gnew wirds? *Journal of Experimental Psychology: Human Perception and Performance*, *24*(4), 1052-1086.

Apgar, V. (1953). A proposal for a new method of evaluation of the newborn infant. *Current Researches in Anesthesia and Analgesia, 32,* 260–267. Original paper retrieved January 28, 2006 from http://apgar.net/virginia/Apgar_Paper.html.

Armstrong, D., & Wilcox, S. (2005). *Vision to voice: The origin of language through gestures.* New York: Oxford University Press.

Asher, J. J. (1969). The total physical response approach to second language learning. *Modern Language Journal, 53,* 3–17.

Asher, J. J. (2003). *Learning another language through actions* (6th ed.). Los Gatos, CA: Sky Oaks Productions, Inc.

Augustine, Saint. (1952). In R. M. Hutchins (Ed.), *Great books of the western world: The confessions of St. Augustine* (Vol. 18), Chicago: Encyclopedia Britannica. (Original work published ca. 401 AD)

Austin, J. L. (1955). *How to do things with words.* Cambridge, MA: Harvard University Press.

Autism Speaks (February 2005). A message from Suzanne and Bob Wright. Retrieved January 28, 2006 from http://www.autismspeaks.org/founders.php.

Badon, L. C., Oller, J. W., Jr., & Oller, S. D. (2005). Enabling literacy in at-risk learners: Decoding surface-form versus attending to meaning and narrative structure. *Psychology of Language and Communication, 9*(1), 5–27.

Badon, L. C., Oller, S. D., & Oller, J. W., Jr. (2005). Qualitative ratings within and across ethnic boundaries of maximally different methods of one on one reading instruction. *Journal of Communication Disorders, 38*(6), 445–457.

Badon, L. C., Oller, S. D., Yan, R. & Oller, J. W., Jr. (2005). Gating walls and bridging gaps: Validity in language teaching, learning, and assessment. *Working Papers in TESOL & Applied Linguistics Teachers College, Columbia University, 5*(1), 1–15.

Bailey, C. J. N. (1973). *Variation and linguistic theory.* Arlington, VA: Center for Applied Linguistics.

Bailey, C. J. N. (1996). *Essays on time-based linguistic analysis.* New York: Oxford University Press.

Ball, E. W., & Blachman, B. A. (1988). Phoneme segmentation training: Effect on reading readiness. *Annals of Dyslexia, 38,* 208–225.

Ball, E. W., & Blachman, B. A. (1991). Does phoneme awareness training in kindergarten make a difference in early word recognition and developmental spelling? *Reading Research Quarterly, 26,* 49–66.

Ball, M. J., & Müller, N. (2005). *Phonetics for communication disorders.* Mahwah, NJ: Lawrence Erlbaum Associates.

Barber, T. E. (1978). Inorganic mercury intoxication reminiscent of amyotrophic lateral sclerosis. *Journal of Occupational and Environmental Medicine, 20*(10), 667–669.

Barlow, M., & Kemmer, S. (2000). *Usage-based models of language.* Stanford, CA: Center for the Study of Language and Information.

Baron-Cohen, S., Tager-Flusberg, H. & Cohen, D.J. (Eds.), (1993). *Understanding other minds: Perspectives from autism.* Oxford: Oxford University Press.

Barsalou, L. W. (2005). Abstraction as dynamic interpretation in perceptual symbol systems. In L. Gershkoff-Stowe & D. Rakison (Eds.), *Building object categories* (389–431). Carnegie Symposium Series. Mahwah, NJ: Erlbaum.

Bates, E. (1976). *Language and context: The acquisition of pragmatics*. New York: Academic Press.

BBC News World Edition. (June 28, 2004). The BBC's Vicki Young: The 4D scan gives a far more detailed picture than normal ultrasounds. Retrieved January 28, 2006, from http://news.bbc.co.uk/2/hi/health/3846525.stm.

Belin, P., Fecteau, S. & Bédard, C. (2004). Thinking the voice: Neural correlates of voice perception. *Trends in Cognitive Sciences, 8*(3), 129–134.

Bellugi, U. (1980). The structure of language: Clues from the similarities between signed and spoken language. In U. Bellugi & M. Studdert-Kennedy (Eds.), *Signed and spoken language: Biological constraints on linguistic form* (pp. 115–140). Dahlem Konferenzen. Weinheim/Deerfield Beach, FL: Verlag Chemie.

Bernard, S., Enayati, A., Redwood, L., Roger, H., & Binstock, T. (2001). Autism: A novel form of mercury poisoning. *Medical Hypotheses, 56*, 462–471.

Berninger, V. W. (2001). Understanding the "lexia" in dyslexia: A multidisciplinary team approach to learning disabilities. *Annals of Dyslexia, 51*, 23–48.

Berthoud-Papandropoulou, I., & Kilcher, H. (2003). Is a false belief statement a lie or a truthful statement? Judgments and explanations of children aged 3 to 8. *Developmental Science 6*(2), 173–177.

Bess, F. H., & Hall, J. W. (1992). *Screening children for auditory function*. Nashville, TN: Bill Wilkerson Center Press.

Best, C., & McRoberts, G. (2003). Infant perception of non-native consonant contrasts that adults assimilate in different ways. *Language & Speech, 46*, 183–216.

Biemer, P. P., & Lyberg, L. E. (2003). *Introduction to survey quality*. Hoboken, NJ: John Wiley & Sons.

Binet, A. (1911). New investigations upon the measure of the intellectual level among school children. *L'Annee Psychologique, 11*, 145–201.

Birdwhistell, R. L. (1970). *Kinesics and content*. Philadelphia: University of Pennsylvania Press.

Birnholz, J. C. (1981). The development of human fetal eye movement patterns. *Science, 213*, 679–681.

Birnholz, J., Stephens, J. C., & Faria, M. (1978). Fetal movement patterns: A possible means of defining neurologic developmental milestones in utero. *American Journal of Roentology, 130*, 537–540.

Blevins, J. (1995). The syllable in phonological theory. In J. Goldsmith, (Ed.), *The handbook of phonological theory* (pp. 206–244). Oxford: Blackwell.

Bloom, K., & Lo, E. (1990). Adult perceptions of vocalizing infants. *Infant Behavior & Development, 13*(2), 209–219.

Bloom, K., Russell, A., & Wassenberg, K. (1987). Turn-taking affects the quality of infant vocalizations. *Journal of Child Language, 14*, 211–227.

Bloom, L. (1970). *Language development: Form and function in emerging grammars*. Cambridge, MA: MIT Press.

Bloomfield, L. (1933). *Language*. London: Allen & Unwin.

Bloomfield, L. & Barnhart, C. L. (1961). *Let's read: A linguistic approach*. Detroit, MI: Wayne State University Press.

Bond, L. A. (1996). Norm- and criterion-referenced testing. *Practical Assessment, Research & Evaluation, 5*(2). Retrieved January 28, 2006 from http://pareonline.net/getvn.asp?v=5&n=2.

Borsboom, D., Mellenbergh, G. J., & van Heerden, J. (2004). The concept of validity. *Psychological Review, 111*, 1061-1071.

Bower, T. G. R. (1971). The object in the world of the infant. *Scientific American, 225*(4), 30-38.

Bower, T. G. R. (1974). Development of infant behavior. *British Medical Bulletin, 30*(2), 175-178.

Bower, T. G. R. (1997). Contingencies, logic, and learning. *The Behavior Analyst, 20*, 141-148.

Bower, T. G. R., Broughton, J. M., & Moore, M. K. (1970). *Perception & Psychophysics, 9*, 193-196.

Bower, T. G. R., & Paterson, J. G. (1973). The separation of place, movement, and object in the world of the infant. *Journal of Experimental Child Psychology, 15*, 161-168.

Bradley, L., & Bryant, P. E. (1983). Categorizing sounds and learning to read—a causal connection. *Nature, 301*, 419-421.

Bradley, L., & Bryant, P. E. (1985). *Rhyme and reason in reading and spelling.* Ann Arbor, MI: University of Michigan.

Bradstreet, J., Geier, D. A., Kartzinel, J. J., Adams, J. B., & Geier, M. R. (2003). A case-control study of mercury burden in children with autistic spectrum disorders. *Journal of American Physicians and Surgeons 8*(3), 76-79.

Braine M.D.S. (1963). The ontogeny of English phrase structure: The first phase. *Language, 395*, 1-13.

Brand, R. J., Baldwin, D. A., & Ashburn, L. A. (2002). Evidence for 'motionese': modifications in mothers' infant-directed action. *Developmental Science, 5*, 72-83.

Breggin, P. R. (1998). *What doctors aren't telling you about stimulants for children.* Monroe, ME: Common Courage Press.

Broca, P. P. (1861). Perte de la parole; ramolissement chronique et destruction partielle du lobe antérieur gauche de cerveau. (Loss of speech: Chronic softening and partial destruction of the left frontal lobe of the brain.) *Bulletins de la Société d'Anthropologie de Paris, 2*, 235-238.

Brookes, H., Slater, A., Quinn, P. C., Lewkowicz, D. J., Hayes, R., & Brown, E. (2001). Three-month-old infants learn arbitrary auditory-visual pairings between voices and faces. *Infant and Child Development, 10*, 75-82.

Brown, H. D. (1994). *Principles of language learning and teaching.* Englewood Cliffs, NJ: Prentice-Hall.

Brown, R. (1973). *A first language: The early stages.* London: George Allen & Unwin, Ltd.

Bruck, M., Lambert, W., & Tucker, G. R. (1977). Cognitive consequence of bilingual schooling: The St. Lambert Project through grade six. *Psycholinguistics, 6*, 13-33.

Bruner, J. S. (1975). From communication to language: A psychological perspective. *Cognition, 3*, 255-287.

Bruner, J. S. (1983) *Child's talk: Learning to use language.* New York: Norton.

Burbacher, T. M., Shen, D. D., Liberato, N., Grant, K. S., Cernichiari, E., & Clarkson, T. (2005). Comparison of blood and brain mercury levels in infant monkeys exposed to methyl mercury or vaccines containing thimerosal. *Environmental Health Perspectives, 113*(8), 1015-1021.

Buros Institute of Mental Measurement. (1938–2005). *Mental measurements yearbook*. Lincoln, NE: Author. Retrieved January 28, 2006 from http://www.unl.edu/buros/bimm/html/catalog.html#mmy.

Buros, O. K. (Ed.). (1970). *Personality tests and reviews.* Highland Park, NJ: Gryphon Press.

Bushnell, I. W. R., Sai, F., & Mullin, J. T. (1989). Neonatal recognition of the mother's face. *British Journal of Developmental Psychology*, 7, 3–15.

Butterfield, L. J. (1962). Practical epigram of the Apgar score, *Journal of the American Medical Association*, July 1962, 353.

Buytendijk, F. J. J. (2002). The first smile of the child. *Phenomenology & Pedagogy*, 6(1), 15–24. Retrieved January 28, 2006 from http://www.phenomenologyonline.com/articles/buytendijk.html. (Originally presented in Dutch by Professor Buytendijk as his inaugural lecture at the University of Nijmegen, the Netherlands, in 1947; Trans. and ed. by Max van Manen.)

Bybee, J. L. (2000). The phonology of the lexicon: Evidence from lexical diffusion. In Barlow & Kemmer (2000, pp. 65–85).

Bybee, J. L. (2001). *Phonology and language use.* New York: Cambridge University Press.

Byrne, B., & Fielding-Barnsley, R. (1989). Phonemic awareness and letter knowledge in the child's acquisition of the alphabetic principle. *Journal of Educational Psychology*, 81, 805–812.

Byrne, B., & Fielding-Barnsley, R. (1993). Evaluation of a program to teach phonemic awareness to young children: A 1-year follow-up. *Journal of Educational Psychology*, 85, 104–111.

Byrne, B., & Fielding-Barnsley, R. (1995). Evaluation of a program to teach phonemic awareness to young children: A 2- and 3-year follow-up and a new preschool trial. *Journal of Educational Psychology*, 87, 488–503.

Calfee, R. C., & Norman, K. A. (1998). Psychological perspectives on the early reading wars: The case of phonological awareness. *Teachers College Record*, 100, 242–274.

Cameron-Faulkner, T., Lieven, E., & Tomasello, M. (2003). A construction-based analysis of child-directed speech. *Cognitive Science*, 27(6), 843–873.

Camras, L. A. (1992). Expressive development and basic emotions, *Cognition & Emotion*, 6(3–4), 269–283.

Capps, L. R., & Pickreign, J. (1993). Language connections in mathematics: A critical part of mathematics instruction. *Arithmetic Teacher*, 41(1), 8–12.

Cargill, E. J., Famula, T. R., Strain, G. M., & Murphy, K. E. (2004). Heritability and segregation analysis of deafness in U.S. Dalmatians. *Genetics*, 166(3), 1385–1393.

Carpenter, M., Call, J. & Tomasello, M. (2002). A new false belief test for 36-month-olds. *British Journal of Developmental Psychology*, 20, 393–420.

Carroll, J. B. (1960). Language development. In C. Harris (Ed.), *Encyclopedia of educational research* (pp. 744-752). New York: Lawrence Erlbaum Associates.

Carroll, J. B. (1971). Language development. In A. Bar-Adon & W. F. Leopold (Eds.), *Child language: A book of readings.* Englewood Cliffs, NJ: Prentice-Hall.

Cattell, R. B., & Cattell, A. K. S. (1933–1973). *Culture fair intelligence test.* Urbana-Champaign, IL: Institute for Personality and Ability Testing.

Centers for Disease Control (2005). Autism spectrum disorders. Retrieved January 28, 2006 from http://www.cdc.gov/ncbddd/factsheets/asd.pdf.

Chafe, W. L. (1980). The flow of consciousness in the production of a narrative. In W. L. Chafe (Ed.), *The pear stories: Cognitive, cultural, and linguistic aspects of narrative production* (pp. 9–50). Norwood, NJ: Ablex.

Chamberlain, D. B. (1996). The fetal senses. Retrieved January 28, 2006 from http://www.birthpsychology.com/lifebefore/fetalsense.html.

Chamberlain, P., & Medeiros-Landurand, P. (1991). Practical considerations for the assessment of LEP students with special needs. In E. Hamayan, & J. S. Damico (Eds.), *Limiting bias in the assessment of bilingual students* (pp. 111–156). Austin, TX: Pro-Ed.

Champe, P. C. & Harvey, R. A (2005). Lippincott's illustrated reviews: Biochemistry. Baltimore, MD: Lippincott Williams & Wilkins.

Chartrand, T. L., & Bargh, J. A. (1999). The Chameleon effect: The perception-behavior link and social interaction. *Journal of Personality and Social Psychology*, *76*(6), 893–910.

Chen, L. (2005). *The acquisition and use of motion event expressions in Chinese*. Unpublished doctoral dissertation, University of Louisiana, Lafayette, Louisiana.

Chen, L., & Oller, J. W., Jr. (2005). High quality sound motion pictures in L2 curricula: Why and how they work. *Canadian Modern Language Review*, *62*(2), 263–284.

Chomsky, N. A. (1957). *Syntactic structures*. The Hague: Mouton.

Chomsky, N. A. (1959). A review of B. F. Skinner's *Verbal behavior*. *Language* *35*(1), 26–58.

Chomsky, N. A. (1965). *Aspects of the theory of syntax*. Cambridge, MA: MIT Press.

Chomsky, N. A. (1972). *Language and mind*. New York: Harcourt, Brace, & World.

Chomsky, N. A. (1975). *Reflections on language*. New York: Pantheon.

Chomsky, N. A. (1980). On cognitive structures and their development: A reply to Piaget. In M. Piatelli-Palmarini, (Ed.), *Language and learning: The debate between Jean Piaget and Noam Chomsky* (pp. 35–54). Cambridge, MA: Harvard University Press.

Chomsky, N. A. (1995). Language and nature. *Mind*, *104*, 1–61.

Chomsky, N. A. (2002). *On nature and language*. New York: Cambridge University Press.

Chomsky, N. A., & Fodor, J. A. (1980). The inductivist fallacy. In M. Piatelli-Palmarini (Ed.), *Language and learning: The debate between Jean Piaget and Noam Chomsky* (pp. 259–275). Cambridge, MA: Harvard University Press.

Chomsky, N. A., & Halle, M. (1968). *The sound pattern of English*. New York: Harper and Row.

Christophe, A., Nespor, M., Guasti, M. T., & Van Ooyen, B. (2003). Prosodic structure and syntactic acquisition: The case of the head-direction parameter. *Developmental Science*, *6*(2), 211–220.

Clark, H. H. (1996). *Using language*. New York: Cambridge University Press.

Clark, H. H., & Clark, E. V. (1977). *Psychology of language: An introduction to psycholinguistics*. New York: Harcourt Brace Jovanovich.

Clark, H. H., & Wilkes-Gibbs, D. (1986). Referring as a collaborative process. *Cognition*, *22*, 1–39.

Clarke, M. A. (1982). On bandwagons, tyranny, and commonsense. *TESOL Quarterly*, *16*(4), 437–448.

Clarke, M. A., Losoff, A., & Rood, D. S. (1982). Untangling referent and reference in linguistic relativity studies: A response. *Language Learning 32*(1), 209-217.

Clay, M. M. (1990). The reading recovery program, 1984-88—coverage, outcomes and Education Board District figures. *New Zealand Journal of Educational Studies, 25*, 61-70.

Cole, M., & Cole, S. (Eds.), (1979). *The making of mind: The autobiography of A.R. Luria.* (pp. 189-225). Cambridge, MA: Harvard University Press.

Condon, W. S., & Ogston, W. D. (1966). Sound film analysis of normal and pathological behavior patterns. *Journal of Nervous and Mental Disease, 143*, 388-347.

Condon, W. S., & Ogston, W. D. (1967). A segmentation of behavior. *Journal of Psychiatric Research, 5*, 221-235.

Condon, W. S., & Sander, L. W. (1974). Synchrony demonstrated between movements of the neonate and adult speech. *Child Development, 45*, 456-462.

Cooper, R. P., Abraham, J., Berman, S., & Staska, M. (1997). The development of infants' preference for motherese. *Infant Behavior & Development, 20*, 477-488.

Cooper, R. P., & Aslin, R. N. (1994). Developmental differences in infant attention to the spectral properties of infant-directed speech. *Child Development, 65*, 1663-1677.

Create Health Center for Reproduction and Advanced Technology. (2001). 3D and 4D ultrasound scans. Retrieved January 28, 2006 from http://www.create health.org/#.

Crowne, D. P. & Marlowe, D. (1964). *The approval motive: Studies in evaluative dependence.* Westport, CT: Greenwood Press.

Crystal, D. (1987). *The Cambridge encyclopedia of language.* Cambridge: Cambridge University Press.

Cummins, J. (1981). The role of primary language development in promoting educational success for language minority students. In California State Department of Education (Ed.), *Schooling and language minority students: A theoretical framework* (pp. 3-49). Los Angeles, CA: Evaluation, Dissemination and Assessment Center, California State University.

Cutler, A. (1994). Segmentation problems, rhythmic solutions. *Lingua, 92*, 81-104.

Damico, J. S., Oller, J. W., Jr., & Storey, M. E. (1983). The diagnosis of language disorders in bilingual children: surface-oriented and pragmatic criteria. *Journal of Speech and Hearing Disorders, 48*, 385-394.

Damper, R. I., Marchand, Y., Adamson, M. J., & Gustafson, K. (1999). Evaluating the pronunciation component of text-to-speech systems for English: A performance comparison of different approaches. *Computer Speech and Language, 13*(2), 155-176.

Davidson, D. (1996). The folly of trying to define truth. *Journal of Philosophy, 93*, 263-278.

Davis, R. L., Verstraeten, T., Gu, D., DeStefano, F., Thompson, R. S., & Chen, R. T. (2000). Infant exposure to thimerosal-containing vaccines and risk for subsequent neurologic and renal disease. *Pediatric Research, 47*(4), 146A-146A 857 Part 2 Suppl. S.

Day, B. (2004). Heightened awareness of communication pitfalls can benefit safety. *ICAO Journal, 59*, 20-22.

Day, B. (2005). ICAO standards and recommended practices: An overview. Retrieved January 25, 2005, from http://www.icao.int/icao/en/anb/meetings/IALS/proceedings/PAPERS/2-Day.pdf

DeCasper, A. J., & Fifer, W. P. (1980). Of human bonding: Newborns prefer their mothers' voices. *Science, 208,* 1174–1176.

Dehaene-Lambertz, G. (1998). Syllable discrimination by premature neonates with or without subcortical lesion. *Developmental Neuropsychology, 14*(4), 579–597.

Dehaene-Lambertz G., & Pena M. (2001). Electrophysiological evidence for automatic phonetic processing in neonates. *Neuroreport, 12,* 3155–3158.

Detenber, B. H., Simons, R. F., & Bennett, G. G. (1997). Roll 'em!: The effects of picture motion on emotional responses. *Journal of Broadcasting and Electronic Media, 21,* 112–126.

deVries, J. I. P., Visser, G. H. A., & Prechtl, H. F. R. (1985). The emergence of fetal behavior: II. Quantitative aspects. *Early Human Development, 12,* 99–120.

Dewey, J. (1916). *Essays in experimental logic.* Chicago: University of Chicago Press.

Dickinson, C., & Givón, T. (2000). The effect of the interlocutor on episodic recall: An experimental study. In Barlow, & Kemmer (2000, pp. 151–196).

Dictionary.LaborLawTalk.com. (N.D.). The Apgar score. Retrieved January 28, 2006 from http://encyclopedia.laborlawtalk.com/Apgar_score.

Dominey, P. F., & Dodane, C. (2004). Indeterminacy in language acquisition: The role of child-directed speech and joint attention. *Journal of Neurolinguistics, 17*(2-3), 121–145.

Dowd, J. M., & Tronick, E. Z. (1986). Temporal coordination of arm movements in early infancy: Do infants move in synchrony with adult speech. *Child Development, 57*(3), 762–776.

Dunn, L. M. (1968). Special education for the mildly retarded: Is much of it justifiable? *Exceptional Children, 35*(1), 5–22.

Easterbrook, M. A., Kisilevsky, B. S., Hains, S. M. J., & Muir, D. W. (1999). Faceness or complexity: Evidence from newborn studies. *Infant Behavior and Development, 22,* 17–35.

Easterbrook, M. A., Kisilevsky, B. S., Muir, D. W., & Laplante, D. P. (1999). Newborns discriminate schematic faces from scrambled faces. *Canadian Journal of Experimental Psychology, 53,* 231–241.

Eilers, R. E., Oller, D. K., Levine, S., Basinger, D., Lynch, M. P., & Urbano, R. (1993). The role of prematurity and socioeconomic status in the onset of canonical babbling in infants. *Infant Behavior and Development, 16,* 297–315.

Eimas, P., Siqueland, E., Jusczyk, P., & Vigorito, J. (1971). Speech perception in infants. *Science, 171,* 303–306.

Einstein, A. (1944). Remarks on Russell's theory of knowledge. In P. A. Schilpp (Ed.), *The philosophy of Bertrand Russell* (pp. 277–291). New York: Tudor.

Einstein, A. (1956) The common language of science. In Author, *Out of my later years* (pp. 111–113). Secaucus, NJ: Citadel Press. (Originally produced as a radio broadcast in 1941)

Ejiri K. (1998). Synchronization between preverbal vocalizations and motor actions in early infancy I: Pre-canonical babbling vocalizations synchronize with rhythmic body movements before the onset of canonical babbling. *Japanese Journal of Psychology, 68,* 433–440.

Ejiri, K., & Masataka, N. (2001). Co-occurrence of preverbal vocal behavior and motor action in early infancy. *Developmental Science, 4,* 40–48.

Elbers, L. (1982). Operating principles in repetitive babbling: A cognitive continuity approach. *Cognition, 12,* 45–63.

Eldadah, Z. A., Grifo, J. A., & Dietz, H. C. (1995) Marfan syndrome as a paradigm for transcription-targeted preimplantation diagnosis of heterozygous mutations. *Nature Medicine, 1,* 798–803.

Ellis, N. C. (2002). Reflections on frequency effects in language acquisition: A response to commentaries. *Studies in Second Language Acquisition, 24,* 297–339.

Enestrom, S., & Hultman, P. (1995). Does amalgam affect the immune-system—a controversial issue. *International Archives of Allergy and Immunology, 106*(3), 180–203.

Fant, G. (1970). *Acoustic theory of speech production: With calculations based on x-ray studies of Russian articulations* (2nd ed.). The Hague: Mouton.

Federal Drug Administration. (2002). Consumer Update: Dental Amalgams. Information retrieved January 28, 2006 from http://www.fda.gov/cdrh/consumer/amalgams.html.

Felton, R. H., & Pepper, P. P. (1995). Early identification and intervention of phonological deficits in kindergarten and early elementary children at risk for reading-disability, *School Psychology Review, 24,* 405–414.

Fénelon, G., Mahieux, F., Huon, R., & Ziégler, M. (2000). Prevalence, Hallucinations in Parkinson's disease: phenomenology and risk factors. *Brain, 123* (4), 733–745.

Ferguson, C. F. (1959). Diglossia. *Word, 15*(2), 325–340.

Ferguson, C. F. (1991). Diglossia revisited. In A. Hudson (Ed.), *Studies in diglossia. Southwest Journal of Linguistics, 10*(1), 214–234.

Ferguson, L. R. (1999). Natural and man-made mutagens and carcinogens in the human diet. *Mutation Research-Genetic Toxicology and Environmental Mutagenesis, 443*(1–2), 1–10.

Ferguson, L. R. (2002). Natural and human-made mutagens and carcinogens in the human *Toxicology, 181,* 79–82.

Fernald, A., Swingley, D., & Pinto, J. P. (2001). When half a word is enough: Infants can recognize spoken words using partial phonetic information. *Child Development, 72,* 1003–1015.

Field, T. M., Cohen, D., Garcia, R., & Greenberg, R. (1984). Mother-stranger face discrimination by the newborn. *Infant Behavior & Development* 7(1), 19–25.

Fifer, W. P., & Moon, C. M. (1994). The role of mother's voice in the organization of brain function in the newborn. *Acta Paediatrica Supplement, 397,* 86–93.

Filipek, P. A., Accardo, P. J., Ashwal, S., Baranek, G. T., Cook, E. H., Jr., Dawson, G., et al. (2000). Practice parameter: Screening and diagnosis of autism. Report of the Quality Standards Subcommittee of the American Academy of Neurology and the Child Neurology Society. *Neurology, 55,* 468–479.

Floccia, C., Christophe, A., & Bertoncini, J. (1997). High-amplitude sucking and newborns: The quest for underlying mechanisms. *Journal of Experimental Child Psychology, 64*(2), 175–198.

Fodor, J. A. (1980). Fixation of belief and concept acquisition. In M. Piatelli-Palmarini (Ed.), *Language and learning: The debate between Jean Piaget and Noam Chomsky* (pp. 147–149). Cambridge, MA: Harvard University Press.

Fogel, A. & Hannan, T. E. (1985). Manual actions of nine- to fifteen-week-old human infants during face-to-face interaction with their mothers. *Child Development, 56*, 1271–1279.

Fogel, A. & Hsu, H-C. (2003). Stability and transitions in mother-infant face-to-face communication during the first 6 months: A microhistorical approach. *Developmental Psychology, 39*(6), 1061–1082.

Forbes, H. S., & Forbes, H. B. (1927). Fetal sense reaction. *Journal of Comparative Psychology, 7*, 353–355.

Fox, H. E., Steinbrecher, M., Pessel, D., Inglis, J.,, & Angel, E. (1978). Maternal ethanol ingestion and the occurrence of human fetal breathing movements. *American Journal of Obstetrics & Gynecology, 132*, 354–358.

Frederiksen, C. H. (1975). Effects of context-induced processing operations on semantic information acquired from discourse. *Cognitive Psychology, 7*(2), 139–166.

Fromkin, V., & Rodman, R. (1973). *An introduction to language*. New York: Harcourt Brace College Publishers.

Fromkin, V., & Rodman, R. (1998). *An introduction to language*. (7th ed.) New York: Harcourt, Brace, Jovanovich. New York: Harcourt Brace College Publishers.

Fry, D. B. (Ed.), (1976). *Acoustic phonetics: A book of basic readings*. Cambridge, MA: Cambridge University Press.

Fuchs, D., & Fuchs, L. S. (2005). Peer-assisted learning strategies: Promoting word recognition, fluency, and reading comprehension in young children. *Journal of Special Education, 39*(1), 34–44.

Fuchs, D., Fuchs, L. S., Thompson, A., Al-Otaiba, S., Yen, L., Yang, N. J., Braun, M., & O'Connor, R. E. (2001). Is reading important in reading-readiness programs? A randomized field trial with teachers as program implementers. *Journal of Educational Psychology, 93*(2), 251–268.

Fuchs, D., Fuchs, L. S., Thompson, A., Al-Otaiba, S., Yen, L., Yang, N. J., Braun, M., & O'Connor, R. E. (2002). Exploring the importance of reading programs for kindergartners with disabilities in mainstream classrooms. *Exceptional Children 68*(3), 295–311.

Gallup, R. Parent and Founder of The Autism Autoimmunity Project, TAAP. Retrieved January 28, 2006 from http://www.taap.info.

Gardner, H. (1983). *Frames of mind: the theory of multiple intelligences*. New York: Basic Books.

Gardner, H. (1993). *Multiple intelligences: The theory in practice*. New York: Basic Books.

Gavrilova, L. A., & Gavrilova, N. S. (2001). The reliability theory of aging and longevity. *Journal of Theoretical Biology, 213*(4), 527–545.

Gavrilova, L.A., & Gavrilova, N. S. (2004). The reliability-engineering approach to the problem of biological aging. Strategies for engineered negligible senescence: Why genuine control of aging may be foreseeable. *Annals of the New York Academy of Sciences 1019*, 509–512.

Geier, D. A., & Geier, M. R. (2004). Neurodevelopmental disorders following thimerosal-containing childhood immunizations: A follow-up analysis. *International Journal of Toxicology, 23*(6), 369–376.

Geier, D. A., & Geier, M. R. (2005a). A case-control study of serious autoimmune adverse events following hepatitis B immunization. *Autoimmunity*, *38*(4), 295–301.

Geier, D. A., & Geier, M. R. (2005b). A two-phased population epidemiological study of the safety of thimerosal-containing vaccines: A follow-up analysis. *Medical Science Monitor*, *11*(4), CR160-CR170.

Geldmacher, D. S. (2003). *Contemporary diagnosis and management of Alzheimer's Disease*. Newtown, PA: Handbooks in Health Care Company.

Gernsbacher, M. A., Varner, K. V., & Faust, M. E. (1990). Investigating general comprehension skill. *Journal of Experimental Psychology: Learning, Memory, and Cognition* 16, 430–445.

Gleitman, L. (1990). The structural source of verb meaning. *Language Acquisition*, *1*, 3–55.

Glenberg, A. M. (1997). What memory is for. *Behavioral and Brain Sciences, 20*, 1–55.

Glenberg, A. M., & Robertson, D. A. (1999). Indexical understanding of instructions. *Discourse Processes* 28(1), 1–26.

Glenberg, A. M., & Robertson, D. A. (2000). Symbol grounding and meaning: A comparison of high-dimensional and embodied theories of meaning. *Journal of Memory and Language 43*(3), 379–401.

Gogate, L. J., Walker-Andrews, A. S., Bahrick, L. E. (2001). The intersensory origins of word comprehension: An ecological-dynamic systems view. *Developmental Science, 4*, 1–18.

Goldberg, A. E. (1995). *Constructions: a construction grammar approach to argument structure*. Chicago, University of Chicago Press.

Goldsmith, J. A. (1990). *Autosegmental and metrical phonology*. Oxford and Cambridge, MA: Basil Blackwell.

Goodman, K. S. (1967). Reading: A psycholinguistic guessing game. *Journal of the Reading Specialist, 6*, 126–135.

Goodman, K. S. (1972). The reading process: Theory and practice. In R. E. Hodges, & E. H. Rudorf (Eds.). *Language and learning to read*. Boston, MA: Houghton Mifflin.

Goodman, K. S. (1993). Does whole-language work: Reply. *The Reading Teacher, 47*, 182–182.

Goodman, K. S. (1996). *On reading*. Portsmouth, NH: Heinemann.

Goodman, K. S., Goodman, Y., & Flores, B. (1979). *Reading in the bilingual classroom: Literacy and biliteracy*. Rosslyn, VA: InterAmerica Research Associates.

Gopnik, A., Capps, L., & Meltzoff, A. N. (in press). Early theories of mind: What the theory theory can tell us about autism. In S. Baron-Cohen, H. Tager-Flusberg, & D.J. Cohen (Eds.), *Understanding other minds: Perspectives from autism and developmental cognitive neuroscience*. Oxford: Oxford University Press.

Gordon, R. A. (1980). Labeling theory, mental retardation, and public policy: Larry P. and other developments since 1974. In W. R. Gove (Ed.), *The labeling of deviance* (pp. 111–174). Beverly Hills, CA: Sage.

Gordon, R. G., Jr. (Ed.), (2005). *Ethnologue: Languages of the world, 15th ed*. Dallas, TX: SIL International. Online version retrieved January 28, 2006 from http://www.ethnologue.com/.

Graesser, A. C., Millis, K. K., & Zwaan, R. A. (1997). Discourse comprehension. *Annual Review of Psychology, 48*, 163–189.

Gratier, M. (2003). Expressive timing and interactional synchrony between mothers and infants: Cultural similarities, cultural differences, and the immigration experience. *Cognitive Development, 18*(4), 533–554.

Grégoire, A. (1948). L'apprentissage du langage. *Lingua, 1*, 162–172.

Grice, H. P. (1975). Logic and conversation. In P. Cole, & J. L. Morgan (Eds.), *Syntax and semantics, 3: Speech acts* (pp. 41–58). New York: Academic Press.

Grimes, B. F., & Grimes, J. E. (Eds.), (2000). *Ethnologue: Languages of the world* (14th ed.). Arlington, TX: Summer Institute of Linguistics.

Gussmann, E. (2002). *Phonology: Analysis and theory*. Cambridge: Cambridge University Press.

Hakuta, K. (1986). *Mirror of language.* Rowley, MA: Newbury House.

Hall, N. (1987). *The emergence of literacy*. Portsmouth, NH: Heinemann Educational Books, Inc.

Halliday, M. A. K. (1978). *Language as social semiotic: The social intterpretation of language and meaning.* London: Edward Arnold.

Halpern, J. (Ed.), (2001). *Outline of Japanese writing system.* Retrieved January 28, 2006 from http://www.kanji.org/kanji/japanese/writing/outline.htm.

Hamayan, E. & Damico, J. S. (Eds.), (1990). *Limiting bias in the assessment of bilingual students.* Austin, TX: Pro-Ed.

Hanna, P. R., Hanna, J. S., Hodges, R. E., & Rudorf, E. H. (1966). *Phoneme-grapheme correspondences as cues to spelling improvement.* Washington, DC: U.S. Department of Health, Education, and Welfare. ED 003 321.

Hasher, L., & Zacks, R. T. (1979). Automatic and effortful processes in memory. *Journal of Experimental Psychology: General, 108*, 356–388.

Havarinasab, S., Haggqvist, B., Bjorn, E., Pollard, K. M., & Hultman, P. (2005). Immunosuppressive and autoimmune effects of thimerosal in mice. *Toxicology and Applied Pharmacology, 204*(2), 109–121.

Havarinasab, S., Lambertsson, L., Qvarnstrom, J., & Hultman, P. (2004). Dose-response study of thimerosal-induced murine systemic autoimmunity. *Toxicology and Applied Pharmacology, 194*(2), 169–179.

Hayashi, A., Tamekawa, Y., Kiritani, S. (2001). Developmental change in auditory preferences for speech stimuli in Japanese infants. *Journal of Speech Language and Hearing Research, 44*(6), 1189–1200.

Hayes-Brown, Z. (1984). Linguistic and communicative assessment of bilingual children. In C. Rivera (Ed.), *Placement procedures in bilingual education: Educational policy and issues* (pp. 40–105). Oxford: Oxford University.

Hecht, H., Vogt, S., & Prinz, W. (2001). Motor learning enhances perceptual judgment: A case for action-perception transfer. *Psychological Research: Psychologische Forschung, 65*, 3–14.

Hepper, P. G., & Shahidullah, B. S. (1994). Development of fetal hearing. *Archives of Disease in Childhood, 71*(2), F81–F87.

Hepper, P. G., Shahidullah, S., & White, R. (1991). Handedness in the human fetus. *Neuropsychologia, 29*(11), 1107–1111.

Herrnstein, R. J. (1973). *IQ in the meritocracy.* Boston: Atlantic-little Brown.

Herrnstein, R. J., & Murray, C. (1994). *The bell curve: Intelligence and class structure in American life.* New York: Free Press.

Hodapp, R. M., Goldfield, E. D., & Boyatzis, C. J. (1984). The use and effectiveness of maternal scaffolding in mother-infant games. *Child Development, 55,* 772-781.

Hofstetter, C. R., Sticht, T. G., & Hofstetter, C. H. (1999). Knowledge, literacy, and power. *Communication Research, 26*(1), 58-80.

Holmgren, K., Lindblom, B., Aurelius, G., Jalling, B., & Zetterstrom, R. (1986). On the phonetics of infant vocalization. In B. Lindblom & R. Zetterstrom (Eds.), *Precursors of early speech* (pp. 51-63). New York: Stockton Press.

Hornykiewicz, O. (1992). From dopamine to Parkinson's disease: A personal research record. In F. Samson, & G. Adelman (Eds.), *The neurosciences: Paths of discovery II* (pp. 125-146). Boston Basel Berlin: Birkhäuser.

Hosp, J. L., & Reschly, D. J. (2004). Disproportionate representation of minority students in special education: Academic, demographic, and economic predictors. *Exceptional Children, 70* (2), 185-199.

Hoxhallari, L., van Daal, V. H. P., & Ellis, N. C. (2004). Learning to read words in Albanian: A skill easily acquired. *Scientific Studies of Reading 8*(2), 153-166.

Hsu, H. C., & Fogel, A. (2003). Social regulatory effects of infant nondistress vocalization on maternal behavior. *Developmental Psychology, 39*(6), 976-991.

Hsu, H. C., Fogel, A., & Cooper, R. B. (2000). Infant vocal development during the first 6 months: Speech quality and melodic complexity. *Infant and Child Development, 9*(1), 1-16.

Hsu, H. C., Fogel, A., & Messinger, D. S. (2001). Infant non-distress vocalization during mother-infant face-to-face interaction: Factors associated with quantitative and qualitative differences. *Infant Behavior & Development, 24,* 107-128.

Hudson, A. (Ed.), (1991). Studies in diglossia. *Southwest Journal of Linguistics, Vol. 10.*

Huff, D., & Geis, I. (1993). *How to lie with statistics.* New York: Norton.

International Dyslexia Association. (2005). Promoting literacy through research, education, and advocacy. Retrieved January 28, 2006 from http://www.inter dys.org/.

International Phonetic Alphabet (1993-1996). Retrieved January 28, 2006 from http://www2.arts.gla.ac.uk/IPA/fullchart.html.

Jaffe, J., Beebe, B., Feldstein, S., Crown, C. L., & Jasnow, M. D. (2001). Rhythms of dialogue in infancy: Coordinated timing in development. *Monographs of the Society for Research in Child Development, 66*(2), 1-132.

Jakobson, R. (1941). *Kindersprache, Aphasie, und allgemeine Lautgesetze.* Uppsala: Almqvist and Wiksell.

Jakobson, R. (1968). *Child language, aphasia, and phonological universals.* The Hague: Mouton.

James, W. (1995). *Pragmatism.* New York: Dover Publications. (Originally published in 1907.)

Jenkins, J. R., Peyton, J. A., Sanders, E. A., & Vadasy, P. F. (2004). Effects of reading decodable texts in supplemental first-grade tutoring. *Scientific Studies of Reading, 8*(1), 53-85.

Jensen, A. R. (1969). How much can we boost IQ and scholastic achievement? *Harvard Educational Review, 39,* 1-123.

Jensen, A. R. (1974). How biased are culture-loaded tests? *Genetic Psychology Monographs, 90,* 185-244.

Jensen, A. R. (1980). *Bias in mental testing.* New York: Free Press.

Jensen, A. R. (1984). Test bias: Concepts and criticisms. C. R. Reynolds & R. T. Brown (Eds.), *Perspectives on bias in mental testing* (pp. 507–586). New York: Plenum Press.

Jensen, A. R. (1995). The differences are real. In R. Jacoby, & N. Glauberman (Eds.), *The bell curve debate: History, documents, opinions* (pp. 617–639). New York: Random House.

Jespersen, O. (1904). *How to learn a foreign language.* London: Allen and Unwin.

Jitendra, A. K., & Rohena-Diaz, E. (1996). Language assessment of students who are linguistically diverse: Why a discrete approach is not the answer. *School Psychology Review, 25,* 40–56.

Johnson, K. (1997). *Acoustic and auditory phonetics.* Malden, MA: Blackwell Publishing.

Jusczyk, P. (1997). *The discovery of spoken language.* Cambridge, MA: MIT Press.

Justice, L., Skibbe, L., Canning, A., & Lankford, C. (2005). Preschoolers, print, and storybooks: An observational study using eye-gaze analysis. *Journal of Research in Reading, 28,* 229–243.

Kako, E. (1999). Elements of syntax in the systems of three language-trained animals. *Animal Learning & Behavior 27*(1), 1–14.

Kant, I. (1964). *The groundwork of the metaphysics of morals* (Trans., H. J. Paton). New York: Harper & Row Publishers. (Original work published in 1785)

Karam, F. X. (1979). Processes of increasing mutual intelligibility between language varieties. *International Journal of Sociolinguistics, 22,* 115–137.

Kasarski E. J., Haley, B., & Gunnerson, D. (1993). GTP-binding proteins in amyotrophic lateral sclerosis cerebrospinal fluid. *Annals of Neurology 34*(2), 297–297.

Kaschak, M. P., & Glenberg, A. M. (2000). Constructing meaning: The role of affordances and grammatical constructions in sentence comprehension. *Journal of Memory and Language 43*(3), 508–529.

Kavasch, E. B. & Baar, K. (1999). *American Indian healing arts herbs, rituals, and remedies for every season of life.* New York: Bantam.

Kave, G. (2005). Standardization and norms for a Hebrew naming test. *Brain & Language, 92*(2), 204–211.

Kaye, K. L., & Bower, T. G. R. (1994). Learning and intermodal transfer of information in newborns. *Psychological Science, 5,* 286–288.

Kemp, D. T. (1978). Stimulated acoustic emissions from within human auditory-system. *Journal of the Acoustical Society of America 64* (5): 1386–1391.

Kennedy, R. F., Jr. (2005). Deadly immunity. Retrieved January 28, 2006 from http://www.commondreams.org/views05/0616-31.htm.

Kenny, D. A., Mohr, C., & Levesque, M. (2001). A social relations partitioning variance of dyadic behavior. *Psychological Bulletin, 127,* 128–141

Kessler, B., & Treiman, R. (2001). Relationships between sounds and letters in English monosyllables. *Journal of Memory and Language 44*(4), 592–617.

Khare, S. S., Ehmann, W. D., Kasarskis, E. J., & Markesbery, W. R. (1990). Trace-element imbalances in amyotrophic-lateral-sclerosis. *Neurotoxicology, 11*(3), 521–532.

Kirby, D. (2005). *Evidence of harm: Mercury in Vaccines and the autism epidemic.* New York: Saint Martin's Press.

Kisilevsky, B. S., Hains, S. M. J., Lee, K., Xie, X., Huang, H. F., Ye, H. H., Zhang, K., &

Wang, Z. P. (2003). Effects of experience on fetal voice recognition. *Psychological Science*, *14*(3), 220–224.

Kolstad, R., Briggs L. D. & Whalen K. (1996). Incorporating language arts into the mathematics curriculum: A literature survey. *Education*, 116(3) 423–429.

Koopmans-van Beinum, F. J., & van der Stelt, J. M. (1986). Early stages in the development of speech movements. In B. Lindblom & R. Zetterstrom (Eds.), *Precursors of early speech* (pp. 37–50). New York: Stockton Press.

Krashen, S. (1985). *The input hypothesis: Issues and implications*. New York: Longman.

Krashen, S. D. (1991). Bilingual education: A focus on current research. *NCBE FOCUS: Occasional Papers in Bilingual Education, Number 3, Spring 1991*. Retrieved January 28, 2006 from http://www.ncela.gwu.edu/pubs/focus/focus3.htm.

Krashen, S. D. (1992). *Fundamentals of language education*. Torrance, CA: Laredo.

Krashen, S.D. & Terrell, T.D. (1983). *The natural approach: Language acquisition in the classroom*. London: Prentice Hall Europe.

Krosnick, J. A. (1999). Survey research. *Annual Review of Psychology*, *50*, 537–567.

Kuhl, P. K., Andruski, J. E., Chistovich, I. A., Chistovich, L. A., Kozhevnikova, E. V., Ryskina, V. L., Stolyarova, E. I., Sundberg, U., & Lacerda, F. (1997). Cross-language analysis of phonetic units in language addressed to infants. *Science*, *277*, 684–686.

Kuhl, P. K., & Meltzoff, A. N. (1982). The bimodal perception of speech in infancy. *Science*, *218* (4577), 1138–1141.

Kuhl, P. K., & Meltzoff, A. N. (1984). The intermodal representation of speech in infants. *Infant Behavior & Development*, 7(3), 361–381.

Kuhl, P. K., & Meltzoff, A. N. (1996). Infant vocalizations in response to speech: Vocal imitation and developmental change. *Journal of the Acoustical Society of America*, *100*, 2425–2438.

Kurath, H. & McDavid, R. I., Jr. (1961). *The pronunciation of English in the Atlantic states*. Ann Arbor, MI: University of Michigan Press.

Labov, W. (1994). *Principles of linguistic change. Volume 1: Internal factors*. Oxford: Blackwell Publishers.

Lachs, L., & Pisoni, D. B. (2004). Crossmodal source identification in speech perception. *Ecological Psychology*, *16*(3), 159–187.

Ladefoged, P. (1996). *Elements of acoustic phonetics* (2nd ed.) Chicago: University of Chicago Press.

Ladefoged, P. (2001). *A course in phonetics*. Stamford, CT: Heinle & Heinle.

Ladefoged, P. (2005). *Vowels and consonants* (2nd ed.). London: Blackwell. (See the vowel and consonant chart retrieved January 28, 2006 from http://hctv.humnet.ucla.edu/departments/linguistics/VowelsandConsonants/vowels/chapter3/amengvowels.html.)

Landau, B., & Gleitman, L. (1985). *Language and experience*. Cambridge, MA: Harvard University Press.

Langacker, R. W. (1987). *Foundations of cognitive grammar, Vol. 1: Theoretical prerequisites*. Stanford, CA: Stanford University Press.

Langacker, R. W. (1991). *Foundations of cognitive grammar, Vol. 2: Descriptive application*. Stanford, CA: Stanford University Press.

Langacker, R. W. (2000). A dynamic usage-based mode. In Barlow, M., & Kemmer, S. (2000, pp. 1–63).

Langlois, J. H., Ritter, J. M., Roggman, L. A., & Vaughn, L. S. (1991). Facial diversity and infant preferences for attractive faces. *Developmental Psychology, 27,* 79–84.

Langlois, J. H., & Roggman, L. A. (1990). Attractive faces are only average. *Psychological Science, 1,* 115–121.

Langlois, J. H., Roggman, L. A., Casey, R. J., Ritter, J. M., Rieser-Danner, L. A., Jenkins, V. Y. (1987). Infant preferences for attractive faces: Rudiments of a stereotype? *Developmental Psychology, 23,* 363–369.

Lefly, D. L., & Pennington, B. F. (1991). Spelling errors and reading fluency in compensated adult dyslexics. *Annals of Dyslexia, 41,* 143–162.

Lehman, D. R., Krosnick, J. A., West, R. L., & Li, F. (1992). The focus of judgment effect: A question of wording due to hypothesis confirmation bias. *Personality and Social Psychology Bulletin, 18*(6), 690–699.

Leibniz, G. W. (1953). The monadology. In G. R. Montgomery (Ed. & Trans.), *Leibniz: Discourse on metaphysics, correspondence with Arnauld, monadology: Philosophical classics religion of science library, No. 52* (2nd ed., pp. 251–272). La Salle, IL: Open Court Publishing. (Original work published 1714.)

Lemke, U., & Zimprich, D. (2005). Longitudinal changes in memory performance and processing speed in old age. *Aging, Neuropsychology, & Cognition, 12*(1) 57–78.

Leong, C. C., Syed, N. I., & Lorscheider, F. L. (2001). Retrograde degeneration of neurite membrane structural integrity of nerve growth cones following in vitro exposure to mercury. *Neuroreport, 12*(4), 733–737.

Lewy-body disease. Retrieved November 16, 2005 from http://ci.columbia.edu/c1182/web/sect_5/c1182_s5_2.html.

Light, L. L., & Burke, D. M. (Eds.), (1988). *Language, memory, and aging.* New York: Cambridge University Press.

Lightman, A. (1993). *Einstein's dreams.* New York: Pantheon Books.

Lin, C-C. (1989). *The structure of English and Chinese narrative written by college students in Taiwan.* Unpublished doctoral dissertation, University of New Mexico, Albuquerque.

Lindh, V., Wiklund, U., & Hakansson, S. (1999). Heel lancing in term new-born infants: An evaluation of pain by frequency domain analysis of heart rate variability. *Pain, 80*(1-2), 143–148.

Locke, J. (1690). *The second treatise of civil government.* Available in its entirety retrieved January 28, 2006 from http://www.constitution.org/jl/2ndtreat.htm.

Locke, J. L. (1983). *Phonological acquisition and change.* New York: Academic Press.

Locke, J. L. (1994). Phases in the child's development of language: The learning that leads to human speech begins in the last trimester of pregnancy—long before they utter a word, infants are talking themselves into a language. *American Scientist 82*(5), 436–445.

Locke, J. L. (2001). First communion: The emergence of vocal relationships. *Social Development, 10,* 294–308.

Lorenzo's Oil, the movie. (2004). Directed by George Miller and staring Nick Nolte and Susan Sarandon as Augusto and Michaela Odone, Universal Studios released the film on DVD in North America on April 6, 2004. Retrieved January 28, 2006 from http://www.myelin.org/themovie.htm. (Originally released in 1984.)

Lorscheider, F. L., Vimy, M. J., & Summers, A. O. (1995). Mercury exposure from "silver" tooth fillings: Emerging evidence questions a traditional dental paradigm. *FASEB Journal, 9*(7), 504–508.

Luria, A. R., & Yudovich, I. F. (1959). *Speech and the development of mental processes in the child: An experimental investigation.* London: Staples Press.

Lyon, G. R. (1995). Toward a definition of dyslexia. *Annals of Dyslexia, 45,* 3–27.

Lyon, G. R. (2001). Toward a definition of dyslexia. *Annals of Dyslexia, 51,* 3–27.

Lyon, G. R., Shaywitz, S. E, & Shaywitz, B. A. (2003) A definition of dyslexia. *Annals of Dyslexia, 53,* 1–14.

MacKain, K., Studdert-Kennedy, M., Spieker, S., & Stern, D. (1983). Infant intermodal speech perception is a left-hemisphere function. *Science, 219,* 1347–1349.

Macnamara, J. (1972). Cognitive basis of language learning in infants. *Psychological Review, 79*(1), 1–13.

MacNeilage, P. F., & Davis, B. L. (1995). The articulatory basis of babbling. *Journal of Speech and Hearing Research, 38,* 1199–1211.

MacNeilage P. F., & Davis B. L. (2000). Deriving speech from nonspeech: A view from ontogeny. *Phonetica, 57*(2–4), 284–296.

MacNeilage, P. F., & Davis, B. L. (2001). Motor mechanisms in speech ontogeny: Phylogenetic, neurobiological and linguistic implications. *Current Opinion in Neurobiology, 11,* 696–700.

MacWhinney, B. (Ed.). (1998). *The emergence of language.* Mahwah, NJ: Erlbaum.

Malinowski, B. (1923). The problem of meaning in primitive languages. In C. K. Ogden & I. A. Richards (Eds.), *The meaning of meaning* (pp. 451–510). London: Routledge & Kegan Paul.

Manning, C. (2004). Beyond memory: Neuropsychological features in differential diagnosis of dementia. *Clinics in Geriatric Medicine, 20*(1), 45–58.

Marchand, Y., & Damper, R. I. (2000). A multistrategy approach to improving pronunciation by analogy. *Computational Linguistics, 26*(2), 195–219.

Masataka, N. (1992). Early ontogeny of vocal behavior of Japanese infants in response to maternal speech. *Child Development, 63,* 1177–1185.

Masataka, N. (1995). The relation between index-finger extension and the acoustic quality of cooing in 3-month-old infants. *Journal of Child Language, 22,* 247–257.

Masataka, N. (1996). Perception of motherese in a signed language by 6-month-old deaf infants. *Developmental Psychology, 32*(5), 874–879.

Masataka, N. (1998). Perception of motherese in Japanese sign language by 6-month-old hearing infants. *Developmental Psychology, 34* (2), 241–246.

Masataka, N. (1999). Preference for infant-directed singing in 2-day-old hearing infants of deaf parents. *Developmental Psychology, 35*(4), 1001–1005.

Masataka N. (2003). *The onset of language.* Cambridge, MA: Cambridge University Press, Kyoto University.

Masataka, N., & Bloom, K. (1994). Acoustic properties that determine adults preferences for 3-month-old infant vocalizations. *Infant Behavior & Development, 17*(4), 461–464.

Mastropieri, D., & Turkewitz, G. (1999). Prenatal experience and neonatal responsiveness to vocal expressions of emotion. *Developmental Psychobiology, 35*(3), 204–214.

Mathews, E. (2001). Provisions for proficiency in common aviation language to be strengthened. *ICAO Journal, 56*(3), 24-26.

Mathews, E. (2003). Language proficiency: effective language training for pilots and air traffic controllers. *ICAO Journal, 58*(4), 7-9.

Mathews, E. (2004). New provisions for English language proficiency are expected to improve aviation safety. *ICAO Journal, 59*(1), 4-6.

Mauch, E., Gebhardt, A., Stiefel, T., Rauer, S., Wagner, U., Laufen, H., & Kornhuber, H. H. (1995). Trace metals in multiple sclerosis. *Neurology Psychiatry and Brain Research, 3*(3), 149-154.

Mayer, M. (1969). *Frog! Where are you?* New York: Dial Press.

McCallum, R. S., Sharp, S., Bell, S. M., & George, T. (2004). Silent versus oral reading comprehension and efficiency. *Psychology in the Schools, 41*(2), 241-246.

McGraw-Hill Science Research Associates. Retrieved January 28, 2006 from http://www.sraonline.com/index.php/home/curriculumsolutions/reading/basicreading/components/810.

McGrother, C. W., Dugmore, C., Phillips, M. J., Raymond, N. T., Garrick, P., & Baird, W. O. (1999). Multiple sclerosis, dental caries, and fillings: A case-control study. *British Dental Journal, 187*(5), 261-264.

McGurk, H., & MacDonald, J. (1976). Hearing lips and seeing voices. *Nature, 264,* 746-748. The McGurk Effect, see the demonstration retrieved January 28, 2006 from http://www.media.uio.no/personer/arntm/McGurk_english.html.

McNeill, D. (1970). *The acquisition of language: The study of developmental psycholinguistics*. New York: Harper & Row.

McNeill D. (1985). So you think gestures are nonverbal? *Psychological Review, 92,* 350-371.

Mell, J. (2004). Language training and testing in aviation need to focus on job-specific competencies. *ICAO Journal, 59*(1), 12-14, 27.

Meltzoff, A. N. (1990). Foundations for developing a concept of self: The role of imitation in relating self to other and the value of social mirroring, social modeling, and self-practice in infancy. In D. Cicchetti & M. Beeghly (Eds.), *The self in transition: Infancy to childhood* (pp. 139-164). Chicago: University of Chicago Press.

Meltzoff, A. N. (1995). Infants' understanding of people and things: From body imitation to folk psychology. In J. L. Bermudez, A. Marcel, N. Eilan (Eds), *The body and the self* (pp. 43-69). Cambridge, MA: MIT Press.

Meltzoff, A. N. (1999). Origins of theory of mind, cognition and communication. *Journal of Communication Disorders, 32,* 251-269.

Meltzoff, A. N., & Borton, R. W. (1979). Inter-modal matching by human neonates. *Nature, 282,* (5737), 403-404.

Meltzoff, A. N., & Moore, M. K. (1977). Imitation of facial and manual gestures by human neonates. *Science, 198,* 75-78.

Meltzoff, A. N., & Moore, M. K. (1997). Explaining facial imitation: A theoretical model. *Early Development & Parenting, 6,* 179-192.

Meltzoff, A. N., & Moore, M. K. (1998). Object presentation, identity, and the paradox of early permanence: Steps toward a new framework. *Infant Behavior & Development, 1998, 21*(2), 201-235.

Menyuk P. (1969). *Sentences children use*. Cambridge, MA: MIT. Press.

Mercer, J. R. (1973). Labeling the retarded. Berkeley, CA: University of California Press.

Mercer, J. R. (1984). What is a racially and culturally nondiscriminatory test? In C. R. Reynolds, & Brown, R. T. (Eds.), *Perspectives on bias in mental testing* (pp. 293–356). New York: Plenum Press.

Messick, S. (1989). Validity. In R. L. Linn (Ed.), *Educational measurement* (pp. 13–103). Washington, DC: American Council on Education and National Council on Measurement in Education.

Messick, S. (1994). The interplay of evidence and consequences in the validation of performance assessments. *Educational Researcher, 23*, 13–23.

Messick, S. (1998). Test validity: A matter of consequence. *Social Indicators Research, 45*, 35–44.

Mitsutomi, M. & O'Brien, K. (2004). The critical components of aviation English. Retrieved January 27, 2006 from http://www.miair.us/icao/Aviation%20English%20concept.pdf.

Montague D. P., & Walker-Andrews, A. S. (2001). Peekaboo: A new look at infants' perception of emotion expressions. *Developmental Psychology, 37*(6), 826–838.

Montgomery, J. K. (1999). Accents and dialects: Creating a national professional statement. *Topics in Language Disorders, 19*(4), 78–86.

Moon, C., Cooper, R. P., & Fifer, W. P. (1993). 2-day-olds prefer their native language. *Infant Behavior & Development, 16*(4), 495–500.

Moore, G. A., & Calkins, S. D. (2004). Infants' vagal regulation in the still-face paradigm is related to dyadic coordination of mother-infant interaction. *Developmental Psychology, 40*(6), 1068–1080.

Morford, J. P. (1996). Insights to language from the study of gesture: A review of research on the gestural communication of non-signing deaf people. *Language and Communication, 16*(2), 165–178.

Morgan, J. L., & Demuth, K. (Eds.). (1996). *Signal to syntax: Bootstrapping from speech to grammar in early acquisition*. Hillsdale, NJ: Lawrence Erlbaum Associates.

Morris, C. W. (1958). Words without meaning: A review of Skinner's *Verbal Behavior. Contemporary Psychology, 3*, 212–214.

Müller, N., & Guendouzi, J. A. (2005). Order and disorder in conversation: Encounters with dementia of the Alzheimer's type. *Clinical Linguistics & Phonetics 19*(5), 393–404.

Mutter, J., Naumann, J., Walach, H., & Daschner, F. (2005). Amalgam risk assessment with coverage of references up to 2005. *Gesundheitswesen, 67*(3), 204–216.

Myelin Project. (2002). Hope for multiple sclerosis, the leukodystrophies, and other myelin disorders. Retrieved January 28, 2006 from http://www.myelin.org/index.htm.

Naigles, L. (1990). Children use syntax to learn verb meanings. *Journal of Child Language, 17*, 357–374.

Naigles, L. R. (2002). Form is easy, meaning is hard: Resolving a paradox in early child language. *Cognition 86*(2), 157–199.

Naigles, L. R. (2004). Comprehension matters: A commentary on "A multiple process solution to the logical problem of language acquisition." *Journal of Child Language, 31*(4), 936–940.

Nasar, S. (2001). *A beautiful mind: The life of mathematical genius and Nobel Laureate John Nash*. New York: Simon & Schuster.

National Multiple Sclerosis Society. (2003). The history of MS. Retrieved January 28, 2006 from http://www.nationalmssociety.org/Brochures-HistoryofMS1.asp.

Nazzi, T., Bertoncini, J., & Mehler, J. (1998). Language discrimination by newborns: Toward an understanding of the role of rhythm. *Journal of Experimental Psychology: Human Perception and Performance*, *24*(3), 756–766.

Nazzi, T., & Ramus, F. (2003). Perception and acquisition of linguistic rhythm by infants. *Speech Communication*, *41*(1), 233–243.

Nelson, K. (Ed.). (1989). *Narratives from the crib*. Cambridge, MA: Harvard University Press.

Nelson, R., Damico, J. S., & Oller, J. W., Jr. (2002, November). Literacy knowledge: Surveying SLP literacy theory and practice. Poster session presented at the annual meeting of the American Speech-Language-Hearing Association, Atlanta, GA.

Nicklas, W. J., Youngster, S. K., Kindt, M. V., & Heikkila, R. E. (1987). MPTP, MPP+ and mitochondrial function. *Life Sciences*, *40*(8), 721–729.

Nicoladis, E. & Genesee, F. (1998). Parental discourse and code-mixing in bilingual children. *International Journal of Bilingualism*, *2*, 85–99.

Ockham, W. (1957). Summa of logic, commentary on the first book of the *Sentences of Peter Lombard*, and explanations of Aristotle's *On Interpretation* (excerpts). In P. Boehner (Ed. and Trans.), *Ockham: Philosophical writings* (pp. 35–46). Indianapolis, IN: Bobbs-Merrill. (Original work published about 1320.)

Ockleford, E. M., Vince, M. A., Layton, C., & Reader, M. R. (1988). Responses of neonates to parents and others voices. *Early Human Development*, *18*(1), 27–36.

Ohta, M., Nagai, Y, Hara, H., & Sasaki, M. (1987). Parental perception of behavioral symptoms in Japanese autistic children. *Journal of Autism and Developmental Disorders*, *17*(4), 549–563.

Ohtsuka, K. & Brewer, W. F. (1992). Discourse organization in the comprehension of temporal-order in narrative texts. *Discourse Processes*, *15*, 317–336.

Oller, D. K. (1980). The emergence of the sounds of speech in infancy. In G. Yeni-Komshian, J., Kavanaugh, & C. Ferguson (Eds.), *Child phonology* (pp. 93–112). New York: Academic Press.

Oller, D. K. (1986). Metaphonology and infant vocalizations. In B. Lindblom & R. Zetterstrom (Eds.), *Precursors of early speech* (pp. 21–35). New York: Stockton.

Oller, D. K. (1995). Development of vocalizations in infancy. In H. Winitz (Ed.), *Human communication and its disorders: A review* (Vol. IV, pp. 1–30). Timonium, MD: York Press, Inc.

Oller, D. K. (2000). *The emergence of the speech capacity*. Mahwah, NJ: Lawrence Erlbaum Associates.

Oller, D. K., Eilers, R. E., & Basinger, D. (2001). Intuitive identification of infant vocal sounds by parents. *Developmental Science*, *4*(1), 49–60.

Oller, D. K., Eilers, R. E., Neal, A. R., & Schwartz, H. K. (1999). Precursors to speech in infancy: The prediction of speech and language disorders. *Journal of Communication Disorders*, *32*(4), 223–245.

Oller, D. K., & Lynch, M. P. (1992). Infant vocalizations and innovations in infraphonology: Toward a broader theory of development and disorders. In C. F.

Ferguson, L. Menn, & C. S. Gammon (Eds)., *Phonological development: Models, research, implications* (pp. 509-536). Timonium, MD: York.

Oller, J. W., Jr. (1975). Pragmatic mappings. *Lingua, 35*, 333-344.

Oller, J. W., Jr. (1976). Evidence for a general language proficiency factor. *Die Neuren Sprachen, 76*, 165-174.

Oller, J. W., Jr. (1979). *Language tests at school: A pragmatic approach*. London: Longman.

Oller, J. W., Jr. (Ed.). (1993). *Methods that work: Ideas for literacy and language teachers*. Boston: Heinle and Heinle Publishers.

Oller, J. W., Jr. (1995). Adding abstract to formal and content schemata: Results of recent work in Peircean semiotics. *Applied Linguistics, 16*(3), 273-306.

Oller, J. W., Jr. (1996). How grammatical relations are determined. In B. Hoffer (Ed.), *The 22nd Linguistic Association of Canada and the United States (LACUS) forum, 1995* (pp. 37-88). Chapel Hill, NC: Linguistic Association of Canada and the United States (series Ed., T. Griffen).

Oller, J. W., Jr. (1997). Monoglottosis: What's wrong with the idea of the meritocracy and its racy cousins? *Applied Linguistics, 18*(4), 467-507.

Oller, J. W., Jr. (November, 2004). *Is mercury poisoning a factor in the increasing prevalence of diagnosed autism spectrum disorders?* Presented at the Geneva Centre for Autism, Tenth International Symposium on Autism, 11-12 November 2004, Toronto.

Oller, J. W., Jr. (2005). Common ground between form and content: The pragmatic solution to the bootstrapping problem. *Modern Language Journal, 89*, 92-114.

Oller, J. W., Jr., Badon, L., & Oller, S. D. (in press). *Communication disorders: A survey across the life-span*. San Diego, CA: Plural Publishing.

Oller, J. W., Jr. & Chen, L. (in press). Episodic organization in discourse and valid measurement in the sciences. *Journal of Quantitative Linguistics*.

Oller, J. W., Jr., Chen, L., Oller, S. D., & Pan, N. (2005). Empirical predictions from a general theory of signs. *Discourse Processes, 40*(2), 115-144.

Oller, J. W., Jr. & Giardetti, J. R. (1999). *Images that work: Creating successful messages in marketing and high stakes communication*. Westport, CT: Quorum Books.

Oller, J. W., Jr., & Jonz, J. (1994). *Cloze and coherence*. Cranbury, New Jersey: Bucknell University Press.

Oller, J. W., Jr., Kim, K., & Choe, Y. (2000a). Applying general sign theory to testing language (verbal) and nonverbal abilities. *Language Testing, 17*(4), 377-396.

Oller, J. W., Jr., Kim, K. & Choe, Y. (2000b). Testing verbal (language) and nonverbal abilities in language minorities: A socio-educational problem in historical perspective. *Language Testing, 17*(3), 341-360.

Oller, J. W., Jr., Kim, K., & Choe, Y. (2001). Can instructions to nonverbal IQ tests be given in pantomime? Additional applications of a general theory of signs. *Semiotica, 133*(1/4), 15-44.

Oller, J. W., Jr., Kim, K., Choe, Y., & Hernandez-Jarvis, L. (2001). Testing verbal (language) and nonverbal abilities in children and adults acquiring a nonprimary language. *Language Testing, 18*(1), 33-54.

Oller, J. W., Jr., & Perkins, K. (1978a). A further comment on language proficiency as a source of variance in certain affective measures. *Language Learning, 28*, 417-423.

Oller, J. W., Jr., & Perkins, Kyle. (Eds.), (1978b). *Language in education: testing the tests.* Rowley, MA: Newbury House.

Oller, J. W., Jr. & Rascón, D. (1999). Applying sign theory to autism. *Clinical Linguistics and Phonetics, 13*(2), 77-112.

Oller, S. D. (2005). Meaning matters: A clinician's/student's guide to general sign theory and its applicability in clinical settings. *Journal of Communication Disorders, 38,* 359-373.

Ortiz, A. A. (1997). Learning disabilities occurring concomitantly with linguistic differences. *Journal of Learning Disabilities, 30*(3), 321-332.

Ortiz, A. A., & Yates, J. R. (1983). Incidence of exceptionality among Hispanics: Implications for manpower planning. *NABE Journal, 7,* 41-54.

Osgood, C. E. (1949). The similarity paradox in human learning: A resolution. *Psychological Review, 56,* 132-143.

Owens, M., & Todt, E. H. (1984). Pain in infancy: Neonatal reaction to a heel lance. *Pain, 20*(21), 77-86.

Oxley, J., Daniloff, R., Pirolli, J., & Roussel, N. (2000). Two fates: The articulatory frame in babbling. *Texas Journal of Audiology and Speech Pathology, 24,* 14-19.

Palarito, K. (2004). Lullaby of the womb: Unborn children hear "melody" of speech, study suggests. Retrieved November 17, 2005 from http://www.hon.ch/News/HSN/517339.html.

Pamphlett, R., & Png, F. Y. (1998). Shrinkage of motor axons following systemic exposure to inorganic mercury. *Journal of Neuropathology and Experimental Neurology, 57*(4), 360-366.

Pamphlett, R., & Waley, P. (1996). Uptake of inorganic mercury by the human brain. *Acta Neuropathologica, 92*(5), 525-527.

Pan, B. A., Rowe, M. L., Singer, J. D., & Snow, C. E. (2005). Maternal correlates of growth in toddler vocabulary production in low-income families. *Child Development, 76*(4), 763-782.

Pan, N. (2004). *The un-universality of phonological awareness: A problem of methodology.* Poster presented at the 10th Symposium of the International Clinical Phonetics and Linguistics Association, Lafayette, February 25-28, 2004.

Pan, N. (2005). *A government phonology approach to the acquisition of syllable structure.* Unpublished doctoral dissertation, University of Louisiana, Lafayette, Louisiana.

Pan, N., & Chen, L. (in press). Phonological/phonemic awareness and reading: A crosslinguistic perspective. *Journal of Multilingual Communication Disorders.*

Pan, N., & Snyder, W. (2003). Setting the parameters of syllable structure in early child Dutch. In B. Beachley, A. Brown, & F. Conlin, (Eds.), *Proceedings of the 27th Annual Boston University Conference on Language Development* (pp. 615-625). Somerville, MA: Cascadilla Press.

Pan, N., & Snyder, W. (2004). Acquisition of /s/-initial clusters: A parametric approach. In A. Brugos, L. Micciulla & C. E. Smith (Eds.), *Proceedings of the 28th Annual Boston University Conference on Language Development* (pp. 436-446). Somerville, MA: Cascadilla Press.

Pan, N., & Snyder, W. (2005). Acquisition of phonological empty categories: A case study of early child Dutch. In A. M. Di Sciullo, & R. Delmonte (Eds.), *UG and external systems.* Amsterdam: John Benjamins.

Papoušek, H. (1994). Intuitive parenting: Arguments for comparative approaches. *Early Development and Parenting, 3,* 1–3.

Parker S. K., Schwartz, B., Todd, J., & Pickering, L. K. (2004). Thimerosal-containing vaccines and autistic spectrum disorder: A critical review of published original data. *Pediatrics, 114*(3), 793–804.

Parker, S., Todd, J., & Schwartz, B. (2005). Thimerosal-containing vaccines and autistic spectrum disorder: A critical review of published original data. *Pediatrics, 115*(1), 200.

Parkinson, J. (1817). *Essay on the shaking palsy.* London: Whittingham & Rowland.

Patterson, M. L., & Werker, J. F. (1999). Matching phonetic information in lips and voice is robust in 4.5-month-old infants. *Infant Behavior & Development, 22,* 237–247.

Patterson, M. L., & Werker J. F. (2003). Two-month-old infants match phonetic information in lips and voice. *Developmental Science 6*(2), 191–196.

Peereman, R., & Content, A. (1997). Orthographic and phonological neighborhoods in naming: Not all neighbors are equally influential in orthographic space. *Journal of Memory and Language, 37*(3), 382–410.

Peiper, A. (1925). Sinnesempfindungen des kindes vor seiner geburt. *Monatsschrift für Kinderheilkunde, 29,* 236.

Peirce, C. S. (1868). Questions concerning certain faculties claimed for man. *Journal of Speculative Philosophy, 2,* 103–114. Retrieved on January 28, 2006 from http://www.peirce.org/writings/p26.html.

Peirce, C. S. (1933). Preface to Book 1: Logic and mathematics. In C. Hartshorne & P. Weiss (Eds.), *Collected papers of Charles Sanders Peirce* (Vol. IV, pp. i–v). Cambridge, MA: Harvard University Press.

Peirce, C. S. (1934). Pragmatism and pragmaticism. In C. Hartshorne & P. Weiss (Eds.), Collected papers of *Charles Sanders Peirce* (Vol. 5, pp. 130–131). Cambridge, MA: Harvard University Press. (Original work published in 1903.)

Peirce, C. S. (1982). Treatise on metaphysics. In M. Fisch, C. J. W. Kloesel, E. C. Moore, D. D. Roberts, L. A. Ziegler, & N. P. Atkinson (Eds.), *Writings of Charles S. Peirce: A chronological edition* (Vol. 1, pp. 57–84). Indianapolis: Indiana University Press. (Original work published in 1861.)

Peng, F. C. C. (2003). Is dementia a disease? *Gerontology, 49*(6), 384–391.

Penn, A. A., & Shatz, C. J. (1999). Brain waves and brain wiring: The role of endogenous and sensory-driven neural activity in development. *Pediatric Research, 45*(4), 447–458.

Pepperberg, I. M., & Gordon, J. D. (2005). Number comprehension by a grey parrot (*Psittacus erithacus*), including a zero-like concept. *Journal of Comparative Psychology 119*(2), 197–209.

Petitto, L. A., Holowka, S., Sergio, L. E., & Ostry, D. (2001). Language rhythms in baby hand movements. *Nature, 413,* 35–36.

Petitto, L. A., & Marentette, P. F. (1991). Babbling in the manual mode: Evidence for the ontogeny of language. *Science, 251,* 1493–1496.

Piaget, J. (1950). *The psychology of intelligence.* London: Routledge and Kegan Paul.

Piaget, J. (1952). *The origins of intelligence in children.* New York: International Universities Press.

Piaget, J. (1954). *The construction of reality in the child*. New York: Basic Books.

Piaget, J. (1962). *Play, dreams and imitation in childhood*. New York: Norton.

Piaget, J. (1970). *Genetic epistemology*. (E. Duckworth, Trans.). New York: Columbia University Press.

Piatelli-Palmarini, M. (Ed.), (1980). *Language and learning: The debate between Jean Piaget and Noam Chomsky*. Cambridge, MA: Harvard University Press.

Pinker, S. (1984). *Language learnability and language development*. Cambridge, MA: Harvard University Press.

Pinker, S. (1987). The bootstrapping problem in language acquisition. In B. MacWhinney (Ed.), *Mechanisms of language acquisition* (pp. 339–441). Hillsdale, NJ: Erlbaum.

Pinker, S. (1989). *Learnability and cognition: The acquisition of argument structure*. Cambridge, MA: MIT Press.

Pinker, S. (1994). How could a child use verb syntax to learn verb semantics? *Lingua*, *92*, 377–410.

Pinker, S. (2000). *The language instinct: How the mind creates language*. New York: Perennial Classics.

Plassman, B. L., & Breitner, J. C. (1996). Recent advances in the genetics of Alzheimer's disease and vascular dementia with an emphasis on gene-environment interactions. *Journal of American Geriatric Society*, *44*(10), 1242–1250.

Platt, O. S., Brambilla, D. J., Rosse, W. F., Milner, P. F., Castro, O. Steinberg, M. H. & Klug, P. P. (1994). Mortality in sickle cell disease: Life expectancy and risk factors for early death. *New England Journal of Medicine*, *330*, 1639–1644.

Polka, L., & Werker, J. F. (1994). Developmental changes in perception of non-native vowel contrasts. *Journal of Experimental Psychology*, *20*, 421–435.

Poplack, S. (1980). "Sometimes I'll start a sentence in English y termino en espanol." *Linguistics*, *18*, 581–616.

Prince, A., & Smolensky, P. (2004). *Optimality theory: Constraint interaction in generative grammar*. Malden, MA: Blackwell Publishing. (Originally published in 1993 by Rutgers University Center for Cognitive Science as Technical Report 2.)

Priner, R., Freeman, S., Perez, R., & Sohmer, H. (2003). The neonate has a temporary conductive hearing loss due to fluid in the middle ear. *Audiology and Neuro-otology*, *8*(2), 100–110.

Prochazkova, J., Sterzl, I., Kucerova, H., Bartova, J., Stejskal, V. D. M. (2004). The beneficial effect of amalgam replacement on health in patients with autoimmunity. *Neuroendocrinology Letters*, *25*(3), 211–218.

Putnam, H. (1975), The meaning of "meaning". In H. Putnam *Mind, language, and reality* (pp. 215–271). Cambridge: Cambridge University Press.

Pylyshyn, Z. W. (2002). Mental imagery: In search of a theory. *Behavioral and Brain Sciences*, *25*, 157–238.

Raising Deaf Kids. (2005). Screening newborns. Retrieved January 28, 2006 from http://www.raisingdeafkids.org/hearingloss/testing/nhs.jsp.

Ramey, C. T., & Ramey, S. L. (1999). *Right from birth: Building your child's foundation for life*. Lanham, MD: Goddard Press.

Ramsay, D. S., & Lewis, M. (1994). Developmental change in infant cortisol and behavioral response to inoculation. *Child Development*, *65*, 1491–1502.

Ramus, F., & Mehler, J. (1999). Language identification with suprasegmental cues: A study based on speech resynthesis. *Journal of the Acoustical Society of America, 105*(1), 512-521.

Ramus, F., Hauser, M. D., Miller, C., Morris, D., & Mehler, J. (2000). Language discrimination by human newborns and by cotton-top tamarin monkeys. *Science, 288* (5464), 349-351.

Rattanavich, S. Walker, R. F. & Oller, J. W., Jr. (1992). *Teaching all the children to read*. London and New York: Open University Press.

Raven, J. C., & Court, J. H. (1938-1983). *Raven progressive matrices*. New York: H. K. Lewis and Company.

Reason, J. T. (1997). *Managing the risks of orgnizational accidents*. Aldershot, Hampshire: Ashgate Publishing Company.

Redhe, O., & Pleva, J. (1994). Recovery from amyotrophic lateral sclerosis and from allergy after removal of dental amalgam fillings. *International Journal of Risk & Safety in Medicine 4*, 229-236.

Reissland, N. (1988). Neonatal imitation in the first hour of life: Observations in rural Nepal. *Developmental Psychology, 24*, 464-469.

Richard-Amato, P. (2003). *Making it happen: From interactive to participatory language teaching theory and practice* (3rd ed.). London: Longman.

Rigo, T. G., Arehole, S., & Hayes, P. A. (1998). Central auditory processing abilities of low-achieving gifted adolescents. *Journal of Secondary Gifted Education, 10*(1), 217-227.

Ritter, J. (1996, January 9). Transcript of crash shows controller error/Review reveals poor English "Over and Over." *USA Today*, p. 7A.

Rivera, C., & Simich, C. (1981). Issues in the assessment of language proficiency of language minority students. *NABE: The Journal for the Association of Bilingual Education, 6*, 19-39.

Rivers, K. O., & Lombardino, L. J. (1998). Generalization of early metalinguistic skills in a phonological decoding study with first-graders at risk for reading failure. *International Journal of Communication Disorders, 33*, 369-391.

Rodrigues, R. J., & White, R. N. (1983). From role play to the real world. In J. W. Oller & P. Richard-Amato (Eds.), *Methods that work: A smorgasbord of ideas for language teachers* (pp. 246-255). Rowley, MA: Newbury House Publishers, Inc.

Roffwarg, H. A., Muzio, J. N. & Dement, W. C. (1966). Ontogenetic development of the human sleep-dream cycle. *Science, 152*, 604-619.

Rommetveit, R. (1979). On codes and dynamic residuals in human communication. In R. Rommetveit & R. M. Blakar (Eds.), *Studies of language, thought, and verbal communication* (pp. 163-175). Orlando, FL: Academic Press.

Rosenblum, L. D., Schmuckler, M. A., & Johnson, J. A. (1997). The McGurk effect in infants. *Perception & Psychophysics, 59*(3), 347-357.

Rosenshine, B. V. (1986). Synthesis of research on explicit teaching. *Educational Leadership, 43*, 60-69.

Rossell, C. (September/October 2000). Educating limited English proficient children. *American Language Review, 4* (5). Retrieved January 28, 2006 from http://languagemagazine.com/internetedition/so2000/rossell.html.

Russell, B. (1948). *Human knowledge: Its scope and limits*. New York: Simon and Schuster.

Rusyniak, D. E., Furbee, R. B., & Pascuzzi, R. (2005). Historical neurotoxins: What we have learned from toxins of the past about diseases of the present. *Neurologic Clinics, 23*(2), 337–352.

Rvachewa, S., Slawinski, E. B., Williams, M., & Green, C. L. (1999). The impact of early onset otitis media on babbling and early language development. *Journal of the Acoustical Society of America, 105*(1), 467–475.

Sacks, H., Schegloff, E. A., & Jefferson, G. (1974). A simplest systematic for organization of turn taking in conversation. *Language, 50*, 696–735.

Sai, F. Z. (2005). The role of the mother's voice in developing mother's face preference: Evidence for intermodal perception at birth. *Infant & Child Development, 14*(1), 1–29.

Sailor, K., Antoine, M., Diaz, M., Kuslansky, G., & Kluger, A. (2004). The effects of Alzheimer's disease on item output in verbal fluency tasks. *Neuropsychology, 18*(2), 306–314.

Salvador, H. S., & Koos, B. J. (1989). Effects of regular and decaffeinated coffee on fetal breathing and heart rate. *American Journal of Obstetrics & Gynecology, 161*(3), 669.

Sanders, W., & Horn, S. (1995). Educational assessment reassessed: The usefulness of standardized and alternative measures of student achievement as indicators for the assessment of educational outcomes. *Education Policy Analysis Archives, 3*(6). Retrieved January 28, 2006 from http://olam.ed.asu.edu/epaa/v3n6.html.

Sapir, E. (1921). *Language: An introduction to the study of speech*. New York: Harcourt Brace.

Sapir, E. (1933/1949). The psychological reality of the phoneme. In D. G. Mandelbaum (Ed.), *Selected writings of Edward Sapir in language, culture and personality*. Berkeley, CA: University of California Press. (Originally published in 1933 as La réalité psychologique des phonèmes. *Journal de Psychologie Normale et Pathologique, 30*, 247–265.)

SAS (Statistical Analysis Systems). Retrieved January 28, 2006 from http://www.sas.com/.

Saussure, F. (1959). *Course in general linguistics*. (C. Bally, A. Sechehaye, & A. Riedlinger, Eds.; W. Baskin, Trans.). New York: Philosophical Library. (Original lecture ca. 1906.)

Savignon, S. J. (1997). *Communicative competence: Theory and classroom practice* (2nd ed.). New York: McGraw-Hill.

Schaal, B., Orgeur, P., & Rognon, C. (1995). Odor sensing in the human fetus: Anatomical, functional, and chemeo-ecological bases. In J-P. Lecanuet, W. P. Fifer, N. A., Krasnegor, & W. P. Smotherman (Eds.), *Fetal development: A psychobiological perspective* (pp. 205–237). Hillsdale, NJ: Lawrence Erlbaum Associates.

Schell, V. J. (1982). Learning partners: Reading and mathematics. *Reading Teacher, 35*, 544–548.

Schmidt, K. L., Cohn, J. F., & Tian, Y. L. (2003). Signal characteristics of spontaneous facial expressions: Automatic movement in solitary and social smiles. *Biological Psychology, 65*(1), 49–66.

Schwartz, R. (1988). Learning to learn vocabulary in content area textbooks. *Journal of Reading*, *32*, 108-117.

Sebeok, T. A., & Umiker-Sebeok, J. (Eds.), (1980). *Speaking of apes: A critical anthology of two-way communication with man*. New York: Plenum.

Selinker, L. (1972). Interlanguage. *International Review of Applied Linguistics*, *10*, 209-231.

Serjeant, G. R. (2005). Mortality from sickle cell disease in Africa. *British Medical Journal*, *330*, 432-433.

Serna, L. A., Forness, S. R., & Nielsen, M. E. (1998). Intervention versus affirmation: Proposed solutions to the problem of disproportionate minority representation in special education. *Journal of Special Education*, *32*(1), 48-51.

Shahidullah, S., & Hepper, P. G. (1992). Hearing in the fetus: Prenatal detection of deafness. *International Journal of Prenatal and Perinatal Studies*, *4*(3/4), 235-240.

Shankweiler, D., Lundquist, E., Dreyer, L.G., & Dickinson, C. C. (1996). Reading and spelling difficulties in high school students: Causes and consequences. *Reading and Writing 8*(3), 267-294.

Shaywitz, S. E., Fletcher, J. M., Holahan, J. M., Shneider, A. E., Marchione, K. E., Stuebing, K. K., Francis, D. J., Pugh, K. R., & Shaywitz, B. A. (1999). Persistence of dyslexia: The Connecticut Longitudinal Study at Adolescence. *Pediatrics*, *104*(6), 1351-1359.

Shenker, B. J., Pankoski, L., Zekavat, A., & Shapiro, I. M. (2002). Mercury-induced apoptosis in human lymphocytes: Caspase activation is linked to redox status. *Antioxidants & Redox Signaling*, *4*(3), 379-389.

Siblerud, R. L. (1992). A comparison of mental-health of multiple-sclerosis patients with silver mercury dental fillings and those with fillings removed. *Psychological Reports*, *70*(3), 1139-1151.

Siblerud, R. L., & Kienholz, E. (1994). Evidence that mercury from silver dental fillings may be an etiologic factor in multiple-sclerosis. *Science of the Total Environment*, *142*(3), 191-205.

Sickle cell anemia. Retrieved January 28, 2006 from http://www.nlm.nih.gov/med lineplus/ency/article/000527.htm.

Simich-Dudgeon, C. (Ed.), (1992). *Proceedings of the Second National Research Symposium on Limited English Proficient Student Issues: Focus on Evaluation and Measurement*. Washington, DC: U.S. Department of Education, Office of Bilingual Education and Minority Language Affairs.

Simons, R. F., Detenber, B. H., Reiss, J. E., & Shults, C. W. (2000). Image motion and context: A between- and within-subjects comparison. *Psychophysiology*, *37*(5), 706-710.

Sims, C. R. & Gray, W. D. (2004). Episodic versus semantic memory: An exploration of models of memory decay in the serial attention paradigm. In M. C. Lovett, C. D. Schunn, C. Lebiere, & P. Munro (Eds.), *Proceedings of the 6th International Conference on Cognitive Modeling—ICCM2004* (pp. 279-284). Pittsburgh, PA: ICCM.

Skinner, B. F. (1957). *Verbal behavior*. New York: Appleton-Century-Crofts.

Skinner, B. F. (1971). *Beyond freedom and dignity*. New York: Knopf.

Skinner, B. F. (2002). *Verbal behavior*. New York: Skinner Foundation. (Originally published in 1957 by Appleton-Century-Crofts.)

Skoyles, J. R. (1998). Speech phones are a replication code. *Medical Hypotheses, 50*(2), 167–173.

Slater, A., Bremner, G., Johnson, S. P., Hayes, R., & Brown, E. (2000). Newborn infants' preference for attractive faces: The role of internal and external facial features. *Infancy, 1*, 265–274.

Slater, A., & Kirby, R. (1998). Innate and learned perceptual abilities in the newborn infant. *Experimental Brain Research, 123*, 90–94.

Slater, A., Mattock, A., Brown, E., & Bremner, J. G. (1991). Form perception at birth: Cohen and Younger (1984) revisited. *Journal of Experimental Child Psychology 51*(3): 395–406.

Slater, A., & Quinn, P. C. (2001). Face recognition in the newborn infant. *Infant and Child Development, 10*, 21–24.

Slater, A., Quinn, P. C., Hayes, R. A., & Brown, E. (2000). The role of facial orientation in newborn infants' preference for attractive faces. *Developmental Science, 3*, 181–185.

Slobin, D. I. (1996). From "thought and language" to "thinking for speaking." In J. Gumperz, J. John, & S. C. Levinson (Eds.), *Rethinking linguistic relativity* (pp. 70–96). Cambridge: Cambridge University Press. Retrieved January 28, 2006 from http://ihd.berkeley.edu/slobinpapers.htm.

Slobin, D. I. (2003). Language and thought online: Cognitive consequences of linguistic relativity. In D. Gentner & S. Goldin-Meadow (Eds.), *Advances in the investigation of language and thought* (pp. 157–192). Cambridge, MA: MIT Press.

Slobin, D. I. (2004). The many ways to search for a frog: Linguistic typology and the expression of motion events. In S. Strömqvist & L. Verhoeven (Eds.), *Relating events in narrative: Typological and contextual perspectives* (pp. 219–257). Mahwah, NJ: Erlbaum.

Smith, F. (1988a). *Joining the literacy club*. Portsmouth, NH: Heinemann.

Smith, F. (1988b). *Understanding reading*. Hillsdale, NJ: Erlbaum.

Smith, F. (1997). *Reading without nonsense*. New York: Teachers College.

Smith, S. L., Gerhardt, K. J., Griffiths, S. K., Huang, X. Y., & Abrams, R. M. (2003). Intelligibility of sentences recorded from the uterus of a pregnant ewe and from the fetal inner ear. *Audiology and Neuro-Otology, 8*(6), 347–353.

Smolensky, P. (1996). On the comprehension/production dilemma in child language. *Linguistic Inquiry, 27*(4), 720–731.

Smotherman, W. P., & Robinson, S. R. (1995). Tracing developmental trajectories into the prenatal period. In J-P. Lecanuet, W. P. Fifer, N. A. Krasnegor, & W. P. Smotherman (Eds.) *Fetal development* (pp. 15–32). Hillsdale, NJ: Lawrence Erlbaum.

Spearman, C. (1904). "General intelligence" objectively determined and measured. *American Journal of Psychology, 15*, 201–293.

Stanback M. L. (1992). Syllable and rime patterns for teaching-reading—analysis of a frequency-based vocabulary of 17,602 words. *Annals of Dyslexia 42*, 196–221.

Stanovich, K. E. (1987). Children's reading and the development of phonological awareness: Introduction. *Merrill-Palmer Quarterly Journal of Developmental Psychology, 33*, U255–U258.

Stanovich, K. E. (1988). Explaining the differences between the dyslexic and the garden-variety poor reader: The phonological-core variable-difference model. *Journal of Learning Disabilities, 21*, 590-604.

Stanovich, K. E. (1992). Speculations on the causes and consequences of individual differences in early reading acquisition. In P. Gough, L. Ehri, & R. Treiman (Eds.), Reading acquisition (pp. 307-342). Hillsdale, NJ: Lawrence Erlbaum Associates.

Stark, R.E. (1980). Prespeech segmental feature development. In G. Yeni-Komshian, J. Kavanaugh, & C. Ferguson (Eds.), *Child Phonology* (pp.73-92). New York: Academic Press.

Statistical Package for the Social Sciences. Retrieved October 22, 2005 from http://www.spss.com/.

Steel, K. P., & Bussoli, T. J. (1999). Deafness genes expressions of surprise. *Trends in Genetics, 15*, 207-211.

Steiner, J. E. (1979). Human facial expressions in response to taste and smell stimulation. *Advances in Child Development and Behavior, 13*, 257-296.

Stern, D. N. (1985). *The interpersonal world of the infant.* New York: Basic Books.

Stevens, S. S. (1968). Measurement, statistics, and the schemapiric view. *Science, 161*(3844), 849-856.

Stevick, E. (1997). *Memory, meaning, and method.* Boston: Heinle & Heinle.

Sticht, T. G. (1972). Learning by listening. In R. O. Freedle & J. B. Carroll (Eds.), *Language comprehension and the acquisition of knowledge* (pp. 285-314). Washington, DC: V. H. Winston and Sons.

Sticht, T. G. (1978). Development of literacy. *Curriculum Inquiry, 8*(4), 341-351.

Sticht, T. G. (1988). Adult literacy education. *Review of Research in Education, 15*, 59-96.

Sticht, T. G. (1995). Untitled. *Reading Research Quarterly, 30*(2), 152-152.

Sticht, T. G., Hofstetter, C. R., & Hofstetter, C. H. (1996). Assessing adult literacy by telephone. *Journal of Literacy Research, 28*(4), 525-559.

Stokoe, W. (1960). *Sign language structure: An outline of the visual communication system of the American deaf. Studies in Linguistics, Occasional Papers 8.* Buffalo, NY: University of Buffalo.

Strange, W., & J. J. Jenkins (1978). Role of linguistic experience in the perception of speech. In R. D. Walk & H. L. Pick (Eds.), *Perception and experience* (pp.125-169). New York: Plenum Press.

Streeter, L. A. (1976). Language perception of 2-month-old infants shows effects of both innate mechanisms and experience. *Nature, 259*, 39-41.

Streri, A., & Gentaz, E. (2003). Cross-modal recognition of shape from hand to eyes in human newborns. *Somatosensory and Motor Research, 20*, 13-18.

Streri, A., & Gentaz, E. (2004). Cross-modal recognition of shape from hand to eyes and handedness in human newborns. *Neuropsychologia, 42*(10), 1365-1369.

Strömqvist, S. & Verhoeven, L. (Eds.). (2004). *Relating events in narrative: Typological and contextual perspectives.* Mahwah, NJ: Lawrence Erlbaum Associates.

Stromswold, K. (2001). The heritability of language: A review and meta-analysis of twin, adoption, and linkage studies. *Language, 77*(4), 647-723.

Su, M., Wakabayashi, K., Kakita, A., Ikuta, F., & Takahashi, H. (1998). Selective involvement of large motor neurons in the spinal cord of rats treated with methyl mercury. *Journal of the Neurological Sciences, 156*(1), 12-17.

Sullivan, M. W., & Lewis, M. (2003). Emotional expressions of young infants and children: A practitioner's primer. *Infants and Young Children, 16*(2), 120–142.

Sweeney, P. J. (1995). Parkinson's-disease: Managing symptoms and preserving function. *Geriatrics, 50*(9), 24–31.

Sweeney, P. J. (2005). Parkinson's disease: An overview. Retrieved January 28, 2006 from http://www.clevelandclinicmeded.com/diseasemanagement/neurology/parkinsons/parkinsons.htm.

Tajani, E., & Ianniruberto, A. (1990). The uncovering of fetal competence. In M. Papini, A. Pasquinelli, & E. A. Gidoni (Eds.), *Development handicap and rehabilitation: Practice and theory* (pp. 3–8). Amsterdam: Elsevier Science Publishers.

Tajima, A. (2004). Fatal miscommunications: English in aviation safety. *World Englishes, 23,* 451–470.

Takei W. (2001). How do deaf infants attain first signs? *Developmental Science, 4*(1), 71–78

Tangel, D. M., & Blachman, B. A. (1992). Effect of phoneme awareness instruction on kindergarten children's invented spelling. *Journal of Reading Behavior, 24,* 233–258.

Tannen, D. (1986). *That's not what I meant!* New York: William Morrow.

Tatsumoto S. (1993). The development of visual co-action in infancy. *Japanese Journal of Psychology, 64,* 173–180.

Tesar, B., & Smolensky, P. (1998). Learnability in optimality theory. *Linguistic Inquiry, 29*(2), 229–268.

Tetnowski, J. A., & Franklin, T. C. (2003). Qualitative research: Implications for description and assessment. *American Journal of Speech-Language Pathology 12*(2), 155–164.

Thelen, E. (2005). Dynamic systems theory and the complexity of change. *Psychoanalytic Dialogues, 15*(2), 255–283.

Thelen, E., & Smith, L. B. (1994). *A dynamic systems approach to the development of cognition and action.* Cambridge, MA: MIT Press.

Tincoff, R., Hauser, M., Tsao, F., Spaepen, G., Ramus, F., & Mehler, J. (2005). The role of speech rhythm in language discrimination: Further tests with a non-human primate. *Developmental Science, 8*(1), 26–35.

Titzer, R. (2005). Your baby can read. Retrieved January 28, 2006 from http://www.infantlearning.com/robert.html.

Tomasello, M. (1992). *First verbs.* London: Cambridge University Press.

Tomasello, M. (2000). First steps toward a usage-based theory of language acquisition. *Cognitive Linguistics, 11*(1–2), 61–82 .

Tomasello, M. (2001). Perceiving intentions and learning words in the second year of life. In M. Tomasello & E. Bates (Eds.), *Language development: The essential readings* (pp. 111–128). Oxford: Blackwell.

Tomasello, M. (2002). The emergence of grammar in early child language. In T. Givón & B. F. Malle (Eds.), *The evolution of language out of pre-language* (pp. 309–328). Amsterdam: John Benjamins and Company.

Tomasello, M. (2003). *Constructing a language: A usage-based theory of language acquisition.* Cambridge, MA: Harvard University Press.

Tomasello M., & Akhtar, N. (2003). What paradox? A response to Naigles (2002). *Cognition, 88* (3), 317–323.

Tomasello, M., & Call, J. (2004). The role of humans in the cognitive development of apes revisited. *Animal Cognition, 7*(4), 213-215.

Torgesen, J. K., Alexander, A. W., Wagner, R. K., Rashotte, C. A., Voeller, K. K. S., & Conway, T. (2001). Intensive remedial instruction for children with severe reading disabilities: Immediate and long-term outcomes from two instructional approaches. *Journal of Learning Disabilities, 34*, 33-58, 78.

Torgesen, J. K., Wagner, R. K., & Roshette, C. A. (1994a). Development of reading-related phonological processing abilities: New evidence of bidirectional causality from a latent variable longitudinal study. *Developmental Psychology, 30*, 73-87.

Torgesen, J. K., Wagner, R. K., & Roshette, C. A. (1994b). Longitudinal studies of phonological processing and reading. *Journal of Learning Disabilities, 27*, 276-286.

Toro, J. M., Trobalon, J. B., & Sebastian-Galles, N. (2003). The use of prosodic cues in language discrimination tasks by rats. *Animal Cognition 6*(2), 131-136.

Toro, J. M., Trobalon, J. B., & Sebastian-Galles, N. (2005). Effects of backward speech and speaker variability in language discrimination by rats. *Journal of Experimental Psychology: Animal Behavior Processes 31*(1), 95-100.

Traumatic Brain Injury. (2005). Retrieved January 28, 2006 from http://catalog.nucleusinc.com/displaymonograph.php?MID=92.

Trehub, S. E. (1976). The discrimination of foreign speech contrasts by infants and adults. *Child Development, 47*, 466-472.

Treiman, R., Mullennix, J., Bijeljacbabic, R., & Richmondwelty, E. D. (1995). The special role of rimes in the description, use, and acquisition of English orthography. *Journal of Experimental Psychology: General, 124*(2), 107-136.

Trevarthen, C., & Aitken, K. J. (2001). Infant intersubjectivity: Research, theory, and clinical applications. *Journal of Child Psychology and Psychiatry and Allied Disciplines, 42*(1), 3-48.

Tulving, E. (1972). Episodic and semantic memory. In E. Tulving & W. Donaldson (Eds.), *Organization of memory* (pp. 381-403). New York: Academic Press.

U.S. Department of Health and Human Services. (no date). *Eleventh report on carcinogens*. Retrieved January 28, 2006 from http://ntp.niehs.nih.gov/ntp/roc/toc11.html.

Uebersax, J. S. (1988). Validity inferences from interobserver agreement. *Psychological Bulletin, 104*, 405-416.

Uebersax, J. S. (1992). A review of modeling approaches for the analysis of observer agreement. *Investigative Radiology, 27*, 738-743.

UN Webcast Archives. (December 31, 2004). Press Conference: UN Secretary-General Kofi Annan and United States Secretary of State Colin Powell update on the relief effort for countries affected by the recent earthquakes and tidal waves in the western Pacific and Indian Oceans, retrieved January 28, 2006 from http://www.un.org/webcast/sg2004.html.

University of Calgary Faculty of Medicine (2002). How mercury causes brain neuron degeneration, retrieved January 28, 2006, from http://commons.ucalgary.ca/mercury/.

Valette, R. M. (1967). *Modern language testing*. New York: Harcourt, Brace, and World.

van der Meer, E., Kruger, F., & Nuthmann, A. (2005). The influence of temporal order information in general event knowledge on language comprehension. *Zeitschrift Fur Psychologie, 213*(3), 142-151.

Velten, H. V. (1943). The growth of phonemic and lexical patterns in infant language. *Language, 19*, 281-292.

Verstraeten, T. (2004). Thimerosal, the Centers for Disease Control and Prevention, and GlaxoSmithKline. *Pediatrics, 113*(4), 932-932.

Verstraeten, T., Davis, R. L., DeStefano, F., Lieu, T. A., Rhodes, P. H., Black, S. B., Shinefield, H., & Chen, R. T. (2003). Safety of thimerosal containing vaccines: A two-phased study of computerized health maintenance organization databases. *Pediatrics, 112*, 1039-1048.

Vigil, N., & Oller, J. W., Jr. (1976). Rule fossilization: a tentative model. *Language Learning, 26*, 281-295.

Vihman, M. M., Macken, M. A., Miller, R., Simmons, H., & Miller, J. (1985). From babbling to speech: A re-assessment of the continuity issue. *Language, 61*(2), 397-445.

Vingerhoets, F. J., Snow, B. J., Tetrud, J. W., Langston, J. W., Schulzer, M., & Calne, D. B. (1994). Positron emission tomographic evidence for progression of human MPTP-induced dopaminergic lesions. *Annals of Neurology, 36*(5),765-770.

Vouloumanos, A., & Werker, J. F. (2004). Tuned to the signal: The privileged status of speech for young infants. *Developmental Science, 7*(3), 270-276.

Vygotsky, L. S. (1962). *Language and thought.* (Ed. and trans. by Eugenia Hanfmann and Gertrude Vakar.) Cambridge, MA: Harvard University Press. (Original work in Russian published in 1934.)

Vygotsky, L. S. (1978). *Mind in society: The development of higher psychological processes.* (Eds. and trans. from the Russian by M. Cole, V. John-Steiner, S. Scribner, & E. Souberman). Cambridge, MA: Harvard University Press. (Original works published in Russian between 1930 and 1935.)

Wagner, R. K., & Torgesen, J. K. (1987). The nature of phonological processing and its causal role in the acquisition of reading skills. *Psychological Bulletin, 101*, 192-212.

Walton, G. E., Bower, N. J. A., & Bower, T. G. R. (1992). Recognition of familiar faces by newborns. *Infant Behavior and Development*, 15, 265-269.

Walton, G. E., & Bower, T. G. R. (1993). Amodal representation of speech in infants. *Infant Behavior & Development, 16*, 233-243.

Watkins, S. C., & Salter, R. D. (2005). Functional connectivity between immune cells mediated by tunneling nanotubules. *Immunity, 23*(3), 309-318.

Watson, J. B. (1925). *Behaviorism.* New York: People's Institute.

Watson, J. D. (1968/1998). *The double helix: A personal account of the discovery of the structure of DNA.* (G. S. Stent, Ed.). New York: Norton.

Watzlawick, P., Beavin, J. B., & Jackson, D. J. (1967). *Pragmatics of human communication.* New York: Norton.

Weber, B. A. (1988). Screening for high-risk infants using Auditory Brainstem Response Audiometry. In F. H. Bess (Ed.), *Hearing impairment in children* (pp. 112-132). Parkton, MD: York Press.

Weinreich, U. (1953). *Languages in contact.* The Hague: Mouton.

Werker, J. F., Cohen, L. B., Lloyd, V. L., Casasola, M., & Stager, C. L. (1998). Acquisition of word-object associations by 14-month-old infants. *Developmental Psychology, 34*(6), 1289-1309.

Werker, J. F., Gilbert, J. H. V., Humphrey, K., & Tees, R. C. (1981).Developmental aspects of cross-language speech perception. *Child Development, 52*, 349-355.

Werker, J. F., & McLeod, P. J. (1989). Infant preference for both male and female infant-directed talk: A developmental study of attentional and affective responsiveness. *Canadian Journal of Psychology, 43*(2), 230-246.

Werker, J. F., Pegg, J. E., & Mcleod, P. J. (1994). A cross-language investigation of infant preference for infant-directed communication. *Infant Behavior & Development, 17*(3), 323-333.

Werker, J. F., & Tees, R. C. (1984). Cross-language speech perception: Evidence for perceptual reorganization during the first year of life. *Infant Behavior and Development, 7*, 49-63.

Werker, J. F., & Tees, R. C. (1999). Influences on infant speech processing: Toward a new synthesis. *Annual Review of Psychology, 50*, 509-535.

Wernicke, C. (1874). *Der aphasiche Symptomenkomplex.* Breslau: Cohn and Weigert. (1977, *The aphasia symptom complex: A psychological study on an anatomical basis. Wernicke's works on aphasia.* The Hague: Mouton.)

Wesseling, R., & Reitsma, P. (2001). Preschool phonological representations and development of reading skills. *Annals of Dyslexia, 51*, 203-229.

White, T. G. (2005). Effects of systematic and strategic analogy-based phonics on grade 2 students' word reading and reading comprehension. *Reading Research Quarterly 40*(2), 234-255.

Wicklund, M. P. (2005). Amyotrophic lateral sclerosis: Possible role of environmental influences. *Neurologic Clinics, 23*(2), 461-484.

Wilcox, S., & Wilcox, P. (1997). *Learning to see: American Sign Language as a second language.* Washington, DC: Gallaudet University Press.

Williams, J. P. (1980). Teaching decoding with an emphasis on phoneme analysis and phoneme blending. *Journal of Educational Psychology, 72*, 1-15.

Wilson, M. (2001). Perceiving imitatible stimuli: Consequences of isomorphism between input and output. *Psychological Bulletin, 127*(4), 543-553.

Wittgenstein, L. (1953). *Philosophical investigations.* New York: Macmillan.

Wittgenstein, L. (1958). *The blue and brown books.* London: Basil Blackwell. (Originally dictated in 1933-1935; information retrieved January 28, 2006 from http://www.philosophypages.com/ph/witt.htm)

Wood N. (1997). Genes and parkinsonism. *Journal of Neurology and Neurosurgical Psychiatry, 62*(4), 305-309.

Woodcock Reading Mastery Test. retrieved January 28, 2006 from http://www.agsnet.com/assessments/bibliography/wrmt.asp.

Yairi, E., Ambrose, N., & Cox, N. (1996). Genetics of stuttering: A critical review. *Journal of Speech Language and Hearing Research, 39*, 771-784.

Young, J. Z. (1978). *Programs of the brain.* London: Oxford University Press.

Zamuner, T. S., Gerken, L., & Hammond, M. (2005). The acquisition of phonology based on input: A closer look at the relation of cross-linguistic and child language data. *Lingua, 115*(10), 1403-1426.

Zlatin, M. (1975). *Explorative mapping of the vocal tract and primitive syllabification in infancy: The first six months.* Paper presented at the American-Speech-Hearing Association Convention, Washington, D.C.

Glossary of Terms

The terms in this Glossary are defined with respect to their use in this book. We have tried to use examples that convey the essential meaning of many technical terms, but the reader may also find it useful to consult a specialized dictionary or other on-line resources.

abstraction: the process or result of isolating the material content associated with hard objects, bodily persons, or relations, by setting the object off from the real or actual contexts in which it is found, for example, if we imagine something that is not present or not real, we use the process of abstraction.

abstractive cycle: the three step process by which the material content of a sign is (1) first noticed or marked by its boundaries, surfaces, edges, or limits, then, (2) separated by movement of the object or observer from its original location within the perceptual context, then, (3) thought of or conceptualized independently of its original context.

achievement test: any test designed to assess or measure the prior learning or knowledge in a particular subject area.

acoustic phonetics: the study of the physical properties of sounds, especially the sounds of speech.

acquiescence response bias: the tendency to agree (rather than disagree) with a perceived assertion or expectation of someone else, especially used in reference to survey-based research.

acronym: a word constructed from the initial letters of a descriptive phrase or name, for example, *laser* for the phrase *Light Amplification by Stimulated Emission of Radiation*.

adinity: an attribute of a predicate system showing how many arguments it normally takes, or how many it has in any given case; for example, "The dog chased the cat" has an adinity of 2 whereas "The farmer chased the dog with a pitchfork" has an adinity of 3.

adrenoleukodystrophy: one of the rare genetically linked diseases that involves the destruction of the myelin sheath that normally insulates nerve fibers; popularized in the film *Lorenzo's Oil* released in 1993. The oil was developed to prevent the buildup of long chains of fatty

acids that are involved in the destruction of myelin. See http://www.
ncbi.nlm.nih.gov/books/bv.fcgi?call=bv.View.ShowSection&rid=gnd
.scction.226 visited on August 20, 2005.

affective disorders: any one of a large class of loosely defined difficulties
severe enough to be regarded as disabilities that affect the emotions,
feelings, personality, and social relations of an individual.

afferent nerves: those that carry sensations and other messages from the
periphery to the spinal column and the brain.

affix: any bound morpheme that is attached to another word, for example, at its beginning (as a prefix) or at its end (as a suffix).

African American Vernacular English: a term applied to a common
variety of American English spoken in the southern states (not exclusively spoken by African Americans).

agent: in grammar, person or other referent in a verb structure that acts
or causes some result or outcome, for example, in the sentence, *The
car door smashed Tom's finger*, the car door would be the agent of the
structure.

algorithm: a sequence of rules or procedures that can be used to solve,
or approximate a computed solution to a given problem.

alphabetic principle: the principle that each letter of the alphabet
stands for a distinct class or system of sounds in the writing system;
also known as the phonemic principle.

alveolar: the articulatory target for the tip of the tongue in producing /t/,
/d/, /s/, and /z/ in English; the gum ridge just behind the upper teeth.

Alzheimer's disease: the most common degenerative disease associated
with aging, characterized by a progressive loss of memory and eventual
inability to understand language and/or perform routine tasks, first
identified and described in 1907 by Alois Alzheimer and still of
unknown causation.

amino acid: the basic building blocks of the protein structures of all living organisms; there are 20 crucial distinct left-handed varieties used in
building the proteins.

amniocentesis: a procedure for extracting a sample of amniotic fluid
from within the sac (placenta) inside the uterus that encloses the
developing baby.

amniotic fluid: the fluid that surrounds the developing baby while it is
contained within the mother's uterus.

amodal: not associated with a particular modality of perception, that is,
fully abstract.

amplitude: the power of a waveform, especially a sound, or the distance
between the maximum peak and the maximum trough of a wave.

amyotrophic lateral sclerosis: a commonly fatal disease of the motor
nerves of unknown causation, first discovered in 1869 by Jean Martin

Charcot, usually detected at first through a general weakness in an extremity that is not associated with any pain; eventually affects such motor processes as speech, swallowing, mobility, and breathing; also known as Lou Gerhig's disease.

anecdotal: known through informal reports of interesting behaviors, in other words, stories or anedotes that tend to be confirmed by others who have observed the same or similar phenomena; sometimes used to mean that the reports characterized in this way cannot be trusted or relied upon.

animate being: any entity that can move on its own initiative or volition.

anterior canals: the front canals of the semicircular canal structure in the vertical plane pointed outward at about 45 degrees from the line of sight looking straight ahead.

apathy: a generalized lack of interest in normal events, activities, and relations that would normally elicit arousal, alertness, or heightened awareness.

aphasia: the loss of the previously acquired ability to use some aspect of language, for example, loss of ability in speech, writing, signing, or even verbal thought and understanding.

appropriateness requirement: the demand that a meaningful symbol must fit the occasion or context of its use.

approval motive: the near-universal tendency of human beings to seek the approval of others in social situations.

approximant: a class of speech sounds where the tongue, lips, vocal folds, or other organs of production come close together but without producing friction, as in the sounds represented by the letters "y" and "r" of *year*, or the "w" and "l" of *well*.

aptitude test: any test designed to assess or measure the ability or capacity to learn a particular skill, or subject matter.

arcuate fasciculus: the roughly rainbow-shaped bundle of fibers that connects the area in the left frontal lobe commonly associated with the production of fluent speech and the area in the left temporal lobe commonly associated with the comprehension of language in its various forms, spoken, written, signed, and so forth.

argument: any distinct referent or signification associated under the scope of one or more predicates.

argument structure: the arrangement of referents or distinct significant elements collected under the scope of a single predicate.

articulation: the result or process of distinct and regular movements of the speech organs, especially the tongue, lips, and jaw, or, in signed languages, the distinct movements of the hands in producing meaningful signs; in education, sometimes applied to the coordination of transitions between grades, schools, or educational programs.

articulators: the movable organs of the body that are used in the production of speech and language. Also, the hands and other body parts involved in the languages of the Deaf.

articulatory phonetics: the study of the ways in which sounds are produced, especially the sounds of speech.

association (semantic memory): any meaning or aspect of knowledge that is activated or comes to mind when some other meaning is represented or suggested.

attention deficit/hyperactivity disorder (ADD/ADHD): a commonly diagnosed condition believed by many to impede a person's ability to focus on a task or to pay attention to someone else; may or may not be accompanied by a tendency to be overactive (so-called "hyperactivity"); commonly treated with various forms of methylphenidate (Ritalin, Adderall, and so forth); see Breggin (1998) on the abuse of these drugs.

attentional gap: the lapse of time between shifting attention from one representation to another; a factor of processing time that causes the perceiver, presumably, to lose track of one representation while constructing or shifting attention to another.

attenuation: the damping, reduction, or muffling of a wave or sound so that it loses power and distinctness.

attitude measurement: any test, survey, or other measurement procedure designed to assess the likes, dislikes, or other psychological, social, or mental dispositions toward a given idea, subject matter, group, language, or what-have-you.

audiologist: someone who is trained to measure hearing acuity and is certified to assess and treat hearing disorders.

audiology: the study of the processes, physiology, and mechanisms of hearing.

auditory brainstem response: abbreviated "ABR," a screening procedure to identify babies with hearing problems; relies on changes in electrical activity of the brain that are measurable at the scalp.

auditory phonetics (perceptual): the study of the impressions made by sounds as they impinge on the ear of a human being or other organism.

autism spectrum disorders: a broad class of disorders usually detected in childhood that are characterized by impaired verbal skills, social relations, and a reduced ability to take other persons, relations, and attitudes into consideration.

autoimmune disease: any disease or condition where the natural systems that normally protect an organism from attacks by bacteria, viruses, and damage from toxins, begin for any reason to mistake its own bodily tissues for invaders and begin to attack and destroy them.

autopsy: an examination of a body after death by a qualified medical examiner or other practitioner.

back-formation: a word formed from another word by removing one of its parts or by proceeding in a direction that is opposite the normal forward process of formation; for example, normally an *acronym*, for instance, is constructed from the initial letters of a series of words and making a pronounceable form of the abbreviation. In back-formation, a phrase is invented from some existing word or name; for example, the name *Apgar* is interpreted as if it were the initial letters of a phrase such as an abbreviation for the *American Pediatric Gross Assessment Record*.

backsliding: the process or result of returning from what appears to be a more advanced and more correct form of speech or language to a less advanced form.

behaviorism: the approach to psychology that observes, describes, and aims to control observable behaviors of organisms by controlling the contingent events that are believed to reinforce or punish those behaviors; in its extreme forms as advocated by B. F. Skinner, for instance, denies that abstract ideas, mind, or meanings are useful concepts.

binaural hearing: the sensations produced by the fact that we have two ears and we can hear sounds in both of them.

biomechanical activity: any action of a living organism that can be explained in part or possibly in whole in terms of skeletal and muscular structures, for example, the opening and closing of the jaw is constrained in part by its shape and the systematic relations of the bones and muscles involved.

blend: in phonics approaches to the teaching of reading, when adjacent letters are joined together and the sounds they represent are pronounced in rapid sequence they are said to be "blended," for example, in the word "blend" the "b-" is joined with "-l-" to form "bl-" which is joined with "-end" to form the word "blend"; a theoretical part of reading that treats letters as if they were actual segments of speech rather than representations of such segments.

blood brain barrier: a system of tiny blood vessels that filter out many harmful substances to keep them from entering the brain and/or spinal column.

bodily kinesthetic intelligence: in the theory of Howard Gardner, the kind of intellectual ability that is associated with articulated and rhythmic movements of the body as in dancing or athletic performances.

bootstrapping: lifting oneself by one's bootstraps, or shoelaces; a metaphor for the performance of any task that appears to be impossible, for example, such as figuring out or learning the meaning of a sign or sign system that we cannot at first understand at all, that is, acquiring a new language.

bottom-up: a term applied to reading processing that begins at the surface-forms of print and works "upward" (in theory) to meanings.

bound morpheme: any morpheme that is attached to another and cannot occur by itself, for instance, the "-s" of "dogs" is a bound morpheme because it cannot occur alone.

bradykinesia: a disease manifested by trembling in the extremities at rest and rigidity of certain muscles producing slowed movement.

breath group: a unit of speech that occurs on a single breath, marked by pauses or breathing at the beginning and end.

Broca's aphasia: a loss of the ability to produce fluent speech.

canonical babbling: repetitive rhythmic babbling that resembles speech in its surface-form, for example, /bababa/, /dadada/, and so forth.

carcinogen: any substance or chemical that produces increased risk of cancer.

cascading effect model of risk: a theoretical description of factors causing difficulties where one result causes another difficulty which in its turn causes yet another resulting in a series of undesirable outcomes; also called the domino model of risk.

categorical imperative: the logical requirement that really abstract concepts, in thought for instance, must retain their meanings while we are thinking, or else we will not be able to know ourselves what it is that we are thinking of. If the ideas associated with a certain color of green could change to red, or to a dog, or to the known universe, or to nothing at all, for instance, and yet be the same idea, how would we be able to tell if we were thinking of that particular color of green?

central nervous system: the brain and spinal cord.

cephalocaudal: literally meaning from head to tail, *cephalo-* being the Greek transliteration for *head* and *-caudal* being the Latin for *tail.*

chameleon effect: the tendency of interlocutors to coordinate and match their movements; for example, to use similar gestures, facial expressions, accents, rhythms, and words, phrases, and so forth.

chelation: the removal of a toxin through medical treatments, for example, as in removing mercury.

chronological order: an arrangement of events into a time sequence according to which happened first, second, third, and so forth.

cleft palate: a condition where the palate does not close, as it does in normal fetal development, leaving an opening in the roof of the mouth.

clinical depression: an abnormal form depressed mood and not a mere temporary downward swing such as might be caused by loss or normal grief.

coda: the part of a syllable that comes after its nucleus, if there is anything after the nucleus, for example, in the word *jinxed* the coda consists of the sequence of consonants shown roughly in the letters "-nxed" or in the phonetic sequence [ŋkst].

code-mixing: the process of using more than one language in the same sentence, possibly with multiple switches back and forth; see code-switching.

code-switching: the process or especially the habit of using more than one language/dialect in producing discourse.

codon: any three of the four sugar bases (adenine, cytosine, guanine, uracil, and thymine) that make up meaningful strings in DNA or RNA specifying any one of the amino acids used in building life's proteins, or signaling one of its ends.

cognitive: having to do with the mind, knowing, and representation.

cognitive momentum: the tendency to complete a thought, inference, or representational process according to expectations, for example, the tendency to expect a certain element to follow on the basis of what has preceded it.

common writing system criterion: one of the criteria applied in judging whether two language/dialects are the same.

comorbid: when two or more undesirable conditions, diseases, or injuries exist in one individual simultaneously.

competency test: any generalized achievement test designed to assess or measure knowledge of subject matter and ability to reason about it that is expected to be achieved, say, when nearing high school graduation, or some other milestone.

complementarity: the sort of relation between nonoverlapping sets or systems that completes, or exhausts, a whole universe of possibilities; for example, things that exist and things that do not exist constitute the universe of possible things and these two sets, things that exist, and things that do not exist, complement each other.

comprehensibility: the extent to which a text or speech (or the producer of the text or speech) can be understood by other its readers or other interpreters.

comprehensiveness: the extent to which a term or concept is generalized and or the range of concepts covered by a vocabulary or system of signs.

concept: the abstract idea of anything real or imagined, including any other concept, that enables us to think of that other thing when it is not present to be perceived. A concept of anything is distinct from its percept by being more abstract and removable from whatever is represented.

concept of identity: the idea, or knowledge if it is true, that a given individual is a unique, nonrepeating, particular entity, with a distinct body, mind, and personality (a self or soul) and a real-life history that extends at least from conception to death.

conceptual: of or pertaining to abstract ideas or the processes involved in forming them.

concordance: in measurement and statistics an index of agreement, especially in ratings or judgments assigned to a task or series of responses.

concrete operational stage: a stage of child development proposed by Piaget characterized by the ability to manipulate objects, for example, to move a toy and then put it back where it was.

connectedness: the property of ordinary perceptual representations (that is, of experience) shown in true narrative representations; the property of ordinary discourse that enables generalized semantic inferences to associations, presuppositions, and implications.

consciousness: the kind of situational awareness that accompanies normal experience when we are awake.

conservation: in Piaget's view of psychology child development, the ability to know and understand that objects or substances moved around, for instance, a liquid poured into a different container, retain their mass, quantity, or other qualities.

consonant: a class of speech sounds that are typically transitional, of short duration, and that do not function as the center of a syllable; typically produced by relatively rapid movement and/or approximation of the articulators so as to produce blockage or even closure of the mouth or other air passageways and/or the production of noise by friction or plosion; contrast with vowel (also see liquid and glide).

consonantal sound: any speech-like sound that has the constrictive or transitional properties of a consonant (contrasts with vocalic sound).

construction: the result or process of putting elements together to build a higher structure. For example, syllables are built up from vowels and consonants; words are built up from syllables; phrases are built up from words; and clauses are built up from phrases or other clauses, and so forth.

content-based approach: any approach to comprehension, teaching, or learning that is based on or that refers to the meaning underlying the surface-forms of representations.

contrastive analysis: a common method applied in assessing the extent to which two languages/dialects are the same or different with respect to form or meaning.

convention: a habit, consistency, repeated pattern, or regularity of use that is produced by the usage of a word or other sign by a community of users.

convention of use: a rule, habit, or regularity of usage that is understood and shared by a community of sign-users.

conventionality requirement: the demand that a meaningful symbol must be applied in a way that is consistent with is normal or regular use by a community of sign-users.

correlation: in statistics, a measure of the extent to which scores on two different tasks tend to differ proportionately and in the same direction from their respective averages; varies between 1 and 0 in absolute value where 0 indicates no correlation and 1 indicates a perfect correlation; can be positive where high scores on A, for instance, tend to correspond to high scores on B, and low scores on A tend to correspond to low scores on B, or negative where low scores on A correspond to high scores on B, and high scores on A correspond to low scores on B.

craniofacial anomalies: any deformity of the head or face of which cleft lip and cleft palate are the best known and the most common.

criterion-referenced test: any test designed to assess or measure the ability or capacity to perform a particular task with a certain level of skill, or to show knowledge at a given level of certain subject matter (commonly referred to as "can do" tests where success shows that the examinee is able to perform a certain task with an independently determined level of skill); contrasted with norm-referenced test.

crossmodal transfer: the process or result of translating information from one sense modality, for example, sight, to another, for example, hearing.

decibel: abbreviated "dB," a ratio of sound pressure levels expressed as 10 times the logarithm of the ratio in the base 10; applied mainly to express the relative power of a sound; the main virtue of this ratio is that it can express a vast range of values in a way that is consistent with perceptions of loudness.

decoding: as applied to literacy, the process of converting a string of letters into a string of speech sounds.

deep structure: the sequential and meaningful relations between the parts of any construction that enable language users to understand and/or produce it.

deglutition: the process or result of swallowing, also, glutition.

deixis: in linguistics and sign theory the process of pointing or indicating or referring to some particular person, object, place, time, or other element of a real or imagined context of experience.

dementia: a loss of brain function caused by damage, disease, toxicity, or some combination of these.

dementia pugilistica: a deterioration of the brain and nervous system owed to blows received in combative sports such as boxing and full-contact karate.

dental amalgam: an alloy of metals including silver and mercury that is commonly used in tooth restoration to fill cavities.

determinacy: the property of true narrative representations that enables the determination of the identity of objects, persons, and histories of experience and behavior; the foundational basis in true narrative representations that also enables the discovery of the pragmatic content of conventional linguistic signs.

diagnosis: the process or result of determining the nature of a problem, difficulty, disorder, or disability.

diagnostic: of or pertaining to the process or result of identifying a level of competence or capacity in a sign-user as shown in the highest attained level of performance that can be observed or demonstrated by an individual or group.

dialect: any variety of any language.

diglossia: the kind of social situation where two language/dialects are used by a given community for different purposes, for example, one may be used at school and in the courts while the other is used in the marketplace, local neighborhood, and at home.

diphthong: a sequence of two or more distinct vocalic elements such as [o] and [u], for instance, in the word *bow* or the [a] and [i] of *buy* as these are pronounced in the most widely spoken dialect of American English.

direct object: the referent that is acted upon directly by the action signified in a verb such as *ate* in *The cat ate the canary*, that is, the canary.

discourse: the result or process of interacting through the signs of one or more languages.

discrete: bounded, characterized by having a sharp onset or beginning and a similarly distinct end or offset.

discriminate: to tell the difference between sensations, percepts, or sensory stimuli of any kind.

discriminated icon: the kind of icon exemplified in a percept; an image or representation of an object that appears to be the object itself.

discriminated index: the result of a successful search for a certain object represented as a hypostatic icon (a fully abstract concept of the object searched for); that is, the result of a search that ends with the discovery of a percept of the object searched for.

discriminated symbol: a repeated syllabic utterance (rhythmic manual sign or written symbol) that is not only distinguished but also recognized as a repetition of a prior utterance (manual sign or written symbol); the recognized surface-form of a given linguistic symbol; this is usually designated as the distinctive sequence of sounds and syllables that constitute the surface-form of the linguistic symbol, for example, for the word *mama* the discriminated symbol can be represented as the distinct phonetic shape of that word as uttered, for example, as [máma], or as the printed form of the word in the letters "mama" provided these forms are recognized as distinct from other possible linguistic surface-forms.

discrimination: the process of marking the boundaries, edges, surfaces, or limits of an object that is perceived with one or more of the senses, for example, by seeing, hearing, touching, tasting, or smelling.

discriminative index: the result of an unsuccessful search for a particular object where the object is not found; this sort of sign consists of an intentional act of searching a location with a particular object in mind (that is, its hypostatic icon) but not connecting with any percept of the object; the discriminative index is uncompleted.

discursive act: any act that involves the surface-forms of discourse whether spoken, heard, manually signed, written, read, or merely thought of.

disequilibration: the result or process of noticing the fact that things are out of balance or that an unexpected inconsistency has come up, for example, surprise is an indicator of disequilibration.

dissolution of communication abilities: the falling apart (that is, loss or destruction) knowledge, skills, and abilities associated especially with language.

DNA: a type of macromolecule, deoxyribonucleic acid, that stores the genetic information that specifies the nature, structure, metabolism, and so forth of a living organism.

domino model of risk: a theoretical description of factors causing difficulties where one result causes another difficulty which in its turn causes yet another resulting in a series of undesirable outcomes; also called the cascading effect model of risk.

dopamine: a neurotransmitter critically involved in the proper firing of motor neurons; deficient in Parkinson's disease.

Down syndrome: a genetic disorder characterized by flattening of the face, wider spacing and slanting of the eyes, a reduced head size, and double jointedness; typically associated with mental retardation.

Duchenne smiling: the sort of smile that is distinguished by cheek raising, spreading, and a friendly and happy squinting of the eyes; the genuine spontaneous kind of smiling named for Guillaume Duchenne who studied its characteristics and identified it as distinct from the kind of professional smiling that shows deliberate politeness without the spontaneity (see Figure 4–1 for an example).

duration: the length of an event, especially a sound or syllable, from its detectable onset or beginning until its offset or ending.

dyad: any arrangement or relation characterized by having two distinct parts, components, or participants as in a conversational dyad (where there are only two interlocutors).

dynamic systems approach: especially in grammar or in the theory, practice, or conception of signs and sign behaviors that accounts for their changing relations over time; contrasts with any static, timeless, or categorical approach to theory or practice; any theory or method of research that takes account of the changing influences of distinct sign systems on each other; for example, certain sensory-motor systems must be in place prior to the development of the first meaningful word.

dyslexia: in general any disorder specifically interfering with the process of reading or learning to read (see the definition of the International Dyslexia Association at http://www.interdys.org/ visited on January 27, 2006 where the term is defined as "a specific learning disability that is neurological in origin. It is characterized by difficulties with accurate and/or fluent word recognition and by poor spelling and decoding abilities. These difficulties typically result from a deficit in the phonological component of language that is often unexpected in relation to other cognitive abilities and the provision of effective classroom instruction. Secondary consequences may include problems in reading comprehension and reduced reading experience that can impede the growth of vocabulary and background knowledge.")

efferent nerves: those that carry messages and commands for movement from the central nervous system and the spinal column to the periphery.

ego-centric particulars: the kind of referring terms that are linked to a person, object, place, time, or other element of a real or imagined context of experience by assuming the viewpoint of a certain observer whether real or imagined.

Einstein's gulf: the logical barrier or gap that separates the world of sensory impressions from the realm of fully abstract ideas, propositions, or meanings.

electroencephalogram (EEG): a recording of brain waves made from electrodes placed on the scalp.

embryo: in humans a term applied to the early stages of a developing individual from conception until the body parts can be easily recognized (formerly until about week 14, but now we know that the normal fetus is well formed prior to the end of week 12).

emergent literacy: the natural behaviors of scribbling, drawing pictures, looking at books, turning pages, being read to, and so on, that precede and that some theoreticians believe naturally develop into literacy.

empiricist tradition: the theory and research emphasizing observable (empirical, sensory) aspects of experience.

endogenous: a structure, signal, or idea that originates from within an organism, model, system, or representation.

endogenous syntactic development: an increase in sign complexity where words or phrases are expanded from within by the subordination of signs within signs, for instance, the addition of the plural marker to "dog" and to "this" to get "these dogs" or the addition of the past tense marker to a verb as in going from "go" to "went" or "walk" to "walked." See morphology.

entrainment: the synchronization in part or in whole of one individual's body rhythms and movements with those of another, as typically seen between speaker and listener when they are fully engaged in conversation.

episodic memory: the ability to represent, store, and later recall particular events that happen in experience; the kind of memory based in actual, pragmatic experience; contrasts with semantic memory.

episodic organization: the tendency for the sequence of clauses and higher structural systems in a discourse to conform to an arrangement that reflects causal relations, the actual time sequence of events, the spatial arrangement of bodily things, or some other transitive relation where the related elements tend to be arranged in the discourse in the same order, A, B, C, . . . and so on, as they tend to have in experience.

error term: in measurement and statistics, the portion of variability in a measure (or test) that cannot be attributed to whatever the measure or test is supposed to assess; the error term is the opposite and complement of its validity; synonymous with unreliability.

ethyl mercury: the form of mercury found in the preservative thimerosal; a known neurotoxin that damages the brain and nervous system.

etiology: the study of causation especially of diseases, disorders, or undesirable conditions.

event-related potential: a measurable change in electrical activity at one or more positions on the scalp believed to be attributable to a particular stimulus or event.

exclusive-we: in grammar, a plural first person pronoun in any language that does not include the listener or listeners among its referents.

exemplar: an instance of the conventional use of a sign that enables the discovery of its significance.

exogenous: a structure, signal, or idea that originates from outside the organism, model, system, or representation.

exogenous syntactic developments: the expansion of signs by attaching them to each other so as to form a higher order sign or a higher relation between signs, for example, as in moving from a referring expression (a zero order predicate) such as "Nunu" to a more complex form involving a first order predicate such as "Nunu bark."

expansion stage: the phase of vocal development in infancy where the infant begins to produce well-differentiated vowels that resemble the range of vowels present in the speech of adults who speak the target language to which the infant is being exposed.

expectancy: the advance preparation to perceive, interpret, or represent a future event based on inference from past or present experience, knowledge, or innate tendencies.

experimental paradigm: a procedure used in one or several experiments that becomes more or less standardized and comes to be applied to a variety of questions with different participants across various contexts, in other words, a class of experiments similar in methods used.

feature: a quality or attribute of some sign or sign element that is usually insufficient to identify it and yet is an element that is detectable as part of it.

fetus: in humans this term is commonly applied to the developing individual during gestation but especially after body parts are recognizable about the end of the first 12 weeks.

fictional representation: a representation that refers to or signifies something that must be imagined, that is, is either not real or not present in the setting where it is to be imagined, for example, Tom Sawyer's raft, or the character himself in the famed stories by Mark Twain.

final position: with respect to a syllable or word, the last position in a string of segments making up that syllable or word.

first order of reference: the association of an utterance or voluntary vocalization with the person who produces it.

first order predicate: a predicate that takes one or more zero order predicate(s) as its arguments zero order predicates as its argument(s), for example, "bark" in "Nunu barks" or the possessive relation shown in "Pop hat" meaning "Pop's hat."

first position (or person): the speaker or producer of a sign or sequence of signs.

fixed vocal signal: the kind of vocalization that is innately determined and relatively invariant, for example, the song produced by a particular kind of bird, or the bark of a dog or seal; a class of voluntary sounds not part of the inventory leading to speech, for example, cries, laughter, groans, and so forth.

flashback: a device commonly used in writing, film-making, or story-telling where events from an earlier time period are reported, portrayed, or otherwise represented out of sequence, that is, a part of the story told as a memory of a character rather than a present experience.

flashforward: a theoretical device rarely used in writing, film-making, or story-telling where events from a future time period relative to the unfolding narrative are reported, portrayed, or otherwise represented before they will occur in the experience of the character(s), in other words, a part of the story told out of sequence as a kind of premonition, a clairvoyant view, an anticipation of the future, rather than as present, ongoing experience.

foreign language: a language that is not spoken in the country or place of reference, for instance, English is a foreign language in central China.

foreign language setting: a context of use or learning where the target language is not spoken in the community outside the classroom or learning context, contrasts with a second language setting.

formal operational stage: the stage of development defined by Piaget where the individual becomes able to perform fully abstract mental operations that can be completely reversed, for instance, multiplying a number, say, n by 10 to get $10n$ and then dividing $10n$ by 10 to get back to n. Contrasted with the concrete operational stage where we can, for instance, drive to town and back again, but we cannot arrive at the same time or place from which we departed. However, the number n (in a formal operation) is still n no matter how we get to it, for example, by counting forward or backward. Of course, practically speaking, the actual operations involved in counting forward and counting backward are not the same.

formant: a concentrated band of acoustic energy originating from the voice or other regular sound source over a range of frequencies that is generated by the shape of one or more resonating cavities.

fossilization: in language acquisition, the process of leveling off or reaching a plateau of development beyond which the sign-user does not further advance.

frame-and-content: the theory that the syllables, and therefore the building blocks of speech, emerge naturally from movements of the jaw while producing voluntary sounds.

free morpheme: a morpheme that can occur as a separate word in discourse, for example, "dog" in "the dog is barking."

free will: the capacity to make a choice between two or more courses of action and to rationally take into account the necessary, likely, or possible outcomes of the choice; also see volition.

frequency: the relative commonness of an event or the number of times per second (or other time interval) that a waveform completes a cycle and repeats itself.

frequency of occurrence: the commonness with which a given word, phrase, or other bit of discourse is repeated.

fricative: the subclass of consonant sounds characterized by the friction of air flowing past the articulators.

fundamental frequency: the lowest frequency, or pitch, of the voice in normal speaking (the pitch that defines the normal depth of the voice in speech).

gender: in grammar, the differentiation of the class of a word or phrase according to whether it is masculine, feminine, or neuter; generally associated with physical gender in pronouns, but arbitrarily associated with content words in many languages.

gender bias: any tendency for males (or females) to be more (or less) affected by a given treatment, diagnosis, disorder, or trait.

genderlect: a language/dialect that tends to be learned and used by either males or females but not both.

General American English: the widespread variety of English spoken throughout the United States in urban centers but especially west of the Mississippi and across most of the northern states; the variety usually preferred in network media presentations.

general intelligence: the common factor known (or believed) to undergird almost all intellectual, mental, psychological, or social tasks that involve reasoning; especially found in language measures aimed at vocabulary knowledge and linguistic reasoning.

general limit of abstraction: the representation of any abstract representation brings us to a general limit of abstraction that cannot be surpassed; there is no level of abstraction above the level already attained when an abstract representation of another already abstract representation is produced.

generalizability: the property of true narrative representations that enables the conventional application of any sign in any such representation to be generalized to any similar context of use exactly to the extent of the similarity across the contexts.

generalization: the process or result by which a concept abstracted from one object is applied to the same object in different settings or to similar objects across settings.

genetic code: the underlying system of correspondences between the codons of DNA and the amino acids that make up life's proteins.

genetic disorders: ones that are caused by or linked to errors or damage to the genes inherited from an individual's ancestors.

genome: the genetic description (or blueprint) that defines the structure, metabolism, and unique character of any organism. See http://www.ornl.gov/sci/techresources/Human_Genome/home.shtml visited January 27, 2006. The human genome consists of about 3 billion base pairs in our DNA.

genotoxic: a characteristic of poisons that damage genes and genetic material.

gestation: the entire period of a pregnancy during which and or the process by which a fertilized egg develops into a viable organism.

gestational age: the time that has elapsed from conception, and prior to the birth of the organism, up to the present time.

glide: the subclass of sounds that are hardly vowels or consonants. They include the transitional sounds that are commonly signified in English by the letters "y" and "w" and that are found in the words *cue*, *you*, *yet*, *wet*, *quick*, *cow*, *boy*, and so on.

glutition: the process or result of swallowing; also, deglutition.

graduation test: any test used as a criterion for advancement in grade, for example, from one level of study to the next, or especially after completion of a major course of study toward a diploma or degree.

grammatical gender: the kind of morphological marking that seems to signify male or female sex but that is often generalized to objects that have no physically obvious male or female parts, for example, in Spanish, "mano" translates as "hand" in English but is invariably feminine gender in Spanish where almost all nouns are marked as masculine or feminine gender. A remnant of gender marking is evident in English where any ship at sea is commonly referred to by the feminine pronoun "she."

grammatical number: the kind of morphological marking that usually signifies whether a referring term signifies one (singular number) or more than one (plural number) logical object as its referent(s).

grammatical person: the kind of morphological marking usually associated with pronouns and often with verbs or other forms that signifies the distinction between the viewpoints of the producer, consumer, and the rest of the world with respect to any given representation, for example, in "I saw him leave," the pronoun "I" signifies the producer of the statement, while "him" signifies someone other than the producer and also distinct from the consumer addressed by the producer.

Grice's maxims: certain rules, principles, or axioms proposed by H. P. Grice (1975) to account for common regularities and expectations in ordinary conversational exchanges.

gustatory: of or pertaining to the sense of taste.

hallucination: the kind of perceptual error, a fictional production of the mind, that is so vivid it may seem to be real to the person who experiences it, for example, the sort of error fallen into by a person who mistakes an imagined event or even a sequence of them for actual perceptions.

hand-eye coordination: the ability to reach, touch, and grasp things that can be seen.

handedness: the tendency to prefer either the right hand, or the left hand, for voluntary actions such as eating with a fork, or throwing a ball.

hemoglobin: a protein containing the red pigment from iron that is crucial to the uptake of oxygen by red blood cells; also involved in keeping them round so that the blood can flow through the small capillaries.

hertz: a unit of measure, abbreviated "Hz," named for Heinrich Rudolf Hertz meaning one cycle per second; a clock has a rate of 1 Hz.

high-amplitude sucking (HAS): a high rate of sucking behavior observed in certain instances by researchers in paradigms where infants control the presentation of stimuli by sucking or not sucking on a specially designed pacifier linked to a computer that records contractions of the baby's mouth.

high saliency: the noticeability of a word, phrase, or bit of discourse usually associated with its amplitude, length, duration, and intensity; may be augmented by the association of a word, phrase, or bit of discourse with an intensely painful, pleasurable, or otherwise memorable experience.

holophrasis: several apparently distinct words that are used by the child as a whole, where the distinct meanings of the components are not distinguished by the child, from "don't go far away" the child stands at the door and produces a simpler sequence of syllables "'on't fa' way" meaning roughly "outside" or "open," or from "Are you thirsty?" the child takes two distorted syllables and produces a single form "ofirs" meaning "water" or "drink."

holophrastic construction: see holophrasis.

homeostasis: the state of equilibrium that is maintained by many of the body's systems, for example, a relatively constant body temperature at 98.6 degrees Fahrenheit, the normal sense of balance, and so forth.

horizontal canals: the canals of the semicircular canal structure that lie roughly in the horizontal plane pointing upward at about a 30 degree angle when the line of sight is straight ahead and on the level.

hypostasis: the process of imagining or thinking of an object when it is not present; the highest level of the abstractive cycle.

hypostatic icon: the image of an object or a sign separated from its contexts of occurrence in the world of experience.

hypostatic index: the kind of sign that connects an object that disappears, a prescinded index, from the perceptual field with the object in spite of the fact that the object in question is no longer perceivable; for example, the kind of index that represents the mosquito that we hear buzzing past our ear and disappearing into the darkness; or the sign that represents the car that passes ours on the highway but that is presumed to still be out there ahead of us on the highway somewhere.

hypostatic symbol: an abstract symbol, especially a linguistic symbol, that comes to be associated with some arbitrary conventional significance in addition to its producer and or consumer, that is, a symbol that acquires tertiary significance.

hypostatize: to abstract by imagining or thinking of an object when it is not present.

icon: the kind of sign that represents its object by resemblance or similarity to it, for example, a picture of a horse must resemble the horse that it is a picture of and so it is an icon just as a bust of Julius Caesar is supposed to look like he looked and is also an icon. The most common examples of icons in our experience are percepts of objects, whole scenes, landscapes, and so on.

identity of indiscernibles: the principle proposed by Gottfried Wilhelm Leibniz [1646–1716] in his *Monadology* arguing that things which cannot be discriminated in any way, that is, cannot be told apart, must be assumed to be the same thing; for example, if a percept of an object does not show any difference whatever from another percept they must be assumed to be percepts of the same thing.

ideographic orthography: a writing system that uses ideas, concepts, or meanings as its point of reference; for example, the symbol "$" when it is used to represent money and the circle with a line through it used to mean negation, are ideographs.

illocutionary force: the pragmatic meaning or significance of a speech act as intended by a speaker.

illusion: a regularly produced perceptual error that occurs when a phenomenon seems to be different than it really is, for example, see the McGurk effect.

immersion program: an approach to nonprimary language instruction, where a whole group of students who speak some language other than the language of instruction are provided an entire educational curriculum in the target language; an approach where study, instruction, and routine communications are carried out in the target language.

immune system: the body's normal defense against attack by microbial invaders.

immunity: the condition of being prepared to defend against a particular disease, bacterium, virus, or toxin.

implication: an inference the pertains to some event or fact not yet in evidence but expected.

inclusive-we: in grammar, a plural first person pronoun in any language that includes the listener or listeners among its referents.

index: the sort of sign that represents its object by being connected with it, for instance, as someone's act of pointing may be sometimes be connected with whatever is pointed at.

inertial state: a relatively unchanging state of motion or location; for example, a train moving on a track approximates an inertial state, as does the same train when it is stopped.

infant-directed speech: signing or speaking that is addressed to an infant; also see motherese.

inferential implication: an interpretation that to facts not yet asserted but that either must or are likely to follow from what has been asserted, for example, if a prisoner is to be hanged at dawn, we may infer by implication that soon after dawn he will be dead.

infrasemiotic system: in general sign theory, any developing relation between sign systems, especially icons with icons, indexes with icons, indexes with indexes, either or both of these with symbols, and so forth, that enables the whole sign hierarchy to become more integrated and connected; that is, any generalizable relation between signs that helps to enable crossmodal transfer.

innate intelligence: the factor(s) in human mental ability that an individual is either born with or that matures over time because of the person's genetic make-up; the portion of variability in scores on tests of mental ability that can be attributed to genetic inheritance.

innateness hypothesis: the idea that a great deal of what human beings know or learn about languages is inborn, in other words, genetically determined by the human genome.

innatist perspective: the theory, sometimes taken for granted and unstated, that a great deal of the human language capacity is unique to human beings and inherited in the genome.

intelligence: the ability to use abstract signs to represent ideas, to reason about them, and to engage in rational thought and discourse.

intelligence test: any test intended mainly for the purpose of assessing a person's mental capacities; in recent years expanded to include a variety of other abilities that are governed by or related to mental abilities.

interactional synchrony: the matching or coordination of rhythmic actions by different persons engaged in conversation or some other discursive interaction.

inter-rater reliability: a statistical (quantitative) measure of the agreement between distinct raters or judges of a given phenomenon, usually reported as a correlation.

interlocutor: a participant in any interaction that takes place through one or more languages.

International Phonetic Alphabet (IPA): a notational system consisting of distinct letters and diacritic marks for representing the sounds of the world's languages (see http://www2.arts.gla.ac.uk/IPA/images/ipachart.gif visited on January 27, 2006).

interpersonal intelligence: one of the varieties (or factors) of mental ability proposed by Howard Gardner (1983/1993), in this case that aspect of mental ability that enables individuals to understand others.

interpretability (practicality): the requirement that the purpose, content, and results of a test, survey, or assessment procedure should be easy to understand and to use; one of the criteria for overall test validity.

intersubjectivity: shared consciousness, or mutual awareness, of interests, objects of attention, or experience, by different interlocutors or persons engaged in communication.

interval scale: the kind of yardstick or measure where each unit of measurement has the same value throughout the test, survey, or measure, for example, where any unit at any position on the scale represents the same value.

intonation: the overall impression created by the changing sound of an utterance, constituted by changes in pitch, loudness, and rhythm.

intrapersonal intelligence: one of the varieties (or factors) of mental ability proposed by Howard Gardner (1983/1993), in this case that aspect of mental ability that enables individuals to understand themselves.

intrinsic reinforcers: positive contingent events that tend to produce a higher rate of response or behavior of a particular sort; for example, infant smiling tends to produce smiling in adults and appears to be an intrinsic reinforcer for smiling behavior.

intuitions of the ideal native speaker: the knowledge of the hypothetical "average" person of his or her first (primary) language, the one learned from birth; the sort of knowledge that enables us to know, for instance, that "the dog bit the man" is a perfectly well-formed possible sentence in English while "dog the man bit the" is badly formed.

isomorphism: having exactly the same form, shape, order, or componential structure in some respect or other.

journal assessment: a qualitative approach to assessment of knowledge, skills, and abilities where the individual to be assessed keeps a kind of diary or journal of activities that can be read, reacted to, and used as an indicator of performance.

kinesics: the knowledge or study of meaningful gestures and bodily movements.

kinesthetic: having to do with any sensation of movement, for example, the way a body or person feels in moving about, for example, the sensations of how the articulators feel when we speak, or how we imagine our body would feel if we were performing a certain action, involves "kinesthetic" representation.

language acquisition device: a hypothetical component of the human mind that enables us to acquire any language.

language acquisition support structure: the community of users and the actions they regularly perform with language that enables most any child to acquire whatever language the child may happen to be exposed to by a suitable community of users.

language community: any group of people who share one or more dialects of some particular language.

language/dialect deficit: the sort of lack or absence of language learning and development that can arise when an individual has been deprived of the opportunity to acquire a language by environmental, physical, or mental limitations.

language/dialect difference: the sort of communication problem created not by an individual but by a context of interaction where a normal and competent individual, knows another language/dialect but fails to understand or to be understood in a communication context because he or she does not yet know the language/dialect of interaction, for example, the individual in question may speak Igbo (or, say, Australian English) while the language of conversation is Chinese (or an American dialect of English), the problems that arise should be attributed to the fact that two different systems (language/dialects) are involved.

language faculty: the innate capacity to learn and use abstract conventional languages that humans have as part of their distinct genetic make-up.

latching: the linking of one turn to the next in a conversational exchange or in any kind of social turn-taking.

lateral development: the kind of sign development that expands within a given level, for example, increasing the number of objects discriminated by distinct percepts would be an example of lateral growth.

lemma: in linguistics, the root or stem of a word as contrasted with any affixes that may be attached; the portion of the word that is normally present when it appears in an unmarked form.

lesion: the place where bodily tissue is damaged by injury, disease, poison, or whatever.

Lewy-body disease: a form of dementia involving memory impairment and reduced ability to plan and carry out complex actions; involves deposits of the protein, alpha synuclein (see http://www.ninds.nih. gov/disorders/dementiawithlewybodies/dementiawithlewybodies.htm visited October 31, 2005); may be a variety of Alzheimer's disease and/or Parkinson's disease.

lexical taxonomy: words in a particular category, for example, colors, or pieces of furniture, or games played with a ball, and so forth.

lexicon: the component of grammar, or of any particular language, that consists of the words, idioms, pat phrases, and verbal routines (for example, "Hello. How are you?" as a telephone greeting, or "Dear X," as the opening of a letter), that can only be learned by discovering their conventional associations within particular contexts of experience and usage.

linear: arranged in a line, or characterized by the properties of numbers that reflect such an arrangement, especially, changes that are like motion along a line; monotonic as contrasted with exponential change.

linguistic neighbor: a form similar in letters, sounds, or meanings to one or more others forms.

linguistic neighborhood: the hypothetical space that is created by forms that are similar with respect to their letters, sounds, or meanings.

liquid: a sound that can function either as a consonant or vowel in American English as commonly designated by the letters "l" and "r" as found in words like *ticker* and *tickle* where they approximate vowels, and in *berry*, *belly*, *rack*, and *lack* where they take on the role of consonants.

literacy: the capacity to read and write or to understand written symbols (derived from the root of the word "letter").

loanword: a word that is taken more or less directly from another language and used in the new system without much change in its surface-form or meaning; for example, the word "perestroika" meaning "restructuring" borrowed from Russian by English speakers, or "hip hop" taken into Russian, Spanish, French, German, and so forth, from English.

locutionary force: the pragmatic meaning or significance of a speech act as generally understood by persons who know the language and conventions deployed in that act.

logarithm: the inverse of an exponent; has the advantage of converting vast differences in quantities to more manageable ones; useful to hearing science in the logarithmic decibel scale to measure both the physical power of sounds and their perceived relative loudness.

logical form: the fully abstract semantic meaning of a construction. The part of the meaning that can be translated or paraphrased. Also see, deep structure.

logico-mathematical intelligence: one of the varieties (or factors) of mental ability proposed by Howard Gardner (1983/1993), in this case that aspect of mental ability that enables individuals to reason logically, especially with abstract symbol systems especially numbers.

logical object: any thing, person, event, relation, scene, or context, whether real or imagined, whether actual, possible, or impossible, that may be the referent of a sign or complex of signs.

logographic orthography: a writing system that uses whole word units as its point of reference; for example, the symbol "%" when it is used to represent "per cent" and the symbol "&" used to represent the word "and" are logographs.

longevity: the relative length of life.

Lou Gehrig's disease: a commonly fatal disease of the motor nerves of unknown causation, first discovered in 1869 by Jean Martin Charcot, usually detected at first through a general weakness in an extremity that is not associated with any pain; eventually affects such motor processes as speech, swallowing, mobility, and breathing; also known as amyotrophic lateral sclerosis.

mastication: the process or result of chewing.

maxim of manner: Grice's principle that interlocutors will normally (or should) avoid being obscure, wordy, or beating around the bush.

maxim of quality: Grice's principle that interlocutors will normally (or should) avoid saying anything known to be false or concerning which there is insufficient knowledge of truth or falsehood.

maxim of quantity: Grice's principle that interlocutors will normally (or should) should be as informative as necessary but not more so.

maxim of relevance: Grice's principle that interlocutors will normally (or should) avoid saying anything not related to the issue(s) under consideration in the present conversation.

McGurk effect: the illusional tendency for listeners to convert an auditory stimulus, for example, the syllable /ba/, to /da/ or /ga/, when the visual image of the speaker appears to be saying /ga/ (see http://www.media.uio.no/personer/arntm/McGurk_english.html visited on August 29, 2005); demonstrates a deep integration and coordination between seeing and hearing of speech.

meaning-oriented approach: any approach to comprehension, teaching, or learning that is based on or that directs attention to the meaning or content underlying the surface-forms of representations.

medial position: with respect to a syllable or word, any position in the middle of a string of segments making up that syllable or word.

Merthiolate: a formerly well-known brand name for thimerosal (also known as thiomersal) used as a topical disinfectant; known in the southern U.S. as "monkey blood."

meshing: the process of integrating forms and meanings through processes of representation, for instance, fitting signs together on the basis of their meanings and functions.

metabolism: the processes and systems of the body involved in the conversion of food into body tissues and various forms of energy.

methamphetamine: an illegal drug known on the streets as an "upper," that is, a stimulant, known to contain toxins that can cause the onset of neurodegenerative conditions such as Parkinson's disease.

methyl mercury: a form of mercury that can be ingested by fish or livestock in contaminated feed or water; known to have caused various widespread incidents of poisoning causing severe, sometimes fatal, neurological damage, for example, it affected many people in Minamata, Japan in 1970.

mimetic: imitative in nature; tending to copy or replicate.

minimal pair contrast: in linguistics, but especially in phonology, the sort of contrast in sounds found between words that differ only in one segment, for example, *pit* and *bit*, or *reek* and *rake*.

mirror image hypothesis: the theory that the loss of knowledge, skills, and abilities, especially those involved in linguistic communication, due to the cumulative damage that becomes increasingly evident with aging tends to be the reverse of the order of their development or acquisition in early childhood.

mistaken representation (error): when the construal of a representation either in constructing it or in interpreting it does not match what was intended.

mnemonic: a technique, gimmick, trick, or procedure to aid memory or recall; for example, a pronounceable word or phrase to facilitate the recall of a list or sequence of other words, phrases, numbers, or whatever; for example, the acrostic *A*ppearance, *P*ulse, *G*rimace, *A*ctivity, and *R*espiration, created from the name *Apgar*, to help users remember the five key elements of the scale invented by Dr. Apgar.

modality: any of the five senses, seeing, hearing, touching, tasting, or smelling; or any particular means of processing a signal, for example, by speaking, listening, reading, or writing.

monad: any arrangement or relation characterized by having only one distinct part, component, or participant; for example, a distinct identity may be thought of as a monad.

monotonic: a singular unchanging tone of a given pitch.

morpheme: the smallest sign in any language that has a distinct meaning or syntactic function, for example, the "-s" of "dogs" signifying plurality, the "-s" of "barks" signifying the third person singular and present or habitual action, or the "to" of "he wants to go" which marks the verb "go" which follows it as an infinitive form.

morphological marker: the surface-form of any morpheme; see morpheme.

morphology: the study of the substructure of words and phrases and especially of morphemes; see morpheme.

mortality: the fact that all organisms inevitably experience sufficient cumulative systemic damage over time to cause death.

mother tongue: the primary or first language of an infant; especially the language of the infant's own mother or primary caregivers.

motherese: a term applied to the speech of a mother to her own infant with all of its special modifications and characteristics, for example, being of higher pitch than normal, slower than adult speech, having exaggerated vowels of greater length and distinctness, and so on.

multimodal sensory impression: any sensation or impression that involves more than one sense, for example, hearing and seeing, or hearing, seeing, and touching, and so on.

multiple intelligences: the theory of mental ability proposed by Howard Gardner (1983/1993) which argues that human intellect can be divided into seven or eight, or more, distinct abilities that are, according to Gardner, not necessarily correlated with each other.

multiple sclerosis: a disease that involves degeneration of the motor nerves believed to have been first described in 1869 by Jean Martin Charcot who is also credited with having discovered amyotrophic lateral sclerosis; one of the diseases that has been linked with mercury poisoning.

musical intelligence: one of the varieties (or factors) of mental ability proposed by Howard Gardner (1983/1993), in this case that aspect of mental ability that enables individuals to appreciate music, recall a melody, produce a pitch, play an instrument, read music, and so forth.

mutual intelligibility criterion: the primary basis for judging whether or not two varieties of a language system represent the same system or two different ones; generally, but not always, if both systems can be understood by their respective speakers they are considered to be varieties (dialects) of the same language, otherwise, different languages.

myelin: a complex structure made up mainly of the proteins actin and tubulin that form the insulating layer enabling nerves to send and receive electrochemical impulses. If the myelin disintegrates the nerves cannot function.

naïve realism: the notion that things are exactly as they seem to be; naïve because of the existence of illusions, hallucinations, and errors, as well as deliberate deceptions in the form of lies.

narrative structure: the tendency for stories to be told, and for conversations, reports, and other discourse forms, to unfold as a sequence of distinct events arranged in a linear sequence from event A, to B, to C, and so forth.

nasal: characterized by reverberation of sound as it passes from the voice through the air exiting through the nose when the mouth is partially or completely closed, especially, as an attribute of sounds that involve the resonance of the nose passages in particular.

nasalized: produced with a noticeable resonance in the cavities of the nose, that is, with nasal resonance.

national boundary criterion: a distant secondary (and rarely applied) basis for judging whether or not two varieties of a language system represent the same system or two different ones; in some cases, if two similar varieties of a language (even mutually intelligible systems in some cases) are on opposite sides of borders (or geographical barriers) separating two nations, the two systems may be considered separate languages.

native language: any language learned from birth forward or in early childhood, also referred to as the *mother tongue*.

neonate: a newborn.

neurodegenerative: having to do with deterioration of nerves or nervous tissues.

neurotoxin: any poison that damages or adversely affects nerve tissues.

nominal: of or pertaining to names, nouns, or referring terms that have a naming or noun-like function.

nominal scale: an on-or-off categorical distinction between one individual case (whatever may be named) and whatever other cases may exist (for example, Bill versus everyone else); in measurement theory sometimes treated as a kind of yardstick with just two positions, for example, 0 and 1, or "yes" and "no."

nondistress vocalizations: any sound produced by the voice or vocal apparatus that is not associated with pain, fear, or other forms of distress.

nonlinear: a representational system is nonlinear if its units do not stand in a one-to-one relation with the units of whatever is represented; for example, an increase of one decibel is barely detectible, while an increase of 10 does not result in a sound 10 times louder, but one twice as loud (so measurement in decibels is nonlinear).

nonprimary language: any language acquired, studied, learned, or used after the first (native or birth) language, or any language other than the one used most of the time.

nonverbal (nonlinguistic) intelligence: in classical theories the kinds of mental ability that supposedly involve reasoning but without the overt use of language; more recently, in his theory of "multiple intelligences," one of the varieties (or factors) of mental ability proposed by Howard Gardner (1983/1993) with roughly the same meaning as in the classical theory except that Gardner argues that this variety of intelligence is uncorrelated with language abilities.

norm-referenced test: any test designed to assess or measure knowledge, skill, or ability relative to the performance of some comparison group (the so-called "norm"); contrasted with criterion-referenced test.

normative: characterized by shared habits, tendencies, or regularities of use, that is, *normal* as in *normal speech and language development.*

noun phrase: any phrase that has a noun as its head or main component part; for example, "the dog" has "dog" as its main component and is a noun phrase for that reason.

null hypothesis: the theory that no relation exists or that a certain outcome will not be found; such a theory can be refuted by a single replicable experiment, but it cannot be proved by any number of experiments.

number: in grammar, the marking of pronouns or other referring terms according to whether they signify one (singular) or more than one (plural) referent(s).

numeracy: the capacity to represent, understand, and reason with numbers.

object: in grammar the referent or part of a verbal construction that receives the action of the verb.

object permanence: the Piagetian concept that infants must learn that an object no longer being perceived still exists.

Ockham's razor: the rule for theory building that entities should not be multiplied beyond necessity; that is, if a simpler theory is possible and adequate, it should be preferred over a more complex one.

onset: the consonantal part at the beginning of syllables that happen to begin with one or more consonants, for instance, *tick*, *trick*, and *strict.*

operant: an action, process, or behavior, or the defining characteristic of such an action, process, or behavior, that controls or produces some contingent outcome or result; for example, the kind of action that causes something else to happen as when sucking on a pacifier causes a stimulus sound or image to change in some way.

oracy: the capacity to represent, understand, and reason by using spoken language.

ordinal scale: the kind of yardstick or measure where the marks on the scale, or the scores, can at least be arranged in a certain order, in other words, distinctions can be made between higher and lower scores.

orthographic: of or pertaining to a writing system or written representation.

orthography: a system of writing or written representation.

otoacoustic emissions: abbreviated "OAE," a screening procedure to identify babies with hearing problems; it detects the sound produced by the inner ear in response to an auditory stimulus (see http://www.raisingdeafkids.org/hearingloss/testing/nhs.jsp, scroll down and click on "Sound Beginnings," visited August 26, 2005).

panic tantrum: the sort of expression of extreme distress displayed by an infant experiencing what appears to be sheer terror as if something awful and frightening has just happened; distinguished from an ordinary anger or frustration tantrum by the notable presence of fear or terror.

Parkinson's disease: a disease, second only to Alzheimer's disease, in incidence affecting the brain and especially motor nerves; first described in detail in 1817 by James Parkinson and linked to the neurotransmitter, dopamine, involved in directing muscle activity, in 1961 by Oleh Hornykiewicz; also linked in the research literature to mercury poisoning.

past morpheme: any surface-form expressing grammatical past tense or the abstraction representing the common meaning or function of such surface-forms in a language; for example, in English the past morpheme assumes the regular forms /-d/, /-t/, and /əd/ as in "begged," "walked," and "waited" and various irregular forms as in "went," "ran," "fell," "came," and so on.

patient: in grammar, the person or thing operated on by the action of the verb, for example, in *The cat ate the canary*, the canary would be the patient or the direct object of the act of eating performed by the cat (the agent).

percept: the icon of an object that is being perceived, for example, when we see a plane in the sky overhead, the plane is represented in a percept that has the shape, sound, size, and so on, of the plane in the distance. Distinct from concept by the fact that a percept cannot be fully dissociated from the object perceived.

perceptual: of or pertaining to the processes of sensation and/or the construction of percepts.

perceptual field: the roughly bounded domain that the senses of a perceiver encompass; the domain within which the senses are capable of noticing differences and producing distinct sensations of the bodily objects contained there.

perfection (completeness): in the grammatical or logical sense, the wholeness, coherence, or unity of an object, event, or representation.

performance testing: the sort of assessment of knowledge, skills, and abilities where attention is paid not so much to the products of tasks but to the dynamic processes that go on while the person(s) being examined are doing the tasks; often also applied to the sorts of tasks found in many so-called nonverbal intelligence tests.

perlocutionary force: the pragmatic meaning or significance of a speech act as it affects the listener, audience, or consumer, that is, the change in the behavior, thinking, or representations of the consumer attributable to the meaning of a given speech act.

personality inventory: typically a battery of questions aimed at assessing the attitudes, preferences, and social traits of an individual; contrasted with tests of knowledge, skills, and abilities associated more commonly with mental or physical traits.

pervasive developmental disorders: a diverse class of disorders that have long-term, cascading effects throughout the life span; at the center of this class are the autism spectrum disorders.

phatic communion: the kind of mutual awareness that does not necessarily involve an exchange of information other than the fact that the interlocutors mutually recognize one another as beings of the same kind, or beings in the same situation; also see intersubjectivity, the chameleon effect, and reciprocity.

phonation: any voluntary speech-like vocalization of early infancy.

phoneme: a theoretical class or system of distinctive sounds within a given language.

phonemic principle: the principle that each letter of the alphabet stands for a distinct class or system of sounds in the writing system; also known as the alphabetic principle.

phonics: an approach to the teaching of literacy based on rules of correspondence between particular letters of the alphabet or sequences of letters with the sounds or sound sequences of a particular language.

phonographic neighbor: a form that resembles others in terms of shared phonological elements but that does not share any common meaning.

phonological awareness: the capacity to represent or the knowledge of the sounds of a particular language as they are represented in the letters of an alphabetic writing system.

phonology: the component of grammar or the study of that component of grammar having to do with its sounds and their combinations.

pitch: the basic underlying frequency of a voiced sound.

pivot-grammar: a proposal from Braine (1963) to treat certain surface-forms as mere points of attachment for other forms; proposed to avoid using the terminology of adult grammars to refer to developing systems of signs in child language development.

placenta: the sac that encloses the developing fetus during pregnancy.

plaque: the extraneous scar-like tissue that replaces the myelin sheath that normally insulates neurons, discovered in 1925 by E. D. Adrian (http://www.firelady40.com/ms/mshistory.html#facts2 visited July 11, 2005).

plural morpheme: any surface-form expressing grammatical number or the abstraction representing the common meaning or function of such surface-forms in a language; for example, in English the plural morpheme assumes the regular forms /-z/, /-s/, and /əz/ as in "dogs," "cats," and "classes" and various irregular forms as in "women," "men," "children," "oxen," and so forth.

plurality: in grammar, the conceptual property of having more than one referent; the conceptual property marked by the plural morpheme.

polyad: any arrangement or relation characterized by having two or more distinct parts, components, or participants as in a relation that connects multiple participants; for example, the businesses in the downtown area, or the planes in a particular portion of airspace under the control of a single air traffic controller, the passengers on a plane, and so on, would constitute polyads, or polyadic relations.

polyglot: a person who knows and uses more than two languages; commonly also called, colloquially and incorrectly, "a linguist."

portfolio assessment: a loosely defined qualitative approach to assessment that collects relevant evidence about the person being assessed into a folder (or "portfolio"); may contain products, work samples, writings by or about the individual, descriptions of work done, letters of reference, a diary, newspaper clippings, E-mail, and so on; see qualitative assessment.

possessive marker: in grammar, the conceptual property of ownership or a similar association between an argument possessor and whatever other argument or attribute may be possessed as marked in the possessive morpheme; for example, the /əz/, /-s/, and /-ez/ of "the dog's collar," "the cat's paw," and "the horse's bridle."

posterior canals: the back canals of the semicircular canal structure in the vertical plane pointed inward at about 45 degrees from the line of sight looking straight ahead.

postnatal: after birth.

postnatal age: the age after birth (contrasts with gestational age).

powers of representation: the capacity to perceive, indicate, refer to, describe, understand, interpret, or otherwise signify things that may be experienced, imagined, or signified by oneself or someone else.

pragmatic: of or pertaining to the practical use of signs or sign systems.

pragmatic bootstrapping: the process or result of attaching an abstract sign or signs to one or more particular referents; that is, the instantiation of a conventional use of a sign by associating it with one or more particular referents.

pragmatic content: the material substance of particular concrete things, situations, events, or relations that is associated with one or more signs.

pragmatic forces: the meanings associated with any given speech act, or more broadly any act of communication.

pragmatic mapping: the dynamic indexical association of one or more abstract general symbols with the particular content of a context or experience.

predicate: any sign that is asserted as true of or appropriate as a description or as applied to or associated with something other than itself, for example, in any naming or referring relation, the name or referring phrase is predicated as applicable to the object (or whatever) is named.

predicate-argument structure: the kind of relation between a verb such as *put* and the things, persons, locations, and so on, with which it may be associated as in, *The man put some gas in his car*.

predication: any discursive utterance produced to assert, express, or otherwise signify a distinct meaning to be associated with one or more arguments or with a context of discourse.

prefix: the sort of bound morpheme that is attached to the beginning of word, for example, the "pre-" in *prefix*.

prenatal: before birth.

preoperational stage: in Piaget's theory a stage loosely defined as involving abstract linguistic representations enabling play and pretense but not yet sufficiently developed so as to enable the child to take full account of the viewpoints of other persons, or to perform reversible operations.

prescind: to separate an object from a location, or a sign from the object that it represents.

prescinded icon: the sort of image required to imagine an object in its former location or in the location where it will end up if it is moved.

prescinded index: the sort of pointing sign that is dynamically moved by the sign-user to connect the different inertial states of an object as it moves about and changes over time.

prescinded symbol: the first distinct syllables and sequences of them (or the first recognizable surface-forms of manual signs) that are produced by the infant; the production of the prescinded symbol is synonymous with canonical babbling.

prescission: the intermediate process of abstraction by which an object is removed from a location, or by which a sign of an object is removed from that object.

presupposition: the process or result of inference that enables us to take account of meanings that are necessary to make sense of a given construction, for example, the statement that *Sandra opened the window* leads to the presupposition that the window was closed prior to her opening it.

presymbolic forms: meaningful words or word-like signs tightly embedded within and associated with a particular activity, for instance, the syllabic sound "hmma" made along with a kissing gesture.

preverbal systems of signs: the icons and indexes that must precede the development of the first conventional symbols.

primary reference: the stage of reference achieved when the infant notices the bodily speaker as the source of speech sounds.

primary stress: the main prominence usually shown in higher pitch, greater length, and greater amplitude, assigned to a syllable, word, phrase, or higher structure. For example, in "George left" the verb "left" would normally receive primary stress.

priming: the result or process in experimental psychology of causing an anticipatory readiness for a subsequent event, form, word, or concept to arise, for example, hearing the word "mother" may cause a readiness to process words related in meaning, such as "sister," "brother," or "father."

probe words: in experimental psychology, a word used to test for a memory or anticipatory readiness for a particular event, form, word, or concept.

productive vocabulary: the conventional signs, especially words, that an individual can produce with their usual conventional meanings in typical contexts of use.

prognosis: the expected or predicted course of a difficulty, disease, or disorder, for example, whether it will get better or worse over time and with or without treatment.

prosodic bootstrapping: the theory that the melody, pitch changes, and the rhythm and stress patterns of speech provide critical information to discovering meanings and syntactic structure.

prosody: the aspect of the surface-forms of speech or signed language that have to do with its contrasting intonations, rhythms, stress patterns, and so on.

protein: any one of thousands of macromolecules that form the basic materials of body tissues; they consist of long sequences of the 20 amino acids that are specified in DNA and RNA and they are crucial to the structures and functions of all living organisms.

protophone: the predecessor of any given sound of speech.

protostructure: the presumed prior structure from which some later structure is derived or from which the later structure develops; for example, the foundation of a building is a kind of protostructure for the building.

prototype: a blueprint, model, or plan for the development of a complex system or construction.

pseudoword (nonce word): any pronounceable sequence of letters that might be a word in a particular language but, by chance, happens not to have any particular meaning in that language, for example, the forms "donk," "kack," and "preel" are pronounceable nonce words in English.

psychiatric disorders: the kind of difficulties or imbalances that are commonly treated by a psychiatrist, often with drugs; however, the boundary between this class of disorders and other difficulties is unclear.

pupil dilation: the opening of the black center of the eye that permits light to enter.

qualitative assessment: any form of so-called "subjective" assessment that emphasizes the holistic judgment of some person or persons (the "subject" or "subjects"), who often participate in and assess the qualities associated with some event, process, or performance by some person or group; commonly contrasted with quantitative assessment.

quantitative assessment: any form of so-called "objective" assessment that emphasizes repeated judgments, ratings, or other measurements that can be counted reliably and validly and that can be related to some other series of events, performances, or processes that are the "objects" of measurement; commonly contrasted with qualitative assessment.

quarantine: confinement within one of the body's systems, as if in a prison, of a potentially harmful entity or toxin so that its potential harm can be reduced, halted, or prevented altogether.

quasi-alphabetic: a characteristic of a writing system that does not fully conform to the alphabetic principle of writing, for example, written English is only a quasi-alphabetic system.

quasivowel: a vowel-like utterance of an infant without any distinctive shaping of the articulators.

rapid eye movements (REM): the kind of movements of the eyes that are characteristic of during deep sleep and dreaming.

ratio scale: the kind of yardstick or measure that enables reliable and valid doubling, halving, or otherwise multiplying or dividing the quantities on the scale.

rationalism: a philosophical outlook that relies on or stresses the role of reason, thought, and intelligence; often contrasted in recent years with behaviorism.

rationalist tradition: the theory and research emphasizing thought, reason, and the mind.

readability formulas: methods of calculating the ease or difficulty of understanding of a written text usually based on the number of syllables per word, the number of words per sentence, the relative commonness of words used in the text, and similar features.

reading aloud: the process of converting written text into a spoken form.

reading competence: the capacity or ability to read.

reading comprehension: the result, process, or measure of a person's capacity to understand what is read.

reading readiness: the hypothetical age at which a child is able to begin to learn to read and write.

receptive vocabulary: the conventional signs, especially words, that an individual can understand in accordance with their usual conventional meanings in typical contexts of use.

reciprocity: mutual interest and sharing within a given sphere of understanding; also see intersubjectivity and the chameleon effect; the result or process of intentional sharing, that is, holding things, relations, or experiences in common.

recognizability requirement: the demand that the surface-form of a meaningful symbol must be produced with sufficient accuracy so that it can be understood in the normal and intended way by the community of sign-users; synonymous with the surface-form requirement.

recommended therapy: the preferred approach to restoration of functions, reduction of damage, or curative treatment for a given difficulty, disability, disorder, or disease.

re-entry: the constructive process or result of learning by associating signs or meanings with a new or old context of experience in such a way as to enrich the understanding of the ongoing stream of experience.

reference: the process or result of linking a name or phrase with the person or thing named or described.

regional dialect: a language variety that is commonly used in a definable geographical area.

relevance: any actual relation to the current subject of discourse, an abstract property of any sign or sequence of signs in a discourse that enables it to be associated with whatever is currently under consideration by real or potential interlocutors.

representation: the process or result of making meaning accessible or present; commonly involves sensation, movement, and/or language.

resonance: the quality of speech sounds, especially vowels, but also including voiced consonants, produced by the voice as it reverberates (literally bounces off the walls) inside the body, especially the throat, mouth, and nose. The particular resonant quality of any given voiced sound is largely a product of the shape of these cavities. The shapes can be changed by opening or closing and by movements especially of the tongue.

response set: the tendency to give an answer consistent with, or the same as, one that has previously been produced.

reversibility: a distinguishing logical property of operations (actions) according to Piaget. Concrete operations, for instance, can be reversed in part. We can move an object back to where it was before. However, formal operations, completely abstract ones, seemingly are completely reversible according to Piaget. For instance, adding 2 to 3 gets us to 5, but we can return to 3 by subtracting 2 from 5.

reversion hypothesis: the idea that sign systems of lower levels are commonly accessible to a sign-user while signs at higher levels than the highest level previously achieved are generally inaccessible; a sign-user may regress at any time to a lower level but the only way to reach a higher level is by painstaking learning and development.

rhythm: the characteristic rate and beat of the syllables of speech in any given language as a result of which different languages sound different when they are spoken, for example, compare Spanish and Greek with English or Mandarin Chinese.

rime: the part of a syllable consisting of its vocalic center and any following consonants, for example, in the word *Faust* the sounds represented by the letters *-aust* would constitute its rime.

risk factor: the supposed or inferred likelihood that infants who do not achieve a certain milestone on schedule will be more likely to develop or be diagnosed with a learning disability or communication disorder later on.

RNA: the gene material consisting of ribonucleic acid that is crucial to the specification of protein structures; the material especially involved in the communication of the instructions for the building of proteins.

satisficing: the tendency to give an answer that suffices to get the surveyor or interviewer to leave the respondent alone; see acquiescence response bias.

second language setting: a context of use or learning where the learner or classroom for language teaching is located within a community that uses the target language.

second order predicate: a predicate that takes (that is, subsumes or is subsumed by) one or more first order predicates as its argument(s).

second position (or person): the consumer or audience to whom a bit of discourse is addressed; when Emeril Lagasse says to his audience in his television program *Emeril Live!*, "So I said to myself, 'Self!' . . . " He is both the first person and the second person in the included quote, but his live audience and the greater television audience stands in the second position.

secondary reference: the stage of reference achieved when the infant begins to distinguish speech addressed to him or herself, or to another infant, as contrasted with speech addressed to an adult; the addressee, consumer, or audience of a speech or sign act whether present or inferred by the infant.

secondary stress: the degree of prominence just lower than primary stress, for example, in "George Lakoff left," primary stress would normally go to the verb "left" and secondary stress to "Lakoff."

self-awareness: the act of a representer representing him or herself and also understanding that representation. This is more complex than it may seem at first. It involves the representer functioning as the primary referent and as the first, second, and third person of a given act of representation.

self-flattery: a known factor of bias in survey procedures where the respondent tends to give the response that makes him or herself look good in his or her own eyes.

self-synchrony: the matching or coordination of rhythmic actions of one sort, for example, gestures, with those of another, for example, speaking, by the same person; for instance, a speaker tends to coordinate distinct facial expressions and changes in tone of voice with phrase boundaries of speech.

semantic: the aspect of meaning that is fully abstract (often conflated and confused with reference which belongs to pragmatic meaning).

semantic association: inferences that apply across contexts of experience, generalize to imagined contexts, and even to representations of unimaginable states of affairs; for example, "a perfectly square circle" would require a circle that is both round and square at the same time.

semantic bootstrapping: the process or result of discovering how to use or understand a new sign by inferring its meaning or use from the meanings of other signs with which the new sign may be associated.

semantic conceptualization: the kind of abstract reasoning, inference, or constructive representation that involves abstract ideas as distinct from particular memories, experiences, or perceptions; sometimes referred to as semantic memory.

semantic feature: an abstract representation of a concept that may be associated with an object or a word, for example, the shape, density, texture, color, of an object, or any of these meanings associated with a word or its referents.

semantic limit of generality: the absolute theoretical limit that is reached when a sign is generalized to all possible instances that are the same as the one at hand, a limit that logically applies exactly to the extent of the similarity and no further.

semantic memory: the abstract knowledge of facts or general inferences from representations that are not associated with any particular experience that may be recalled from the past, for example, knowing whether you are male or female, the shape of a brick, how many states there are in the United States, the colors of the flag are typically thought to be semantic bits of knowledge or memory; contrasts with episodic memory.

semantic value: the abstract and general meaning of a sign that applies across all the contexts that may exist or be imagined where that sign might conceivably be applied.

semicircular canals: principal parts inner ear that are involved in our sense of balance.

senescence: the deterioration that occurs over time because of the cumulative effects of injuries, diseases, poisons, and genetic errors; a Latin-based word for aging.

sensitivity: in binary decision-making, for example, whether a person has or does not have a certain disease, disorder, or risk factor, the percentage of true positive judgments of a measure, test, or assessment procedure.

sensorimotor stage: the first postnatal stage of development in Piaget's theory in which the infant represents itself, other persons, and so forth in terms of sensations and movements.

shifters: Edward Sapir's term for words whose meaning depends on the viewpoint of the person using the word; for example, "I" and "you" change in meaning depending on who is producing the words.

sickle cell anemia: a disease caused by a defect in the gene that specifies the hemoglobin protein causing red blood cells to be deformed into a sickle shape, or, better, a quarter moon shape, that interferes with circulation because the blood cells with the deformed shape tend to clog up the smallest capillaries.

sign: the surface-form of any representation.

sign cycle: the growth of sign systems beginning in icons, moving to indexes, and finally to more and more abstract symbols; the process by which icons are used in constructing indexes which in their turn are used in constructing symbols; all of which are subsequently used to enrich the experience of the objects, relations, and meanings that they represent.

sign hierarchy: the vast layered system of signs that a normal human being achieves at full maturity.

sign system: the dynamic relation between a sign and its meanings (semantic and pragmatic).

signed language: the language system used by a Deaf community. May be applied to a manually signed version of a particular spoken language, such as Manually Signed English, but we use the term to apply to such distinct language systems as American Signed Language, which is as different from Signed English as English is from Chinese.

significance: the abstract or concrete meaning of a sign.

silent period: a time of quiescence when no advancement in a particular level of sign systems seems to be occurring; for example, in foreign language acquisition, the time during which learners typically do not speak in the foreign language but hear it spoken by others.

silent reading: the kind of understanding and interpretation of written text(s) that does not involve production of any spoken forms of the words or symbols involved.

sincerity maxim: another name for Grice's maxim of quality, the principle that interlocutors normally do, or should, be sincere in what they say, in other words, avoid saying anything known to be false or concerning which there is insufficient knowledge of truth or falsehood.

social action: any action that is shared with or that affects the lives and comprehension of other persons whether intentionally or not; the sort of action that invariably involves shared sign systems.

social dialect: a language variety that is defined by factors such as age, gender, income, social status, or educational background.

sound pressure level (SPL): the ratio of the normal pressure of the still air relative to the fluctuations produced by a sound wave moving through it.

spatial intelligence: one of the varieties (or factors) of mental ability proposed by Howard Gardner (1983/1993), in this case supposedly that aspect of mental ability that enables individuals to reason about and negotiate relations between bodily things in space.

specificity: in binary decision-making, for example, whether a person has or does not have a certain disease, disorder, or risk factor, the percentage of true negative judgments of a measure, test, or assessment procedure.

spectral properties: the relative concentrations of energy in a waveform, especially, the formant of speech as distributed over distinct frequencies of the sound spectrum.

spectrogram: the visible output of a spectrograph giving a visual display of the intensity of concentrations of sound energy, especially in a stream of speech, over a range of frequencies from approximately 1 cycle per second up to either 4,000 (a narrow band spectrogram) or up to 8,000 cycles per second (in a broadband spectrogram).

spectrograph: a device for converting the sound energy, especially of speech, into a visual display where the vertical axis shows the frequency of sounds expressed in vibrations per second, the horizontal axis shows time, and the relative darkness of the marks on the output, called a spectrogram, show concentrations of sound energy.

speech act: an intentional act that implicitly or explicitly involves speaking, such as making a request, refusing an invitation, offering an apology, and so forth.

speech-language pathology: the field of study that deals with communication difficulties, disorders, and disabilities that affect speech and language, also, historically includes swallowing disorders and all those that affect speech and language even indirectly.

standardized test: any test for which the procedures of test construction, administration, and analysis are supposed to be consistently applied in a prescribed ("standardized") manner; commonly these tests are norm-referenced tests, however, criterion-referenced tests and even qualitative assessment procedures can be standardized.

stress pattern: the variability in the relative prominence of syllables, words, and phrases, owing to loudness, relative pitch, and length; where syllable (or other stress) stress normally is signaled by the stressed element being louder, higher pitched, and longer in duration.

stress-timed: a rhythmic characteristic of a language such as English, Dutch, German, and Mandarin, where the rhythm of speech in that language is determined by where the stress is placed in syllabic structures, stressed elements being lengthened and unstressed ones being relatively shorter.

stroke: damage to the brain caused by release of fluids in the especially associated with internal bleeding.

subject: in grammar the part of a verbal construction that precedes the verb, *the visitor* in *The visitor was bitten by the dog* but *the dog* in *the dog bit the visitor*; in traditional grammar, whatever a predicate may be asserted of or applied to.

submersion program: an unplanned approach to nonprimary language instruction where the student is simply mainstreamed with other children or language users who already know the target language and where all study, instruction, and routine communications are conducted in the target language; contrasts with immersion program.

substance: the material of which any logical object whether appearing as a solid, liquid, gas, or some combination of these, is made; especially, the bodily part of the object or the aspect that is noticeable to the senses of seeing, hearing, touching, tasting, and/or smelling.

suffix: a morphological affix that changes the form, meaning, or function of a word or other morpheme and that is added to the end of it.

surface-form: the part of a representation that can be perceived.

surface-form requirement: the demand that the surface-form of a meaningful symbol must be produced with sufficient accuracy so that it can be understood in the normal and intended way by the community of sign-users; synonymous with the recognizability requirement.

surface-oriented approach: any approach to comprehension, teaching, or learning that directs attention to the sensible, perceivable, forms of representations, that is, their letters, sounds, rhythms, and so on, that can be seen, heard, touched, or otherwise sensed; contrasts with approaches that look to abstract and general meanings, or the conventional associations of surface-forms with actual facts of experience and with abstract meanings.

Swiss cheese model of risk: a model of human risk factors proposed by James Reason where successive layers of cheese represent protections against risk and the holes in the layers represent errors, oversights, or weaknesses in the barriers; when the holes in the layers of cheese line up, accidents occur.

syllabary: a writing system that uses syllables (rather than sound segments, words, or concepts) as its units of reference.

syllabic sequences: sounds made by the voice that have the repetitive rhythm and some of the qualities of speech.

syllable: the smallest pronounceable unit of speech. Also, each part in a stream of speech that receives a beat.

syllable-timed: a rhythmic characteristic of a language such as Spanish, Italian, or Japanese, where the rhythm of speech in that language is determined by the fact that syllables tend to be of about the same length.

symbol: a sign that serves as such only by its conventional association with its meaning or object, for example, a name is a symbol but so is any word, phrase, sentence, or discourse.

symptomology: the patter of characteristic signs (symptoms) associated with a given difficulty, disorder, disability, or especially with a disease.

synchronization: the coordination and partial matching of two or more distinct rhythms across modalities, persons, and groups in discursive interactions.

syntactic bootstrapping: the process or result of discovering how to use or understand a new sign by inferring its meaning or use from its co-occurrence in particular sequences with other known signs or structures.

syntactic function: any distinct use of a sign to indicate how it is to be regarded relative to other signs in the stream of discourse, for example, the word "to" in "he wants to go" serves the syntactic function of setting up an expectation for an infinitive to follow.

syntactic limit of diminishing returns: the period of development where the syntax already acquired by the child becomes sufficient to meet essentially all the desired distinctions in surface-forms; that is, the point in time where there is no longer any pragmatic motivation to amplify the syntax further.

syntax: the aspect of linguistic structure that pertains to the sequence of elements in a stream of speech or any other form of discourse.

synthetic speech: speech that is produced by a machine, computer, or some process associated with a mechanism (not human speech).

target language: the language that an individual or group is learning or trying to learn.

task-based language teaching/testing strategy: any approach to language teaching or testing where the focus is shifted somewhat from the learner, classroom, or testing context to one or more tasks that have to be performed, for example, reporting a series of events, ordering a meal at a restaurant, explaining the rules of a game, negotiating a contract or a treaty, translating court documents, and so forth.

tertiary reference: the stage of reference achieved when the infant begins to associate a referent or significance other than the producer or consumer of a speech or sign act with its surface-form; synonymous with linguistic reference.

theory of markedness: the theory proposed by Bailey (1973, 1996) leading to the conclusion that the marking added to an existing sign makes it more complex and requires the construction of the marked form prior to the addition of the marking.

thimerosal: a preservative that kills all living cells especially aimed at the bacteria that might infect a cut, exposed mucous membrane, or a vaccine used in inoculating groups of individuals; consists of almost 50% ethyl mercury, a potent neurotoxin; also known as thiomersal and under the brand name of Merthiolate.

thiomersal: a preservative that kills all living cells especially aimed at the bacteria that might infect a cut, exposed mucous membrane, or a vaccine used in inoculating groups of individuals; consists of 49% ethyl mercury, a potent neurotoxin; also known as thimerosal and under the brand name of Merthiolate.

third order predicate: a predicate that takes (that is, subsumes or is subsumed by) one or more second order predicate(s) as its arguments.

third position (or person): the logical position occupied by anyone other than the speaker (producer) or listener (intended consumer) of a bit of discourse. In grammar the third person is someone spoken about rather than to.

token: the distinct and nonrepeatable surface-form of an abstract sign or meaning.

top-down: a term applied to reading processing that begins with meanings and works "downward" from that abstract level toward the surface-forms of print.

total physical response strategy (TPR): an approach to nonprimary language instruction where the student carries out commands of an instructor that require movements of the body, for example, stand up, sit down, turn around, give the ball to Mary, put the red canvass bag in the back seat of the car, and so forth.

toxicity: the condition resulting from an accumulation of poisons, that is, of toxins.

toxin: any poisonous substance.

transitive: in grammar the syntactic property of a verb that links an actor through some action with something acted upon.

transitive relation: in logic and in ordinary experience, any relation where if A has that relation to B and B has it to C, A must also have the same relation to C; the most widely known relations of this kind are chronological ones, causal ones, and spatial relations.

translucent: allowing light to pass through but not transparent.

trauma: the result or process of damage owed to an injury usually caused by physical impact of a blunt object leading to bruising with or without penetration of bodily tissues.

traumatic brain injury: the kind of damage caused by a blow to the head resulting in bruising and internal injury to the brain; can be caused by a sudden deceleration of motion or violent shaking which bruises the soft brain tissues against the harder bone of the skull.

triad: any arrangement or relation characterized by having three distinct parts, components, or participants; sign relations are typically at least triadic in their complexity.

trimester: any one of the three nearly equal time periods of three months each in the normally 9-month human pregnancy prior to the birth of an infant; the first trimester consists of months 1 to 3 of the pregnancy, the second trimester, months 4 to 7, and the third trimester, months 7 to 9.

true narrative representation: a perception, report, or story-like representation that unfolds or develops over time and that is faithful to the facts that it purports to represent; that is, any story, report, or story-like representation that happens to be as true as it purports to be of whatever it purports to be a representation of.

truth maxim: another name for Grice's maxim of quality, the principle that interlocutors normally do, or should, be truthful in what they say, in other words, that they should avoid saying anything known to be false or concerning which there is insufficient knowledge of its truth or falsehood; also known as the sincerity maxim.

tubulin: the protein that forms a tiny pipe-like insulating sheath (a micro-tubule) that surrounds each neuron at it grows outward from a nerve cell connecting it with other cells and enabling it to function in sensation and movement.

turn-taking: the process by which speaker and hearer exchange roles in the course of a conversation or in any social interaction.

ultrasound video: a digitized moving real time picture or recording that is created by bouncing a sound waves of very high frequency (20,000 cycles per second or more) off of the surfaces of a body.

umami: a taste distinct from sweet, sour, salty, or bitter, associated with the amino acid, glutamate (the taste in the synthetic product known as *monosodium glutamate*, or MSG); discovered by Kikunae Ikeda of Tokyo Imperial University in 1907 (see http://www.glutamate.org/media/glutamate.htm visited January 30, 2006).

unity of coherence: the kind of harmony that is achieved when essentially all the facts in evidence concerning a particular perception, assertion, or discourse fit a given interpretation and none of them conflict with that interpretation.

universal grammar: the deep structural properties that are (or are hypothesized to be) shared across all languages.

unreliability: in measurement and statistics, the portion of variability in a measure (or test) that cannot be attributed to whatever the measure or test is supposed to assess; synonymous with the error term and the opposite and complement of validity.

validity: in measurement and statistics, the portion of variability in a measure (or test) that can be attributed to whatever the procedure is supposed to measure; that is, that portion of the variance in the measurement procedure that is associated with whatever it is supposed to be associated with.

variegated babbling: repetitive rhythmic babbling that resembles speech in its surface-form and that goes one step beyond canonical babbling by producing multiple distinct syllables, for example, /badaga/, /gadaba/, and so on.

vascular system: the system of blood vessels consisting of the veins, arteries, and the heart that are involved in the circulation of the blood as well as the lymph ducts.

vegetative sounds: involuntary sounds including burps, grunts, coughs, and sneezes that are not believed to be any part of the sounds leading to the inventory of voluntary speech sounds; those that are commonly produced involuntarily (though they can sometimes by brought under voluntary control) by the body of a normal human being or infant, for example, by burping, passing gas, coughing, sneezing, wheezing, swallowing, slurping, slobbering, blowing bubbles, raspberries, and so forth.

velar: the point of articulation associated with the phonemes /k/ and /g/, or the quality of sounds that are produced by proximity or contact of the back of the tongue with that point of articulation, for example, the /l/ in the word *fool* as it is normally pronounced in most dialects of English has this quality.

verb: in grammar, the part of speech that expresses action, being, state of being, or the undergoing of some action, for example, in *The dog* chased *the cat*, *The dog* is *a Rottweiler*, *The dog* is *lost*, and *The dog* got *fleas* we have examples of each possibility, respectively.

verb phrase: a phrase defined as having a verb as its main component or head, for example, in the command, "He put the drink on the bar" the verb, according to some theories of grammar, subordinates "the drink on the bar"; any phrase whose principal, defining, or head element is a verb.

verbal fluency: a supposed trait of language learners judged by the number of different words in a given subject area that an individual can produce within a limited time frame, for instance, usually one to three minutes; a concept commonly used in assessments done in speech-language pathology; also called vocabulary fluency.

verbal (linguistic) intelligence: in classical theories, the kind of mental ability and reasoning that involves the knowledge of and or the use of language; in Howard Gardner's theory of "multiple intelligences" (1983/1993), merely one of the seven or eight varieties (or factors) of mental ability; contrasted especially with nonverbal (nonlinguistic) intelligence in the classical theories and with all other varieties of intelligence in Gardner's theory.

verbal modifier: at the two-word stage of development, any form that has a verb-like function with respect to any form (usually a noun-like zero order predicate) with which it is associated, for example, in *baby up* meaning "pick baby up," or *Mimi house* meaning "let's go to the house where Mimi is," the element that receives primary stress can usually be taken as the comment or verb-like element.

vertical development: the kind of sign development that advances from one level to the next higher level, for example, advancing from percepts to images of percepts would be an example of vertical growth.

vestibular: of or pertaining to the *vestibule* in the inner ear, which, together with the semicircular canals, enables our sense of balance; the vestibule in particular works like a carpenter's level letting us know our orientation relative to the pull of gravity toward the center of the earth.

vocabulary fluency: a supposed trait of language learners judged by the number of different words in a given subject area that an individual can produce within a limited time frame, for example, usually one to three minutes; a concept commonly used in assessments done in speech-language pathology; also called verbal fluency.

vocabulary spurt: the seemingly sudden increase in the number of words the child produces with comprehension; normally occurs about months 18 to 20.

vocal imitation: copying in some way the sounds or shapes of the mouth and lips of another person; the process or result of copying or trying to produce a sound similar to one produced by someone else, or by some other sound maker or voice.

vocalic sound: a sound made with the voice that can be extended for the whole length of a single breath; of or pertaining to the sound of a vowel, or vowel-like sound.

vocative: a form used to call someone's attention.

voicing: the quality of vowels and of consonants such as those typically represented by the letters b, d, g, z, j, r, l, that is produced by vibration of the vocal folds.

volition: the capacity to choose between possible courses of action and to rationally take into account the necessary, likely, or possible outcomes; also see free will.

volitional control: deliberate or intentional control, causation, or shaping by the willful action of a person or animate being.

vowel: a class of relatively steady state usually voiced sounds that are differentiated mainly by the shape of the oral cavities subject to opening, closing, tongue position front or back, and the presence or absence of lip rounding or flattening; the center or nucleus of a syllable; the part that gets the beat or that carries the voicing; the part that can be extended until you run out of breath.

vowel space: defined as the relative distance between vowels in any given language/dialect or in the speech of a particular speaker; can be defined in terms of the habits of articulation of a particular speaker or group, or in terms of the physical properties of the waveforms of the sounds produced; a greater distance between vowels defines a greater vowel space.

Wernicke's aphasia: a loss of the ability to understand the meanings associated with speech, writing, signing, or other forms of language.

whole-language approach: any approach to comprehension, teaching, or learning that is based on or that refers to the meaning of all the surface-forms involved in any given text.

whole-word approach: any approach to comprehension, teaching, or learning that is based on or that refers to word sized chunks of text rather than the individual letters that make up or represent those words.

xenobiotic: any foreign substance or chemical introduced into a living cell.

zero order predicate: the kind of discursive unit that is so closely associated with its meaning that the word and the meaning seem to be the same thing.

zone of proximal development: the highest level at which an individual can function with the assistance of a more expert person.

Index of Authors, Subjects, and Technical Terms